Measurement and Evaluation In Physical Education and Exercise Science

Related Benjamin Cummings Kinesiology Titles

Anshel, *Sport Psychology: from Theory to Practice,* Fourth Edition (2003)

Bishop, *Fitness through Aerobics,* Fifth Edition (2002)

Darst/Pangrazi, *Dynamic Physical Education for Secondary School Students,* Fourth Edition (2002)

Darst/Pangrazi, *Lesson Plans for Dynamic Physical Education for Secondary School Students,* Fourth Edition (2002)

Freeman, *Physical Education and Sport in a Changing Society,* Sixth Edition (2001)

Fronske, *Teaching Cues for Sport Skills,* Second Edition (2001)

Fronske/Wilson, *Teaching Cues for Basic Sports Skills for Elementary and Middle School Children* (2002)

Hastie, *Teaching for Lifetime Physical Activity Through Quality High School Education* (2003)

Harris/Pittman/Waller/Dark, *Social Dance from Dance a While,* Second Edition (2003)

Horvat/Eichstaedt/Kalakian/Croce, *Developmental/Adapted Physical Education,* Fourth Edition (2003)

Housh/Housh/Johnson, *Introduction to Exercise Science,* Second Edition (2003)

Mosston/Ashworth, *Teaching Physical Education,* Fifth Edition (2002)

Pangrazi, *Dynamic Physical Education for Elementary School Children,* Thirteenth Edition (2001)

Pangrazi, *Lesson Plans for Dynamic Physical Education for Elementary School Children,* Thirteenth Edition (2001)

Plowman/Smith, *Exercise Physiology for Health, Fitness, and Performance,* Second Edition (2003)

Powers/Dodd, *Total Fitness and Wellness,* Brief Edition (2003)

Powers/Dodd, *Total Fitness and Wellness,* Third Edition (2003)

Schmottlach/McManama, *Physical Education Activity Handbook,* Tenth Edition (2002)

Silva/Stevens, *Psychological Foundations of Sport* (2002)

Check out these and other Benjamin Cummings health and kinesiology titles at www.aw.com/bc.

Measurement and Evaluation In Physical Education and Exercise Science

FOURTH EDITION

Alan C. Lacy
Illinois State University

Douglas N. Hastad
University of Wisconsin—LaCrosse

Benjamin
Cummings

San Francisco   Boston   New York
Cape Town   Hong Kong   London   Madrid   Mexico City
Montreal   Munich   Paris   Singapore   Sydney   Tokyo   Toronto

Publisher: Daryl Fox

Acquisitions Editor: Deirdre McGill

Publishing Assistant: Michelle Cadden

Managing Editor: Wendy Earl

Production Editor: Janet Vail

Cover Design: Yvo Riezebos

Text Design: Brad Greene Design

Copyeditor: Anna Reynolds Trabucco

Compositor: Brad Greene Design

Manufacturing Buyer: Stacey Weinberger

Marketing Manager: Sandy Lindelof

Library of Congress Cataloging-in-Publication Data

Lacy, Alan C.
  Measurement and evaluation in physical education and exercise science
/ Alan C. Lacy and Douglas N. Hastad.--4th ed.
      p. cm.
Previous edition has main entry under Hastad, Douglas N.
Includes bibliographical references and index.
    ISBN 0-321-10302-5
  1. Physical fitness--Testing. I. Hastad, Douglas N. II. Title.
    GV436 .H35 2002
    613.7--dc21

                                                    2002073870

ISBN 0-321-10302-5

2 3 4 5 6 7 8 9 10—PBT—06 05 04 03

www.aw.com/bc

To our students, the future physical education and exercise science professionals, who will deliver programs to educate our society about the countless benefits of engaging in physically active lifestyles.

Contents

Chapter 1

Introduction to Measurement and Evaluation 1

continued

CHAPTER 5

Measuring Health-Related Physical Fitness and Physical Activity 104

continued

CHAPTER 6
Measuring Psychomotor Skills 171

CHAPTER 7

Measuring Cognitive Knowledge 251

continued

CHAPTER 9

Alternative Assessment 313

CHAPTER 12
Measurement and Evaluation in Activity-Based Settings 414

continued

Chapter 12, continued

*T*he fourth edition of *Measurement and Evaluation in Physical Education and Exercise Science* is intended to provide connections between theory and practice in the realm of measurement and evaluation in activity settings. The major focus of the book is to provide a practical approach to measurement and evaluation activities as they apply to physical education in the schools (K–12) as well as exercise science in nonschool settings.

A pervasive theme of the textbook is that measurement and evaluation activities should be an integral part of both physical education and exercise science activity settings and should enhance any program. In fact, no program can be of the best quality without effective measurement and evaluation strategies in place.

The book intends to provide basic introductory information concerning measurement and evaluation, examine measurement possibilities in the various learning domains (health-related physical fitness, psychomotor, cognitive, and affective domains), and how these measurement activities can be used to evaluate and improve programs in school and nonschool settings. The book clearly articulates the role of measurement and evaluation in program development and assessment.

The fourth edition continues to provide in-depth information concerning assessment in school settings while expanding information on measurement and evaluation of adults and older adults in activity-based programs. A new chapter, Chapter 9—*Alternative Assessment,* has been added along with major revisions in Chapter 1—*Introduction to Measurement and Evaluation,* Chapter 5—*Measuring Health-Related Physical Fitness Physical Activity,* Chapter 6—*Measuring Psychomotor Skills,* and Chapter 8—*Measuring Affective Behaviors.* Finally, Chapter 12—*Measurement and Evaluation in Activity-Based Settings*—synthesizes information from all preceding chapters to suggest practical assessment models applicable to school and nonschool settings.

The textbook as a whole has been updated and revised to reflect current trends, new tests, and technological advances. Chapter 1 includes upgrades on current trends including Healthy People 2010 initiatives and alternative assessment. Chapter 2 has been revised to include not only physical education curriculum development but also applications for activity-based program development and evaluation. This is an important chapter to emphasize the role of measurement and evaluation with program development and links directly with Chapter 12. In combination, these chapters provide a unique emphasis on practical development and application of measurement and evaluation models.

Based on the suggestions of reviewers, Chapter 3 has been broken into four sections—displaying your data, descriptive and the normal curve, correlation and regression, and tests for differences. Information has been added on multiple correlation/regression and 2-way ANOVA, and references for Microsoft Excel® and SPSS for Windows® are included. Chapter 4 addresses the critical issues of validity, reliability, and objectivity and a variety of administrative concerns that should be considered in test selection.

Chapter 5 has been largely rewritten and presents updated information on physical activity and physical fitness. Separated into two major sections, the first section of the chapter focuses on assessing health-related physical fitness and physical activity in K–12 populations. It includes upgraded information on the FITNESSGRAM, ACTIVITYGRAM, and the President's Challenge. A discussion is presented on process vs. product of fitness, various factors that impact fitness test performance, and implications for uses of fitness testing. Testing students with disabilities is also discussed. A second major section, written by Dr. Kristen Lagally, discusses fitness testing protocols for adults, including older adults. Purposes of fitness testing for adults, measurement techniques, and test batteries specific for adult populations are detailed. Chapter 6 has also been revised and split into two major sections. One section focuses on testing skill-related physical fitness while the other section highlights a variety of tests designed to test specific sports skills.

Chapter 7 addresses issues pertaining to the measurement of the cognitive domain and discusses the importance of this often overlooked area in school and non-school settings. Chapter 8 focuses on assessment of affective behaviors. This chapter has major revisions as some instruments were deleted and others added to make the information applicable to both school and nonschool settings. Measurement tools used in activity settings to assess attitudes toward physical activity, activity interests, motivation, self-concept, and social competence are included.

Chapter 9, written by Dr. Margo Coleman, is new to this edition and presents excellent information on alternative assessment strategies. Since alternative assessment (also known as authentic assessment) has become a very important topic in the last 5–10 years, this is a timely and important addition to the text. These assessment strategies offer viable alternatives to traditional assessment strategies. This chapter presents authentic assessment strategies, outlines how to write rubrics, and gives examples as to how these strategies can be used to measure health-related fitness, psychomotor, cognitive, and affective areas. Chapter 10 focuses on issues related to grading and includes a new section on assessing students with disabilities.

Chapter 11 emphasizes the use of systematic observation techniques to provide tools for self-evaluation of teaching and coaching. The use of such techniques in non-school settings is discussed. New information on the Behavioral Evaluation Strategy and Taxonomy (BEST) system is presented to illustrate usage of technology in evaluating instruction. Chapter 12 combines two former chapters from the third edition with a major revision featuring information on measurement and evaluation applications in non-school settings being new material. This chapter is organized into a major section focusing on assessment models in school settings that includes information on assessment of students with disabilities and teacher self-evaluation. A new section focusing on measurement and evaluation models applicable to adult fitness programs has been written by Dr. Kristen Lagally. This information is directly related to the major section that she authored in Chapter 5. Case studies are presented in both sections to illustrate practical application of material presented previously in the textbook.

As with the third edition, all chapters begin with concise objectives and a list of key words and conclude with a summary and a series of discussion questions designed to assist students in reviewing key points and synthesizing information presented. The fourth edition continues to be accompanied by an Instructors' Manual that includes a sample syllabus, discussion points, lecture topics, suggested student learning activities, and an updated test bank featuring fill-in-the-blank, true/false, and multiple choice questions for each chapter.

ACKNOWLEDGMENTS

*T*here are many individuals who have made contributions to this textbook. Without their help, all the revisions and updates in the fourth edition would not have been possible.

The efforts and suggestions made by each of the reviewers are certainly appreciated. Thanks to Bower L. Johnston, Jr. of Tennessee Tech University, Dave Fleming of University of Florida, and V. Dianne Ulibarri of Michigan State University. The contributions of reviewers of past editions are also acknowledged as well.

Benjamin Cummings has published the fourth edition of this textbook. Thanks to Deidre McGill and Michelle Cadden for their efforts in bringing this book to fruition. Appreciation is also extended to Janet Vail and her staff for their contributions in the production of the textbook.

Special acknowledgements must go to Margo Coleman and Kristen Lagally for providing their expertise in their contributions to this textbook. Dr. Lagally wrote major sections in Chapters 5 and 12 pertaining to measurement and evaluation of adult fitness, while Dr. Coleman is the author of Chapter 9 on alternative assessment. Both did an excellent job in their writing and also provided excellent counsel in other aspects of producing this textbook.

Thanks also to Gale Wheatley and Gayle White for their many contributions to the production of the text. Their work in securing permissions, making copies, proof-reading, mailing manuscripts, and in countless other tasks were invaluable to me. They were diligent, patient, and persistent in their work, and it is appreciated.

Finally, I want to acknowledge the contributions of my co-author, Doug Hastad, in the previous three editions of this textbook. Without his leadership, this textbook would never have come to fruition. Now serving as Chancellor of the University of Wisconsin—La Crosse, Doug's duties in this administrative role did not allow him to make new contributions to the fourth edition. Nevertheless, his work on past editions is very much alive in this edition. He has been a good friend and colleague, and I thank him for cajoling me into writing a book with him many years ago. Last but not least, I must acknowledge Dr. Robert Pangrazi, Dr. Paul Darst, and Dr. Chuck Corbin for their mentorship, friendship, and professional contributions that have so much influenced our work on not only this textbook but also in many other professional endeavors.

CHAPTER 1

Introduction to Measurement and Evaluation

Key Terms

alternative assessment

event tasks

evaluation

measurement

National Association for Sport and Physical Education (NASPE)

National Physical Education Standards: A Guide to Content and Assessment

Outcomes of Quality Physical Education Programs

parental reports

portfolio

qualitative

quantitative

reliability

student journals

test

validity

Objectives

1. Define and understand the relationship among test, measurement, and evaluation.
2. Discuss measurement and evaluation from a historical perspective.
3. Identify current trends that impact measurement and evaluation practices.
4. List and describe various ways that measurement and evaluation can be used in conjunction with student performance.
5. List and describe various ways that measurement and evaluation can be used in conjunction with teacher performance.
6. List and describe ways that measurement and evaluation can be used in activity-based settings outside the school.

As you begin reading this textbook, you probably have never had a class in measurement and evaluation. At your institution, it may be called "assessment." For purposes of this textbook, we will consider assessment and evaluation to mean the same thing. Whatever your class is called, this course will include important information for you to learn and understand. Measurement and evaluation are critical to program assessment and development. As a teacher, coach, athletic trainer, fitness instructor, or in some other activity-based profession, you will use measurement and evaluation to do your job and improve your program. In fact, whether you realize it or not, you use measurement and evaluation every day.

Here is an example of how you use measurement and evaluation. You probably have an alarm clock in your bedroom. Some of you probably could use more than one! When that alarm goes off in the morning and you squint open your eyes to see what time it is, you have just used measurement. The clock measures the time. If you decide you can push the snooze button and sleep a few more minutes, you have done an evaluation. You have looked at the measurement that the clock provides and evaluated that you can sleep ten more minutes and still make it to class on time. There are countless other ways you use measurement to make reasoned decisions in your daily routine. When you drive a car down the highway, you check the gas gauge to measure how much fuel you have left. You look at the road sign to see how far it is to the next town (another measurement) and evaluate when you need to fill your gasoline tank. Hopefully, you are getting the point that measurement and evaluation are integral to daily activities. Can you give another example of measurement and evaluation in your daily routine?

In every activity-based setting, measurement and evaluation are used. Think about how an exercise clinician uses measurement to plan an exercise program for a client and evaluate the progress of that individual. Athletic trainers have set protocols for evaluating injuries and use measurement to chart progress of their athlete's rehabilitation. Physical education teachers use fitness tests to measure components of fitness and make fitness evaluations based on the results. Coaches collect a variety of statistical information on their athletes and teams on which to base evaluation of performance. We hope you can begin to understand why the information that is going to be covered in this book is so important for you to incorporate in whatever activity-based profession you are pursuing

Measurement and evaluation practices should not be done as isolated activities. Rather they should always be done with a purpose in mind that is connected to the objectives and goals of your program. Measurement and evaluation should be integrated into the overall program and should enable activity-based professionals to make informed decisions related to their work.

As you can see from the examples above, measurement and evaluation are interrelated processes. Generally speaking, measurement is the task of administering a test for the purpose of obtaining a quantifiable score. The number of abdominal curls successfully completed in one minute, the distance run in 12 minutes, the number of questions answered correctly on a written examination, and the score attained on a personality inventory are some examples of **quantitative** information derived from measurement techniques. Assigning "very good" to an individual's performance or rating a team's performance on the basketball floor as "average" are examples of **qualitative** measurement information.

Physical educators and exercise scientists have at their disposal a variety of measurement tools to assist in the acquisition of useful data about performance in the psychomotor, fitness, cognitive, and affective domains. Improved testing procedures also assist administrators and supervisors in systematically quantifying information pertaining to program effectiveness. The wide variety of physical activity programs in nonschool settings has created multiple possibilities for measurement and evaluation techniques. Some of these applications require the use of sophisticated testing instruments and others rely on standard procedures already used in the school setting.

Evaluation refers to the translation of test results into meaningful information that will aid physical education and exercise science professionals in making judgments and unbiased decisions about the data obtained through measurement. Results of physical fitness testing that show below average performance by students may cause the physical education teacher to alter program offerings. Because of poor hitting, a baseball coach may decide to rotate his or her line-up. Similarly, an exercise physiologist may develop, after a particular testing protocol on the treadmill, a personalized exercise regimen for a client. In these cases, the results of measurement were used for evaluative purposes and the results of the evaluation caused a decision to be rendered and a change to occur.

Thus, evaluation translates test results into meaningful information. Measurement, evaluation, and decision making are intertwined. It is important that reliable, solid, objective measurement take place to be used in making sound evaluation upon which a decision can be based. Measurement precedes evaluation, and evaluation precedes decision making. With respect to physical education and exercise science, decisions need to be based on measurement techniques that can be carefully evaluated.

It is important to remember that physical education has gained a place of prominence and partnership with other facets of the educational curriculum in direct proportion to the development and refinement of its measurement and evaluation techniques. Likewise, activity programs in nonschool settings are rapidly attaining credibility in the area of health promotion and disease prevention. If physical education and nonschool exercise programs are to survive and flourish, it is imperative that physical educators and exercise specialists rely on measurement and evaluative techniques in the decision-making process.

Definitions of Test, Measurement, and Evaluation

Many terms in the area of measurement and evaluation are closely related, and terms may at times be used interchangeably and improperly in informal discussion. Though many terms will be introduced throughout this textbook, it is important to establish some operational definitions of basic terminology before embarking on further topics. It is critical for you to understand the interrelationships and differences between test, measurement, and evaluation.

Test

Three terms that are used interchangeably are *test, examination,* and *quiz*. Each of these words refers to a type of instrument or procedure that measures attributes or properties of an individual. In most subject areas, these terms refer to some type of paper-and-pencil instruments used to measure content knowledge. A "quiz" is most often thought of as a brief version of a test, while "examination" carries the connotation of a lengthy, comprehensive testing process.

In physical education, there is a need to test content knowledge, fitness levels, motor skills, and attitudes and feelings related to physical activity. Paper-and-pencil quizzes and examinations can certainly be administered in many circumstances, but because of the wide variety of areas to be measured, the term "test" is most appropriate for the majority of physical education situations. Thus, in this textbook, **test** is an all-encompassing term that refers to instruments, protocols, or techniques used to measure a quantity or quality of properties or attributes of interest. In physical education, properties or attributes included in areas such as cognitive knowledge, components of fitness, values, general motor skills, and motor skills specific to certain sports are subject to testing. Many types of tests may be effectively utilized in physical education settings. For example, students' knowledge of fitness concepts or understanding of a particular sport's rules and strategies may be measured with written tests. Certain questionnaires or inventories may be used to measure attitudes or feelings about physical activity. A shuttle run can measure agility; a 40-yard sprint can test running speed; the 12-minute run is commonly used to test cardiovascular endurance. Numerous tests have been designed to measure particular sports skills such as serving in tennis or dribbling in basketball.

Whatever test is chosen, it is crucial that it meet the criteria of being a valid and reliable test for the group being measured. The **reliability** of the test refers to the precision, consistency, or repeatability of the measurement, while the **validity** of a test is the degree to which it measures what it purports to measure. The concepts of validity and reliability will be discussed in detail in Chapter 4.

Measurement

After choosing or constructing an appropriate test, the next step is to administer the chosen measuring instrument. During the administration of this test, measurement takes place when a score is obtained. **Measurement** is the process of collecting data on the property or attribute of interest. Measurement should be as precise, reliable, and objective as possible, and the results expressed in a numerical form that indicates the quantity of the property or attribute being measured. If a multiple-choice test is administered on the rules and strategies of tennis, then the student's knowledge should be reflected by the score on the test. This score serves as a measurement of the individual student's knowledge of the topic. When a sprint is used as a test of running speed, the performance is measured by timing the trials. The final measurement in seconds will indicate how much running speed each particular sprinter possesses.

It is important to remember that an appropriate test must be chosen and properly administered before any confidence can be placed in the final measurement. Even a highly valid and reliable test will yield inaccurate measurements if the administration of the test is carried out under varied conditions. The environment of the test must be as controlled as possible, with a standardized plan of administration followed to ensure accuracy of measurement.

Evaluation

Evaluation is the process of interpreting the collected measurement and determining some worth or value. Evaluation can also be called assessment. The two terms are synonymous. Often this interpretation of worth will be done by comparing results to predetermined criteria or objectives. Without the availability of tests and the resulting measurements and norms to be used for comparison, the evaluative process would lack crucial information necessary for informed and impartial decisions.

Without the evaluative processes, the scores collected would have little value. With some tests, the criterion by which to judge the score is common knowledge. If a college sprinter runs 100 meters in 9.4 seconds, a value judgment, or evaluation, of this time can be made based on our knowledge of performances in this event. Evaluations resulting from measurements in other tests may not be as simple. On a treadmill stress test, a 45-year-old female is measured to have a maximal oxygen uptake of

60 millimeters of oxygen per kilogram of body weight. How would you evaluate that measurement? Is her cardiovascular condition good, fair, or bad?

By comparing the results of this test with similar scores, you would be able to evaluate the cardiovascular condition of this subject. However, without administering the test and completing the measurement, you would have no basis for evaluation. Thus, it becomes obvious that the selection of the test and the measurement process are integral to evaluation.

There is no substitute for good judgment and common sense in choosing the testing instrument and in attaining and evaluating the measurement. Though we strive for objectivity, evaluation is a judgment. If there were no place for judgment in the measurement and evaluation process, people could be replaced by computers. Nevertheless, there is no place for judgments that are made without supporting quantitative data in today's educational process.

Relationships Among Test, Measurement, and Evaluation

From the preceding definitions and accompanying discussion, it should be obvious that the terms *test, measurement,* and *evaluation* are interrelated but not synonymous. Tests are specific instruments of measurement. Administering the test is a process of measurement; without tests, measurement would be impossible. The quantitative data resulting from the test represent the measurement.

Measurement is a technique necessary for evaluation. Measurement represents status of a certain attribute or property and is a terminal process. Evaluation is a broader term representing a more complex process than the other two, and many times will be expressed in qualitative terms. Evaluation determines the extent to which objectives are met and is an ongoing and continuous process. By comparing measurements and comparing them to objectives, it is possible to form conclusions based on sound judgment and rationale to improve the quality of the activity-based program.

In summary, tests are tools or instruments of measurement; measurement is a major step in evaluation; and evaluation is an all-encompassing process that makes qualitative decisions based on quantitative data derived from tests and measurement.

Historical Perspective

The origin of testing and measurement coincides with that period of history often cited as the beginning of formal physical education, the mid-1800s. The appointment of Dr. Edward Hitchcock, in 1861, to the position of director of the department of hygiene and physical education at Amherst College gave academic status to the discipline of physical education. Of more important historical significance, Dr. Hitchcock's work in the science of anthropometrics (body symmetry and proportion) introduced a quantifiable and objective approach to physical education. The pioneer efforts of Hitchcock and other medical doctors turned physical educators marked the beginning of an era in which measurement was developed, implemented, and promoted.

1860–1900

During the period from 1860 to 1880, measurement techniques were most commonly used in the continued study of anthropometrics and the resulting longitudinal studies

Figure 1.1 Physical education class.

to develop normative data about the physical dimensions and growth patterns of youth. Dr. Dudley Sargent of Harvard University devised more than 40 different anthropometric measurements. While his research was used to describe the "typical" college male and female, Sargent went one step further in the process of using data: from obtained measurements, he prescribed a program of exercises for individuals. Although Sargent's efforts were reported in journals and in a manual on measurement and testing, his impact was greatest on American youth. His testing system was adopted by public schools, colleges, and the YMCA. There is no doubt that the use of measurement in physical education contributed to its rise to a more respected position in the overall educational scheme during the latter part of the nineteenth century.

Around 1880, the use of measurement in the field of physical education broadened to include more than the study of anthropometrics. The high interest in competitive athletics and strength development to improve performance caused leaders in physical education to focus attention on capacities of performance rather than on body symmetry. Sargent devised a battery of tests measuring the strength of the arms, legs, back, grip, and vital capacity. This test battery, known as the *Intercollegiate Strength Test*, became an integral component of intercollegiate competition.

As the medical profession made advances in the areas of cardiac and respiratory function, physical educators began to tap newly acquired knowledge and sought methods of testing the cardiovascular efficiency of the body. Results of these studies suggested a relationship between the functional capacity of the body during movement and the efficiency of the heart and circulatory system. From its birth in the late 1800s, assessment of the cardiorespiratory system has matured into one of the most vital areas associated with physical education.

1900–1940

In the beginning of the twentieth century, public schools and colleges began to introduce achievement tests into their curricula. Using tests for the purposes of assigning a grade and classifying students by skill level marked the beginning of an application practice widely used today (Figure 1.1). In the area of physical education, this period was marked by further refinement of strength testing and the onset of achievement tests. No longer was strength considered the prime factor in performance. Measures of muscular endurance and speed were found to be independent of strength and identified as variables that enhanced athletic performance. Test batteries that measured the endurance of various muscle groups were developed.

The 1920s were particularly significant for the area of measurement and evaluation. New statistical techniques were developed and more precise methods to construct tests became available. Reliability, validity, and objectivity of tests were enhanced. The development of tests to measure motor ability and capacity flourished. The public's increased interest in sport spawned a wide assortment of skills tests designed to measure selected components of athletic performance. Standards of performance once arbitrarily assigned were now clearly and accurately defined. Modern test construction continues to be modeled on what was learned in the 1920s.

The concept of measuring social skills was also introduced in the 1920s. Since physical education and sport programs claimed to positively affect the social competence of participants, efforts to measure such effects were necessary. Rating scales and inventories to assess social and moral attributes were developed. The assessment of social qualities is often overlooked, but is nevertheless a viable measurement area, important in the overall evaluation of physical education and sport programs.

1940–1980

World War II prompted a renewed national concern for physical fitness. College and public school physical education curricula responded to the need for physically fit citizens by shifting program emphasis from a sports orientation to physical training. Not surprisingly, a change in the focus of measurement in physical education accompanied this trend toward physical fitness. New physical fitness tests, developed at a rapid rate and designed to meet the needs of a nation at war, could be easily administered to large groups, and scores could be quickly tabulated and interpreted. While initially devised for the various branches of the armed forces, many items included in these test batteries evolved into appropriate tools for today's practitioner.

Though the major thrust in physical education and measurement techniques following World War II was away from fitness testing and back to a more eclectic course and study emphasis, the United States' involvement in the Korean conflict brought with it a resurgence of physical training of U.S. youth. Of greater programmatic significance, however, were the results of the Kraus-Weber tests of minimal muscular strength. These tests were used in a project that compared the minimum muscular strength of European and U.S. youth. The findings reported that U.S. youth were dramatically less fit than their European counterparts. The outgrowth of this study was the establishment of the President's Council on Youth Fitness and the development of the AAHPER (American Association for Health, Physical Education, and Recreation) Youth Fitness Test.

It is arguable that the successful launching of Sputnik I by the Soviets in 1957 had greater impact on U.S. education than any other single event in history. Almost overnight, schools shifted educational philosophy. Science courses quickly became the core of most academic programs. This trend, of course, prompted a rethinking about the place of nonscientific disciplines in the total curriculum. Physical education's place in the overall educational scheme was in jeopardy. In response to criticism about its apparent lack of a scientific knowledge base, and in an attempt to establish quantifiable evidence to retain programs, university physical education departments began undertaking various empirically based research projects. This research was aided by a dramatic increase in funding for facilities and equipment for scientific investigations during the 1960s. Further, graduate programs in physical education experienced rapidly increasing enrollments. These factors, coupled with advancing technology, contributed to the need for enhanced measurement and evaluation techniques in physical education.

In many respects, physical education prospered during the 1970s. Enrollment in school and college programs reached all-time highs. External and internal funds were available to support programs, and the demand for teachers remained high during the early part of the decade. Equipment used for measurement and evaluation became more sophisticated and reasonably priced. Physical education programs seemed secure, but this was not the case for long. The dawn of the 1980s brought with it declining enrollments, budget cuts, drastic decreases in federal and state grant funds, the elimination of school and college teaching positions, and a rethinking about how educational programs should be held accountable. State and local governments were under pressure to improve the quality of education for students. Physical education was not exempted from these eroding factors.

1980–Present

Physical education in the 1980s was characterized by relaxed requirements in the schools. Many school districts began to reduce the time devoted to physical education that once was a vital part of the curriculum. Fewer students in the United States were taking high school physical education than during the mid-1970s. The U.S. Centers for Disease Control (1991) reported that of a sample of students in grades 9–12 only 48 percent were enrolled in physical education classes during 1985. This compared to 65 percent in 1984 (*Chicago Tribune*, 1991). Not surprisingly, this trend was accompanied by a "dramatic decline in the fitness of the nation's youth" (AAHPERD, 1990, p. 1). The total enrollment of school-age youth reached its long-predicted low in the latter part of the decade. During this period the general public was demanding greater accountability of school boards and schools. Physical education programs needed to provide quantifiable evidence of demonstrated improvement and progress toward goals.

In the 1980s and early 1990s physical educators and exercise scientists began to establish clearer definitions for what it means to be physically fit and physically educated. Physical education and exercise programs began to encourage students and clients to develop higher levels of basic fitness and physical competence as needed for many work situations and active leisure participation. Improving student/client health-related fitness components of cardiorespiratory endurance, muscular strength and endurance, flexibility, and body composition became prominent goals. Beyond broadening the general public's understanding of what it means to be physically fit, exercise professionals and physical educators began to develop programs that would take into account variations in an individual's level of fitness. This meant more personal attention for clients and more focused exercise programs to attain specific goals. In addition to improving health-related fitness as measured by selected fitness tests, programs began to recognize the value of having clients and students better understand the importance of being physically fit (NASPE, 1995). Programs developed written materials that better described the why and how of fitness. The ultimate goal was no longer to simply develop fitness. Rather, it was becoming increasingly important to assist the student and client in developing the ability and willingness to accept responsibility for personal fitness. Measurement and evaluation were critical procedures in this process.

Today, activity-based programs must justify their existence with quantifiable outcomes—no longer are we able to develop or continue programs that are supported only on philosophical beliefs and professional opinion. To this end, physical educators and exercise scientists must seek and properly use methods and techniques to gather data to support programs. During the past 125 years, activity-based professions have taken great steps forward, and many of these steps coincided with advances in research, measurement, and evaluation. To continue to progress, practitioners must recognize the importance of measurement and evaluation techniques in developing effective physical education programs, promoting adult health and fitness programs, and generally moving the American public toward a more active lifestyle. Intervention in the early years will facilitate the commitment to an active and healthy lifestyle.

Current Trends

While measurement and evaluation in physical education and exercise science has had a somewhat fragmented history, a clearer perspective of the purpose of measurement and evaluation in the educational scheme is emerging. Current events suggest that physical education and other physical activity-based programs are at a crossroads. Reacting properly and with expediency to current trends could greatly solidify the position of physical education within the educational experience and further broaden exercise science's extension into the private sector. Understandably, measurement and evaluation play important roles in the response to each trend.

Public Health Initiatives

Professionals in all activity-based professions are impacted by public health initiatives. In many cases, these initiatives provide powerful rationale for our programs and dovetail nicely with programmatic objectives. The most recent national initiative is *Healthy People 2010* (U.S. Department of Health and Human Services, 2000), which includes a comprehensive health promotion and disease prevention agenda. It is designed to improve the health of all people in the United States during the first decade of the twenty-first century. Like the preceding *Healthy People 2000* (U.S. Department of Health and Human Services, 1990) initiative, *Healthy People 2010* is committed to a single, overarching purpose: promoting health and preventing illness, disability, and premature death

Healthy People 2010 builds on initiatives pursued over the past two decades. In 1979, *Healthy People: The Surgeon General's Report on Health Promotion and Disease Prevention* provided national goals for reducing premature deaths and preserving independence for older adults. In 1980 another report, *Promoting Health/Preventing Disease: Objectives for the Nation*, set forth 226 targeted health objectives for the nation to achieve over the next 10 years. *Healthy People 2000: National Health Promotion and Disease Prevention Objectives*, released in 1990, identified health improvement goals and objectives to be reached by the year 2000. The *Healthy People 2010* initiative continues in this tradition as an instrument to improve health for the first decade of the twenty-first century.

Healthy People 2010 is designed to increase quality and years of healthy life and eliminate health disparities. One of the major focus areas is physical activity. Regular physical activity throughout life is important for maintaining a healthy body, enhancing psychological well-being, and preventing premature death. In 1999, 65 percent of adolescents engaged in the recommended amount of physical activity. In 1997, only 15 percent of adults performed the recommended amount of physical activity, and 40 percent of adults engaged in no leisure-time physical activity (U.S. Department of Health and Human Services, 2000).

Regular physical activity is associated with lower death rates for adults of any age, even when only moderate levels of physical activity are performed. Regular physical activity decreases the risk of death from heart disease, lowers the risk of developing diabetes, and is associated with a decreased risk of colon cancer. Regular physical activity helps prevent high blood pressure and helps reduce blood pressure in persons with elevated levels.

Professionals in all activity-based professions should be aware of this public initiative. Promoting activity to improve the health status of our society should be a goal of both school and nonschool programs. Linkage of programmatic goals to the goals of initiatives such as this can be very advantageous in promoting the accomplishments of your program. Funding sources in the form of grants may be available to enhance the budgets of your operation. Physical educators and exercise scientists can use measurement and evaluation strategies to illustrate how they can contribute to meeting the goals of this ambitious public health agenda.

Increased Accountability for School-Based Programs

The verification of educational attainment is an essential application of measurement and evaluation. The 1990s witnessed a renewal of eductional reform. At the heart of this revival is the public's growing interest in greater educational effectiveness. For example, never before in the history of education have legislators, boards of education, and the general public placed such a premium on the quality of student that schools and colleges produce. Most states are requiring undergraduate students to pass preprofessional exams before entering the sequence of teacher preparation courses; states are implementing competency tests for certified teachers; and local boards are demanding that teachers be held accountable for their performance and the achievement of their students. Declining physical fitness scores, increasing numbers of obese individuals, and poor health habits do little to exempt physical education from critical review.

In response to the demand for increased accountability and to strengthen curricular offerings in physical education, the **National Association for Sport and Physical Education (NASPE)** sponsored a project resulting in **Outcomes of Quality Physical Education Programs** (1992) that includes 20 outcome statements (Box 1.1) culminating in a definition of a physically educated person. The definition includes five major focus areas, specifying that a physically educated person has learned skills necessary to perform a variety of physical activities, is physically fit, participates in regular physical activity, knows the implications of and the benefits from involvement in physical activities, and values physical activity and its contribution to a healthful lifestyle.

Follow-up work to the Outcomes Project has been the development and adoption of the *Moving into the Future: National Physical Education Standards: A Guide to Content and Assessment* (1995). Content standards from this document are shown in Box 1.2. Content standards specify what students should know and be able to do and are roughly equivalent to "student learning outcomes" or "student objectives." These

Box 1.1 Outcome statements from the National Association for Sport and Physical Education (NASPE) Outcomes Project.

The physically educated person:

- **HAS learned skills necessary to perform a variety of physical activities**
1. . . . moves using concepts of body awareness, space awareness, effort, and relationships.
2. . . . demonstrates competence in a variety of manipulative, locomotor, and non-locomotor skills.
3. . . . demonstrates competence in combinations of manipulative, locomotor, and nonlocomotor skills performed individually and with others.
4. . . . demonstrates competence in many different forms of physical activity.
5. . . . demonstrates proficiency in a few forms of physical activity.
6. . . . has learned how to learn new skills.

- **IS physically fit**
7. . . . assesses, achieves, and maintains physical fitness.
8. . . . designs safe, personal fitness programs in accordance with principles of training and conditioning.

- **DOES participate regularly in physical activity**
9. . . . participates in health-enhancing physical activity at least three times a week.
10. . . . selects and regularly participates in lifetime physical activities.

- **KNOWS the implications of and the benefits from involvement in physical activities**
11. . . . identifies the benefits, costs, and obligations associated with regular participation in physical activity.
12. . . . recognizes the risk and safety factors associated with regular participation in physical activity.
13. . . . applies concepts and principles to the development of motor skills.
14. . . . understands that wellness involves more than being physically fit.
15. . . . knows the rules, strategies, and appropriate behaviors for selected physical activities.
16. . . . recognizes that participation in physical activity can lead to multicultural and international understanding.
17. . . . understands that physical activity provides the opportunity for enjoyment, self-expression, and communication.

- **VALUES physical activity and its contributions to a healthful lifestyle**
18. . . . appreciates the relationships with others that result from participation in physical activity.
19. . . . respects the role that regular physical activity plays in the pursuit of life-long health and well-being.
20. . . . cherishes the feelings that result from regular participation in physical activity.

Reprinted from Outcomes of Quality Physical Education Programs (1992) with permission from the National Association for Sport and Physical Education (NASPE), 1900 Association Drive, Reston, VA 20191-1599.

Box 1.2 Content standards in physical education.

A physically educated student:
1. Demonstrates competency in many and proficiency in a few movement forms.
2. Applies movement concepts and principles to the learning and development of motor skills.
3. Exhibits a physically active lifestyle.
4. Achieves and maintains a health-enhancing level of physical fitness.
5. Demonstrates responsible personal and social behavior in physical activity settings.
6. Demonstrates understanding and respect for differences among people in physical activity settings.
7. Understands that physical activity provides opportunities for enjoyment, challenge, self-expression, and social interaction.

From *Moving into the Future: National Physical Education Standards: A Guide to Content and Assessment* (1995) published by the National Association for Sport and Physical Education.

---

content standards, sample benchmarks, and assessment examples have been developed for grades K–12 at two-year intervals. An example of Content Standard #1 for the fourth grade is given in Box 1.3. Since standards are of little use without precise guidelines to judge whether they have been achieved, NASPE has provided teachers with valid and reliable methods of assessing student progress toward attaining the standards. A major benefit of comprehensive standards and accompanying assessments is that they provide strong rationale that physical education is not "academically soft." The standards show the uninformed that there are meaningful and important areas of achievement in physical education and that these levels of achievement can be measured. These projects provide in-depth illustration of how curricular goals and assessment should be aligned so that the measurement and evaluation activities are relevant and meaningful to students.

Box 1.3 Fourth Grade Content Standard #1, Benchmarks, and Assessment Examples.

1. Demonstrates competency in many movement forms and proficiency in a few movements forms.

Fourth grade students should be able to demonstrate refined fundamental patterns. Attainment of mature motor patterns for the basic locomotor, nonlocomotor, and selected isolated manipultive skills (throwing, catching, striking) is an expected exit outcome for fourth grade students. Variations of skills and skill combinations are performed in increasingly dynamic and complex environments (e.g., performing manipulative tasks while dodging, performing a gymnastics sequence with a partner, performing a formal dance to music). In addition, students should be able to acquire some specialized skills basic to a movement form (i.e., basketball chest pass, soccer dribble, fielding a softball with a glove) and to use those skills with a partner.

Box 1.3 continued

The emphasis for the fourth grade student is to:

- Demonstrate mature form in all locomotor patterns and selected manipulative and nonlocomotor skills.
- Adapt a skill to the demands of a dynamic, unpredictable environment.
- Acquire beginning skills of a few specialized movement forms.
- Combine movement skills in applied settings.

Sample Benchmarks:

1. Throws, catches, and kicks using mature form.
2. Dribbles and passes a basketball to a moving receiver.
3. Balances with control on a variety of objects (balance board, large apparatus, skates).
4. Develops and refines a gymnastics sequence demonstrating smooth transitions.
5. Develops and refines a creative dance sequence in a repeatable pattern.
6. Jumps and lands for height/distance using mature form.

Assessment Examples:

1. Teacher observation—observational record.

Students are asked to receive and send a basketball pass to a partner on the move. The teacher observes the passing and uses a checklist to annotate the performance.

Criteria for Assessment:

a. Receives the pass and sends it in one motion.
b. Passes ahead of the moving player (receiver does not have to stop).
c. Receiving student cuts into a space to receive the pass.

2. Event task—observational record

Students are asked to combine a balance, a roll, and a traveling action into a gymnastics sequence. The sequence must include all the components and a clear beginning and ending.

Criteria for Assessment:

a. Exhibits a balance, a roll, and a traveling action during the performance.
b. Demonstrates a clear beginning and ending to the sequence.
c. Demonstrates smooth transitions between the various skills.

3. Peer observation

Have partners observe the preparatory phase of a designated skill in an attempt to ascertain the correct use of critical elements. For example, student A will throw a ball toward a target 5 times using the overhand pattern while student B observes the performance, focusing on a single critical element during the preparatory phase (e.g., opposite foot forward, side to target, arm pulled way back). The observing student gives a "thumb up" if the critical element is correct; if incorrect, the observing student tells what is needed to improve the movement.

Criteria for Assessment:

a. Thrower displays the critical element that is the focus of the observation.
b. Observer makes an accurate judgment on the performance.

Reprinted from Outcomes of Quality Physical Education Programs (1992) with permission from the National Association for Sport and Physical Education (NASPE), 1900 Association Drive, Reston, VA 20191-1599.

Alternative Assessments

While traditional assessment of physical fitness, sport skills, knowledge, and psychosocial characteristics still should be utilized, alternative assessment techniques are being implemented to complement or sometimes replace traditional written, fitness, or skills testing. A short description of a sampling of alternative assessment strategies as detailed in the NASPE (1995) document follows.

Portfolios are collections of a student's work assembled over time. They include various pieces of evidence documenting student achievement of a goal. If the goal was to learn to play soccer, a portfolio might include such things as evidence of playing on a recreational team, a list of drills practiced at home three times a week, a videotape of game play, a critique of offensive and defensive strategies observed in a soccer game, etc.

Parental reports provide a record of student participation of some form of out-of-class performance. These reports may refer to play choices, purposeful practice, formal activities such as sports clubs or lessons in a sport, or family activities. They can include anecdotal information and the signature of the person who observed the out-of-class performance.

Event tasks are performance tasks that can be completed within 50 minutes. The task is written broadly enough so that there are a variety of correct answers or solutions. An example might be to have a group of students develop a tumbling routine that could serve as a demonstration of skills learned in physical education or plan a five-minute routine that could be presented in a school assembly.

Student journals provide a student record of participation, results, feelings, and perceptions about events. Entries should be made on a regular basis and serve as indicators of success, failure, enjoyment, or other intangible products of participation. Entries should not be judged as right or wrong, as students describe both positive and negative experiences. Self-analysis and reflections about personal performance are often included. This type of activity can provide valuable insight about students' social and psychological perspective concerning their participation and performance in activity.

The four alternative assessment techniques described above are examples of a variety of alternative assessment methods presented in the NASPE (1995) document. A detailed discussion of these and other alternative assessment strategies is presented in Chapter 9.

Rapid Technological Advancements

The continuous development of software and hardware technologies continues to open new possibilities for measurement and evaluation to be utilized. Undoubtedly, by the time this textbook is published, new technologies will have been introduced that impact the professional lives of physical educators, athletic trainers, fitness leaders, and other exercise science professionals. Forbus and Fiorentino (2001) suggest that technology can be considered from three perspectives: hardware, software, and networks. Each type is distinct, yet depends on the others. Hardware includes mainframes, servers, desktop computers, laptop computers, and handheld computers. Digital and video cameras and various types of projection systems can also be classified as hardware. Software is defined as computer programs that perform specific functions. Networks include local area networks (LANs) that allow users to interface and exchange files. The Internet is a network of networks and the World Wide Web has revolutionized our access to information.

Physiological responses can be readily monitored by electronic apparatus. Using sophisticated scientific equipment to obtain computer-generated readouts of heart rate, oxygen consumption, blood pressure, and other variables associated with cardiovascular efficiency is becoming a common learning experience for undergraduate students. Improvements in the area of high-speed cinematography, e.g., allowing simultaneous computer analysis of movement in several planes, are responsible for the rapid advancement of knowledge of motor behavior and biomechanics. Human performance laboratories at colleges and universities are strengthening teaching and research components of physical education programs through the acquisition of laboratory equipment (Figure 1.2).

Outside of exercise science laboratories, many products based on technology have been developed for the practitioner. Contemporary

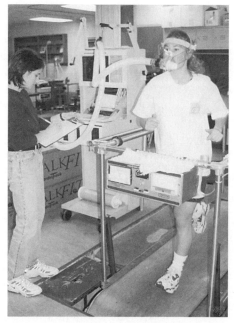

Figure 1.2 Human performance laboratory, University of Wisconsin—LaCrosse.

physical education programs use technology in such ways as recording data and providing fitness profiles for students, utilizing heart rate monitors to measure and provide feedback about the duration and intensity of activity, providing nutrition software for individual dietary analysis, and skinfold calipers that provide a digitized reading of body composition measures. Exercise equipment has become increasingly sophisticated with elliptical trainers, treadmills, and bicycle ergometers providing a variety of statistical data that measures the amount of work being accomplished on the workout apparatus.

Powerful desktop and laptop personal computers provide opportunities for such tasks as word processing, using spreadsheets, creating charts and graphs with ease, and preparing materials for presentations. Many professionals are beginning to utilize hand-held computers to help them be more efficient in their work as well. Specialized software packages have been developed for record keeping in athletic training, for collecting data on teacher and student behaviors in physical education settings, and for collecting game and seasonal statistical data for athletic teams in a variety of sports. The sophisticated technology that is available today and being developed for tomorrow clearly impacts the ways that measurement and evaluation strategies can be incorporated into all activity-based settings.

Continued Growth of Activity-Based Programs

In recent years there has been a marked trend toward the establishment of enterprises offering directed programs of exercise. Private health clubs, fitness centers, and exercise studios have targeted the sedentary adult population as a viable market. Many corporations and businesses have established extensive on-site workout facilities for their employees. Exercise and wellness programs are often linked with local hospitals and sports medicine clinics. Undergraduate and graduate programs in fitness leadership have flourished in response to this trend. Students in these programs are usually required to successfully complete a program of study in exercise science. Central to the program is a course in measurement and evaluation. It is important to respond to the expanding perspectives on physical education and the variety of nonteaching careers that are available to students in movement-based programs.

Providing personalized testing and evaluation on selected human performance parameters is a vital aspect of many of these programs. The types of assessment procedures vary from simple fitness and psychomotor tests to sophisticated protocols such as underwater weighing, submaximal stress tests, and, in some cases, blood analysis. Whatever the type, personal health evaluation is an essential and attractive feature of most nonschool physical activity-based programs. Chapter 12 provides a broader discussion of measurement and evaluation in the nonschool setting.

Use of Systematic Observation Instruments

The use of systematic observation instrumentation, which will be discussed in detail in Chapter 11, has contributed more quantifiable information about teacher and student behavior than any other measurement technique. The development of descriptive analytic techniques has enabled physical educators to collect and isolate specific objective data about such teacher and student behaviors as appropriateness, productivity, activity, management, negative reactions, and rates of information feedback. Systematic observation relies on procedures that measure the number of events, duration of the events, and/or occurrence of events over time. Specifically, systematic observation allows a trained person following stated guidelines and procedures to observe, record, and analyze interactions with the assurance that others viewing the same sequence of events would agree with the recorded data. There are a number of systems currently being used throughout the country to analyze teacher and student behaviors during organized physical activity. These types of systems can be used effectively for self-evaluation purposes.

Uses of Measurement and Evaluation in Physical Education

It would be impossible to have quality physical education without utilizing measurement and evaluation strategies. Good teachers should test continuously to measure and evaluate in order to gain insights about student progress and the effectiveness of instruction. The process of measurement and evaluation is not an end unto itself. Everything in a program should have a purpose, with the measurement providing data with which to evaluate predetermined objectives. Student outcomes can be measured and evaluated in relation to objectives concerning skills, fitness, knowledge, and values included in the curriculum. Program effectiveness, including teaching behaviors and curricular offerings, can also be evaluated based on this information. With this perspective established, more specific uses of measurement and evaluation regarding student and teacher performance in physical education can be detailed.

Student Performance

Measurement undertaken in conjunction with student performance can take many forms, with tests running the gamut from simple to complex. Whatever the scope of the measurement, a certain amount of data is critical to giving both the teacher and the student needed information about whether objectives are being met. The effective teacher can use measurement in a variety of ways to have an impact on the student.

Diagnosis In certain physical education settings, it is appropriate to use measurement tools for diagnosis of specific student competencies. By diagnosing weaknesses, the teacher is able to concentrate on these areas to help the student learn. Diagnosis is obviously important in improving motor skills and in pinpointing cognitive areas that need to be emphasized and can be effective in areas concerning health-related physical fitness. Perhaps more important, it can enable the teacher to plan and instruct more effectively. It furnishes the teacher information with which to formulate objectives and determine curricular content. If particular weaknesses surface, remedial programs can be prescribed after the students are assessed.

Classification Related to the issue of diagnosis is the measurement strategy of classification. From an educational standpoint, it is sometimes advantageous to divide students into either homogeneous or heterogeneous groups based on some attribute. An obvious example of this is in sport when coaches use performance to group players into teams (e.g., varsity, junior varsity). Certain units of instruction might be taught most effectively to groups of students with similar abilities, while other units of instruction may be taught more effectively if student groups comprise a wide range of abilities. Decisions regarding classification by group are based on the teacher's philosophy, unit objectives, the nature of the unit, and the type of students involved.

Achievement Perhaps the most important role of measurement is that of determining student achievement. Achievement is not to be confused with improvement. Achievement refers to the final ability level at a designated point in time, often coinciding with the end of a unit. The measurement of achievement is normally made relative to some standard or criterion.

The achievement of an individual student gives information to the teacher and student about the level of performance. The collective achievement of a group or class of students supplies data needed to evaluate teacher effectiveness and determine whether the objectives of the program are being met.

Improvement Improvement is the difference in performance between an initial point and a later point in time. Improvement may be measured over the length of an individual unit, semester, or year. Information concerning improvement in a given area can be valuable to both the teacher and the student. It is particularly encouraging for a student with low initial levels of a certain attribute to be able to measure his or her progress.

Assessing improvement is a viable role of measurement and, in some instances, can be implemented into a grading scheme. However, the teacher must be aware of the inequities of grading on improvement in the case of students who exhibit outstanding initial performance levels and so may not be able to show dramatic gains. It would seem that the best reason to measure improvement is to provide encouragement and information on performance to less skilled members of the group.

Motivation   Measurement of different facets of physical education can provide an important motivation factor. For example, if skill tests are given at the beginning and end of a unit, many students will be motivated to try to improve their performance scores. Likewise, if an examination on rules and strategies of a sport is announced, this may motivate students to learn material that they might not otherwise study.

There are occasions when physical educators encourage students to monitor their performance levels through self-testing activities. For example, youngsters could be encouraged to complete some or all of the items included on a health-related fitness test battery. Self-assessment of levels of performance on the distance run, skinfold, sit-and-reach, sit-up, or pull-up tests is a useful approach to keep students up-to-date on their progress toward goals. A word of caution should be mentioned. Educators must always be aware of the situation in which a student might become frustrated by the lack of improvement and/or poor performance. If a student is not meeting personal expectations or is obviously deficient compared to classmates, the process of measuring this weakness might serve to discourage rather than to motivate the student.

Teacher Performance

Measurement and evaluation can perform a variety of roles in relation to the performance of the teacher. Determining grades, assessing improvement, and motivating students are a few examples of ways in which measurement and evaluation can aid teacher effectiveness. Teachers can utilize measurement procedures to evaluate their students, themselves, and their programs. A competent teacher views this process as a way to evaluate students in a fair and consistent manner and as a vehicle for program development and an opportunity for professional growth.

Assignment of Grades   When measurement and evaluation are mentioned, most physical educators immediately think of the grading process, since measurement is used for grading more than for any other purpose. Grades should convey a sense of achievement and status as compared with the stated objectives of the curriculum. The construction/selection of proper measuring instruments to gather information on students becomes integral to the grading process.

The teacher should have a strong rationale and supporting evidence to justify why certain grades are assigned to particular students. There are several methods of grading, and setting up an equitable system to assign grades is not a task to be undertaken lightly. Chapter 10 examines the many facets of grading to be considered by the physical education teacher. The point to be made at this time is that assignment of grades in an accountable manner is a major component of teacher performance. Without measurement and evaluation procedures, this would be impossible.

Evaluation of Units of Instruction   Student achievement in individual units of instruction may be measured and compared with the predetermined objectives of the unit. The teacher is then able to make an evaluation of the unit based on this information. This evaluation may affect several areas. Teaching performance comes under scrutiny; if students did not achieve as well as was expected, then course content and teaching methods may need to be altered; or perhaps the objectives of the unit need to be modified to reflect more realistic expectations. All instruments used for measurement during the unit should be examined to determine if they accurately assess student achievement.

Evaluation of the Curriculum   The cumulative evaluation of the individual units in comparison with general or global curricular objectives provides information for teachers and administrators to use in assessing the effectiveness of the overall program. This broad-based evaluation may result in modifying the length of a unit, adding or dropping a unit from the curriculum, forming the rationale for procuring equipment and/or facilities, or justifying the request for additional faculty members.

The evaluation of curriculum should be ongoing, and the results of the process should be incorporated into the program. A curriculum must be continually modified to meet the changing needs of students. If a program is allowed to continue the status quo, then it runs the chance of becoming stagnant and outdated. Constant fine-tuning can help ensure a dynamic physical education curriculum based on sound education philosophy. Without a solid measurement and evaluation foundation, this process cannot be effective.

Teacher Effectiveness   Measurement instruments may be utilized to determine teacher effectiveness by assessing student performance or by direct observation of the teaching–learning setting. If a majority of students fails to meet desired objectives in a unit, then certainly teacher effectiveness could be questioned. However, valid reasons other than the effectiveness of the teacher may contribute to this situation. A particularly unskilled group of students and/or unrealistic objectives could be the root of the problem. No doubt, the teaching style and resultant learning environment that is created should be evaluated on a regular basis as well, regardless of levels of student achievement. This assessment may be in the form of a self-evaluation, peer evaluation, or formal evaluation by an administrator.

With the advent of systematic observation instrumentation, behaviors of teachers in the teaching–learning environment can be observed, coded, and quantified. This type of measurement offers objective insights to teachers by which they can evaluate and improve their teaching style. Teaching behaviors such as the praise-to-scold ratio, use of first names and instructional feedback, and management of time can be crucial to creating an environment in which students have the best chance for success.

Student behaviors as they relate to teaching effectiveness may also be measured. For example, time on task has been identified as a crucial element of learning, so it is possible now to measure the amount of time that students are actively engaged in appropriate versus inappropriate activities. Student interactions may also be observed and quantified.

Traditionally, teacher effectiveness was measured by subjective means such as rating scales and anecdotal records. With the development of objective observation systems, these subjective methods are of limited value. Chapter 11 is devoted to a thorough discussion of systematic observation of teacher and student behaviors.

Public Relations   Physical educators should use every opportunity to publicize the contributions that a quality physical education program can make. If by using measurement it can be demonstrated that the program is meeting worthwhile objectives, continued support for physical education is more likely. It is well worth the effort to publicize outstanding fitness scores of physical education students to other students, administrators, parents, and the general community. Physical educators should take advantage of every chance to justify their place in the curriculum of contemporary schools.

Uses of Measurement and Evaluation In Nonschool Settings

You just finished reading about uses of measurement and evaluation in school settings. If you skipped over that part because you are not planning to teach, you need to go back and review this section. The basic uses of measurement and evaluation are applicable in any activity-based setting. Though there may be specific learning domains and objectives for physical education programs in schools, many of the same domains and objectives are transferable to other activity-based settings as well. Many academic programs are preparing professionals in such fields as athletic training, cardiac rehabilitation, fitness leadership, sports management, and therapeutic recreation. Graduates from such programs can be employed in hospital settings, sports medicine clinics, community recreation programs, private fitness clubs, corporate fitness settings, university wellness programs, and many other activity-based settings.

Similar to measurement and evaluation strategies in school settings, the professional in nonschool activity settings will need to diagnose and classify the clients. A variety of measurement protocols are specific to athletic training as well as to exercise settings. Baseline levels of performance will need to be established using valid and reliable testing procedures. Similarly, improvements in performance must be monitored using appropriate measurement and evaluation procedures. Based on this improvement, a client's exercise program may be modified or a patient's rehabilitation regimen can be changed or discontinued. Certainly, the client or patient can be motivated by periodic feedback on his or her performance. This motivation will hopefully lead to high levels of adherence to regular activity patterns.

Measurement and evaluation strategies must also be used for effective administration of a program. Employee performance must be evaluated. Facility usage is an important area to measure and evaluate. Just as in physical education, data carefully collected from your programs can be used to effectively market and promote your efforts. Finally, it is crucial to support budgetary requests with statistical data to justify the requests. Without this type of justification, it will be very difficult to garner additional resources for your program. Without carefully planned and administered measurement and evaluation procedures, it is impossible to have a quality program. It is absolutely critical that you incorporate appropriate testing protocols into your program and use the collected data to make informed administrative decisions. Chapters 5 and 12 will provide more specific details about measurement and evaluation in activity-based settings outside the school.

SUMMARY

The purpose of this chapter is to provide an overview and orientation to the interconnections of measurement and evaluation practices in delivering quality activity-based programs in school and nonschool settings. Definitions of *test, measurement,* and *evaluation* and their interdependent nature are presented and are crucial for you to understand.

An historical background of measurement and evaluation in our field is given to provide you with an understanding of the development of assessment, as we know it today. Current trends that directly influence the importance of sound measurement and evaluation practices are also discussed.

The multifaceted uses of measurement and evaluation in quality K–12 physical education programs are examined from the perspective of both student performance and teacher performance. Similarly, the multiple uses of measurement and evaluation in nonschool activity-based programs are also presented. Parallels between their uses in school versus nonschool programs are illustrated

No matter which activity-based profession you are interested in, it is hoped that the crucial nature of the role of measurement and evaluation in the physical education and exercise science professions will become increasingly clear as you progress through this textbook. The ability to appropriately use sound measurement and evaluation protocols and procedures is critical for you to be successful in your chosen activity-based profession.

Discussion Questions

1. How did the work of Edward Hitchcock and Dudley Sargent contribute to the development of measurement and evaluation in physical education from 1860 until the turn of the twentieth century?

2. What is the interrelationship between test, measurement, and evaluation?

3. What significant events in history had an impact on the evolution of measurement and evaluation procedures from 1900 to 1970?

4. What were the significant events in the 1970s, 1980s, and 1990s in which the measurement and evaluation process helped portray the fitness status of our nation's school-age youth?

5. What current trends have a direct relationship to the importance of measurement and evaluation in physical education and exercise science?

6. What is the role of measurement and evaluation in assessing student performance in physical education?

7. How can measurement and evaluation procedures be used in relation to the performance of the teacher?

8. How can measurement and evaluation procedures be used in exercise and sport settings outside the school?

References

American Alliance for Health, Physical Education, Recreation, and Dance (1992). *Outcome of quality physical education programs*. Reston, VA: AAHPERD.

American Alliance for Health, Physical Education, Recreation, and Dance (1990). Poor student test scores give boost to fitness education awareness in California. *Update*, p. 1, March.

Centers for Disease Control (1991). Participation of high school students in school physical education—United States, 1990. *Morbidity and Mortality Weekly Report* 40: 607–615.

Chicago Tribune. (1991). Physical education classes shrinking. *Chicago Tribune*, p. 22, September 8.

Forbus, W., and Fiorentino, L. (2001). Two approaches for acquiring technology skills in professional practice programs. *The Chronicle of Physical Education in Higher Education*, 12(2): 3, 14–15, May.

Melagrano, V. J. (1994). Portfolio assessment: Documenting authentic student learning. *Journal of Physical Education, Recreation, and Dance* 65: 50–61.

National Association for Sport and Physical Education (1995). Moving into the future: National Standards for Physical Education. St. Louis: Mosby.

U.S. Department of Health and Human Services. *Healthy People 2010: Understanding and Improving Health.* 2nd ed. Washington, DC: U.S. Government Printing Office, November 2000.

U. S. Department of Health and Human Services. (1990). *Promoting health/ preventing disease: Year 2000 objectives for the nation.* Washington, DC: Author.

U.S. Department of Health and Human Services (1990). *Standards and criteria for the development and evaluation of comprehensive federal physical fitness programs.* Washington, DC: U.S. Department of Health and Human Services.

Zessoules, R., and Gardner, H. (1991). Authentic assessment: Beyond the buzzword and to the classroom. In V. Perrone (Ed.), *Expanding student assessment* (pp. 47–71). Alexandria, VA: Association for Supervision and Curriculum Development.

REPRESENTATIVE READINGS

Baumgartner, T., and Jackson, A. (1999). *Measurement for evaluation in physical education and exercise science.* 6th ed. Boston: WCB/McGraw-Hill.

Johnson, B. L., and Nelson, J. K. (1986). *Practical measurements for evaluation in physical education.* 4th ed. Minneapolis, MN: Burgess.

Kraus, H., and Hirschland, R. P. (1954). Minimum muscular fitness tests in school children. *The Research Quarterly* 25: 178–188.

Miller D. K. (2001). *Measurement by the physical educator: Why and how.* 4th ed. Boston: WCB/McGraw-Hill.

Morrow, J., Jackson, A., Disch, J., and Mood, D. (2000). *Measurement and evaluation in human performance.* 2nd ed. Champaign. IL: Human Kinetics Press.

Nelson, M. A. (1991). The role of physical education and children's activity in the public health. *Research Quarterly for Exercise and Sport* 62: 148–150.

Pangrazi, R. P. (2001). *Dynamic physical education for elementary school children.* 13th ed. Boston: Allyn and Bacon.

Ross, J. G., and Pate, R. R. (1987). The national children and youth fitness study II: A summary of findings. *JOPERD* 58(9): 51–56.

Symons, C. W., and Gascoigne, J. L. (1990). The nation's health objectives—A means to schoolwide fitness advocacy. *JOPERD* 61(6): 59–63.

CHAPTER 2

Linking Program Development with Measurement and Evaluation

Key Terms

activity interest surveys

affective domain

cognitive domain

curriculum development

health-related physical fitness domain

learning domain

mission statement

needs assessment

outcome statements

performance-based objectives

physical fitness

program goals

psychomotor domain

sports-related fitness

unit outcomes

Objectives

1. Characterize the four learning domains associated with physical education and exercise science and analyze them from the perspective of different activity settings.
2. Understand how to plan a needs assessment and cite occasions for use.
3. Identify and describe the five steps of program development and understand the role of measurement and evaluation in this process.
4. Distinguish relationships among program goals, outcome statements, and performance-based objectives.
5. Discuss the ongoing nature of the program development process.
6. Articulate the relationship of measurement and evaluation procedures to program development.

When preparing for a career in physical education or exercise science professions, measurement and evaluation are typically not something that you consider when you think of preparatory coursework. However, understanding the basic tenets of measurement and evaluation and incorporating them into your professional life is fundamental to being productive. Whatever activity-based profession you may enter, you simply cannot do your job without measurement and evaluation. The assessment activities that you do with individual students/clients are one important area of measurement and evaluation, but the crucial nature of incorporating these types of activities into program assessment, development, and improvement is often not recognized by professionals in activity-based settings.

The planning of the curriculum, the subsequent delivery of the activities, and the effectiveness of the overall physical education program are seldom discussed in relationship to measurement and evaluation practices. One of the shortcomings of many measurement and evaluation courses is that they do not sufficiently address practical issues relevant to the contemporary physical educator. Many practitioners never consider their measurement and evaluation practices as tools to use in improving their programs.

In exercise science settings, measurement and evaluation activities are also critical to program development and continuity. In athletic training, physical therapy, adult fitness settings, and other exercise science environments, the use of measurement and evaluation is the foundation of the program. For instance, in fitness settings, a client typically undergoes an initial screening to assess current levels of body composition, cardiovascular endurance, and flexibility. An exercise program is then designed based on this initial assessment, and the individual's progress is monitored as she or he progresses through the program.

Without measurement and evaluation of the components of health-related physical fitness, there would be no way to ascertain initial fitness levels, monitor the program, or know when the person had met prescribed goals. The same sort of model would typically be used in athletic training for assessing injury, monitoring the effectiveness of rehabilitation, and knowing when an athlete should be released to return to activity. Beyond these individual programs, program administrators can use measurement and evaluation to assess total program goals by looking at collective outcomes of all clients currently engaged in the program.

The physical education curriculum also should provide experiences that promote students' growth and development. These activities need to be planned and categorized based on their contributions to the various learning domains. The traditional learning domains—cognitive, affective, and psychomotor—represent logical classifications for directed learning. This conceptualization of the learning domains, as related to physical education, needs to be upgraded to include a fourth domain: health-related physical fitness.

Traditionally, the exercise science professions do not typically think of the learning domains in their work. We suggest that these domains can be as applicable to working with athletes and adult clients as they are in teaching K–12 students. The material in this chapter will suggest ways in which these learning domains are pertinent to activity-based professionals as well as K–12 physical educators.

The ultimate success of a school or nonschool program depends on your effectiveness in helping students or clients achieve goals related to each of the four learning domains. Planning and implementing various learning experiences is a multiphase, ongoing process that relies on quantitative and qualitative data to assist in determining the effectiveness of learning experiences. In this era of accountability, measurement and evaluation are inextricably linked to decisions made concerning program development. Practitioners need to become more familiar with assessment tools that can be used to measure performance in each of the four domains.

Thus, the main purpose of this chapter is to discuss and emphasize the natural connections between the program development and the measurement and evaluation processes. To do this, it is first necessary to identify and briefly describe each of the four learning domains integral to physical education and exercise science. Each of these domains, and its appropriate measurement and evaluation procedures, is presented in depth in subsequent chapters. A five-step approach to program development is then presented, emphasizing the role of measurement and evaluation in each step.

The Four Learning Domains

Program structure should provide educational experiences that foster growth and development in the four learning domains of physical education and exercise science: health-related physical fitness, psychomotor, cognitive, and affective. Each **learning domain** should be viewed as a sphere in which certain outcomes are targeted for attainment through specific planned activities. An individual's progress toward objectives in each domain can and should be monitored. Chapters 5–8 describe specific measurement tools and strategies that can be used appropriately to measure performance or qualities associated with each of the four domains. The establishment of goals in these domains is equally important in school and nonschool settings.

Health-Related Physical Fitness Domain

A review of curriculum as well as measurement and evaluation texts shows that most authors include health-related physical fitness within the psychomotor domain. However, it is proposed in this textbook that program development and accompanying measurement techniques could be more effective and easily understood if the health-related physical fitness domain and the psychomotor domain were viewed as separate realms. Proposed initially by Annarino, Cowell, and Hazelton (1980), this view is a logical way to classify learning domains in activity-based settings. The increased emphasis on health-related fitness as determined by the surge of interest in fitness activities for a lifetime, the *Healthy People 2010* initiative, and the number of texts devoted specifically to health fitness also support the emergence of a separate learning domain.

The **health-related physical fitness domain** is characterized by those aspects of physical fitness that affect an individual's functional health and physical well-being. The importance of good eating and activity habits to increase the chances for good health has received much publicity in recent years. Regular aerobic exercise, combined with good nutrition, helps prevent hypokinetic conditions such as cardiovascular disease, low back pain, obesity, and hypertension. The importance of emphasizing these areas warrants it being included as a separate domain. In adult fitness settings, health-related physical fitness is clearly a primary goal.

Despite the public interest, much confusion still exists about the term **physical fitness**. Some textbooks include health-related physical fitness tests, such as the FITNESSGRAM (1999), in the psychomotor domain. Some physical fitness test batteries still being used include tests of speed, agility, quickness, and jumping ability. While these are important skills for playing competitive or recreational sports, they have little bearing on maintaining good health for a lifetime. In order to distinguish these tests of athletic skills from those of health-related fitness, we can classify them as measuring **sports-related fitness**. Sports-related fitness tests also should be included in measurement and evaluation schemes, but it should be remembered that they are more appropriately grouped in the psychomotor domain. In adult fitness settings, sports-related fitness is seldom emphasized or tested, while athletic trainers may have a need for it.

It is becoming accepted practice for physical fitness testing to emphasize health-related components, including body composition (ratio of leanness to fatness), cardiovascular efficiency, muscular strength and endurance, and flexibility of the lower back and posterior thigh areas. To avoid confusion with the sports-related fitness components and to ensure proper emphasis of the health-related components, a separate learning domain is not only helpful, but necessary. Chapter 5 describes the components of health-related physical fitness and discusses tests designed to measure cardiovascular fitness, muscular strength and endurance, flexibility, and body composition for both K–12 and adult populations.

Psychomotor Domain

The **psychomotor domain** includes fundamental movement patterns that are sports-related and emphasizes specialized skills needed in particular sports. Sports-related fitness components include balance, speed, agility, coordination, and power associated with quality performance in sport. Sports-related fitness can also be called skill-related fitness. The terms are interchangeable. Of the four demains, this one is more specific to school settings than to nonschool settings. Typically, adult fitness settings would not include sport skill development as a goal.

While the psychomotor domain includes traits specific to general motor ability tests, test batteries are also available to measure skills that are specific to a particular sport. Therefore, sports skills are also included in the psychomotor domain. The ability to shoot free throws in basketball, putt a golf ball, or serve a tennis ball can be measured in a very accurate way. Chapter 6 identifies and discusses specific facets of skill fitness and describes various assessment techniques to evaluate general motor ability and specific sports skills. Chapter 9 presents alternative assessment practices also used to evaluate sports skills.

Cognitive Domain

Though not often associated with physical education by the general public and many physical educators, the cognitive domain is a critical area that should be addressed in the measurement and evaluation scheme. The **cognitive domain** includes processes of acquiring and using knowledge such as thinking, recognizing, memorizing and recalling, creating, and understanding. The classification of educational objectives for this domain is typically linked to Bloom's *Taxonomy of Educational Objectives* (1956). The various levels of Bloom's taxonomy represent an ascending order of cognitive processes. These hierarchical levels can be matched to students' cognitive abilities at the various stages of development in order to provide proper cognitive activities and realistic objectives.

Inasmuch as there is a renewed emphasis on the importance of teaching the how and why of physical activity, it is necessary to develop proper techniques designed to measure and evaluate performance in the cognitive domain. A knowledge of the rules, strategies, skill techniques, safety procedures, equipment, and the underlying concepts of movement and fitness should be addressed in the program. The use of valid and reliable procedures allows us to know if students are achieving in the cognitive area. Chapter 7 describes how to construct, administer, and evaluate a written test.

Exercise science professionals do not typically consider the cognitive domain in their work in a formal way. It would be quite uncommon to see someone taking a written exam in a health club or sports medicine clinic. Nevertheless, most activity-based professionals want their clients to have an understanding of their program. For instance, one way to motivate an athlete to adhere to a rehabilitation regimen is to educate that athlete about why it is important that he or she stays with the program. If the athlete understands the basic underlying purposes of the treatment regimen, then he or she will be much more likely to adhere to the program. Similarly, an exercise clinician wants clients to understand the benefits of their program so as to motivate them to maintain their workout habits. This also helps clients learn how to work out on the various workout apparatuses in a safe manner. This is another form of the cognitive domain. Though you may not give a test, you will monitor the exerciser until you are certain that she or he understands the safety procedures. Logically, developing a checklist for your client to keep a record of that person's understanding of safe operation would be a wise thing to have in the client's personal files. This is a form of cognitive measurement that would be used to evaluate the exerciser's cognitive knowledge. This could also serve as a form of protection against lawsuits if a client was injured during a workout.

Coaches want athletes to understand all the rules of their sport in order to play effectively. Think about all the offensive and defensive strategies and plays that a basketball or football player needs to know. Softball and baseball players have to learn to read the signs that their coaches give them when they are batting or in the field. Coaches and players spend hours of practice time learning what to do in competition. This is the cognitive domain! Maybe they do not call it that, but it is crucial to their performance. Some coaches actually give quizzes to their players over scouting reports and their assignments. We hope you get the point that the cognitive domain is important in all activity-based settings and should not be neglected in planning program goals.

Affective Domain

The **affective domain** includes development of socioemotional skills, good sportsmanship, cooperation, self-concept, and positive attitudes toward physical activity. Within the wide scope of activity-based settings, there are lofty goals about improving areas associated with the affective domain. Nevertheless, little has been done to substantiate these claims or hold practitioners accountable in this area. Virtually every set of goals or objectives in physical education contains statements concerning the affective domain; however, these objectives are seldom measured and evaluated in an objective and quantifiable manner. If objectives about such things as improving attitudes toward physical activity are included, then these areas should be included in the measurement and evaluation scheme.

Affective goals are not typically associated with activity-based settings outside schools and organized athletics. We would advocate that exercise science professionals should put more emphasis on this area. If you want to make positive impacts on your clients, then you must ensure that they enjoy their program and feel enriched by it. If this is not the case, it is unlikely that they will be your clients for very long! Knowing how your clients feel about their program can help you make it more effective. The perceptions of the exerciser or athlete in rehabilitation are important for you to understand. The Borg Perceived Exertion Scale is one example of an affective domain assessment typically used in exercise settings. The use of journals and exercise logs can also be classified in the affective area. Thus, the use of affective measurement and evaluation strategies should be carefully considered for activity programs outside of the K–12 environment.

The assessment of the affective domain can be accomplished with measurement tools such as attitudinal surveys, sociometric inventories, self-concept scales, and value appraisals. Chapter 8 provides a thorough explanation of the affective domain and identifies various measurement tools that can provide objective information about the areas included in the affective domain. Chapter 9 also provides insight into alternative assessments in this domain.

Needs Assessment

Prior to any stage of program development, an assessment should be conducted to determine the needs of the program. These needs may be classified according to philosophical beliefs, content requirements, fitness levels, or students' performance. The procedure used to identify strengths and weaknesses associated with the various aspects of the program, a critical tool for obtaining information important to program decision making, is called a **needs assessment**.

In physical education, a needs assessment is a process for determining the appropriateness of the goals for the program, teacher, or student and for determining what specific activities to include in a physical education curriculum. In nonschool settings, needs assessments can take the form of initial screening of injuries, fitness levels, etc. This initial assessment forms the basis for subsequent treatments or fitness prescriptions. Even though general program goals are broad and easily understood, the specific unit outcomes and performance-based student objectives should be geared toward the needs of the particular program or students involved. The needs assessment may also serve as an initial pretest to obtain baseline data, which enables the progress of the students to be regularly monitored and evaluated through periodic testing during the unit, semester, or year. Whatever the format, the needs assessment is clearly based on sound measurement and evaluation practices.

Through comparative procedures, results of the assessment are translated into more meaningful descriptive data. This information can then be utilized to determine the relative status of the program, teacher effectiveness, and student performance in relation to expected standards.

For example, a needs assessment could be conducted to determine the health-related physical fitness status of the students in a particular school. The FITNESS-GRAM test battery (1999) could be administered to students during the fall. Raw scores could be collected and means calculated for each age and gender. Group means could be compared to national standards. The relationship of the group means to the national criteria would provide information about the relative health-related physical fitness status of youth in the school. Based on this comparison, the physical education teacher would have the information necessary to draw conclusions regarding the health-related physical fitness needs of the students.

The prevalence and sophistication of assessment tools make the type and extent of information that can be obtained about the program, teachers, and students almost

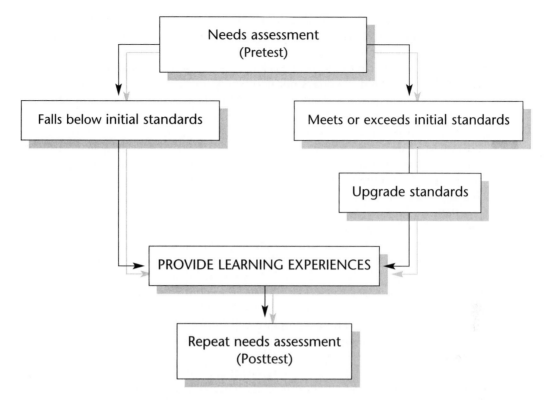

Figure 2.1 Map for conducting need assessment.

limitless. Remember, the needs assessment can be utilized to evaluate any of the four learning domains associated with physical education. See Figure 2.1 for an outline for conducting a needs assessment. Once the needs have been determined, physical educators and exercise science practitioners can rely on the results of recent scientific findings to assist in the selection of appropriate activities to best meet those needs.

The importance and utility of the needs assessment should not be underestimated. Both physical educators and exercise science practitioners are encouraged to implement a needs assessment during any phase of program development, always keeping in mind that the quantifiable information derived from a needs assessment can be useful in making the transition from one phase of curriculum development to the next.

Program Development

An active plan of program development should be in place in any activity-based setting. Whether the setting is K–12 physical education, athletic training, adult fitness, or some other activity-based program, a sound programmatic foundation is crucial. The steps of program development are the same in these different activity-based environments. The role of measurement and evaluation is integral in the development and maintenance of any type of program.

Many physical education textbooks are dedicated to **curriculum development**, with each offering a different approach to the teaching of physical education. Despite this variety, most long-term goals for physical education are the same. What differs is the approach to achieve those goals. Lack of agreement among nationally recognized experts in curriculum design does not necessarily imply that physical education curriculum development is fragmented and unrefined. Rather, it typifies the pattern of curriculum development in virtually all subject areas and suggests that more than one approach can achieve the same outcome.

Similarly, various activity-based programs outside school settings will obviously have different approaches associated with their respective settings. These approaches are driven by differing philosophies, varying needs of the clientele, whether they are profit or nonprofit entities, and by the other characteristics of the particular setting. Nevertheless, the basic steps of program development are still applicable, and measurement and evaluation is involved in each step.

Programmatic decision making is neither an exact science nor a simple operation, yet it is essential to the successful functioning of any program. There should be a systematic plan in place to guide the decision-making process. Whereas program management theories suggest differing steps associated with program development and assessment, there are steps in the process that are common to virtually all models. These steps are: (1) establishing a program philosophy; (2) developing program goals; (3) planning program activities; (4) delivering the program; and (5) evaluating and improving the program.

These five steps of program development should flow in a sequential pattern. Although the procedures for the respective steps vary, each of the five steps depends upon measurement and evaluation techniques to provide information essential to the decision-making process. For example, establishing a realistic philosophical approach requires a database that accurately depicts the parameters (budget, facilities, equipment, supplies, and so on) that characterize the program. The successes of steps two through four, which deal with program goals, activities, and delivery, depend on qualitative and quantitative information that accurately indicates the status of each stage of program development. The final phase, evaluating and improving the program, also needs to work from a baseline of quantifiable and qualitative information if subsequent alterations in program are to be recommended and successfully implemented. Each of these steps is discussed below.

Step 1: Establishing a Program Philosophy

Perhaps the most important task confronting physical educators and exercise science practitioners during the various stages of program building is establishing a realistic philosophical approach. The philosophical aims of a program are the foundation on which the other phases of program development are built. Certainly, not everyone endorses the same philosophical beliefs. However, no matter what the activity-based setting, several philosophical aims would likely be included in any quality program. There should be: a goal of providing optimal participation for your clientele, whether they be student, athlete, or adult exercisers; efforts to educate the participants about the benefits of regular activity; rules, skills, and strategies of the activity, and equipment and safety issues; an emphasis on creating positive, successful activity-based settings that focus on life-long activities; and a commitment to systematic evaluation and improvement of all facets of the program. Measurement and evaluation are not readily associated with the development of a program philosophy. Nevertheless, some measurement techniques provide invaluable assistance in the process of finalizing the philosophical aims.

Activity interest surveys provide important information related to diversity and balance of program offerings. These surveys should take into account facilities, equipment, administrative policies, and so on. Results of such a survey are often surprising and may offer suggestions on new activities that can be included to update the program. For instance, a survey of physical education programs can yield helpful information about innovations in curriculum design. By studying program offerings in an objective way, a determination can be made as to whether a curriculum is sufficiently diverse to meet the philosophical aims of a physical education program. Similar surveys can be used to gather valuable information for nonschool programs.

The philosophy of a program should reflect the characteristics and needs of the participants. A clear understanding of the various attributes and stages of development of your clientele and the relationship of these attributes to the domains of physical education provide a basis for philosophical decisions. Research provides excellent descriptive information on the general characteristics and developmental stages of school-age youth. The best way to collect specific information about students is to utilize selected performance tests to measure the current status of students. Knowing the status of the students makes it possible to construct the curricular framework to accommodate the characteristics and needs of the students. Similarly, research has been completed on differences between men and women in the exercise environment at various ages of adulthood. Increasing information is available about characteristics of geriatric populations. With shifting demographics, activity-based professionals should be prepared to work with clients of all ages. The needs and interests of these various populations can differ greatly and may affect the development or modification of programmatic philosophy.

A dilemma in forming philosophical aims for a program is knowing how much emphasis to put on the various learning domains. Should more concern be displayed toward the health-related fitness levels, cognitive understanding, motor skill development, or the attitudes and socioemotional skills of the participants? Which domain is most important and, as a result, receives more emphasis? Though all domains are certainly important, formal needs assessment may indicate that a particular area needs more emphasis. This type of decision influences many later decisions made in regard to program planning and the measurement and evaluation model.

Part of the philosophical underpinnings of a quality physical education program should be the expectations of teacher performance. Too often, all of the attention centers on student expectations, and teacher performance is taken for granted. Certain teacher behaviors promote an effective teaching–learning environment and facilitate the management of students in physical education. High rates of specific, positive feedback to students; high rates of using students' first names; an active teaching style; low percentages of management activities; and high rates of appropriate on-task student behaviors are examples of behaviors that indicate effective teaching. Systematic observation procedures enable us to measure and analyze behaviors in physical education in a quantifiable and objective way. Chapter 11 describes systematic observation procedures that can be readily implemented in the physical education setting.

While it is more common to consider the assessment of teaching performance, it is equally important to evaluate performance of exercise and fitness professionals, athletic trainers, and coaches. Clearly, the interactions and types of feedback that these professionals provide their clients and athletes impact the quality of their program. Philosophically, we are obligated to find ways to effectively assess these activity professionals as well as teachers. Many of the systematic observation procedures suggested for teachers in Chapter 11 can also be used in other activity settings with minimal modifications.

A logical end to developing a program philosophy is to prepare a **mission statement.** A mission statement should succinctly describe the program philosophy. Most physical education curricula, athletic departments, profit and not-for-profit exercise and fitness organizations have specific mission statements or statements of philosophy. Unfortunately, in many cases the practitioners delivering the program do not know the mission statement and, thus, do not base day-to-day decisions on this foundational philosophy. It is crucial that the philosophy of a program be clearly stated, understood, and used in making programmatic decisions by program administrators and practitioners alike.

Philosophically, an ongoing evaluation of any activity-based program is essential. Properly chosen measurement tools based on philosophical tenets should be utilized to provide a basis for this evaluation to take place. The primary purpose of the evaluation is to determine if program objectives are being achieved. Because various constituencies demand accountability, the concept of ongoing evaluation based on sound measurement procedures assumes even more importance. This evaluation should focus on the performance of the participants as well as the activity professional. The evaluation model should enable program administrators to make decisions on successful and unsuccessful facets of the activity program. Areas of deficiency then can be corrected, and what is judged as satisfactory can be retained and enhanced.

Step 2: Developing Program Goals

Once a realistic philosophical approach to the program has been developed, it becomes appropriate to develop global program goals that are challenging, yet attainable and realistic. This is the second step of program development. **Program goals** evolve from the fundamental philosophical aims and serve as the primary link between the philosophy and activities of the program. Failure to develop and attain predetermined program goals makes any type of accountability difficult and places the program in jeopardy of being cut back or eliminated.

Similar to the process that leads to establishing a program philosophy, Step 2 depends on proper techniques of measurement and evaluation to develop attainable program goals. To evaluate whether program goals have been attained obviously is a function of sound measurement procedures. Determining the degree to which program goals are being met is vital to the process and is best achieved through objective inquiry.

Many of the same areas in which needs assessments are used to determine philosophical aims are also used to formulate program goals. Written activity-based goals cannot be finalized without investigating participant needs, characteristics, and interests. A predetermined set of program goals provides an overview of expectancies of the program. Program goals should be measurable and realistic and lend themselves to objective assessment.

The program goals should be somewhat broad and provide a holistic overview of what the program seeks to accomplish. Not only should these goals evolve naturally from the programmatic mission, but they should also be linked with the planned program activities (Step 3). Program goals should reflect the learning domains. In physical education curricula, there should be goals that are specific to each of the four domains. In adult fitness programs, it may be appropriate that goals would not include much emphasis, if any, on the psychomotor domain but would include definite goals in the health-related physical fitness, cognitive, and affective domains.

It is advisable to write goals specific to a single domain. If you write a goal that combines two domains, it becomes more difficult to assess properly. For instance, a poorly stated goal would be:

Understand the importance of health-related physical fitness and the benefits of an active lifestyle and display a positive attitude toward physical activity.

This goal combines the cognitive domain (understand the importance...) and the affective domain (display a positive attitude...). While meeting the cognitive goal might lead to the accomplishment of the affective goal, it is possible to do one without the other. It also would require different measurement techniques to assess each domain. In writing program goals, you may have more than one goal for a particular domain but develop the goals so they are specific to a single domain.

The following list is a good example of program goals for a physical education program. These goals could also be easily modified to fit the needs of other activity-based settings. Consider these goals and decide if others should be added. How would you modify these goals to make them apply to an employee fitness program in a corporate setting?

1. Establish and maintain health-related physical fitness.
2. Develop competence in movement.
3. Understand the importance of health-related physical fitness and the benefits of an active lifestyle.
4. Comprehend the rules, strategies, techniques, and safety procedures associated with games and sports.
5. Develop socioemotional skills.
6. Display a positive attitude toward physical activity.

Step 3: Planning Program Activities

As noted earlier, the program goals are broad and global in nature. After Step 2 is completed, the tasks of choosing activities, sequencing activities in a logical order, and determining desirable outcomes for each activity make up Step 3. Just as measurement and evaluation play an integral part in the first two steps, they also are crucial to this step.

Information on participant needs, characteristics, and interests is critical in the selection of units. Availability of facilities and equipment, number and length of units, instructor expertise, balance of activities, and climate also must be considered when selecting and sequencing activities. In school settings, the activities should be organized in a horizontal progression during any given school year and in a vertical progression from grades K–12.

In schools, **unit outcomes** are developed for activities to serve as targets for students and teachers during the individual activity and can be linked to any of the program goals. For example, assume we are defining unit outcomes for a seventh grade basketball unit. A unit outcome could be

The student will learn the fundamentals of shooting a free throw.

This unit outcome is directly linked to the program goal of developing competence of movement, which in basketball includes the ability to shoot free throws.

From this example, one can readily see that there could be a number of unit outcomes. Remember that the length of the unit, the age of the students, their initial competence, the size of class, and many other factors will affect what can be accomplished. Since unit outcomes are related to attainable program goals, make certain that the unit outcomes are attainable as well.

In nonschool activity settings, activities can include many different things according to the setting. In athletic training, the rehabilitation program for the athlete must be planned. The individualized workouts prepared for clients in adult fitness settings should be carefully prepared. Planning workouts for athletic teams is work that coaches do to prepare for the competitive season. Similar to unit outcomes in the school physical education program, it would be very appropriate to have more specific **outcome statements** prepared that would be used to assess the progress made by the client or athlete. These types of statements should be more specific but clearly related to program goals (Step 2) and philosophy (Step 1). Thought must be given to how these outcome statements can be measured and evaluated as the program is being delivered.

Step 4: Delivering the Program

After the activities for the program have been carefully planned, it is time to implement these activities by delivering the program to your participants. In the case of school physical education programs, the activities of your program are included in your curriculum plan. This yearly curriculum plan tells you what activities (units) will be offered, when they will be offered, and how long each unit will last. The curriculum plan will include unit outcomes. Within unit outcomes, there should be **performance-based objectives** linked to the unit outcomes. Performance-based objectives break unit outcomes into measurable and observable terms.

Care must be taken in writing these objectives so that expectancies of the students are clear. Also called behavioral objectives, performance-based objectives are statements about what the student should be able to perform. An example of a performance-based objective is

The student will be able to make 5 of 10 free throws.

The achievement of this performance-based objective has obvious evaluative implications on the unit outcome stated previously. Because of this relationship, the achievement of the performance-based objective also has influence on the related program goal. The achievement-based objective is crucial to the measurement and evaluation scheme of the overall program.

A series of performance-based objectives written for different levels of competence can furnish a more complete evaluation picture for a given task. For instance, the example above could be stated with different criteria: "3 free throws of 10" or "7 free throws of 10."

Performance-based objectives can and should be written for each of the four learning domains. The clarity of performance-based objectives and the accurate measurement of student outcomes based on these objectives provide the basis for evaluating achievement.

Just as consideration of performance objectives is critical in school settings, the continual assessment of a client or athlete's progress in other activity settings is an integral part of delivering the program. The athletic trainer will constantly monitor the progress of an athlete rehabilitating an injury and make modifications as necessary based on assessments and professional observations. The exercise clinician should use assessment techniques to ensure that participants are feeling successful and positive about participating in the program. The delivery of the program can be modified if necessary based on this information. Coaches constantly assess their teams in practice situations. When the competitive season arrives, game performance becomes the key assessment for athletic performance. How can anyone coach without using measurement and evaluation techniques? During the season the coach and athletes make constant adjustments based on specific performance outcomes. Effective goal-setting strategies used as motivators by exercise leaders, coaches, and athletic trainers are based on specific, measurable performance outcome statements. Thus, measurement and evaluation play an essential role in the effective delivery of programs in all activity-based settings. The effectiveness of any program should be evaluated in light of the achievement of the participants.

Step 5: Evaluating and Improving the Program

The final step of the program development process is concerned with a complete evaluation of the program after it has been delivered so that the program can be constantly scrutinized and improved. In academic settings, the logical time to do this is at the end of a school year or semester. In coaching, evaluations are typically made at the conclusion of competition in the off-season. In adult fitness settings, program evaluations often occur at the end of the fiscal year. Athletic training programs have evolved into year-round endeavors, but annual evaluations tend to occur in the late spring or summer. Whenever these program evaluations are made, they need to be done systematically and regularly.

This fifth step of program evaluation actually involves all five steps of program development. It provides an opportunity to examine all facets of the program. Based on data collected during the delivery of the program, evaluations can be made of the achievement of the participants. These evaluations are directly linked to performance objectives associated with program delivery (Step 4), outcome statements related to program planning (Step 3), program goals (Step 2), and program philosophy (Step 1).

Step 5 follows this evaluation model. If areas of the program need improvement, it may be necessary to return to any or all of the previous four steps to make changes. Addressing Step 5 can directly affect any of the first four steps of program development. Figure 2.2 illustrates this concept.

Evaluating the effectiveness of the program is an ongoing process, since a program never should be in its final form. It continually needs to be fine-tuned for improvement and to remain current. Measuring the performance of participants, sur-

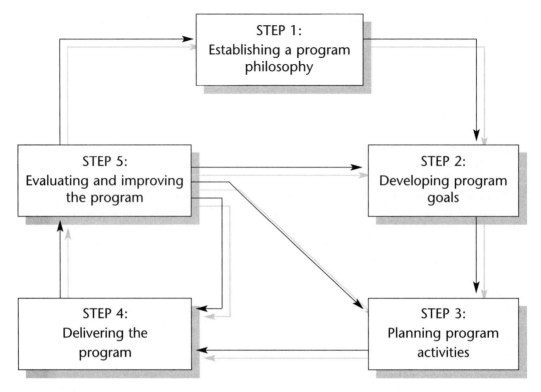

Figure 2.2 The ongoing program development process.

veying their interests, and assessing their needs are all sources of information for program evaluation. A periodic evaluation, usually yearly, is done based on the information gathered from measurement procedures in each of the first four steps. The evaluation includes each of the four learning domains.

After quantifiable and objective information is gathered, qualitative judgments based on sound logic and the data collected are made to evaluate and improve the program. Some activities will be added, others will be dropped, and still others will undergo various types of modification. The utilization of information collected from the variety of measurement procedures is critical to programmatic decision making. With the wide range of available measurement tools, it would be foolish to make any decisions concerning the program without making full use of these assessment procedures. It is impossible to construct and maintain a quality program without having a solid measurement and evaluation model.

SUMMARY

The primary goal of this chapter is to establish the critical linkages between measurement and evaluation strategies and program development processes in physical education and exercise science. The five steps of program development and the role of measurement and evaluation in each step are presented. The importance of the program development process as dynamic rather than static is discussed.

Measurement and evaluation are critical components of this ongoing program development process. Informed decisions in any phase depend on sound measurement and evaluation strategies. Accuracy of measurement followed up with sound evaluation are essential to ensuring initial and continued quality in school and non-school programs.

DISCUSSION QUESTIONS

1. Describe each of the four learning domains in physical education and exercise science. Explain what measurement and evaluation procedures could be used to assess achievement in each domain.

2. Provide a rationale for the treatment of health-related physical fitness as a separate learning domain. Include a discussion about the differences between health-related fitness and sports-related fitness in your answer.

3. Which learning domain merits the most instructional time in physical education during the year? The least? Give reasons for your opinions.

4. Provide examples of situations in which a needs assessment should be used. How often should a needs assessment be conducted?

5. Select any step in program development. What are the various ways measurement and evaluation strategies can be used to make informed decisions about the status of this step?

6. Explain how Step 5 of program development is related to the previous four steps. In your answer discuss how the relationship among the five steps affects program development as an ongoing process.

REFERENCES

Annarino, A. A., Cowell, C. C., and Hazelton, H. W. (1980). *Curriculum theory and design in physical education*. St. Louis, MO: C. V. Mosby.

Bloom, B., Englehart, M., Furst, E., and Kratwohl, D. (1956). *Taxonomy of educational objectives: The classification of educational goals, handbook 1: Cognitive domain*. New York: Longmans, Green.

Cooper Institute for Aerobics Research (1999). *FITNESSGRAM: Test Administration Manual*. 2nd edition. Champaign, IL: Human Kinetics.

CHAPTER 3

Basic Statistics

Key Terms

abscissa

apparent limits

bar graph

ceiling effect

continuous data

correlation

correlation coefficient

cumulative frequency
    graph

discrete data

frequency polygon

grouped frequency
    distribution

histogram

interval

leptokurtic

mean

median

mode

multiple correlation

multiple regression

nominal

normal curve

one-way ANOVA

ordinal

ordinate

Pearson product-
    moment
    correlation

percentile

platykurtic

range

ratio

real limits

scattergram

simple frequency
    distribution

simple regression

skewed

Spearman rho rank-
    order correlation

standard deviation

standard scores

statistics

T-score

t-test for dependent
    samples

t-test for
    independent
    samples

two-way ANOVA

variance

z-score

Objectives

1. Classify data according to the four measurement levels.

2. Recognize and use data display techniques.

3. Identify, understand the role of, and calculate the measures of central tendency and the measures of variability.

4. Describe the properties of the normal curve.

5. Give the general properties of standard scores and transform raw scores into percentile ranks, z-scores, and T-scores.

6. Utilize appropriate correlational procedures to ascertain relationships between sets of data.

7. Develop simple regression formulas from sets of data with high correlation coefficients.

8. Provide a rudimentary explanation of appropriate applications for t-tests, one-way ANOVA, and two-way ANOVA.

This chapter is designed as a basic guide to the most common statistical procedures used in physical education and exercise science. Very little theory is presented, and the "cookbook" approach to the statistical operations included is geared to helping the practitioner feel comfortable with the various techniques. Many statistical textbooks present in-depth theoretical explanations if the student desires more information. For students who are apprehensive about studying statistics, they should discard any preconceived ideas and approach this chapter with an open mind. The only mathematical skills needed to master the statistical procedures presented are the basic computational skills of addition, subtraction, multiplication, and division. A pocket calculator will make it easier to complete the steps involved in the various procedures.

At the mention of the word "statistics," people exhibit a variety of reactions—cynicism, suspicion, awe, anxiety. A popular notion sees statistics as numerical information that may be manipulated to defend any position while appearing analytical and objective. True, statistics can be used in this way, but keep in mind that nonsense may be expressed verbally as well as statistically. A knowledge of logic is a good defense against verbal nonsense. By the same token, a basic knowledge of statistics is a good safeguard against numerical nonsense.

With advances in technology and the availability of a variety of programs, it is much less cumbersome for the practitioner to maintain databases, generate statistics, graphically represent sets of scores, and highlight participant and program successes. Spreadsheet programs such as Microsoft Excel and statistical programs now available for personal computers such as SPSS for Windows make statistical analyses easy to do. However, it is still important that you have a basic understanding of the concepts of the various statistical analyses. Thus, the examples in this chapter that show you how to calculate descriptive statistics by hand are designed to help with your conceptual understanding. Once the concepts are clear, you are certainly encouraged to use programmable calculators or data analysis programs to facilitate efficient handling of your data. A listing of resources to provide further information in computer applications is given later in the chapter.

Simply defined, **statistics** is the science of collecting, classifying, presenting, and interpreting numerical data. A basic knowledge of statistics helps to organize and analyze data collected, or measured, from tests. For instance, it is common for a curl-up test to be administered as a part of fitness testing. The teacher administers the test to all the students in her classes. This could easily be 150 students or more. All scores are recorded, but raw data in this form means very little to the teacher or the students. What kind of information does the teacher need to make these data meaningful?

An average score for all students would certainly be helpful, as would average scores per class or by age and gender. By looking at the highest score and the lowest score, the teacher gets an idea of the spread of the scores or the range of ability of students in the group. If students are to be tested later in the year, improvement can also be calculated. All of this information is statistical in nature and helps the teacher and student understand the results of the curl-up test. Without statistical procedures, this information would be meaningless.

Levels of Measurement

Prospective physical education teachers and exercise science practitioners should become familiar with the four levels of measurement: nominal, ordinal, interval, and ratio. These four kinds of measurement represent different levels of precision in gathering data and measuring variables. An understanding of the differences in these levels of measurement is basic to using various statistical procedures properly. Certain statistical procedures assume a specific level of measurement, and if this criterion is not met, then the data will be analyzed in an improper manner, resulting in misinterpretation.

Nominal Level

The **nominal** level is the simplest and least precise of the four measurement scales. Numbers are often assigned for the sole purpose of differentiating an attribute or property of one object from another. The following are examples of a nominal level of measurement with numbers assigned for identification:

Basketball jersey #34

Interstate Highway 20

Locker #80

Nominal measurements do not always assign numbers for differentiation. Rather than numbers, letters of the alphabet or names can easily be assigned. Gender is differentiated by male and female; male could be assigned M and female assigned F. Eye color can be identified by the terms *blue, brown, gray,* or *hazel.* Nationality can be American, Canadian, or Mexican. By totalling the number of each nationality, a frequency count for each category can be reported.

Other than a frequency count, no other calculation can be made with nominal measures. Locker #80 and locker #40 are merely two different lockers that are assigned numbers for identification. No arithmetic procedures would be appropriate for these locker numbers. No comparisons between #40 and #80 can be made. Locker #40 is not viewed as being smaller than locker #80. A Social Security number is a nominal measurement that identifies a person as distinct from other people. As simple as the nominal scale is, it is a form of measurement that is very useful in making differentiation between objects or people and in reporting the frequency of something that occurs or exists.

Ordinal Level

The **ordinal** level of measurement is more precise than the nominal level because it has the property of order. The numbers assigned represent relative amounts of the quality or attribute being measured. A differentiation between one object and another can be made as with nominal measurement, but ordinal measurement also specifies the direction of the difference. Thus, one can say "more than" or "less than."

If a student did more sit-ups than anyone in the class, that student's name would be first on a list showing order of scores. The statement can be made that this student did "more sit-ups than the second-place student." Similarly, the second-place student did "more than the third-place student." Without knowing the actual scores, it cannot be known how many is "more than." The top-ranked student may have done 60 sit-ups, the second-ranked student 59, while the third-ranked student may have done 55. Though first place is one place higher than second place, and second place is one place higher than third place, the differences between the raw scores of the three students are not equal.

This is an important level of measurement, but it does not allow for meaningful arithmetic calculations to be made. As illustrated by the sit-up example above, ordinal differences do not imply equal differences in the amount of the attribute being measured. Ranking teams or players is common in physical education and athletics. Any type of ranking is an example of ordinal measurement.

Assigning Ranks to Raw Data   If two scores are identical, then those scores logically should share the same rank. The scores below represent the score of a 10-point pop quiz. In the example, the score "6" occurs twice and shares the rank of 3.5.

Score	Rank
9	1
7	2
6	3.5
6	3.5
5	5
3	6
2	7

If three scores are the same, then their shared rank would be the middle rank of the three.

Score	Rank
9	1
8	2
7	3
6	5
6	5
6	5
5	7
4	8

Interval Level

Scores at the **interval** level are more precise than nominal and ordinal data. With data at the interval level, the equal differences in measurements reflect equal differences in the amount of the characteristic being assessed. In an interval scale, the zero point of the interval scale is arbitrary, but it does not represent absence of the attribute. A temperature scale is an example of an interval level measurement. If it is 0 degrees outside, the measurement does not reflect absence of temperature. The temperature can go below zero as well. However, a change in the temperature from 0° to 4° F is the same amount of difference if the temperature changes from 72° to 76° F. Calendar time is also an example of an interval measurement scale.

With interval data, calculations are meaningful. Arithmetic operations can be done, but ratio statements cannot be made. For instance, is 80° F twice as hot as 40° F? Because there is no value in an interval scale that represents absence of an attribute, in this case temperature, ratio statements of this sort are incorrect; 80° F is 40° F warmer than the temperature of 40° F, but it does not represent a temperature that is twice as hot.

Ratio Level

The most precise and most useful of all levels is that of **ratio** measurement. It has all the same characteristics of the interval scale with the added advantage of having an absolute zero that reflects absence of the attribute or quality being measured. Because of the absolute zero quality, ratio statements such as "twice as high" or "half as fast" have meaning.

Assume that a student took an exam that had 100 possible points. If she scored 90 on the exam and a classmate scored 45, one score is twice as high as the other. If someone scored zero on the exam, the score reflects the fact that the person did not get any answers correct. A child who is three feet tall is only half as tall as an adult who is six feet tall. With ratio level data, this type of statement is meaningful. Fortunately, most measurements in physical education and exercise science settings are ratio in nature so that arithmetic operations can be calculated and comparative statements can be made.

SECTION 1—DISPLAYING YOUR DATA

Frequency Distributions

Frequency distributions are a simple way to present a set of collected scores in an organized way. Frequency refers to how often a score occurs. Distribution refers to how the scores are dispersed. When data such as test scores are collected, the result is usually a list of unorganized numbers. Listed below is a short list of raw scores from a one-minute curl-up test.

41, 22, 40, 38, 58, 44, 49, 15, 28, 46, 35, 55, 33

For any interpretation of the scores to be made, it is helpful to organize it into some type of logical format. The most common method of organization is to list the scores in rank order fashion as shown below:

58, 55, 49, 46, 44, 41, 40, 38, 35, 33, 28, 22, 15

Simple Frequency Distribution

With a larger amount of curl-up scores, a similar list can be made to show each score separately:

58, 55, 54, 50, 49, 48, 46, 45, 44, 43, 42, 41, 40, 40, 40, 40, 39, 39, 39, 39, 38, 38, 38, 38, 38, 38, 37, 37, 37, 37, 37, 36, 36, 36, 36, 35, 35, 34, 34, 34, 34, 34, 34, 34, 33, 33, 33, 33, 33, 33, 32, 32, 32, 32, 31, 31, 31, 31, 31, 30, 30, 30, 29, 29, 29, 29, 28, 28, 28, 28, 27, 27, 27, 26, 26, 26, 26, 25, 25, 24, 24, 24, 23, 22, 22, 22, 21, 21, 20, 19, 18, 17, 16, 15, 15, 13, 12, 10, 9

However, to avoid a long, cumbersome list of numbers such as this, it is helpful to form the numbers into a **simple frequency distribution**. The first step is to rank the scores from best to worst in order to gain additional information about the relative position of each score in the list. In most cases, the highest score is the best. In some situations, however, lower scores represent better results. For instance, faster (lower) times in the 100-meter dash and lower golf scores represent better performance. Typically, a lower resting heart rate represents better cardiovascular fitness. Then add a frequency column (f) to indicate how many times each score (X) occurred. Table 3.1 illustrates the long list of individual scores shown above transformed into a simple frequency distribution. The "N = 100" indicates that 100 scores are in this group of data. By briefly examining the simple frequency distribution, one can see which scores occurred most often and least often and how the scores are dispersed throughout the range of scores. Even though the simple frequency distribution is more compact than a long listing of individual scores, it is sometimes advantageous to use another method to summarize data.

Grouped Frequency Distribution

Sometimes it is more convenient to create a **grouped frequency distribution**. Grouped frequency distributions further compact the data and are particularly appropriate for large groups of data. The first step is to decide how many groups should be formed and what size the interval should be for a group to adequately display the data. A rule that should almost always be followed is that there should be somewhere between 10 and 20 groups. Fewer than 10 groups will result in too many scores in each group and will obscure important data patterns, while more than 20 groups can cause too few or even zero scores to be in each group and make it difficult to see trends in data. Generally, try to keep the number of groups around 15.

By locating the highest and lowest curl-up scores in the data, the spread of the scores, called the **range**, can be determined. In the example used in Table 3.1, the

Table 3.1 Simple frequency distribution for curl-up scores on one-minute test.

X	f	X	f	X	f
58	1	38	6	24	3
55	1	37	5	23	1
54	1	36	4	22	3
50	1	35	2	21	2
49	1	34	7	20	1
48	1	33	5	19	1
46	1	32	4	18	1
45	2	31	5	17	1
44	1	30	3	16	1
43	1	29	4	15	2
42	1	28	4	13	1
41	2	27	3	12	1
40	4	26	4	10	1
39	4	25	2	9	1
				N = 100	

lowest score is 9 and the highest score is 58. Thus, the range is 49, which can be rounded to 50. Knowing that it is desirable to have between 10 and 20 groups, divide those two numbers into 50. This will help determine the interval for each group and the number of groups to be formed.

$$50 \div 10 = 5$$
$$50 \div 20 = 2.5$$

The interval size should be a whole number, and it is advantageous for the whole number to be odd. The previous calculation tells us that the interval should be between 2.5 and 5. Since the interval should be both whole and odd, our choice is either 3 or 5. An interval of 5 will be used, although either of the two interval values would suffice.

Next, the limits of the interval must be determined for the set of data. The lowest number in the group should be a multiple of the interval. Since 9 is the lowest score, the limit for the lowest group would be 5, and the interval for the lowest group would be 5–9. The next group would be 10–14, followed by 15–19, and so on. When the group intervals are established, tally the number of scores that fall into each interval. Table 3.2 lists a group frequency distribution for the curl-up scores.

The group limits discussed above, called **apparent limits**, are adequate as long as all the data are in whole numbers, called **discrete data**. Since partial curl-ups are not counted, results of a curl-up test would be an example of discrete data. However, a large amount of data in physical education can be in decimal form, known as **continuous data**. The **real limits** of the 5–9 interval would be 4.5 and 9.49 if the data were in continuous form. The apparent limits are used for convenience, but we must remember that the real limit is .5 below the lower apparent limit and .49 above the upper apparent limit. For example, a score of 14.5 would fall into the 15–19 group while a score of 14.49 would be placed in the 10–14 group.

Table 3.2 Grouped frequency distribution for curl-up scores on one-minute test.

Group X	f
55–59	2
50–54	2
45–49	5
40–44	9
35–39	21
30–34	24
25–29	17
20–24	10
15–19	6
10–14	3
5–9	1
	N = 100

Graphical Representation of Data

Graphs provide a visual representation of data and often present data in a more meaningful form than tables of numbers. In many situations, the old adage "a picture is worth a thousand words" can be adapted to "a graph is worth a thousand numbers." Graphs are particularly useful in comparing two sets of data or in illustrating a trend.

Usually, the frequency is placed on the Y-axis, or the **ordinate**, and the scores are placed on the X-axis, or the **abscissa**. The most common type of graph is the **histogram**, which is usually based on data from a group frequency distribution. Note that the frequency is placed on the Y-axis, or the ordinate, and the raw scores are placed on the X-axis, or the abscissa. By looking at relative heights of the various bars, one can quickly note the distribution of scores. The histogram in Figure 3.1 is based on the data in Table 3.2 and depicts grouped frequency distribution of curl-up scores on a one-minute test.

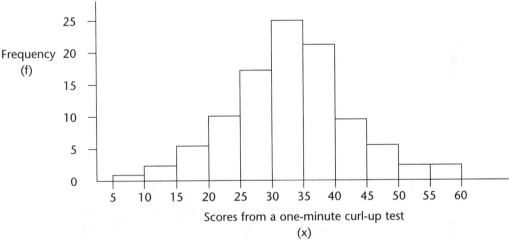

Figure 3.1 Histogram.

A **frequency polygon** is another type of graph that is used frequently to display data. Either the frequency polygon or histogram can be used to depict the same data. Figure 3.2 illustrates the same curl-up scores used in Figure 3.1 in a frequency polygon.

Another graph similar to the histogram is the **bar graph**. The difference in the two is that the bars are separated on a bar graph. Figure 3.3 shows scoring results of a conference basketball season on a bar graph.

If a physical education teacher wanted to determine cumulative frequencies and percentiles, these could be calculated and graphed for a visual representation. Table 3.3 shows cumulative frequencies and percentiles for the set of curl-up scores found in the grouped frequency distribution shown in Table 3.2. The cumulative frequencies are derived by starting at the lowest interval and adding each successive higher group interval to the total frequency below. By looking at the lowest interval, 5–9, a frequency of 1 is noted, and when added to the frequency of the next interval, 10–14, which is 3, the cumulative frequency is 4. This process continues through each group interval.

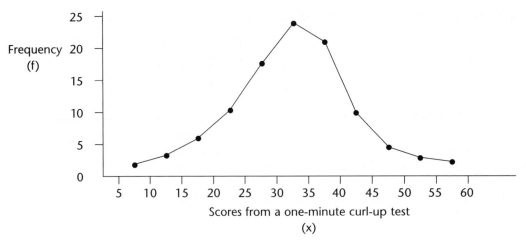

Figure 3.2 Frequency polygon.

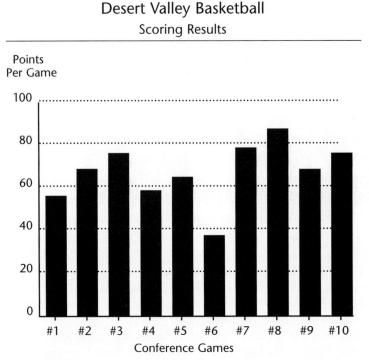

Figure 3.3 Bar graph.

The cumulative percentiles are calculated by dividing each cumulative frequency by the total number of scores in the distribution. For example, group interval 25–29 has a cumulative frequency of 37. This number divided by 100 yields the cumulative percentile of this interval, 37 percent. More information about calculating percentiles from raw scores is provided later in the chapter.

Table 3.3 Cumulative frequencies (Cum f) and percentiles (Cum %) for a grouped frequency distribution.

Group X	f	CUM f	CUM %
55–59	2	100	100
50–54	2	98	98
45–49	5	96	96
40–44	9	91	91
35–39	21	82	82
30–34	24	61	61
25–29	17	37	37
20–24	10	20	20
15–19	6	10	10
10–14	3	4	4
5–9	1	1	1
	N = 100		

A **cumulative frequency graph** can be constructed from this type of information. This type of graph shows the number of students who scored at or below a certain score. This curve can be plotted using scores on the abscissa and cumulative frequency on the ordinate. The upper limits for each group interval should be used to plot the graph. A cumulative frequency graph depicting the data in Table 3.3 is shown in Figure 3.4.

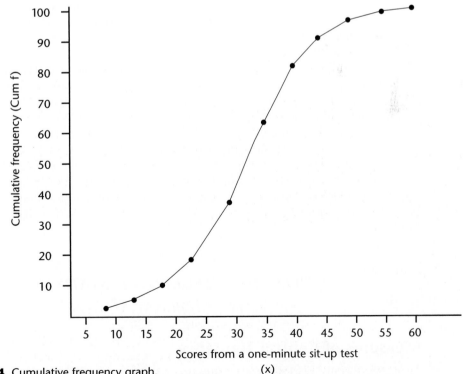

Figure 3.4 Cumulative frequency graph.

Symmetry and Skewness

When scores are plotted on the various graphs, as has been discussed in previous sections, many different types of curves can result. The most common curve is the **normal curve**. This symmetrical, bilateral, bell-shaped curve theoretically occurs when a large number of scores are normally distributed on each end of the curve. The typical normal curve is shown in Figure 3.5.

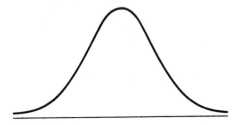

Figure 3.5 Normal curves.

Both ends, or tails, of the curve are symmetrical, and they represent extremely low or high scores in the distribution. Most scores are at the middle of the scale with very few scores falling at the ends. However, many sets of data are not normally distributed, which results in several variations of the normal curve.

If the range of scores in the distribution is limited, which results in the extreme scores being closer to the middle, the curve is steeper and called **leptokurtic**. If the scores of the group are spread out with fewer scores in the middle, the resulting flatter curve is called **platykurtic**. Illustrations of these two curves are shown in Figure 3.6. Notice that either of these conditions can be created artificially by compressing or spreading the scale of scores on the abscissa.

While leptokurtic or platykurtic variations of the normal curve are still symmetrical, distributions of scores have a disproportionate number of scores that do not fall in the middle of the distribution. This causes the tails of the curve to be asymmetrical. For data of this sort, the frequency is described as being **skewed**. With skewed data, the high point, or the hump, of the curve will be shifted to the left or right with a longer than normal tail going the opposite direction. If most scores in a group are high on a test and a small number do poorly, the high point of the curve shifts to the right with a longer tail to the left. This type of distribution is skewed negatively, or skewed to the left. A curve that has the hump to the left and the longer tail to the right is skewed positively, or to the right. Examples of skewed curves are also shown in Figure 3.6.

SECTION 2—DESCRIPTIVE STATISTICS AND THE NORMAL CURVE

Measures of Central Tendency

Measures of central tendency are numerical values that describe the middle or cen-

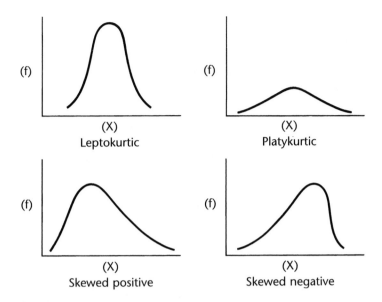

Figure 3.6 Leptokurtic, platykurtic, skewed positive, and skewed negative curves.

tral characteristics of a set of scores. If measures of central tendency are known, any given score can be compared to the middle scores. If a student takes an exam and attains a score of 85, that score provides some information about the student's performance. If the average score on the exam was 70, then additional important information is available to use in evaluating individual test results. Measures of central tendency allow a score to be compared with the group of scores.

Mode

The simplest measure of central tendency is the **mode**. The mode of a group of scores is the score that occurs the most often. If the variable measured assumes a normal or near normal curve distribution, the mode will be near the middle of the curve and be fairly representative of the middle scores.

In a simple frequency distribution, the mode is easily identifiable; it is the score with highest frequency. In the distribution of sit-up scores in Table 3.1, the mode is 34. In a grouped frequency distribution, the mode is considered the midpoint of the interval with the highest frequency. Some groups may have two or more modes if several scores tie for the highest occurrence in a set of scores.

There are several advantages in using the mode over other measures of central tendency: It is easy to identify, no calculations are necessary, and it gives a quick estimate of the center of the group that is fairly accurate when the distribution is normal. Disadvantages in using the mode are as follows: it is a terminal statistic—that is, it does not give information that can be used for further calculation; it is unstable compared to other measures of central tendency, since it can change depending on the methods of grouping the intervals; and it disregards extreme scores and does not reflect their number, their size, or the distance from the center of the group. Notice in the two groups of scores below that the mode is 80 in both.

95, 90, 90, 90, 85, 85, 80, 80, 80, 80, 75, 75, 75, 70, 70
99, 99, 90, 85, 85, 80, 80, 80, 80, 70, 70, 50, 45, 45, 20

Because the mode is not a precise measure of central tendency, it is the same in two groups of numbers that are quite different.

Median

The **median** of a group of scores is the point at which half of the scores are below and half are above. It represents the 50th percentile in the group of scores. If the number of scores in the group is odd, the median is the middle score. If the number of scores is even, the median falls between the middle two scores. Thus, the median of the scores 4, 5, 6, 7, 8 would be 6, while the median of the scores 4, 5, 6, 7, 8, 9 would be 6.5. The median can be used with ordinal, interval, or ratio data.

Like the mode, the median is unaffected by extreme scores. The calculation of the median does not take into consideration the value of the scores. It is based on the number of scores and their rank order. Consider the example of nine employees making $20,000 a year and the owner making $200,000 a year. In this case, the mode and the median are both $20,000. They are unaffected by the size of the extreme score.

In the example above, the median would be more representative than the average salary of the central tendency of the group. The average salary, $38,000, of the company would not be as accurate, because of the extreme score. When the distribution is skewed with extreme scores, it is more appropriate to use the median. The lack of effect by extreme scores on the median can also be a disadvantage in certain instances. Because the median does not consider the size of the scores, important information given by the data is lost. Another disadvantage is that the median is also a terminal statistic so that no further calculations can be made to divulge more information about the data.

Mean

The numerical average of a group of numbers is the **mean**, which is calculated by adding all the scores and dividing by the total number of scores. The mean is not always a whole number—it is continuous rather than discrete. The mean is the most commonly used measure of central tendency.

Unlike the mode and median, the calculation of the mean considers both the number of scores and their size. It gives weight to each of the scores according to its relative distance from other scores in the group. Because of this feature, it is the most sensitive of all central measures. Slight changes in some of the scores in the group will probably not affect the mode or median, but even minor changes in any score will be reflected in the mean. Thus, the chief advantage of the mean is that it considers all information about the data. Further, it is not a terminal statistic because it provides a basis for many additional calculations that yield even more information.

The critical disadvantage of the mean is that it is very sensitive to extreme scores. When one or more of the scores is extreme, the mean is pulled toward that extreme and may not represent the true central measure of the group. The example cited concerning the nine employees making $20,000 per year with the employer making

$200,000 illustrates this characteristic of the mean. The mean of $38,000 would not accurately represent the central tendency of this group of salaries.

The mean assumes at least a level of measurement that is either interval or ratio. Whereas the mode requires only nominal measures and the median assumes an ordinal level, the mean cannot be calculated with these levels of measurement. The mode and median can be applied to interval/ratio data, but since the mean uses the greatest amount of information about the data, it is the most stable.

The formula for finding the mean ($\bar{X}$) with ungrouped data is shown in Formula 3.1.

FORMULA 3.1 Calculation of mean for ungrouped data

$$\bar{X} = \frac{\Sigma X}{N}$$

where
ΣX is the sum of all scores
N is the total number of scores

Table 3.4 shows scores for 13 students from a one-minute curl-up test and illustrates the calculation of the mean with Formula 3.1.

Table 3.4 Calculation of the mean for ungrouped data.

X	
58	
55	
49	
46	$\bar{X} = \dfrac{\Sigma X}{N}$
44	
41	
40	$\bar{X} = \dfrac{504}{13}$
38	
35	
33	$\bar{X} = 38.77$
28	
22	
15	
$\Sigma X = 504$	$N = 13$

When calculating the mean for a simple frequency distribution, as illustrated in Table 3.5, a slight modification is made in the formula. Instead of taking the sum of the 13 individual scores, multiply the frequency (f) by the score and add the products to find the sum of all scores. Note also that N is calculated by adding the f column, since this represents the total number of scores. The formula for finding the mean of data listed in a frequency distribution is listed below (Formula 3.2):

FORMULA 3.2 Calculation of mean for frequency distribution

$$\bar{X} = \frac{\Sigma fX}{N}$$

Table 3.5 lists data from a one-minute curl-up test in a simple frequency distribution to illustrate the use of this formula.

Table 3.5 Calculation of the mean for a simple frequency distribution.

X	f	fX	
58	1	58	
55	1	55	
49	2	98	$\bar{X} = \frac{\Sigma fX}{N}$
44	4	176	
41	5	205	
40	7	280	$\bar{X} = \frac{1777}{49}$
38	6	228	
35	6	210	
33	7	231	$\bar{X} = 36.27$
28	5	140	
22	3	66	
15	2	30	
	N = 49	ΣfX = 1777	

The formula for calculating the mean of a simple frequency distribution is also used when figuring the mean for a grouped frequency distribution. Since all scores are not known in this situation, let the midpoint of each interval represent X. The midpoint is the median of the interval in question. For example, the midpoint of the 5–9 interval is 7. The computation for the mean of a grouped frequency distribution is illustrated in Table 3.6.

By assuming that the midpoint represents all the scores in the particular group interval, a small amount of accuracy is sacrificed. Actually, the sum of the original 100 scores used in this example (see Table 3.1) is 3210. When this sum is divided by 100 (N), the true mean is 32.1. This type of small error can be tolerated for the sake of convenience. The examples used to illustrate calculation of the mean can be done easily on a hand-held calculator. If there is a need to store the data or if you are working with large numbers of scores, you are advised to use SPSS for Windows, Microsoft Excel, or some other similar program available for personal computers to do the statistical work for you. Once you understand the conceptual basis of calculating the mean as well as other statistics presented in this chapter, there is no need to calculate them by hand when sophisticated statistical programs are available.

Table 3.6   Calculation of the mean for a grouped frequency distribution.

Group X	Mid-X	f	fX	
55–59	57	2	114	$\bar{X} = \dfrac{\Sigma fX}{N}$
50–54	52	2	104	
45–49	47	5	235	
40–44	42	9	378	
35–39	37	21	777	$\bar{X} = \dfrac{3200}{100}$
30–34	32	24	768	
25–29	27	17	459	
20–24	22	10	220	$\bar{X} = 32$
15–19	17	6	102	
10–14	12	3	36	
5–9	7	1	7	
		N = 100	ΣfX = 3200	

Measures of Variability

Knowing the mean, median, and mode gives little information about the variability of the scores. After determining the central tendencies of a set of data, information about the variability, or the spread, of the scores is desirable. The scores of the group can be clustered or spread out around the mean. Normal, leptokurtic, and platykurtic curves (see Figure 3.6) illustrate these situations.

When the variability of data is known, it allows for further analysis of the scores to be made, as well as a comparison of two groups of scores. Typically, the means of two sets of data are compared when, in fact, it may be more appropriate to compare the variability of the groups, especially when the means are similar but the scores are decidedly different. Like measures of central tendency, several statistical methods give information about the variability of scores in a group.

Range

The range gives a quick estimate about the spread of scores in a list of data. At best, it is a rough estimate of the variability of the group but offers an advantage because it is easily calculated. The range is the difference between the highest and lowest score in the group. Because it is determined by only two scores in the group and is, thus, directly affected by an extreme score, it is not a sensitive indicator of the variability.

The range has been previously mentioned in reference to determining appropriate intervals for grouped frequency distributions. When grouped frequency distributions are illustrated with graphs, the range is typically placed on the abscissa, with the frequency on the ordinate. When large groups of scores are collected from normal populations, these graphs are usually in the form of a normal curve.

Variance

Another method of examining the spread of the scores is by determining the distance of each score from the mean, called the deviation from the mean. If the mean of the group of scores is 5, and one of the scores (X) is 7, then the deviation from the mean is +2. If another score is 3, then the deviation is –2. The deviation score is derived by subtracting the mean from the raw score $(X-\bar{X})$. Notice in the example below that the mean is 5, and the sum of all deviation scores equals zero. When the mean is correct, the sum of the deviations will equal zero. This is a good way to check the accuracy of the mean.

Group 1			*Group 2*	
X	$X-\bar{X}$		X	$X-\bar{X}$
7	+2		9	+4
6	+1		7	+2
5	0		5	0
4	–1		3	–2
3	–2		1	–4
X = 25			X = 25	
N = 5			N = 5	
$\bar{X}$ = 5			$\bar{X}$ = 5	

The scores in Group 2 have a greater spread around the mean as reflected in the higher deviation scores. If the signs are ignored and only the absolute number of units from the mean is considered, the total deviation $\Sigma(X-\bar{X})$ is indicative of the variability of the group. Total deviation around the mean for Group 1 is 6 and for Group 2 is 12. If the $\Sigma(X-\bar{X})$ is divided by the number of scores (N) in the group, the resultant value for Group 1 is 1.2 and for Group 2, 2.4. This value is called the average deviation. It should be noted that the range for Group 1 is 4 while the range for Group 2 is 8. This range corresponds perfectly to the average deviation for each group.

Though this statistic gives information about the variability of the scores, it is a terminal statistic because it is mathematically incorrect to ignore the positive and negative values. Because of this, the average deviation is not often utilized other than to help conceptualize variance and standard deviation. A mathematical way of eliminating the negative numbers is to square the deviation scores of each score. By performing this simple operation, all the squared deviation scores, i.e. $(X-\bar{X})$, would be expressed in positive numbers.

By adding all the $(X-\bar{X})^2$ values, we find the sum of squared deviation scores $\Sigma(X-\bar{X})^2$ from the mean. When the $\Sigma(X-\bar{X})^2$ is divided by N, the statistic called the **variance** has been calculated. Thus, the formula for variance is given in Formula 3.3.

FORMULA 3.3 Calculation of the variance

$$s^2 = \frac{\Sigma(X-\bar{X})^2}{N}$$

where
s^2 = variance
X = score
$\bar{X}$ = mean
N = total number of scores

Below, a third column for $(X-\bar{X})^2$ is added to our example to illustrate how the variance (s^2) is derived.

	Group 1			*Group 2*	
X	$X-\bar{X}$	$(X-\bar{X})^2$	X	$X-\bar{X}$	$(X-\bar{X})^2$
7	+2	4	9	+4	16
6	+1	1	7	+2	4
5	0	0	5	0	0
4	−1	1	3	−2	4
3	−2	4	1	−4	16

X = 25	$\Sigma(X-\bar{X})^2 = 10$	X = 25	$\Sigma(X-\bar{X})^2 = 40$
N = 5		N = 5	
$\bar{X}$ = 5		$\bar{X}$ = 5	

$$s^2 = \frac{\Sigma(X-\bar{X})^2}{N} \qquad\qquad s^2 = \frac{\Sigma(X-\bar{X})^2}{N}$$

$$s^2 = \frac{10}{5} \qquad\qquad s^2 = \frac{40}{5}$$

$$s^2 = 2 \qquad\qquad s^2 = 8$$

The s^2 is an accurate indicator of variability of a group of scores. Unfortunately, s^2 is expressed in squared units.

Standard Deviation

The problem of squared units can easily be remedied by taking the square root of the variance, which is called the **standard deviation** (s). Just as the mean is the most commonly used measure of central tendency, the standard deviation is the most common statistic of measures of variability. Thus, the previous sections on average deviation and variance have been leading to the concept of standard deviation. Remember that in calculating the variance, the deviation scores were squared to eliminate the negative signs. To eliminate the squared units that represent the value of the variance, it is logical to take the square root. Therefore, the deviation formula for calculating the standard deviation for a group of scores is given in Formula 3.4.

FORMULA 3.4 Calculation of standard deviation (deviation method)

$$s = \sqrt{\frac{\Sigma(X-\bar{X})^2}{N}}$$

The standard deviation for Group 1 and Group 2 is calculated with the deviation formula as follows:

$$\text{Group 1} \qquad\qquad \text{Group 2}$$

$$s = \sqrt{\frac{\Sigma(X-\overline{X})^2}{N}} \qquad\qquad s = \sqrt{\frac{\Sigma(X-\overline{X})^2}{N}}$$

$$s = \sqrt{\frac{10}{5}} \qquad\qquad s = \sqrt{\frac{40}{5}}$$

$$s = \sqrt{2} \qquad\qquad s = \sqrt{8}$$

$$s = 1.41 \qquad\qquad s = 2.82$$

The standard deviation values for both groups remain consistent with the range. If the standard deviation for a group of scores is small, then this indicates that the deviations of the scores from the mean are small. There could still be extreme scores in the set of data, but a majority of scores are clustered near the mean. As the standard deviation becomes larger, the scores of the group are spread farther from the mean. A leptokurtic curve would have a small standard deviation, while a platykurtic curve would have a larger standard deviation.

This statistic gives an accurate and mathematically correct description of the variability of the group. It is the most commonly used measure of variability since many advanced statistical applications are based on the mean and standard deviation of a set of data. It is also quite useful in its applications to the normal curve and standard scores. These applications will be discussed later in this chapter.

In statistics, the symbol "σ" is often used to represent the standard deviation of a population, while "s" is used to represent the standard deviation of a sample selected from that population. For convenience and because it is appropriate for the statistical scope of this textbook, the symbol "s" will be used in this chapter.

Similarly, in formulas for standard deviation for a sample selected from a population, N–1 may be used in the denominator. If the standard deviation is calculated for specific groups, or populations, it is appropriate to use N in the denominator. Since most applications for the practitioner in physical education and the exercise sciences are with specific groups rather than samples, all standard deviation formulas in this textbook use N in the denominator.

The method for calculating the standard deviation used in the examples above is called the "deviation method." The steps entailed in using this method offer a conceptual framework underlying the standard deviation statistic. When the mean is a whole number and there are a small number of scores in the group, the deviation method is an effective way to calculate the standard deviation. Although the deviation method is of value to help understand the derivation of the standard deviation, it is rarely used for computational purposes. When the mean is a fractional number and a large number of cases is in the group, the "raw score method" is much easier than the deviation method.

Use of a hand-held calculator will expedite the calculations necessary for the raw score method. The raw score formula for calculating the standard deviation for ungrouped data is given in Formula 3.5.

FORMULA 3.5 Calculation of standard deviation for ungrouped data
(raw score method)

$$s = \sqrt{\frac{N\Sigma X^2 - (\Sigma X)^2}{N\,(N)}}$$

Table 3.7 illustrates the use of this formula.

Table 3.7 Calculation of standard deviation with ungrouped data.

X	X^2
16	256
14	196
13	169
11	121
10	100
8	64
7	49
5	25
4	16
2	4
$\Sigma X = 90$	$\Sigma X^2 = 1000$
$N = 10$	

The steps in computing the standard deviation for these data are as follows:

1. Determine N by counting the total number of scores.
2. Determine the sum of (ΣX).
3. Create an X^2 column by squaring each score.
4. Sum the X^2 column to calculate ΣX^2.
5. Substitute the values into the formula and solve for s.

$$s = \sqrt{\frac{N\Sigma X^2 - (\Sigma X)^2}{N\,(N)}}$$

$$s = \sqrt{\frac{10(1000) - (90)^2}{10(10)}}$$

$$s = \sqrt{\frac{10{,}000 - 8100}{100}}$$

$$s = \sqrt{\frac{1900}{100}}$$

$$s = \sqrt{19}$$

$$s = 4.36$$

The same steps can be followed to calculate the s for a simple or grouped frequency distribution, except the frequency column must be included in the computation. The raw score formula for a frequency distribution would be as given in Formula 3.6.

FORMULA 3.6 Calculation of standard deviation for a frequency distribution (raw score method)

$$s = \sqrt{\frac{N\Sigma fX^2 - (\Sigma fX)^2}{N(N)}}$$

Table 3.8 illustrates the computations involved in finding the standard deviation for a frequency distribution.

Table 3.8 Calculation of standard deviation from frequency distribution.

X	f	fX	x2	fX2
16	1	16	256	256
14	2	28	196	392
13	4	52	169	676
11	5	55	121	605
10	5	50	100	500
8	7	56	64	448
7	6	42	49	294
5	4	20	25	100
4	3	12	16	48
2	2	4	4	8
	N = 39	ΣfX = 335		ΣfX^2 = 3327

The steps in computing the standard deviation for these data are as follows:
1. Determine N by adding the frequency (f) column.
2. Multiply f by X to create the fX column.
3. Add the fX column to determine ΣfX.
4. Square scores in the X column to create the X^2 column.
5. Multiply f by X^2 to create the fX^2 column.
6. Add the fX^2 column.
7. Substitute the values into the formula and solve for s.

$$s = \sqrt{\frac{N\Sigma fX^2 - (\Sigma fX)^2}{N(N)}}$$

$$s = \sqrt{\frac{39(3327) - (335)^2}{39(39)}}$$

$$s = \sqrt{\frac{129,753 - 112,225}{1521}}$$

$$s = \sqrt{\frac{17,528}{1521}}$$

$$s = \sqrt{11.52}$$

$$s = 3.39$$

When a grouped frequency distribution is involved, the midpoint of each interval serves as the value in the X column. Otherwise, the computations are the same for both types of frequency distributions.

There are other methods of calculating the standard deviation for different groups of scores. Unless there is a relatively small group of data, it is desirable to utilize a programmable desk calculator or statistical software such as SPSS for Windows or Microsoft Excel to derive the standard deviation. In situations where the standard deviation is calculated by hand, the raw score method is an effective choice.

When the standard deviation and the mean are known for a set of data, it is easier to analyze the group of scores. The average score as well as the spread of the scores helps describe the data. A better understanding of what these statistics mean should evolve as the relationship of these statistics and the properties of the normal curve are discussed.

Properties of the Normal Curve

The normal frequency distribution curve, known as the normal curve, was mentioned briefly earlier in this chapter. After presenting the measures of central tendency and variability, it is now appropriate to further discuss the properties of the normal curve. The normal curve represents a theoretical distribution of data based on a mathematical formula. Shown in Figure 3.7, the normal curve suggests that, for normally distributed interval/ratio data, the scores will be symmetrically distributed around the mean. The scores cluster in the vicinity of the mean and gradually taper off in the tails of the curve. The tails of the curve never reach the baseline so that it allows infinite variation in either direction.

The center of a perfectly normal curve is the highest point of the curve representing the greatest frequency of scores. As such, it also represents the mode, median, and mean of the group of scores. This center point divides the curve in half so that 50 percent of the scores fall above and 50 percent fall below the mean. The standard deviation of the curve is measured along the baseline. (See Figure 3.7.)

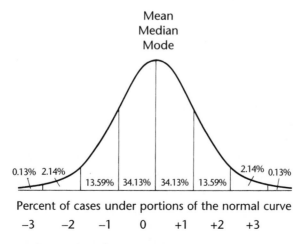

Figure 3.7 Mean, median, and mode in normal curve.

The properties of the normal curve are such that practically all scores (99.74 percent) will fall ±3 standard deviations from the mean. Further, 95.44 percent of all scores will occur within ±2 standard deviation units from the mean, while 68.26 percent are found ±1 standard deviation from the mean.

Standard Scores

The direct result of measurement is the raw score. These raw scores may reflect time, distance, weight, number of successful attempts, and so on. In most instances, raw scores from one set of data are not directly comparable to scores from another set of data. If a student runs 1.5 miles in 11:45 minutes and does 48 sit-ups in one minute, which is better? A track athlete ran 400 meters in 55 seconds and threw the discus a distance of 129 feet. In which event was the performance superior?

Without more information about these raw scores, it is impossible to make any meaningful comparisons. Seconds in the 400-meter run and feet in the discus throw cannot be logically compared. By knowing more about the set of scores, **standard scores** can be calculated that provide a commonality, which allows meaningful comparisons of different sets to be made. Several types of standard scores may be used. The most widely used types are the percentile rank, the z-score, and the T-score.

Percentile Rank

One of the most common statistics, and certainly the most popular standard score, is the **percentile**. Most people in the general public have some understanding of percentiles. As a result, practitioners in physical education and the exercise sciences find this statistical method to be particularly useful in interpreting scores. Percentile rank provides a quick comparison with all other scores in the group.

A score at the 66.7th percentile is equal to or surpasses at least two-thirds of the scores in the group. A 90th percentile score indicates that a score is equal to or better than 9 of 10 scores earned on the particular test. If a student scores in the 25th percentile on a test of aerobic endurance, then three-quarters of the persons who took the test had a better performance than that student.

Using percentile rank, it becomes possible to compare raw scores from different sets of data. If 400 meters is run in 55 seconds and is in the 71st percentile, and the discus is thrown 129 feet and is in the 64th percentile, then it is obvious which is the best performance.

Since the 50th percentile is, by definition, the median for the group of scores, information about the relative value of any percentile rank is known. The mathematical conversion of raw scores to standard scores, such as a percentile, allows logical comparisons to be made and is a common technique in statistics.

As discussed previously in the chapter, percentiles can be calculated from frequency distributions. When scores are arranged in a simple frequency distribution, it is necessary to determine how many scores are equal to or below the raw score in question. Consider the following data:

Group X	f	Cum f	Cum %
23–25	3	66	100
20–22	7	63	95
17–19	15	56	85
14–16	19	41	62
11–13	11	22	33
8–10	9	11	14
5–7	2	2	1
	N = 66		

By creating the cumulative frequency (Cum f) and cumulative percentile (Cum %) columns, the percentile for each group of scores can be ascertained. For instance, 22 scores are equal to or lower than the group of scores from 11 to 13. By dividing that number found in the cumulative frequency column for the 11–13 group by the total number of scores (N = 66), it can be calculated that this group of scores is at the 33rd percentile.

Suppose the exact percentile rank of a score in the 11–13 interval is needed. For instance, what is the percentile rank for the score of 12? For a more exact calculation of percentile rank, Formula 3.7 can be used:

FORMULA 3.7 Calculation of percentile rank

$$\text{Percentile of rank score} = 100 \left[\frac{(\text{score} - \text{LRL of group})}{i} \times (\text{f of group}) + (\text{cum f of the group below}) \right] \div N$$

The values to be substituted into the formula to calculate the percentile rank of the raw score of 12 are as follows:

score = 12

LRL (lower real limits) of group = 10.5

i (size of interval of group) = 3

f (frequency) of group = 11

cum f (cumulative frequency) of group below = 11

N (total number of scores) = 66

The formula used for this calculation may look complex. However, by making the necessary substitutions from the grouped frequency distribution as shown, it is a simple task to calculate the percentile rank of 12.

$$\text{Percentile of score} = 100 \left[\frac{(\text{score} - \text{LRL of group})}{i} \times (\text{f of group}) + (\text{cum f of the group below}) \right] \div N$$

$$\text{Percentile of } 12 = 100 \left[\frac{12-10.5}{3} \times 11 + 11 \right] \div 66$$

$$\text{Percentile of } 12 = 100 \left[\frac{1.5}{3} \times 11 + 11 \right] \div 66$$

$$\text{Percentile of } 12 = 100 [.5 \times 11 + 11] \div 66$$

$$\text{Percentile of } 12 = 100 [5.5 + 11] \div 66$$

$$\text{Percentile of } 12 = 100 [16.5] \div 66$$

$$\text{Percentile of } 12 = 1650 \div 66$$

$$\text{Percentile of } 12 = 25$$

It is also possible to calculate the score that corresponds to a specific percentile rank. Using the same grouped frequency distribution data, suppose it were desirable to know the score that falls at the 75th percentile. Formula 3.8 can be used to make this calculation:

FORMULA 3.8 Calculation of score corresponding to percentile rank

$$\text{Score} = (\text{LRL of group}) + i \left[\frac{(\text{nth case}) - \left(\begin{array}{c} \text{cum f of} \\ \text{group below} \end{array} \right)}{\text{f of group}} \right]$$

The values to be substituted into this formula are as follows:

nth case = 75% of N = .75 2 66 = 49.5

cum f of group below = 41 (In the Cum f column, this is the cum f of the group that does not exceed the nth case.)

f of group = 15 (In the Cum % column, it can be noted that the 75th percentile falls in the 35–39 group.)

i (interval of group) = 3

LRL (lower real limit) of group = 16.5

The calculation of this sample problem is as follows:

$$\text{Score} = (\text{LRL of group}) + i \left[\frac{(\text{nth case}) - (\text{cum f of group below})}{\text{f of group}} \right]$$

$$\text{Score} = 16.5 + 3 \left[\frac{(49.5) - (41)}{15} \right]$$

$$\text{Score} = 16.5 + 3 \left[\frac{8.5}{15} \right]$$

$$\text{Score} = 16.5 + 3 [.57]$$

$$\text{Score} = 16.5 + 1.71$$

$$\text{Score} = 18.21$$

Thus, the score from the data that corresponds to the 75th percentile would be 18.21.

Though percentile ranks are a very useful statistical tool, some limitations exist. Percentile ranks are ordinal in nature and, as such, represent a terminal statistic. They cannot be added or subtracted logically. Equal differences in percentile ranks do not represent equal differences in the corresponding raw scores. Percentiles are based on the number of scores on a particular test. In a normal frequency distribution, it is much more difficult to improve from the 90th to the 95th percentile than to improve from the 45th to the 50th percentile. Because there are so many scores, a small improvement in the raw score in the middle of the group could be a relatively large jump in percentile rank. The opposite holds true on the extreme ends of the scale. This phenomenon is called a **ceiling effect**.

In Figure 3.8, note that a student who improved from 30 sit-ups to 35 sit-ups shows an improvement from the 50th percentile to the 74th percentile. A student who had a better initial performance of 45 sit-ups, 96th percentile, and improved to 50 sit-ups shows an increase to the 98th percentile. Though both students improved by five sit-ups, the resultant percentile ranks can be deceiving. This example shows that percentile ranks should be used with caution when considering improvement in performance.

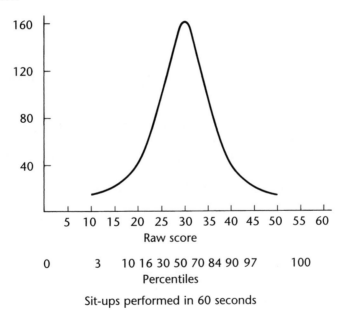

Figure 3.8 Illustration of ceiling effect.

Z-Score

A standard score that is expressed in terms of standard deviation units on a normal curve is called a **z-score**. A z-score indicates how far from the mean the raw score is located. The farther above the mean the raw score is, the higher the z-score will be. If the score is lower than the mean of the group, the z-score will be negative. The mean of a group of scores is represented by a z-score of 0. If the mean and standard deviation of the group of scores are known, the z-score for any raw score in the group can be calculated using Formula 3.9.

FORMULA 3.9 Calculation of z-score

$$z = \frac{X - \bar{X}}{s}$$

In a group of scores with a mean of 50 and a standard deviation of 6, what would be the z-score value of the raw score of 59? By applying Formula 3.9, the z-score for 59 can be calculated as follows:

$$z = \frac{X - \bar{X}}{s}$$

$$z = \frac{59 - 50}{6}$$

$$z = \frac{9}{6}$$

$$z = 1.5$$

The z-score of 1.5 represents a raw score that is 1.5 standard deviation units above the mean. A raw score smaller than the mean will always result in a negative z-score unless the lower score represents the better performance.

In physical education, exercise science, and athletics, there are certain tests in which a lower score is better. Golf scores, time in any type of race, and percentage of body fat are examples. In these situations, subtract the raw score from the mean in the numerator of the equation. Thus, the equation is as shown in Formula 3.10.

FORMULA 3.10 Calculation of z-score when lower score represents better performance

$$z = \frac{\bar{X} - X}{s}$$

If the mean for a group of golf scores is 86.8 with a standard deviation of 9.4, what is the z-score for a raw score of 79?

$$z = \frac{\bar{X} - X}{s}$$

$$z = \frac{86.8 - 79}{9.4}$$

$$z = \frac{7.8}{9.4}$$

$$z = .83$$

A z-score is useful in comparing scores in two separate distributions. The raw scores may represent time in the 50-yard dash and distance in the standing long jump. By converting both raw scores to z-scores, there is a basis for comparison to determine which is the best score. The size of the z-score also gives important information about how far above or below the mean the score is located.

With the properties of the normal curve in mind (see Figure 3.7), the z-score gives information about what percent of scores of the population falls between the z-score and the mean. A z-score of 1.0 represents one standard deviation unit above the mean. It is characteristic of the normal curve that exactly 34.13 percent of the population of scores lies between the mean and one standard deviation unit.

Since 50 percent of the scores lie on each side of the mean, it can be deduced that a z-score of 1.0 is equal to or better than 84.13 percent of the scores in the distribution. This assumes that the group of scores is normally distributed. Table 3.9 shows the percentage of area that falls between the mean and any z-score in a group. The far left-hand column represents z-values to the nearest tenth. The figures across the top represent the hundredths value. If the z-score was 1.57, then move down the left-hand column to 1.5 and then across the table to the .07 column. The number located by this procedure should be 0.4418. This means that 44.18 percent of the area of the normal curve lies between the mean and the z-score of 1.57.

Because the normal curve is symmetrical, 44.18 percent of the area of the normal curve lies between the mean and a z-score of −1.57. Further, 88.36 percent of the area lies between the z-scores of 1.57 and −1.57.

T-Score

Another type of standard score derived from the z-score is the **T-score**. Because the z-score is usually a fractional number and half of the z-scores are negative numbers, it is sometimes desirable to transform the z-score into a T-score. The value for a T-score is represented by a positive, whole number, which may help students or parents comprehend the meaning of the standard score. To calculate the T-score, Formula 3.11 is used:

FORMULA 3.11 Calculation of T-score

$$T = 10 \left(\frac{X - \bar{X}}{s}\right) + 50$$

or

$$T = 10z + 50$$

Using this formula, convert a z-score of −1.2 to the corresponding T-score. Simply multiply the z-score by 10 and add 50. The substitutions into the formula above should read

$$T = 10z + 50$$
$$T = 10 \, (-1.2) + 50$$
$$T = -12 + 50$$
$$T = 38$$

Table 3.9 The normal distribution.

Percentage area under the standard normal curve from 0 to z
(shown shaded) is the value found in the body of the table.

z	0.00	0.01	0.02	0.03	0.04	0.05	0.06	0.07	0.08	0.09
0.0	0.0000	0.0040	0.0080	0.0120	0.0160	0.0199	0.0239	0.0279	0.0319	0.0359
0.1	0.0398	0.0438	0.0478	0.0517	0.0557	0.0596	0.0636	0.0675	0.0714	0.0753
0.2	0.0793	0.0832	0.0871	0.0910	0.0948	0.0987	0.1026	0.1064	0.1103	0.1141
0.3	0.1179	0.1217	0.1255	0.1293	0.1331	0.1368	0.1406	0.1443	0.1480	0.1517
0.4	0.1554	0.1591	0.1628	0.1664	0.1700	0.1736	0.1772	0.1808	0.1844	0.1879
0.5	0.1915	0.1950	0.1985	0.2019	0.2054	0.2088	0.2123	0.2157	0.2190	0.2224
0.6	0.2257	0.2291	0.2324	0.2357	0.2389	0.2422	0.2454	0.2486	0.2517	0.2549
0.7	0.2580	0.2611	0.2642	0.2673	0.2704	0.2734	0.2764	0.2794	0.2823	0.2852
0.8	0.2881	0.2910	0.2939	0.2967	0.2995	0.3023	0.3051	0.3078	0.3106	0.3133
0.9	0.3159	0.3186	0.3212	0.3238	0.3264	0.3289	0.3315	0.3340	0.3365	0.3389
1.0	0.3413	0.3438	0.3461	0.3485	0.3508	0.3531	0.3554	0.3577	0.3599	0.3621
1.1	0.3643	0.3665	0.3686	0.3708	0.3729	0.3749	0.3770	0.3790	0.3810	0.3830
1.2	0.3849	0.3869	0.3888	0.3907	0.3925	0.3944	0.3962	0.3980	0.3997	0.4015
1.3	0.4032	0.4049	0.4066	0.4082	0.4099	0.4115	0.4131	0.4147	0.4162	0.4177
1.4	0.4192	0.4207	0.4222	0.4236	0.4251	0.4265	0.4279	0.4292	0.4306	0.4319
1.5	0.4332	0.4345	0.4357	0.4370	0.4382	0.4394	0.4406	0.4418	0.4429	0.4441
1.6	0.4452	0.4463	0.4474	0.4484	0.4495	0.4505	0.4515	0.4525	0.4535	0.4545
1.7	0.4554	0.4564	0.4573	0.4582	0.4591	0.4599	0.4608	0.4616	0.4625	0.4633
1.8	0.4641	0.4649	0.4656	0.4664	0.4671	0.4678	0.4686	0.4693	0.4699	0.4706
1.9	0.4713	0.4719	0.4726	0.4732	0.4738	0.4744	0.4750	0.4756	0.4761	0.4767
2.0	0.4772	0.4778	0.4783	0.4788	0.4793	0.4798	0.4803	0.4808	0.4812	0.4817
2.1	0.4821	0.4826	0.4830	0.4834	0.4838	0.4842	0.4846	0.4850	0.4854	0.4857
2.2	0.4861	0.4864	0.4868	0.4871	0.4875	0.4878	0.4881	0.4884	0.4887	0.4890
2.3	0.4893	0.4896	0.4898	0.4901	0.4904	0.4906	0.4909	0.4911	0.4913	0.4916
2.4	0.4918	0.4920	0.4922	0.4925	0.4927	0.4929	0.4931	0.4932	0.4934	0.4936
2.5	0.4938	0.4940	0.4941	0.4943	0.4945	0.4946	0.4948	0.4949	0.4951	0.4952
2.6	0.4953	0.4955	0.4956	0.4957	0.4959	0.4960	0.4961	0.4962	0.4963	0.4964
2.7	0.4965	0.4966	0.4967	0.4968	0.4969	0.4970	0.4971	0.4972	0.4973	0.4974
2.8	0.4974	0.4975	0.4976	0.4977	0.4977	0.4978	0.4979	0.4979	0.4980	0.4981
2.9	0.4981	0.4982	0.4982	0.4983	0.4984	0.4984	0.4985	0.4985	0.4986	0.4986
3.0	0.4987	0.4987	0.4987	0.4988	0.4988	0.4989	0.4989	0.4989	0.4990	0.4990

Abridged from Table 9 in *Biometrika Tables for Statisticians*, Vol. 1 (3rd ed.), edited by E. S. Pearson and H. O. Hartley, 1966, New York: Cambridge. Reprinted by permission of E. J. Snell for and on behalf of the Biometrika Trustees, London, England.

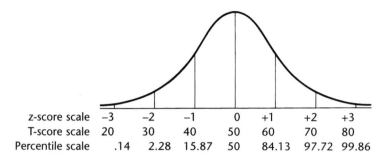

z-score scale	−3	−2	−1	0	+1	+2	+3
T-score scale	20	30	40	50	60	70	80
Percentile scale		.14	2.28	15.87	50	84.13	97.72	99.86

Figure 3.9 Normal curve with standard score scales.

While a distribution of z-scores has a mean of zero and a standard deviation of 1, the T-score distribution has a mean of 50 and a standard deviation of 10. This means that a z-score of −1.0 is equivalent to a T-score of 40, a z-score of 0 is the same as a T-score of 50, and a z-score of 1.0 corresponds to a T-score of 60. T-scores are used because it is sometimes easier to conceptualize standard scores from 0 to 100 with a mean of 50. It is rare to have a T-score less than 20 or higher than 80 since these represent a −3 and a +3 standard deviation from the mean. Figure 3.9 should clarify the relationships between the various standard scores that have been discussed in the previous sections. As noted in the figure, a z-score of 1.0, a T-score of 60, and a percentile score of 84.13 percent are equivalent. These various scales represent different ways to compare raw scores in standard score formats.

SECTION 3—CORRELATION AND REGRESSION

Correlation

The statistical technique of correlation can be quite valuable in physical education. The concept of **correlation** refers to the relationship between two variables. The **correlation coefficient** is the statistic that represents the relationship, or association, between the variables. When information is desired about the relationship between one set of values and another set of values, a correlation procedure is employed. To use correlation, two or more variables from the same population are required. When more than two variables are examined, multiple correlation procedures are appropriate. The discussion in this chapter will be limited to correlation between two variables.

Consider a group of 30 physical education students. What type of relationship is there between the height and weight of these 30 students? In most circumstances, the taller a student is, the more he or she weighs. This illustrates a positive correlation. Similarly, when variable X is smaller and variable Y also decreases, this also represents a positive correlation. A perfect positive correlation coefficient would be +1.00. The correlation coefficient can never be larger than this value.

Suppose the same group of 30 students were timed in the 50-yard dash and measured in the long jump. Usually the faster a person can sprint, the better long jumper he or she will be. Thus, the lower the time (variable X) in the 50-yard dash, the greater the distance (variable Y) in the long jump. As variable X gets smaller, variable Y gets larger. This is an example of a negative correlation. A perfect negative correlation coefficient would be –1.00. A correlation coefficient can never be lower than this value.

Thus, the correlation coefficient that represents the relationship between two sets of variables is always between –1.00 and +1.00. If two sets of values have absolutely no relationship, then the correlation coefficient would be 0. Correlation coefficients of –1.00, +1.00, or 0 are rarely obtained. A correlation of –.75 indicates just as strong a relationship between the two variables as +.75. As the correlation coefficient approaches 0 from either the positive or negative side, it is an indication of less relationship between the variables. Therefore, a –.50 correlation coefficient indicates a stronger relationship between two sets of variables than a +.49.

As the correlation coefficient nears +1 or –1, there is a stronger linear relationship between the variables in question. A visual description of the correlation coefficient may be shown on a graph called a **scattergram** (see Figure 3.10). The X variable is placed on the abscissa, and the Y variable on the ordinate. By plotting the points for each subject on variables X and Y, a pattern of points will emerge. If the pattern formed is linear, the relationship between variables is great, and the correlation coefficient will be high. A perfectly straight line would represent a +1.00 or –1.00 correlation coefficient. Figure 3.10 includes several scattergrams to illustrate the various relationships between variables.

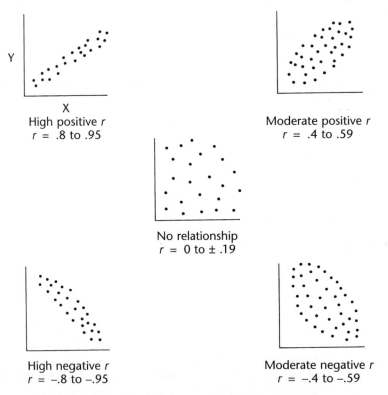

Figure 3.10 Scattergrams representing various correlation coefficients.

Safrit and Wood (1995) present general guidelines on how the size of the correlation coefficient should be interpreted. They are

± .80 – 1.00 High

± .60 – 0.79 Moderately high

± .40 – 0.59 Moderate

± .20 – 0.39 Low

± .00 – 0.19 No relationship

The correlation coefficient for the relationship between two sets of variables can be squared to interpret the amount of shared variance between the two sets of data. Thus, if the correlation between pull-ups and chin-ups is .9, the shared variance is .81. This can be interpreted to mean that the two sets of data have 81 percent shared variance, or overlap. These two sets of data are highly related by one or more common characteristics, which can be logically assumed to be strength of the arms and shoulders.

It should be emphasized that highly correlated variables show a strong relationship, or association between the two sets of variables. However, high correlation never proves causation. Being tall does not cause someone to be heavy nor does being short guarantee weighing less. A very fast sprinter may be a poor long jumper. If a correlation coefficient is high enough, it can have some predictive potential. Unless there is a perfect correlation, however, the prediction cannot be foolproof.

Spearman Rho Rank-Order Correlation

When one or both groups of data involved in a correlation procedure are at the ordinal level of measurement, then the **Spearman rho rank-order correlation** should be used. Team rankings and order of finish in tournaments are examples of ordinal data often used in physical education. If one group of scores happens to be interval or ratio data, change them to the ordinal level by rank ordering them before using the Spearman rho formula.

Suppose a racquetball instructor gave a serving test that yielded a raw score at the ratio level and then had a single round-robin class tournament at the end of the unit. The teacher wants to know if the scores on the serving test correlate highly with the final ranking in the class tournament.

To calculate the Spearman rho rank-order correlation, Formula 3.12 is used.

FORMULA 3.12 Spearman rho rank = order correlation

$$r' = 1 - \frac{6\Sigma d^2}{N(N^2 - 1)}$$

Table 3.10 illustrates the calculation of a Spearman rho rank-order correlation coefficient.

The correlation coefficient in this calculation is .66. This represents a moderately high relationship between the results of the serving test and finish in the class standings.

Table 3.10 Calculation of Spearman rho rank-order correlation coefficient.

Serving Score (X)	Rank X	Rank of Finish (Y)	d	d²
95	1	2	−1	1
92	2	4	−2	4
88	3	1	2	4
87	4	5	−1	1
85	5	8	−3	9
82	6	3	3	9
80	7	9	−2	4
77	8	10	−2	4
75	9	7	2	4
72	10	6	4	16
N = 10			$\Sigma d = 0$	$\Sigma d^2 = 56$

The steps in computing the Spearman rho rank-order correlation coefficient are as follows:

1. Determine N by counting the number of paired scores, N = 10.
2. Convert the raw scores on the serving test to ordinal data.
3. Subtract the rank of variable Y from the rank of variable X to create the d column, d = Rank X − Rank Y. If subtraction is done correctly, the Σd will always be zero.
4. Square each value of d to create the d² column and add the d² values, $\Sigma d^2 = 56$.
5. Substitute the values into the formula to solve for r'.

$$r' = 1 - \frac{6\Sigma d^2}{N(N^2-1)}$$

$$r' = 1 - \frac{6(56)}{10(10^2-1)}$$

$$r' = 1 - \frac{336}{10(100-1)}$$

$$r' = 1 - \frac{336}{10(99)}$$

$$r' = 1 - \frac{336}{990}$$

$$r' = 1 - .34$$

$$r' = .66$$

Pearson Product-Moment Correlation

If the two sets of variables in question are represented by interval or ratio data, then the **Pearson product-moment correlation** method should be used. The correlation coefficient value derived from this procedure is represented by the symbol *r*. When using correlation procedures, 30 or more subjects are desirable so that extreme scores of one subject do not affect the coefficient. For convenience, the examples included here will have fewer subjects.

The raw score formula for the Pearson product-moment correlation is shown in Formula 3.13.

FORMULA 3.13 Calculation of Pearson product-moment correlation

$$r = \frac{N\Sigma XY - \Sigma X \Sigma Y}{\sqrt{[N\Sigma X^2 - (\Sigma X)^2][N\Sigma Y^2 - (\Sigma Y)^2]}}$$

Though the formula may appear complex, it is simply a matter of substituting the proper values and completing the calculation. The use of a hand-held calculator makes this task easier. Table 3.11 shows the scores attained by 10 students on pull-up and chin-up tests. By surveying the scores and from intuition, it is easy to note a positive relationship between the scores. By implementing the raw score formula, the exact nature of the relationship between the scores on these two tests can be calculated.

A correlation coefficient of .985 represents a high positive relationship between pull-ups and chin-ups.

The data in the Pearson product-moment correlation example (Table 3.11) can be changed to ordinal data by ranking each set of data. If this were done, the Spearman rho formula could be utilized. The coefficients for the two correlation techniques would not be identical, but they would be very similar, because when ratio scores are converted to ordinal scores, less information is known about the original ratio-level scores.

In summary, when two sets of scores are collected from the same set of subjects, the relationship between the two variables can be estimated using a correlation procedure. The Pearson product-moment method is used with interval or ratio data and is usually preferred since it utilizes a higher level of measurement. However, if ordinal data are involved, the Spearman rho formula should be used. Correlation procedures provide the basis for more important applications in physical education and the exercise sciences. When there is a high correlation coefficient, regression equations can be developed to make meaningful predictions from known data. In Chapter 4, validity and reliability of tests are discussed. Correlation procedures play an integral role in establishing validity and reliability of tests used in both school and nonschool settings. As mentioned earlier, correlations are more meaningful and accurate when a larger number of scores is collected. Since large amounts of data are typically used, we recommend the use of statistical programs available for use on a personal computer to expedite calculations of correlation coeggicients.

Regression

Using the mean and standard deviation from the sets of data for two variables having a high correlation coefficient, it is possible to predict the value of variable Y from variable X and vice versa. When working with two sets of data, this process is known as **simple regression**. The higher the correlation coefficient, the more accurate will be the prediction of the regression equation. While regression equations can be calculated for two sets of data with a moderate or low correlation coefficient, it makes little sense to do so since they would reflect a wide range of possible error in the prediction. Only when the correlation coefficient is ±1.00 is the resulting prediction

Table 3.11 Calculation of Pearson product-moment correlation.

Pull-Ups (X)	Chin-Ups (Y)	X2	Y2	XY
10	13	100	169	130
16	20	256	400	320
4	6	16	36	24
8	11	64	121	88
9	11	81	121	99
6	10	36	100	60
1	2	1	4	2
12	15	144	225	180
7	8	49	64	56
5	6	25	36	30
$\Sigma X = 78$	$\Sigma Y = 102$	$\Sigma X^2 = 772$	$\Sigma Y^2 = 1276$	$\Sigma XY = 989$

The steps in computing the Pearson product-moment correlation coefficient are as follows:

1. Determine N by counting the number of pairs of scores. In this example, $N = 10$.
2. Add column X, $\Sigma X = 78$.
3. Add column Y, $\Sigma Y = 102$.
4. Create an X^2 column by squaring each score in the X column and add the X^2 column, $\Sigma X^2 = 772$.
5. Create a Y^2 column by squaring each score in the Y column and add the Y^2 column, $\Sigma Y^2 = 1276$.
6. Multiply each X score by the corresponding Y score to create an XY column and add the XY column, $\Sigma XY = 989$.
7. Substitute the values into the formula and solve for r.

$$r = \frac{N\Sigma XY - \Sigma X \Sigma Y}{\sqrt{[N\Sigma X^2 - (\Sigma X)^2][N\Sigma Y^2 - (\Sigma Y)^2]}}$$

$$r = \frac{10(989) - 78(102)}{\sqrt{[10(772) - (78)^2][10(1276) - (102)^2]}}$$

$$r = \frac{9890 - 7956}{\sqrt{(7720 - 6084)(12{,}760 - 10{,}404)}}$$

$$r = \frac{1934}{\sqrt{(1636)(2356)}}$$

$$r = \frac{1934}{\sqrt{3{,}854{,}416}}$$

$$r = \frac{1934}{1963.27}$$

$$r = .985$$

from the regression equation completely accurate. However, when the correlation is high (±.8 or higher), the range of error for the predicted values is relatively small.

A simple regression is also called a linear regression since the analysis tries to find a straight line that best fits the data from variable X and variable Y. Formula 3.14 for a simple regression analysis is the formula for a straight line.

FORMULA 3.14 Calculation of simple regression
_____

$$Y' = a + bX$$

The values to be substituted into this formula are as follows:

Y' = predicted value of variable Y
a = Y intercept (where line crosses the Y axis)
b = slope of the regression line
X = known value of variable X

Before applying the formula, calculate the slope (b) and the Y intercept. Formula 3.15 is used for calculating the slope (b).

FORMULA 3.15 Calculation of the slope
_____

$$b = r\left(\frac{s_Y}{s_X}\right)$$

r = correlation coefficient
s_Y = standard deviation of variable Y
s_X = standard deviation of variable X

The formula for calculating the Y intercept (a) is as follows:

FORMULA 3.16 Calculation of the Y intercept
_____

$$a = \bar{Y} - b\bar{X}$$

$\bar{Y}$ = mean of variable Y
$\bar{X}$ = mean of variable X
b = slope

Using the data from the previous Pearson product-moment correlation example (Table 3.11), r is calculated as .985. For variable X (pull-ups), the mean is 7.8 and the standard deviation is 4.04. For variable Y (chin-ups), the mean is 10.2 and the standard deviation is 4.85. With this information, the calculation of a regression equation allows an accurate prediction of how many chin-ups a student can do when the number of pull-ups that student is capable of doing is known. For instance, if a student can do 15 pull-ups, how many chin-ups could a teacher expect the student to do? To answer this question using regression analysis, calculate as follows:

1. Calculate the mean and standard deviation for each set of data. Since these procedures were performed previously in this chapter, the values are provided.

2. Calculate the Pearson product-moment correlation coefficient. This was done in Table 3.11.

3. Calculate the slope (b).

$$b = r\left(\frac{s_y}{s_x}\right)$$

$$b = .985\left(\frac{4.85}{4.04}\right)$$

$$b = .985(1.2)$$

$$b = 1.18$$

4. Calculate the Y intercept (a).

$$a = \bar{Y} - b\bar{X}$$

$$a = 10.2 - 1.18(7.8)$$

$$a = 10.2 - 9.22$$

$$a = .98$$

5. Using the regression formula, compute Y′ (called "Y prime"), which is the predicted number of chin-ups the student will be able to complete.

$$Y' = a + bX$$

$$Y' = .98 + 1.18 (15)$$

$$Y' = .98 + 17.7$$

$$Y' = 18.68$$

The Y′ value of 18.68 is a prediction of the number of chin-ups the student can do. Since fractional chin-ups would not be counted, the predicted Y value can be rounded to 19. Remember that while there is some margin of error in the prediction, the closer the correlation coefficient is to ±1.00, the more accurate the prediction is. The exact standard error of the estimate can be calculated for any regression equation, but this information is beyond the intended scope of this chapter. The reader should refer to a textbook with more advanced statistical procedures for a discussion of determining confidence intervals for regression analysis.

This introduction to simple or linear regression is based on working with only two sets of variables. This is quite common in physical education and the exercise sciences. For instance, predicting a person's maximal oxygen uptake based on results of a 12-minute run test would be based on simple regression. Completing a 12-minute run test is much simpler, cheaper, and more time efficient than a maximal oxygen uptake test protocol. While giving up a small amount of accuracy is a disadvantage, the advantages far outweigh this disadvantage in many situations.

Multiple Correlation/Regression

The previous section has explained simple correlation and regression. As described, these prediction equations are based on predicting one variable (Y) based on the actual results of another variable (X). A prediction formula based on a single measure X may not be as accurate as we would hope for predicting an individual's score on measure Y. A more complex and accurate prediction formula can be developed using multiple measures to predict a measure of Y. Thus, variables X_1, X_2, and X_3 might be used to predict Y. This can be called **multiple correlation, multiple regression**, or multiple prediction. The terms are interchangeable. A multiple regression equation will have a single Y intercept (a) and multiple slopes (b) associated with the X variables. If there were three predictor variables, the formula would take the form of:

$$Y' = a + b_1X_1 = b_2X_2 + b_3X_3$$

If there were only two predictor variables, the formula would be:

$$Y' = a + b_1X_1 = b_2X_2$$

The calculation of a multiple correlation formula is much more complicated than for simple regression. Because of the complexity of the calculations, you should use statistical programs such as SPSS for Windows in developing multiple regression equations. This is not typical of the statistical work that the practitioner would find necessary to do. The practitioner, however, needs to understand how to use these formulas that researchers have developed. One of the most common applications is the use of skinfold measurement. If a skinfold measurement were done at the chest, abdominal, and thigh sites to measure millimeters of fat, then the three variables would be used to predict the percentage of body fat. This prediction of body fat would be based on a high multiple correlation coefficient of skinfold sites to underwater weighing procedures of determining body fat. A number of prediction equations for body composition based on multiple-site skinfold measurements have been developed and are commonly used in both school and nonschool activity settings.

Thus far, all discussions of both simple prediction and multiple prediction formulas are based on linear relationships. You should be aware that there are also nonlinear relationships used to develop prediction formulas. Some statistical programs have a polynomial regression option that allow for the computation of curvilinear relationship. This more advanced statistical concept is beyond the intended scope of this textbook.

SECTION 4—TESTS FOR DIFFERENCES

The previous section of this chapter has dealt with the relationship, or correlation, between sets of data. In some situations, it is desirable to know if significant differences exist between groups of scores. A number of different statistical tests are appropriate to use based on a number of different factors. Among these factors are the number of groups involved, number of subjects in the groups, and sampling procedures used for selection of subjects within the groups. Many other research design and methodological factors are also involved in determining differences between groups. In addition, the student needs a thorough conceptual knowledge of probability theory, assumptions underlying the tests, hypothesis testing, and other more advanced statistical concepts to interpret the results of these tests used to determine differences between groups.

These areas of information are typically included in introductory statistics and research methods courses. Entire textbooks are devoted to these areas. While it is important that a student recognize the existence of such tests, a cursory examination of the tests and their accompanying formulas can often lead to misuse and faulty interpretations of results. Clearly, an introductory measurement and evaluation textbook such as this one cannot present the depth of information necessary for the reader to have sufficient knowledge to use and interpret these tests properly. Thus, the following brief descriptions of two types of t-tests—simple analysis of variance (ANOVA) and two-way ANOVA—are intended to provide the reader with an introduction to the role and function of these commonly used statistical procedures. They are referred to as inferential statistics because results can be inferred to apply to the population from which the sample was selected.

t-Tests

t-test for Independent Samples

A **t-test for independent samples** can be used to determine if there are differences between the sets of scores from two groups of subjects taking the same test. Suppose a physical education teacher wants to examine whether being in physical education class improves the cardiorespiratory fitness levels of students. In this hypothetical situation, two groups of 31 students are randomly selected from the entire 10th grade population at a school. One group of 31 students enrolls in daily physical education class during the year, while the other group does not take physical education. At the end of the year, the 12-minute run/walk test is administered to all students to measure cardiorespiratory fitness. In the 12-minute run/walk, the score on the test is the number of yards covered in 12 minutes.

The PE group has a mean score of 2400 yards, with a standard deviation of 300, while the non-PE group has a mean score of 2150, with a standard deviation of 375. The t-test for independent samples can be used to determine if there is a statistically significant difference in the results of the two groups in the 12-minute run/walk test. In some cases, small differences in the mean can be statistically significant, while in other sets of data, larger differences are not significant. The calculation of statistical significance takes into account sample size and variability of group scores. Thus, the t-test takes into account not only the difference in the means of the two groups, but also the difference in the variability of the scores.

The steps for calculating this type of t-test using the data above are as follows:

1. Calculate the standard error of the difference between the means ($S_{d\bar{x}}$) using the standard deviations of the two groups. The formula is

$$S_{d\bar{x}} = \sqrt{\frac{N_1 s_1{}^2 + N_2 s_2{}^2}{N_1 + N_2 - 2}\left(\frac{1}{N_1} + \frac{1}{N_2}\right)}$$

where s_1 is the standard deviation of the PE group

s_2 is the standard deviation of the non-PE group

N_1 is the size of the PE group

N_2 is the size of the non-PE group

By substituting the values, the $S_{d\bar{x}}$ is calculated as follows:

$$S_{d\bar{x}} = \sqrt{\frac{31(300^2) + 31(375^2)}{31 + 31 - 2}\left(\frac{1}{31} + \frac{1}{31}\right)}$$

$$S_{d\bar{x}} = \sqrt{\frac{31(90,000) + 31(140,625)}{60}(.032 + .032)}$$

$$S_{d\bar{x}} = \sqrt{\frac{2,790,000 + 4,359,375}{60}(.064)}$$

$$S_{d\bar{x}} = \sqrt{\frac{7,149,375}{60}(.064)}$$

$$S_{d\bar{x}} = \sqrt{119,156.25\ (.064)}$$

$$S_{d\bar{x}} = \sqrt{7626}$$

$$= 87.32$$

2. Calculate the t-value by using the following formula:

$$t = \frac{\bar{X}_1 - \bar{X}_2}{S_{d\bar{x}}}$$

where X_1 is the mean of the PE group

X_2 is the mean of the non-PE group

S_{dx} is the standard error of difference between means

By substituting the appropriate values, the t-value is calculated as follows:

$$t = \frac{2400 - 2150}{87.32}$$

$$t = \frac{250}{87.32}$$

$$t = 2.86$$

3. Determine the degrees of freedom (df) by adding the two numbers of scores in each group and subtracting 2 (df = $N_1 + N_2 - 2$). In this example the df are calculated as follows:

df = 31 + 31 − 2 = 62 − 2 = 60

4. Refer to Table 3.12, which is an abbreviated table of the critical values of t. The t-value in this sample problem is 2.86. If this obtained value is greater than the table value, it is concluded that the means are significantly different from one another. To use this table, the degrees of freedom must be known and a level of significance must be selected. The .05 level of significance should be used. This level indicates a 95 percent probability that the conclusions being reached by the t-test are actually true (5 chances out of 100 not true). In physical education and exercise science, .05 is typically used. By checking Table 3.12 for 60 degrees of freedom at the .05 level, you can see that the critical value is 2.00. Since the t-value of 2.86 exceeds the critical value of 2.00, it can be concluded that there is a significant difference in cardiorespiratory fitness in the two groups.

t-test for Dependent Samples

A second type of t-test is the **t-test for dependent samples**. When a group of subjects is measured on two different occasions (usually a pretest and posttest situation), this test can be used to see if significant differences exist between the two sets of scores. This t-test is done in a manner similar to the independent t-test, the difference being that the two sets of scores are related. The two most common designs for this type of t-test are repeated measures and matched pairs. Repeated measures typically uses a pretest and a posttest to generate two groups of scores from one set of subjects. Matched pairs deliberately matches subjects according to one or more variables and then assigns them to two different groups. In either case, the two groups are not independent of each other.

If a fitness instructor assesses a group of 20 clients prior to prescribing an exercise program, the assessment (pretest) typically includes body composition testing. After the clients are involved in a supervised exercise program for eight weeks, a second body composition assessment (posttest) might be done. A repeated measures t-test would determine if any significant changes in body composition occurred for the group. The t-value would be calculated the same way as the example given for independent samples, except that the values for the means and standard deviations would come from the pretest and posttest data. Another slight difference is that the degrees of freedom are calculated by using the formula $df = n - 1$. Thus, for this example, the degrees of freedom would be 19.

If a football coach wants to experiment with two different off-season strength training regimens, the matched pairs t-test can be used. The coach can match pairs of players by their one-repetition bench press maximum and their weight at the start of off-season. For instance, the coach might match two players weighing 270 pounds each and both able to bench press 300 pounds. By repeating this type of matching with 25 pairs of players and splitting them into two matched groups of 25 players, the coach creates two groups equally matched on bench press strength and weight. Each group would go through a different weight training regimen in the off-season workouts. At the end of the off-season, the players would be tested for their bench press maximum again. This data collected at the end of the off-season would form two groups of scores for the t-test computation. Degrees of freedom for this type of dependent t-test are calculated with the number of pairs − 1 (N − 1) being the formula. Thus, if the coach were to match 25 pairs of players and assign them to separate groups, the degrees of freedom would be 24.

Table 3.12 Critical value of t.

Degrees of freedom	Level of significance (two-tailed)	
	.05	.01
1	12.71	63.66
2	4.30	9.93
3	3.18	5.84
4	2.78	4.60
5	2.57	4.03
6	2.45	3.71
7	2.37	3.50
8	2.31	3.36
9	2.26	3.25
10	2.23	3.17
11	2.20	3.11
12	2.18	3.06
13	2.16	3.01
14	2.15	2.98
15	2.13	2.95
16	2.12	2.92
17	2.11	2.90
18	2.10	2.89
19	2.09	2.86
20	2.08	2.85
25	2.06	2.79
30	2.04	2.75
40	2.02	2.70
60	2.00	2.66

Analysis of Variance (ANOVA)

One-Way Analysis of Variance

The **one-way ANOVA** is an extension of the t-test for independent samples. Recall that the t-test is used when two groups of scores are involved. The one-way ANOVA test is used when there are three or more groups. Suppose a secondary physical education instructor wants to know if the type of curricular offerings makes a difference in student attitudes toward physical activity. In this sample, three different 10th grade classes might be taught physical education with the same instructional methods but different curricular design. Group A might participate only in team sports for the semester. Group B might participate only in lifetime sports during the same semester, while Group C is involved in a curriculum that alternates a team sports unit with a lifetime sports unit. It would be time-consuming and statistically incorrect to do three different t-tests (A–B, A–C, B–C).

The one-way ANOVA enables the practitioner to compare the differences among the three groups in one statistical procedure. In the example above, a fourth group

(group D) could be formed that took no physical education at all. Again, multiple t-tests (A–B, A–C, A–D, B–C, B–D, C–D) should not be computed. Rather, a 1 (attitude scores) x 4 (groups) ANOVA would be the proper test for significant differences. If the ANOVA procedure indicates significant differences, it is then necessary to use a post hoc test (i.e., Scheffe test for multiple comparisons) to ascertain exactly which groups are significantly different from the others.

Two-Way Analysis of Variance

In the one-way ANOVA presented above, there were four different groups of students from which data were collected on their attitudes toward physical activity. In this research design, data would be collected after the students had experienced the various physical education curricula. Data would be collected for the fourth group (group D), which was not enrolled in physical education, at the same time. Thus, the data is collected after the specific curricula experienced might have created differing attitudes toward physical activity. A stronger research design for this question would employ both a pretest and a posttest, rather than just the posttest used in the one-way ANOVA. This would require a **two-way ANOVA** to analyze the data.

By testing all four groups prior to the three groups (A, B, C) of students experiencing the curricular delivery, data on student attitudes are collected prior to the experiment. The data collection at the end of the experiment would be the posttest. Thus, each student would take the inventory to assess attitudes toward physical activity twice. Because each student takes the inventory twice, this is known as a repeated measure. The statistical analysis allows the experimenter to see if there are differences between groups at the end of the experiment just as the one-way ANOVA did. However, the data can be analyzed a second way as well. Each group can be checked to see if there were differences between the pretest and the posttest. Thus, changes both between groups and within groups can be analyzed. This is why this analysis is called a two-way ANOVA. It is a 2 (tests) x 4 (groups) repeated measures ANOVA design used to measure possible effects of curricular delivery on attitudes toward physical activity. Interactions between tests and groups are also calculated. If significant interactions were found, a post hoc test for multiple comparisons would need to be used. Further discussion of this interaction effect is beyond the scope of this textbook.

This brief overview of tests for significant differences between groups indicates the breadth of this area of statistics. The four statistics described are but a few of the statistical procedures used to determine significant differences. Other procedures include Chi-square, three-way ANOVA, and multiple analysis of variance (MANOVA). With the broad array of concepts and procedures included in this area of statistics, it is important that you realize that the information provided in this textbook is introductory in nature. The examples discussed provide illustrations to help the reader understand possible applications of these statistical procedures. Although more detailed information is beyond the intended scope of this textbook, in-depth study of this area would be beneficial to any person in the physical education or exercise science professions.

Computer Applications

With the rapid technological advances in personal computers resulting in greater power, speed, and storage, it is now possible for practitioners to utilize programs to create databases, generate statistical analyses, and create a variety of different types of graphs to highlight data. Two of the most popular options are SPSS for Windows and Microsoft Excel. Both are powerful programs that enable the proficient user to analyze data quickly and easily. All of the statistics presented in this chapter can be calculated with these programs. Though it is beyond the scope of this textbook to provide tutorials in their use, it is likely that you have access to these programs on your campus through institutional site licenses.

A wide variety of books and CD-ROM programs offer tutorials for using these programs. If you are interested in exploring some of these resources, the listing below is a sample of the many products that are available.

Meehan, A., and Werner, C. (2000). *Elementary data analysis using Microsoft Excel*. New York: McGraw-Hill.

Sincrich, T., Levine, D., and Stephan, D. (2002). *Practical statistics by example using Microsoft Excel and Minitab*. 2nd ed. Upper Saddle River, NJ: Prentice-Hall.

SPSS. (2002). *SPSS 11.0 Guide to Data Analysis*. Upper Saddle River, NJ: Prentice-Hall.

SPSS. (2002). *SPSS 11.0 for Windows Brief Guide*. Upper Saddle River, NJ: Prentice-Hall.

SPSS. (2002). *SPSS 11.0 for Windows Student Version*. Upper Saddle River, NJ: Prentice-Hall.

Velleman, P. (2002). *ActivStats for Microsoft Excel*. Boston: Addison Wesley.

Velleman, P. (2002). *ActivStats for SPSSl 2001–2002*. Boston: Addison Wesley.

Because of the popularity of these programs, they are updated regularly. By searching the Internet, you can easily determine the latest version of these programs. You are encouraged to develop skills in using this type of program. Check at your institution and see if credit courses or noncredit short courses are available. The time that you invest in learning how to use your personal computer to collect, analyze, graphically depict, and store your data will pay great dividends as you pursue your activity-based career.

SUMMARY

This chapter examines basic statistical terminology and techniques that are important to practitioners in physical education and exercise science. A number of statistical concepts are presented, including levels of measurement, frequency distribution, graphical presentation of the data, measures of central tendency, measures of variability, properties of the normal curve, standard scores, correlational procedures, simple regression, and tests for differences between groups. An understanding of this information should prepare the reader for more in-depth understanding of the issues in the chapters that follow.

DISCUSSION QUESTIONS

1. Describe the characteristics of the four levels of measurement. Give an example of each. Why is it important to understand the differences in these levels of measurement?

2. What are the advantages of using data display techniques to illustrate results of a test? What are some different methods of illustrating data?

3. List five characteristics of the normal curve.

4. Explain what is meant by the term "correlation." How can the use of correlational procedures help in teaching physical education?

5. Give the definition of a standard score. How are standard scores used in analyzing performance on tests given in physical education?

6. Below is a set of data representing measurement to the nearest millimeter of tricep skinfold of 7th grade boys:

4, 7, 13, 12, 10, 6, 7, 17, 9, 8, 13, 21, 6, 9, 10, 9, 8, 7, 5, 9, 15, 17, 19,

8, 9, 10, 7, 4, 20, 10, 9, 15, 12, 18, 12, 8, 9, 9, 11, 10, 7, 8, 15, 6, 19, 10,

9, 9, 7, 13, 12, 8, 22, 10, 5, 8, 9, 11, 13, 15, 19, 17, 11, 9, 8, 9, 10, 11, 7,

9, 14, 7, 16, 10, 9, 8, 9, 6, 14, 11, 12, 9, 8, 15, 6, 10, 17

Complete the following using the above data:
a. Organize the data into a grouped frequency distribution.
b. Draw a histogram of the data.
c. Draw a frequency polygon of the data.
d. Calculate cumulative frequency and cumulative percentiles for the data.
e. From the grouped frequency distribution, find the mode, median, and range.
f. From the grouped frequency distribution, calculate mean and standard deviation.
g. Transform the raw scores of 7, 10, 13, and 16 into corresponding z-scores, T-scores, and percentiles.

7. Calculate the correlation coefficient for the following sets of scores.

X (Pull-ups)	Y (Push-ups)
3	12
12	30
7	27
10	37
5	21
9	35
6	21
1	9
4	17
0	4

8. From the data above, using simple regression procedures, predict how many push-ups can be done by a student who is able to complete 8 pull-ups.

REFERENCE

Safrit, M. J., and Wood, Terry M. (1995) *Introduction to measurement in physical education and exercise science*. 3rd ed. St. Louis, MO: Times Mirror/Mosby.

REPRESENTATIVE READINGS

Bluman, Allan. (1998). *Elementary statistics: A step by step approach*. New York: McGraw-Hill.
Hopkins, K., Hopkins, B., and Glass, G. (1996). *Basic statistics for the behavioral sciences*. 3rd ed. Boston: Allyn and Bacon.
Triola, M. (2002). *Essentials of statistics*. 8th ed. Boston: Addison Wesley.
Vincent, W. J. (1995). *Statistics in kinesiology*. 2nd ed. Champaign, IL: Human Kinetics.

CHAPTER 4

Criteria for Test Selection

Key Terms

alternate form reliability

concurrent validity

construct validity

content validity

criterion measure

discrimination

face validity

independence

learning effect

norms

objectivity

odd-even reliability

predictive validity

relevant

reliability

Spearman-Brown prophecy formula

split-half reliability

test-retest reliability

validity

Objectives

1. Understand methods of establishing validity of various types of testing instruments.

2. Understand methods of establishing reliability of various types of testing instruments.

3. Explain the relationship between the validity, reliability, and objectivity of a testing instrument.

4. Discuss administrative concerns involved with selection of appropriate testing instruments.

5. Realize the importance of thorough planning for the administration of the test to ensure the collection of valid scores.

W hen the term "test" is mentioned, the thought of paper and pencil examinations taken in most classes usually comes to mind. While this is an important type of testing in the cognitive area, other types of tests exist to assess components of health and skill-related fitness, measure specific sports skills, and determine attitudes and feelings related to physical activity that are important in physical education and exercise science. One of the responsibilities of physical educators or other exercise professionals is to select appropriate test instruments based on certain criteria. This chapter presents criteria critical to the effectiveness of any type of test.

A "test" has been defined as an instrument, protocol, or technique used to measure a quantity or quality of properties or attributes of interest. A wide variety of tests is available to evaluate content in the various domains of physical education and exercise science. In some cases, it may be necessary to construct a test to measure some trait or attribute if an appropriate test is not available. Whether the instructor is constructing a test or using an existing one, certain characteristics, or criteria, are necessary if the measurements from the test are to be useful. These criteria are validity, reliability, and objectivity.

Validity

A test is said to possess **validity** if it accurately measures the attribute that it is designed to measure. This may seem to be a simple idea, but surprisingly, many tests being used lack this crucial quality. If a student won the class ladder tournament in racquetball but did not score well on the battery of racquetball skills test, then it is likely that the tests administered were not indicative of racquetball skill. Assuming that the tests were administered correctly, the battery of tests was not a valid measure of racquetball skill. Conversely, a student who is a mediocre player scoring high on a skills test would cast doubts on the validity of the particular test.

Suppose an instructor scheduled an examination on the statistical concepts presented in the previous chapter. When the students receive a copy of the test, they notice that all the questions pertain to the measures of central tendency. Would this be a valid test regarding their knowledge of Chapter 3? It might be a valid test of knowledge specific to the mode, median, and mean, but it would not measure the knowledge of the information included in the whole chapter. Thus, it would lack validity. It would not measure what it was supposed to measure.

Validity of tests can be established using either a qualitative or quantitative approach. Although numerical techniques can be included, the qualitative approach depends upon the use of common sense and logic in making subjective judgments about the test in question. The quantitative approach is a data-based approach that involves calculating correlation coefficients to determine the validity. Choosing a procedure for establishing the validity of a test often depends on the type of test being administered. With this in mind, five procedures for establishing validity will be discussed, starting with qualitative, or data-free, techniques and followed by the more powerful quantitative, or data-based, methods.

Face Validity

The weakest procedure for establishing validity is called **face validity**. This argument is based on cursory examination of the testing instrument to see if it measures what it purports to measure. Because face validity is based on subjectivity, it does not present a strong argument for validity. The nature of some tests, however, allows them to be validated by this means.

If an instructor wanted to test the ability of a group of students to shoot free throws in basketball, the obvious test would be to let the students shoot a predetermined number of free throws and count the number of successful attempts. Certainly, this test would measure what it intended to measure. Logic tells the instructor that this is a valid way to test the ability to shoot free throws. No other more powerful procedure for determining validity needs to be considered.

Suppose an instructor wanted to give a written examination of fitness concepts and prepared a 50-item test. After reading the exam, it is noticed that all the items refer in some way to the concepts of fitness. If face validity is accepted, then this test would be considered valid. However, this type of logic contains pitfalls that demand more than a superficial examination to ensure validity. The test may contain an overabundance of questions in one area of fitness or contain questions that are poorly written. These weaknesses would cause the scores to reflect inaccurately the student's comprehension, or lack thereof, of the fitness concepts covered in class. Consider the next type of validity procedure to understand why face validity is not acceptable in this situation.

Content Validity

For many assessment techniques used in physical education or fitness settings (e.g., certain questionnaires, attitude surveys), **content validity** is the strongest method available. To establish content validity of an instrument, a more in-depth study is made of the test to ensure the representativeness of the items. Content validity argues that there is a rationale for each item based on what the instrument is designed to measure. The test items should represent the educational objectives of the unit.

When some type of physical performance is being measured, content validity can be established by logically determining the actions and demands made by the particular performance. The "content" of swimming 25 yards is a valid test for swimming speed. On closer inspection, however, some physical performance tests may not measure what they are intended to measure.

Suppose a test were constructed to measure the ability to throw a softball. The students being tested throw at the target from a distance of 25 feet. One might consider this a valid test until realizing that from that distance a person could hit the target and have a high score on the test without exhibiting good throwing form or velocity. Consequently, the "content" of this test does not test all facets of softball throwing ability, so it is not valid for measuring overall softball throwing ability.

Construct Validity

A statistical extension of content validity is called **construct validity**. To use this procedure, one must first locate two groups that are known to differ significantly on the variable, or construct, being tested. A test is then administered to both groups to determine if there is a significant statistical difference between the scores in the groups. If there is no significant difference, then the test is not valid. Because extreme groups are normally used in determining construct validity, it is, at best, evidence of a general level of validity.

Concurrent Validity

A stronger quantitative procedure for establishing validity is called **concurrent validity**. To use this method, one must have a known valid instrument to measure the variable of interest. Both the established test and the new test are administered to the same students. The results of the two tests are then correlated. A high correlation coefficient shows concurrent validity. The higher the correlation coefficient, the stronger the rationale is for the validity of the new test.

Concurrent validity procedures provide an estimate of the validity of the test. Few tests are perfectly valid. A weakness of the previous procedures discussed is that they assume an "either/or" stance on the validity of a test and provide no estimate—either they are valid or they are not. Because quantitative procedures can give an estimated degree of validity, they provide a stronger, more powerful argument for validity.

If a new test is easier to administer, less expensive, requires less equipment, or is in some way more adaptable to local needs, then there is good reason to develop and validate it. For instance, a maximal oxygen uptake treadmill test has proved to be a valid way to measure cardiorespiratory endurance. This type of test requires thousands of dollars' worth of equipment, several people to administer it properly, and is time-consuming. Therefore, it is not practical for mass testing in schools and colleges. However, other tests of cardiorespiratory endurance, such as the 12-minute run, have shown high concurrent validity to treadmill testing. Additionally, the 12-minute run can be administered inexpensively to a large number of people in field situations. Though it may not be as accurate as the more sophisticated treadmill test, it is an excellent test for most needs.

Predictive Validity

The final method for establishing validity is **predictive validity**. This procedure can provide more powerful evidence of validity than any of the techniques that have been previously discussed. If an instrument has strong predictive validity, its scores will correlate highly with some type of measure in the future. Predictive validity is considered the ultimate evidence of an instrument's validity when the instrument predicts the behavior it seeks to measure.

For example, based on the score of a valid test, one should be able to predict how well a person will perform in the future in a competitive situation. Thus, to establish predictive validity, we correlate the scores on the test with performance in a game or meet. If the correlation coefficient is .80 or above, that is a strong argument for the predictive validity of the test. Unfortunately, this procedure is time-consuming and requires longitudinal study of the variable in question; that is, the subjects must be followed to the actual performance in the future.

Reliability

A test that gives consistent results is said to possess **reliability**. If a class of students takes the same test on two different days, the scores obtained should be about the same. A reliable test will yield data that are stable, repeatable, and precise. Some qualities or attributes can be measured more reliably than others. A person's height or weight can be measured precisely, and several trials are not likely to show much variation. Conversely, time on a mile run will fluctuate over several trials.

To ensure reliability, measurement techniques and conditions should be standardized to reduce measurement error. For example, consider what would happen to scores on a sit-up test if it were administered the first time on a gym floor and the next time on cushioned gym mats. Less than precise directions, inconsistent scoring procedures, different equipment, and different environmental conditions are examples of factors that can affect test reliability and the value of the scores collected. The subject's motivational state and general health, the presence of an audience, and length of the test are other elements that can affect reliability.

Because vastly different types of tests are given in physical education and exercise science, a number of different methods have been developed to estimate the reliability of testing instruments. To determine the reliability of a test, at least two sets of scores must be obtained. Three procedures for establishing reliability are presented below.

Test-Retest Reliability

The **test-retest reliability** procedure is exactly what the name implies. By administering the test, the first set of data is produced. After an appropriate period of time, the test is administered again in conditions as much the same as possible. The two sets of data are correlated to determine the reliability coefficient. Thus, this technique requires administering the same test to the same subjects on two separate occasions.

The tricky part of this procedure is to determine what is an "appropriate period of time" between the test and retest. The time interval between tests must consider the relationship between the variable being measured and factors such as maturation, learning, or changes in physical condition. The test-retest procedure is a good way to determine reliability for tests measuring stable information or measuring a variable or characteristic that is slow to change or develop.

If the test in question is a physical performance test, it can be given on the same day (e.g., free throw test) or on separate days (e.g., 12-minute run) if fatigue is a factor. In some physical performance tests, learning may take place during the first trial that would cause improvement in the second trial. Could this "learning effect" be a cause of concern in a free throw test? If "learning effect" is probable, then the test-retest may not be effective for estimating reliability.

In many types of written tests, students can remember the questions and their answers. If enough time elapses so that they forget the items on the test, there is a chance that the level of knowledge may have changed. The same is true for instruments that measure changeable traits such as attitudes and values. In these instances, other procedures to estimate reliability may be more appropriate.

Alternate Form Reliability

The **alternate form reliability** procedure requires two equivalent forms of the test in question. The two tests should be of the same length with the same type of questions included on both instruments. The same group of respondents is given both tests. Depending on whether fatigue is a factor, the tests may be administered consecutively or with a suitable interval of rest. Intervals should be short, however, to avoid any change in condition or learning that would compromise reliability.

It is important to alternate the order in which the forms are administered. Part of the group should take form 1 first, followed by form 2, while the other half should take form 2 followed by form 1. This alternation protects against fatigue and boredom distorting the scores of the second test.

After both forms have been scored, the correlation of the scores on forms 1 and 2 can be calculated to determine the reliability of the instrument. The biggest problem with this method is that it is difficult enough to develop one testing instrument, and alternate form reliability requires the formulation of two tests. In most instances, it is not practical for teachers to devote this much time to test construction.

Split-Half or Odd-Even Reliability

A third procedure, called **split-half** or **odd-even reliability**, can alleviate some of the problems encountered in the alternate form reliability and the test-retest methods. This technique is often used with written tests but can also be used with physical performance tests when an even number of trials are given. The advantage of this procedure is that it requires only one administration of one instrument to the group of respondents. The instrument is either split in half or the odd and even items are separated to form two sets of scores from the test. The two sets of scores are then correlated to estimate the reliability of the instrument.

The odd-even version is generally preferred because it ensures that fatigue or boredom will not bias scores, and more importantly, both sets of questions will be representative of the test. If the split-half procedure is used, it creates the possibility that each half of the test covers different material or one is easier than the other. The odd-even split eliminates this concern.

A major problem with this procedure is that, generally, greater length provides more reliability in an instrument. If reliability is related to the number of items on the instrument, then splitting the instrument in half can reduce its reliability. Because of this situation, a procedure called the **Spearman-Brown prophecy formula** was developed. This formula uses the actual reliability coefficient obtained from the correlation of the two halves of the instrument to predict the reliability of the entire instrument. It is given in Formula 4.1.

FORMULA 4.1 Spearman-Brown Prophecy Formula

$$\text{Reliability of whole test} = \frac{2 \ (\text{reliability of } \tfrac{1}{2} \text{ test})}{1 + (\text{reliability of } \tfrac{1}{2} \text{ test})}$$

As an example, assume that after administering an exam, it was scored by separating the odd and even questions. The correlation computed between the odd and even scores was .70. Using the formula shown above, the estimated reliability of the whole test would be calculated as follows:

$$\text{Reliability of whole test} = \frac{2(.70)}{1+.70} = \frac{1.40}{1.70} = .82$$

As illustrated, the reliability of the whole test is estimated to be higher (.82) than the correlation between the odd and even scores (.70). The odd-even method followed by the Spearman-Brown prophecy formula is one of the most frequently used procedures to estimate reliability.

Objectivity

A third criterion for a good test is **objectivity**. Objectivity is a type of reliability that concerns the administration of tests. Giving directions, scoring, and behavior of the administrator can affect the reliability of a test. If a test is administered and scored independently by two people, the resulting scores should be similar. The only differing condition of the two testing procedures is *who* administered the test.

Suppose a group of students was given a pull-up test on successive days by two different teachers. On the first day, the administrator of the test allowed students to kick and swing on the bar to help perform their pull-ups. The teacher on the second day did not allow this technique. If the scores from the first trial and second trial were correlated, the coefficient would probably not be very high. This would be due to the lack of objectivity during the two test administrations.

Tests that measure height, weight, or length, or that use counting, are usually highly objective. Two timers with accurate stopwatches should be able to measure the same runner in an accurate and objective way. Similarly, two testers independently measuring the high jump or long jump on the same attempt should be able to obtain the same reading.

When tests have a high degree of subjectivity, such as the judging of diving or the form of a golf swing, objectivity coefficients are typically lower. Rating scales are frequently used in physical education and athletic settings. Unless properly constructed with specific criteria in mind, these rating scales can be very subjective. This is caused by a difference in interpretation or bias, usually unintentional, on the part of the judges. To increase the objectivity of the judging, a **criterion measure** is used, which is based on detailed specifics of the skill to be performed and how it should be judged. When a teacher is evaluating form of a sport skill in a class, the evaluation should be based on a criterion list to improve the objectivity of the analysis.

Written tests involving true/false, matching, or multiple choice questions can be graded in a highly objective manner since the answer given is clearly right or wrong. Objectivity can become more of a problem on essay questions. If two different graders evaluate an essay answer, it is likely that they will give differing amounts of credit. This problem can be alleviated somewhat by composing a criterion answer and scoring the question based on specific points mentioned in the criterion.

Objectivity also depends on the clarity of directions. The test administrator must understand how to properly administer the test, and the students must understand how the test is performed and how it will be scored. A trial test is often appropriate to ensure that testing and scoring procedures are clear. By carefully planning the test and conscientiously following the protocol for test administration and scoring, objectivity of the test can be improved. Results of a test that are biased by a lack of objectivity waste the time and efforts of both the students and the teacher and are of little value in evaluating students.

Validity, Reliability, and Objectivity in Alternative Assessment

In many physical education settings, classes are large and time is limited. Rather than a formalized skills test, teachers often use alternative assessment techniques, described in Chapter 9, of observing students in actual game situations to evaluate student performance. This observation made in the actual context of the game actually provides a more realistic appraisal of student outcomes, with the bonus of being time efficient. However, the teacher must be aware of systematically applying the same performance criteria to all students to maintain objectivity. While alternative assessment offers exciting opportunities for evaluating students, the standards for validity and reliability must be satisfied. These measurement concepts, as they apply to alternative assessment, are presented in Chapter 9.

In alternative assessment, examples of student performance, not highly inferential estimates provided by group testing, are used to measure learning. For instance, student performance in real game settings is assessed rather than assessing skill with a more artificial skills test. Alternative assessment is ongoing and can include many types of documentation. Performance samples, anecdotal reports, student journals or logs, and fitness profiles are some of the things included in alternative assessment that may be compiled in a portfolio. More detailed information concerning alternative assessment is in Chapter 9.

Relationship Between Validity, Reliability, and Objectivity

For a test to yield results that are an accurate reflection of the ability or attribute being measured, it must possess the characteristics of validity, reliability, and objectivity. A definite relationship exists among these three criteria.

There is a one-way relationship between validity and reliability. A test may be reliable but not valid. An instrument might give consistent results but not measure what it claims to measure. However, a test cannot be valid if it is not reliable. If a test cannot provide stable and repeatable results, it is not possible for it to be valid. The reliability of a test should be established before examining the validity of the instrument. In a sense, a test's degree of reliability places a ceiling on how valid the instrument can be.

As stated earlier, objectivity is related to reliability. Without objectivity, an instrument will lack reliability. Thus, the relationship between objectivity and validity is the same as between reliability and validity. An instrument may be objective without being valid but cannot be valid without being objective. Therefore, both objectivity and reliability are prerequisites to validity. To summarize, if a test is to be of any value, it must yield the same results regardless of who administers it; it must measure the quality or attribute in a stable and repeatable manner; and it must measure the quality or attribute that it claims to measure.

Administrative Concerns in Test Selection

Because activity performance tests are generally more complex than written tests and the time period available to physical education is usually shorter than that of other academic classes, other criteria must also be met if a test is to be useful. Even a valid, reliable, and objective test may be eliminated from consideration if it fails to address some of these additional administrative concerns.

For a testing program to be effective, it is necessary to avoid the pitfall of selecting tests that, due to a particular teaching situation, may cause logistical nightmares. A careless approach to test administration can result in invalid scores. Because testing in physical education should consume no more than 10 percent of the total instructional time, it becomes only prudent to select tests that are compatible with various aspects of the overall program. Therefore, during the curricular planning stages, several practical criteria for selecting a test and planning for test administration need to be considered. In nonschool activity settings, most of the same administrative concerns for test selection should be the same as in school environments. Test results are essential to client evaluation, program planning, and program assessment.

After acceptable validity, reliability, and objectivity of a test have been determined, it is the responsibility of the program planners to identify factors that affect the efficiency and management of the testing program. Only after thorough deliberations about these factors should a test or testing program be considered for inclusion in the yearly physical education program.

Relevance

Program planning should include educational activities that are designed to achieve stated goals and objectives. To be meaningful, the selection of tests should be relevant, or linked, to measurement of program, unit, student, or teacher goals and the specific learning experiences planned to achieve those goals. Further, tests should require that participants use proper technique, adhere to the rules of the activity, and perform skills associated with the activity. For example, a tennis serve test that does not demand that the performer execute a proper toss and legal foot placement is not requiring proper technique.

Outcome statements, learning activities, and testing programs associated with the activity program should be closely linked. Simply testing for the sake of testing has no place in a physical education program, particularly when the viability of a physical education program may rest on test scores to show success in meeting predetermined objectives.

The National Association for Sport and Physical Education (NASPE) sponsored a project resulting in *Outcomes of Quality Physical Education Programs* (1992) that includes 20 outcome statements that were expanded into sample benchmarks for selected grade levels. To complement this work, *Moving Into the Future: National Physical Education Standards—A Guide to Content and Assessment* (1995) was completed to clarify content standards and provide assessment guidelines. These two related projects illustrate how curricular goals and assessment should be aligned so that measurement and evaluation activities are relevant and meaningful to the students.

Educational Value

As an integral part of the education process, testing should not just be an evaluation process, but a learning experience for the students and clients as well. As a result of test taking, they should learn something about themselves and the qualities being assessed. A key feature of contemporary health and fitness test batteries is their educational component. The *FITNESSGRAM* provides a comprehensive health-related physical fitness test battery accompanied by educational materials. Student knowledge and attitudes about physical fitness are considered more important than actual results of the test administration. Test results can be used to profile the level of physical performance capacities, thereby broadening the student's awareness of, and interest in, personal health and functional well-being. On a written test, it is feasible that students can learn facts or concepts by comparing their responses with the answer key. In clinical exercise settings, clinicians should educate their clients about the underlying reasons for the test and the meaning of the results.

Many software packages are available that offer tutorials about physical fitness, nutrition, sports, and health. Often these learning packages contain review questions that give students or clients an opportunity to test their knowledge about a particular topic. Utilizing the computer in testing can be an effective method to assist participants in learning. It also can be a way to greatly reduce the amount of formal time dedicated to testing. Keep in mind that testing can be educational and that allowing it to become separate from instruction can be deleterious to the overall program.

Economy

Tests should be economically feasible in terms of equipment and personnel. Because school districts do not have the financial resources to purchase elaborate instruments, machines, and high-tech equipment that measure human performance with great precision, it is imperative that the tests selected be affordable. This is one reason that the FITNESSGRAM is such a popular test battery. Each test requires minimal monetary expenditure for equipment and supplies.

Equipment and materials are not the only cost factor associated with test administration. To ensure valid results, tests need to be monitored by trained individuals. Since most test batteries contain several items, it is economical to have more than one person available to function as a test administrator. When students, parents, college students, or other teachers assist in testing, time must be devoted to training them. A test that takes a great deal of time to complete, demands a high degree of skill and experience to administer, and requires extensive training and practice time may not be a judicious use of personnel.

Time

Tests should be administered in a relatively short period of time. With the demands placed on teacher accountability, it is appropriate that the majority of time in physical education be devoted to learning experiences designed to meet predetermined objectives. Recognizing this, most experts in program design and measurement recommend that formal testing programs consume no more than 10 percent of total instructional time (Baumgartner and Jackson, 1999; Barrow, McGee, and Tritschler, 1989; and Johnson and Nelson, 1986). The task of test selection based on the availability of time becomes increasingly difficult in situations in which instructional units are short, and time for instruction and practice is at a premium. As we know, the validity and reliability of a test often depend on the administration of a certain number of trials. Deviating from the standard instructions may cause invalid results. Compromising the testing program by offering an abbreviated version of a particular test can result in gathering useless data and wasting valuable class time.

While tests that require precise equipment may be costly in terms of dollars, they also may take a significant amount of time to administer. Other tests may need extensive preliminary arrangements, such as lines drawn on the floor, stations set up at various locations throughout the test area, specific dimensions marked on the playing field, or other tasks that take time. The bottom line is that all tests demand some set-up time. Always be aware of the time allocated for testing and select tests accordingly.

Enjoyment

Tests should be a nonthreatening and relatively enjoyable experience. Most people have experienced anxiety and apprehension associated with taking a test. These feelings are often due to a threatening environment. Particularly with physical performance tests, test administrators need to take measures to ensure that the testing session is as enjoyable as possible and in no way discourages participation in physical activity. When participants enjoy taking a test and understand why they are being tested, they may become motivated to do well. A person who wants to improve her time on the mile run may be motivated by the fact that a faster time reflects a higher level of cardiovascular functioning.

Enjoyability is related to comfort. Providing mats for tests that require students to be on the floor, ensuring pleasant climatic conditions, and planning on privacy for certain tests are examples of how teachers can make the testing environment more comfortable. Even though certain cardiorespiratory endurance tests and other maximum-effort tests can be uncomfortable, participants can learn to view them as challenging and important. Also, if a test is too repetitive, extremely easy or difficult, or viewed as unimportant, the chances of it being an enjoyable experience are diminished.

Norms

Selection of tests should be made only after considering the availability of current normative tables. **Norms** are values representative of a particular population. These values are usually reported as the mean and percentile equivalents of performance scores on a standardized test. In physical education, normative tables are available for many tests that measure performance in the physical and psychomotor learning domains. While results of tests of cognition and affective behavior lack a normative database, the scores may be either compared to an existing standard or used to determine change over a period of time.

Normative tables provide the means to compare individual performance with a larger population. These comparisons can provide valuable information to assist the test administrator and participant in determining the relationship of individual performance scores to scores of others of the same age and gender. If comparisons show students scoring below the national average, it is probably necessary to seriously review the existing curriculum. While the categorization of norms according to age and gender is common, some normative tables further classify scores by height and weight. Since these maturational factors affect physical performance, it is only prudent to consider them when making comparisons of performance scores. The important point to remember is that norms are a reflection of a specific group from which the norms were compiled and should be interpreted accordingly. For example, completing 60 sit-ups in one minute would not be as impressive if done by a high school senior as if performed by a second grade youngster. Similarly, norms based on the performance of secondary girls are not appropriate for kindergarten boys.

Several other important factors should be considered before using norms. Specifically, the adequacy of the norms must be evaluated.

1. The normative database should include a sufficiently large number of subjects. Generally, the larger the sample, the more closely it represents the total population. Though there is no clear-cut rule indicating how large the sample should be, any normative table with fewer than several hundred scores for each age, sex, and test should be interpreted with caution.

2. The normative database should be representative of the performance of the population for which it was devised. Sampling a population that is in some way unique could result in erroneous interpretation of obtained scores. For example, using performance scores of college football players to develop norms for a particular test of minimal muscular strength and endurance would result in disproportionately high norms and would not be representative of the general population. To allow for a fair interpretation of student scores, comparisons should be made with a similar population.

3. The directions and manner of scoring need to be clear enough to ensure that the procedures used to administer the test are identical to those used in compiling the norms. If the procedures are different, any attempt to compare scores legitimately is impossible.

4. The geographic location of the population should be considered in devising the norms. Climate, socioeconomic level, cultural influence, and other environmental conditions could bias the sample. Variation in the norms can be controlled somewhat by devising local norms. Using computers, tables generated from raw performance scores can be quickly compiled and formatted into normative tables that display the percentile equivalents for the range of scores.

5. Norms should be current and updated on a regular basis. Computers allow for frequent revision. Maintaining a current bank of raw scores and revising the norms on a yearly basis will take into account the ever-changing characteristics and abilities of exercise participants.

Discrimination

A test must take into account the wide range of performance capacities and abilities of test takers and should place a score on a continuum and be sensitive enough to make discriminations among all people taking the test. **Discrimination** refers to the ability of a test to differentiate between good, average, and poor performance. In selecting a test, an instructor may wish to choose one that is difficult enough so that no student receives a perfect score, but easy enough so that no student receives a zero. For example, assessment of percentage of body fat allows each student an opportunity to receive a score. That score falls along a continuum that discriminates among individuals who are extremely lean and those who are extremely fat. Similarly, a student completing a softball throw for distance will receive a perfomance score that falls somewhere between an extremely short distance and an extremely long distance.

Tests that allow for a score of zero are problematic and may not truly discriminate among the performances of those who take them, as Baumgartner and Jackson (1999) demonstrate:

> *Consider the problem of students' receiving the minimum or maximum score. How would you determine who is the better student: Although two students who receive a zero on a pull-up test are both weak, they are probably not equal in strength per pound of body weight. Remember, however, that the fact that no student receives a perfect score or a zero is no guarantee that a test discriminates satisfactorily; conversely, the fact that someone does receive a perfect score or a zero is no guarantee that the test is a poor one.*

Finding a test that totally discriminates among students' performance scores is a difficult task. The FITNESSGRAM test battery is one such test. Each test item is designed to measure the qualities of a function, along a continuum from severely deficient to high levels of functional capacity.

Independence

Usually a single test is insufficient to measure the overall physical abilities or performance capacities of an individual. To obtain an overall profile of a student's physical skills or physical fitness requires administration of a test battery, composed of several tests that are each designed to measure a specific component. There should be **independence** between the tests included in the battery. Each test should be independent of, or unrelated to, other items in the battery. Having students run the 50-yard dash, 100-yard dash, and the 100-meter dash to measure running speed would be a waste of time. Each of these tests is a true measure of running speed, and hence highly related. Giving just one of the tests would provide all the information necessary to determine running speed performance.

If the measures in a test battery are independent, the correlation (see Chapter 3) between them is low. When scores from two tests are highly correlated, they are probably measuring the same trait and lack independence. The practice of using related tests to measure performance is not only time-consuming, but also unfair to students who consistently score poorly on tests that measure that particular trait. When two (or more) tests in a battery are not independent (i.e., they are highly correlated), retain only the one that is most appropriate for the situation.

Gender Appropriateness

Tests should take into account the differences between males and females in such a way that the process does not bias in favor of one gender or another. In selecting and administering tests, instructors should be continually aware of the inherent differences that exist between males and females. From a physiological perspective, males generally have more muscular strength and endurance, are taller and heavier, possess a lower percentage of body fat, and display greater cardiovascular endurance. On the other hand, females tend to have greater flexibility, rhythmic coordination, and buoyancy.

Test administrators need to develop procedures for assessment and evaluation that take into account these differences in a nondiscriminating way. Administering tests with available norms allows the comparison of raw performance scores with those of others of the same age and sex. This type of evaluative procedure is more acceptable than having a criterion-referenced scale that applies to all test takers, regardless of gender. Differences attributed to gender are pertinent only on measures of physical ability or functional capacity and need not be a concern when selecting a test to measure abilities or behavior traits associated with the cognitive or affective learning domains.

Reliance on Another's Performance

One person's test score should not depend on the performance of another person. The practice of administering tests that require interaction among participants during the test trials with the results of that interaction being recorded as a test score should be avoided. Suppose a teacher was interested in testing students' ability to catch the forward pass in football. Using another student as the thrower could result in inconsistent throws. In this case, the performance score, the number of caught balls, would depend on the ability of another person.

Performances should be based entirely on a person's abilities and not those of classmates or other individuals. Skills tests for such sports as racquetball, tennis, and basketball should be constructed so that an individual's ability is measured and the score is not biased by interaction with another person.

Safety

Tests should always be selected that can be conducted in a safe environment and that are not inherently dangerous. Criteria to be considered in determining whether a test is safe include station site, the potential for students to overexert, and the capabilities of students. Selecting a safe site to conduct tests of motor ability or physical fitness is important. Most of the time this means exercising good judgment and common sense. Finding a smooth, unlittered outdoor area for the distance run, providing mats for the sit-up test, and securing spotters for tests of balance are examples of prudent measures to make the testing site as safe as possible. The use of marking devices that are soft, unbreakable, and highly visible is recommended. Fluorescent boundary cones are much preferred to chairs, bottles, or portable metal standards.

On tests of physical performance, the test taker should be encouraged to do as well as possible. However, safeguards need to be provided that will protect against the likelihood of participants overexerting themselves to the extent of causing injury. All tests of flexibility require that a muscle, or group of muscles, be stretched as far as possible. To prevent the injury of muscle tissue during the test, a warm-up session stretching the particular muscle group to be tested should be conducted immediately before test administration.

Protecting participants from overexertion is a result of proper planning and thorough knowledge of the purposes of the test. As a general rule, physical education teachers should consult with the school nurse prior to administering any strenuous test. This assists the teacher in identifying students who may have health problems that should prohibit participation. In adult activity settings, thorough screening and medical clearance are essential prior to testing. Proper conditioning should precede the administration of tests that require great efforts of muscular strength and endurance or cardiovascular expenditure.

Maturation is a factor that affects test performance. Expecting young children to perform at the same level as high school students on measures of strength and endurance is ludicrous. Similarly, working with older adults warrants caution. Asking people to perform skills on a test at a higher level than they are capable of could jeopardize their safety. Be sure to check the age appropriateness of the test prior to final test selection and be familiar with the abilities of participants before placing them in a testing situation.

The tester also needs to be knowledgeable about the test and the characteristics to be measured if the environment is to be safe. If the test administrator does not understand potential dangers associated with the test, problems could arise. In order to secure a safe testing environment, the tester must know what to do and how to do it.

Testing Large Groups

Generally, exercise clinicians and athletic trainers do not have to test large groups. However, physical education teachers are usually responsible for more participants in testing situations. Planning, organizing, and actual testing to accommodate such large numbers seems overwhelming. Selecting tests under these circumstances can be made easier if attention is given to tests that lend themselves to mass testability. With large classes it is imperative that students be measured as quickly, yet accurately, as possible. This can be accomplished by testing students successively or simultaneously. For example, a large number of students can be tested in a single class period in physical performance tests such as the flexed arm hang, pull-ups, sit-and-reach, and shuttle run. Using the partner system, half of the class can be tested at the same time. Having a partner count the number of sit-ups correctly completed in a given time period or keeping track of elapsed time on a distance run are examples of how administration time can be reduced by simultaneously testing large numbers of students. Using the school nurse, other teachers, aides, parents, or local college students to assist in test administration is another way to reduce the time associated with testing large numbers of students. Another feature of simultaneous testing is that it keeps most students occupied and discourages class disruptions resulting from inactivity.

Ease of Scoring, Interpreting, and Reporting

A test should allow for easy and accurate scoring and should be used as a self-assessment technique by students. Selecting tests that can be easily scored on specially designed forms or that provide software for quick and accurate interpretation and reporting are time-saving procedures and should be considered. While important to test administration, ease of scoring should not be the primary factor in test selection. It should, however, be considered if the test is to be utilized for educational purposes. For instance, a sit-and-reach apparatus could be located in a particular area of the school and made available for students to self-test their flexibility. Similarly, a tumbling mat with permanently marked distance increments could be used by students to regularly monitor their performance on a standing long jump.

As previously discussed, if a test is to provide valid and reliable results, the test administrator must follow the standardized instructions. Deviating from the proper procedures will result in worthless scores. Learning correct test procedures and developing an understanding of assessment instruments used to measure the learning domains in physical education is crucial. Attending training sessions or working with someone who is familiar with the test are good ways to acquire the knowledge and skills to conduct a testing session. Participants can learn how to administer many of the physical performance tests simply through the process of taking the test. Tutoring sessions and brief training episodes are opportunities to provide test takers with the skills needed to benefit from self-testing. If one of the major goals is to develop knowledge and understanding about the value of physical activity, then participants must be taught self-appraisal techniques.

Planning Test Administration

Once the assessment instruments to be used in the activity-based program have been determined, planning for the testing session can begin. Proper planning increases the likelihood of smooth and efficient testing sessions and of obtaining valid and reliable scores. Several suggestions related to test selection, administration, scoring, and objectivity have already been discussed in this chapter. Specific organizational hints are also provided in Chapters 5–8 along with the directions for each of the tests presented in those chapters. However, some general recommendations for planning are given here.

Securing Materials and Preparing the Testing Area

Proper use of space, equipment, and supplies reduces the amount of time required for administering the test. Competent test administration begins with compiling a detailed list of needed test equipment, supplies, and other necessary materials. Planning for appropriate utilization of space can reduce set-up time, ensure a safer environment, eliminate confusion, and minimize crowding.

Equipment and Supplies The test directions should indicate the type and amount of equipment and supplies necessary for administration of the test. While materials vary among tests, items usually needed include stopwatches, tape measures, signs, pencils, score cards, tumbling mats, and boundary cones. Examples of specialized items include hand dynamometers, skinfold calipers, and a sit-and-reach apparatus. Remember, all necessary equipment and supplies should be in their proper location before the testing session. Scurrying around during the test session looking for necessary items is a waste of precious time. Be prepared!

Testing Area Because the condition of a test area can affect performance, the area to be used should be a safe environment in which to conduct a test. A properly prepared test area eliminates hazards to test takers' safety. Advance preparation to ensure safety includes mowing the field, sweeping the asphalt area, trimming border shrubs, replacing burned-out light fixtures, cleaning the floor, and repairing the walls.

Arrangement of the Testing Area Proper sequential ordering of test items is essential and requires careful advance preparation. If the standardized instructions detail a specific arrangement for the testing area, then that blueprint must be precisely followed. If not, establish an order and arrangement that meets the needs of the testing program. Several factors should be kept in mind as plans are made. First, the sequence of test items should be arranged to offset fatigue and provide functional rest periods for students. For example, strenuous tests should not be administered in succession. Alternating a fatigue test with a test requiring minimal locomotor movement is an appropriate practice. As a standard rule, distance runs should not be scheduled first. In fact, distance runs can serve as an exciting culminating experience to a testing program. Second, the number of possible test stations may be limited by availability of equipment and supplies. If more than one piece of necessary equipment is available, however, test time can be decreased by increasing the number of test stations used for the particular activity. Third, test situations should be clearly marked and students made aware of the rotational sequence before beginning the tests. Finally, the tester needs to know how long it takes to administer each of the tests. A test that requires a particularly long time to administer may be handled best by using multiple test sites.

Knowledge of the Test

As a test administrator, the instructor should have a thorough knowledge of the test and a precise understanding of its administrative procedures. It also helps if the students are familiar with the test and know its purpose. If the instructor is inexperienced with a particular test, it may be helpful to write out a list of all the instructional and organizational procedures. Knowing the number of trials, exact measurement techniques, and recommended organizational procedures associated with each test ensures accuracy of scores and allows judicious use of valuable class time. If a test will not take the entire class period, the instructor should plan some instructional activity for the remaining time.

Recording the Scores

Recording scores with large groups of students in school settings can be challenging. The manner in which raw scores are recorded on score cards is integral to the efficiency of the testing program. Scoring forms should be designed and printed in advance of the test session. Many test batteries have preprinted score cards available. Adopting these forms may save time and serve the purpose. Keep in mind, however, that a cost is usually associated with requesting these forms.

In most cases, the instructor will be responsible for devising the score sheet used in recording the individual performance scores. Two common types of score cards are the class roll sheet and the individual score card.

Class Roll Sheet   The class roll sheet contains the names of all members of a particular class. Usually alphabetized by last name, this sheet provides spaces to record the scores that students achieve on all tests as well as to report other pertinent data (e.g., age, height, weight, sex). This type of form is appropriate when one test administrator is responsible for the recording of all raw scores. Because all the names are listed in a sequential manner, use of a class roll sheet facilitates the time taken to record scores. In addition, posting scores on sheets gives students the opportunity to readily view their performance on the different tests in relation to others in their class. Having all the raw scores on sheets also expedites the conversion from raw scores to percentile equivalents. The likelihood of misplacing any student's performance scores is also decreased by using roll sheets.

Individual Score Card The most popular, and perhaps the best, way to record students' test scores is to use an individual score card. Even in the elementary schools, the individual score card offers numerous advantages. If the students are tested in the order in which the score cards are arranged, the tester does not have to look through a long list of names. Trained assistants in the form of parents, college students, or members of the class can accurately record raw scores. With individual score cards, students have an opportunity to become more aware of their performance and to share in the testing procedure. They can examine and reflect on their performance scores and have a better idea of their achievement status. Posting normative tables on a convenient bulletin board will allow students to receive immediate feedback regarding their relative performance.

The design and contents of the card depend, of course, on the test or test battery selected. Space should be provided for information such as the student's name, age, height, weight, class, homeroom, and teacher. Generally, the 5" x 8" index card provides enough space for all the necessary categories.

Training Testers

An important step in the testing process is the training of testers. Simply because a person reads the instruction manual does not guarantee that the directions are understood. Some tests, such as body composition, also require proficiency on the part of the tester. In this case, the tester must be skilled with the skinfold calipers in order to obtain accurate and reliable readings of subcutaneous fat. To better prepare testers and assistants, practice sessions should be conducted with a sample of subjects. These sessions can be used to clarify instructions, standardize procedures, and develop technical skills necessary to administer the test. The advent of several new batteries of physical fitness and performance tests has prompted many schools and districts to devote inservice workshop time to training physical education personnel in methods and procedures associated with test administration. While the use of paraprofessionals, college students, parents, and class members as assistants for testing is encouraged, it is advisable to conduct formal practice sessions so they become familiar with their responsibilities.

Practicing Test Items

A primary source of measurement error is not allowing participants the opportunity to become familiar with and practice test items. Reliability, the ability of a test to consistently measure what it is supposed to measure, depends on whether a student has practiced the skills related to the test. Most people perform better in a test on the second administration since they are familiar with techniques and protocols of the test from the first administration. This is the **learning effect**. The second score is more indicative of true abilities. Thus, it is important to become thoroughly familiar with the test before the scores are actually collected to evaluate participants' proficiency.

Test takers should be informed well in advance of upcoming tests so that they can prepare accordingly. In the 1.5-mile run, for instance, it is important to understand the concept of pace, be aware of optimal pace, and have experience in running for an extended duration. In another case, improved muscular strength and endurance as measured by free weight lifting may be related more to efficiency and familiarity with the technique than to actual strength gains.

Participants should be given ample time to develop some degree of physical fitness prior to taking tests that require extreme physical exertion. For example, expecting the students to complete a distance run test the first week of classes is unacceptable practice from a medical point of view and may also promote resentment and poor attitudes toward physical education and activity.

Warming Up

An initial period of 5–10 minutes should be devoted to physiologically and psychologically preparing for taking a test. Proper warm-up and stretching exercises may also help prevent muscle and joint injury, which could occur as a result of maximum effort on a test. The warm-up is not only a safety precaution but it also improves performance on tests. Some tests are specific in nature and require a special kind of warm-up. The sit-and-reach test to measure flexibility of the lower back and posterior thigh requires a thorough warm-up session to prepare those particular muscle groups for the actual test. Remember, it is the responsibility of the test administrator to properly warm up test takers for each of the test items. Make certain that participants do not cool down as they wait their turn to perform the test.

Standardizing Instructions

Once the test site has been designed and procedures determined, it is time to develop specific instructions. Most tests require two types of directions, one for the test administrators and the other for the test takers. Instructions for testers contain information related to explanation, demonstration, administration, and scoring of the test. Instructions for participants include how to perform the test, hints on techniques to improve scores, and other information. These directions should be standardized and prepared in written form. Caution must be taken that some test takers are not given different or additional information about what is considered good performance or suggested goals. Though viewed as motivating, this type of information may also have a deleterious effect on performance.

Converting, Interpreting, and Evaluating the Results

The reason for testing students is to obtain meaningful information about their abilities. Once obtained, this information can be used in a variety of ways to enhance program and individual performance. Interestingly, many activity professionals test for the sake of satisfying an imposed administrative mandate and fail to complete the final stage of test administration—converting, interpreting, and evaluating the results.

Converting Scores   Recording scores is usually a simple process of placing raw scores onto roll sheets or individual score cards. However, scores in raw form are generally meaningless and difficult to interpret. Therefore, it sometimes becomes necessary to convert raw scores into standard scores. Chapter 3 describes different types of standard scores and their calculations.

The most common procedure for obtaining a standard score is converting a raw score to a percentile equivalent. Percentile scores describe the individual's performance relative to the performance of others in the same age and gender categories. Some normative tables even classify scores according to height and weight.

Interpreting Scores   Once the scores have been converted to a more meaningful standard score, the next phase of the posttest procedure is interpretation of the results. Participants should always be apprised of their performance and made aware of the meaning of the results. A score of 32 centimeters on the sit-and-reach test is more easily interpreted by a 12-year-old girl if she knows that her performance is at the 60th percentile. She can translate this to mean that her performance on this test of flexibility is better than 60 percent of the population of same-age and -gender students who made up the normative sample. Many software programs can also quickly convert raw scores into percentile equivalents and provide immediate feedback in the form of a personalized fitness profile. The use of local norms is an asset, especially when students have a working knowledge of norms and have ready access to them. Interpretation of standard scores enables monitoring of the participant's progress and can identify strengths and weaknesses.

Evaluating Scores   A vital phase of the posttest procedure is the evaluation of scores in relation to the process and product. This follow-up procedure usually results in the refocus of aims or goals of the program and a concomitant change in the process used to attain stated goals. For example, if students in a school district display poor performance relative to national percentile equivalents on a test of cardiorespiratory fitness, physical educators could rightfully redirect the program to attain higher levels of cardiorespiratory performance. To do so would require the inclusion of more vigorous learning activities in the curriculum. Always be mindful that evaluation is an ongoing process designed to improve the standards of the program.

SUMMARY

This chapter deals with many criteria that a teacher or exercise science professional must consider in selecting testing instruments. Because of the many types of tests available, the practitioner must be aware of the various pitfalls in test selection and administration that can contaminate the results.

A portion of the chapter presents the concepts of validity, reliability, and objectivity. Regardless of the type of test, any instrument must possess these critical characteristics. It is important that the reader understand these criteria for test selection and their interrelationships.

Even if a test possesses these three characteristics, many other concerns must be considered in test selection. A test may be valid, reliable, and objective, yet not meet the needs of a particular situation. A detailed listing of additional administrative concerns is presented and discussed.

Once it is determined that a test is valid, reliable, and objective and that it satisfies other criteria specific to the testing situation, careful planning of the test administration is necessary to ensure the accuracy of the results. No matter how good a test is, it will yield scores of little value if it is not administered properly.

A number of steps important to test administration are presented as suggestions for good planning. It should be emphasized that there is no substitute for common sense in selecting and properly administering a test. Hopefully, the information in this chapter, coupled with a healthy dose of common sense, will simplify the task of test selection and administration and ensure scores that reflect the true abilities and/or attributes of the persons being tested.

DISCUSSION QUESTIONS

1. What are two qualitative methods for determining validity of a testing instrument? Describe testing instruments for which it would be appropriate to use these procedures.

2. What are three quantitative methods of determining validity of a testing instrument? Describe testing instruments for which it would be necessary to use these methods.

3. What are four methods used to determine the reliability of a test? Compare and contrast the advantages and disadvantages of each of these procedures. Give an example of when it would be appropriate to use each of these methods.

4. What is the one-way relationship between validity and reliability of a testing instrument?

5. What are some administrative concerns that a practitioner should have when selecting a test? Which are most important and why?

6. Thorough planning is essential when preparing to administer a test. What things should a practitioner consider to ensure valid scores when planning the test?

REFERENCES

American Alliance for Health, Physical Education, Recreation, and Dance. (1992). *Outcomes of quality physical education programs.* Reston, VA.

Barrow, H. M., McGee, R., and Tritschler, K. (1989). *Measurement in physical education and sport.* 4th ed. Philadelphia, PA: Lea and Febiger.

Baumgartner, T., and Jackson, A. (1999). *Measurement for evaluation in physical education and exercise science.* 6th ed. Boston: WCB-McGraw Hill.

Johnson, B. L., and Nelson, J. K. (1986). *Practical measurements for evaluation in physical education.* 4th ed. Edina, MN: Burgess Publishing.

National Association for Sport and Physical Education. (1995). *Moving into the future: National physical education standards—A guide to content and assessment.* St. Louis: Mosby.

REPRESENTATIVE READINGS

Crowl, T. K. (1986). *Fundamentals of research: A practical guide for educators and special educators.* Columbus, OH: Publishing Horizons.

Cooper Institute for Aerobic Research. (1999). *The FITNESSGRAM: Test Administration Manual.* 2nd ed. Champaign, IL: Human Kinetics Press.

Morrow, J., Jackson, A., Disch J., and Mood, D. (2000). *Measurement and evaluation in human performance.* 2nd ed. Champaign, IL: Human Kinetics Press.

Thomas, J., and Nelson, J. (1996). *Research methods in physical activity.* 3rd ed. Champaign, IL: Human Kinetics Press.

CHAPTER 5

Measuring Health-Related Physical Fitness and Physical Activity

Key Terms

blood pressure
body composition
cardiorespiratory fitness
densitometry
distance run
environmental factors
extension
fat weight
field-based tests
flexibility
flexion
functional fitness
genetic endowment
health-related physical fitness
heart rate
lean weight
lifestyle factors
maturation
muscular endurance
muscular strength
perceived exertion
physical activity
Physical Activity Readiness
    Questionnaire (PAR-Q)
physical fitness
physiological fitness
risk stratification
skill-related physical fitness
special populations
trainability

Objectives

1. Articulate the relationship between physical activity and physical fitness.
2. Tell the differences between physiological fitness, health-related physical fitness, and skill-related physical fitness.
3. Describe the components of health-related physical fitness and discuss the relationship of each to an individual's physical health and well-being.
4. Understand the importance of incorporating learning experiences that are designed to develop health-related physical fitness.
5. Recognize and describe the importance of valuing and assessing the process of physical activity.
6. Identify valid and reliable tests used to measure components of health-related physical fitness.
7. Follow standardized procedures in administering tests that measure various components of health-related physical fitness.
8. Identify differences in the assessment of health-related physical fitness in younger and older populations.
9. Identify pretest considerations for adult fitness testing.
10. Compare and contrast adult fitness testing batteries.

In Chapter 2, a rationale for including health-related physical fitness as a fourth learning domain was presented. Traditionally, learning domains have included the affective, cognitive, and psychomotor domains. Many have included health-related physical fitness in the psychomotor domain. Based on the increasing recognition of the importance of the health-related physical fitness area, we feel that it is critical to consider this area separately. Further, we strongly suggest that activity professionals in both school and nonschool programs consider the learning domains in planning their programs. These learning domains are as pertinent to adults and athletes in activity settings as they are to K–12 students in physical education.

From an historical perspective, the objectives of physical education and physical activity programs have reflected scientific evidence concerning the relationship of physical skills, fitness, and activity to societal health and well-being. In the last fifty years, we have seen programs move from emphasizing muscular strength and endurance in the 1950s to skill-related fitness in the 1960s and 1970s (Welk and Wood, 2000). In the 1980s, the focus shifted to health-related fitness. The research of the 1990s suggests that the perspective on exercise, fitness, and physical activity must shift from vigorous exercise prescriptions to more moderate and wide-ranging physical activities. The report, *Physical Activity and Health: A Report from the Surgeon General* (1996), states that virtually all people will benefit from regular physical activity. As we enter the first decade of this millennium, there is a clear shift to the promotion of physical activity and the positive impact that moderate physical activity can have on health status.

The Surgeon General's Report (1996) summarized the research findings and concluded that moderate physical activity can substantially reduce the risk of developing or dying from heart disease, diabetes, colon cancer, and high blood pressure. On average, individuals who are physically active outlive people who are inactive. Blair and his colleagues (1989) conducted a comprehensive study that investigated the relationship between physical fitness and the risk of dying. The following conclusions were reported:

1. Death rates for the least fit men were 3.4 times higher than for the most fit men and for the least fit women, 4.6 times higher than for the most fit women.

2. Higher levels of physical fitness were beneficial even in those with other risk factors such as high blood pressure, elevated cholesterol levels, history of cigarette smoking, and family history of heart disease.

3. Cancer death rates were much lower in physically fit men and women.

4. Even moderate levels of exercise will result in a fitness level associated with a greatly reduced risk of disease.

Despite the overwhelming evidence about the benefits of a physically active lifestyle, only about 23 percent of American adults report regular, vigorous physical activity for 20 minutes or longer for 3 or more days a week. More alarming, 40 percent of adults do not participate in *any* type of physical activity. The Surgeon General's report on physical activity and health (1996) recommends an accumulation of 30 minutes of moderate activity on most days of the week.

Children are the most physically active segment of our society (Rowland, 1990). During teenage years, the rate of physical activity declines dramatically. This decline is particularly pronounced for female adolescents. While there are many psychosocial and physiological variables that contribute to this decline, it is a serious source of concern for activity professionals. The trend toward sedentary living continues into adulthood in our society.

This lack of physical activity promotes obesity. Obesity has become an epidemic of serious consequences in our country. Government statistics show that 56.4 percent of Americans are overweight and 19.8 percent are categorized as obese (Mokdad et al., 2001). In 1991, those numbers were 45 percent and 12 percent, respectively. The health consequences of carrying extra pounds include increased incidence of type 2 diabetes, high blood pressure, and increased risk of cardiovascular disease. Children and adolescents are following this societal trend as they are becoming fatter than their counterparts of past decades.

Physical health and well-being are undeniably associated with an active lifestyle. Promotion of increased physical activity as a means of disease prevention as well as prevention of obesity, lower back pain, and degenerative diseases and processes is critical (American College of Sports Medicine, 1993). As such, physical education and exercise science become valuable means to enhance the functional health of American society.

Two of the primary goals of our programs are to develop and maintain a level of health-related physical fitness commensurate with an individual's needs and to promote the value of a physically active lifestyle. To meet these programmatic goals, school and nonschool activity-based programs must include a strong emphasis on activity promotion. Physical activity in the daily lifestyle will help improve the health-related physical fitness status of our students and clients. Physical fitness should be considered a subset of physical activity. Methods of assessing both physical activity and health-related physical fitness are crucial to effective programs. This chapter will include methods of measuring physical activity and fitness for K–12 and adult populations.

Physical Activity and Physical Fitness

The emphasis of this chapter is on the measurement of health-related physical fitness. Chapter 6 focuses on measurement of skill-related physical fitness. It is important that you know which area of physical fitness you want to measure so that you can select the most appropriate test battery. Before presenting the selected measurement techniques and test batteries, the brief discussion below will help you have a clearer understanding of the relationship of physical activity and physical fitness. Further, the information below should help you understand the different categories of physical fitness.

Physical activity can be defined as body movement that is produced by the contraction of skeletal muscle and that substantially increases energy expenditure (USDHHS, 1996; Bouchard et al., 1990). Selected forms of physical activity pertinent to physical education and exercise science are exercise, sports, leisure activities, and dance. Physical activity is a process, which includes these subcategories, while physical fitness is a product. **Physical fitness** is a product of physical activity that includes a set of attributes that people have or achieve relating to their ability to perform physical activity (USDHHS, 1996). **Physiological fitness** includes nonperformance components of physical fitness that relate to biological systems that are influenced by one's level of habitual physical activity (Bouchard et al., 1990). **Health-related physical fitness** consists of those components of physical fitness that have a relationship with good health (ACSM, 1998). **Skill-related physical fitness** consists of those components of physical fitness that have a relationship with enhanced performance in sports and motor skills. Bouchard, Shephard, and Stephens presented a comprehensive model of physical fitness that lists components of each of these categories of physical fitness. Each of these components is a product that is related to the process of being physically active. This model is shown in Table 5.1 and is consistent with contemporary definitions (ACSM, 1998; USDHHS, 1996; USDHHS, 2000).

Table 5.1 Dimensions of physical fitness.

Physiological	Health-Related	Skill-Related
Metabolic	Body composition	Agility
Morphological	Cardiorespiratory fitness	Balance
Bone integrity	Flexibility	Coordination
	Muscular endurance	Power
	Muscular strength	Speed
		Reaction time

Source: Corbin, C., Pangrazi, R., and Frank, D. (2000). *President's Council on Physical Fitness and Sports Research Digest.* 3(9).

Components of Health-Related Physical Fitness

Until 1980, distinctions were not commonly made between health-related physical fitness and skill-related physical fitness. The AAHPERD Health-Related Physical Fitness Test (1980) represented one of the first school-based tests that separated the components. Prior to that time, most test batteries given to K–12 youth had a mix of health-related and skill-related components. In contemporary activity settings, it is important to differentiate between the types of physical fitness. This dichotomy clearly shows that health-related physical fitness is related to functional health and well-being, while skill-related physical fitness is related to physical performance and athletic ability. It should be noted that health-related physical fitness is foundational to skill-related physical fitness. Definitions of the specific components of health-related physical fitness (USDHHS, 1996) are as follows:

Body composition relates to the relative amounts of muscle, fat, bone, and other vital parts of the body. This component of physical fitness can be measured by hydrostatic (underwater) weighing in a laboratory setting or in the field with skinfold calipers. There are a variety of other methods of assessing body composition, including formulas to calculate body mass index (BMI). Whereas other field tests of health-related fitness involve some type of performance such as running, stretching, or a muscular exercise, body composition is the only nonperformance component of health-related physical fitness.

Cardiorespiratory fitness relates to the ability of the circulatory and respiratory systems to supply oxygen during sustained physical activity. Cardiorespiratory fitness is also known as cardiovascular fitness, cardiovascular endurance, or aerobic fitness. A maximal oxygen uptake test in a laboratory setting is the best measure of this component. Commonly administered field tests are the mile run, the 12-minute run, the PACER run, and various bicycle ergometer, treadmill, and step tests.

Flexibility relates to the range of motion available at the joint. Flexibility is specific to each joint of the body. Therefore, there is no general test of flexibility like there is for cardiorespiratory fitness. Flexibility can be measured in the laboratory with devices such as a goniometer or in field settings. In the field, the sit-and-reach box is commonly used to measure flexibility of the low back and hamstring. Good flexibility in these areas is generally associated with less risk of low back pain.

Muscular endurance relates to the muscle's ability to continue to perform without fatigue. Like flexibility, muscular endurance is specific to each major muscle group of the body. Laboratory and field tests are similar and are based on the number of repetitions (e.g., push-ups, chin-ups, abdominal curls) that can be performed by the specific muscle group.

Muscular strength relates to the ability of the muscle to exert force. Muscular strength is also specific in nature. Laboratory and field tests are similar and involve the amount of maximum resistance the subject can overcome one time (one repetition maximum—1 RM). One-RM tests are usually conducted on weight resistance machines. A typical muscular strength test would be the 1-RM bench press. Strength can also be measured by dynamometers.

The remainder of this chapter will provide descriptions of health-related physical fitness tests. It is important that tests be chosen with the appropriate population in mind. The chapter is broken into two major sections. The first section describes testing for K–12 populations and the other major section is dedicated to the testing of adult populations.

SECTION 1—TESTING CHILDREN AND YOUTH IN SCHOOLS

In order to understand the purpose and philosophy of fitness testing in the school setting today, it will be helpful to briefly review the history of fitness testing over the past fifty years. In the early 1950s, data was reported that indicated that European children had superior fitness levels to their American counterparts. This led to the development of the first fitness test battery widely used in the schools, the American Alliance of Health, Physical Education, Recreation, and Dance (AAHPERD) Youth Fitness Test (1958). The test items were selected by logic and not validated by research. In 1975, the straight-leg sit-up was replaced by a bent-leg sit-up and the softball throw was eliminated. In 1976, national norms were completed. Items for this test included pull-ups (boys) or flexed arm hang (girls), a 1-minute bent-leg sit-up, shuttle run, standing long jump, 50-yard dash, and 600-yard run. You can see that this test includes a mixture of health-related and skill-related components of physical fitness. It is also important to note that student performance was compared to national norms and that there was an award system for outstanding performance on all test items.

The AAHPERD Health-Related Physical Fitness Test (1980, 1984) was developed by a joint committee of experts over a five-year period. It was the first test that included only test items pertaining to health-related components. It included a distance run, body composition by measuring triceps and the subscapular skinfold site, 1-minute modified bent-knee curl-up, and the sit-and-reach test. Normative data was developed for these test items. The vision of the developers of this test concerning the importance of health-related fitness has proved to be on target. Nevertheless, this test never gained widespread popularity and perhaps was a bit ahead of its time. It represented a radical departure from previous fitness test batteries. Many teachers continued to use the AAHPERD Youth Fitness Test during the 1980s rather than switch to this test.

The Fit Youth Today (1986) test battery was notable because it included the first major educational program to accompany the fitness test protocols. It was endorsed by the American College of Sports Medicine (ACSM) and included a 20-minute steady state run, a 2-minute bent-knee curl-up, sit-and-reach test, and body composition using the triceps and medial calf skinfold sites. It was also the first test to introduce criterion-referenced standards rather than using normative standards. This test was used regionally but never reached national popularity.

Prior to 1987, the President's Council on Physical Fitness used the AAHPERD Youth Fitness Test. In 1987, the council established its own test called the President's Challenge (1987). While other tests were moving toward criterion standards, this test battery continued to use normative standards and included heavy emphasis on an awards program. Students had to reach the 85th percentile or better in all test items to win the Presidential Physical Fitness Award and the 50th percentile to receive the Participant Physical Fitness Award. The test items included pull-ups or flexed arm hang, sit-and-reach or V-sit, one-mile run, and the shuttle run (a skill-related component). More recently, the President's Challenge has introduced an additional Health Fitness Award based on achieving specific criteria in the five health-related components.

In the late 1980s, AAHPERD (1988) introduced the Physical Best test battery. It included a one-mile run, sit and reach, pull-ups, modified sit-ups, and body composition (tricep and medial calf). It also included a significant educational package and utilized criterion standards. This test was the successor to the AAHPERD Health-Related Physical Fitness test battery. At about the same time the Physical Best test battery was being introduced, the FITNESSGRAM® was being developed by a team of professionals at the Cooper Institute for Aerobics Research (CIAR). This test battery also included criterion standards and provided teachers with software to generate test results and fitness profiles for students. It measured basically the same health-related components as Physical Best but provided more options. In 1993, AAHPERD and the CIAR agreed to merge their programs. AAHPERD provides the Physical Best educational materials and the FITNESSGRAM is used as the test battery to assess health-related physical fitness. Detailed information on FITNESSGRAM is provided later in the chapter.

From this brief historical synopsis, you can see that fitness testing has changed significantly, especially in the past 20 years. As you have just read, numerous test batteries were being introduced in the 1980s. This led to confusion in the schools as teachers and administrators grappled with changing philosophies and emphases. Test batteries evolved from testing both health-related and skill-related components to assessing exclusively health-related components. The emphasis now is clearly on health-related physical fitness. There is also a much greater focus on the educational materials that accompany the fitness assessment since it is realized that all assessment should be educational and meaningful to students. Current trends also promote physical activity by emphasizing criterion-based testing and de-emphasizing reward systems based on fitness performance. Naturally, there is extensive computerized support in contemporary test programs, with plans under way to launch Web-based support for FITNESSGRAM in the near future.

Considerations About Fitness Testing

The overall goal of fitness testing should be to promote the enjoyment of regular physical activity and to provide comprehensive fitness and activity assessments of children and adolescents. The fitness testing procedures should be educational and meaningful to the students. They should be able to understand their fitness test results as they relate to their health and well-being throughout their life. Your fitness testing results should be used not only to educate students but also to motivate them to lead active lifestyles. Further, test results can be used to publicize the goals and accomplishments of your program. Student improvements should be highlighted. When choosing a fitness test battery and administering the test, you should always consider the objectives of your program and tailor your efforts to meet these objectives.

Process or Product

As mentioned earlier in the chapter, physical activity is a process that is related to the product of physical fitness. It is important that fitness testing programs be geared to the promotion of physical activity. The focus of fitness experiences and testing should be on helping students clearly understand the relationship between good health and activity. This means that criterion-referenced health standards should be emphasized rather than normative standards in which students are compared to each other. These criterion-referenced health standards help the students understand what level of fitness is necessary for good health. To be meaningful, fitness testing should reveal which students are healthy and which are at risk. It allows students the opportunity to decide whether they need to improve their health status. Test results with criterion standards provide meaningful information on which students can make thoughtful decisions that affect the quality of their lives.

For many years, physical educators focused their attention on the product of physical fitness. More recently, the emphasis has changed to encouraging physical activity (process). One of the implications to this approach is to de-emphasize award systems. Rewards for fitness test performance reinforce the product of fitness. We should be trying to motivate all students to be physically active. A majority of students will find it difficult, if not impossible, to earn awards for high performance. Students who do exceedingly well on these tests will certainly be reinforced without external rewards. Many students, no matter how hard they might try or how much training they do, will not be able to score at a high percentile on all tests. If awards systems are used, they should recognize students for regular participation in activity.

Factors in Fitness Test Performance

There are many factors that impact the performance of physical fitness tests. Research findings clearly indicate that **genetic endowment** is a major factor in physical fitness test scores. Bouchard and Perusse (1994) reported that biological inheritance was associated with approximately 29 percent of habitual physical activity, 25 percent of cardiorespiratory fitness, 30 percent of muscular fitness, and 25 percent of percent body fat. *It is important to realize that not all students will be equally successful even if exposed to regular physical activity.* Because of genetic predispositon, some students will score higher on fitness tests. **Trainability** is also inherited (Bouchard et al., 1992). This means that some individuals can make large improvements with training while others do not respond in such significant ways. For example, student A and student B do the same activities throughout the semester. Student A shows dramatic improvements, while student B does not. This would indicate that student A inherited a system that responds well to training. It is important to realize that student B will also receive benefits of training and improve in fitness tests, but it will likely take longer. It is also likely that student B will never achieve the fitness level of student A.

Lifestyle and environmental factors can also make a difference. **Lifestyle factors** such as nutrition, sleeping patterns, and activity outside of school can certainly affect test scores. **Environmental factors** such as heat, humidity, and pollution can also impact test scores. A final factor that must be recognized is **maturation**. Anyone who has worked with children and youth know that they mature at different rates. Generally, the more mature child will perform in fitness tests better than the less mature child even though they are the same age and gender.

Undoubtedly, the amount of physical activity in which students engage impacts physical fitness scores. The relationship between physical activity and physical fitness is lower than most professionals realize. Morrow and Freedson (1994) reported that the typical relationship between activity and measured oxygen consumption in adolescence is less than r = .20. Thus, you must understand that many other factors also are major determinants of performance on fitness tests. The powerful influences of heredity, maturation, lifestyle, and environmental factors must be recognized.

For many years, physical educators focused their attention on the product of physical fitness. In the last decade, the attention has changed to encouraging physical activity. Recognizing the difference between the product of physical fitness and the process of physical activity is crucial. This differentiation should be taught to students as well. Given the nature of the relationship between physical fitness and physical activity, it is important that the emphasis in physical education be on physical activity rather than on physical fitness test scores. This is a major reason why it is recommended that criterion-referenced tests be used in schools rather than normative tests and that rewards for performance should be discouraged.

Normative Data

Although the use of criterion-referenced physical fitness test batteries is the current trend and the recommended choice, an awareness of normative data can still be helpful to physical educators. Safrit and Looney (1992) point out that normative data from fitness testing of school-aged children can be valuable for identifying the current status of individuals compared to other students of the same age and gender, identifying excellence in test performance, and in program evaluation. Results of the National Children and Youth Fitness Studies (NCYFS) (Ross, Dotson, Gilbert, and Katz, 1985; Ross et al., 1987) established sound normative data on youth fitness. Whereas other normative studies were derived from "convenience samples" of K–12 students, the NCYFS developed norms from a national probability sample. This sampling procedure was used to create data that is most representative of children and youth in the United States. Tables 5.2 through 5.6 illustrate percentile norms for the fitness tests given in conjunction with the NCYFS.

Table 5.2 Percentile norms for males and females on distance runs (min:sec).

Male percentile	Age (years)												
	6	7	8	9	10	11	12	13	14	15	16	17	18
90	4:27	4:11	8:46	8:10	8:13	7:25	7:13	6:48	6:27	6:23	6:13	6:08	6:10
75	4:52	4:33	9:29	9:00	8:48	8:02	7:53	7:14	7:08	6:52	6:39	6:40	6:42
50	5:23	5:00	10:39	10:10	9:52	9:03	8:48	8:04	7:51	7:30	7:27	7:31	7:35
25	5:58	5:35	12:14	11:44	11:00	10:32	10:13	9:06	9:10	8:30	8:18	8:37	8:34
10	6:40	6:20	14:05	13:37	12:27	12:07	11:48	10:38	10:34	10:13	9:36	10:43	10:50
Female percentile													
90	4:46	4:32	9:39	9:08	9:09	8:45	8:34	8:27	8:11	8:23	8:28	8:20	8:22
75	5:13	4:54	10:23	9:50	10:09	9:56	9:52	9:30	9:16	9:28	9:25	9:26	9:31
50	5:44	5:25	11:32	11:13	11:14	11:15	10:58	10:52	10:32	10:46	10:34	10:34	10:51
25	6:14	6:01	12:59	12:45	12:52	12:54	12:33	12:17	11:49	12:18	12:10	12:03	12:14
10	6:51	6:38	14:48	14:31	14:20	14:35	14:07	13:45	13:13	14:07	13:42	13:46	15:18

Note: Subjects aged 6 to 7 run 1/2 mi; others run 1 mi.

Table 5.3 Percentile norms for males and females for sum of skinfolds (mm)

Male percentile	Age (years)												
	6	7	8	9	10	11	12	13	14	15	16	17	18
90	12	12	12	12	12	12	12	11	12	12	12	13	13
75	14	14	14	15	14	14	14	13	13	14	14	14	15
50	16	17	18	21	17	18	17	17	17	17	17	17	18
25	20	22	24	29	24	25	24	23	22	22	22	22	24
10	27	32	37	40	35	36	38	34	33	32	30	30	30
Female percentile													
90	15	15	15	16	13	14	15	15	17	19	19	20	19
75	18	18	19	20	16	17	18	19	20	23	22	23	22
50	21	22	24	26	20	21	22	24	26	28	26	28	27
25	27	28	33	35	27	30	29	31	33	34	33	36	34
10	33	37	43	45	36	40	40	43	40	43	42	42	42

Note: For subjects aged 6 to 9, values represent the sum of triceps and calf skinfolds; for other subjects, values are the sum of triceps and subscapular skinfolds.

Table 5.4 Percentile norms for males and females on the 1-minute bent-knee sit-up test (number completed)

Male	Age (years)												
percentile	6	7	8	9	10	11	12	13	14	15	16	17	18
90	28	32	35	39	47	48	50	52	52	53	55	56	54
75	24	28	30	33	40	41	44	46	47	48	49	50	50
50	19	23	26	28	34	36	38	40	41	42	43	43	43
25	14	18	20	23	28	30	32	32	35	36	38	37	36
10	9	12	15	16	22	22	25	28	30	31	32	31	31
Female percentile													
90	28	33	34	36	43	42	46	46	47	45	49	47	47
75	23	27	29	31	37	37	40	40	41	40	40	40	40
50	18	21	25	26	31	32	33	33	35	35	35	36	35
25	14	16	19	21	25	26	28	27	29	30	30	30	30
10	6	11	13	15	20	20	21	21	23	24	23	24	24

Table 5.5 Percentile norms for males and females on the pull-up test (number completed)

Male	Age (years)												
percentile	6	7	8	9	10	11	12	13	14	15	16	17	18
90	15	19	20	20	8	8	8	10	12	14	14	15	16
75	10	13	14	15	4	5	5	7	8	10	12	12	13
50	6	8	10	10	1	2	3	4	5	7	9	9	10
25	3	4	6	6	0	0	0	1	2	4	6	5	6
10	1	1	3	3	0	0	0	0	0	1	2	2	3
Female percentile													
90	2	13	16	17	17	3	3	2	2	2	2	2	2
75	1	9	11	11	12	1	1	1	1	1	1	1	1
50	0	6	7	8	9	0	0	0	0	0	0	0	0
25	0	3	4	4	4	0	0	0	0	0	0	0	0
10	0	0	1	1	1	0	0	0	0	0	0	0	0

Note: Subjects aged 6 to 9 performed modified pull-ups.

Table 5.6 Percentile norms for males and females on the sit-and-reach test (inches)

Male percentile	Age (years)												
	6	7	8	9	10	11	12	13	14	15	16	17	18
90	16.0	16.0	16.0	15.5	16.0	16.5	16.0	16.5	17.5	18.0	19.0	19.5	19.5
75	15.0	15.0	14.5	14.5	14.5	15.0	15.0	15.0	15.5	16.5	17.0	17.5	17.5
50	13.5	13.5	13.5	13.0	13.5	13.0	13.0	13.0	13.5	14.0	15.0	15.5	15.0
25	12.0	11.5	11.5	11.0	11.5	11.5	11.0	11.0	11.0	12.0	13.0	13.0	13.0
10	10.5	10.0	9.5	9.5	10.0	9.5	8.5	9.0	9.0	9.5	10.0	10.5	10.0
Female percentile													
90	16.5	17.0	17.0	17.0	17.5	18.0	19.0	20.0	19.5	20.0	20.5	20.5	20.5
75	15.5	16.0	16.0	16.0	16.5	16.5	17.0	18.0	18.5	19.0	19.0	19.0	19.0
50	14.0	14.5	14.0	14.0	14.5	15.0	15.5	16.0	17.0	17.0	17.5	18.0	17.5
25	12.5	13.0	12.5	12.5	13.0	13.0	14.0	14.0	15.0	15.5	16.0	15.5	15.5
10	11.5	11.5	11.0	11.0	10.5	11.5	12.0	12.0	12.5	13.5	14.0	13.5	13.0

Reprinted from the 56(1): 62–66 and 58(9): 66–70 *Journal of Physical Education, Recreation & Dance*, a publication of the American Alliance of Health, Physical Education, Recreation and Dance, 1900 Association Dr., Reston, VA 20191.

Measurement of Health-Related Physical Fitness in School Settings

There are many different methods of measuring the various components of health-related physical fitness. Each component can be measured in different ways. Some measurement techniques require laboratory settings with expensive equipment that are not feasible in school settings. Fortunately, there are field tests used in schools that can be carried out with minimal equipment and facilities. The selection of the appropriate test is dependent on many factors (see Chapter 4). Care should be taken to choose a test that is valid, age-appropriate, and most advantageous to your particular testing situation.

Measuring Body Composition

Basically, total body weight can be divided into two components, fat weight and lean weight. **Lean weight** comprises all organ tissue, muscle, and bone. **Fat weight** refers to the body tissue that can be defined as chemically fat. Percent body fat, or the percent of total weight represented by fat weight, is the index used to describe individual body composition. For example, a youngster who weighs 100 pounds and whose body composition is 20 percent fat, has a fat weight of 20 pounds and a lean weight of 80 pounds.

Measuring fatness and leanness of the body has been of interest to physical educators for years. Measuring body composition is important because being misinformed about healthful body fat levels or having a distorted body image may result in physiological and psychological problems (Thomas and Whitehead, 1993).

Researchers have developed many methods to assess and evaluate body composition. Historically, educators and scientists have used height and weight ratios to determine overweight, making the assumption that overweight and overfat were synonymous. We now know that overweight and overfat are not interchangeable terms. Overweight is defined as a condition that exists when people's weight is in excess of recommended limits for their body type. Overfatness refers to a state of poor health that results from possessing an unacceptable ratio of fat to lean body mass. For example, many athletes participating in sports that require a great deal of strength to be successful (e.g., football, shot put, discus throw) would be classified as overweight according to age-height-weight scales, when in fact their body composition indicates that they are lean. Their apparent overweight is related to heavy bone structure and high amounts of muscle tissue. Because of the misinterpretations associated with the definitional differences between overweight and overfat, methods other than weight/height ratio should be used to quantify the fat component of total body weight (AAHPERD, 1984).

Body composition is measured in laboratory settings with hydrostatic (underwater) weighing techniques. Population-specific skinfold formulas have been developed using concurrent validity techniques with hydrostatic weighing. These skinfold measurements provide a reasonable estimate of body composition if measurements are taken properly. A skinfold consists of a double layer of skin and subcutaneous fat (see Figure 5.1). Measurement is usually taken on the right side of the body with the subject standing. Typical skinfold measurement sites include the abdomen, calf, scapula, suprailiac, thigh, and triceps. In school settings, the typical skinfold sites used for assessing body composition are the triceps and medial calf. Body mass index (BMI) formulas have also been developed and are appropriately used in some situations.

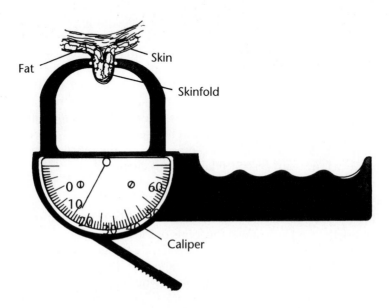

Figure 5.1 Measuring body fat with skinfold caliper.

Measuring Cardiorespiratory Fitness

The relationship between cardiorespiratory fitness and health is well documented. Increases in cardiorespiratory fitness permit a higher quality of life by increasing the rate at which energy can be provided to support work and play activities. Individuals with higher levels of cardiorespiratory fitness can accomplish more physical work in a given period of time and can complete work tasks with less physiological stress than persons with low levels of cardiorespiratory fitness.

Cardiorespiratory fitness involves numerous physiological variables. No single measurement protocol can be expected to accurately evaluate every variable associated with the cardiorespiratory system. The laboratory test that has earned the widest acceptance as a composite measure of cardiorespiratory fitness is direct measurement of maximal aerobic power. This measurement is reported in terms of maximal oxygen uptake relative to body weight.

Maximal oxygen uptake (usually identified as VO_{2max}) is the greatest rate at which oxygen can be consumed during exercise at sea level. This precise measurement is typically expressed as milliliters of oxygen consumed per kilogram of body weight per minute (ml. $kg^{-1}min^{-1}$) and represents an overall indicator of the functional capacity of the cardiorespiratory system. Exercise physiology classes provide more detailed discussions regarding cardiorespiratory fitness and introduce laboratory methods used to directly measure VO_{2max}. Powers and Hawley (1997) and McArdle, Katch, and Katch (2000) serve as good references and provide background on the procedures associated with measuring cardiorespiratory fitness in a laboratory setting. In this chapter assessment of cardiorespiratory fitness will be confined to field-based tests.

Field-based tests refer to assessment protocols that can be conducted away from the confines of the laboratory. Because the setting is less restricting than the laboratory, procedures are less sophisticated, accommodate larger numbers of subjects, and are significantly less expensive and time-consuming. Losses in precision and accuracy are offset by gains in practicality.

The most widely used approach in school settings to field measurement of cardiorespiratory fitness is the **distance run**. Distance runs are similar to VO_{2max} in that subjects are encouraged to expend maximum effort. Distance runs typically used are the one-mile run, 12-minute run/walk test, and the PACER run. Even though distance runs are dependent on other factors, such as body composition and running efficiency, these tests of long duration can be used to accurately estimate cardiorespiratory fitness. Field-based tests that can be used by the practitioner to measure cardiorespiratory fitness are described later in this chapter.

Measuring Flexibility

Flexibility is a measure of the range of motion available at a joint or group of joints. Individuals who can freely move the joints of the ankles, knees, hips, wrists, elbows, and shoulders without stiffness are said to have good flexibility. They can move better and enjoy their activities more. Most important, people who display high degrees of flexibility seem to be healthier than those who do not.

In the past, flexibility has been the most ignored component of health-related physical fitness. Recently, however, there has been a resurgence of interest in exer-

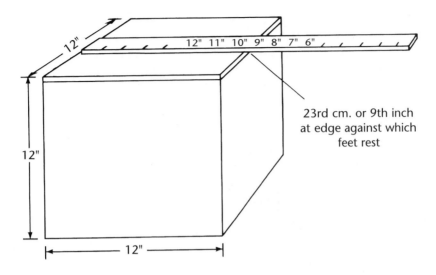

12"

12" 11" 10" 9" 8" 7" 6"

12"

12"

23rd cm. or 9th inch
at edge against which
feet rest

12"

Figure 5.2 Schematic drawing of constructed sit-and-reach apparatus.

cise and physical activity designed to promote and develop flexibility. Research has shown that lower back–posterior thigh flexibility is important for the prevention and rehabilitation of lower back disorders. Lower back pain and muscular tension are significant health problems for the American population. In fact, it has been estimated that 30 to 70 percent of the population has suffered from recurrent back problems (Corbin, Lindsey, and Welk, 2000). As a result of back pain, 2 million people cannot hold jobs. It is the most frequent cause of inactivity in people under 45; even teenagers report backaches.

Flexibility varies among individuals, and great differences can occur among the joints of one person. Structure as well as the amount of muscle and fatty tissue around the joint can affect the range of motion. Measuring and evaluating flexibility is usually discussed in terms of *flexion* or *extension*. **Flexion** occurs when the angle of the body with its articulations is decreased through movement. Getting the lower leg in position to punt a football by moving it backward and upward to the upper leg is an example of flexion. Angle increase of the body in relationship to its articulations is referred to as **extension**. Extending the lower leg to punt the football is an example of extension. Tests of flexibility may be used to determine potential in a particular athletic activity, assess change of flexibility performance as part of a physical education unit or rehabilitation process, and diagnose joint or muscular dysfunction.

There is no general flexibility test because flexibility is joint specific. The most common type of flexibility test used in health-related physical fitness test batteries is the sit-and-reach test. Typically, a sit-and-reach apparatus (see Figure 5.2) is used to measure flexibility of the low back and posterior thigh. Though there are variations of this test, the measurement of the flexibility of the low back and posterior thigh is standard in recent test batteries.

Measuring Muscular Endurance

Muscular endurance is the ability of the muscles to work for extended periods of time without undue fatigue. Endurance prevents unwanted fatigue in daily routines and during sport and leisure opportunities. Muscular endurance is specific to various muscle groups, so different tests must be designed.

The assessment of muscular endurance in health-related physical fitness batteries invariably includes a test of endurance of the abdominal muscles. There are variations (modified sit-ups, curl-ups) of the test to measure this area that will be covered later in this chapter. Pull-ups, flexed arm hang, and push-ups are used in various test batteries to test endurance of arm and shoulder muscles.

Measuring Muscular Strength

Muscular strength is the amount of force a muscle can exert. Strength is measured by the amount of force produced from a single maximal effort. Like flexibility and muscular endurance, strength is specific to various muscles and muscle groups. Thus, a variety of muscular strength tests have been developed.

It can be argued that the tests listed previously in the muscular endurance category also measure muscular strength. In these tests, strength and endurance are used to perform the tests. While not included in recommended health-related physical fitness testing batteries used in schools, the 1 RM bench press to measure upper body strength (see Figure 5.3) is commonly used in physical education settings. The measurement of lower body strength using the 1 RM squat is used in athletic settings but is not commonly used elsewhere because of safety factors. A leg press on a weight machine can be a suitable substitute in some situations.

Figure 5.3 Bench press.

Test Batteries for School Settings

Fitness testing has undergone significant changes in recent years. Once dedicated to measuring skills, test items now focus on components of health-related physical fitness. Most test batteries currently in use evaluate performance on the basis of its relationship to a criterion or standard rather than to the group being tested. Normative information, while useful to profile group performance, is assuming a less prominent role in judging the fitness of individuals. With the movement toward the use of standards has come a movement to encourage and recognize improvement and alteration of activity behavior, rather than merely performance. The reader is reminded that this movement toward criterion-referenced scores reflects the fact that there is little correlation between activity and fitness test results. It is important, therefore, to reinforce behavior rather than simply a score. With this rapidly changing focus in fitness testing comes the responsibility for educators and program administrators to remain up-to-date on testing, philosophies, goals, and procedures.

Choosing a battery of test items rather than individually selected tests can be advantageous. First, often a test battery has been checked for reliability and validity and efforts have been made to avoid testing the same component twice. Second, batteries may provide a way to calculate an overall score for each participant. And finally, test batteries can serve as common denominators among schools within the same locale. In selecting a fitness test battery, you should look for a package that includes comprehensive educational materials, technology support, economic feasibility, ease of administration, and appropriate recognition systems.

President's Challenge

The President's Challenge (2001) is a fitness test battery that includes a variety of options from which to choose. This testing program offers the Physical Fitness program with three levels of awards, the Health Fitness Award, and the Presidential Active Lifestyle Award.

The Physical Fitness program is the traditional physical fitness program that includes: curl-ups or partial curl-ups, endurance run/walk, V-sit reach or sit-and-reach option, right-angle push-ups or pull-ups option, and shuttle run. It should be noted that the shuttle run is a skill-related tests, while the other four items are health-related. There are three levels of awards available for children and youth depending on their level of physical fitness:

The Presidential Fitness Award—must score at or above the 85th percentile on all five items.

The National Physical Fitness Award—must score at or above the 50th percentile on all five items.

The Participant Fitness Award—scores fall below the 50th percentile on one or more items.

Given the research on factors affecting fitness test scores presented earlier in this section of this chapter, the Physical Fitness program is not recommended by the authors of this textbook. We would advocate a test battery that did not mix health-related and skill-related test items, used criteria rather than normative standards, and did not emphasize a rewards system. Nevertheless, this test is used in some schools, and you should know about its existence.

The Health Fitness Award can be earned by students whose test scores meet health criteria standards on the following five items: partial curl-up, one-mile run/walk with distance adjustments for age, V-sit reach or sit-and-reach option, right-angle push-ups or pull-ups option, and body mass index. The standards are shown in Table 5.7. We recommend this option for testing rather than the Physical Fitness program if you are using the President's Challenge. Even with the Health Fitness option, we advocate downplaying the awards system.

The newest component developed by President's Challenge is the Presidential Active Lifestyle Award. This award recognizes students who are regularly physically active. Students who are active for 60 minutes per day, five days a week for six weeks are eligible for the award. Activities that cause all or most of the body to move, causing increased heart rate and respiration, can be done alone, in groups, and inside or outside of school. The activity can be done for a continual 60 minutes or accumulated in shorter segments throughout the day. An activity log is kept by the student to document activity. It must be verified by a supervising adult. A second way to earn this award is by using a pedometer. The pedometer is used to measure steps throughout the day. A student must reach 11,000 steps per day, five days a week for six weeks to qualify for the award. The latest addition to the President's Challenge recognizes the process of activity rather than the product.

More information on the specifics of the President's Challenge is available at www.indiana.edu/~preschal.

FITNESSGRAM

We believe that the FITNESSGRAM (1999) is the best program available for testing children and youth and recommend its use. Developed by the Cooper Institute for Aerobics Research, it is a comprehensive health-related physical fitness testing program that uses criterion-referenced standards. Upper and lower healthy fitness zones are included for each test as target criteria. It provides computer software for recording scores and generating reports for students. It does not advocate use of an award program that focuses on fitness performance. The FITNESSGRAM is accompanied by comprehensive educational materials produced by the American Alliance of Health, Physical Education, Recreation, and Dance (AAHPERD) called Physical Best. The program also includes a new module called ACTIVITYGRAM. It is the most comprehensive package currently available to teachers and is used throughout the country.

FITNESSGRAM and ACTIVITYGRAM are designed to help students learn about concepts of physical activity and physical fitness. This type of approach should increase the chances of your students pursuing an active lifestyle as adults. FITNESS-GRAM is designed to provide personal information about physical fitness and help students learn to plan lifetime activity programs. Emphases are on learning to self-assess fitness levels, making accurate interpretations about the results, and learning to plan personalized programs. The ACTIVITYGRAM provides personal information about general levels of activity and helps teach ways to be physically active. It also can help students become more aware of their activity patterns and make appropriate interventions to be more active.

Table 5.7 Qualifying standards for the Health Fitness Award.

	Age	Partial Curl-Ups (#)	Endurance Run (min:sec)	V-Sit Reach OR (in)	Sit and Reach (cm)	Rt.-Angle Push-Ups OR (#)	Pull-Ups (#)	BMI (range)
BOYS								
	6	12	2:30 ⎫ 1/4 Mile	1	21	3	1	13.3–19.5
	7	12	2:20 ⎭	1	21	4	1	13.3–19.5
	8	15	4:45 ⎫ 1/4 Mile	1	21	5	1	13.4–20.5
	9	15	4:35 ⎭	1	21	6	1	13.7–21.4
	10	20	9:30	1	21	7	1	14.0–22.5
	11	20	9:00	1	21	8	2	14.0–23.7
	12	20	9:00	1	21	9	2	14.8–24.1
	13	25	8:00 ⎬ 1 Mile	1	21	10	2	15.4–24.7
	14	25	8:00	1	21	12	3	16.1–25.4
	15	30	7:30	1	21	14	4	16.6–26.4
	16	30	7:30	1	21	16	5	17.2–26.8
	17	30	7:30	1	21	18	6	17.7–27.5
GIRLS								
	6	12	2:50 ⎫ 1/4 Mile	2	23	3	1	13.1–19.6
	7	12	2:40 ⎭	2	23	4	1	13.1–19.6
	8	15	5:35 ⎫ 1/4 Mile	2	23	5	1	13.2–20.7
	9	15	5:25 ⎭	2	23	6	1	13.5–21.4
	10	20	10:00	2	23	7	1	13.8–22.5
	11	20	10:00	2	23	7	1	14.1–23.2
	12	20	10:30	2	23	8	1	14.7–24.2
	13	25	10:30 ⎬ 1 Mile	3	25	7	1	15.5–25.3
	14	25	10:30	3	25	7	1	16.2–25.3
	15	30	10:00	3	25	7	1	16.6–26.5
	16	30	10:00	3	25	7	1	16.8–26.5
	17	30	10:00	3	25	7	1	17.1–26.9

Source: President's Challenge (2001). www.indiana.edu/~preschal. Bloomington, IN..

FITNESSGRAM tests the components of health-related physical fitness. On most components, several options are provided, with recommendations. The items of the test battery are (1) one-mile walk/run, a multistage 20-meter shuttle run called the PACER to measure cardiorespiratory capacity or a walk test for secondary students; (2) skinfold thickness or body mass index to measure body composition; (3) timed curl-up test to measure abdominal strength and muscular endurance; (4) the trunk lift to measure trunk extensor strength and flexibility; (5) 90-degree push-ups, modified pull-ups, pull-ups, or flexed arm hang to measure muscular strength and endurance of the upper body; and (6) back-saver sit-and-reach or shoulder stretch to measure flexibility.

Age Level: Ages 17+

Norms: Results of the FITNESSGRAM are communicated in the form of desirable health standards.

Test Area: Any spacious gymnasium or multipurpose room and outdoor area are suitable for administering the test battery.

Test 1: One-Mile Walk/Run (Recommended)

Instructions: Students are instructed to run/walk the one-mile distance as fast as possible. Students begin on the command "Ready, start."

Equipment Needed: Stopwatch, pencil and scoresheet, and boundary markers for the running area.

Scoring Procedure: The time taken to cover the one-mile distance is recorded in minutes and seconds. Students in grades K–3 should not be timed but should simply complete the distance.

Organizational Hints: Instruction emphasizing pacing and practice should precede test administration. Administering the test under conditions of high temperature and/or humidity or windy conditions should be avoided. A proper warm-up should precede test administration. It is important that a system be devised to accurately count laps and record times (e.g., partnering with older children).

The Progressive Aerobic Cardiovascular Endurance Run—PACER (Recommended for K–3)

Instructions: A 20-meter course is marked with boundary cones and a taped line at each end. Each student should have a space for running that is 40–60 inches wide. A PACER audiotape (includes music and prerecorded beeping sound) is used and students are to run the distance of the marked area and touch the line before the beep on the audiotape sounds. At the sound of the beep, students reverse direction and run back to the other taped line. Students who get to the line before the beep must wait for the beep before running in the other direction. Students continue this pattern until they have twice failed to reach the line before the beep sounds. Two missed arrivals constitutes completion of the test.

Equipment Needed: Tape playback machine with good volume, PACER tape, boundary cones, masking tape, pencils, and score sheets.

Scoring Procedure: A partner should record the lap number on a predesigned score sheet. The reported score is the total number of laps completed.

Organizational Hints: Students should be encouraged to pace themselves. When testing groups of students, older students or adults can be used to assist in the scorekeeping. Students who have twice missed the pace should depart the testing area being careful not to interfere with others still running.

Walk Test (Alternative for 13 Years and Older)

Instructions: On the start signal, students are instructed to complete a one-mile walk as fast as possible while maintaining a constant walking pace for the entire distance.

Equipment Needed: Stopwatch, pencil and score sheet, and boundary markers for the walking area.

Scoring Procedure: At the finish of the one-mile walk, the students count their heart rate for 15 seconds. The walk time and the heart rate are entered into the FITNESS-GRAM software, and an estimated maximum volume of oxygen uptake is estimated.

Organizational Hints: Instruction and practice on pacing need to be given prior to the test administration. Extreme weather conditions can affect scores. Avoid giving the test on high-temperature and/or high-humidity days or in windy conditions.

Test 2: Skinfold (Recommended)

Instructions: The triceps and the medial calf are the two sites for the skinfold test.

The proper sequence for administering the skinfold tests consists of firmly grasping the skinfold between the thumb and forefinger and lifting it away. Place the skinfold caliper one-half inch below the skinfold. Slowly release the pressure on the caliper trigger so the pinchers can gently exert full tension on the skinfold and then read the scale.

The medial calf skinfold site is taken on the inside of the right calf at the level of maximal calf girth. The student should put his or her right foot on a bench or chair and relax the muscle (see Figure 5.4).

The triceps skinfold is measured over the triceps muscle on the right arm halfway between the olecranon process of the elbow and the acromial process on the top of the shoulder and parallel to the longitudinal axis of the upper arm (see Figure 5.5).

FITNESSGRAM Report

Using the software that accompanies the test battery, students or teachers can generate reports of fitness testing in the form of a fitness profile. The report shows the healthy fitness zones for each item tested and sends messages to students about their scores. The report also asks three questions specific to aerobic, strength, and flexibility

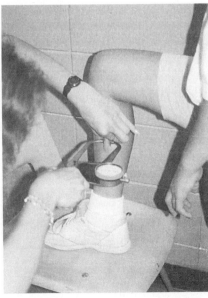

Figure 5.4 Calf skinfold.

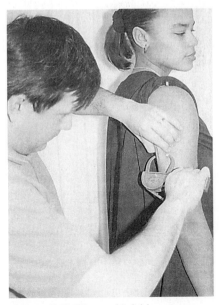

Figure 5.5 Triceps skinfold.

activities and two questions about activity participation in physical education. Based on the responses, individualized feedback is provided to the students about their activity patterns. This type of report is both educational and an excellent way to promote physical activity. It helps inform parents, teachers in other subject areas, and administrators about the positive contribution of your physical education program. A sample of the FITNESSGRAM report is shown in Figure 5.6.

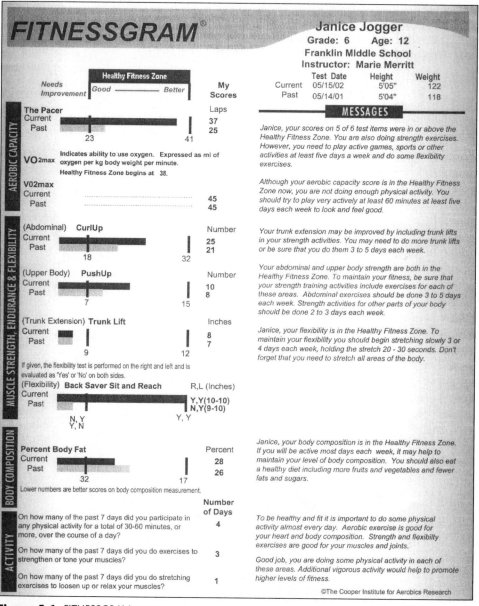

Figure 5.6 *FITNESSGRAM* report.
Source: The Cooper Institute for Aerobics Research. Dallas, TX.

Equipment Needed: Skinfold caliper and bench.

Scoring Procedure: The median of three measurements for each site is recorded as the student's score.

Organizational Hints: All measurements are taken on the right side of the body. Skinfolds should be measured in a setting that assures privacy for the child. When possible, it is suggested that the same tester administer all skinfold measurements.

Body Mass Index (Optional)

Instructions: The body mass index (BMI) is defined as the ratio of body weight (measured in kilograms) and the square of the height (measured in meters). Body weight is measured with the individual clad in lightweight shorts and shirt. Reading is recorded to the nearest 0.5 kilogram. Standing height is measured with the individual in stocking feet, fully erect, and stretched to full height while keeping the heels flat on the floor. The body mass index is determined as follows:

$$\text{BMI} = \text{Body weight (Kg)} / \text{Height (m)}^2$$

Test 3: Curl-Up (Required)

Instructions: Students lie on their back on a mat or piece of carpet, with legs bent at the knee (approximately 140° angle). Legs should be slightly apart, arms straight and parallel to the trunk with palms of hands resting on the mat or carpet, and fingers stretched out. The head is in contact with the hands of a partner sitting or kneeling at the student's head. When the student has assumed the correct start position, another partner places the appropriate measuring strip on the mat under the student's knees so that the fingertips are resting on the edge of the measuring strip. Figure 5.7 shows the start and up positions for this test and the responsibilities of each partner. On the command "Go" the student curls up slowly, sliding the fingers across the measuring strip until they reach the other side of the strip, then returns to the start position (head returns to contact the partner's hands on the floor). This movement should be slow and deliberate (approximately 20 curl-ups per minute or one every three seconds). The

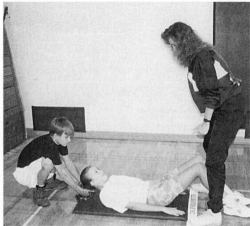

Figure 5.7 Curl-up.

teacher should call the cadence for the class. The student maintains this pattern without pausing until completing 75 curl-ups or becoming unable to continue.

Equipment Needed: Stopwatch or prerecorded audiotape to monitor cadence, mat or piece of carpet, FITNESSGRAM measuring strip, and pencils and scoresheets.

Scoring Procedure: The number of correctly performed curl-ups is recorded as the score.

Organizational Hints: Students should be placed in groups of three with one student designated to secure the measuring strip, another to place his/her hands under the head of the test taker, and the third to do the curl-up. The upward movement should consist of a flattening of the lower back followed by a slow curl of the upper spine. A curl-up is considered completed when the back of the head returns to the partner's hands.

Test 4: Trunk Lift (Required)

Instructions: The student lies face down on a mat or piece of carpet. Hands are placed under thighs and toes are pointed. The student is instructed to slowly lift the upper body off the floor to a maximum height of 12 inches. See Figure 5.8.

Equipment Needed: Mat or piece of carpet and a yardstick or 12-inch ruler.

Scoring Procedure: The greatest height maintained by the student's chin from the mat/carpet, recorded to the nearest inch, is the score, with the better of two trials recorded. Maximum score is 12 inches.

Organizational Hints: Students should be encouraged to use slow, static movements to attain the highest score. Marking the yardstick/ruler at 6 inches and 12 inches will be helpful in accurately measuring the chin height.

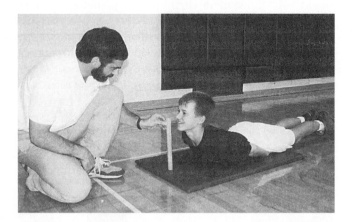

Figure 5.8 Trunk lift.

Test 5: 90-Degree Push-Up (Recommended)

Instructions: The student is instructed to complete as many push-ups as possible, keeping time with the cadence provided by the audiotape. Figure 5.9 shows the correct up and down positions for the push-up.

Equipment Needed: Mat or piece of carpet and PACER test audiotape to indicate cadence.

Scoring Procedure: The total number of push-ups completed successfully is recorded as the score.

Organizational Hints: A partner should be used to count. Incorrectly completed push-ups, usually the result of knees touching floor, swaying of back, inability to fully extend arms, or failing to bend arms to 90°, should not be counted.

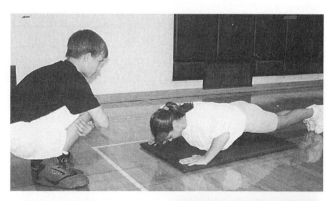

Figure 5.9 90-degree push-up.

Modified Pull-Up (Optional)

Instructions: Student lies on back with shoulders directly under the bar, which is set 1–2 inches above the student's reach. An elastic band is positioned approximately 7–8 inches below and parallel to the bar. Using an overhand grip and from the down position, the student pulls up on the bar until chin is above the elastic band. Legs should remain straight and heels on the floor throughout this upward movement. Upon completing the pull-up, the student returns to the start position. Figure 5.10 shows the start and up positions for this test.

Equipment Needed: Modified pull-up apparatus, elastic band, mat or piece of carpet, and pencils and scoresheets.

Scoring Procedure: The number of correctly completed modified pull-ups is recorded as the score.

Organizational Hints: Movement should be rhythmical and continuous. Resting or stopping is not allowed.

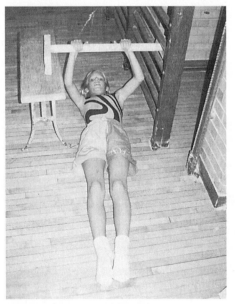

Figure 5.10 Modified pull-up.

Pull-Up (Optional)

Instructions: The student hangs from a horizontal bar with arms and legs fully extended and feet off the floor. The hands grasp the bar with palms away from the body. Once the body is still the student pulls up with the arms until the chin is over the bar, then lowers the body to the starting position. This movement is repeated as many times as possible.

Equipment Needed: A horizontal bar approximately 1.5 inches in diameter. This bar should be of adequate height or adjustable to accommodate the tallest person in class. Figure 5.11 shows the down and up positions for the pull-up.

Scoring Procedure: The number of successfully completed pull-ups (chin over bar) is recorded as the student's score.

Organizational Hints: This option should not be selected for students unable to complete one pull-up. Pull-ups should be completed smoothly and with minimal horizontal motion. Test administrators may lift the student to reach the bar and assist in minimizing unnecessary movement by placing their arms across the front of the student's thighs. Legs must remain fully extended throughout the test.

Flexed-Arm Hang (Optional)

Instructions: Instructions for the flexed-arm hang are given later in this chapter. The stopwatch is stopped if the head tilts backward to keep the chin above the bar or when the chin touches or falls below the bar.

Equipment Needed: A horizontal bar approximately 1.5 inches in diameter. This bar should be of adequate height or adjustable to accommodate the tallest person in class. A stopwatch is required.

Figure 5.11 Pull-up.

Scoring Procedure: The score is the number of seconds (to the nearest second) the student holds the hanging position, with one trial only.

Organizational Hints: The height of the bar should be adjusted for each student, as necessary, to be approximately equal to the standing height of the student. Spotters should be positioned in front of and behind the student. The timer should start the stopwatch as soon as the student is free from both spotters' assistance and assumes the flexed-arm hang position. Knees must not be raised and kicking is not permitted.

Test 6: Back-Saver Sit-and-Reach Test (Recommended)

Instructions: The student sits on the floor, shoes off, with one leg extended so the bottom of the foot is flat against the box. The other leg is bent at the knee with the foot flat on the floor 2–3 inches to the side of the extended leg. Arms are extended over the measuring scale with one hand on top of the other, palms down, finger pads on fingernails. Keeping palms down, the student reaches forward along the scale four times and holds the fourth reach for one second. Repeat with other side. Figure 5.12 shows the hold positions for one side of the body.

Equipment Needed: Solid box, 12 inches tall and 9 inches long (any width). Measuring scale is marked on top of box with 9-inch mark at far end and zero-inch mark at end near student.

Scoring Procedure: The number of inches (rounded to nearest inch) reached for each side is recorded. Maximum score per side is 12 inches.

Organizational Hints: To keep the student's extended leg from bending, the tester may place one hand on the student's knee. The student's hips should remain square with the box.

Figure 5.12 Back-saver sit-and-reach test.

Shoulder Stretch (Optional)

Instructions: Student reaches with right hand over right shoulder and down the back. At the same time, the student places the left hand behind the back and reaches up, trying to touch the fingers of the right hand. Figure 5.13 shows shoulder stretch for right side.

Equipment Needed: None necessary.

Scoring Procedure: The test is scored pass/fail. If the student is able to touch the fingers of opposite hands, the score is recorded as pass.

Organizational Hints: A partner should be used to determine touch. A proper warm-up should precede the test.

ACTIVITYGRAM

The ACTIVITYGRAM assessment is a three-day recall of physical activity. It includes each 30-minute block of time between the hours of 7:00 AM and 11:00 PM. The student is asked for the name of the activity that was done during the 30 minutes, if the activity was done for all or part of the 30 minutes, and a rating of intensity of the activity (rest, light, moderate, vigorous).

The ACTIVITYGRAM report is generated by using the software that has been developed to complement the program. The report includes minutes of activity per day, times of activities across each day, and an

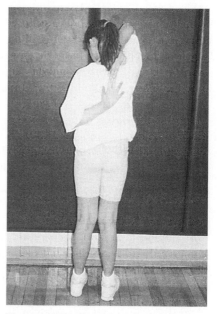

Figure 5.13 Shoulder stretch.

activity analysis utilizing the activity pyramid. A sample activity report is included in Figure 5.14.

More information on FITNESSGRAM is available from the Cooper Institute for Aerobics Research (www.cooperinst.org). FITNESSGRAM is endorsed by the AAH-PERD. Materials for FITNESSGRAM and Physical Best are available from www.americanfitness.net.

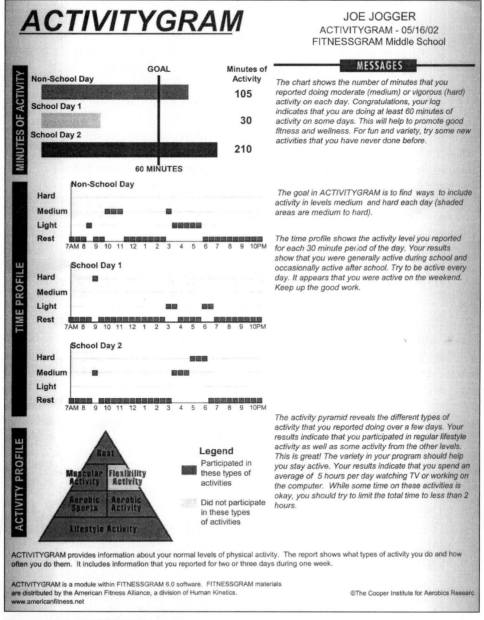

Figure 5.14 *ACTIVITYGRAM* report.
Source: The Cooper Institute for Aerobics Research. Dallas, TX.

Testing Students with Disabilities

The development of physical fitness and the promotion of physical activity are important for students with special needs for the same reasons they are important to other individuals. It is imperative that all children are given the chance to be fit and active. The health-related components of physical fitness for students with disabilities can be assessed with the same test batteries previously presented. Modifications of the test may need to be made depending on the nature of the disability. Remember that the process of physical activity should be emphasis rather than the fitness test performance. There is value in participating in the testing procedure to stress the importance of being active. As test items are modified, you can no longer compare the score with other scores derived from taking the test without the modification.

FITNESSGRAM Modifications for Special Populations (1999)

(Cooper Institute for Aerobics Research, 1999)

Test batteries that measure components of health-related fitness have been identified and described. Each of the tests is intended for students who are not disabled. Since health-related fitness is important for everyone, practitioners should be able to modify the tests to meet the particular fitness needs of students or clients with disabilities.

The FITNESSGRAM illustrates how the health-related physical fitness of students with disabilities can be effectively evaluated. Educators should keep in mind that valid and reliable measures of fitness are only obtained when the subject understands each of the tests. Therefore, it is important when working with students with disabilities to allow ample practice time for each test and to be sure that verbal instructions are understood. Suggestions for modifying the FITNESSGRAM for individuals with disabilities are briefly described in the following sections.

Aerobic Capacity

Certain physical conditions may prevent a student from running. For example, youngsters may be restricted to the use of a wheelchair, some individuals may require braces, others may have severe visual impairment. Some individuals, although capable of running, may have cystic fibrosis, serious coronary conditions, or acute asthma. In these cases, the practitioner should use some form of submaximal test of aerobic capacity.

Recommendation: Use large-muscle exercises such as swimming, stationary bicycling, propelling the wheelchair, or walking/treadmill. Refer to *The FITNESSGRAM Test Administration Manual* (Cooper Institute for Aerobics Research, 1999) for specific information regarding test modification. Initial scores can be used as baseline data to measure future progress.

Body Composition

The FITNESSGRAM uses the triceps and calf skinfolds. Normally, these procedures are appropriate for individuals with disabilities. There are, however, certain circumstances in which different measures should be used. For example, skinfold measurements should not be taken if scar tissue is present at the site or if the site is otherwise used as a location for medical injections. Limbs that display muscle atrophy also should not be used as skinfold sites. Finally, measures can be made on the left side if problems exist on the right.

Muscle Strength, Endurance, and Flexibility

There may be occasions when the teacher needs to assess the strength, endurance, and flexibility of students with motor control problems. In these cases, it is important that the teacher remember that any repeated movement may be used to assess these components of fitness. The key is to ask students to reproduce the movement as many times as possible. Students should be encouraged to maintain a rhythmic pace and pause not longer than two seconds between repetitions. Scores obtained can be used as baseline data for subsequent tests to evaluate students' progress.

Brockport Physical Fitness Test (Winnick and Short, 1999)

Project Target was a funded project that enabled the development of a health-related physical fitness test with criterion-referenced standards for individuals with disabilities, aged 10–17. As a result of this project the Brockport Physical Fitness Test was designed. There are 27 test items in the Brockport test, but four items can generally be used to measure health-related physical fitness of young persons with disabilities.

The test was designed primarily for individuals with amputations, blindness, cerebral palsy, congenital anomalies, mental retardation, and spinal cord injury. It can, however, be used for youth aged 10–17 with other disabilities or in the general population. Guidelines are provided in the test manual about how to modify the items for various populations. There are also standards for each age, gender, and population.

Equipment needed for this test include an audiocassette player, PACER audiotape, tape measure, cones, electronic heart monitor (recommended), stopwatch, skinfold caliper, barbells and weights, gym mat, chair, adjustable horizontal bar, grip dynamometer, sturdy armchair, yardstick, standard wheelchair ramp, sit-and-reach box, and a sturdy table.

There are test components in aerobic functioning (4 test options), body composition (2 test options), musculoskeletal functioning—muscular strength and endurance (16 test options), and musculoskeletal functioning—flexibility (5 test options). The test manual with complete descriptions of each of these options is available at www.americanfitness.net.

Organizational Hints: This assessment should be conducted at the same time other testing procedures are being administered. Often, a school nurse is responsible for taking these measurements. Arrangements can sometimes be made for the nurse to maintain records of the students and identify those who appear to exhibit disproportionate growth patterns.

Measuring Physical Activity of Students

Physical inactivity contributes to more than 250,000 deaths each year. Based on a wealth of information, the American Heart Association now lists a sedentary lifestyle as an official major risk factor for coronary heart disease. As might be expected, increased levels of habitual physical activity are associated with lower all-cause death rates. Even so, only one in four adult Americans is active at the level recommended for health benefits (ACSM, 1993). Much evidence suggests that teenagers are not as active as children. And even at the elementary school, there are concerns about the activity level of children (Ross, Pate, Caspersen, Damberg, and Svilar, 1987).

Regardless of age, physical activity influences the degree of health-related physical fitness. The extent to which it directly affects health fitness depends on a number of factors. Some variables, such as heredity, growth, development, and diet, to name a few, are nearly impossible for the practitioner to consider in the typical health fitness evaluation. It is unwise to merely deduce that because a youngster demonstrates health fitness she must be active. Physical activity generally increases health-related fitness, but the idea that activity builds fitness may lead teachers or exercise practitioners to believe that individuals who score well on fitness tests are active and those who do not score well are inactive (Pangrazi and Corbin, 1993).

Because of this relationship, it is increasingly more important to devote attention to valuing and assessing the process of physical activity. If physical educators are attempting to promote an active lifestyle among students, then there must be a means to measure the results of their efforts. These tactics can be stand-alone efforts but should be woven into the fabric of a health-related physical fitness test.

Following are some suggestions and recommendations that incorporate the assessment of physical activity into the evaluation of health-related physical fitness in the physical education environment.

1. Fitness experiences and testing should help students clearly understand the relationship between good health fitness and physical activity. Employ strategies that encourage activity and participation.

2. Criterion-referenced standards should be emphasized rather than normative standards that compare students to each other. Criterion-referenced standards that convey a level of health allow students to decide whether they need to alter their physical activity in order to improve their health fitness.

3. Avoid concluding that low fitness scores mean that the student is inactive. The result of this may negatively influence youngsters' self-esteem and deter them from activity.

4. Work with students to help them assess their level of activity outside the school. Activities such as keeping an activity diary of type and extent of exercise, using computer programs to calculate caloric consumption and expenditure, and following a specially designed fitness regime are examples of measurable homework activities that students can complete for physical education. By doing so, individuals will be able to ascertain a pattern of behavior over time. This is useful for individuals to better understand their actual activities, thus enhancing their decision-making process.

5. Consider employing a self-testing procedure. This allows students an opportunity to work together to develop fitness profiles. The goal is to teach students the process of fitness testing so they will be able to evaluate their health status during adulthood (Pangrazi and Corbin, 1993).

Given the recognition of the benefits of moderate physical activity to the general health and well-being of people, there has been a resultant increase in promoting physical activity. Certainly this should be the case in physical education classes. As a result of this promotion, much attention has been given in recent years to the accurate measurement of physical activity.

Earlier in the chapter, the issue of measurement of physical activity was discussed in both the President's Challenge and the ACTIVITYGRAM. Both test batteries made use of different forms of physical activity recall logs that are classified as a self-report. The President's Challenge also suggests the use of pedometers to monitor activity. The advantages of using pedometers in physical education include relatively inexpensive costs, valid assessment of activity, and the ability to document changes in activity (Beighle, Pangrazi, and Vincent, 2001). Heart rate monitors have also increased in use as teachers have used them as a valuable assessment and educational tool. Direct observation and accelerometers are also used for activity measurement. While there are advantages and disadvantages to each of these methods (see Trost, 2001; Welk and Wood, 2000), each has been used to measure physical activity. Welk and Wood (2000) also provide several good examples of self-report and physical activity questionnaires. Effective contemporary physical educators should make use of these methods of assessing physical activity to enhance their programs.

Section 2—Testing Adult Populations

Purposes of Adult Fitness Testing

It is probably reasonable to assume that most adults who are already participating in or are starting to participate in an exercise program do so, at least in part, because they want to improve their health-related physical fitness. The best way to improve health-related physical fitness is through an exercise program designed specifically to meet the needs of each individual participant. Fitness testing is essential in order to develop and refine an individualized exercise program, because it provides information regarding your client's current fitness level. From fitness testing results, you can identify strengths and weaknesses, which are used as the basis for setting reasonable and attainable fitness goals. In addition, baseline exercise testing results can be compared with follow-up testing results and used as a means for evaluating the effectiveness of an exercise program, and for providing motivation to continue the exercise program.

Pre-Exercise Testing Considerations

Pre-Exercise Health Evaluation

A pre-exercise health evaluation is imperative to ensure the safety of the participant during exercise testing. Pre-exercise health evaluations help to identify individuals who require medical clearance prior to exercise, such as those who are at increased risk for disease or who have an existing disease or other medical concerns. At minimum, pre-exercise health screening should include administration of the **Physical Activity Readiness Questionnaire (PAR-Q)** (Figure 5.15) (Canadian Society, 1994). The PAR-Q was designed to identify individuals who require medical clearance prior to participating in fitness testing or an exercise program. If a participant answers "yes" to any of the seven PAR-Q questions, he or she should obtain medical clearance prior to performing fitness testing.

Physical Activity Readiness
Questionnaire - PAR-Q
(revised 1994)

PAR – Q & YOU

(A Questionnaire for People Aged 15 to 69)

Regular physical activity is fun and healthy, and increasingly more people are starting to become more active every day. Being more **active is very safe** for most people. However, some people should check with their doctor before they start becoming much more physically active.

If you are planning to become much more physically active than you are now, start by answering the seven questions in the box below. **If you are** between the ages of 15 and 69, the PAR-Q will tell you if you should check with your doctor before you start. If you are over **69 years of age**, and you are not used to being very active, check with your doctor.

Common sense is your best guide when you answer these questions. Please read the questions carefully and answer each one honestly: check YES or NO.

YES	NO	
☐	☐	1. Has your doctor ever said that you have a heart condition <u>and</u> that you should only do physical activity recommended by a doctor?
☐	☐	2. Do you feel pain in your chest when you do physical activity?
☐	☐	3. In the past month, have you had chest pain when you were not doing physical activity?
☐	☐	4. Do you lose your balance because of dizziness or do you ever lose consciousness?
☐	☐	5. Do you have a bone or joint problem that could be made worse by a change in your physical activity?
☐	☐	6. Is your doctor currently prescribing drugs (for example, water pills) for your blood pressure or heart condition?
☐	☐	7. Do you know of <u>any other reason</u> why you should not do physical activity?

If

you

answered

YES to one or more questions

Talk with your doctor by phone or in person BEFORE you start becoming much more physically active or BEFORE you have a fitness appraisal. Tell your doctor about the PAR-Q and which questions you answered YES.

- You may be able to do any activity you want - as long as you start slowly and build up gradually. Or, you may need to restrict your activities to those which are safe for you. Talk with your doctor about the kinds of activities you wish to participate in and follow his/her advice.
- Find out which community programs are safe and helpful for you.

NO to all questions
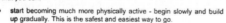

If you answered NO honestly to all PAR-Q questions, you can be reasonably sure that you can:

- start becoming much more physically active - begin slowly and build up gradually. This is the safest and easiest way to go.
- take part in a fitness appraisal - this is an excellent way to determine your basic fitness so that you can plan the best way for you to live actively.

DELAY BECOMING MUCH MORE ACTIVE:
- If you are not feeling well because of temporary illness such as a cold or a fever – wait until you feel better; or
- If you are or may be pregnant – talk to your doctor before you start becoming more active.

Please note: If your health changes so that you then answer YES to any of the above questions, tell your fitness or health professional. Ask whether you should change your physical activity plan.

<u>Informed Use of the PAR-Q</u>: The Canadian Society for Exercise Physiology, Health Canada, and their agents assume no liability for persons who undertake physical activity, and **if in doubt** after completing this questionnaire, consult your doctor prior to physical activity.

> **You are encouraged to copy the PAR-Q but only if you use the entire form**

NOTE: If the PAR-Q is being given to a person before he or she participates in a physical activity program or a fitness appraisal, this section may be used for legal or *administrative purposes.*

    I have read, understood and completed this questionnaire. Any questions I had were answered to my full satisfaction.

NAME _____

SIGNATURE _____ DATE _____

SIGNATURE OF PARENT _____ WITNESS _____

or GUARDIAN (for participants under the age of majority)

continued on other side...

© *Canadian* Society for Exercise Physiology
Société. canadienne de physiologie de l'exercice

Supported by: Health Santé
Canada Canada

Figure 5.15 PAR-Q.

Reprinted from the 1994 revised version of the Physical Activity Readiness Questionnaire (PAR-Q and YOU). PAR-Q is a copyrighted, pre-exercise screen owned by the Canadian Society for Exercise Physiology.

In addition to the PAR-Q, pretest screening may include an evaluation of the participant's risk factors for development of coronary artery disease (Table 5.8), as well as of the signs and symptoms associated with cardiovascular, metabolic, or pulmonary disease (e.g., pain related to ischemia, dizziness, tachycardia, shortness of breath) (ACSM, 2000). The results from these evaluations allow you to develop a **risk stratification** for the participant that can be used to make decisions regarding the need for medical clearance prior to and supervision during exercise testing. Participants are classified as low, moderate, or high risk based on the likelihood of an untoward event during physical activity (ACSM, 2000). A *low-risk* individual is asymptomatic and has no more than one risk factor. Low-risk individuals do not require medical clearance or supervision to participate in physical activity. A *moderate-risk* individual is a male aged 45 years or older or a female aged 55 years or older with two or more risk factors. The ACSM recommends that these individuals obtain medical clearance prior to participating in vigorous exercise and that a physician be present if the individual participates in maximal exercise testing. A *high-risk* individual has one or more signs or symptoms of disease or known cardiovascular, metabolic, or pulmonary disease. The ACSM recommends that high-risk individuals obtain medical clearance prior to any physical activity and that a physician be present during all exercise testing.

Table 5.8 Positive* coronary artery disease risk factors.

Cigarette smoking	Current or quit within past 6 months
Family history (first-degree relative)	Coronary artery disease or MI in male relative < 55 years of age Coronary artery disease or MI in female relative < 65 years of age
Hypertension	≥ 140/90 mm Hg
Hypercholesterolemia	Total cholesterol > 200 mg/dL LDL cholesterol > 130 mg/dL HDL cholesterol < 35 mg/dL
Impaired fasting glucose	≥ 100 mg/dL on 2 occasions
Obesity	BMI ≥ 30 kg/m²
Sedentary lifestyle	

*High HDL cholesterol (> 60 mg/dL) is considered a negative risk factor. Adapted from ACSM (2000)

Source: American College of Sports Medicine (2000). *ACSM's Guidelines for Exercise Testing and Prescription*, 6th ed. Philadelphia: Lippincott Williams & Wilkins.

Fitness Testing Order

If all five health-related fitness components are assessed in one session, the following testing order is recommended (ACSM, 2000):

- Resting measurements (heart rate, blood pressure, body composition)
- Cardiorespiratory endurance
- Muscular strength and endurance
- Flexibility

Measurement of Health-Related Physical Fitness

Measuring Body Composition

Total body weight is composed of both fat tissue and fat-free tissue. Most body composition assessment methods provide an estimate of percent body fat, which is used as an indicator of health risk. Body fat in excess of the healthy levels (obesity) is associated with hypertension, type 2 diabetes, and hyperlipidemia (National Institutes of Health [NIH], 1985). Too little body fat may interfere with normal physiological functions. Maintaining optimal levels of body fat (Table 5.9) is therefore essential for maintaining good health. There are several laboratory and field techniques that can be used to assess body composition. Each technique differs in cost, time, and equipment requirements, accuracy, and complexity.

Densitometry

The criterion standard for assessing body composition is a laboratory procedure called **densitometry**, which provides a measure of whole body density that is used to estimate percent fat. Body density (Db) equals body mass divided by body volume. *Body mass* is body weight on land. *Body volume* is slightly more complex to measure and requires a technique called hydrostatic (underwater) weighing (Figure 5.16). This technique is based on Archimedes' principle, which states that the weight a body loses under water equals the weight of the water it displaces. *Body volume* is calculated from the loss of weight in water, or the difference between land weight and underwater weight. The density of the water as well as the volume of air left in the lungs (residual volume) after a maximal expiration must also be taken into consideration.

Db is calculated from the following formula:

$$\text{Body Density (Db)} = \frac{\text{Weight in air}}{\left[\dfrac{\text{Weight in air} - \text{Weight in water}}{\text{Density of water}} - \text{Residual volume} \right]}$$
(mass/volume)

Once Db is known, percent body fat can be estimated using either of the following two equations:

Siri (1961) equation:

$$(4.95/\text{Db} - 4.50) \times 100 = \% \text{ Body Fat}$$

Brozek, Grande, Anderson, and Keys (1963) equation:

$$(4.57/\text{Db} - 4.142) \times 100 = \% \text{ Body Fat}$$

Anthropometric Measurements

In field settings where underwater weighing is impractical, an anthropometric assessment such as skinfolds, body mass index, or waist-to-hip circumference may be used to assess body composition.

Skinfold Measurements The skinfold technique is widely used because it has been shown to be valid and reliable, and requires minimal equipment (skinfold calipers).

Table 5.9 Body fat standards.

	Men	Women
At risk	≤ 5%	≤ 8%
Below average	6–14%	9–22%
Average	15%	23%
Above average	16–24%	24–31%
At risk	≥ 25%	≥ 32%

Source: Lohman, T. G. (1992). *Advances in Body Composition Assessment* (Champaign, IL: Human Kinetics Press), 80.

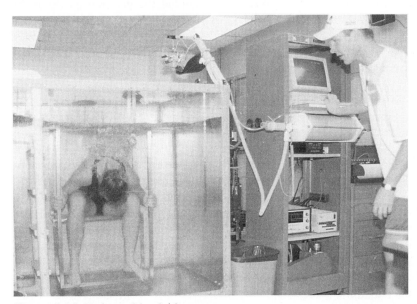

Figure 5.16 Hydrostatic weighing.

This technique is also relatively easy to perform, but does require extensive practice in order to achieve optimal measurement accuracy and reliability.

Skinfold measurements assess the thickness of the subcutaneous body fat at specific sites. The abdomen, triceps, chest, subscapular, suprailiac, thigh, and midaxillary are common skinfold sites for adults. Descriptions of these sites are provided below (ACSM, 2000).

Abdomen	2 cm to the right of the umbilicus, vertical
Triceps	Posterior midline of upper arm, halfway between the acromion and olecranon processes, vertical
Chest	Half the distance between the anterior axillary line and the nipple for males, one third of the distance for females, diagonal

Subscapular	1 to 2 cm below the inferior angle of the scapula, diagonal
Midaxillary	On the midaxillary line at the level of the xiphoid process, vertical
Suprailiac	In line with the natural angle of the iliac crest, diagonal
Thigh	On the anterior midline of the thigh, halfway between the top of the patella and the inguinal crease, vertical

The sum of the thicknesses from each site is used to determine body density or percent body fat. Numerous equations can be used to predict body density and percent fat from skinfold measurements. We have included the generalized three-site equations adapted from Jackson and Pollock (1985), which are appropriate for a wide range of people; however, choosing an equation specific to the participant's gender, age, and ethnicity may improve prediction accuracy. For a comprehensive list of population-specific equations, please refer to Heyward and Stolarczyk (1996).

Three-Site Generalized Skinfold Equations

Men: (skinfold sites—chest, abdomen, and thigh)

Body Density = 1.10938 − 0.0008267(sum of 3 skinfolds) + 0.0000016(sum of three skinfolds)2 − 0.0002574 (age)

Women: (skinfold sites—triceps, suprailiac, and thigh)

Body Density = 1.099421 − 0.0009929(sum of 3 skinfolds) + 0.0000023(sum of three skinfolds)2 − 0.0001392(age)

Once Db is known, percent body fat can be estimated using the Siri and Brozek et al. equations given above. Population-specific equations for converting body density to percent fat can also be used. Please refer to Heyward and Stolarczyk (1996) for a list of available equations.

If the correct equation is used, the accuracy of estimating body fat from skinfolds is approximately ± 3.5%. To ensure this prediction accuracy, correct procedures must be followed. The ACSM (2000) recommends the following procedures for measuring skinfolds:

1. Take all measurements on the right side of the body.

2. Place calipers 1 cm away from thumb and finger and perpendicular to the fold. Maintain pinch while reading the caliper and wait 1 to 2 seconds before reading the caliper.

3. Take at least 2 measurements at each site. Measurements should be within 1 to 2 mm of each other; if not, redo measurements. Allow some time for skin to regain thickness between measurements at one site. The best way to do this is to rotate through measurement sites.

4. Train with a skilled technician and practice on a variety of individuals.

Body Mass Index   The body mass index (BMI) is calculated by dividing body weight in kilograms by height in meters squared (kg/m^2). Although BMI does not provide an assessment of percent fat, it has been shown to correlate with the measurement of body fat from densitometry ($r = 0.70$) (Heyward, 1996). The ACSM provides the following classifications based on BMI:

Normal	18.5 to 24.9
Overweight	25.0 to 29.9
Obese	> 30.0

Waist-to-Hip Circumference   When assessing health risk related to excess body fat, the patterning of fat on the body is an important factor to consider. Those with excessive body fat on the upper body, particularly in the abdominal area, have an increased risk of hypertension, diabetes, heart attack, and stroke when compared to those with excessive fat on the lower body (Bray and Gray, 1988). The waist-to-hip ratio (WHR) provides a method for assessing fat patterning. Waist circumference is measured at the narrowest part of the torso and divided by the hip circumference, which is measured at the maximum circumference around the buttocks (Callaway et al., 1988). Health risk is very high for young males and females when the WHR is equal to or greater than 0.94 and 0.82, respectively (Bray and Gray, 1988).

Measuring Cardiorespiratory Fitness
Cardiorespiratory Fitness Tests

VO_{2max} is considered to be the single best measure of cardiorespiratory fitness. It can be assessed using maximal or submaximal exercise tests. Maximal tests in which oxygen uptake is measured directly require expensive equipment and trained personnel, and are therefore most commonly performed in research and clinical settings. VO_{2max} can also be predicted from a maximal exercise test by using the maximum exercise time achieved on a maximal treadmill test (Heyward, 1998), or maximal power output achieved on a cycle ergometer. These prediction methods are fairly accurate and do not require measurement of respiratory gases.

However, due to equipment and time limitations, submaximal tests are chosen over maximal tests in most adult fitness testing settings. Submaximal tests are also less effortful and safer for the client than maximal tests, and have been shown to have acceptable validity. Submaximal exercise tests usually consist of one (single-stage) or more (multistage) submaximal exercise intensities. The heart rate response during each stage is assessed and used to estimate VO_{2max}. This prediction procedure is based on the linear relationship that exists among heart rate, workload, and VO_2. The VO_{2max} estimated from a submaximal test can be compared to normative data (Table 5.10).

There are numerous submaximal test protocols that can be used to estimate VO_{2max}. For adult fitness testing, the most popular modes for submaximal testing are the cycle ergometer and the bench step. Although cycle ergometry and step tests are considered field-based tests, they do require specific equipment, and the number of people that can be tested at one time is limited, particularly for cycle ergometer

Table 5.10 Maximal oxygen uptake (ml•kg-min^{-1}) classifications.

Women

Age	Poor	Fair	Good	Excellent	Superior
20–29	≤ 31	32–34	35–37	38–41	42+
30–39	≤ 29	30–32	33–35	36–39	40+
40–49	≤ 27	28–30	31–32	33–36	37+
50–59	≤ 24	25–27	28–29	30–32	33+
60–69	≤ 23	24–25	26–27	28–31	32+

Men

Age	Poor	Fair	Good	Excellent	Superior
20–29	≤ 37	38–41	42–44	45–48	49+
30–39	≤ 35	36–39	40–42	43–47	48+
40–49	≤ 33	34–37	38–40	41–44	45+
50–59	≤ 30	31–34	35–37	38–41	42+
60–69	≤ 26	27–30	31–34	35–38	39+

Source: *The Physical Fitness Specialist Manual,* The Cooper Institute for Aerobics Research, Dallas, TX, revised 2002, reprinted with permission.

testing. For these reasons, cycle ergometer and step tests may be more appropriately labeled as field/laboratory tests. When a cycle ergometer or step is not available, other "true" field tests can be used to measure cardiorespiratory fitness, such as the Rockport Fitness Walking Test or the 1.5-mile run test.

Submaximal Cycle Ergometer Tests Blood pressure, heart rate, and perceived exertion are measured during cycle ergometer cardiorespiratory exercise tests in order to monitor the participant's physiological and perceptual responses to exercise (Heyward, 1998). These data are also used to predict VO_{2max} (e.g., heart rate) or to develop an exercise prescription (e.g., heart rate and/or perceived exertion) following the exercise test. Because it is important that these variables be assessed accurately, a brief description of the procedures is provided below.

   Blood pressure is a measure of the pressure in the arteries exerted by the blood. The highest pressure, or *systolic* blood pressure, is the pressure in the arteries during contraction of the heart (systole). The lowest pressure, or *diastolic* blood pressure, is the pressure in the arteries when the heart is filling (diastole). A blood pressure cuff, sphygmomanometer and stethoscope are needed to measure blood pressure. The blood pressure cuff is placed around the upper arm so that the midline of the cuff is over the brachial artery pulse (Reeves, 1995). The cuff should be inflated slightly higher than the expected systolic pressure to restrict blood flow. Slowly releasing the cuff allows blood flow to resume. The systolic blood pressure is the pressure at which the first sounds of blood flow are heard. The diastolic blood pressure is the pressure at which the sounds of blood flow cease. Readings are recorded in mm Hg. For more detailed instructions on blood pressure assessment, please refer to Reeves (1995).

Resting blood pressure should be assessed prior to exercise, but after the participant has been seated quietly for five minutes. An average resting blood pressure can range between 110 and 140 mm Hg (systolic) and 60 and 80 mm Hg (diastolic) (Heyward, 1998). An individual with a resting blood pressure >140/90 mm Hg measured on two occasions would be classified as hypertensive. When included as part of an exercise test, blood pressure is usually assessed every 2–3 minutes, depending on the test protocol. It is normal for systolic blood pressure to increase with increasing exercise intensity; however, diastolic blood pressure usually does not change significantly during exercise.

As you read through the cardiorespiratory fitness tests that follow, you will find that **heart rate** is a key variable for the prediction of maximal oxygen uptake for each of the tests. You can measure heart rate by palpating the pulse at the brachial or radial arteries, or by using electrocardiography or heart rate monitors. When palpating, be sure to use the middle and index fingers rather than the thumb, as it has a pulse of its own. Resting heart rate should be counted for one minute by means of a stethoscope prior to exercise and following a 5- to 10-minute seated rest. During exercise tests, the pulse is usually palpated for 10 to 15 seconds and then the heart rate in beats•min^{-1} is determined by multiplying by 6 or 4, respectively. Resting heart rates usually fall between 60 and 100 beats•min^{-1}, and heart rate should increase with increasing exercise intensity.

Perceived exertion is defined as the subjective intensity of the effort, strain, discomfort, or fatigue experienced during an exercise task (Noble and Robertson, 1996). Ratings of perceived exertion (RPE) are most commonly assessed using the original category RPE scale (6–20) or the category-ratio RPE scale (0–10) (Table 5.11). Ratings from these scales are highly correlated with heart rate and work rate during exercise. Assessing perceived exertion during exercise testing can provide information regarding the participant's exercise tolerance and can signal impending fatigue. Perceived exertion data from an exercise test can also be used to develop an exercise prescription. To ensure rating accuracy, it is important that participants be familiarized with the use of the RPE scale prior to exercise testing. At minimum, the instructions should include a definition of perceived exertion and an explanation of the range of sensations from the scale chosen (Noble and Robertson, 1996). For instance, when using the 6–20 scale, it should be explained to the participant what feelings of exertion a "7" represents, and what feelings of exertion a "19" represents. A common definition for a 7 is the least exertion ever experienced (e.g., getting up off of a couch), while a 19 is defined as the greatest exertion ever experienced (e.g., sprinting as fast as possible).

When performing submaximal cycle ergometer tests, the ACSM (2000) recommends that appropriate warm-up and recovery periods be provided, heart rate be monitored every minute, and blood pressure and RPE be monitored near the end of every stage.

Astrand-Rhyming Test (Astrand and Rhyming, 1954)
Purpose: To predict maximal oxygen uptake.

Table 5.11 Ratings of perceived exertion scales.

6–20 Category scale		CR–10 scale		
6	No exertion at all	0	Nothing at all	"No I"
7	Extremely light	0.3		
8		0.5	Extremely weak	Just noticeable
9	Very light	0.7		
10		1.0	Very weak	
11	Light	1.5		
12		2.0	Weak	Light
13	Somewhat hard	2.5		
14		3.0	Moderate	
15	Hard (heavy)	4.0		
16		5.0	Strong	Heavy
17	Very hard	6.0		
18		7.0	Very strong	
19	Extremely hard	8.0		
20	Maximal exertion	9.0		
		10.0	Extremely Strong	"Strongest I"
		11.0		
		•	Absolute Maximum	Highest Possible

Source: Borg, Gunnar (1998). The Borg RPE Scale® from *Borg's Perceived Exertion and Pain Scales.* Champaign, IL: Human Kinetics Press, 31.

Equipment Needed: Cycle ergometer, metronome, stopwatch, blood pressure apparatus, RPE chart.

Test Area: Area suitable to accommodate a cycle ergometer and two testers.

Procedures: The bicycle seat should be set at a comfortable height. The metronome should be set at 100 bpm so that the pedal rate is maintained at 50 rpm. A 2–3 minute warm-up with a work rate less than the chosen testing work rate is appropriate. The suggested work rate is based on gender and fitness status as follows:

Males (unconditioned): 300 or 600 kgm/min (1 or 2 kp)

Males (conditioned): 600 or 900 kgm/min (2 or 3 kp)

Females (unconditioned): 300 or 450 kgm/min (1 or 1.5 kp)

Females (conditioned): 450 or 600 kgm/min (1.5 or 2 kp)

The goal is to obtain HR values between 125 and 170 bpm. Participants perform at the selected work rate for six minutes, and HR is measured during the fifth and sixth minutes of work. Blood pressure and RPE should be measured in the sixth minute.

Prediction Procedures: VO_{2max} is estimated from the Astrand-Rhyming nomogram (Figure 5.17) using work rate and average heart rate from minutes 5 and 6. This value must then be adjusted for age by multiplying the VO_{2max} value by the following correction factors:

Age	Correction Factor
15	1.10
25	1.00
35	0.87
40	0.83
45	0.78
50	0.75
55	0.71
60	0.68
65	0.65

VO_{2max} Calculation:

Predicted VO_{2max} (nomogram) = _____ x _____ (correction) = _____ $L \cdot min^{-1}$

To convert to $ml \cdot kg \cdot min^{-1}$, multiply the above number by 1000 to obtain $ml \cdot min^{-1}$, and then divide by the participant's body weight in kilograms.

Organizational Hints: The choice of workload is important because a workload that is either too easy or too difficult for the participant may not elicit a heart rate within the target zone, preventing estimation of VO_{2max} from the nomogram. Be sure to determine the participant's fitness level prior to testing and use that information to guide your choice of workload. For instance, if the participant were a highly trained cyclist, the higher work rate would be an appropriate choice. Conversely, if the participant cycles on a recreational basis, it may be more appropriate to choose the lower of the two possible work rates.

YMCA Cycle Ergometer Test (Golding, Myers, and Sinning, 1989)

Purpose: To predict maximal physical working capacity and maximal oxygen uptake.

Equipment Needed: Cycle ergometer, metronome, stopwatch, blood pressure apparatus, RPE chart, scoring graph.

Test Area: Area suitable to accommodate a cycle ergometer and two testers.

Procedures: Determine and record the participant's age-predicted maximal heart rate (APMHR) and 85% of the APMHR. The bicycle seat should be set at a comfortable height. The metronome should be set at 100 bpm so that pedal rate is maintained at 50 rpm. Workload should be set according to the guidelines found in Figure 5.18. The participant should work at each workload for at least 3 minutes. Heart rate should be determined during the second and third minutes in each stage, and blood pressure and RPE should be assessed near the end of the stage. If the final two heart rates differ by more than 6 bpm, the participant should continue at that work rate until heart rate stabilizes. Heart rate and work rate are recorded. The goal is to obtain heart rates from at least two consecutive stages that fall between 110 bpm and 85 percent of the APMHR. The heart rates from these two stages are then used to predict maximal work rate from the scoring graph.

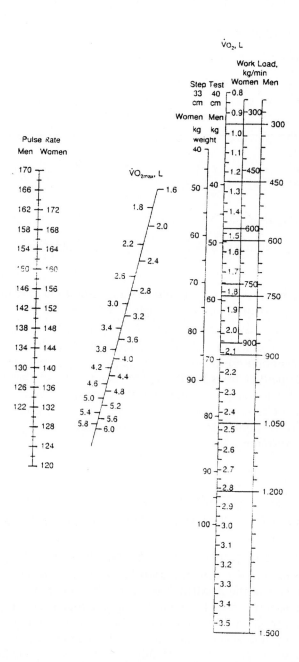

Figure 5.17 Modified Astrand-Rhyming nomogram.

Source: Astrand, P–O., and Rhyming, I. (1954). A nomogram for calculation of aerobic capacity (physical fitness) from pulse rate during submaximal work. *Journal of Applied Physiology.* 7:218–221. Reprinted by permission.

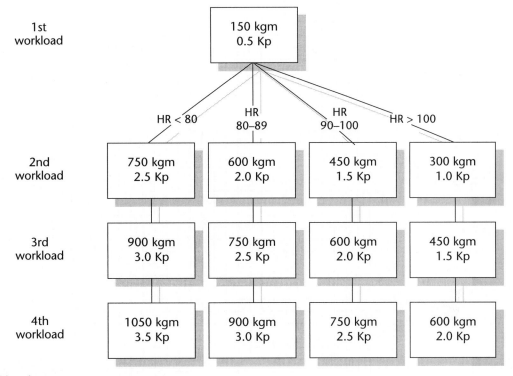

Directions:

1. Set the first workload at 150 kgm/min (0.5 Kp).

2. If the HR in the third min is
   ▶ less than (<) 80, set the second load at 750 kgm (2.5 Kp);
   ▶ 80 to 89, set the second load at 600 kgm (2.0 Kp);
   ▶ 90 to 100, set the second load at 450 kgm (1.5 Kp);
   ▶ greater than (>) 100, set the second load at 300 kgm (1.0 Kp).

3. Set the third and fourth (if required) loads according to the loads in the columns below the second loads.

Reprinted from *Y's Way to Physical Fitness,* 3rd Edition with permission of the YMCA of the USA, 101 N. Wacker Drive, Chicago, IL 60606.

Figure 5.18 YMCA workload guidelines.

Prediction Procedures: The results of the test should be plotted on the scoring graph (Figure 5.19), according to the directions in the rectangular box.

Organizational Hints: If the heart rate during the initial stage was greater than 110 bpm, the third workload need not be performed. Additionally, a fourth workload is conducted only if the participant's heart rate response to the second and third workloads did not fall within the target range.

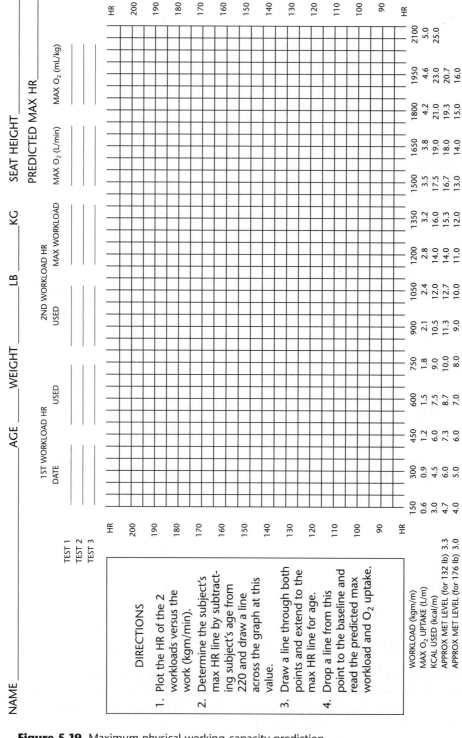

Figure 5.19 Maximum physical working capacity prediction.

Step Tests VO_{2max} can be predicted from the heart rate response to one or a series of stepping work rates. However, the most commonly used step tests determine cardiovascular fitness based on recovery heart rate following a single stepping work rate. One such test, McArdle's 3-minute step test, is described below. The following is a list of other similar step tests:

1. LSU Step Test (Nelson, 1976)

2. Kasch Pulse Recovery Test (Kasch and Boyer, 1968)

3. YMCA 3-Minute Step Test (Golding et al., 1989)

McArdle's 3-Minute Step Test (McArdle, Katch, and Katch, 2001)

Purpose: To predict maximal oxygen uptake.

Equipment Needed: Step or bench 16.25 inches high (standard gymnasium bleachers are appropriate substitutes), metronome, stopwatch, and calculator.

Test Area: An area spacious enough to accommodate a bench step and tester.

Procedures: The participant steps up and down on the step or bench in a 2-count-up, 2-count-down manner for 3 minutes. Females step at a rate of 22 steps per minute, males at 24 steps per minute. The beat is established by a metronome at a rate of 88 and 96 beats•min^{-1} for females and males, respectively. At the conclusion of the 3-minute stepping, the participant remains standing while the pulse rate is counted for a 15-second period beginning 5 seconds after the end of the stepping (5–20 seconds of recovery). Figure 5.20 shows the phases of this test.

Prediction Procedures: The 15-second heart rate value is converted to beats•min-1 and the following equations are used to determine predicted VO_{2max}:

Figure 5.20 McArdle step test.

Men: VO_{2max} (ml•kg•min^{-1}) = 111.33 – 0.42(HR in beats•min^{-1})

Women: VO_{2max} (ml•kg•min^{-1}) = 65.81 – 0.1847(HR in beats•min^{-1})

Walking/Running Tests Walking/running tests can be performed with large groups of people anywhere a track or other flat, measurable area is available. Prediction of VO_{2max} from these tests is based on some or all of the following variables: the time to complete the walk/run, age, gender, body weight, and heart rate. Although easy to administer, these tests are not without disadvantages. The results are highly dependent upon the individual's motivation. Furthermore, the running tests in particular can be considered maximal because the individual is asked to give an all-out effort. As such, it may be inappropriate to administer these tests with a sedentary or high-risk individual.

Rockport Fitness Walking Test (Kline et al., 1987)

Purpose: To determine cardiovascular fitness.

Equipment Needed: Stopwatch.

Test Area: A running track is preferred, but any large open flat area suitable for walking that can be accurately measured will suffice.

Procedures: Start the stopwatch and begin walking. Walk one mile as quickly as possible. Record the time it takes to walk the mile and immediately determine your 15-second heart rate. Multiply this number by 4 to obtain the heart rate per minute.

Prediction Procedures: The time it takes to walk one mile and the heart rate recorded immediately at the end of the walk is used to determine cardiorespiratory fitness from the charts in Figure 5.21.

You can also predict maximal oxygen uptake from this test by using the one-minute walk time and heart rate per minute in the following calculation (Kline et al., 1987):

$$VO_{2max} = 6.9652 + 0.0091 \times \text{(weight)} - 0.0257\text{(age)} + 0.5955\text{(gender)}$$
$$\text{(L•min}^{-1}) - 0.2240\text{(mile walk time)} - 0.0115\text{(heart rate)}$$

Weight in lbs.

Age in years

Gender: male = 1, female = 0

Heart rate in beats•min^{-1} measured during last quarter mile of the walk

Walk time in minutes and hundredths of a minute

To convert to ml•kg•min^{-1}, multiply the VO_{2max} in L•min^{-1} by 1000, and then divide by body weight in kg.

1.5-Mile Run Test

Purpose: To predict maximal oxygen uptake.

Equipment needed: Stopwatch or digital watch and a calculator.

Test area: An outdoor running track is preferred, but any large open flat area suitable for running that can be accurately measured will suffice.

Find Your Fitness Level

The information in the following charts pertains to both the nontreadmill walker as well as the treadmill walker.

Turn to the appropriate Rockport Fitness Walking Test™ chart according to your age and sex. These show the established fitness norms from the American Heart Association.

Using your Relative Fitness Level chart, find your time in minutes and your heart rate per minute. Follow these lines until they meet and mark this point on the chart. This point is designed to tell you how fit you are compared to other individuals of your same age and sex. For example, if your mark places you in the "above average" section of the chart, you are in better shape than the average person in your category.

The charts are based on weights of 170 lbs. for men and 125 lbs. for women. If you weigh substantially less, your relative cardiovascular fitness level will be slightly underestimated. Conversely, if you weigh substantially more, your relative cardiovascular fitness level will be slightly overestimated.

——— Age 20–29 ———

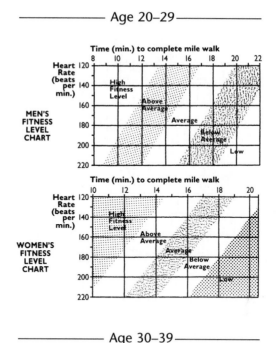

——— Age 30–39 ———

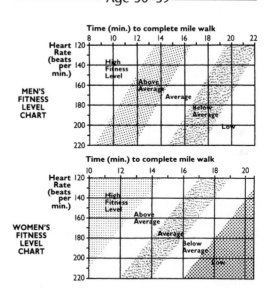

Figure 5.21 The Rockport "Fitness Walking Test."

(continued)

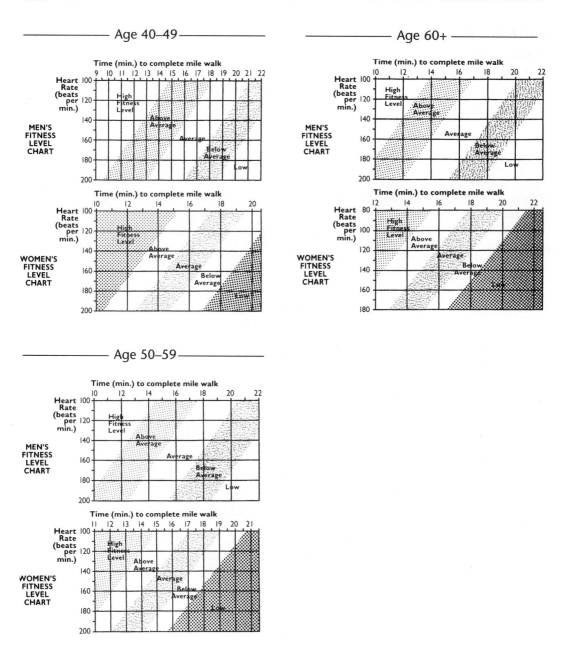

Figure 5.21 The Rockport "Fitness Walking Test" *continued.*

Procedures: Participants should run 1.5-miles in the shortest period of time possible.

Prediction Procedures: The time for the run is recorded in minutes. The following equation is used to predict VO_{2max} in ml•kg•min^{-1}(George, Verhs, Allsen, Fellingham, and Fisher, 1993):

VO_{2max} =   88.02 + 3.716(gender) − 0.1656(weight) − 2.767(time)

Gender: males = 1, females = 0

Body weight in kg

Total run time in minutes

Maximal Cardiorespiratory Fitness Testing

As mentioned previously, maximal oxygen uptake can be directly measured during a maximal exercise test or estimated from the results of a maximal exercise test. The most commonly used modes for maximal exercise testing are stationary cycling and treadmill walking and running. Maximal tests are usually multistage, graded exercise tests (GXTs), which means that the individual will exercise at gradually increasing submaximal workloads. Heart rate, blood pressure, and RPE should be assessed during each stage of the test. VO_{2max} is measured when the oxygen uptake fails to increase by more than 150 ml•min-1 in spite of an increase in workload. When oxygen uptake is not being directly measured, the test is terminated when RPE is greater than 17, when heart rate fails to increase with increasing exercise intensity, or when the participant asks to stop (ACSM, 2000). Many maximal cycle ergometer and treadmill protocols have been developed to assess VO_{2max}. The protocol you choose should be appropriate for your client's age, gender, and fitness status. For more information on maximal exercise testing protocols, please refer to Heyward (1998) or ACSM (2000).

Measuring Flexibility

Flexibility is the range of motion available at a joint or group of joints. Gymnasts and dancers require excellent flexibility, and most other athletes benefit from optimizing flexibility. Good flexibility is important for nonathletes as well, as it may help to prevent lower back pain and enhance the ability to perform activities of daily living. Remember that flexibility is joint specific. The tests listed here do not provide information regarding whole-body flexibility, but rather assess the flexibility of a given joint. There are currently no valid tests of overall flexibility.

YMCA Sit-and-Reach Test (Golding et al., 1989)

Purpose: To measure the flexibility of the lower back and hamstring muscles.

Equipment needed: Yardstick and masking tape (or sit-and-reach box).

Test area: An area large enough to accommodate a yardstick, participant, and tester.

Procedures: It is recommended that the participant perform a brief warm-up that includes some stretches. The yardstick should be placed on the floor. Place a piece of tape at the 15-inch mark. The participant should sit with his or her heels touching the edge of the tape about 10 to 12 inches apart. The participant should reach forward slowly as far as possible with fingertips overlapping. The position should be held for a moment while the measurement is recorded. Repeat three times and use the highest score. Figure 5.22 illustrates this technique. If a sit-and-reach box is used, the participant should sit facing the box with the legs extended and the soles of the feet against the box. The procedures are the same as above.

Scoring Procedures: The most distant point reached (in inches or cm) is compared to the norms for this test (Table 5.12). The best reach of three trials should be used to score. These norms are based on a box in which the starting point is at 26 cm. Subtract 3 cm from each normative value if you are using a box that starts at 23 cm.

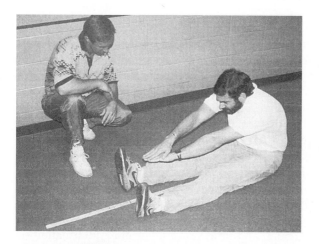

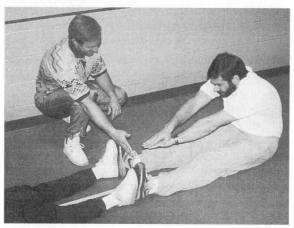

Figure 5.22 Sit-and-reach using yardstick.

Table 5.12 Norms (in inches) for the YMCA sit-and-reach test.

	Age (years)					
Males	**18–25**	**26–35**	**36–45**	**46–55**	**56–65**	**66+**
Excellent	26–20	25–20	24–19	23–19	21–17	20–17
Good	20–18	19–18	19–17	17–16	17–15	15–13
Above average	18–17	17–16	17–15	15–14	13	13–11
Average	16–15	16–15	15–13	13–12	11	11–9
Below average	14–13	14–12	13–11	11–10	9	9–8
Poor	12–10	12–10	11–9	9–7	7–5	7–5
Females						
Excellent	27–24	26–23	25–22	24–21	23–20	22–20
Good	23–21	22–20	21–19	20–18	19–18	19–18
Above average	21–20	20–19	19–17	18–17	17–16	17–16
Average	19–18	18	17–16	16–15	15	15–14
Below average	18–17	17–16	15–14	15–14	14–13	13–12
Poor	16–14	15–14	13–11	13–11	12–10	11–9

Sources: Reprinted and adapted with permission of the YMCA of the USA, 101 N. Wacker Drive, Chicago, IL 60606.

Measuring Muscular Endurance

Dynamic muscular endurance is assessed by establishing the number of repetitions of a given exercise that can be performed using submaximal resistance. The curl-up and the push-up tests are common field tests that assess local muscular endurance.

YMCA 1-Minute Timed Sit-up Test (Golding et al., 1989)

Purpose: To assess abdominal endurance.

Equipment Needed: Stopwatch and mat or towel.

Procedures: The participant should lie on her or his back with knees bent and feet flat on the floor. The hands are placed behind the head with elbows out to the sides to start. To complete one repetition, the participant touches the elbow to the opposite knee and returns to the starting position. A partner holds the participant's feet to keep them in contact with the floor at all times, and also counts the number of repetitions performed in one minute's time. Figure 5.23 illustrates the phases of this test.

Scoring Procedures: Compare the number of repetitions performed with correct form to the norms for males and females in Table 5.13.

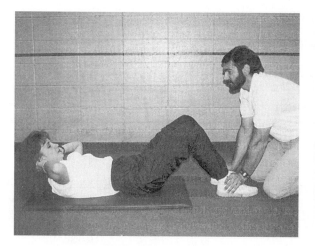
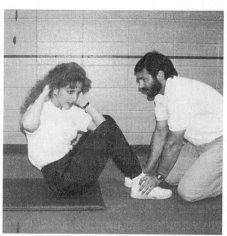

Figure 5.23 Sit-up.

Table 5.13 Norms for the 1-minute sit-up test.

	Age (years)					
Males	**18–25**	**26–35**	**36–45**	**46–55**	**56–65**	**66+**
Excellent	60–50	55–46	50–42	50–36	42–32	40–29
Good	48–45	45–41	40–36	33–29	29–26	26–22
Above average	42–40	38–36	34–30	28–25	24–21	21–20
Average	38–36	34–32	29–28	24–22	20–17	18–16
Below average	34–32	30–29	26–24	21–18	16–13	14–12
Poor	30–26	28–24	22–18	17–13	12–9	10–8
Females						
Excellent	55–44	54–40	50–34	42–28	38–25	36–24
Good	41–37	37–33	30–27	25–22	21–18	22–18
Above average	36–33	32–29	26–24	21–18	17–13	16–14
Average	32–29	28–25	22–20	17–14	12–10	13–11
Below average	28–25	24–21	18–16	13–10	9–7	10–6
Poor	24–20	20–16	14–10	9–6	6–4	4–2

Source: Reprinted and adapted with permission of the YMCA of the USA, 101 N. Wacker Drive, Chicago, IL 60606.

Table 5.14 Norms for the push-up test.

	Age (years)					
Males	**15–19**	**20–29**	**30–39**	**40–49**	**50–59**	**60–69**
Excellent	≥ 39	≥ 36	≥ 30	≥ 22	≥ 21	≥ 18
Very good	29–38	29–35	22–29	17–21	13–20	11–17
Good	23–28	22–23	17–21	13–16	10–12	8–10
Fair	18–22	17–21	12–16	10–12	7–9	5–7
Needs improvement	≤ 17	≤ 16	≤ 11	≤ 9	≤ 6	≤ 4
Females						
Excellent	≥ 33	≥ 30	≥ 27	≥ 24	≥ 21	≥ 17
Very good	25–32	21–29	20–26	15–23	11–20	12–16
Good	18–24	15–20	13–19	11–14	7–10	5–11
Fair	12–17	10–14	8–12	5–10	2–6	1–4
Needs improvement	≤ 11	≤ 9	≤ 7	≤ 4	≤ 1	≤ 1

Source: The Canadian Physical Activity, Fitness & Lifestyle Appraisal: CSEP's Plan for Healthy Active Living, 2nd edition, 1998: Reprinted with permission from the Canadian Society for Exercise Physiology.

Push-up Test to Exhaustion (Canadian Standardized Test of Fitness, 1986)

Purpose: To assess upper-body endurance.

Equipment Needed: Mat or towel.

Procedures: Males should perform this test with the palms and toes touching the ground. Females can modify this position by placing the knees on the ground. The participant lowers the body until the chin touches the mat, maintaining a straight back and returning to a straight-arm position.

Scoring Procedures: Compare the number of correct repetitions performed with correct form and without rest to the norms for males and females in Table 5.14.

Measuring Muscular Strength

Muscular strength is determined by assessing the maximal amount of resistance (one-repetition maximum, or 1 RM) that an individual can lift one time. One-RM tests focus on specific muscle groups, so performing several 1 RM tests using different muscle groups may provide a better picture of overall body strength than a single 1 RM test. A common test for upper body strength is the bench press 1 RM, and for lower body strength is the leg press 1 RM. Although 1 RM testing is considered the gold standard, this type of testing involves trial and error that often requires a great deal of time, as well as effort on the part of the participant. The hand grip dynamometer test is often used to assess strength when these factors are a concern.

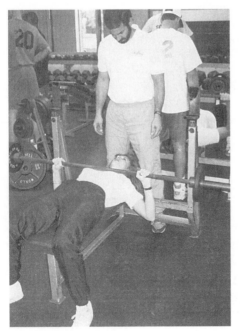 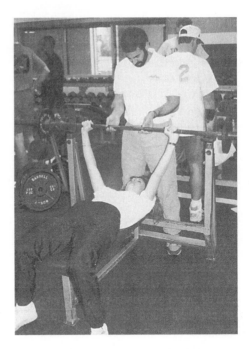

Figure 5.24 Bench press.

One-Repetition Maximum (1 RM) Testing

Purpose: To assess muscular strength.

Equipment Needed: Weightlifting bench, barbells, and plates.

Procedures: The ACSM (2000) recommends the following procedures for performing bench press 1 RM testing:

1. Have the participant perform a warm-up at 40–60 percent of the estimated maximum. Provide a rest period during which the participant stretches lightly.

2. Have the participant perform 3 to 5 repetitions at 60–80 percent of the estimated maximum.

3. Based on the success of the previous lift, add 5–10 pounds and ask the participant to attempt another lift. If this lift is successfully completed, wait 3–5 minutes, add 5–10 additional pounds, and have the participant attempt another lift. Continue until the participant fails an attempt, and use the last weight successfully completed as the 1 RM. Be sure that a spotter is available throughout the test. Figure 5.24 illustrates the phases of this test.

4. Divide the 1 RM weight by the participant's body weight.

5. Compare the 1 RM/body weight ratio to the norms in Table 5.15. The norms are based on a 1 RM test performed using Universal® weight machines. Results may vary if 1 RM testing is performed with different equipment, such as free weights.

Table 5.15 1 RM/body weight ratio norms.

A. Upper-Body Strength (1 RM Bench Press)

	Age (years)				
Males	**20-29**	**30-39**	**40-49**	**50-59**	**60-69**
Above average	1.48+	1.24+	1.10+	.97+	.89+
Average	1.06	.93	.84	.75	.68
Below average	.93	.83	.76	.68	.63
Females					
Above average	.90+	.76+	.71+	.61+	.64+
Average	.65	.57	.52	.46	.45
Below average	.56	.51	.47	.42	.40

B. Leg Strength (1 RM Leg Press)

	Age (years)				
Males	**20-29**	**30-39**	**40-49**	**50-59**	**60-69**
Above average	2.27+	2.07+	1.92+	1.80+	1.73+
Average	1.91	1.71	1.62	1.52	1.43
Below average	1.74	1.59	1.51	1.39	1.30
Females					
Above average	1.82+	1.61+	1.48+	1.37+	1.32+
Average	1.44	1.27	1.18	1.05	.99
Below average	1.27	1.15	1.08	.95	.88

Source: The Physical Fitness Specialist Manual, The Cooper Institute for Aerobics Research, Dallas, TX, revised 2002, reprinted with permission.

Grip Strength Test with Hand Dynamometer
(Canadian Society for Exercise Physiology, 1996)

Purpose: To assess static strength of grip (squeezing) muscles.

Equipment Needed: Hand-grip dynamometer.

Procedures: The dynamometer should be adjusted to fit the participant's hand-grip size. The participant should assume a slightly bent forward position, with the hand tested in front, not touching the body. The arm can be slightly bent. The participant should perform an all-out gripping effort for a few seconds, while keeping the arm stationary. Have the participant perform 2–4 trials for each arm. Record the scores for each in kilograms and add the highest scores for both arms.

Scoring Procedures: The maximum scores in kilograms for the right and left hands are added together and compared to the norms in Table 5.16.

Table 5.16 Grip-strength norms (in kg) for combined right and left hand.

	Age (years)					
Males	**15–19**	**20–29**	**30–39**	**40–49**	**50–59**	**60–69**
Excellent	≥ 113	≥ 124	≥ 123	≥ 119	≥ 110	≥ 102
Very good	103–112	113–123	113–122	110–118	102–109	93–101
Good	95–102	106–112	105–112	102–109	96–101	93–101
Fair	84–94	97–105	97–104	94–101	87–95	86–92
Needs improvement	≤ 83	≤ 96	≤ 96	≤ 54	≤ 86	≤ 78
Females						
Excellent	≥ 71	≥ 71	≥ 73	≥ 73	≥ 65	≥ 60
Very good	64–70	65–70	66–72	65–72	59–64	54–59
Good	59–63	61–64	61–65	59–64	55–58	51–53
Fair	54–58	55–60	56–60	55–58	51–54	48–50
Needs improvement	≤ 53	≤ 54	≤ 55	≤ 54	≤ 50	≤ 47

Source: The Canadian Physical Activity, Fitness & Lifestyle Appraisal: CSEP's Plan for Healthy Active Living,
2nd edition, 1998. Reprinted with permission from the Canadian Society for Exercise Physiology.

Health-Related Fitness Testing Batteries for Adults

The ACSM and YMCA have developed test batteries that include assessments for each of the five health-related fitness components. Both batteries require minimal equipment and personnel, and can be performed in most adult fitness settings.

ACSM Fitness Testing Battery (ACSM, 1998b)

The tests included in the ACSM battery are "true" field tests, and can be performed almost anywhere. Because of the minimal time and equipment required, this battery would be particularly useful to exercise professionals who train clients in their homes, or have limited testing equipment. Additionally, this testing battery is less invasive than others because skinfold caliper assessment is not a component. Instead, body mass index and waist-to-hip ratio are included to provide information regarding health risk associated with excess body fat. For more information on the ACSM testing battery, it is suggested that the reader obtain a copy of the ACSM Fitness Book (ACSM, 1998b).

Each of the following tests used in the ACSM testing battery has been described earlier in this chapter:

1. Rockport one-mile walk (cardiorespiratory endurance)
2. Push-up test (muscular fitness)
3. Sit-and-reach test (flexibility)
4. Body mass index and waist-to-hip ratio (body composition)

Equipment Needed: Track or other flat, measured (one-mile) surface, stopwatch, yardstick, adhesive tape, calculator, and anthropometric tape.

YMCA Fitness Testing Battery (Golding et al., 1989)

Although several of the components require laboratory equipment, the YMCA test battery is designed to minimize testing time and is relatively easy to administer, score, and interpret. When compared to the ACSM test battery, the YMCA test battery is more comprehensive; however, it requires more time, equipment, and experienced testing personnel. The components and suggested tests are given below. Any test procedures that deviate from previously described tests in this chapter are noted with an asterisk and briefly explained. Normative data may also differ if test procedures differ. For more information on test procedures and norms, it is suggested that the reader obtain a copy of the text *Y's Way to Physical Fitness* (Golding et al., 1989).

1. Height
2. Weight
3. Resting heart rate
4. Resting blood pressure
5. *Body composition. A four-site skinfold test (triceps, abdomen, ilium, and calf) is recommended.
6. Cardiorespiratory fitness. The YMCA bicycle ergometer test is recommended, but a 3-minute step test may be more appropriate when testing large groups of individuals.
7. Flexibility. Sit-and-reach test.
8. *Muscular strength. Bench press using a 35-pound barbell for women and an 80-pound barbell for men. The participant is asked to complete as many repetitions as possible keeping time with a 60-beat-per-minute count on the metronome. The test is terminated when the rhythm is broken or the participant fails to reach full extension. The number of successful repetitions is recorded as the score.
9. Muscular endurance. One-minute timed sit-ups.

Equipment Needed: Anthropometric tape, scale, stethoscope, blood pressure cuff with sphygmomanometer, skinfold caliper, bicycle ergometer, yardstick, adhesive tape, barbell and weights, metronome, bench for bench press, and mat or carpet square for sit-ups.

Fitness Battery for Older Adults

Older adults (those aged 65 years or older) often have different fitness goals than younger adults. The focus of a fitness program for older adults may be maintaining or increasing **functional fitness**, or the *physical capacity to perform normal everyday activities safely and independently without undue fatigue* (Rikli and Jones, 2001). As life expectancy for people at age 65 has increased, so has the risk of spending an increased number of years with disability, possibly unable to perform normal daily activities (Institute of Medicine, 1990). However, age-related declines in functional fitness can be prevented or reversed through physical activity. If functional fitness is assessed and weaknesses are detected early through fitness testing, then appropriate physical activity programs can be developed to improve functional fitness and reduce disability in later years.

The tests used to evaluate physical fitness in young adults are often unsafe or too difficult for older adults. Rikli and Jones (2001) have developed a fitness testing battery appropriate for older adults that includes measures of upper- and lower-body strength and flexibility, cardiorespiratory endurance, agility, and balance. The assessments can be performed at home with minimal time and equipment. The test items are safe to administer to community-residing older adults, provided that:

- They have not been advised by their doctors not to exercise.
- They do not have congestive heart failure.
- They are not currently experiencing joint pain, chest pain, dizziness, or exertional angina (chest tightness, pressure, pain, heaviness) during exercise.
- They do not have uncontrolled high blood pressure greater than 160/100 mm Hg.

Older Adult Fitness Test Items (Rikli and Jones, 2001)

Prior to testing, a warm-up and stretching period should be provided to the participant. A demonstration of each test is also recommended. Once the battery is complete, the results can be compared to the normal range of scores for men and women (Table 5.17). A score above the normal range is considered "above average" and a score below the range is considered "below average."

30-Second Chair Stand

Purpose: To assess lower-body strength.

Equipment Needed: Stopwatch and straight-back or folding chair with seat height of 17 in (43.18 cm).

Procedures: The chair should be placed against the wall to prevent it from moving during the test. The participant should sit in the middle of the chair with feet flat on the floor and arms crossed at the wrist and held against the chest. The goal is for the participant to complete as many full stands as possible in 30 seconds. The participant should rise to a full stand when you say "go," and then return to a fully seated position. This constitutes one repetition.

Scoring Procedures: The total number of stands in 30 seconds is the score.

Arm Curl Test

Purpose: To measure upper-body strength.

Equipment Needed: Stopwatch, straight-back or folding chair with no arms, 5-lb. dumbbell for women and 8-lb. dumbell for men.

Procedures: The participant sits on the chair with back straight and feet flat on the floor. The dominant side of the body should be close to the corresponding edge of the chair. The weight is at the participant's side with the arm extended, and in the dominant hand. From the down position, the weight is curled up with the palm gradually rotating to a facing-up opposition during flexion. The weight is then returned to the extended down position. The goal is for the participant to perform as many curls as

Table 5.17 Older Adult Fitness Test Normal Range of Scores.

Women*	60–64	65–69	70–74	75–79	80–84	85–89	90–94
Chair stand test (# of stands)	12–17	11–16	10–15	10–15	9–14	8–13	4–11
Arm curl test (# of reps)	13–19	12–18	12–17	11–17	10–16	10–15	8–13
6–minute walk test** (# of yards)	545–660	500–635	480–615	435–585	385–540	340–510	275–440
2–minute step test (# of steps)	75–107	73–107	68–101	68–100	60–90	55–85	44–72
Chair sit–and–reach test (inches +/–)	–0.5/+5.0	–0.5/+4.5	–1.0/+4.0	–1.5/+3.5	–2.0/+3.0	–2.5/+2.5	–4.5/+1.0
Back scratch test† (inches +/–)	–3.0/+1.5	–3.5/+1.5	–4.0/+1.0	–5.0/+0.5	–5.5/+0.0	–7.0/+1.0	–8.0/+1.0
8–foot up–and–go test (seconds)	6.0–4.4	6.4–4.8	7.1–4.9	7.4–5.2	8.7–5.7	9.6–6.2	11.5–7.3
Men*	**60–64**	**65–69**	**70–74**	**75–79**	**80–84**	**85–89**	**90–94**
Chair stand test (# of stands)	14–19	12–18	12–17	11–17	10–15	8–14	7–12
Arm curl test (# of reps)	16–22	15–21	14–21	13–19	13–19	11–17	10–14
6–minute walk test** (# of yards)	610–735	560–700	545–680	470–640	445–605	380–570	305–500
2–minute step test (# of steps)	87–115	86–116	80–110	73–109	71–103	59–91	52–86
Chair sit–and–reach test (inches +/–)	–2.5/+4.0	–3.0/+3.0	– 3.0/+3.0	–4.0/+2.0	–5.5/+1.5	–5.5/+0.5	–6.5/+0.5
Back scratch test† (inches +/–)	–6.5/+0.0	–7.5/+1.0	–8.0/+1.0	–9.0/+2.0	–9.5/+2.0	– 9.5/+3.0	–10.5/+4.0
8–foot up–and–go test (seconds)	5.6–3.8	5.9–4.3	6.2–4.4	7.2–4.6	7.6–5.2	8.9–5.5	10.0–6.2

*Normal range of scores is defined as the middle 50 percent of each age group. Scores above the range would be considered "above average" for the age group and those below the range would be "below average."

**Scores are rounded to the nearest five yards.

†Scores are rounded to the nearest half–inch.

Source: R. E. Rikli & C. J. Jones, 2001, *Senior Fitness Test Manual* (Champaign, IL: Human Kinetics), 143.

possible in 30 seconds. Participant starts on the signal "go." The weight should move through the full range of motion, with the upper arm still throughout the test.

Scoring Procedure: The total number of arm curls performed in 30 seconds is the score.

6-Minute Walk Test

Purpose: To assess aerobic endurance.

Equipment Needed: Long measuring tape, two stopwatches, four cones, masking tape, magic marker, 12 to 15 popsicle sticks per person, chairs in case people need to rest, name tags.

Procedures: This test requires some setup. Mark off in 5-yard segments a flat, 50-yard rectangular area (20 yards by 5 yards). The inside corners of the measured distance should be marked with cones, and the 5-yard lines marked with masking tape or chalk. Two or more participants should be tested at a time to standardize the motivation. Starting (and stopping) times are staggered 10 seconds apart to encourage participants to walk at their own pace and not in clusters or pairs. Numbers (using name tags) are placed on participants to indicate the order for starting and stopping. On the signal "go" the participant begins walking as fast as possible (no running) around the course covering as much distance as possible in the 6-minute time limit. To keep track of distance walked, partners give popsicle sticks to participants each time they complete a lap. The timer should move to the inside of the marked area after everyone has started. Remaining time should be called out when the test is about half done, and when 2 minutes are left. Participants can rest on chairs if necessary, but time continues to run. When the participant's 6 minutes has elapsed, he/she should move to the right (to the closest 5-yard marker) and step in place to cool down.

Scoring Procedures: The score is the number of yards walked (to the nearest 5 yards) in 6 minutes.

2-Minute Step Test

Purpose: An alternative test of aerobic endurance.

Equipment Needed: Stopwatch, piece of string about 30 in (76.2 cm) long, masking tape, tally counter if available to help count steps.

Procedures: First determine the proper stepping height by finding the midway point between the kneecap and the iliac crest. Use a tape measure or piece of string to measure and mark the point on the thigh with a piece of tape. Transfer the tape to the appropriate height on a wall or chair to monitor step height. The participant begins stepping in place when you say "go." The tester should count the number of times the right knee reaches the height target in 2 minutes. If proper knee height cannot be maintained, ask the participant to stop or slow down until he/she can regain proper form. Keep the time running through rest periods. To prevent falls, the participant can place on hand on a table or chair.

Scoring Procedures: The number of full steps (i.e., number of times the right knee reaches the proper height) is the score.

Chair Sit-and-Reach Test

Purpose: To assess lower-body flexibility.

Equipment Needed: Folding chair with seat height of 17 in. (43.18 cm) and legs that angle forward to prevent tipping, and an 18-in. ruler.

Procedures: The participant should sit with the crease between the top of the leg and the buttocks even with the edge of the chair seat. One leg is bent with the foot flat on the floor. The other leg is extended straight forward with the heel on the floor and the foot flexed at 90 degrees. Keeping the leg as straight as possible, the participant should reach forward slowly as far as possible. If the leg starts to bend, ask the participant to move slowly back until the knee is straight. The maximum reach must be held for 2 seconds. The participant can practice on both legs to see which produces the better score. Record only the score for this leg.

Scoring Procedures: Measure the distance from the tips of the middle fingers to the top of the shoe to the nearest half inch (centimeter). The midpoint at the top of the shoe represents the zero point so that a reach that doesn't make it to the toe is recorded as a minus score. A reach beyond that point is a plus score, and only to that point is zero. Administer two trials and record both, but use the highest as the final score.

Back Scratch Test

Purpose: To assess upper-body flexibility.

Equipment Needed: 18-in. ruler.

Procedures: While standing, the participant should place the preferred hand, palm down and fingers extended, over the same shoulder, reaching down as far as possible (elbow pointing up). The other arm is placed around the back of the waist with the palm up, reaching upward in an attempt to touch or overlap the extended middle fingers of both hands. The tester may assist in directing the two middle fingers toward each other, provided the participant's hands are not moved. Participants are not permitted to grab their fingers and pull. The participant can practice to determine the preferred hand and can be given two practice trials before the scoring trial.

Scoring Procedures: Administer two test trials and record both scores to the nearest half inch. Measure the distance of overlap or distance between the middle fingers, using the best score. If the fingers do not touch, a minus score is given. A zero is given if the fingers just touch, and a plus score if the fingers overlap.

Eight-Foot Up-and-Go Test

Purpose: To assess agility and dynamic balance.

Equipment Needed: Stopwatch, folding chair with 17-in. (43.18-cm) seat height, tape measure, and cone.

Procedures: Set the chair against the wall facing a cone marker exactly 8 feet away (measure from the back of the cone to a point on the floor even with the front edge of the chair). Provide some space beyond the cone so the participant can turn around easily. The participant should start by sitting in the chair with back straight, hands on the thighs, and feet flat on the floor with one slightly in front of the other. On the signal "go," the participant rises from the chair and walks as quickly as possible around the cone, and sits back down in the chair. Start the timer as soon as you say "go," even if the person has not yet started to move. Stop the timer when the person sits back down.

Scoring Procedures: After a practice trial, administer two trials and use the fastest time as the score. The score is the time from "go" to the return to a seated position in the chair.

Testing Special Populations

The term **special populations** refers to individuals with a disability, impairment, or handicap. Physical activity is as beneficial for special populations as it is for able-bodied individuals, and may slow down the progression of certain conditions or attenuate the effects of others. As with able-bodied individuals, fitness testing is essential in order to develop an appropriate individualized physical activity program for the disabled. In his book *Fitness in Special Populations*, Shephard (1990) recommends that fitness testing for special populations include assessments similar to those for able-bodied individuals, such as assessments of anaerobic power and capacity, aerobic power, muscle strength and endurance, body composition, and flexibility. Although research on fitness testing procedures for special populations is limited, Shephard (1990) provides information on fitness assessment and modifications for adults who are wheelchair-disabled, deaf, blind, or mentally retarded.

Measuring Physical Activity of Adults

The Surgeon General's report on physical activity and health states that moderate physical activity (e.g., 30 minutes on most days of the week) can provide significant health benefits (USDHHS, 1996). With increased awareness of the importance of physical activity has come an increased emphasis on the assessment of physical activity in research, school, and health/fitness settings.

Valid and reliable physical activity measurement is challenging because of the numerous dimensions of physical activity (Kriska and Caspersen, 1997). An accurate assessment must consider the intensity, frequency, and duration of the activity. Common field techniques consist of recall surveys, diaries and logs (self-report), and direct observer monitoring, or monitoring of heart rate or body motion (direct monitoring) (USDHHS, 1996). Self-report tools would be considered true field techniques, requiring only an interviewer and copies of the instrument. A collection of physical activity questionnaires suitable for adolescents, adults, and older adults is provided in the supplement to *Medicine and Science in Sports and Exercise*, June 1997 issue. Each questionnaire differs in complexity, the types of activities assessed (e.g., leisure, job-related, household), the time frame assessed (e.g., week, month, year), and the method of assessment (e.g., self-, interviewer-administered). The goal of the assessment would determine the questionnaire selected, but in general, the questionnaires can provide information regarding the amount of time spent in physical activity or calories expended from physical activity over a given time period. The results can then be compared to the ACSM (2000) recommendations for minimum caloric expenditure to achieve health benefits (1000 kcal/week), or to caloric expenditure data collected previously. This information is useful in assessing or prescribing changes in physical activity patterns that may impact health status.

SUMMARY

This chapter focuses on the assessment of health-related physical fitness and physical activity for child, youth, adult, and older adult populations. The assessment of this area is placed in the context of current research that extols the benefits of regular physical activity. The relationship between physical activity and physical fitness is explained, and the differences between physiological fitness, health-related physical fitness, and skill-related physical fitness are examined. The components of health-related physical fitness—body composition, cardiorespiratory fitness, flexibility, muscular endurance, and muscular strength—are identified and defined. Test batteries appropriate for K–12 students, adults, and older adults are presented with these components of health-related physical fitness in mind. The tests presented are age appropriate, represent current research findings, require little expense, and are simple to administer. Emphasis is placed on linking the choice of measurement tools with the objectives of the particular activity-based setting. The importance of emphasizing the process of physical activity rather than the product of the test performance is noted. Suggestions and recommendations to incorporate the assessment of physical activity into the evaluation of health-related physical fitness are presented.

DISCUSSION QUESTIONS

1. Discuss recent research findings that explain the relationship of physical activity and good health. What implications does this have on physical activity professionals and the role of testing health-related physical fitness?

2. Explain the relationship between the process of physical activity and the product of physical fitness.

3. Discuss the differences between physiological fitness, health-related physical fitness, and skill-related physical fitness.

4. Define the components of health-related physical fitness and identify two ways that each component is typically measured.

5. Outline a history of physical fitness testing of school populations in the past fifty years. What are important contemporary trends in fitness testing?

6. What factors impact performance on physical fitness tests? What implications do these factors have on the type of emphasis that should be placed on fitness testing results?

7. Compare and contrast the President's Challenge with the FITNESSGRAM test battery. Which test would be your choice to use, and why?

8. Describe test batteries that can be used when testing children with disabilities.

9. What is the minimum pre-exercise health evaluation that should be performed prior to adult fitness testing? What are other pretest considerations? Why are these important?

10. What are the differences between the ACSM and YMCA fitness testing batteries for adults? Which battery would you choose, and why?

11. How do fitness tests for older adults and younger adults differ?

12. What methodologies can be used to assess the physical activity of students and adults?

REFERENCES

American Alliance for Health, Physical Education, Recreation, and Dance. (1980). *Health related physical fitness test manual.* Reston, VA.

_____. (1994). *Technical manual: Health related physical fitness.* Reston, VA.

_____. (1998). *Physical best: The American Alliance physical fitness education and assessment program.* Reston, VA.

American Alliance of Health, Physical Education, and Recreation. (1958). *Youth fitness test manual.* Reston, VA.

American College of Sports Medicine. (1993). *The Role of Physical Activity and Prevention in Health Care Reform in the United States.* Presented to House Ways and Means Subcommittee in Health, October 26, 1993.

_____. (2000). *ACSM's guidelines for exercise testing and prescription.* (6th ed.) Philadelphia: Lippincott Williams & Wilkins.

_____. (1998). Position stand: The recommended quantity and quality of exercise for developing and maintaining cardiorespiratory and muscular fitness, and flexibility in healthy adults. *Medicine & Science in Sports & Exercise.* 30 (6).

_____. (1998b). *ACSM fitness book.* 2nd ed. Champaign, IL: Human Kinetics Press.

American Health and Fitness Foundation, Inc. (1986). *FYT-FIT youth today.* Austin, TX.

Åstrand, P-O., and Rhyming, I. (1954). A nomogram for calculation of aerobic capacity (physical fitness) from pulse rate during submaximal work. *Journal of Applied Physiology.* 7:218–221.

Beighle, A., Pangrazi, R., and Vincent, S. (2001). Pedometers, physical activity, and accountability. *Journal of Health, Physical Education, Recreation, and Dance.* 72 (9): 16–19, 36.

Blair, S., Kuhl, H., Pattenbarger, R., Clark, D., Cooper, K., and Gibbons, L. (1989). Physical fitness and all-cause mortality: A prospective study of healthy men and women. *Journal of the American Medical Association* 262:2395–2401.

Bouchard, C. (1990). Discussion: Heredity, fitness, and health. In C. Bouchard, R. Shephard, T. Stephens, J. Sutton, and B. McPherson (Eds.). *Exercise, fitness, and health.* Champaign, IL: Human Kinetics Press.

Bouchard, C., Dionne, F., Simoneau, J., and Boulay, M. (1992). Genetics of aerobic and anaerobic performance. *Exercise and Sport Sciences Reviews.* 20, 27–58.

Bouchard, C., and Perusse, L. (1994). Heredity, activity level, and health. In C. Bouchard, R. Shephard, and T. Stephens (Eds.). *Physical activity, fitness, and health: International proceedings and consensus statement.* 106–118. Champaign, IL: Human Kinetics Press.

Bray, G. A., and Gray, D. S. (1988). Obesity. Part I—Pathogenesis. *Western Journal of Medicine.* 149:429–441.

Brozek, J., Grande, F., Anderson, J. T., and Keys, A. (1963). Densiometric analysis of body composition: Revision of some quantitative assumptions. *Annals of the New York Academy of Sciences.* 110:113–140.

Callaway, C. W., Chumlea, W. C., Bouchard, C., Himes, J. H., Lohman, T. G., Martin, A. D., Mitchell, D. C., Mueller, W. H., Roche, A. F., and Seefeldt, V. D. (1988). Circumferences. In T. G. Lohman, A. F. Roche, and R. Martorell (Eds.). *Anthropometric standardization reference manual.* 39–54. Champaign, IL: Human Kinetics Press.

Canadian Society for Exercise Physiology. (1996). *The Canadian physical activity, fitness & lifestyle appraisal.* Ottawa, Ontario: Author.

Canadian Standardized Test of Fitness Operations Manual. (1986). 3rd ed. Ottawa, Ontario: Fitness and Amateur Sport Canada.

Cooper Institute for Aerobics Research. (1999). *FITNESSGRAM test administration manual.* 2nd ed. Champaign, IL: Human Kinetics Press.

Corbin, C., Lindsey, R., and Welk, G. (2000). *Concepts of physical fitness.* 10th ed. Boston: McGraw-Hill.

Corbin, C., Pangrazi, R., and Frank, D. (2000). *President's Council on Physical Fitness and Sports Research Digest.* 3 (9), 1–8.

Fox, E. L., and Mathews, D. K. (1981). *The physiological basis of physical education and athletics.* 3rd ed. Philadelphia, PA: Saunders College Publishing.

George, J. D., Vehrs, P. R., Allsen, P. E., Fellingham, G. W., and Fisher, A. G. (1993). VO_{2max} estimation from a submaximal 1-mile track jog for fit college-age individuals. *Medicine & Science in Sports & Exercise.* 25:401–406.

Golding, L., Myers, C., and Sinning, W. (1989). *Y's way to physical fitness.* Champaign, IL: Human Kinetics Press.

Heyward, V. H. (1998). *Advanced fitness assessment and exercise prescription.* 3rd ed. Champaign, IL: Human Kinetics Press.

Heyward, V. H., and Stolarczyk, L. M. (1996). *Applied body composition assessment.* Champaign, IL: Human Kinetics Press.

Institute of Medicine, Division of Health Promotion and Disease Prevention. (1990). *The second fifty years: Promoting health and preventing disability.* Washington, DC: National Academy Press.

Jackson, A. S., and Pollock, M. L. (1985). Practical assessment of body composition. *The Physician and Sportsmedicine.* 13:76–90.

Kasch, F. W., and Boyer, J. L. (1968). *Adult fitness: Principles and practices.* Palo Alto, CA: Mayfield Publishing.

Kline, G., Porcari, J., Hintermeister, R., Freedson, P., Ward, A., McCarron, R., Ross, J., and Rippe, J. (1987). Estimation of VO_{2max} from a one-mile track walk, gender, age, and body weight. *Medicine and Science in Sports and Exercise.* 19(3):253–259.

Kriska, A. M., and Caspersen, C. J. (1997). Introduction to a collection of physical activity questionnaires. *Medicine and Science in Sports and Exercise.* 29(6):S5–S9.

Laporte, R., Montoye, H., and Caspersen, C. (1985). Assessment of physical activity in epidemiologic research: Problems and prospects. *Public Health Reports.* 100:131–146.

McArdle, W. D., Katch, F. I., and Katch, V. L. (2000). *Essentials of exercise physiology.* 2nd ed. Baltimore, MD: Lippincott, Williams & Wilkins.

—————. (2001). *Exercise physiology: Energy, nutrition, and human performance.* 5th ed. Baltimore, MD: Lippincott, Williams & Wilkins.

Mokdad, A., Bowman, B., Ford, E., Vinicor, F., Marks, J., and Koplan, J. (2001). The continuing epidemics of obesity and diabetes in the United States. *Journal of the American Medical Association.* 286: 1195–1200.

Morrow, J., and Freedson, P. (1994). Relationship between habitual physical activity and aerobic fitness in adolescents. *Pediatric Exercise Science.* 6: 315–329.

National Institutes of Health. (1985). Health implications of obesity: National Institutes of Health consensus development statement. *Annals of Internal Medicine.* 103: 1073–1077.

Nelson, J. K. (1976). Fitness testing as an educational process. In Jan Broekhoff, Ed. *Physical education, sports and the sciences.* Eugene, OR: Microform Publications pp. 65–74.

Noble, B. J., and Robertson, R. J. (1996). *Perceived exertion.* Champaign, IL: Human Kinetics Press.

Pangrazi, R., and Corbin, C. (1993). Physical fitness questions teachers ask. *Journal of Health, Physical Education, Recreation, and Dance.* 64 (7): 14–19.

Powers, S. K., and Howley, E. T. (1997). *Exercise physiology: Theory and application to fitness and performance.* 3rd ed. Madison, WI: Brown & Benchmark.

President's Challenge. (2001). http://www.indiana.edu/~preschal. Bloomington, Indiana.

Reeves, R. A. (1995). Deos this patient have hypertension? How to measure blood pressure. *Journal of the American Medical Association.* 273: 1211–1218.

Rikli, R. E., and Jones, C. J. (2001). *Senior fitness test manual.* Champaign, IL: Human Kinetics Press.

Ross., J., Dotson, C., Gilbert, G., and Katz, S. (1985). New standards for fitness measurement. *Journal of Health, Physical Education, Recreation, and Dance.* 56 (1): 62–66.

Ross, J., Pate, R., Delby, L., Gold, R., and Svilar, M. (1987). New health-related fitness norms. *Journal of Health, Physical Education, Recreation, and Dance.* 58 (9): 66–70.

Safrit, M., and Looney, M. (1992). Should the punishment fit the crime? A measurement dilemma. *Research Quarterly for Exercise and Sport.* 63:124–127.

Shephard, R. J. (1990). *Fitness in special populations.* 61–79. Champaign, IL: Human Kinetics Press.

Siri, W. E. (1961). Body composition from fluid space and density. In J. Brozek and A. Henschel (Eds.). *Techniques for measuring body composition.* 223–224. Washington, DC: National Academy of Sciences.

Thomas, D. Q., and Whitehead, J. R. (1993). Body composition assessment—some practical answers to teachers' questions. *Journal of Physical Education, Recreation, and Dance.* May–June, pp. 16–19.

Trost, S. (2001). Objective measurement of physical activity in youth: Current issues, future directions. *Exercise and Sport Sciences Reviews.* 29 (1), 32–36.

U.S. Department of Health and Human Services (USDHHS). (1996). *Physical activity and health: A report from the Surgeon General.* Atlanta: U.S. Department of Health and Human Services, Centers for Disease Control and Prevention, National Center for Chronic Disease Prevention and Health Promotion.

_____. (2000). *Healthy People 2000: National health promotion and disease prevention objectives.* Washington, DC: U.S. Department of Health and Human Services.

Welk, G., and Wood, K. (2000). Physical activity assessments in physical education: A practical review of instruments and their use in the curriculum. *Journal of Health, Physical Education, Recreation, and Dance.* 71 (1): 30–40.

Winnick, J., and Short, F. (1999). *The Brockport physical fitness test manual.* Champaign, IL: Human Kinetics Press.

REPRESENTATIVE READINGS

American College of Sports Medicine. (1998). *ACSM's resource manual for guidelines for exercise testing and prescription.* 3rd ed. Baltimore, MD: Lippincott, Williams & Wilkins.

Baumgartner, T., and Jackson, A. (1999). *Measurement for evaluation in physical education and exercise science.* 6th ed. Boston: McGraw-Hill.

Kriska, A. M., and Caspersen, C. J. (Eds.). (1997). *A collection of physical activity questionnaires for health-related research.* [Supplement]. *Medicine and Science in Sports and Exercise.* 29 (6).

Miller, D. (2001). *Measurement by the physical educator: Why and how.* 4th ed. Boston: McGraw-Hill.

Morrow, J., Jackson, A., Disch, J., and Mood, D. (2000). *Measurement and evaluation in human performance.* 2nd ed. Champaign, IL: Human Kinetics Press.

Piscopo, J. (1985). *Fitness and aging.* New York: Macmillan Publishing Company.

CHAPTER 6

Measuring Psychomotor Skills

Key Terms

agility

balance

body management competence

coordination

dynamic balance

fundamental skills

higher skill attainment

power

reaction time

skill-related physical fitness

specialized skills

speed

static balance

Objectives

1. Define psychomotor performance and cite fundamental skills associated with general motor ability and sports.

2. Describe the sequence in which children acquire physical skills.

3. Understand and discuss considerations for testing specific to the psychomotor domain.

4. Articulate the various ways that results of psychomotor tests can be appropriately used.

5. Explain components of skill-related physical fitness and state examples of how each can be measured and evaluated.

6. Describe psychomotor test batteries appropriate for use with students with disabilities.

7. Make well-informed choices of psychomotor tests for assessing skill-related physical fitness and specific sports skills.

8. Administer selected tests to measure general motor ability, selected team sports skills, and individual sports skills.

The psychomotor domain encompasses the area of skill-related physical fitness and the development of specific sports skills. The development of basic motor proficiencies and specific sport skills is a goal of virtually every K–12 physical education program. You will recall that in the previous chapter, clear distinctions were made between health-related and **skill-related physical fitness** (see Table 5.1). Components of skill-related physical fitness include agility, balance, coordination, power, reaction time, and speed. These skill-related components form the basis for developing skills related to particular sports. Thus, skill-related physical fitness is also sometimes referred to as sports-related physical fitness. The development of the components of skill-related physical fitness is directly related to the specific development of sport skills associated with various team, individual, and dual sports.

Typically, the psychomotor domain is emphasized within the K–12 physical education setting much more than in adult activity settings. In clinical exercise settings like private health clubs, corporate fitness, hospital-based activity programs, and community fitness, the emphasis is almost exclusively on health-related physical fitness. Resistive weight training, aerobic dance, aerobic workouts on various workout machines (e.g., treadmill, elliptical trainer, recumbent bicycle ergometers), and water exercise are the backbone of these programs. Some programs may offer racquetball, tennis, golf, or sport activities to participants. However, the participants who choose these activities are typically already skilled and little emphasis is placed on skill development. Perhaps programs such as these should have a greater psychomotor emphasis, but that is not the case at present.

Thus, the emphasis on measuring psychomotor skills in this chapter will focus on school settings. However, the principles for testing sports skills and skill-related physical fitness would be much the same if used with adult participants. The exercise science professional can easily adapt this information to apply to nonschool activity settings. This may be particularly important as many activity programs are moving from an exclusive focus on adult clientele and are actively promoting family fitness and programs for youth. Even if you do not plan a career in teaching in the K–12 setting, you should be able to work with youth in a variety of nonschool settings as an exercise science professional.

A primary goal of physical education is to develop movement competence. As physical educators, we must recognize that the essence of physical activity is movement and our task is to teach students how to become skillful movers. Whether it is by providing learning experiences that teach kindergarten children fundamental locomotor movements, teaching middle school youngsters how to play racquet sports, or refining complex techniques associated with selected sports, one of the primary roles of the physical educator is to develop and improve performance in the psychomotor domain.

In the elementary school, children should learn how to competently manage their bodies and develop useful physical skills (Pangrazi, 2001). The hierarchy of skill development depends on the early acquisition of fundamental movement competencies. There are four stages in this hierarchy, the first of which is body management competence. **Body management competence** is achieved when a child learns how to control the body in personal space, in general space in relation to others, and while working with an object or an apparatus. To accomplish this requires repeated opportunity for practice and for experimentation with a wide variety of basic movement challenges. After youngsters are able to effectively demonstrate appropriate body management using good standards of posture and body mechanics, they are ready to move into stage two of skill acquisition: fundamental skill development.

Fundamental skills are the basic skills that children require to function in their environment. Classified into three groups—locomotor, nonlocomotor, and manipulative—these skills are stressed in the primary grades and are periodically reviewed in the intermediate grades. Locomotor skills get the body from one place to another or propel the body upward in a vertical manner. The eight basic locomotor movements are walking, running, hopping, jumping, galloping, sliding, leaping, and skipping. Nonlocomotor movements are those executed in place, without appreciable movement or utilization of space. Examples of nonlocomotor movement include bending, twisting, swaying, shaking, and bouncing. Hand-eye or foot-eye skills in which an individual handles some kind of object with one or more body parts are referred to as manipulative skills. Manipulation of objects leads to better coordination and tracking skills, which are important to the development of specialized skills, the third stage of skill development.

Specialized skills are those used in sports and other units of activity taught in physical education. Rhythmic activities, gymnastics, swimming, individual sports, team sports, fitness routines, rope jumping, and so on are examples of areas that require a foundation of fundamental skills. Many of these skills have critical points of technique and strongly emphasize correct performance. Only after students have acquired specialized skills can they be successful in the fourth stage of skill development: higher skill attainment.

Higher skill attainment usually is accomplished after an individual possesses a firm foundation of body management, fundamental skills, and specialized skills and expresses a willingness to participate in activities that will further refine selected skills. Intramural sports, organized youth sports, and interschool competition are a few examples of areas in which children may seek higher skill attainment.

From a psychomotor perspective, most students in junior and senior high school require movement opportunities associated with stages three and four of the hierarchy of skill attainment. By the time a youngster makes the transition from the elementary school to the middle school, learning experiences in physical education to enhance psychomotor development should focus on specialized skills and higher skill attainment. Junior and senior high school physical educators should begin to counsel students on procedures and opportunities for developing physical skills outside the school program. As students' skill levels improve, so does their interest in voluntary participation in physical activity.

Students need to be aware that physical skill development is not easy and demands long, continuous effort before visible dividends are returned. The notion that skill attainment is easy must be discouraged. A more realistic premise that physical activity can be enjoyed throughout life and that skill practice will result in enhanced performance must be emphasized. The use of practical assessment techniques at all grade levels will assist the practitioner in evaluating students and will provide a basis on which students can better view their progress toward higher skill attainment.

The relationship between physical skill development and physical fitness development may be confusing, especially to a beginning teacher. As we discussed earlier, physical fitness has taken on a multidimensional definition. To be more effective in meeting the needs of students, curricular decision making in physical education should offer students planned experiences throughout the K–12 period in both the health-related physical fitness domain and the psychomotor domain. Chapter 5 focused on the health-related physical fitness domain by providing a definition of health-related physical fitness and a look at tests to measure and evaluate a student's health and physical well-being. This chapter is designed to do the same for the psychomotor domain. The remainder of this chapter provides a clear definition of skill-related physical fitness and its components and suggests practical tests of motor ability and sports skills. It is important to note that testing should not take priority over teaching. First and foremost, teachers and directors of activity programs need to focus energy and time on instruction. Measurement and evaluation are to be used to assist the instructional process, not detract from it.

Considerations for Testing

Testing in physical education requires considerable teacher planning. Paying careful attention to test administration details, simulating actual testing situations prior to working with students, and practicing can often save much time and avoid unnecessary repetition. These and other practical suggestions can improve testing conditions and will often result in more reliable outcomes when working with all students. These suggestions should supplement, not replace, those already discussed in Chapter 4.

1. *Provide the necessary encouragement and incentive for maximum effort.* Various forms of incentives are often necessary to motivate all students when performing physical/motor tests. Unless otherwise stated in the standardized test directions, verbal encouragement is recommended when testing most students. The strength of verbal incentive will be different for various circumstances and students. Some students may perform best following a few quiet words of encouragement from the teacher, while others will demonstrate maximum effort when given loud cheers throughout their entire performance by the teacher and/or peers.

2. *Get to know each student.* Teachers who are familiar with their students can generally recognize performance that is less than maximum. This is important when testing, since anything less than maximum would not be a valid indicator of a student's ability. Teachers must be able to recognize when students are not "giving it their best." It also is helpful to obtain as much observational data as possible about students. Although it may require more time, teachers should learn as much as they can about all students in their classes. This may necessitate talking with other teachers and parents. For example, the physical education teacher may discover medical or physical problems that could affect performance and/or attitude by talking with a school nurse or a physical or occupational therapist. The time taken to get to know each student will be a good investment. In addition to significant others, the student is also a valuable source of information for testing and performance.

3. *Provide accurate, motivating, and thorough demonstrations.* Most standardized physical education test items permit a demonstration by the teacher. This demonstration is very important for all students. If given only verbal directions, many students will not understand the test item and what performance is expected of them. A proper demonstration provides additional opportunity to learn what is required through a visual image. A demonstration also allows the teacher to experience the physical demands of the test. The physical demonstration can reinforce a verbal description of items that require specific techniques or standards. A demonstration may also alleviate possible fears students have about certain test items.

4. *Avoid potentially embarrassing situations.* The nature of much testing in physical education, if not implemented with proper preparation, sensitivity, and common sense, can result in embarrassment for some students. This can have very damaging and long-lasting negative consequences. For example, a student with severe obesity may not be able to perform well. If administered in the usual group testing situation, these events could be devastating to a student's self-concept. A more individualized approach to testing can avoid these results. Care should be

taken when testing students with disabilities. Teachers should be aware of all students' unique conditions and arrange appropriate testing situations. Preservation and enhancement of the student's self-concept should be an important consideration in any testing situation.

5. *Test in a nonthreatening environment.* All possible efforts should be made to make the testing environment relaxed and familiar to students—all students. One way to achieve this is to have present authority figures (teachers, aides, or parents) who are in close contact with the students on a regular basis and who can, if trained properly, assist with testing. Having "extra hands" available when testing will likely make everyone's job easier and the process more time efficient. Persons familiar with students are more likely to know if performance levels represent maximum efforts or if certain individuals are "sandbagging" or inhibited for some reason. Also, most students react better to encouragement or a friendly challenge from a familiar face than from a stranger. It may be difficult for a new person in a situation to determine if a student is in a bad mood, is not feeling well, or is affected by the presence of a newcomer. In addition to having familiar persons present, the testing location should be nonthreatening. Generally, it is best to test students in areas that they recognize. Some students do not react favorably to new locations and this can affect their behavior and test results. If a site different from the usual instructional setting is used for testing, students should have an opportunity to become oriented to the new location before testing takes place. The time spent, however, will be a good investment in obtaining valid and reliable test results.

6. *Practice or simulate unique items or testing conditions.* Several test items included in this chapter require administrative procedures that are different from those in many regular physical education instruments. The item itself may not be very different, but its performance by students may require different movements or execution. It is recommended that teachers simulate or actually perform these items themselves prior to testing students. These simulations allow teachers to experience the movements that students will have to perform and will help avoid many problems during the actual test administration. Based on these simulations, teachers can help students by giving performance tips. Not only will experiencing actual testing situations assist teachers in giving advice and suggestions to students, but it will also show students that the teacher really knows what it is like to perform under their circumstances.

7. *Recognize contraindicated activities.* Many students possess certain characteristics that require careful attention when performing physical activity. For example, a student with exercise-induced asthma is generally required to take a specific type of medication and do a slow, gradual warm-up prior to participation in cardiorespiratory endurance or sustained aerobic activities. Teachers must be aware of these situations and understand the implications associated with various conditions and participation in physical activity. These conditions are usually discussed in detail in an adapted physical education course but are mentioned here to remind physical education teachers about the importance of constant communication with parents, classroom teachers, and school medical personnel. The regular physical education teacher must implement a communication system

with medical and health professionals to stay informed about students with unique conditions. Physical education teachers knowledgeable about common medical conditions are better able to handle the "blanket" medical excuse, which often inappropriately excuses a student from physical education testing and/or class. Students with disabilities should not be excused unnecessarily from physical education programs. If a student is unable to participate in the regular physical education program because of a disability or temporary condition, a specially designed or adapted physical education program must be implemented. Thorough knowledge of the physical activity implications of various medical and health conditions by physical education teachers, coupled with communication among parents, medical personnel, and school staff, can result in physical education testing and instructional programs that benefit all students. Students must participate in physical education to derive its benefits. Physical education teachers are the professional advocates for consistent participation of all students.

Uses of Psychomotor Tests

Because a primary goal of the physical education program is to improve the physical skill of students, it makes sense that a majority of class time be dedicated to skill practice. Further, if most of the class time is devoted to skill practice, then testing should include measures of the skill components that have been practiced. The actual selection of a skills test may be decided on the basis of one or more selected criteria. Considerations in using and selecting skills tests are as follows:

1. *Validity and reliability.* As discussed in previous chapters, two of the primary criteria in selecting a test are validity and reliability. If a particular test is the most valid and reliable instrument representing the skill that the teacher wants to measure, then it should be used.

2. *Classifying students into learning groups.* Placing students of similar abilities together for practice sessions is considered an appropriate teaching strategy. Homogenous grouping permits more desirable teaching situations from the standpoint of practice through drilling. Lessons then can be planned with the strengths and weaknesses of all students in class considered. Having students work with classmates of similar abilities allows for individualized instruction and facilitates skill improvement and a positive learning situation. The teacher is able to structure situations that challenge students of varying abilities, and students are placed in a setting in which they are working with someone of similar ability. And as we know, playing against someone who is far better, or worse, does little to enhance skill or foster a positive attitude toward that particular activity. Youngsters appreciate fairness, enjoy competing with other students of similar athletic ability, and favor homogenous grouping (Lockhart and Mott, 1951).

3. *Inclusion in a comprehensive test of skill-related physical fitness.* Oftentimes physical educators want to obtain a composite profile of motor skill performance. Although several test batteries measure general motor ability, in most instances some items of a test battery are not related to skills taught in a particular unit of instruction. When this is the case, instructors may wish to utilize individual tests

that measure skills emphasized in class. Each test selected becomes part of a more useful whole.

4. *Assessing performance to predict potential in different sport activities.* There may be youths who do not realize their potential for success in sport and/or athletics. The results of assessment may help them recognize their innate potential. Armed with this information, a youngster may feel more confident about seeking participation in interschool or intraschool sport competition.

5. *Motivating students to higher levels of skill performance.* Youth can be motivated to achieve through knowledge of results and goal setting. The results of skill assessment can serve to provide the quantitative base upon which students monitor their progress. Trying to set a personal best on a test is a typical response of youth. The motivation to excel is greatly diminished unless a previous score or a criterion is available.

6. *Determining student achievement and grades.* As in other subject areas, testing may be used in physical education to monitor progress and assist in grading.

7. *Developing class profiles.* The content of yearly programs in physical education does not change much from one year to the next. Modifications in learning experiences are usually in response to recent research findings, state mandates, and new ideas. Since much of what a physical educator does is repeated on an annual basis, it is sometimes helpful to use tests for the purpose of profiling student performance. Establishing a rudimentary form of a normative database can assist the instructor in evaluating the skill performance of students. Comparing classes from different years or sections on similar test items can provide information useful in evaluating, developing, maintaining, or modifying the program.

8. *Measuring the effectiveness of a specific unit of instruction.* A test designed to measure specific student outcomes will provide a quantifiable appraisal of the effectiveness of instruction. Student learning, the primary goal of all teachers, can only be measured and monitored through assessment.

9. *Diagnosing injury or deficiency.* Some tests of skill can be used to determine the level of function associated with a particular aspect of skill-related physical fitness. Motor skill deficiencies apparent in the instructional setting may be more objectively viewed after an assessment session. Diagnosing a youngster's weaknesses in motor skill performance can assist in developing a series of meaningful and appropriate learning experiences.

10. *As a teaching aid to supplement class instruction.* Testing should be an educational experience. Once students become familiar with the test procedures they can periodically conduct their own self-tests, which allows them to monitor performance at their convenience. Teachers can even require students to complete tests during nonclass time. Many skill tests can be completed without the aid of an instructor and can be used as educational tools.

11. *Explaining the physical education program to various publics.* In this era of accountability, the use of test results to explain a program to various constituencies is crucial. Parents, administrators, and other groups can better understand the strengths and weaknesses of a program if it can be explained in quantifiable terms. Tests that have a normative database may help describe the effectiveness

of the program. Comparing the performance of students on a specific skills test with other students of the same age and sex may be more easily understood by noneducators and nonphysical educators than simply reporting scores.

From the preceding list, we have seen that tests of skill-related physical fitness may be used for many purposes. It is important that any testing be used in a humane manner. Students should not feel undue pressure to perform at a high level. Rather, they should be encouraged to participate and demonstrate improvement. Regardless of the reason that tests are being used, physical education teachers have the opportunity to select and administer many different types of motor skills tests. The following sections provide a wide variety of skills tests designed to assess the various components of skill-related physical fitness.

SECTION 1—TESTING SKILL-RELATED PHYSICAL FITNESS

As discussed in Chapter 5, there are many factors that impact a student's ability to do well on health-related physical fitness tests. These include genetic endowment, trainability, lifestyle factors, environmental factors, and maturation. It is logical to assume that these same factors would impact results of tests included in the psychomotor domain. In fact, it can be argued that these factors can play a larger role in skill-related and sports skills testing than in health-related fitness testing. We know that certain students are naturally more gifted when it comes to coordination, agility, balance, speed, and quickness.

Although most students can make some improvement with training on the components of health-related physical fitness, it is more difficult for students to improve such things as speed and quickness in the physical education setting. Because of heredity, certain students are predisposed to doing well in areas of skill-related fitness. It follows that some students can learn skills in specific sports quickly and do well on sports skills tests. Lifestyle and environmental factors play an important role in the development of skills in time outside of class. The maturation of a student also plays a critical role in psychomotor test performance. Thus, it is important that the physical educator recognize these factors in developing grading schemes based on skill assessment and when determining the appropriate emphasis on the process of the test versus the product of the test. Please review the discussion on process versus product in Chapter 5 if you do not immediately recall it.

Components of Skill-Related Physical Fitness

To be successful in sports requires more than an optimal level of health-related physical fitness. An individual must possess qualities of function that enable him to perform sports skills. The particular attributes that assist an individual in displaying athletic prowess, but are not related to the degree of functional health, are referred to as skill-related physical fitness components. Basketball, football, and baseball are some of the more obvious sports that require harmonious interaction among various body parts. To be successful at receiving a pass while driving for a lay-up, taking a pitch-out from the quarterback, or fielding a ground ball hit to deep shortstop requires coordination. While coordination is essential for performance of certain athletic skills, it is not related to the overall health and well-being of an individual. In addition to coordination, six components of skill-related physical fitness are also clearly related to sport performance but are not directly linked to the health of an individual. The assessment of these components is important as the physical educator makes ongoing evaluations of progress toward program and student goals:

Agility is the ability to rapidly and accurately change the position of the body in space. Springboard diving, wrestling, and dynamic gymnastic moves are examples of activities that require agility.

Balance is the maintenance of equilibrium while stationary or moving. Performing a handstand, walking a balance beam, and maintaining a stable position throughout the golf swing are examples of skills that require balance.

Coordination is the ability to simultaneously perform multiple motor tasks smoothly and accurately. Hitting a return in tennis, juggling several objects, batting a pitched baseball, or punting a football are examples of athletic skills that require coordination.

Power is the ability to exert maximum force in a minimum length of time. Weight lifting and football blocking are examples.

Reaction time is the duration between the stimulation and the response to the stimulation. A swimmer's response to the starting gun or a tennis player's reaction to a booming serve are examples of situations that require short reaction times.

Speed is the ability to perform a movement in a short period of time. It is advantageous for a sprinter on a track team or a wide receiver on a football team to possess speed.

Measuring Agility

Agility enables an individual to rapidly and precisely alter the position and direction of the body and is an important ingredient for success in a wide variety of sports. Racquetball, for instance, requires participants to make sudden changes in court positioning in response to the ball coming off the wall. A basketball player must possess agility to guard an opponent. In soccer, a player must constantly be prepared to change direction in order to move with the ball.

Traditionally, agility has been viewed as inexorably linked to heredity. To a certain extent, this is a valid assumption. However, research has confirmed that agility may be improved through practice, training, and instruction (Bennett, 1956). Findings from other research studies indicate a positive correlation between physical growth and agility in boys and girls at the primary grade level (Seils, 1951). As children get older this linear relationship between agility and growth continues in boys, but reverses in girls. At about 14 years of age, girls' agility begins to decline, while boys begin to make significant gains (Espenschade, 1947). Thus, a person's level of agility is probably a combined result of heredity, training, and experience.

An agile person can quickly and efficiently mobilize the large muscle groups of the body in order to make rapid changes in direction of movement. These rapid changes in movement have been measured by such tests as zig-zag runs, side-steps, and obstacle runs. Agility assumes a vital role in predicting the success of an individual in sport and physical activity. Through appropriate testing, the physical educator can determine which students are most agile and which ones require additional practice to better perform an activity.

The following are examples of field-based tests that may be used by the practitioner to measure agility.

Illinois Agility Run (Cureton, 1951)

Purpose: The purpose of this test is to measure agility.

Description: The Illinois Agility Run is a valid and reliable means of assessing agility. It is relatively easy to administer and requires little equipment and setup. Figure 6.1 depicts the layout of the test area and appropriate floor markings.

Instructions: The student assumes a prone position with hands at the sides of the chest and on the starting line. On the command "Go," the student stands up and sprints 30 feet to the first turning point. At the turning point, with at least one foot crossing the turning point, the student reverses direction and sprints diagonally back toward the starting line. After reaching the starting line, the student begins to zig-zag through the chairs in such a way so as to return to the starting line. Upon completing the zig-zag through the chairs, the student sprints toward the final turning point. At this point, a stop and reverse is repeated and the student runs full speed across the finish line.

Validity: Correlation coefficients ranging from .33 to .46 were obtained with other measures of agility (Cureton, 1947; O'Connor and Cureton, 1945).

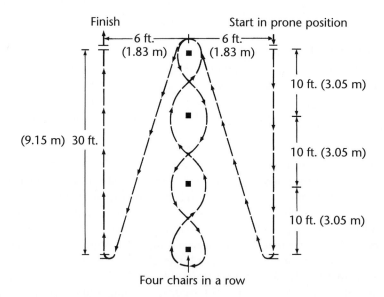

Figure 6.1 Diagram for Illinois agility run.

From Thomas K. Cureton, *Physical Fitness of Champion* Athletes. Urbana, IL: University of Illinois Press, 1951, p. 68. Reprinted by permission.

Reliability: The reliability coefficients ranged from .77 to .92, which suggest a high degree of consistency (Cureton, 1947; O'Connor and Cureton, 1945).

Age Level: Ages 6–adult.

Test Area: Any smooth flat area spacious enough to accommodate the movement.

Equipment Needed: Four chairs and a stopwatch.

Scoring Procedure: The time to the nearest half second is recorded as the student's score. If time permits, the best of three trials should be considered the score.

Norms: Standard score tables are available for young boys ages 7–13 and high school girls in Cureton (1964) and O'Connor and Cureton (1945), respectively.

Organizational Hints: Students should be given time to become acquainted with the path of the test. The test should be taken in court shoes or bare feet.

Side-Stepping (State of North Carolina, 1977)

Purpose: The purpose of this test is to measure agility.

Instructions: Two parallel lines are marked on the floor 12 feet apart. The student assumes a starting position with one foot touching one of the lines. On the command "Go," the student moves sideward with a side-step (sliding) toward the other line. Once the lead foot has crossed the other line, the student repeats the action back to the starting line and continues back and forth until time is called. The student must face the same direction throughout the test and the feet must not cross.

Validity: Face validity is assumed.

Reliability: Not reported.

Age Level: Ages 6–adult.

Test Area: Any smooth flat area is suitable.

Equipment Needed: Tape to mark the lines and a stopwatch.

Scoring Procedure: One point is scored each time the student touches a line. The total number of lines touched in 30 seconds is recorded as the score.

Norms: Normative tables for this test can be found in Table 6.1.

Organizational Hints: Utilizing an assistant to count lines touched and record the score is helpful.

Squat Thrust

Purpose: The purpose of this test is to measure how fast the position of the body can be changed.

Instructions: The student assumes a standing position. On the signal to start, the student moves to a squat position (Count 1), a front-leaning rest position (Count 2), return to a squat position (Count 3), and returns to the starting position (Count 4). Figure 6.2 shows the sequence of the movement. This movement is repeated as rapidly as possible until the signal to stop is given.

Validity: An r of .553 was reported for boys and .341 for girls.

Reliability: A correlation coefficient of .92 has been reported.

Age Level: Ages 10–adult.

Table 6.1 Percentile norms for side-step.*

BOYS

Percentile	9	10	11	12	13	14	15	16	17
95	19	19	20	21	23	23	25	23	26
90	17	18	19	19	21	21	23	22	25
85	16	17	18	20	20	22	21	23	23
80	15		17	18	19	20	21		22
75		16		18	19		20	20	21
70			16	17	18	19			
65	14	15	15	16	17	18	19	19	20
60					16	17	18		
55	13	14		15	16			18	19
50			15			16	18	17	18
45		14		16	17	17		17	18
40	12	13	13	14	15	16	17		17
35		12		14	15	16	16	16	
30	11		12	13	14	15	16	16	16
25				13	14	15	15	15	16
20	10	11	11	12	13	14	15	14	15
15	9	10	11	12	13	14	14	14	14
10	8	9	10	11	11	13	13	13	12
5	7	8	9	10	10	11	11	10	10

GIRLS

Percentile	9	10	11	12	13	14	15	16	17
95	18	19	21	20	20	21	21	21	21
90	16	17	18	18	19	19	20	19	20
85	15	16	17	17	18		19	18	
80			16	17		18	18	17	19
75	14	15			17	17			18
70	14		15	16		17	17	17	
65					16			16	
60		14				16		16	16
55	13		14	15			16		
50	13	13	14	15	15	15	15	15	15
45			13	14	15	15	15		15
40	12		13	14		15	15	14	
35		12		13					14
30	11	11	12	13	14	14	14	13	14
25					13		13	12	13
20	10	10	11	12	13	13	13	12	13
15	9	9	10	11	12	12	13	11	11
10	8	8	9	11	11	12	11	10	11
5	7	7	7	8	10	11	10	9	10

*Gaps (spaces with no numbers) indicate same number as above gap applies.

Reprinted by permission of the North Carolina State Department of Public Instruction (1977), Raleigh, North Carolina.

Figure 6.2 Sequence for squat thrust.

Test Area: Any smooth flat area free from debris is suitable for mass testing.

Equipment Needed: A stopwatch.

Scoring Procedure: Each movement is considered a part. For example, the squat position is counted as one, moving to the front-leaning rest position is two, and so on. The number of successfully executed movements completed in 10 seconds is recorded as the student's score.

Organizational Hints: Points may be deducted for improper execution of the movement, which includes the following: (1) moving the feet to the rear (or standing upright) before the hands are placed flat on the floor, (2) failing to assume a front-leaning rest position (i.e., swayed back or piked position), and (3) assuming a non-erect standing position with the head down.

Shuttle Run (AAHPER, 1976)

Purpose: The purpose of this test is to measure speed and agility.

Description: This test assesses those components of skill fitness requiring quick and accurate movement of muscles.

Instructions: Two blocks of wood 2 inches by 2 inches by 4 inches are placed side by side on a line 30 feet from the starting line. On the command to start, the student runs from behind the starting line to retrieve one of the blocks. After placing it behind the starting line, the student runs to pick up the second block and carries it back across the starting line. Two trials are given, with rest allowed between them.

Validity: Face validity is assumed.

Reliability: Not reported in the AAHPER booklet.

Age Level: Ages 9–adult.

Test Area: Any smooth flat area free of debris is suitable for administering this test.

Equipment Needed: Marking tape, a stopwatch, and two blocks of wood 2 inches by 2 inches by 4 inches.

Scoring Procedure: The time taken to correctly retrieve both blocks is recorded in seconds to the nearest tenth. The better time of the two trials is reported as the student's score.

Norms: Criterion-referenced norms for this test can be found in Table 6.2.

Organizational Hints: Dropping or throwing a block disqualifies the subject for that particular trial. Youngsters should be given adequate time to warm up prior to taking this test.

Table 6.2 Criterion-referenced standards (85th percentile) for shuttle run: boys and girls ages 10–17.

	BOYS		GIRLS
Age	Shuttle Run	Age	Shuttle Run
10	10.4 sec.	10	10.8 sec.
11	10.3 sec.	11	10.6 sec.
12	10.0 sec.	12	10.5 sec.
13	9.9 sec.	13	10.5 sec.
14	9.6 sec.	14	10.4 sec.
15	9.4 sec.	15	10.5 sec.
16	9.2 sec.	16	10.4 sec.
17	9.1 sec.	17	10.4 sec.

Reprinted by permission of the President's Council on Physical Fitness and Sports (1976), Washington, DC.

Measuring Balance

Balance is a vital component of efficient motor response and can be classified into two types, static and dynamic. **Static balance** is the ability to maintain equilibrium while in a stationary position. Remaining virtually motionless in a posed position while on the balance beam or standing on one's hands are examples of tasks requiring static balance. **Dynamic balance** is the ability to move through space in a steady and stable manner. Examples of movement requiring dynamic balance include activities such as tumbling, stunts, skating, and swimming. Both types of balance are important in everyday movement patterns and standing, as well as selected sports skills.

The ability to maintain balance is related to several factors. First of all, balance is a function of the mechanisms of the inner ear. These organs, called semicircular canals, affect the ability of an individual to maintain proper balance. Proper balance is also affected by an individual's ability to sense or "feel" the skill or movement. Many times we hear people say such things as, "She certainly has a feel for performing the floor exercise" or "He can't be knocked off his feet because of his exceptional balance." In these cases, it is likely that the persons in question do indeed have a kinesthetic sense for stability. Finally, balance is affected by visual perception. Those individuals who are able to visualize the body's position during a movement are more likely to maintain proper balance than those who cannot. Controlling and coordinating all these factors are essential to skills requiring balance.

Balance appears to be task-specific and differs from most other motor skills in that performance does not demonstrate marked improvement with age. Most studies of balance use static (one foot standing) and dynamic (beam walking) tests of balance. In the case of static balance, ability usually increases with age. Research on the static balance abilities of children shows a linear trend toward improved performance from ages 2 through 12 (De Oreo, 1971; Van Slooten, 1973). Prior to age 2, children generally are not able to perform a one-foot static balance task, probably because of their still-developing abilities to maintain a controlled upright posture. De Oreo (1980) suggests that distinct boy/girl differences are not evident in static balance performance as with other motor performance tasks. In fact, girls tend to be more proficient in balance-related activities until about age 7 or 8, whereupon the boys catch up. Both sexes level off in performance around age 8, prior to a surge in abilities from ages 9 to 12. This increase, however, is small when compared to increases in other skills. Cratty and Martin (1969) found boys to be superior to girls in balance performance between the ages of 6 and 7, but no significant differences occurred beyond this age. Studies of dynamic balance also show only a slight improvement with age. Govatos (1966) and Keogh (1965) found that girls performed better than boys on tests of dynamic balance between the ages of 7 and 11.

A person who is able to maintain a stationary position or control the body while moving displays the characteristic of good balance, which is an important skill for participation in physical activity or sport. As such, ascertaining the level of performance for balance may be useful for the physical educator. Examples of field-based tests that can be used by the physical educator to measure balance are provided in the following section.

Stork Stand

Purpose: The purpose of this test is to measure the ability to balance in a stationary, upright position supported on the ball of the foot of the dominant leg.

Description: This is a test of static balance.

Instructions: The student stands erect on the dominant foot, placing the opposite foot flat on the medial (inside) part of the supporting knee, with the hands on hips. On the signal to begin, the subject raises the heel of the support foot off the floor and maintains this position as long as possible, as pictured in Figure 6.3.

Safrit (1990) describes a variation of this test in which the performers do not raise themselves on the ball of the foot.

Validity: Face validity is accepted.

Reliability: Test-retest reliability coefficients range from .85 to .87.

Age Level: Ages 6–adult.

Test Area: Any smooth, flat area away from a wall is suitable for administration of this test.

Equipment Needed: Stopwatch.

Scoring Procedure: The highest of three trials is recorded to the nearest second.

Norms: Not available for K–12. Norms for college-age students are reported in Johnson and Nelson (1986).

Organizational Hints: This test also serves as a challenge activity to practice the skill of balancing. Subjects may be tested in pairs by having one person perform and the other monitor the seconds as they are called aloud by the test administrator.

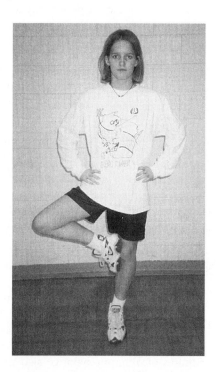

Figure 6.3 Stork stand.

Balance Beam Walk (Jensen and Hirst, 1980)

Purpose: The purpose of this test is to measure the student's ability to balance while walking on a balance beam.

Description: This is a test of dynamic balance.

Instructions: The student is instructed to stand at one end of a four-inch-wide balance beam. When ready, the student begins to slowly walk (one foot in front of the other) the full length of the beam, pausing at the end for five seconds, turning 180 degrees, and returning to the starting point. Three trials are given.

Validity: Face validity is accepted.

Reliability: Not reported.

Age Level: Ages 6–adult.

Test Area: Any smooth, flat area with ample space to place the beam is suitable.

Equipment Needed: A standard balance beam.

Scoring Procedure: Pass-fail.

Norms: Not reported.

Organizational Hints: The participant should be encouraged to move at a steady pace. Using a low beam (4–6 inches off the ground) provides a safer setting than the typical Olympic-height beam.

Measuring Coordination

Coordination is the ability to integrate separate motor systems with varying sensory modalities to produce efficient movement patterns (Gallahue, 1982). The more complex the movement pattern or sequence of patterns, the greater the degree of coordination necessary for successful performance. Although all movements use visual information in one way or another, some commonly accepted examples of gross visual-motor skills are throwing, catching, kicking, striking, and ball bouncing. Coordination is interrelated with other skill-related fitness components, such as balance, speed, reaction time, and agility, but not closely affiliated with muscular strength, endurance, or power. In sum, coordinated movement is that which is rhythmical, properly sequenced, and devoid of any superfluous actions.

Common movement patterns that require coordination are any skills that use foot-eye or hand-eye interaction. Each of these actions is characterized by incorporating visual information with some form of limb action. The success of the movement depends on the accuracy of the visual system. These skills usually involve an object such as a ball, bat, or racquet.

The development of coordinative skills is gradual, linearly related to age, and dependent on visual and motor maturation. Performance on tests of coordination tends to be superior for boys when compared with girls (Frederick, 1977; Van Slooten, 1973). Gross body coordination in children is associated with moving the body rapidly while performing various fundamental skills. Peterson et al. (1974) have reported a strong relationship among measures of the shuttle run, 30-yard dash, basic locomotor movement, and the standing long jump and gross body coordination. Charts depicting the various developmental stages associated with skills requiring coordination can be found in Corbin (1980), Gallahue (1982), Zaichkowsky, Zaichkowsky, and Martinek (1980), and other texts on motor development.

A person who displays coordination can hit a pitched ball, return a shot in badminton, catch a thrown ball on the run, harmoniously integrate multiple gross motor actions into a smooth movement pattern, and so on. Since it depends on maturation, the degree of coordination changes regularly and at times, rapidly. Carefully observing students performing fundamental skills during an instructional unit can assist the physical educator in evaluating the relative levels of coordination. Because of the interrelatedness of coordination with the skill components of balance, agility, reaction time, and speed, a physical education teacher can utilize results of tests in these areas to make evaluative statements regarding the level of coordination exhibited by students. A more effective means to assess coordination, however, is through selected test batteries that have been specifically designed to measure coordination. An example of a field-based test battery that can be used by the practitioner to measure coordination is discussed in the following section.

Body Coordination Test (Schilling and Kiphard, 1976)

Purpose: The purpose of this test battery is to measure total body control and coordination in children.

Description: This battery consists of four homogeneous subtests and was originally designed to identify motor retardation in children 5–14 years old.

Test 1: Balance (Backward)

Task: Backward balancing, three times per beam.

Equipment: Three balance beams.

Practice Trial: Administrator demonstrates the task by walking forward and backward on the wide beam. The child has one practice trial walking forward and backward on each beam. When balance is lost on the practice trial the child steps back on the beam at that point and resumes the practice trial, covering the entire length of the beam.

Test Trials: After the practice trial on the appropriate beam, the tester asks the child to do as well as he or she can by going backward only (starting with the widest beam). There will be three trials per beam for a total of nine trials.

Instructions: "If you touch the floor with your foot you must start again from the beginning. Now begin going backward. I will count each step." The tester should call each step in a loud voice.

Scoring Procedure: One point is awarded for each backward step taken on the balance beam starting with the second step. The first step does not count. A maximum of 8 points can be awarded per trial. If the child travels the beam in less than 8 steps, 8 points are still awarded. Maximum score (3 beams x 3 trials x 8 points) = 72.

Test 2: Hopping

Task: Hopping on one leg to and over foam blocks, maintaining balance.

Equipment: 12 foam rubber blocks, masking tape, tape measure.

Practice Trials: Administrator demonstrates task by hopping on one leg to a foam rubber block, hopping over it on the same leg, and proceeding for at least two more hops (about 10 feet total). The children are shown that the blocks are soft. Two practice trials are allowed for each leg (five hops). A five-year-old child is given the practice trials without a block. If the child succeeds, one block is added for the first test trial. This rule applies separately for each leg. Children 6 years of age and older do two practice trials per leg, using one block. However, if the child fails the first practice trial, the block is removed. If the child succeeds, the appropriate number of blocks are added for the test trial.

Test Trials: A child starts the test trial at a block height determined by age and success on practice trials.

Starting levels:

5 years—0 blocks

6 years—1 block

7 and 8 years—3 blocks

9 and 10 years—5 blocks

11–14 years—7 blocks

If a child seven years or older does not succeed at the starting height, the first trial is started using one block. A child is given three chances to perform the task.

Instructions: "Start hopping on one leg, hop over the blocks, and hop at least two more times on the same leg. Do not touch the floor with your other leg."

Scoring Procedure: Three points are awarded each for levels 0–12 (13 levels) if the child succeeds on the first trial. Two points are awarded for success on the second trial and 1 point for success on the third trial. Failure occurs when (1) the opposite leg touches the floor; (2) the blocks are kicked over; or (3) after hopping over the pile, fewer than two hops are taken. The test is terminated when the child fails to accumulate 5 points on two successive trials. A maximum of 39 points may be awarded per leg for a total score of 78.

Test 3: Lateral Jumping

Task: Lateral jumping as rapidly as possible for 15 seconds.

Equipment: Stopwatch and small wooden beam.

Practice Trial: Administrator demonstrates task by jumping laterally over the beam with two feet together. The student has five practice jumps.

Instructions: "Stand near the beam, feet together. On 'go,' jump across and back as quickly as possible until I say 'stop'." If the child touches the beam, the attempt is counted as successful; however, the child should be encouraged to try clearing the beam, feet together.

Scoring Procedure: Each jump across the beam (side A to side B) is worth one point. There are two trials, each across and back, with each lasting 15 seconds.

Test 4: Lateral Movement

Task: Moving laterally as rapidly as possible.

Equipment: Two platforms (25 cm x 25 cm), stopwatch, masking tape.

Practice Trials: Administrator explains the position of the platforms (12.5 cm apart). The student steps on right platform, picks up the platform to the left using both hands, and places it on the right side. The student then steps on this platform and picks up the left platform, and so on. Allow one practice trial of three to five shifts emphasizing speed as well as the importance of proper positioning of the platform (for maximum scores). Note: If a child wishes to work toward the left it is permissible. Movement in a straight line should be encouraged.

Test Trials: Two trials, each of 20 seconds duration, are allowed with 70 seconds allowed between trials. The test administrator counts points aloud and assumes a position 7 to 10 feet from the child, moving laterally with the child.

Instructions: "Step on this platform. Take the other with both hands and place it on your other side. Now step on this platform. Do this as quickly as possible. I will count your score. Go when I say 'go' and stop when I say 'stop'."

Scoring Procedure: Score consists of shifts of the platform and shifts of the body within a 20-second time interval. The first point is awarded when the platform touches the floor at the right side of the body. The second point is awarded when the child has stepped on the "next" platform with both feet. A third point is given when the platform is placed on the right, and so on.

Note: If the child is distracted by noise, the trial is discontinued. If the child stumbles, falls, touches the floor with a hand or foot, or takes the free platform with only one hand, the trial continues but no point is awarded for the error. The child should be encouraged to keep going on the task. The total score is the sum of the two trials.

Validity: Reported coefficients range from .50 to .60.

Reliability: The reliability of the individual test items ranges from .65 to .87. For the entire test, the reliability is .90, which suggests that the composite score should be used.

Age Level: Ages 6–14 years old.

Test Area: Classroom space or larger with ample area for four testing stations.

Norms: Not available.

Measuring Speed and Reaction Time

Speed and quick reaction time are essential elements for successful performance in most sports skills. Speed is the ability to perform a movement in a short period of time. Reaction time is the time it takes to respond to a stimulus. Specifically, it is the elapsed time between the presentation of a stimulus and the movement of the body, body parts, or an object.

At first glance, speed and reaction time may seem to be two separate elements. While a sprinter may be slow getting out of the blocks in response to the starter's gun, he or she may be able to compensate with his or her sprinting ability. Similarly, a hitter in baseball may be slow on the base paths, but possess the reaction time to move the bat into position to hit a pitched ball. The instances that show the separateness of speed and reaction time are many; however, it is apparent that a relationship exists between speed and reaction time. Reaction time affects total speed of movement. A sprinter who reduces the time to get out of the blocks improves the total running time. A running back with quick reaction time improves his effectiveness by increasing his overall speed.

Speed of forward movement is generally measured through various tests of running speed. Running speed tends to increase as the child gets older, and generally sex differences favor boys. Frederick (1977) found that speed, as measured by the 20-yard dash, was linearly related to age in a group of 3- to 5-year-old children. Milne, Seefeldt, and Reuschlein (1976) reported that running speed varied among children in kindergarten through second grade, and boys' performance scores were significantly better than girls'. Di Nucci (1976) found that age and sex differences favored boys on a number of running tasks with 6- to 8-year-olds. Keogh (1965) indicated that boys and girls were similar in running speed at ages 6 and 7, but boys were superior from age 8 to 12. Both boys and girls improve on measures of running speed until age 12, whereupon girls tend to level off in their performance and boys tend to continue improving throughout the adolescent years (AAHPER, 1976).

Reaction time has been found to decrease (get faster) in children as they get older. Cratty's (1979) review suggested that simple reaction time is approximately twice as long in 5-year-old children as it is in adults for an identical task and that there is rapid improvement in reaction time from age 3 to age 5. These differences in performance are likely due to maturation of the neurological mechanisms and differences in the information processing capabilities of children and adults. Fulton and Hubbard (1975) reported that reaction times of boys and girls ages 9 to 17 improved significantly with age, with girls demonstrating consistently faster times. Speed of movement also improved significantly with age, with boys being faster.

Speed, like reaction time, can be measured in the laboratory setting using sophisticated cinematography techniques or in field-based settings using reliable and valid tests. In most cases, the physical educator is not able to fund the expensive, technologically advanced equipment designed to measure speed and/or reaction time. Nevertheless, using some simple measuring devices (usually a stopwatch and meter stick), the physical educator can conduct meaningful and accurate assessment of the skill-related physical fitness components of speed and reaction time. Examples of field-based tests that can be used by the practitioner to measure speed and reaction time are provided in the following section.

50-Yard Dash (AAHPER, 1976)

Purpose: The purpose of this test is to measure forward running speed.

Description: This is perhaps the most valid field test for predicting speed. Results can be used to establish ability groups on the basis of speed.

Instructions: The student assumes a ready position behind the marked starting line. The sequence for the command to start is (1) "Take your mark," (2) "Get set," (3) "Go." On the command "Go," the student runs 50 yards as fast as possible.

Validity: Construct validity has been established for this test.

Reliability: Test-retest reliability coefficients for this particular test ranged from .86 (Fleishman, 1964) to .94 (Jackson and Baumgartner, 1969).

Age Level: Ages 6–adult.

Test Area: A smooth, flat running area at least 75 yards in length, marked off with starting and finishing lines 50 yards apart, is suitable for this test.

Equipment Needed: Stopwatch and marking tape.

Scoring Procedure: The amount of time elapsed between the start and the moment the student crosses the finish line is the recorded score. Time is reported to the nearest tenth of a second.

Norms: This test is part of the AAHPER Youth Fitness Test Battery. Criterion-referenced norms for this battery are in Table 6.3.

Organizational Hints: The teacher should be positioned at the finish line and should simultaneously lower the arm from a raised position and shout "Go" to signal the start. Using an assistant to record the time (to the nearest tenth of a second) will allow more efficient test administration.

Table 6.3 Criterion-referenced standards (85th percentile) for 50-yard dash: boys and girls ages 10–17.

	BOYS		GIRLS
Age	50-Yard Dash	Age	50-Yard Dash
10	7.4 sec.	10	7.5 sec.
11	7.4 sec.	11	7.6 sec.
12	7.0 sec.	12	7.5 sec.
13	6.9 sec.	13	7.5 sec.
14	6.6 sec.	14	7.4 sec.
15	6.4 sec.	15	7.5 sec.
16	6.2 sec.	16	7.5 sec.
17	6.1 sec.	17	7.5 sec.

Reprinted by permission of the President's Council on Physical Fitness and Sports (1976), Washington, DC.

Hand Reaction Time Test

Purpose: The purpose of this test is to measure the reaction time of the thumb and forefinger.

Description: The test requires the student to react to a randomly dropped falling ruler by catching it with the thumb and forefinger.

Instructions: The student sits in a chair next to a table, with the elbow and lower arm resting on the table. The heel of the hand rests on the table so that only the fingers and thumb extend beyond the edge of the table. The test administrator holds the ruler from the very top, allowing the lower end of the ruler at the 1″ mark to dangle between the thumb and forefinger of the subject. The student is instructed to concentrate on the ruler. The test administrator signals "Ready." After this command the administrator has up to 10 seconds to release the ruler. Once the ruler is dropped, the student pinches the thumb and forefinger together as quickly as possible (Figure 6.4). Twenty trials are administered.

Validity: Construct validity was established for this test.

Reliability: Johnson and Nelson (1986) reported a test-retest reliability coefficient of .89 for a similar test.

Age Level: Ages 6–adult.

Test Area: Any area large enough to comfortably accommodate a table and two chairs.

Equipment Needed: Ruler, chairs, and table.

Scoring Procedure: The point at which the top of the forefinger and thumb crosses the ruler is the initial value. One inch is subtracted from this reading on the ruler, since the starting position was at the one-inch line. The student's score is the sum of the middle 10 scores. The lower the total score, the faster the reaction time.

Norms: Not available.

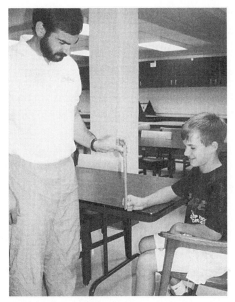 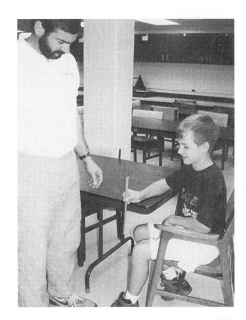

Figure 6.4 Hand reaction.

Organizational Hints: When the ruler is positioned, it should not touch the thumb or index finger of the subject. The time between the ready command and ruler release should be varied.

Test Batteries to Measure Skill-Related Physical Fitness

This section describes various batteries of tests designed to provide a composite picture of a student's performance on test items associated with the psychomotor domain. Theoretically, a comprehensive test to measure skill-related fitness would represent all factors that influence athletic performance. This, of course, is not the case. The sophistication and magnitude of such a test is unrealistic and, to date, not available. Nevertheless, test batteries are available that provide information about the performance of students on selected items of skill-related physical fitness. In general, the batteries cited comprise tests that measure performance in the areas of agility, balance, coordination, reaction time, and speed.

Tests described in this section were selected based on the criteria discussed in Chapter 4. The selected test batteries can be easily administered; require little training; are economically feasible for the public school setting; measure traits that provide useful information to the student, teacher, and parents; have displayed longevity; and contain normative information. These are viable tools for any organization wishing to initiate an assessment protocol to profile the composite motor ability of students. The tests are functional and objective in measuring components of skill-related physical fitness. Teachers should consider program objectives and other variables (see Chapter 2) in selecting a battery that is appropriate for a particular situation. Examples of field-based test batteries that can be used by the physical educator to measure skill-related physical fitness are provided in the following section.

North Carolina Motor Fitness Battery (State of North Carolina, 1977)

Purpose: The purpose of this test battery is to measure achievement in the psychomotor domain. Specifically, individual tests measure components of strength, speed, endurance, agility, and power.

Description: This battery comprises five tests: sit-ups, side-stepping, standing broad jump, modified pull-ups, and squat thrust (Figure 6.5). Students should be divided into five groups and rotated from station to station so that no student will be utilizing the same muscle groups in succession.

Validity: Not reported. Face validity is assumed. Several test items are similar to other tests that have reported validity coefficients.

Reliability: Not reported for the test battery.

Age Level: Boys and girls ages 9–18.

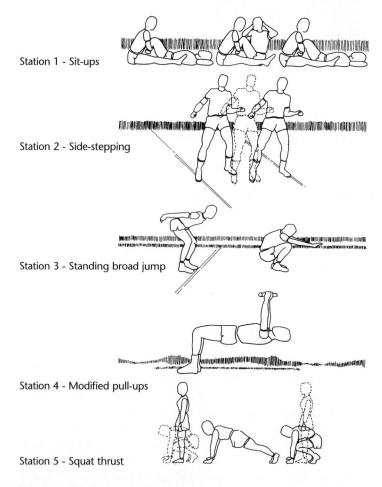

Figure 6.5 North Carolina motor fitness battery.

Reprinted by permission of the North Carolina State Department of Public Instruction, Raleigh, North Carolina.

Norms: Percentile norms are found in Tables 6.1 and 6.4–6.7 regarding test items.

Test Area: The entire test battery should utilize a mass testing format that has students rotating from station to station in a predetermined order. A large multipurpose room or gymnasium would provide appropriate space to administer this battery.

Test 1: Sit-Ups

Instructions: The student lies on the back with fingers clasped behind the neck and elbows touching the floor. Knees should be flexed, feet flat on the floor, with a partner stabilizing the feet. The student sits up, turns the trunk, touches one elbow to the opposite knee, and returns to the starting position. This movement is repeated with the student alternately touching knees with opposite elbows. Students must be reminded to return to the original starting position with the elbows touching the floor. Arching the back on the return should be discouraged (Figure 6.5).

Equipment Needed: Mat and stopwatch.

Scoring Procedure: The score is the number of sit-ups correctly completed (returning to original down position) in 30 seconds.

Organizational Hints: The test administrator can administer this test from a central position. To ensure uniformity in performance, students should have a chance to practice the test.

Test 2: Side-Stepping

Instructions: The student assumes a standing position with one foot touching one of two sidelines spaced 12 feet apart. On the command to "Go," the student moves sideward with a side-step (sliding), leading with the foot nearest the line that is being approached until that line is crossed with one foot. The movement is repeated to the other line in the same manner, and so on for 30 seconds. The student must face the same direction throughout the test.

Equipment Needed: Marking tape and a stopwatch.

Scoring Procedure: The score is the number of sidelines touched in the 30-second period.

Organizational Hints: Students should perform the test in proper court shoes or barefoot.

Test 3: Standing Broad Jump

Instructions: The student assumes a starting (semicrouched) position behind the take-off line with feet approximately shoulder-width apart. When ready, the student takes off on two feet and jumps as far as possible. Students should be encouraged to swing their arms and flex their legs at the knees in preparation for the jump. The distance is measured from the point where the body touches nearest the take-off line to the take-off line. Three consecutive trials are permitted.

Equipment Needed: Measuring tape (12 foot), tumbling mats for use on hard surface or jumping pit for outdoor use, marking tape.

Scoring Procedure: The distance jumped on the best of the three trials is recorded to the nearest inch.

Table 6.4 Percentile norms for sit-ups.

BOYS

Age/Percentile	9	10	11	12	13	14	15	16	17
95	24	25	26	27	30	30	31	33	33
90	21	23	24	25	27	28	30	30	32
85	20	21	23	24	26	27	28	29	31
80	19	20	22	23	25	26	27	28	30
75	18	19	21	22	24	25	26	27	29
70	17	18	20	21	23	25		26	28
65			19		22	24	25	25	27
60	16	17		20	21	23	24		26
55	15	16	18	19		22		24	25
50			17	18	20		23	22	
45	14	15	16	17		21	22	23	24
40	13				19	20	21		23
35		14	15	16	18			21	21
30	12	13	14	15	17	19	20		20
25		12	13	14	16	18		20	19
20	11	11	12	13	15	17	19	19	
15	10	10	11	12	14	16	17	17	18
10	8	8	10	11	13	14	16	16	
5	5	6	7	9	10	12	13	14	15

GIRLS

Age/Percentile	9	10	11	12	13	14	15	16	17
95	20	22	23	25	25	25	25	24	23
90	19	20	22	23	23	23	23	22	22
85	17	18	20	21	21	22	22	21	22
80	16	17	19	20	20	21	21	20	20
75	15	16	18	19	19	20	20	19	19
70			17	18			19	18	
65	15				18	19		17	19
60	14	14	16	17	17	18	18		
55	13		15	16	17			16	18
50	13	13	14		16	17	17		
45	12	12	13	15	15	16	16	15	17
40	11	11		14	15		15	14	16
35		11	12	13	14	15			
30	10		12	13	13	14	14	13	15
25		10	11	12	12	13		12	13
20	9	9	10	11	11	12	13	11	
15	7	8	9	9	10	11	11	10	12
10	6	6	8	8	9	9	10	9	9
5	3	3	5	7	8	9	7	6	7

Reprinted by permission of the North Carolina State Department of Public Instruction (1977), Raleigh, North Carolina.

Table 6.5 Percentile norms for standing broad jump.

BOYS

Age Percentile	9	10	11	12	13	14	15	16	17
95	70	72	75	80	85	92	96	97	98
90	66	68	71	75	80	87	91	94	96
85	63	66	69	72	78	84	89	92	94
80	61	64	67	71	76	82	87	90	93
75	60	62	65	69	74	80	85	88	92
70	59	61	64	67	73	78	83	86	91
65	58	60	63	66	72	77	82	85	87
60	57	59	62	65	71	75	81	83	86
55	55	58	61	64	69	74	79	82	85
50	54	57	59	63	68	72	78	80	83
45	53	55	58	61	66	71	76	78	82
40	52	54	57	60	65	70	75	76	81
35	50	53	56	59	64	69	74	74	79
30	49	52	54	58	62	67	72	73	78
25	48	50	53	56	61	65	71	72	75
20	46	49	51	54	59	63	69	70	74
15	44	47	50	52	56	61	66	68	72
10	41	45	47	49	53	59	63	63	70
5	38	41	41	41	46	54	56	60	63

GIRLS

Age Percentile	9	10	11	12	13	14	15	16	17
95	63	66	71	73	74	75	79	77	76
90	60	62	67	70	72	72	75	76	73
85	58	60	65	68	69	70	73	73	72
80	56	58	63	66	67	68	71	71	71
75	54	57	61	64	66	66	68	68	70
70	53	55	60	63	64	65	67	66	68
65	51	54	59	61	63	64	66	63	
60	51	53	58	60	62	62	64	61	67
55	50	52	56	59	61	61	63		66
50	49	50	55	58	60	60	62	60	64
45	48	49	54	57	59	59	60	59	63
40	47	48	53	56	58	58	59	57	62
35	46	47	51	54	56	57	58	55	59
30	45	46	49	53	55	55	57	54	56
25	43	44	48	50	53	54	56	53	51
20	41	43	46	49	52	52	54	51	50
15	39	40	44	47	50	50	52	49	48
10	37	37	42	44	47	48	48	47	46
5	35	34	38	38	42	44	44	44	41

Reprinted by permission of the North Carolina State Department of Public Instruction (1977), Raleigh, North Carolina.

Table 6.6 Percentile norms for modified pull-ups.

BOYS

Age	9	10	11	12	13	14	15	16	17
Percentile									
95	29	31	34	36	36	36	36	36	36
90	26	28	30	31	32	33	33	34	34
85	24	26	28	29	30	31	32	33	32
80	23	25	26	27	28	30	30	31	31
75	21	23	24	25	26	28	29	30	30
70	20	22	23	24	24	27	28	28	29
65	19	21	21	23	23	25	27	27	28
60	18	20		22	21	24	26	26	26
55	17	19	20	20	20	23	24	25	
50	16	18	19	19	19	22	23	24	25
45	15	17	18	18	18	20	22	23	24
40	14	16	17	17	17	19	21	21	23
35	13	15	16	16	16	18	20	20	21
30	12	14	15	15	14	16	18	18	20
25	10	12	14	13	13	15	17	17	19
20	8	11	12	12	11	12	15	16	17
15	5	9	11	10	9	11	13	14	15
10	3	6	9	8	6	8	10	12	12
5	1	2	3	3	3	4	7	8	9

GIRLS

Age	9	10	11	12	13	14	15	16	17
Percentile									
95	26	29	31	30	29	30	33	25	30
90	24	26	27	27	25	25	28	24	25
85	22	23	23	24	24	23	25	20	23
80	20	21	21	22	21	22	23	19	
75	19	19	20	21	19	21	22	18	21
70	18	18	19	20	18	20	21	17	20
65	17	17	18	19	17	19	20	16	
60	16	16	17	18	16	18	19		14
55	15	15	16	17	15	17	18	15	13
50	14	14	15	16		16	16	14	12
45	13	13	14	15	14	15		13	11
40	12	12	13	14	13	14	15	12	10
35	11	11	12	13	12	13	14	11	
30	10	10	11	11	11	12	13	10	9
25	9	9	10	10	10	11	11	8	8
20	8	7	9	9	9	10	10	5	7
15	6	5	7	7	7	9	8	4	6
10	3	3	4	5	5	7	6	3	5
5	1	1	1	1	2	4	3	1	4

Reprinted by permission of the North Carolina State Department of Public Instruction (1977), Raleigh, North Carolina.

Table 6.7 Percentile norms for squat thrust.

BOYS

Percentile	9	10	11	12	13	14	15	16	17
95	22	20	20	22	23	24	24	23	24
90	19	18	18	19	21	21	22	21	22
85	17	17	17	18	20	20	21		21
80	16	16	16	17	19		20	20	20
75	15	15				19			
70			15	16	18		19	19	
65	14	14				18		18	19
60			14	15	17		18		
55						17			18
50	13	13	13		16		17	17	
45				14		16			17
40	12	12	12		15			16	
35				13		15	16		16
30	11	11	11		14			15	
25				12		14	15		15
20	10	10	10	11	13			14	14
15	9	9	9	10	12	13	14	13	14
10	8	8	8	9	10	11	13	12	13
5	6	6	6	7	8	10	11	10	9

GIRLS

Percentile	9	10	11	12	13	14	15	16	17
95	20	19	18	20	20	20	19	18	19
90	18	17	17	18	18	18	18	18	18
85	16	16	16	17	17	17	17	17	17
80	15	15	15	16	16	16	16	16	
75				15					
70	14	14	14		15	15	15	15	16
65									
60	13	13	13	14				14	
55					14	14	14		15
50		12		13	13	13		13	14
45			12				13		
40	12			12		13			13
35		11			12			12	12
30	11		11	11		12	12		11
25		10			11		11		10
20	10		10	10	10	11		11	
15	9	9	9	9	9	10		10	9
10	8	8	8	8	8	9	10	9	8
5	6	6	7	6	6	7	7	5	3

Reprinted by permission of the North Carolina State Department of Public Instruction (1977), Raleigh, North Carolina.

Organizational Hints: The test administrator should be kneeling in the landing area in order to be able to accurately mark the distance jumped. An assistant to help record scores is beneficial. If mats are used, students not being tested should be positioned on the corners to keep mats from sliding on the floor.

Test 4: Modified Pull-Ups

Instructions: The student lies on his or her back with shoulders positioned directly under a horizontal bar that is 30 inches from the floor. Using a palms-away grip to grasp the bar and keeping feet flat on the floor to create a straight line from the knees to head, the student pulls up with the arms until they are completely bent and the chest and chin are touching the bar, then lowers to the original position. No rest is allowed between pull-ups, feet must be kept under knees, the body must remain rigid, and arms must be fully extended on return to the starting position.

Equipment Needed: Two chairs to support the bar, one horizontal bar approximately six feet in length, a stopwatch, and a tumbling mat or piece of carpet.

Scoring Procedure: The number of successfully completed pull-ups performed in 30 seconds is recorded as the score.

Organizational Hints: Students should be positioned in each chair to hold the chinning bar in place while the student is performing the test. An assistant should be used to spot and carefully monitor the subject.

Test 5: Squat Thrust

Instructions: Students assume an upright standing position. On the signal to begin, they drop to a squat position with the hands flat on the floor about shoulder-width apart (count 1); fully extend the legs back, keeping them together, and assume a front-leaning rest position (count 2); pull legs to the squat position (count 3); and return to the start position (count 4). The squat position must be maintained before thrusting legs back for count 2. The exercise must be continuous with no resting allowed (see Figure 6.2).

Equipment Needed: A stopwatch.

Scoring Procedure: The score is the number of fully completed repetitions in 30 seconds.

Organizational Hints: Using a partner system enables half the group to perform this test at a time.

Texas Physical Motor Fitness/Developmental Tests (American Heart Association in Texas and Governor's Commission on Physical Fitness, 1986)

Purpose: This is a battery of tests designed to assist teachers to determine the physical and motor abilities of students.

Description: The program comprises two test batteries that measure motor fitness and motor development, respectively. The motor fitness test consists of two items: the shuttle run and standing long jump. The motor development test comprises seven items and measures dynamic balance, static balance, kicking, throwing, catching, body awareness, and posture. The motor development battery is optional but is recommended as an aid to help teachers identify motor development deficiencies that could adversely affect a youngster's participation in physical activity in later years. The motor development test is described here to provide an example of an assessment instrument that can help provide a profile depicting the developmental stages of children and secure information essential to curriculum development.

Validity: Face validity is accepted for all items.

Reliability: Not reported.

Age Level: 5–9 years.

Norms: Tables 6.8 and 6.9 provide normative information regarding two motor fitness tests.

Test Area: Any smooth, safe indoor or outdoor area spacious enough to accommodate testing stations is appropriate.

Table 6.8 Percentile norms for Texas Motor Fitness Test: boys ages 5–9.

	STANDING LONG JUMP (in inches)					SHUTTLE RUN TIME (in seconds)				
Percentile	5	6	7	8	9	5	6	7	8	9
95	50	58	63	65	69	6.29	5.55	5.53	5.41	5.32
90	47	55	59	63	67	6.54	5.79	5.75	5.64	5.49
85	46	54	58	61	66	6.79	6.03	5.97	5.87	5.66
80	45	53	58	59	65	7.04	6.27	6.19	6.10	5.83
75	44	51	55	57	62	7.29	6.51	6.41	6.33	6.00
70	43	50	53	56	60	7.54	6.75	6.63	6.56	6.17
65	41	47	51	55	58	7.79	6.99	6.85	6.79	6.34
60	39	45	50	55	57	8.04	7.23	7.07	7.02	6.51
55	38	42	47	52	54	8.29	7.47	7.29	7.25	6.68
50	38	40	45	49	51	8.54	7.71	7.51	7.48	6.85
45	36	37	41	46	49	8.79	7.95	7.73	7.71	7.02
40	35	35	37	43	47	9.03	8.19	7.95	7.94	7.19
35	31	32	35	41	43	9.28	8.43	8.17	8.17	7.36
30	28	30	34	39	40	9.53	8.67	8.39	8.40	7.53
25	27	28	31	38	39	9.78	8.91	8.61	8.63	7.70
20	25	27	28	37	39	10.03	9.15	8.83	8.86	7.87
15	23	26	27	36	38	10.28	9.39	9.05	9.07	8.04
10	22	25	27	35	38	10.53	9.63	9.27	9.32	8.21
5	20	23	25	34	36	10.79	9.87	9.49	9.55	8.38

Reprinted by permission of The American Heart Association of Texas and Governor's Commission on Physical Education, Texas Affiliate (1986), Fort Worth, Texas.

Table 6.9 Percentile norms for Texas Motor Fitness Test: girls ages 5–9.

Percentile	STANDING LONG JUMP (in inches)					SHUTTLE RUN TIME (in seconds)				
	5	6	7	8	9	5	6	7	8	9
95	50	55	62	66	66	6.84	6.26	6.13	6.25	5.76
90	46	53	59	62	63	7.08	6.52	6.36	6.40	5.92
85	45	52	58	60	62	7.32	6.78	6.59	6.55	6.08
80	45	52	57	59	61	7.56	7.04	6.82	6.70	6.24
75	44	50	56	58	60	7.80	7.30	7.05	6.85	6.40
70	43	47	55	57	59	8.04	7.56	7.28	7.00	6.56
65	41	45	52	56	57	8.28	7.82	7.51	7.15	6.72
60	39	42	49	55	56	8.52	8.08	7.74	7.30	6.88
55	38	40	46	51	53	8.76	8.34	7.97	7.45	7.04
50	37	39	43	47	51	9.00	8.60	8.20	7.60	7.20
45	35	37	40	45	48	9.24	8.86	8.43	7.75	7.36
40	34	35	37	44	46	9.48	9.12	8.66	7.90	7.52
35	30	32	35	42	43	9.72	9.38	8.89	8.05	7.68
30	26	30	34	40	41	9.96	9.64	9.12	8.20	7.84
25	25	29	31	38	40	10.20	9.90	9.35	8.35	8.00
20	25	28	29	36	39	10.44	10.16	9.58	8.50	8.16
15	24	27	28	32	38	10.68	10.42	9.81	8.65	8.32
10	23	25	27	29	37	10.92	10.68	10.04	8.80	8.48
5	18	21	25	27	34	11.16	10.94	10.27	8.95	8.64

Reprinted by permission of The American Heart Association of Texas and Governor's Commission on Physical Education, Texas Affiliate (1986), Fort Worth, Texas.

Motor Fitness Test: Shuttle Run

Instructions: The student is positioned behind a start/finish line. On the command to start, the student runs to retrieve an eraser located behind a line 17 yards from the start line. As the student passes the timing line, located 2 yards from the start/finish line, the teacher starts the stopwatch. The watch is stopped as the student crosses the start/finish line. One trial is permitted.

Equipment Needed: Stopwatch, marking tape, measuring tape, and standard chalkboard eraser.

Scoring Procedure: The elapsed time from the student first crossing the timing line until running through the start/finish line is recorded to the nearest hundredth of a second.

Organizational Hints: Proper footwear should be worn. A digital readout stopwatch is best suited to give accurate reading to the nearest hundredth of a second.

Students should be given an opportunity to practice the test and should be encouraged to run through the finish line rather than stop at it.

Motor Fitness Test: Standing Long Jump

Instructions: The student assumes a starting (semicrouched) position behind the take-off line with feet approximately shoulder-width apart. When ready, the student takes off on two feet and jumps as far as possible. Students should be encouraged to swing their arms and flex their legs at the knees in preparation for the jump. The distance is measured from the point where the body touches nearest the take-off line (usually the back of the heels) to the take-off line. Two consecutive trials are permitted.

Equipment Needed: Measuring tape (12 foot), tumbling mats for use on hard surface or jumping pit for outdoor use, marking tape.

Scoring Procedure: The distance jumped on the better of the two trials is recorded to the nearest inch.

Organizational Hints: The test administrator should be kneeling in the landing area in order to accurately mark the distance jumped. An assistant to help record scores is beneficial. If mats are used, students not being tested should be positioned on the corners to keep the mat from sliding on the floor.

Motor Development Test: Walking a Line Forward/Backward

Instructions: The student stands at one end of a one-inch-wide line with one foot in front of the other, heel to toe. The student is requested to walk forward for six consecutive steps, always making sure that the heel of the front foot touches the toes of the back foot. Upon completing the forward walk, the student walks backward, heel to toe, for six consecutive steps. A second trial (for each test) is administered only if the student fails to achieve maximum points on the first trial.

Equipment Needed: Marking tape.

Scoring Procedure: The number of correctly executed steps (forward and backward) is recorded as the student's score (maximum score is 12).

Organizational Hints: If the student does not maintain a heel-to-toe step or steps off the line, the test should be repeated. Proper demonstration helps the students understand how they are to walk.

Motor Development Test: Standing with Eyes Open/Closed

Instructions: This test consists of three sets of two static balance challenges. First, the student assumes a standing position with one foot in front of the other (heel touching toes) on a one-inch-wide line on the floor. The stopwatch is started when the student has established balance and can hold that position. The student repeats this test with eyes closed. In the second set of this test, the student is instructed to stand with only the right foot on the line and the left foot bent at the knee, with the left foot resting on the medial side of the right knee area (stork stand). The stopwatch is started when the student has assumed the starting position. The student repeats the test with the eyes closed. The third set of two tests is a repeat of the second set but balanced on the left foot. Two trials are permitted for each of these six tests. The maximum score possible for any of the six tests is 10 seconds.

Equipment Needed: Stopwatch and marking tape.

Scoring Procedure: The better of two trials for each test is recorded to the nearest second (maximum of 10).

Organizational Hints: On the one-foot balances, the student is allowed one warning for improper positioning of the bent leg. If the student drops the leg below a 45-degree angle a second time, the test is stopped. The supporting foot must be in contact with the line at all times.

Motor Development Test: Kicking a Ball

Instructions: The student stands approximately 15–20 feet from the instructor, who rolls the ball to the child and observes the kicking pattern. Indicating which foot the student uses to kick the ball, the number of proper kicking techniques observed is recorded. Five consecutive trials are given.

Equipment Needed: 8.5-inch playground ball.

Scoring Procedure: One point is awarded for each of the following behaviors: steps toward the ball before kicking, foot contacts center of the ball, leg is fully extended at contact, and leg continues to follow through after contact. The number of observed behaviors (maximum of four) is recorded for each trial.

Organizational Hints: Student assistants can be used to retrieve balls.

Motor Development Test: Throwing a Ball

Instructions: The student stands approximately 15 feet from the instructor and, using an overhand motion, throws a tennis ball to the instructor. The throwing hand and the number of proper throwing techniques observed are recorded. Five consecutive trials are administered.

Equipment Needed: Tennis balls.

Scoring Procedure: One point each is awarded for the following: holds the tennis ball with tips of fingers; stands with feet slightly spread, with foot opposite the throwing arm in a forward position; steps forward with the opposite foot when throwing; and follows through with arm fully extended. A score is recorded for each of the five trials.

Organizational Hints: Student assistants can be used to retrieve balls.

Motor Development Test: Catching a Ball

Instructions: The student holds a standard playground ball (8.5 inch) with hands positioned on each side of ball at waist level in front of the body. The student drops and catches the ball with the instructor observing. Five trials are given.

Equipment Needed: 8.5-inch playground ball.

Scoring Procedure: The number of correct behaviors is recorded for each of the five trials. One point is scored for each of the following: elbows bent and in front of body, flight of ball watched throughout bounce and catch, ball caught entirely with hands, and the ball does not bounce higher than the shoulders. Record the correct number of observed behaviors for each trial (maximum of 4).

Motor Development Test: Body Awareness

Instructions: The following sequence of instructions should be given to students: "Touch each of the body parts I ask you to touch. Touch your nose. Touch your mouth. Touch your foot. Touch your right shoulder. Touch your left ear. Touch your left knee with your right hand. Touch your right elbow with your left hand."

Equipment Needed: None.

Scoring Procedure: One point is awarded for each correct response (maximum of 7 points).

Organizational Hints: To prevent children from overhearing the sequence, the test should be administered privately to one child at a time.

Motor Development Test: Posture

Instructions: The student assumes a standing position on a piece of tape located two feet from the modified posture grid (see Figure 6.6). The instructor is positioned approximately 15 feet directly behind the child in order to view the student's posture and the grid on the wall. The teacher should observe the position of the child's head, shoulders, and hips in relation to the grid. Specifically, the instructor is checking to see whether the head is tilted left or right, whether one shoulder is high or low, and whether either hip is high or low. The student is asked to stand sideways so the instructor can check if the head is tipped forward or backward in relation to the line. Any misalignments should be recorded on a scoresheet according to the following codes:

Posterior View Codes

Head:	HTL (head tilt left)	HTR (head tilt right)
Shoulder:	LSL (left shoulder low)	RSL (right shoulder low)
	LSH (left shoulder high)	RSH (right shoulder high)
Hips:	LHL (left hip low)	RHL (right hip low)
	LHH (left hip high)	RHH (right hip high)

Lateral View Codes

Head:	HTF (head tilt forward)	HTB (head tilt backward)

Equipment Needed: Modified posture grid (see Figure 6.6).

Scoring Procedure: No numeric rating is derived from this test. This test serves as an appraisal of posture and records appropriate misalignments.

Organizational Hints: The grid can be painted or constructed with tape on the gym wall. Youngsters should be encouraged to assume a comfortable position when taking this test.

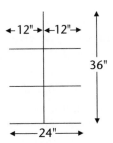

Figure 6.6 Modified posture grid.

Test Batteries for Students with Disabilities

The availability and quality of tests that measure various physical and motor characteristics among students with disabilities have improved dramatically in the past 20 years. This reflects recognition of the need for individual student and program improvements, as well as various state and federal education mandates. Tests range from comprehensive motor development batteries containing over 120 items to practical field-based physical fitness instruments composed of five items.

Tests used in physical education for students with disabilities must be carefully selected. Teachers should ensure that the test chosen is designed to measure the specific components of interest. Because many tests contain items that measure performance in several domains, it may require some very careful picking and choosing among tests to arrive at the best compilation of items for particular students. Of course, only tests with acceptable validity, reliability, and objectivity should be used.

The tests and specific items described below are a very small representation of those that are commonly used with special populations in physical education. Inclusion in this chapter does not indicate that these are the tests of choice for all students. The selection of tests for students with disabilities requires teachers to make informed decisions about measurement based on many factors, including the curriculum, Individualized Education Program goals and objectives, and abilities of students.

In many cases, the test descriptions in this chapter have been abbreviated for space purposes. It is important to note that when any test is used for measurement, placement, and/or programming purposes, the original source should be obtained and properly used. The original documents generally contain detailed descriptions of test development, norms, score sheets, interpretation, and other pertinent information. Certain test items that have already been described elsewhere in this text will not be repeated in this chapter unless unique administrative considerations exist for students with disabilities.

The following section presents selected tests designed to measure physical fitness attributes of students with disabilities. The specific group of students that the tests are designed for is identified in section subheadings. Readers should note that the terms or categories of disabilities identified in the section title will often differ from state to state and even within states or school districts. Many students with mild and moderate mental retardation are mainstreamed or integrated into regular physical education. These students will generally be able to perform most test items used with their nondisabled peers. Motivating and giving clear demonstrations by the teacher are especially useful techniques in assessing students with mental retardation (Eichstaedt and Lavay, 1992).

Motor Fitness Testing Manual for the Moderately Mentally Retarded (Johnson and Londree, 1976)

Purpose: The purpose of this test is to measure selected physical fitness and motor ability characteristics of students with moderate mental retardation.

Description: Physical fitness and motor ability components measured are arm and shoulder strength, abdominal strength, leg power and coordination, arm power and coordination, and running speed. Test items consist of flexed-arm hang, sit-ups, standing long jump, softball throw for distance, 50-yard dash, and 300-yard run/walk.

Flexed-Arm Hang

Instructions: The student is placed at a horizontal bar and uses an overhand (palms away from face) grip to hold the body in position with the chin above, but not touching, the bar. A stopwatch is started once this position is attained and is stopped when the chin touches the bar, falls below the level of the bar, or maintains its height by tilting the head backward. Figure 6.7 depicts proper positioning for the flexed-arm hang.

Equipment: Horizontal bar (chinning bar), mat, and stopwatch.

Scoring Procedure: The score is the number of seconds the student successfully holds the proper flexed-arm hang position.

Organizational Hints: Determine if the student understands that the object of the task is to keep the chin above the bar as long as possible. Check the grip to be sure the palms are facing away from the body. Hands should be approximately shoulder-width apart and no wider. Diameter of bar should not be too large for student's grip. The spotter and timer ideally should be two different persons. Assure the student that there is no danger of a fall. This can be accomplished by lightly touching the student on the waist as the position is held. This touch must not offer any support to aid scoring performance. Use a bar height that does not intimidate students. Adjustable bar units are commercially available or can be constructed. An assistant who is able to move the child to the starting position and serve as a spotter will aid test administration. Give verbal encouragement to "stay up" as long as possible while the student performs.

Figure 6.7 Flexed arm hang.

Sit-Ups

Instructions: A supine, flexed-knee position (knees bent less than 90 degrees) is assumed with soles of the feet flat on mat, heels not more than 12 inches from the buttocks, and hands placed behind the neck with fingers interlocked. The feet are held in contact with the floor by a partner. On the command "Go," the student curls up and touches one elbow to the opposite knee, reclines, and repeats the sit-up motion by bringing the opposite elbow up to the other knee. The student continues this alternate elbow-to-knee curl-up action until time has expired.

Equipment: Stopwatch and mat.

Scoring Procedure: The score is the total number of sit-ups properly performed in one 30-second trial. One sit-up is counted each time an elbow touches a knee. Sit-ups are not counted if the student does not start from a completely reclined position with elbows on mat, the elbow is not touched to the opposite knee, or the fingers come apart behind the neck.

Organizational Hints: Do not permit upward hip thrusts that result in the lower back losing contact with the mat. The student holding down the feet should be strong enough to maintain the person in proper position. Do not allow the student to pull against the neck or back of head with the hands when raising the body to sit-up position. Placing arms/hands across the chest instead may help avoid possible neck hyperextension. Emphasize the curling motion of the upper body as the sit-up is being performed. Encourage students to pace themselves.

Standing Long Jump

Instructions: Prepare a jumping area by making a restraining line and lines parallel to this line every inch for about 120 inches. Another way to design this jump area is to make a start line and secure a tape measure on the floor perpendicular to the line. The student stands facing forward just behind the jumping line with feet about shoulder-width apart. Body movements in preparation for the jump are permitted as long as the feet do not move. Generally these movements include flexion and extension of the knees, swinging of the arms forward and backward, or a strong thrust off the feet as the jump is initiated. The jump is made with both feet leaving the surface and landing at the same time. Allow students sufficient warm-up jumps in order to determine how many jumps are necessary to achieve a maximum performance. With this population, it may be necessary to prepare for testing with weekly charting of 20 to 25 jumps at one time in order to determine how many practices are necessary for optimal jumps.

Equipment: Floor or flat outdoor surface and tape measure or premeasured surface.

Scoring Procedure: Record the best of three trials to the nearest inch. If several practice jumps are administered as discussed above, be sure the student knows which of the three trials is to be measured. For proper performance, both feet must leave the surface and land together. Measurement is made from the restraining line to the heel of the foot closest to the line or other part of the body that touches the surface nearest the take-off line. Do not count a jump if the student moves feet just prior to jumping.

Organizational Hints: Mark the landing point as soon as possible because there is a tendency to move forward with momentum. The take-off and landing surfaces should be secure and not able to slide in any direction (anchor a mat or other movable surface). Place a marker at the spot of the initial or longest jump to help motivate the student on subsequent trials. Encourage students to swing their arms and to jump "out" instead of "up." Often students will not understand this task and jump more vertically than horizontally.

Softball Throw for Distance

Instructions: The student stands behind a restraining line and throws a softball overhand as far as possible. Three trials are permitted for the test. Students should have a proper warm-up prior to testing, which should include throwing at increasingly longer distances. It is recommended that a procedure similar to that used with the standing long jump be used to determine how many practice throws are necessary for the student to attain a maximum performance. A simple charting procedure during practice sessions will tell at what point, or after how many practice throws, the student performs optimally.

Equipment: A large open field or indoor facility, tape measure, a minimum of three softballs (12 inch), and materials to make restraining line.

Scoring Procedure: Record to the nearest foot the distance of the farthest throw. Throws must be overhand. Students can make any type of approach to the throwing line but cannot step over it during or after the throw.

Organizational Hints: Assign one or two persons to retrieve balls. Use a long tape measure for accurate assessment. Keep side areas clear during testing to avoid possible injury from stray balls. Have extra balls available for practice and efficient testing.

50-Yard Dash

Instructions: Two students stand behind a starting line and assume a "set" position. The timer stands at the finish line with arms extended sideways. The signal "Go" is given by the timer bringing her arms down briskly. The timer should have a stopwatch in each hand in order to time the two runners.

Equipment: Two stopwatches and a straight distance of at least 60 yards that is smooth and solid.

Scoring Procedure: One trial is administered. The score is the elapsed time between the "Go" signal and when the student passes the finish line with the body—not the head or arms.

Organizational Hints: Positioning someone at the starting line to assist the runners is helpful. Practice the signals "Set" and "Go" prior to administration of the actual test. Encourage students to run as fast as possible until they reach the finish line. Pair runners of equal or near-equal speed so they do not become frustrated. Remind students to run in a straight path. It may help to have lanes or markers for this purpose. Be sure all students understand they should run "as fast as they can."

300-Yard Run/Walk

Instructions: On the signal, "Ready, go," 5 to 10 students in a single row, and from a standing start, run 300 yards as fast as possible. Some students may be unable to run the entire 300 yards, but walking is preferred to stopping, so students may complete the test at widely varying times.

Equipment: A track or solid and smooth surface on which the distance can be marked and a stopwatch.

Scoring Procedure: The elapsed time the student takes to complete the distance is recorded to the nearest second.

Organizational Hints: This test should be administered after students have had practice in distance running and instruction in pacing. Verbal encouragement should be given.

Test of Gross Motor Development—2 (Ulrich, 2000)

Purpose: The purpose of this test is to measure locomotor and object control gross motor skills.

Description: Locomotor subtest skills assessed are the run, gallop, hop, leap, horizontal jump, and slide. Object-control subtest skills tested are striking a stationary ball, stationary dribble, catch, kick, overhand throw, and underhand roll.

Populations: Preschool and elementary school-age students, including those in special education classes.

Validity: Content validity was established by expert judgment. Construct validity was determined by factor analysis of the 12 gross motor skills performed by the standardization population. Additional construct validation was established by analysis of cross-age performance and comparisons between subjects with and without mental retardation.

Reliability: Test-retest reliability coefficients ranged from .84 to .99.

Age Level: Males and females, ages 3–10.

Norms: Standard scores and percentiles by age for the locomotor and object control subtests are presented. A separate table allows calculation of a Gross Motor Developmental Quotient (GMDQ).

Test Area: A gymnasium, room, or open space at least 60 feet by 30 feet.

Subtest 1: Locomotor Skills

Run

Instructions: The student is instructed to run fast between two marked lines 50 feet apart. The student should run on a line for the full length. Repeat a second trial.

Equipment: Some type of marking for lines and a minimum of 50 feet of clear space in a straight line.

Scoring Procedure: Students are given credit for: (1) a brief period in which both feet are off the ground; (2) arms moving in opposition to legs, elbows bent; (3) foot placement near or on the line (not flat-footed); and (4) nonsupport leg bent approximately 90 degrees (close to buttocks).

Organizational Hints: Inform students that they do not have to run with their feet on the line. This is a "guideline" only. Observe the performance from both the side and rear. Have at least 10 feet of clear space at the ends of the running path.

Gallop

Instructions: Mark two lines 25 feet apart with tape in 2 cones. Instruct students to gallop from one line to the other. Repeat a second trial by galloping back to the original line.

Equipment: A minimum of 25 feet of open space in a straight line and tape on two cones.

Scoring Procedure: Students are given credit for: (1) arms bent and lifted to waist level; (2) a step forward with the lead foot followed by a step with the trailing foot to a position adjacent to or behind the lead foot; (3) brief period in which both feet are off the ground; and (4) maintains a rhythm pattern for four consecutive gallops.

Organizational Hints: Observe performance from both the side and rear of the student. The tester may have to tap or touch the right and left leg if the student is not yet able to determine left from right.

Hop

Instructions: Students are told to hop on a preferred foot three times, then three times on the other foot. Repeat a second trial.

Equipment: A minimum of 15 feet of open space in a straight line.

Scoring Procedure: Students are given credit for: (1) nonsupport leg swinging in pendular fashion to produce force; (2) foot of nonsupport leg being bent and carried in back of body; (3) arm flexed and swinging forward to produce force; (4) takes off and lands three consecutive times on preferred foot; and (5) takes off and lands three times on nonpreferred foot.

Organizational Hints: Administer this item in clear, safe space, since balance is required.

Leap

Instructions: Place a beanbag on the floor. Attach a piece of tape on the floor so it is parallel to and 10 feet away from the beanbag. Have the child stand on the tape and run up and leap over the beanbag. Repeat a second trial.

Equipment: A minimum of 20 feet of clear space, a beanbag, and tape.

Scoring Procedure: Students are given credit for: (1) taking off on one foot and landing on the opposite foot; (2) a period where both feet are off the ground longer than running; and (3) forward reach with the arm opposite the lead foot.

Organizational Hints: Observe from the students' side.

Horizontal Jump

Instructions: The student stands behind a line that is marked off with tape or by other means and told to "jump far." Figure 6.8 depicts a student performing this test. Repeat a second trial.

Equipment: A minimum of 10 feet of open space and masking tape.

Figure 6.8 Horizontal jump.

Scoring Procedure: Students are given credit for: (1) preparatory movement including flexion of both knees with arms extended behind the body; (2) arms extending forcefully forward and upward, reaching full extension above head; (3) taking off and landing on both feet simultaneously; and (4) arms being brought downward during landing.

Organizational Hints: Observe from the side and front on different trials. Be sure that students do not step over the starting line as they initiate the jump.

Slide

Instructions: Two lines are marked off 30 feet apart. Students are told to slide from one line to another three times facing the same direction.

Equipment: A minimum of 30 feet of open space and masking tape.

Scoring Procedure: Students are given credit for: (1) turning the body sideways to the desired direction of travel; (2) a step sideways followed by a slide of the trailing foot to a point next to the lead foot; (3) a short period in which both feet are off the floor; and (4) ability to slide to the right and to the left (this criterion does not require performance of the other three).

Organizational Hints: Remind students to keep their heads up while sliding. Areas to side of slide course should be clear of equipment or other objects.

Subtest 2: Object-Control Skills
Striking a Stationary Ball

Instructions: Place the ball on the batting tee at the child's belt level. Tell the child to hit the ball hard. Repeat a second trial.

Equipment: A 4-inch lightweight ball, a plastic bat, and a batting tee.

Scoring Procedure: Students are given credit for: (1) dominant hand grips bat above nondominant hand; (2) nonpreferred side of body faces the imaginary tosser with feet parallel; (3) hip and shoulder rotation during swing; (4) transfers body weight to front foot; and (5) bat contacts ball.

Organizational Hints: Position students so that balls are not hit into other testing areas. Hit into a wall or net if possible.

Stationary Dribble

Instructions: Tell the child to dribble the ball four times without moving his or her feet, using one hand, and then stop by catching the ball. Repeat a second trial.

Equipment: An 8- to 10-inch playground ball for children ages 3 to 5; a basketball for children ages 6 to 10, and a flat, hard surface.

Scoring Procedure: Students are given credit for: (1) contacts the ball with one hand at about belt level; (2) pushes ball with fingertips (not a slap); (3) ball contacts surface in front of or to the outside of foot on the preferred side; and (4) maintains control of the ball for four consecutive bounces without having to move the feet to retrieve it.

Organizational Hints: Inflate the ball properly. Remind the students that they can look at the ball while bouncing. Do not restrict students by telling them they must stay in one spot.

Catch

Instructions: Student and tosser stand behind lines 15 feet apart. Ball is tossed underhand to student with a slight arc. Instruct student to "catch it with your hands." To be scored, tosses must be between shoulders and waist.

Equipment: A 4-inch plastic ball, 15 feet of clear space, and masking tape.

Scoring Procedure: Students are given credit for: (1) preparation, in which elbows are flexed and hands are in front of body; (2) arms extending in preparation for ball contact; and (3) catching and controlling the ball by hands only.

Organizational Hints: Tosser should stand in an open area, free of any visually confusing background against which the student might lose sight of the ball. Do not position student right on the 15-foot line because students often think they have to stand on a specific spot. Have two or three balls available to use time efficiently. Let students feel the ball to alleviate any fear of being hurt by a hard ball.

Kick

Instructions: Mark off two lines, one 20 feet away from a wall and one 30 feet from the wall. Tell the student to stand on the line that is 30 feet from the wall and place the ball on the bean bag on the other line. Instruct the student to kick the ball "hard" toward the wall (see Figure 6.9).

Figure 6.9 Kicking a ball.

Equipment: A plastic playground ball (8 to 10 inch), a bean bag, 30 feet of clear straight space, and masking tape.

Scoring Procedure: Students are given credit for: (1) a rapid and continuous approach to the ball; (2) an elongated stride or leap immediately prior to ball contact; (3) nonkicking foot placed even with or slightly in back of the ball; and (4) kicks ball with instep of preferred foot (shoelaces) or toe.

Organizational Hints: Observe from side and front during separate trials. Have more than one ball available for kicking. Place the ball on a bean bag to keep it stationary during kicking.

Overhand Throw

Instructions: Instruct student to throw the ball "hard" at the wall.

Equipment: A tennis ball, a wall, and about 20 feet of space.

Scoring Procedure: Students are given credit for: (1) a downward arc of the throwing arm to initiate the windup; (2) rotation of hip and shoulder to a point where the nondominant side faces an imaginary target; (3) transferring weight by stepping with the foot opposite the throwing hand; and (4) follow-through beyond ball release diagonally across body toward the side opposite the throwing hand.

Organizational Hints: Tell students they do not have to stand on a line when throwing. Some students may need a reminder to throw the ball overhand. Have extra balls ready for throwing. Encourage students to look at the target when throwing.

Underhand Roll

Instructions: Place two cones against a wall so they are 4 feet apart. Attach a piece of tape on the floor 20 feet from the wall. Tell the child to roll the ball hard so that it goes between the cones. Repeat a second trial.

Equipment: Tennis ball for children aged 3 to 6, a softball for children aged 7 to 10, two cones, tape, and 25 feet of clear space.

Scoring Procedure: Students are given credit for: (1) preferred hand swings down and back, reaching behind the trunk while chest faces cones; (2) strides forward with foot opposite the preferred hand toward the cones; (3) bends knees to lower body; and (4) releases ball close to the floor so ball does not bounce more than 4 inches high.

Section 2—Testing Specific Sport Skills

Tests measuring psychomotor performance can be either fitness component-specific (i.e., agility, balance, coordination, power, speed, or reaction time) or sport-specific (e.g., badminton, baseball). It may be argued that many of the psychomotor tests discussed in the first portion of this chapter measure performance attributes associated with specific sport skills. However, evaluating units of instruction that teach techniques of certain sports is usually best accomplished by administering tests that require utilization of the objects and implements used in that particular sport. In other words, if a youngster is taught how to hit an overhead clear in badminton and is expected to perform it, then assessment should measure that sport skill. Similarly, if accuracy is emphasized in throwing a football, then tests measuring that goal should be utilized. Specific teaching situations will dictate the type of test or tests to use. When selecting tests of specific sport skills, educators should not use a skill test that does not meet the evaluation needs or the essential criteria of validity, reliability, and objectivity.

For the sake of clarity, the remainder of the chapter has been divided into two parts: tests for team sports and tests for individual and dual sports. The scope of this text is not sufficient to cover all the sports skills tests on the market. The tests selected represent only a small portion of the total number of sports skills tests in the literature, but are well suited for use in the schools. For additional tests see *Assessing Sport Skills* by Strand and Wilson (1993).

Team Sports

The following section describes tests designed to assess specific skill performance in team sports.

Measuring Baseball/Softball Skills
AAHPER Softball Skills Tests for Boys and Girls (1966)
Purpose: The purpose of these test batteries is to measure fundamental skills associated with the sports of baseball and softball.

Description: The test batteries are similar for boys and girls. The primary difference between the two batteries is that the throwing for accuracy and underhand pitching distances are shorter for girls. Otherwise each battery consists of the following: base running, catching fly balls, fielding ground balls, fungo hitting, overhand throw for accuracy, softball throw for distance, speed throw, and underhand pitching.

Validity: Face validity accepted.

Reliability: Tests with reported coefficients of less than .70 were not included in the skills test.

Age Level: Boys and girls ages 10–18.

Norms: Reported in AAHPER Softball Skills Tests (1966).

Test Area: Large gymnasium with wall space, and an outdoor area.

Test 1: Base Running
Instructions: The student assumes a standing position in the batting box. On the command "Hit," the student swings the bat, drops the bat, and runs the base paths in the proper sequence. Two trials are given.

Equipment Needed: Stopwatch, bat, and bases.

Scoring Procedure: The score is the elapsed time from the command "Hit" to the student touching home plate. The better of the two trials is recorded to the nearest tenth of a second.

Organizational Hints: In order for the trial to count, the student must touch all the bases.

Test 2: Catching Fly Balls

Instructions: The student assumes a ready position at second base, which is the middle point of a 60-foot by 60-foot marked-off square (catching zone). A ball is thrown in the air, clearing a rope (8 feet high) fastened between two standards, which are located 5 feet in front of home plate toward the student. The ball is thrown at regular speed and targeted to land somewhere inside the catching zone. Each student is given two trials of 10 balls each.

Equipment Needed: Approximately 15 softballs, fluorescent boundary cones, tape measure, and bases.

Scoring Procedure: The number of balls successfully caught during the two trials is recorded as the student's score.

Organizational Hints: No practice trials are allowed. Approximately one-third of the balls should be thrown to the left of second base, one-third to the right, and one-third at second base.

Test 3: Fielding Ground Balls

Instructions: The student assumes a ready position at least 50 feet from the thrower. On the signal to begin, the thrower begins throwing ground balls toward the student. The student attempts to successfully field each ball, holding it momentarily before tossing it aside. Twenty ground balls constitute the number of trials for the test. One practice trial is permitted.

Equipment Needed: Approximately 15 softballs, fluorescent boundary cones to mark off fielding area, and 100-foot tape measure.

Scoring Procedure: The number of successfully fielded ground balls is recorded as the student's score.

Organizational Hints: Throws should be made at five-second intervals. Each throw must hit the ground inside the first 25-foot restraining line (Figure 6.10). Some variation in speed and direction of the throw is encouraged.

Test 4: Fungo Hitting

Instructions: The student is instructed to stand at home plate, toss the ball into the air, and hit it alternately to right and left field. This process continues until 10 balls have been hit to each field. Practice trials are allowed to each side.

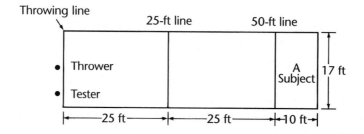

Figure 6.10 Layout for fielding ground balls.

Reprinted by permission of the American Alliance for Health, Physical Education, Recreation, and Dance, Reston, Virginia.

Equipment Needed: Bat and approximately 15 softballs.

Scoring Procedure: A fly ball to the designated field is worth two points, a ground ball one point. Two consecutive misses to the same field count as a trial. The score is the sum of the point values earned for each trial up to a maximum of 40 points.

Organizational Hints: If the bat touches the ball it is counted as a trial. Hits to right and left field must pass between first and second, or second and third base, respectively.

Test 5: Overhand Throw for Accuracy

Instructions: The student throws the ball in an overhand manner at a circular target from a distance of 65 feet for boys or 40 feet for girls. Ten trials are allowed.

Equipment Needed: Softballs and target(s) with the following dimensions: Three concentric circles with 1-inch lines: the center circle is 24 inches in diameter, the second circle is 48 inches in diameter, and the outer circle is 72 inches in diameter. The bottom of the outer circle is 36 inches from the floor.

Scoring Procedure: A ball hitting in the center circle is worth three points, second circle two points, and the outer circle one point. The sum of the points accumulated in 10 throws is the score.

Organizational Hints: Balls hitting on the line are awarded the higher point value. One or two practice throws are allowed.

Test 6: Softball Throw for Distance

Instructions: The student assumes a position in front of a restraining line six feet from the throwing line. Staying within these lines, the student is instructed to throw the softball as far as possible. Three trials are given.

Equipment Needed: Softballs, 250-foot tape measure, and boundary cones.

Scoring Procedure: The farthest of the three trials is recorded to the nearest foot.

Organizational Hints: The measurement of distance is made at right angles from the point of landing to the throwing line (the tape does not have to be moved in an arc to measure each throw). Each throw should be marked with a stake or some other visible but not easily moved object.

Test 7: Speed Throw

Instructions: The student assumes a ready position behind a restraining line located nine feet from a smooth wall. On the signal to "Go," the student throws the ball (overhand) against the wall and catches it on the rebound. This sequence is repeated until 15 hits against the wall have been completed. Two trials are given.

Equipment Needed: Softballs, stopwatch, measuring tape, and marking tape.

Scoring Procedure: The score is the time elapsed between hitting the wall with the first ball and the 15th. The better of two trials is recorded to the nearest tenth of a second.

Organizational Hints: All throws must be made from behind the restraining line. If the ball eludes the student completely, a retrial may be given.

Test 8: Underhand Pitching

Instructions: The student pitches the ball underhand at a rectangular target. Boys stand behind a 46-foot restraining line, girls behind a 38-foot restraining line. Fifteen trials are allowed.

Equipment Needed: Marking tape, measuring tape, softballs, and a rectangular target(s) constructed according to the following dimensions: The outer borders measure 42 by 29 inches wide and enclose an inner rectangle measuring 30 by 17 inches.

Scoring Procedure: Balls hitting the center area of the target count two points, balls hitting the outer area count one point. The sum of the points made on 15 pitches is recorded as the student's score.

Organizational Hints: One practice trial is allowed before the 15 pitches. The student must keep one foot on the restraining line while stepping forward to throw the ball toward the target.

For information on other tests measuring softball and baseball skills, see the *Representative Reading* list at the end of the chapter.

Measuring Basketball Skills

AAHPERD Basketball Skills Test (1984)

Purpose: The purpose of this test battery is to measure student performance of selected basketball skills.

Description: The test battery consists of four items: control dribble, defensive movement, passing, and speed spot shooting.

Validity: Juried validity ratings for test items ranged from .65 to .95.

Reliability: Intraclass reliability coefficients testing boys and girls separately ranged from .82 to .97 for all items.

Age Level: Males and females ages 10 through college.

Norms: Normative information is provided in the AAHPERD manual.

Test Area: Gymnasium with smooth court space and basketball goals.

Test 1: Control Dribble

Instructions: On the signal to start, the student begins dribbling with the nondominant hand from the nondominant side of starting cone A to the nondominant side of the center cone B and proceeds through the course as depicted in Figure 6.11, using either hand for dribbling. A practice trial is followed by two timed trials.

Equipment Needed: A basketball, stopwatch, and six fluorescent boundary cones.

Scoring Procedure: The score for each trial will be the elapsed time required to correctly complete the course. Scores should be recorded to the nearest tenth of a second for each trial. The final score is the sum of the two trials.

Organizational Hints: The stopwatch is stopped as soon as the student passes both feet across the finishing line. Any ball-handling violation (i.e., traveling or double dribbling) results in a retake of that particular trial. Movement in the wrong direction around the cone also results in a retake of the trial.

Test 2: Defensive Movement

Instructions: The student assumes a defensive position (legs flexed at the knees with feet spread) on point A, facing away from the basket. On the signal "Ready, go,"

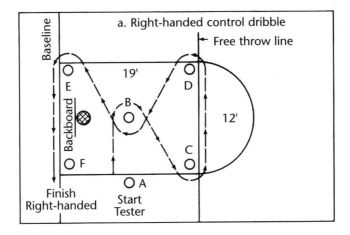

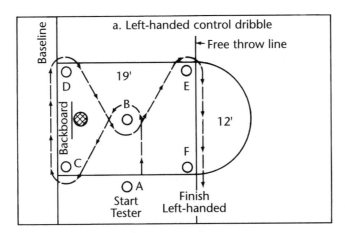

Figure 6.11 Layout for control dribble.

Reprinted by permission of the American Alliance for Health, Physical Education, Recreation, and Dance, Reston, Virginia.

the student slides to the left to point B, touches the floor outside the free throw lane with the left hand, performs a drop step (Figure 6.12) and slides to point C and touches the floor outside the free throw lane with the right hand. The student continues through the course as mapped out in Figure 6.13 until both feet cross the finish line (diagonal return to point A). A practice trial is followed by two timed trials.

Equipment Needed: Stopwatch, measuring tape, and marking tape.

Scoring Procedure: The sum of the elapsed time for each trial is recorded as the student's score. Each trial is recorded to the nearest tenth of a second.

Organizational Hints: Crossing the feet or turning and running are considered faults and result in a retake of the trial. The drop step must occur after the hand touches outside the free throw lane.

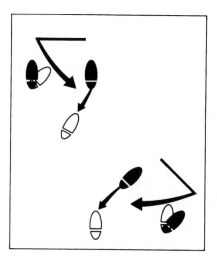

Figure 6.12 Foot positioning for defensive drop-step maneuver.

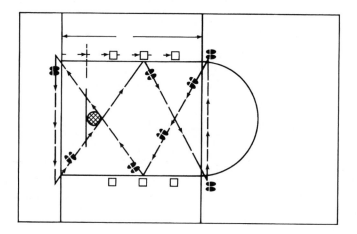

Figure 6.13 Layout for defensive movement.

Reprinted by permission of the American Alliance for Health, Physical Education, Recreation, and Dance, Reston, Virginia.

Test 3: Passing

Instructions: The student stands behind a restraining line, facing the wall, holding a basketball. On the signal "Ready, go," the student executes a chest pass toward the first target, retrieves the ball while moving into position facing the second target, and executes a chest pass toward target B. This sequence is continued until the student reaches target F. At target F, the student completes two passes toward the target and reverses the sequence back to target E, D, and so on. Figure 6.14 diagrams the arrangement for the wall pass test. One practice trial is followed by two timed 30-second trials.

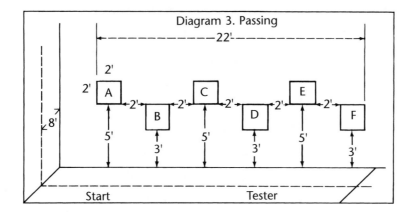

Figure 6.14 Layout for basketball wall pass.

Reprinted by permission of the American Alliance for Health, Physical Education, Recreation, and Dance, Reston, Virginia.

Equipment Needed: A basketball, stopwatch, tape measure, and marking tape.

Scoring Procedure: Each pass hitting the target or the outline counts two points. A pass hitting wall space between the targets counts one point. The sum of points earned in each trial is recorded as the student's score.

Organizational Hints: Executing the pass in front of the restraining line results in no points for that pass. Passes other than chest passes are not allowed. Targets must be passed at in proper sequence.

Test 4: Speed Spot Shooting

Instructions: The student assumes a ready position behind any one of five shooting spots appropriate for the age and grade. Shooting spots are 9 feet from the basket for grades 5 and 6, 12 feet for grades 7–9, and 15 feet for grades 10–12. Figure 6.15 shows the placement of the shooting spots. On the signal "Ready, go," the student shoots at the basketball goal, rebounds the ball, dribbles to another shooting spot, and shoots. The student must attempt at least one shot from each of the five spots. A maximum of four lay-ups are allowed during a trial, but no two may be in succession. A practice trial is followed by two timed 60-second trials.

Equipment Needed: Stopwatch, basketball, tape measure, and marking tape.

Scoring Procedure: Two points are awarded for each shot made. One point is awarded for each shot not made that hits the rim on its downward flight. The total points accumulated for both of the trials is recorded as the student's score.

Organizational Hints: The student must have at least one foot behind the line when executing the shot. A scorecard that allows easy recording of shots taken facilitates scoring. Any ball-handling violation that precedes a shot negates the score of that attempt. Any lay-up in excess of four or immediately following a lay-up is scored as zero.

For information on other tests that measure basketball skills, see the *Representative Readings* list at the end of the chapter.

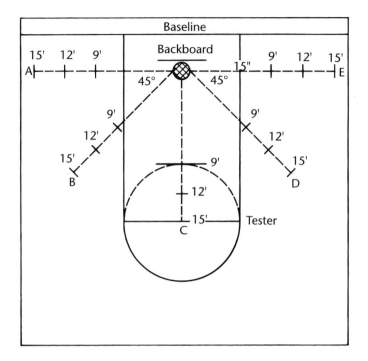

Figure 6.15 Layout and example for speed spot shooting.

Diagrams reprinted by permission of the American Alliance for Health, Physical Education, Recreation, and Dance, Reston, Virginia.

Measuring Football Skills
AAHPER Football Skills Test (1966)
Purpose: The purpose of this test battery is to measure selected performance skills associated with the sport of football.

Description: The items selected for presentation in this text consist of the following tests: ball-changing zigzag run, catching the forward pass, football pass for accuracy, football punt for distance, forward pass for distance, kickoff, pull-out, and 50-yard dash with football.

Validity: Face validity is accepted.

Reliability: Not reported.

Age Level: Ages 10–18. Originally designed for boys.

Norms: Normative information is available in the AAHPER testing manual for boys ages 10–18.

Test Area: A large indoor area and smooth outdoor area free of debris.

Test 1: Ball-Changing Zigzag Run
Instructions: The student assumes a starting position behind a restraining line holding a football under the right arm. On the signal "Go," the student runs in a zigzag pattern through a series of five cones placed in a straight line 10 feet apart, changing the location of the ball to the outside arm as each cone is passed. The student circles the last (fifth) cone and repeats the in-and-out pattern back to the starting line. Two trials are given.

Equipment Needed: Stopwatch, football, tape measure, and five cones.

Scoring Procedure: The elapsed time from the signal "Go," until the student crosses the starting line on the return run is recorded to the nearest tenth of a second. The faster of the two trials is recorded as the student's score.

Organizational Hints: Touching a cone results in a retake of that particular trial. After switching the ball to the other arm, the free arm should be extended in a stiff-arm position.

Test 2: Catching the Forward Pass
Instructions: The student assumes a ready position 9 feet to the left of the center on a line of scrimmage. On a signal, the student runs straight for 30 feet and turns at a 90-degree angle to the left and continues the pattern. A passer located 15 feet behind the center passes the football to the receiver. Ten passes are thrown. The same procedure is followed with the student lined up 9 feet to the right of center, running a pattern 30 feet straight downfield and cutting to the right. Figure 6.16 depicts the field specifications for this particular test.

Equipment Needed: Boundary cones to mark the starting point, cutting point, and passing point, and footballs.

Scoring Procedure: One point is awarded for each pass caught. The total number of passes caught is recorded as the student's score.

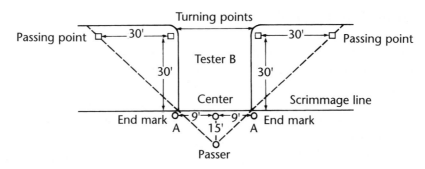

"A" is the starting position of the subject.

Figure 6.16 Layout for the AAHPER football forward pass catching test.

From *AAHPER Football Skills Test Manual,* Washington, DC: American Alliance for Health, Physical Education, Recreation, 1966. Reprinted by permission.

Organizational Hints: The passer should be skilled in throwing a football. A passing point should be located 30 feet to the outside of each cutting point. Poorly thrown balls result in a retake of that trial. The ball should be thrown slightly above head height.

Test 3: Football Pass for Accuracy

Instructions: The student assumes a standing position behind a restraining line located 15 yards from a target that is hung on the wall. Specifications for this target are the same as for the baseball throw for accuracy, previously discussed in this chapter. The student attempts 10 passes at the target. One sequence of 10 trials is given.

Equipment Needed: Target, measuring tape, marking tape, and footballs.

Scoring Procedure: Three points are awarded for a hit in the inner circle, two for the middle circle, and one for the outer circle. Throws hitting on the line are awarded the higher point value. The sum of 10 trials is recorded as the student's score.

Organizational Hints: To simulate a game situation, students should be encouraged to move either left or right before throwing. Students must remain behind the restraining line while throwing.

Test 4: Football Punt for Distance

Instructions: The student assumes a position in front of a restraining line which is six feet from the punting line. Staying within these lines, the student is instructed to punt the football as far as possible. Three trials are given.

Equipment Needed: Footballs, 200-foot tape measure, and boundary cones.

Scoring Procedure: The farthest of the three trials is recorded to the nearest foot.

Organizational Hints: The measurement of distance is made at right angles from the point of landing to the punting line (the tape does not have to be moved in an arc to measure each throw). Each punt should be marked with a stake or some other visible but not easily moved object.

Test 5: Forward Pass for Distance

Instructions: The student assumes a position in front of a restraining line which is six feet from the passing line. Staying within these lines, the student is instructed to pass the football as far as possible. Three trials are given.

Equipment Needed: Footballs, 200-foot tape measure, and boundary cones.

Scoring Procedure: The farthest of the three trials is recorded to the nearest foot.

Organizational Hints: The measurement of distance is made at right angles from the point of landing to the passing line (the tape does not have to be moved in an arc to measure each throw). Each pass should be marked with a stake or some other visible but not easily moved object.

Test 6: Kickoff

Instructions: A football is placed on a kicking tee so that it tilts slightly back toward the kicker. The player kicks the ball as far as possible downfield. Three trials are given.

Equipment Needed: Footballs, 200-foot tape measure, kicking tee, and boundary cones.

Scoring Procedure: The farthest of the three trials is recorded to the nearest foot.

Organizational Hints: The measurement of distance is made at right angles from the point of landing to the kicking line (the tape does not have to be moved in an arc to measure each throw). Each kick should be marked with a stake or some other visible but not easily moved object. The student may take as long a run up to the ball as desired.

Test 7: Pull-out

Instructions: The student assumes a set position (football stance). On the signal "Go," the student pulls out to the right, runs around a goal post (or cone) located 9 feet 3 inches from the starting position, and straight downfield for 30 feet. Two trials are given.

Equipment Needed: Stopwatch, tape measure, and boundary cones.

Scoring Procedure: The score is the elapsed time from the signal "Go" until the student crosses the finish line. The better of the two trials is recorded.

Organizational Hints: The finish line should be clearly marked. A boundary cone may be substituted for a goal post.

Test 8: 50-Yard Dash with Football

Instructions: The student assumes a ready position behind a starting line and, on the command "Go," runs 50 yards carrying the football under the arm. Two trials are given.

Equipment Needed: Stopwatch, football, measuring tape, and boundary cones.

Scoring Procedure: The amount of time elapsed between the start and the moment the student crosses the finish line is the score. The better of two trials is recorded.

Organizational Hints: The testing area should be a smooth, safe area free of debris.

For information on other tests that measure football skills, see the *Representative Readings* list at the end of the chapter.

Measuring Soccer Skills

The McDonald Soccer Test (1951)

Purpose: The purpose of this test is to measure general soccer ability.

Description: The test requires the student to display the fundamental skills of accurate kicking, ball control, and ability to receive a moving ball.

Validity: Validity coefficients derived by correlating coaches' ratings of playing abilities with test scores ranged from .63 to .94.

Reliability: Not reported for this test.

Age Level: Originally designed for college men and women, this test is also appropriate for high school boys and girls.

Norms: Not available for high school students.

Test Area: A smooth, flat area free of debris and long grass is suitable for this test.

Instructions: The student assumes a position behind a restraining line located nine feet from a wall, which is at least 30 feet wide by 11.5 feet high. On the signal to start, the student kicks the ball against the wall as many times as possible in 30 seconds. The student is allowed to retrieve the ball with any part of the body and return it to a position behind the restraining line. All kicks must occur from behind the restraining line. Four trials are given.

Equipment Needed: Wall space, three soccer balls, stopwatch, boundary cones or marking tape, and a tape measure.

Scoring Procedure: The highest number of successful kicks for one of the four trials is recorded as the student's score.

Organizational Hints: Two spare soccer balls should be placed along the nine-foot restraining line and may be used if the kicked ball gets out of control. The student may kick the ball on the fly or on the bounce.

Soccer Battery (Yeagley, 1972)

Purpose: The purpose of this test is to measure fundamental soccer skills of novice participants.

Description: The battery consists of the following four test items: dribbling, heading, juggling, and wall volleying.

Validity: A multiple correlation derived from comparing juried ratings with test scores was .78.

Reliability: Reliability coefficients ranged from .64 to .91.

Age Level: Originally administered to college physical education majors, this test battery is appropriate for use with youth 10–18 years old.

Norms: Not available.

Test Area: Gymnasium with ample wall space.

Test 1: Dribble

Instructions: The student assumes a ready position behind a restraining line. On the signal "Go," the student dribbles the soccer ball through the obstacle course described in Figures 6.17 and 6.18. Two trials are given.

Figure 6.17 Soccer ball dribble.

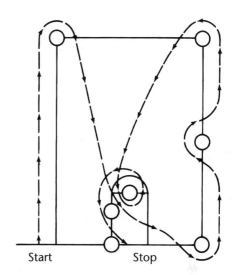

Figure 6.18 Layout for soccer ball dribble.
Reprinted by permission of J. L. Yeagley, Indiana University, Bloomington, Indiana.

Equipment Needed: Soccer ball, stopwatch, and boundary cones.

Scoring Procedure: The time elapsed from the signal "Go," until the student crosses the finish line and brings the ball to a complete halt is recorded to the nearest tenth of a second. The best of two trials is recorded as the student's score.

Organizational Hints: While the course outline must be followed, a student is not penalized for touching or moving an obstacle with the feet or ball.

Test 2: Heading

Instructions: The student assumes a standing position on the inside of the backcourt portion of the center circle area of a basketball floor. Using the midcourt line as the restraining line, the student attempts to head a thrown soccer ball into the specified scoring area. Figure 6.19 shows the configuration for this test. Three tosses each are made from points A and C and four tosses from point B for a total of 10 attempts.

Equipment Needed: Several soccer balls and marking tape.

Scoring Procedure: The sum of points earned on all 10 trials is recorded as the student's score.

Organizational Hints: We suggest that the distance be reduced from the heading area to the scoring area for youngsters. The toss should be made in a soft manner, reaching a height of no more than 15 feet. Any balls landing on the line are awarded the higher point value. The teacher should use caution and good judgment if employing this test at the elementary school level so as to reduce the potential for neck injury.

ABC Serving station

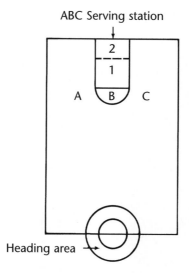

Figure 6.19 Layout for heading test.
Reprinted by permission of J. L. Yeagley, Indiana University, Bloomington, Indiana.

Test 3: Juggling

Instructions: The student assumes a standing position holding a soccer ball in the hands. On the signal "Go," the student bounces the ball on the floor and attempts to juggle the ball with the feet (or other parts of the body except the arms and hands) as many times as possible in 30 seconds. Two trials are given.

Equipment Needed: Stopwatch and soccer ball.

Scoring Procedure: The total number of legal juggles in 30 seconds is recorded. The better of two trials is reported as the student's score.

Organizational Hints: The half-court area of a basketball court serves as the testing area. One point is deducted each time the student touches the ball with arms or hands. The ball is allowed to bounce on the floor.

Test 4: Wall Volley

Instructions: The student assumes a standing position behind a restraining line, which is located 15 feet from a smooth wall. Figure 6.20 describes the set-up specifications for this test. On the signal "Go," the student kicks the ball at the wall as many times as possible in 30 seconds. Two trials are given.

Equipment Needed: Stopwatch, marking tape, tape measure, and soccer ball.

Scoring Procedure: The total number of legal kicks during the 30-second period is recorded. The student's score is the better of the two trials.

Organizational Hints: Failure to keep the nonkicking foot behind the restraining line results in no credit for that attempt. Extra balls should be readily available in case the student loses control of the ball.

For information on other tests that measure soccer skills, see the *Representative Readings* list at the end of the chapter.

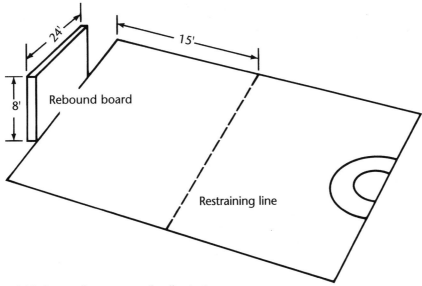

Figure 6.20 Layout for soccer wall-volley test.

Reprinted by permission of J. L. Yeagley, Indiana University, Bloomington, Indiana.

Measuring Volleyball Skills

AAHPER Volleyball Skills Test (1965)

Purpose: The purpose of this test battery is to measure student performance of selected volleyball skills.

Description: The test battery comprises the following four items: passing, serving, setting, and volleying.

Validity: Not reported.

Reliability: Not reported.

Age Level: Ages 10–18.

Norms: Normative information for each of the four tests is available in the testing manual.

Test Area: Gymnasium with unobstructed wall space.

Test 1: Passing

Instructions: The student assumes a ready position within the 10- by 6-foot passing area located near midcourt. From this position, the student attempts to successfully pass a ball thrown over the net into one of the marked landing areas. Figure 6.21 shows the court diagram for this test. Twenty trials are given.

Equipment Needed: Volleyball net, marking tape, and volleyballs.

Scoring Procedure: One point is awarded for a ball landing in the marked area.

Organizational Hints: The trials should be alternated, aiming first at the right target, then at the left, and so on. No points are awarded for a ball hitting the net or landing outside the marked landing area.

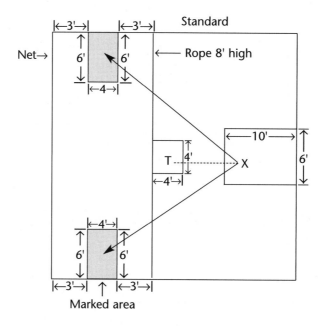

Figure 6.21 Layout for volleyball passing test.

Reprinted by permission of the American Alliance for Health, Physical Education, Recreation, and Dance, Reston, Virginia.

Test 2: Serving

Instructions: The student assumes a standing position behind the serving line midway between the corners and serves the volleyball over the net, attempting to land the ball in areas worth the most points. Figure 6.22 shows the position of the server and the respective point values for marked areas. Ten trials are given.

Equipment Needed: Volleyball net, marking tape, and volleyballs.

Scoring Procedure: The total points accumulated in the 10 trials is reported as the student's score.

Organizational Hints: The distance from serving line to net should be shortened from 30 feet to 20 feet for children younger than 12 years of age.

Test 3: Setting

Instructions: The student assumes a ready position inside one of the six-by-five-foot receiving areas located near the net at approximately midcourt and attempts to set a ball thrown from a designated area over the net into the six-by-four-foot target area. Ten consecutive trials are given to the right side and ten to the left. Figure 6.23 indicates the specifications for the testing area.

Equipment Needed: Volleyball net, marking tape, tape measure, and volleyballs.

Scoring Procedure: One point is awarded for each ball landing in the targeted area. The total score is the sum of hits from both the left and right sides.

Organizational Hints: Any throw that does not land within the setting area may be repeated.

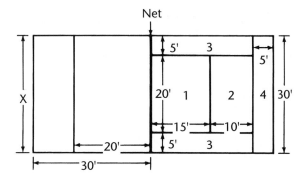

Figure 6.22 Layout for volleyball service test.

Reprinted by permission of the American Alliance for Health, Physical Education, Recreation, and Dance, Reston, Virginia.

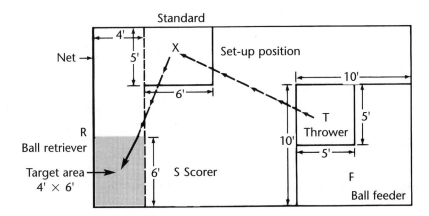

Figure 6.23 Layout and example for volleyball setting test.

Diagram reprinted by permission of the American Alliance for Health, Physical Education, Recreation, and Dance, Reston, Virginia.

Test 4: Volleying

Instructions: The student assumes a ready position next to a wall with volleyball in hand. The student begins the test by throwing the ball against the wall and attempting to hit the ball into a target area that is 5 feet wide, 3 to 4 feet long, and 11 feet from the floor. Figure 6.24 shows the specifications for the testing area. One 60-second trial is given.

Equipment Needed: Volleyball, stopwatch, marking tape, and tape measure.

Scoring Procedure: The number of volleys landing in the target area during the one-minute time limit is recorded as the student's score.

Organizational Hints: If the student catches or loses control of the ball, the test must be restarted by throwing the ball against the wall. Only legal hits are allowed.

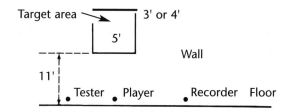

Figure 6.24 Layout for volleyball volleying test.

Reprinted by permission of the American Alliance for Health, Physical Education, Recreation, and Dance, Reston, Virginia.

High Wall-Volley Test (Cunningham and Garrison, 1968)

Purpose: The purpose of this test is to measure the student's ability to pass the ball into a target area.

Description: This test is similar to the volleying test for the AAHPER Volleyball Skills Battery.

Validity: Validity coefficients derived from judges' ratings of the test ranged from .62 to .72.

Reliability: The test-retest reliability coefficient for college women was .87.

Age Level: Although the test was originally devised for college women, it is appropriate to use with youth ages 10–adult.

Norms: Not available.

Test Area: Gymnasium area with unobstructed wall space and at least a 20-foot ceiling.

Instructions: The student stands anywhere in front of a target composed of a 3-foot horizontal line located 10 feet from the floor and two 3-foot vertical lines connected to the end of the horizontal line. Using legal hits, the student attempts to pass and volley a ball into the target area as many times as possible in 30 seconds. Two trials are given.

Equipment Needed: Volleyball, tape measure, and marking tape.

Scoring Procedure: One point is scored each time the ball hits in the target area or on the lines, including extensions of the 3-foot vertical lines. To be counted, the hit must be legal. The student's score is the better of the two trials.

Organizational Hints: If the student loses control of the ball, it may be retrieved and the student may start by tossing the ball off the wall. The student should rest between trials.

For more information on other tests measuring volleyball skills, see the *Representative Readings* list at the end of the chapter.

Individual and Dual Sports

The following sections describe tests that are designed to assess specific skill performance in individual and dual sports.

Measuring Badminton Skills

French Short-Serve Test (Scott, Carpenter, French, and Kuhl, 1941)

Purpose: The purpose of this test is to measure the student's ability to execute a badminton serve accurately, short, and low.

Validity: A validity coefficient of .66 was obtained using a criterion of ladder tournament rankings.

Reliability: Reported correlational coefficients range from .51 to .96.

Age Level: Ages 10–college.

Norms: Not reported.

Test Area: A regulation badminton court with appropriate target markings.

Instructions: The student stands behind the short service line and executes 20 consecutive legal short serves, attempting to hit the shuttlecock between the rope (strung the length of the net and 20 inches above it) and the net and land it in the target area shown in Figure 6.25. Two practice trials are permitted.

Equipment Needed: Tape measure, two dozen shuttlecocks, badminton racquets, rope to stretch above the net, and marking tape.

Scoring Procedure: The score is recorded for each successful serve that passes between the rope and net and lands in the target area. No points are awarded for serves that fail to pass between the net and the rope or shuttlecocks landing outside the target area. Twenty trials are administered. The total accumulated points are recorded as the student's score.

Organizational Hints: The rope used should be highly visible to assist in determining the flight of the shuttlecock. If the shuttlecock hits the rope, it is re-served and counts as a retrial.

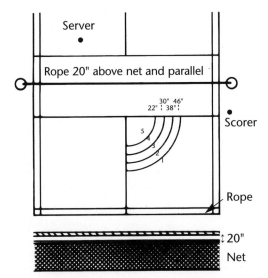

Figure 6.25 Layout for French short-serve test.

Reprinted by permission of the American Alliance for Health, Physical Education, Recreation, and Dance, Reston, Virginia.

Badminton Wall-Volley Test (Lockhart and McPherson, 1949)

Purpose: The purpose of this test is to measure the performer's ability to volley a badminton shuttlecock.

Validity: Reported validity coefficients range from .60 to .90.

Reliability: A test-retest reliability coefficient of .90 was reported using college women.

Age Level: This test was originally devised for use with college women, although it could also be used with youth ages 12–18.

Norms: Normative information can be found in the original source.

Test Area: Gymnasium with unobstructed wall space. Figure 6.26 shows the floor and wall markings for this test.

Instructions: The student stands behind a restraining line located 6 feet 6 inches from the wall. On the signal "Go," the student executes a legal serve above the net line on the wall and volleys the shuttlecock continuously for 30 seconds. Three 30-second trials are administered.

Equipment Needed: Badminton racquet, new shuttlecocks, stopwatch, tape measure, and marking tape.

Scoring Procedure: The number of legal volleys accumulated during each of the three trials is recorded as the student's score. Placing the shuttlecock in play with a serve does not count as a hit.

Organizational Hints: Only shots that are hit from behind the restraining line are counted. If the player loses control of the volley, it may be restarted with a legal serve. Rest times are permitted between trials.

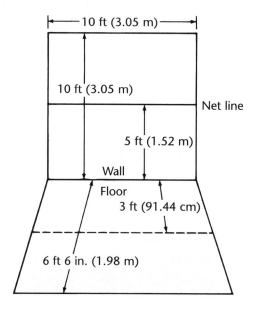

Figure 6.26 Layout for badminton wall-volley test.

Reprinted by permission of the American Alliance for Health, Physical Education, Recreation, and Dance, Reston, Virginia.

Poole Long-Serve Test (Poole and Nelson, 1970)

Purpose: The purpose of this test is to assess the student's ability to serve high and deep into the opposing backcourt.

Validity: A validity coefficient of .51 was derived using the results of tournament play as a criterion measure.

Reliability: A correlational coefficient of .81 was obtained using the test-retest method.

Age Level: Originally designed for college students, this test may also be used with high school students.

Norms: Not available.

Test Area: Regulation badminton court.

Instructions: The student assumes a position behind the short service line and attempts to serve the shuttlecock over the extended racquet of an assistant standing in a marked area 11 feet from the net (see Figure 6.27) into the five marked target zones. Twelve trials are given.

Equipment Needed: Badminton racquet, two dozen shuttlecocks, tape measure, and marking tape.

Scoring Procedure: The point value of the target area in which each shuttlecock lands is recorded for each attempt. The sum of the 10 best trials is recorded as the student's score.

Organizational Hints: Shuttlecocks landing on a line are awarded the higher point value. One point is deducted for any shuttlecock failing to clear the racquet of the opponent (point 0).

For information on other tests that measure badminton skills, see the *Representative Readings* list at the end of the chapter.

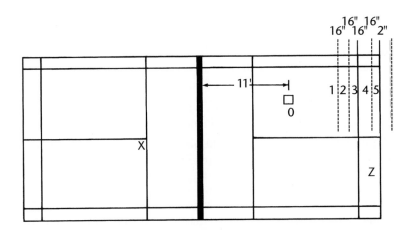

Figure 6.27 Layout for Poole long-serve test.

From *Practical Measurements for Evaluation in Physical Education* by Johnson and Nelson. Copyright © 1986 by MacMillian Publishing Company. Reprinted by permission of MacMillian Publishing Company.

Measuring Golf Skills

Green Golf Skills Test Battery (Green, East, and Hensley, 1987)

Purpose: The purpose of this test battery is to measure the fundamental skill components of golf: chipping, pitching, putting, and using the approach shot.

Description: The full battery of four test items was designed to measure golfing ability in college males and females, but it appears to be appropriate for high school–age youth. To reduce administrative time, shortened versions of the test may be utilized. The two most accurate predictors of overall golfing ability are the middle-distance shot and chip shot.

Validity: Using the score from 36 holes of golf as the criterion measure, a validity coefficient for the four-item test battery was reported as .77.

Reliability: Reliability coefficients for each of the four test items ranged from .65 to .93.

Age Level: High school through college-age youth.

Norms: Percentile norms for college-age men and women are available in the original source.

Test Area: Outdoor area with putting green.

Test 1: Chip Shot

Instructions: The student is instructed to chip six golf balls toward the flagstick from a line 10 feet from the edge of a flat green and 35 feet from the flagstick. Six trials are given.

Equipment Needed: Golf balls, golf clubs, measuring tape, and flagstick.

Scoring Procedure: The sum of the measured distance (to the nearest foot) between the point at which each of the chip shots came to rest and the flagstick is recorded as the student's score.

Organizational Hints: Students are allowed to change clubs any time during the test.

Test 2: Long Putt

Instructions: The student assumes a putting position over one of six balls equally spaced around the cup on a circle with a 25-foot radius. Students are instructed to putt the first ball as close as possible to the hole (or into the hole) and proceed in a clockwise manner to the next ball, and so on, until all six balls have been stroked.

Equipment Needed: Golf balls, putters, measuring tape, and hole.

Scoring Procedure: The student's score is the sum of the measured distance (to the nearest inch) that each putt came to rest from the cup for all six attempts.

Organizational Hints: Students should be encouraged to putt the ball as close as possible or into the hole. Be sure to remove balls from the green after each student's trial.

Test 3: Middle-Distance Shot

Instructions: Students are instructed to hit four golf balls down a smooth, open fairway toward a line of flags placed as targets across the fairway. Target flags for females should be placed 110 yards from the teeing area and 140 yards for males. Four shots are given.

Equipment Needed: Golf balls, 10 flagsticks or boundary cones, measuring tape, and golf clubs (middle to short irons).

Scoring Procedure: The score is the sum of the measured perpendicular distance (to the nearest yard) from the line of flags at which each ball came to rest.

Organizational Hints: Students are allowed to change clubs any time during the test. For safety purposes, the scoring should take place after the student has completed hitting all four shots. The students should be encouraged to use a full swing.

Test 4: Pitch Shot

Instructions: Students are positioned behind a restraining line 40 yards from a simulated green marked with a flagstick and instructed to pitch six golf balls toward a flagstick using either a seven, eight, or nine iron, pitching wedge, or sand wedge.

Equipment Needed: Golf balls, seven, eight, or nine irons, pitching and sand wedges, measuring tape, and flagsticks or boundary cones.

Scoring Procedure: The student's recorded score is the sum of the measured distance (to the nearest foot) from the flagstick at which each of the six pitch shots came to rest.

Organizational Hints: To avoid unnecessary damage due to repeated landings, a simulated green that provides a soft landing area should be used. Balls should be scored and removed from the impact area after each attempt. Students are allowed to change clubs any time during the test.

Indoor Golf Skill Test (Shick and Berg, 1983)

Purpose: The purpose of this test is to measure the golf skills ability of junior high school boys.

Validity: Using a criterion measure of the best of three scores reported for a par-three nine-hole course, a validity coefficient of .84 was reported.

Reliability: A reliability coefficient of .91 was obtained using the test-retest method.

Age Level: Junior high school–age through college.

Norms: None available.

Test Area: This test can be conducted either outside or inside in a small gymnasium or multipurpose area.

Instructions: The student is instructed to hit a plastic golf ball off a driving mat, with a five iron, as far as possible toward a boundary cone located 68 feet from the hitting area directly in front of the student. Figure 6.28 shows the arrangement for the target and scoring zones. Two practice trials are followed by 20 test trials.

Equipment Needed: Several five irons (at least one left-handed), fluorescent boundary cone to mark target and scoring zones, tape measure, marking tape or rope, and driving mat.

Scoring Procedure: The score for each trial is the point value of the area where the ball first hits. Balls landing on a line are given the higher (or highest, if at an intersection of three scoring areas) point value. Balls that travel beyond the scoring areas are awarded either a 4 or 6 depending on the line of flight. Any topped ball passing through the target area is awarded one point. A "whiff," or a ball landing outside the target areas, scores 0. The student's score is the sum of all 20 trials.

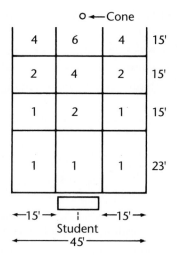

Figure 6.28 Layout for indoor golf test.

Reprinted by permission of the American Alliance for Health, Physical Education, Recreation, and Dance, Reston, Virginia.

Organizational Hints: It is possible to have two or more stations in a gymnasium. The safest and best vantage point for the scorer is a position on either side of the scoring area where the 1 and 2 zones meet.

For information on other tests that measure golf skills, see the *Representative Readings* list at the end of the chapter.

Measuring Racquetball Skills

Racquetball Skills Test (Hensley, East, and Stillwell, 1979)

Purpose: The purpose of this test is to measure the speed and power components of racquetball.

Description: The test battery consists of the following two test items: a short wall-volley test (speed component) and a long wall-volley test (power component).

Validity: Using instructors' ratings of students as the criterion measure, the validity coefficients for men and women combined were .79 for the short wall-volley test and .86 for the long wall-volley test.

Reliability: The estimated reliability of the short wall-volley test for the sum of trials over two days was determined to be .76 for men and .86 for women. Correlational coefficients for the long wall-volley test were .85 for men and .82 for women.

Age Level: Originally designed for college students, this test is appropriate for use with high school students.

Norms: College T-score norms for men and women are available in the original source.

Test Area: Racquetball court.

Test 1: Short Wall-Volley Test

Instructions: The participant stands behind the short service line, drops the ball, and volleys it against the front wall for 30 seconds. A one-minute practice period is followed by two 30-second trials.

Equipment Needed: Racquetball racquet, four new regulation racquetballs, marking tape, and a stopwatch.

Scoring Procedure: One point is awarded each time the ball legally hits the front wall during the 30-second period. The recorded score is the sum of legal hits of the two trials. No points are awarded when the participant steps over the restraining line to hit the ball or when the ball skips on the floor on the way to the wall.

Organizational Hints: There are no restrictions on the number of times the ball bounces before being volleyed. The participant may retrieve the ball in the front court but must return to a position behind the restraining line to put it back in play. Any type of stroke can be used to keep the ball in play. The scorer should be in the court and have two additional balls available in case the original is put out of play. The stopwatch is started when the dropped ball hits the floor for the first time.

Test 2: Long Wall-Volley Test

Instructions: The long wall-volley test is administered in the same manner as the short wall-volley test except for the location of the student on the court. For this test, the participant must volley the ball from behind a restraining line located 12 feet behind and parallel to the short service line.

Equipment: Racquetball racquet, four new regulation racquetballs, marking tape, and a stopwatch.

Scoring Procedure: One point is awarded for each time the ball legally hits the front wall during the 30-second period. The recorded score is the sum of legal hits of the two trials. No points are awarded when the participant steps over the restraining line to hit the ball or when the ball skips on the floor on the way to the wall.

Organizational Hints: Same as in the short volley test, except that the two extra balls may be conveniently placed in the backwall corners.

Measuring Tennis Skills

Revision of the Dyer Backboard Test (Hewitt, 1965)

Purpose: The purpose of this test is to measure the rallying and serving ability of students.

Validity: Converted *r*'s ranged from .68 to .73 for beginners and .84 to .89 for advanced players.

Reliability: Test-retest procedures resulted in correlational coefficients of .82 for beginners and .93 for advanced players.

Age Level: Ages 12 through college.

Norms: Not reported.

Test Area: A smooth gymnasium wall or rebound wall at least 20 feet high and 20 feet wide.

Instructions: The student takes two tennis balls and assumes a position behind a restraining line located 20 feet from unobstructed wall space. When ready, the student serves a tennis ball so it hits above the marked net line on the wall and continues to rally using any type of ground or volley stroke. Three 30-second trials are given.

Equipment Needed: Basket of tennis balls, tennis racquets, marking tape, tape measure, and a stopwatch.

Scoring Procedure: One point is scored each time the ball is hit above the three-foot net line on the wall (balls hitting on the line are considered good). No point is awarded if the student steps over the restraining line while executing the shot. The sum of the three trials is recorded as the student's score.

Organizational Hints: If the student loses control of the rally, one of the spare balls should be put in play by serving. This serve does not count as a point and no points are deducted for using the additional tennis balls. Lines on the wall should be one inch wide. A warm-up period on an adjacent wall area is allowed.

Hewitt's Tennis Achievement Test (1966)

Purpose: The purpose of this test battery is to measure the student's skill at executing ground strokes and serving the tennis ball.

Description: The battery consists of the following three items: test for forehand and backhand drive, service placement, and speed of service.

Validity: Coefficients ranged from .52 to .93.

Reliability: Correlational coefficients ranged from .75 to .93.

Age Level: The test is appropriate for high school through college students.

Norms: Normative information is available in the original source.

Test Area: Tennis court.

Test 1: Forehand and Backhand Drive Test

Instructions: The student assumes a position at the baseline at point X (Figure 6.29), while the test administrator stands on the other side of the net on the center service line at point Y. Using a tennis racquet, the test administrator hits five practice balls to the student's forehand just beyond the service court. The student moves into proper position and attempts to return the ball over the net and under a seven-foot-high rope, strung above the net parallel to it, so the ball lands as near to the baseline as possible in one of the target zones. Figure 6.29 shows the placement of the scoring zones for this test. Ten trials are given. The test is repeated to the backhand side.

Equipment Needed: A basket of tennis balls, tennis racquet, measuring tape, 7' x 2" x 2" poles, rope to span above net, and marking tape.

Scoring Procedure: The point values earned for each hit (forehand and backhand side) are totaled. The student's score is the sum of these values. Balls hit long, wide, or into the net are scored as 0. Shots that pass over the seven-foot rope and land in a scoring area are counted one-half of the score for that area. All lets are repeated.

Organizational Hints: To ensure consistency, the same test administrator should hit balls to all students.

Test 2: Service Placement Test

Instructions: The right service court is marked according to specifications described in Figure 6.30. A rope seven feet from the ground is strung directly over the net. After a 10-minute warm-up, the student serves 10 balls into the marked right service court. The ball must pass through the area marked by the top of the net and the rope.

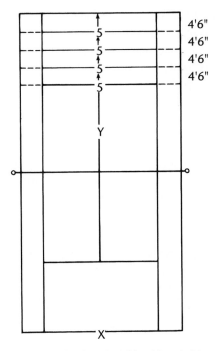

Figure 6.29 Layout for Hewitt's tennis forehand and backhand drive test.

Reprinted by permission of the American Alliance for Health, Physical Education, Recreation, and Dance, Reston, Virginia.

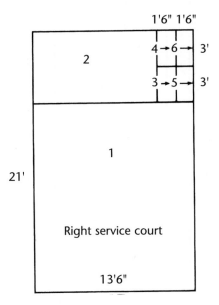

Figure 6.30 Layout for Hewitt's service placement test.

Reprinted by permission of the American Alliance for Health, Physical Education, Recreation, and Dance, Reston, Virginia.

Equipment Needed: A basket of tennis balls, tennis racquet, measuring tape, two-inch-square poles seven feet long, and marking tape.

Scoring Procedure: The point value for the target zone in which the ball hits is the score. The sum of the 10 trials is recorded as the student's score.

Organizational Hints: The instructor should demonstrate the proper service technique prior to administering the test.

Test 3: Speed of Service Test

Instructions: After considerable experimentation, it was determined that the distance a served ball traveled between its first and second bounce was a determinant of the speed of the ball. The court is marked in accordance with specifications detailed in Figure 6.31. This test should be conducted simultaneously with the Service Placement Test and should use the same rules.

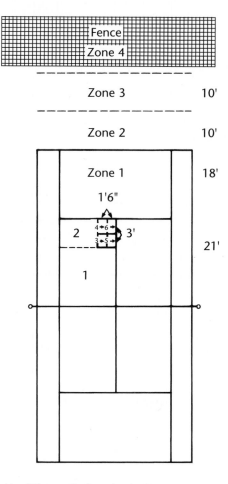

Figure 6.31 Layout for Hewitt's speed of service test.

Reprinted by permission of the American Alliance for Health, Physical Education, Recreation, and Dance, Reston, Virginia.

Equipment Needed: A basket of tennis balls, tennis racquet, measuring tape, two-inch-square poles seven feet long, rope, and marking tape.

Scoring Procedure: The target zone in which the ball hits on its second bounce (after a good serve) is noted. The point values for each serve are recorded. The sum of the 10 trials is recorded as the student's score.

For information on other tests that measure tennis skills, see the *Representative Readings* list at the end of the chapter.

Using Alternative Assessments

The wide variety of tests presented in this chapter represents instruments that can be used to quantitatively assess sports-related physical fitness and specific sports skills. Some of the tests are simple to administer and others require more time-consuming procedures. Specifically, some tests require more setup than others. There are many considerations about what tests you choose to assess your students. Please recall that Chapter 4 provided a long list of considerations in choosing a test.

Many teachers utilize alternative assessments to measure the psychomotor domain in addition to or instead of the tests presented previously in this chapter. These alternative assessments are generally based on well-constructed rating scales or checklists that have carefully worded rubrics to ensure validity and reliability of assessment. They are qualitative in nature and can provide formative assessment. Detailed information is provided in Chapter 9 on alternative assessment strategies.

As an example, suppose you are teaching a three-week basketball unit in a middle school setting. Your students come to your class on a daily basis, and you have a coed class of 35 students. It is likely that unit outcomes would include emphasis on the skills of passing, dribbling, and shooting. As you have learned, there is a battery of skills tests designed to measure these skills. However, you may choose to develop a rubric for rating these skills and observe students in drills and game situations to rate their skill proficiency. This may be more time efficient than organizing and testing 35 students. It is certainly possible that you can combine both quantitative and qualitative assessments in your unit. Many of the skills test batteries make excellent stations that can be used for students to do self-evaluation or peer evaluations. Likewise, the qualitative rating scales that are developed for alternative assessments can also be used for self-evaluation or peer evaluations.

You should be able to choose and effectively use many different types of assessment to assist your students in achieving the objectives of your program. You should use both the quantitative tests presented in this chapter and the qualitative methods presented in Chapter 9. When you finish reading Chapter 9, you should have a clear idea of how to incorporate alternative assessment strategies in your teaching.

SUMMARY

This chapter has focused on measuring sports-related physical fitness and specific sports skills that are included in the psychomotor domain. The field-based tests that are included have information about their purpose, instructions, validity and reliability, appropriate age level, testing materials and areas, scoring procedures, norms when available, and organizational hints. Section 1 of the chapter dealt with measuring skill-related physical fitness. Components of skill-related fitness were presented, and selected field tests to measure these components were described. Test batteries to assess skill-related physical fitness were also presented. Test batteries used in assessing skill-related physical fitness for students with disabilities were also detailed. Section 2 of the chapter highlights tests to measure specific sport skills. The tests cited in this chapter are appropriate for K–12 settings, require little expense, and are easy to administer.

DISCUSSION QUESTIONS

1. Psychomotor performance can be divided into sports-related physical fitness and specific sports skills. Explain the difference in these two main categories of psychomotor performance.

2. What are the fundamental skills necessary for children to acquire? In what order does the mastery of these skills usually occur?

3. What are some major considerations for psychomotor testing of which you should be aware when assessing students?

4. Provide an explanation about the appropriate uses of the results of psychomotor tests.

5. List and briefly describe the components of skill-related physical fitness. What variables or factors come into play with students in demonstrating competence in these various components?

6. What test battery would you choose for measuring general motor ability of students in a fifth grade physical education class? What choices would you make for students with disabilities that might be mainstreamed into your class?

7. Cite disadvantages and advantages of incorporating tests to measure specific sports skills into the physical education curriculum at the elementary school level, at the middle school level, and at the high school level.

8. Other than using specific sports skills tests, what options does a teacher have to assess student performance?

REFERENCES

American Alliance for Health, Physical Education, Recreation, and Dance. (1984). *AAHPERD skills test manual: basketball for boys and girls*. Reston, VA.

American Association for Health, Physical Education, and Recreation. (1965). *AAHPER skills test manual—volleyball for boys and girls*. Washington, DC.

_____. (1966). *AAHPER skills test manual for football*. Washington, DC.

_____. (1966). *AAHPER skills test manual—softball for boys*. Washington, DC.

_____. (1966). *AAHPER skills test manual—softball for girls*. Washington, DC.

_____. (1976). *AAHPER youth fitness test manual*. Reston, VA.

American Heart Association in Texas, and Governor's Commission on Physical Fitness. (1986). *Texas physical and motor fitness development program*. Austin, TX.

Barrow, H. M. (1954). Test of motor ability for college men. *Research Quarterly* 25:253–60.

Bass, R. I. (1939). An analysis of the components of tests of semi-circular canal function and of static and dynamic balance. *Research Quarterly* 10:33–42.

Bennett, C. L. (1956). Relative contributions of modern dance, folk dance, basketball, and swimming to motor abilities of college women. *Research Quarterly* 27:256–57.

Corbin, C. B., ed. (1980). *A textbook of motor development.* 2nd ed. Dubuque, IA: Wm. C. Brown.

Corbin, C. B., and Lindsey, R. (1988) *Concepts of physical fitness with laboratories.* 6th ed. Dubuque, IA: Wm. C. Brown.

Cratty, B. J. (1979). *Perceptual and motor development in infants and children.* Englewood Cliffs, NJ: Prentice-Hall.

Cratty, B. J., and Martin, M. M. (1969). *Perceptual-motor efficiency in children.* Philadelphia, PA: Lea and Febiger.

Cunningham, P., and Garrison, P. (1968). High wall volley test for women's volleyball. *Research Quarterly* 39:486–90.

Cureton, T. K. (1947). *Physical fitness appraisal and guidance.* St. Louis, MO: C. V. Mosby.

_____. (1951). *Physical fitness of champion athletes.* Urbana, IL: University of Illinois Press.

_____. (1964). Improving the physical fitness of youth. *Monographs of the Society for Research in Child Development* 4 (Serial No. 95, 29).

De Oreo, K. L. (1971). *Dynamic and static balance in preschool children.* Unpublished doctoral dissertation, University of Illinois.

_____. (1980). Performance of fundamental motor tasks. In C. B. Corbin, ed., *A textbook of motor development.* Dubuque, IA: Wm. C. Brown.

Di Nucci, J. M. (1976). Gross motor performance: A comprehensive analysis of age and sex differences between boys and girls ages six to nine years. In J. Broekhoff, ed., *Physical education, sports and the sciences.* Eugene, OR: Microform Publications, University of Oregon.

Eichstaedt, C., and Lavay, B. (1992). *Physical activity for individuals with mental retardation: Infancy through adulthood.* Champaign, IL: Human Kinetics Press.

Espenschade, A. (1947). Development of motor coordination in boys and girls. *Research Quarterly* 18:30–43.

Fleishman, E. A. (1964). *The structure and measurement of physical fitness.* Englewood Cliffs, NJ: Prentice-Hall.

Frederick, S. D. (1977). *Performance of selected motor tasks by three, four and five year old children.* Unpublished doctoral dissertation, Indiana University.

Fulton, C. D., and Hubbard, A. W. (1975). Effects of puberty on reaction and movement times. *Research Quarterly* 46:335–44.

Gallahue, D. L. (1982). *Understanding motor development in children.* New York: Wiley.

Gates, D. D., and Sheffield, R. P. (1940). Tests of change of direction as measurement of different kinds of motor ability in boys of the 7th, 8th, and 9th grades. *Research Quarterly* 11:136–74.

Govatos, L. A. (1966). Sex differences in children's motor performance. In *Collected papers of the eleventh interinstitutionalized seminar in child development.* Dearborn, MI: Michigan Education Department.

Green, K. H., East., W. B., and Hensley, L. D. (1987). A golf skills test battery for college males and females. *Research Quarterly for Exercise and Sport* 58:72–76.

Hensley, L. D., East, W. B., and Stillwell, J. L. (1979). A racquetball skills test. *Research Quarterly* 50:114–18.

Hewitt, J. E. (1965). Revision of the Dyer backboard tennis test. *Research Quarterly* 36:153–57.

――――――. (1966). Hewitt's tennis achievement test. *Research Quarterly* 37:231–37.

Jackson, A. B., and Baumgartner, T. A. (1969). Measurement schedules of sprint running. *Research Quarterly* 40:708–11.

Jensen, C. R., and Hirst, C. C. (1980). *Measurement in physical education and athletics.* New York: Macmillan.

Johnson, B. L., and Leach, J. (1968). *A modification of the Bass test of dynamic balance.* Unpublished study, East Texas State University, Commerce.

Johnson, L., and Londree, B. (1976). *Motor fitness testing manual for the moderately mentally retarded.* Reston, VA: AAHPERD.

Johnson, B. L., and Nelson, J. K. (1986). *Practical measurements for evaluation in physical education.* 4th ed. New York: Macmillan.

Keogh, J. F. (1965). *Motor performance of elementary school children.* Los Angeles: University of California.

Kilday, K., and Latchaw, M. (1961). *Study of motor ability in ninth grade boys.* Unpublished manuscript, University of California at Los Angeles.

Lockhart, A., and McPherson, F. A. (1949). The development of a test of badminton playing ability. *Research Quarterly* 20:402–05.

Lockhart, A., and Mott, J. A. (1951). An experiment in homogeneous grouping and its effect on achievement in sports fundamentals. *Research Quarterly* 22.

McCloy, C. H., and Young, N. D. (1954). *Measurements in health and physical education.* 3rd ed. New York: Appleton-Century-Crofts.

McDonald, L. G. (1951). The construction of a kicking skill test as an index of general soccer ability. Unpublished master's thesis, Springfield College, Massachusetts.

Milne, C., Seefeldt, V., and Reuschlein, P. (1976). Relationship between grade, sex, race and motor performance in young children. *Research Quarterly* 47:726–30.

O'Connor, M. F., and Cureton, T. K. (1945). Motor fitness tests for high school girls. *Research Quarterly* 16:302–14.

Pangrazi, R. P. (2001). *Dynamic physical education for elementary school children.* 13th ed. San Francisco: Benjamin Cummings.

Peterson, K. L., et al. (1974). *Factor analyses of motor performance for kindergarten, first, and second grade children: A tentative solution.* Paper presented at the Annual Convention of AAHPER, March, Anaheim, CA.

Poole, J., and Nelson, J. K. (1970). *Construction of a badminton skills test battery.* Unpublished manuscript, Louisiana State University, Baton Rouge.

Schilling, F., and Kiphard, E. J. (1976). The body coordination test. *Journal of Health, Physical Education, and Recreation* 47:37.

Scott, M. G. (1939). The assessment of motor abilities of college women through objective tests. *Research Quarterly* 10:63–83.

Scott, M. G., Carpenter, A., French, E., and Kuhl, L. (1941). Achievement examinations in badminton. *Research Quarterly* 12:242–53.

Seils, L. G. (1951). Agility-performance and physical growth. *Research Quarterly* 22:244.

Shick, J., and Berg, N. G. (1983). Indoor golf skill test for junior high school boys. *Research Quarterly for Exercise and Sport* 54:75–78.

State of North Carolina. (1977). *North Carolina motor fitness battery*. Raleigh, NC: Department of Public Instruction.

Strand, B., and Wilson, R. (1993). *Assessing sports skills*. Champaign, IL: Human Kinetics Press.

Ulrich, D. (2000). *Test of motor development-2*. 2nd ed. The Psychological Corporation. http://www.tpc-international.com/occu/TGMD2.htm.

Van Slooten, P. H. (1973). *Performance of selected motor-coordination tests by young boys and girls in six socio-economic groups*. Unpublished doctoral dissertation, Indiana University, Bloomington.

Yeagley, J. (1972). *Soccer skills test*. Unpublished manuscript, Indiana University, Bloomington.

Zaichkowsky, L. D., Zaichkowsky, L. B., and Martinek, T. J. (1980). *Growth and development: The child and physical activity*. St. Louis, MO: C. V. Mosby.

REPRESENTATIVE READINGS

Baumgartner, T., and Jackson, A. (1999). *Measurement for evaluation in physical education and exercise science*. Boston: McGraw-Hill.

Collins, D., and Hodges, P. (1978). *A comprehensive guide to sports skills test and measurement*. Springfield, IL: Charles C. Thomas.

Badminton Skills Tests

Beverlein, M. A. (1970). *A skill test for the drop shot in badminton*. Unpublished master's thesis, Southern Illinois University, Carbondale.

Hicks, J. V. (1967). *The construction and evaluation of a battery of five badminton skill tests*. Unpublished doctoral dissertation, Texas Woman's University, Denton.

Johnson, R. M. (1967). *Determination of the validity and reliability of the badminton placement test*. Unpublished master's thesis, University of Oregon, Eugene.

Kowert, E. A. (1968). *Construction of a badminton ability test battery for men*. Unpublished master's thesis, University of Iowa, Iowa City.

Popp, P. (1970). *The development of a diagnostic test to determine badminton playing ability*. Unpublished master's thesis, University of Washington, Seattle.

Basketball Skills Tests

Barrow, H. M. (1959). Basketball skill test. *Physical Educator* 16:26–27.

Cunningham, P. (1964). *Measuring basketball playing ability of high school girls*. Unpublished doctoral dissertation, University of Iowa, Iowa City.

Gilbert, R. R. (1968). *A study of selected variables in predicting basketball players*. Unpublished master's thesis, Springfield College, Massachusetts.

Mathews, L. E. (1963). *A battery of basketball skills tests for high school boys*. Unpublished master's thesis, University of Oregon, Eugene.

Moffit, D. (1970). *A measure of basketball skill for fifth and sixth grade boys*. Unpublished master's thesis, Central Washington State College, Ellensburg.

Plinke, J. F. (1966). *The development of basketball physical skill potential test batteries by height categories*. Unpublished doctoral dissertation, Indiana University, Bloomington.

Walter, R. J. (1968). *A comparison between two selected evaluative techniques for measuring basketball skill*. Unpublished master's thesis, Western Illinois University, Macomb.

Football Skills Tests

Cowell, C. C., and Ismail, A. H. (1961). Validity of a football rating scale and its relationship to social integration and academic ability. *Research Quarterly* 32:461–67.

Lee, R. C. (1965). *A battery of tests to predict football potential.* Unpublished master's thesis, University of Utah, Salt Lake City.

May, L. D. (1972). *A study of the measurement of potential football ability in high school players.* Unpublished master's thesis, Texas Tech University, Lubbock.

McDavid, R. F. (1978). Predicting potential in football players. *Research Quarterly* 49:98–104.

Sells, T. D. (1977). *Selected movement and anthropometric variables of football defensive tackles.* Unpublished doctoral dissertation, Indiana University, Bloomington.

Golf Skills Tests

Brown, H. S. (1969). A test battery for evaluating golf skills. *Texas AHPER Journal* 4:28–29.

Cochrane, J. F. (1960). *The construction of an indoor golf skills test as a measure of golfing ability.* Unpublished master's thesis, University of Minnesota, Minneapolis.

Cotten, D. J., Thomas, J. R., and Plaster, T. (1972). *A plastic ball test for golf iron skill.* Paper presented at AAHPER National Conference, March, Houston, TX.

McKee, M. E. (1950). A test for the full-swing shot in golf. *Research Quarterly* 21:40–46.

Thompson, D. H. (1969). Immediate external feedback in the learning of golf skills. *Research Quarterly* 40:589–94.

Vanderhoof, E. R. (1956). *Beginning golf achievement tests.* Unpublished master's thesis, University of Iowa, Iowa City.

West, C., and Thorpe, J. A. (1968). Construction and validation of an eight-iron approach test. *Research Quarterly* 39:115–120.

Racquetball Skills Tests

Buschner, C. A. (1976). *The validation of a racquetball skills test for college men.* Unpublished doctoral dissertation, Oklahoma State University, Stillwater.

Karpman, M. B., and Isaacs, L. D. (1979). An improved racquetball test. *Research Quarterly* 50:526–27.

Shannon, J., Brothers, J., and Ishee, J. (1991). Quick and effective skills test for racquetball. *Strategies,* November/December 1991: 24–25.

Soccer Skills Tests

Crew, V. N. (1968). *A skill test battery for use in service program soccer classes at the university level.* Unpublished master's thesis, University of Oregon, Eugene.

MacKenzie, J. (1968). *The evaluation of a battery of soccer skill tests as an aid to classification of general soccer ability.* Unpublished master's thesis, University of Massachusetts, Amherst.

Mitchell, J. R. (1963). *The modification of the McDonald Soccer Skill Test for upper elementary school boys.* Unpublished master's thesis, University of Oregon, Eugene.

Streck, B. (1961). *An analysis of the McDonald Soccer Skill Test as applied to junior high school girls.* Unpublished master's thesis, Fort Hays State College, Kansas.

Softball/Baseball Skills Tests

Cale, A. A. (1962). *The investigation and analysis of softball skill tests for college women.* Unpublished master's thesis, University of Maryland, College Park.

Elrod, J. M. (1969). *Construction of a softball skill test battery for high school boys*. Unpublished master's thesis, Louisiana State University, Baton Rouge.

Everett, P. W. (1952). The prediction of baseball ability. *Research Quarterly* 23:15–19.

Fox, M. G. (1954). A test of softball batting ability. *Research Quarterly* 25:26–27.

Kelson, R. E. (1953). Baseball classification plan for boys. *Research Quarterly* 24:304–07.

Shick, J. (1970). Battery of defensive softball skills test for college women. *Research Quarterly* 41:82–87.

Sopa, A. (1967). *The construction and standardization of skill tests to measure achievement in specific softball playing abilities*. Unpublished master's thesis, University of North Carolina, Greensboro.

Tennis Skills Tests

Avery, C. A.; Richardson, P. A.; and Jackson, A. W. (1979). A practical tennis serve test: Measurement of skill under simulated game conditions. *Research Quarterly* 50:554–64.

Cotton, D. J., and Nixon, J. (1968). A comparison of two methods of teaching the tennis serve. *Research Quarterly* 39:929–31.

DiGennaro, J. (1969). Construction of forehand drive, backhand drive, and serve tennis tests. *Research Quarterly* 40:496–501.

Elliot, B. C. (1982). Tennis: The influence of grip tightness on reaction impulse and rebound velocity. *Medicine and Science in Sports and Exercise* 14:348–52.

Hubbell, N. C. (1960). A battery of tennis skill tests for college women. Unpublished master's thesis, Texas Woman's University, Denton.

Kemp, J., and Vincent, M. F., (1968). Kemp-Vincent Rally Test of Tennis Skill. *Research Quarterly* 39:1000–04.

Powers, S. K., and Walker, R. (1982). Physiological and anatomical characteristics of outstanding female junior tennis players. *Research Quarterly for Exercise and Sport* 53:172–75.

Purcell, K. (1981). A tennis forehand–backhand drive skill test which measures ball control and stroke firmness. *Research Quarterly for Exercise and Sport* 52:238–45.

Volleyball Skills Tests

Brumbach, W. (1967). *Beginning volleyball: A syllabus for teachers*. Rev. ed. Eugene, OR: University of Oregon.

Clifton, M. (1962). Single hit volley test for women's volleyball. *Research Quarterly* 33:208–11.

Comeaux, B. A. (1974). *Development of a volleyball selection test battery for girls*. Unpublished master's thesis, Lamar University, Beaumont, Texas.

Farrow, B. E. (1970). *Development of a volleyball selection test battery*. Unpublished master's thesis, Lamar University, Beaumont, Texas.

Johnson, J. A. (1967). *The development of a volleyball skill test for high school girls*. Unpublished master's thesis, Illinois State University, Bloomington-Normal.

Kronquist, R. A., and Brumbach, W. B. (1968). A modification of the Brady volleyball skill test for high school boys. *Research Quarterly* 39:116–120.

Liba, M. R., and Stauff, M. R. (1963). A test for the volleyball pass. *Research Quarterly* 34:56–63.

Michalski, R. A. (1963). *Construction of an objective skill test for the underhand volleyball serve*. Unpublished master's thesis, University of Iowa, Iowa City.

Morrow, J. R., Jackson, A. B., Hosler, W. W., and Kachurik, J. K. (1979). The importance of strength, speed, and body size for team success in women's intercollegiate volleyball. *Research Quarterly* 50:429–37.

Puhl, J., Case, S., Fleck, S., and VanHandel, P. (1982). Physical and physiological characteristics of elite volleyball players. *Research Quarterly for Exercise and Sport* 53:257–62.

Ryan, M. F. (1969). *A study of tests for the volleyball serve.* Unpublished master's thesis, University of Wisconsin, Madison.

Shaveley, M. (1960). Volleyball skill tests for girls. In Division of Girls' and Women's Sports *Selected Volleyball Articles.* Washington, DC: American Association for Health, Physical Education, and Recreation.

Spence, D. W., Disch, J. G., Fred, H. L., and Coleman, A. E. (1980). Descriptive profiles of highly skilled women volleyball players. *Medicine and Science in Sports and Exercise* 12:299–302.

Thorpe, J., and West, C. (1967). A volleyball skills chart with attainment levels for selected skills. In *DGWS Volleyball Guide 1967–69.* Washington, DC: American Association for Health, Physical Education, and Recreation.

CHAPTER 7

Measuring
Cognitive Knowledge

Key Terms

answer

cognitive domain

difficulty index

discrimination index

distractor

essay test questions

halo effect

item analysis

item function

objective test questions

qualitative item analysis

quantitative item analysis

semiobjective test questions

stem

table of specifications

taxonomy of educational objectives

Objectives

1. Understand the importance of proper measurement and evaluation procedures regarding the cognitive domain in activity-based programs.

2. Demonstrate the ability to write test items that match stated objectives of the particular unit.

3. Explain the roles and relationship of the taxonomy of educational objectives and the table of specifications in test construction.

4. Compare the relative advantages and disadvantages of various types of test items (e.g., true/false, multiple choice, essay).

5. Perform quantitative item analysis using the difficulty index, discrimination index, and item function to improve the validity of a test.

6. Describe qualitative item analysis and discuss how it can be used to improve the validity of a test

A s discussed in Chapter 2, the **cognitive domain** includes intellectual abilities and skills ranging from rote memory tasks to the synthesis and evaluation of complex information. Because physical education is generally an activity-oriented discipline that emphasizes physical skills and physical fitness, administrators, teachers, parents, and students seldom link physical education with the cognitive domain. Likewise, the cognitive domain is often overlooked in other activity-based settings. In many instances, little thought or planning is given to ensuring that the individual client in an exercise science setting is receiving and comprehending information needed to understand the treatments, training, and fitness program in which he or she is involved. One of the biggest challenges in the health fitness industry is to motivate clients to adhere to their programs for an extended period of time. Many participants drop out within the first six weeks of a program. Ideally, the individuals in these programs should make lifestyle changes and pursue activity and exercise for a lifetime. Individuals who understand the importance of exercising, eating in moderation, breaking the smoking habit, and so forth, are much more likely to carry out their programs. Athletic trainers, physical therapists, exercise clinicians, and other exercise science practitioners should realize the motivational value of increasing the knowledge as well as health fitness levels of their clients. For this to happen, there must be a strong educational component to the program. Without planned measurement and evaluation procedures in place, the exercise science specialist cannot assess the cognitive component of the programs.

It is understandable that people outside the discipline might associate physical education solely with the contributions it can make to the psychomotor and health fitness domains. However, it is not as easily understood why trained physical educators so often neglect the critical cognitive components of physical education. The cognitive domain is an important area that should be addressed in a quality program at any level. Though the cognitive area is almost always included in the stated objectives of the program, the measurement and evaluation procedures concerning these objectives are often inadequate.

Learning the rules and strategies of a game, knowing the history of a sport, recognizing the benefits of various forms of exercise, designing a dance routine, analyzing and making corrections in the performance of a sports skill, understanding established safety procedures, and planning personalized fitness programs are examples of cognitive activities in physical education and exercise science. Understanding these things can help motivate a person to better performance in a selected activity. Establishing this cognitive link is critical in any good program.

In other subject disciplines, the cognitive domain is the major emphasis. Homework assignments, class activities, and written examinations in mathematics, science, social studies, and English are commonplace in the measurement and evaluation schemes of these disciplines. There is no reason why physical educators cannot use the same strategies to assess cognitive objectives in their field. This is not to suggest that physical education should move from the gymnasium to the classroom. Physical education must continue to emphasize skill/fitness goals in motor activity settings, but it should include strategies to ensure that students also gain a fundamental knowledge about the sports and fitness activities in which they participate.

In many secondary physical education settings, conceptual classes on wellness and exercise are being added into the curriculum. These classes are usually one semester long and teach students through a planned sequence of lecture and activities important information concerning proper exercise, body composition, nutrition, stress control, and other wellness topics. The cognitive component is a critical part of these classes. Even in lower elementary levels, physical education includes important information concerning healthy lifestyle habits. It is essential that the teacher have some measurement strategies in place to assess how much of the information is being processed and comprehended by students at any level.

In other activity-based settings, it may not be desirable to use formalized tests to assess cognitive achievement. However, surveys and questionnaires can be designed to determine clients' knowledge levels. Ensuring the validity of these instruments is as important as making sure tests given in school settings are well constructed. The same procedures for constructing tests can be applied to designing instruments to be used in nonschool settings. It would be desirable in most cases to assess a client's knowledge as she enters the program and then use follow-up assessments to monitor the client's progress in the cognitive area. Ideally, upon leaving a program each person should have the knowledge to continue the program without the supervision of the exercise science practitioner.

Measuring Cognitive Achievement

School Settings

Homework

There are several ways to measure the cognitive achievement of students. Students may complete projects or homework assignments relative to cognitive goals. Though these types of activities are certainly desirable, they should not be the only criteria for evaluation. There are a variety of homework assignments that can be given to students. Mitchell, Barton, and Stanne (2000) point out that homework can be cognitive, psychomotor, or affective by nature. If a student were given a homework assignment of charting how many free throws out of 50 attempts the student can make outside of class, this would be a psychomotor assignment. An assignment to watch a basketball game, observe "good" and "bad" sport instances, and to write a short paper summarizing the observations would fall into the affective category. Cognitive assignments can include such things as take-home exams, worksheets, puzzles, or a game analysis of an observed sporting event. Obviously, the sophistication of a homework assignment can differ dramatically between elementary, middle school, and high school students. Since the focus of this chapter is assessing the cognitive domain, we will focus our discussion on the role of homework in that area.

There are certain issues to consider when planning assignments done outside of class. Projects and homework assignments done away from the teacher's supervision are not always a true reflection of the work of the individual student. The student may enlist the aid of parents or help from other students. This is not necessarily bad, but overdependence on this type of work for measurement purposes may lead to invalid evaluations. The real value of outside assignments is to familiarize students with the material to meet educational objectives and, in some situations, prepare them for tests that are given under the supervision of the teacher.

For homework assignments to be effective in meeting objectives in the cognitive domain, they must be carefully planned in accordance with the needs and characteristics of your students. The teacher should clearly present the nature of the assignment, encourage student questions, make certain that the assignment is linked to student performance objectives, and give prompt feedback to students after the homework assignment is turned in. Students will consider homework assignments more important if they are graded by the teacher rather than by themselves or their peers. Although homework can be time consuming to plan and grade, the benefits of such tasks are numerous. The assignment should increase student achievement because it increases the students' time with the subject matter. It provides academic credibility of physical education to students, parents, teachers in other disciplines, and administrators. It provides a method by which to assess cognitive objectives other than formal testing procedures. Finally, creative homework assignments can motivate students to be active outside of the physical education class. It can help students make meaningful connections between physical education content and their lives outside of school.

Research on homework (Mitchell, Barton, and Stanne, 2000) has identified four major factors that influence the effectiveness of such assignments with increased student productivity.

- The homework assignments must be directly linked to class objectives and content that is covered in class.

- Homework must be designed with consideration of students' cognitive abilities and motivation.

- Positive parental attitudes and a supportive home environment are critical to successful completion of homework assignments.

- Holding students accountable for completing homework assignments is crucial.

Tests

Examinations may be oral or written. If oral examinations are used, only one student can be tested at a time. Because of the size of most classes, oral examinations are impractical except in unusual cases. It is generally recommended that the written examination be the major basis of measuring students' knowledge. The use of written examinations with content that matches the stated cognitive objectives provides a way to evaluate how well the objectives are being accomplished. When properly constructed and administered, the examination should provide valid data that accurately reflect the cognitive achievement of the individual student as well as a means of evaluating students' knowledge relative to the stated objectives.

You must consider the cognitive development of your students when designing exams. The reading and writing skills of students obviously affect the type of test to give or whether it is appropriate to give formal tests. Generally, it is not advisable to use written exams with K–3 students. Upper elementary aged students can answer objective and short-answer essay questions at lower cognitive levels. Developmentally, middle school and high school students can be expected to display the ability to apply, analyze, synthesize, and evaluate information. Thus, cognitive objectives and assignments should reflect these more mature cognitive processes.

The written test provides important feedback to the teacher as to whether students are meeting the cognitive objectives. If a majority of a class fails to perform to expectations, this may indicate some shortcoming on the part of the instructor. The test might be too difficult for various reasons: Not enough time was devoted to cognitive aspects of the unit in class; homework and class activities did not prepare students adequately for the test; and so forth. Without the results of the written test, the teacher may not be aware of any problems and, thus, be unable to make necessary adjustments in future units.

Scheduling and administering a written test can be an effective way to encourage students to learn about a given subject. If no tests are given, most students will not study extensively enough to gain an understanding of the material. Further, when the students are given immediate results of their performance on a written examination, they are more likely to learn from their mistakes and be reinforced for their correct responses.

Some students are not highly successful at motor skill activities but excel in cognitive work. Homework assignments, projects, and written tests give this type of student an opportunity for success in physical education, which may stimulate greater efforts in other areas of physical education. Students should be given the opportunity to demonstrate their knowledge in physical education and be positively reinforced by good performance.

It is sometimes a good strategy to give a test and let the students grade their own tests and make necessary corrections. This type of self-test would not be used for grading purposes but is valuable because it allows students to evaluate themselves and, in some cases, motivates them to learn material on which they did poorly. The self-test might be a shortened version of sample questions that the students could expect on upcoming tests. This is good preparation for an examination that will be administered for grading purposes.

Nonschool Settings

In nonschool settings, which also should include emphasis on the cognitive domain, giving formalized tests is an option, but may not be the best choice. Whereas a physical education teacher may have a large number of students, the typical exercise science setting does not have as many clients assigned to a practitioner. Also, schools are on set schedules, while programs in nonschool settings are ongoing. For these reasons, surveys and questionnaires may be a better method for checking clients' knowledge. In many cases, an oral questionnaire may be the most desirable option. Whatever method is chosen, the exercise science specialist should make every effort to ensure the validity of the technique being used. The same type of planning that this chapter details concerning test construction should be applied in the design of nonschool surveys or questionnaires. Planned measurement and evaluation strategies that articulate the goals of the program should be in place to assess not only the progress of individual clients, but also the program's effectiveness.

Planning the Written Test

Planning a written test is an important step in an evaluation scheme because the resulting examination must have content validity. In order for a test to be valid, the test items should match the instructional objectives. To ensure that a test will have content validity, an educator must link the learning outcome and conditions specified in the test question to the learning outcome and conditions described in the performance objective (Kubiszyn and Borich, 1984).

Matching Test Items to Objectives

Test items must be written with stated objectives in mind, and those objectives should match the learning objectives. Test items should not be easier or more difficult than the learning objectives. The process of matching test items to objectives may seem somewhat difficult, but with careful planning and a little practice, a teacher can write appropriate test items. Listed below are some examples of test items that do not match the objective. Teachers sometimes make the mistake of including test items that are more difficult than the objective. For example,

Objective: Identify activities and sports as being primarily aerobic or anaerobic in nature.

Test Item: Explain why jogging is considered an aerobic activity.

In this case, the objective asks only for identification of various activities as aerobic or anaerobic, yet the test question asks for an explanation. If the explanation is considered important, it should be included in the objective.

Often, test items are much easier than the objective. For example,

Objective: From memory, draw a tennis court and label the lines.

Test Item: Given the following diagram of the playing surface, label the lines of a tennis court.

In this case, the test item would not accurately measure the achievement of the objective. The test question does not require the student to recall and draw the court.

The best way to gain an accurate measurement of achievement is to ask students to demonstrate mastery of the subject matter in a way that is consistent with the objectives.

Objective: Describe how to "block out" when rebounding in basketball.

Test Item: When rebounding in basketball, explain how to "block out."

If a student can answer this test item satisfactorily, then the teacher can be certain that the objective has been achieved.

Though the examples given refer to test items in a short-answer format, the same guidelines of matching test items with objectives apply to all types of test items, including multiple choice, true/false, matching, and essay. By taking care to match the learning outcome and conditions of the objective and the test item, regardless of format, teachers can ensure content validity.

Taxonomy of Educational Objectives

Cognitive objectives can be stated in terms that range from simple to complex. If an objective requires a student to memorize material, it is relatively simple compared to an objective that requires a student to synthesize information to make an evaluation of some type. The more advanced a student is, the more advanced the objective should become. The **taxonomy of educational objectives** devised by Bloom, Englehart, Hill, Furst, and Krathwohl (1956) is the most popular system of classifying the levels of cognitive complexity. It delineates six levels of varying complexity from the knowledge level (simplest) to the evaluation level (most complex). Figure 7.1 illustrates the various levels of the taxonomy.

According to Bloom et al. (1956), the taxonomy levels are hierarchical in that the higher level objectives include the lower level objectives. Thus, if an objective is written at the application level, the successful completion of this objective would require cognitive processes to take place at the comprehension and knowledge levels as well as the application level. Each level of the taxonomy of objectives has different characteristics, which are described below with examples of verbs usually associated with the different levels.

Knowledge (recalling information)

Objectives at the knowledge level involve recognition and recall. Test items ask students to remember such items as facts, rules, and definitions. Some verbs that are used with the knowledge level are:

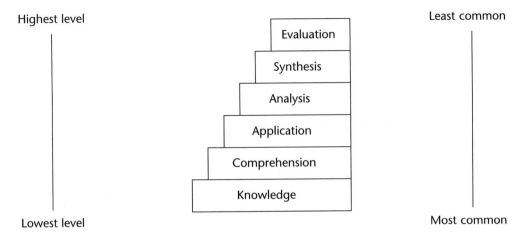

Figure 7.1 Taxonomy of educational objectives: cognitive domain.

From *Educational Testing and Measurement: Classroom Application and Practice,* 3rd ed., by Tom Kubiszyn and Gary Borich. Copyright © 1990 by Scott, Foresman and Company. Reprinted by permission of HarperCollins Publishers.

list	name	label	demonstrate
match	select	define	tell
recite	state	recall	locate

Terms such as *who, what, where, when,* and *why* are often included in test items at the knowledge level.

Sample objective: The student will be able to define "aerobic" and "anaerobic" in terms of exercise.

Comprehension (understanding information)

Some level of understanding is required for meeting objectives at the comprehension level, which is considered the lowest level of understanding. To demonstrate comprehension, a student must use knowledge to interpret, restate, or draw conclusions. Some verbs commonly used with this level of objectives are:

translate	explain	infer	change
estimate	predict	paraphrase	rephase
distinguish	summarize	defend	transform

Sample objective: The student will be able to explain the difference between aerobic exercise and anaerobic exercise.

Application (using facts and rules)

Objectives at this cognitive level require students to use learning in a variety of settings. Application questions present the problem in a different and often applied context. This means the student cannot rely on the question or the context to decide what prior knowledge must be used to solve the problem. Some verbs used in conjunction with the application level are:

develop	organize	modify	group
solve	apply	use	illustrate
employ	produce	prepare	classify

Sample objective: The student will be able to apply the principles of exercise in planning an aerobic workout.

Analysis (separating a whole into parts)

Analysis-level objectives require the student to identify parts or elements, discover interactions or relationships, point out errors of inference or contradictions, or differentiate among facts, opinions, and conclusions. Questions at this level often call for the student to compare and contrast ideas or distinguish relationships. Verbs found in analysis objectives include:

analyze	examine	determine	associate
outline	relate	point out	compare
divide	deduce	diagram	contrast

Sample objective: Examine the sport of racquetball in terms of the contributions it can make to the various components of physical fitness.

Synthesis (combining ideas to form a whole)

Objectives written at the synthesis level involve producing something original or unique. Synthesis might involve rearrangement and combining of elements to construct a new whole. Some verbs that describe learning outcomes at the synthesis level are:

construct	hypothesize	modify	compose
formulate	create	plan	categorize
devise	invent	design	predict

Sample objective: Plan a progressive exercise program for a three-month time frame designed to improve cardiovascular fitness and body composition.

Evaluation (developing opinions, judgments, or decisions)

This level of cognition is the most advanced of all levels because all other levels of cognitive activity are prerequisite to making an evaluation. Objectives written at this level require a student to make judgments about methods, materials, ideas, performance, or products with a specific purpose. Test items at this level ask the student to provide a rationale for such judgments. Verbs associated with objectives and test items at the evaluation level include:

assess	evaluate	prioritize	estimate
appraise	interpret	judge	rate
defend	justify	critique	revise

Sample objective: Evaluate the quality of the exercise programs at a local fitness spa.

Table of Specifications

As we have seen, educational objectives should be written at different levels of the taxonomy and test items should match the objectives. Test items testing student achievement of the objectives should, therefore, represent similar levels of the cognitive domain.

An important step in test planning is making sure that test items and objectives are written at the different levels of the cognitive taxonomy. In order to do this, a **table of specifications** may be created to help the teacher include all details necessary to construct a valid test. This table is analogous to a builder using a blueprint for constructing a building. This blueprint of test construction guides the teacher in selecting items for the test. A good test will include items representative of not just one level of the cognitive taxonomy but items covering several levels of cognitive complexity.

A table of specifications aids the teacher in sampling all the important content areas that a given test covers. Everyone, at some point in his academic career, has taken an exam that did not reflect what was covered and emphasized in class activities. Tests such as these are unfair and do not measure a student's knowledge of the subject. Using a table of specifications can alleviate this problem.

This method of planning a written exam can also be an invaluable aid in planning and organizing instruction because the blueprint should be established before a unit is started. The objectives of the course, the class activities used to meet those objectives, the actual presentation and sequence of the activities, and the testing strategies to measure the degree to which these objectives are met must be thought out in advance so that teaching can be organized and efficient. Minor changes are expected as the unit progresses, but severe alterations from an overall unit plan should seldom be necessary.

An example of a table of specifications is shown in Table 7.1. Steps for constructing such a table are as follows:

1. Determine the educational objectives for the unit.

2. Determine the weighting of the educational objectives in terms of the level of cognitive thinking that is required. For example,

Knowledge	25%
Comprehension	10%
Application	35%
Analysis	20%
Synthesis	5%
Evaluation	5%

3. Determine the approximate time spent in each of the content areas of the specific unit. For instance,

History	5%
Rules	25%
Equipment	5%
Etiquette	10%
Skill and Technique	35%
Strategies	20%

Table 7.1 Table of specifications for 100-point test in beginning tennis.

			COGNITIVE LEVELS						
			Knowledge 25%	Comprehension 10%	Application 35%	Analysis 20%	Synthesis 5%	Evaluation 5%	Total number of points for each content area
CONTENT AREAS	History	5%	1.25	.5	1.75	1.0	.25	.25	5
	Rules	25%	6.25	2.5	8.75	5.0	1.25	1.25	25
	Equipment	5%	1.25	.5	1.75	1.0	.25	.25	5
	Etiquette	10%	2.5	1.0	3.5	2.0	.5	.5	10
	Skill & technique	35%	8.75	3.5	12.25	7.0	1.75	1.75	35
	Strategies	20%	5.0	2.0	7.0	4.0	1.0	1.0	20
	Total number of points for each cognitive level		25	10	35	20	5	5	100

4. After the percentages for cognitive levels and content areas have been determined, set up the table of specifications. The course content areas and their weighting are listed down the left side of the table and the levels of cognition and their weighting are listed across the top.

5. The weight for any cell in the table is determined by multiplying the intersecting values from the left side and top of the cell. For example, the first cell represents knowledge (25 percent) and history (5 percent). Thus, the weighting of the cell would be .25 x .05 = .0125. This figure is multiplied by the number of intended items on the exam to determine how many items should come from this cell. The test illustrated in Table 7.1 has 100 items; therefore, .0125 x 100 = 1.25. Since it is not possible to ask .25 of a question, the weighting of each cell should be used as a guide when writing test items.

6. Adding the values in each cell across each row gives the total number of items for each area of course content. Adding the values in each cell down each column totals the number of items for each cognitive level.

This table of specifications helps the test writer use content areas to implement the different cognitive levels of the educational objectives. A general rule to follow when weighting cognitive levels is to weight introductory-level tests predominantly at the knowledge, comprehension, and application levels. If classes are at the intermediate and/or the advanced levels, the analysis, synthesis, and evaluation levels should be emphasized. It should also be pointed out that items designed to require the higher levels of cognition are more difficult to construct. Good knowledge and comprehension questions are easier to write than synthesis and evaluation items. However, the extra time it takes to construct higher-level questions pays off as a better designed test to measure cognitive achievement.

Previously in this chapter, we mentioned the importance of content validity in written examinations. By constructing a table of specifications, a teacher ensures that the written test meets the criteria for content validity. As we have seen, constructing a valid test involves a lot of thought and time to do it right. Unfortunately, many teachers do not take the time to do it right. As a result, tests used often do not reflect objectives and content covered in the unit. However, if teachers are interested in developing quality physical education programs that are useful to the students and to the school, they will realize that the time and effort it takes to construct a valid test is a worthwhile investment.

Selection of Test Items

Ayers (2001) provides some excellent guidelines for initial test development and selection of test items:

- Provide clear instructions.
- Avoid the use of trick questions or questions that include trivial details.
- Balance the use of gender across all items.
- Balance the use of ethnicity to represent all students.
- Avoid the use of stereotypes in dress, names, activities, physical appearances, etc.

Many teachers typically overlook the last three guidelines as they word their test items. Many schools have a wide diversity of ethnic groups and cultures. It is all right to use common names like "Thomas" and "Sarah" in test questions, but representing something other than European American students should also be done (e.g., Shantrell, Manuel, Ariel, Rashad, Yoshio). Teachers should also strive to use non-stereotypical examples (girls in wrestling or boys in dance) in test items with equal emphasis on male and female references.

After making decisions about the content areas of the written test, a teacher must decide the format of the test and begin to write test items. Many times the nature of the content area dictates the format of the test items. Certain types of subject matter lend themselves to multiple choice or true/false format, while an essay-type question is better suited for other types of content information. Generally, higher level cognitive objectives require essay-type questions, while lower level cognitive objectives can be tested with matching, true/false, and multiple choice questions. Mood (1980) classified the different types of test questions into three general categories: objective, semiobjective, and essay. **Objective test questions** are free from any subjective judgment during grading. True/false, matching, and multiple-choice test items are classified as objective. **Semiobjective test questions** include completion and short-answer items. They are so named because very little organization of information is needed on the student's part, and the response is checked to see if it matches the correct answer. Some subjectivity may be included when partial credit is awarded, but grading procedures are usually similar to these for objective questions. When answering **essay test questions**, the student must formulate a response that is graded in a subjective manner because judgmental decisions must be made about the response.

Mood (1980) further points out that subjectivity is present in every test, regardless of the type of questions used. The decisions about the content of the test as well as the format involves subjective decisions on the part of the instructor. Because subjectivity involves the biases and experiences of just one person, the amount of subjectivity should be reduced as much as possible in the construction and grading of tests. The use of a table of specifications and the revision of test items after a test is given are two ways to reduce subjectivity.

Knowledge of the advantages and disadvantages of various types of test items is also crucial to the construction of a valid test. Since the teacher has a choice of several types of questions, this knowledge is essential. The following sections discuss the advantages and disadvantages of various test-item formats and give suggestions for writing different types of questions.

True/False

The true/false format is an objective and convenient method of testing. The true/false item consists of a statement that gives a student the choice of two possible answers. It is not time consuming to write this type of question, and it is easy to score in an objective manner. Further, it allows coverage of a wide range of material, some of which may not be appropriately covered with another type of question. Alternate forms of the true/false format are answering yes/no or right/wrong. The true/false format may also be modified by asking the student to correct the false statements.

The disadvantage of the true/false format is that it encourages guessing. Sometimes students who actually know the material better will interpret the question and "read too much" into the statement causing mistakes that a weaker student will not make. True/false questions tend to test isolated facts (knowledge level) rather than concepts that require higher levels of cognition.

The following guidelines are suggested when writing true/false questions:

1. Clearly explain the desired way of marking true and false answers before the students begin the test. Writing out "true" or "false" can eliminate any confusion in handwriting between a "T" and an "F." Another way to prevent confusion when scoring the exam is to provide a "T" and an "F" on the test sheet and have students circle their response.

2. Make sure that true and false statements are about the same length. There is a tendency for true statements to be lengthier than false statements. Use relatively short statements and eliminate excessive words.

3. Include approximately the same number of true and false items or slightly more false items. Since students have a tendency to mark "true" when they are uncertain, the false statements usually discriminate better.

4. Use statements that are clearly true or clearly false. However, false statements should not be discernible to the uninformed.

5. Avoid the following:

   a. complex or ambiguous statements

   b. double-negative statements

   c. determiners such as never, always, sometimes, or often

    d. items straight from the text that are used out of context

    e. placing items so that answers are in a systematic order

Matching

The use of matching items is another popular and convenient objective format for testing. They can be used to cover a wide range of material in relatively little space. Like true/false questions, they are quick to write and easy to grade. The matching format consists of two columns of words or phrases, and the student must match each item in one column with the appropriate item in the other. A disadvantage of matching items is that they only test a student's recognition of the material.

When writing matching items, the following guidelines should be followed:

1. It is important that each list include items similar to one another. For example, a list might include dates, names, or terminology but should not mix these things together.

2. A matching section should include about 10–12 items in the description list. The option list should include more items than the description list to inhibit using a process of elimination for selection. Every distractor in the option list should be a plausible alternative.

3. There should be only one correct choice for each item in the description list and an alternative from the option list should only be used once.

4. The items in both lists should be arranged in some systematic fashion, usually alphabetically.

5. Each item in the description list should be numbered and each item in the option list should be lettered.

Multiple Choice

Another common objective format is the multiple choice question. This format is a little more complex than those previously discussed. Three components make up the multiple choice question: the stem, the distractors, and the answer. The **stem** is an incomplete sentence or a question; the **distractors** are the incorrect options; and the **answer** is the correct option.

A unique characteristic of multiple choice questions is that they can be written to measure levels of cognition higher than the knowledge level. The multiple choice format has several other advantages: The questions are easy to grade, can cover almost all types of materials, and can be used at virtually all levels of education. Properly written, they discourage guessing more than do other objective formats.

There are disadvantages to this type of question as well. Even though multiple choice questions can cover higher levels of cognition, they often emphasize isolated facts. They are time consuming and difficult to prepare when done properly. Writing good distractors can be particularly troublesome. As a rule of thumb, if difficulties arise with devising adequate distractors, it may be that the material being tested lends itself to another format.

The stem of the multiple choice item should clearly identify the problem in a concise way. Often the use of questions as a stem is more effective than using an incomplete sentence. If the stem is an incomplete sentence, the distractors must be written in a form to conform to the stem. If written in a question form, the alternatives must only conform to each other. A test-wise student will be able to eliminate distractors if there are clues in the content of the question. For example, if the stem ends with the word "an," then the student can deduce that the correct response must start with a word starting with a vowel. In cases such as this, the stem should be ended with "a/an" so as not to give any hints.

Other suggestions for using multiple choice items are as follows:

1. When possible, the stem should be written in positive terms rather than stated in a negative way.

2. Three or four distractors should be written plus the correct answer for each item. It is not necessary to have the same number of distractors on every question. The distractors should be written in parallel form and be related to the stem in a plausible way.

3. Distractors such as "none of the above," "all of the above," and "both b. and c." should be used sparingly, if at all. There should be one alternative that is clearly the correct answer.

4. The distractors and correct answer should be about the same length. The more similar the content of options, the more difficult the item becomes.

5. The correct answer should be listed with near equal frequency in each of the possible positions of a, b, c, d, and e in the list of options. Any sort of pattern that would help the student guess the right answer should be avoided.

6. Ambiguity of distractors can be reduced by having others with knowledge of the test material review it and by modifying or eliminating troublesome test items after administering the test.

7. Giving the correct answer for one question in the stem of another question should be guarded against.

Completion Items

Completion items are a commonly used semiobjective format on a written test. With this type of question, the student is expected to fill in the blank to answer the test question. This type of item reduces the problem of guessing, and it also requires the student to recall specific information rather than recognize it. In order to complete this type of test, the student must study more intensely.

Although this type of item is easy to prepare, it requires the teacher to subjectively decide which areas are to be tested. With some completion items, there may be more than one correct response, which can complicate grading procedures. This causes the grader to make some subjective judgments about the answer, hence the grading procedure is less objective. However, when writing items so that only one answer is correct, the completion items tend to test isolated facts in the material.

For the completion item format, the following guidelines are suggested:

1. When possible, items should require a single-word answer or a brief, definitive statement. Avoid indefinite statements that can be answered correctly by several responses.

2. Limit the number of blanks in the question so that the item does not become indefinite.

3. Prevent awkward sentences by constructing the item so that the blank is located near the end of the statement.

4. Be sure the item clearly defines the problem for the person taking the test. Use precise language to accurately formulate the subject matter of the question.

5. If the correct answer is stated numerically, indicate the unit of measurement and desired accuracy to be expressed.

6. Make sure all blanks are the same length in each question and use "a/an" before blanks to avoid giving any inadvertent hints.

Short-Answer Questions

Sometimes the short-answer question, another semiobjective test format, can be used in place of completion questions if ambiguity becomes a problem. When the short-answer format is used, it is critical that the respondent understand the limits concerning the length of the answer. The advantages and disadvantages of this format are similar to those of the completion item questions. It is recommended that the short-answer format only be used when there is clearly a correct answer that can be given in one or two words.

Essay

Unlike objective and semiobjective formats in which the student selects an answer, the essay format requires the student to supply the answer by mentally outlining and composing a response that may be quite extensive. Depending upon the essay question, the student may be required to organize, analyze, synthesize, and evaluate information. In short, any or all levels of cognition may be required to make a suitable response.

Like the objective and semiobjective test items previously discussed, essay items can be well constructed and clearly written or poorly constructed and vague. Well-constructed essay questions try to test complex cognitive skills of the students. They ask a student to use information to analyze and evaluate novel situations or provide opportunities for originality and innovation in application and problem solving. A poorly constructed essay question may require the student only to recall information as it was presented in lecture or in assigned reading, or it may be so poorly written that the student does not know what is expected as a satisfactory response.

Properly written essay questions have several advantages over questions in the objective and semiobjective formats. First, because a smaller number of questions is required, an essay test is quicker to construct. Second, when students prepare for an essay test, they must study larger units of information rather than memorize isolated facts. Third, responses to essay questions allow freedom of expression linked with higher order cognitive processes. Students are able to write answers on controversial issues that reflect attitudes and opinions based upon synthesis and evaluation of pertinent information. Fourth, because the student must supply the answer, guessing is eliminated.

However, a number of problems are also associated with essay tests. The major disadvantage of an essay test is the subjectivity of grading. Two different graders may give widely divergent amounts of credit for a certain answer. The same teacher might grade the same question differently on two different occasions. Essay tests are difficult to score because there are often several pages of student handwriting to read and evaluate. Misspellings, grammatical errors, and poor handwriting are elements that can influence grading. In some cases, longer essay answers receive higher marks, which causes students to adopt a rambling, all-inclusive style of writing. Another grading problem is the **halo effect**, in which a teacher forms an opinion of a student's ability and is influenced by that opinion when grading the student's paper. Because a large number of items is not feasible on an essay examination, sampling all areas of instructional content can be a problem. From a student and teacher point of view, fatigue can be more of a problem than with objective items, since it takes longer to answer and grade most essay tests.

A number of procedures can alleviate the lack of reliability in grading essay items. The following steps are suggested by Kubiszyn and Borich (1984):

1. Write good essay items. Phrase the questions so that the cognitive processes required to answer the question are clear. Set restrictions on response length.

2. When appropriate, use several restricted-range questions rather than a single extended-range question. This will help scoring reliability and ensure a wider range of content to be covered. Restricted-range questions are those covering less information and requiring a shorter answer; extended-range questions are broader, requiring a more extensive answer.

3. Specify in advance what is expected in the response and use a predetermined grading scheme. Preparing an ideal answer to the question will help identify the specific criteria for a good answer. Write the ideal response to the question and grade based on this criterion answer.

4. Make sure that the scoring scheme is used consistently. Do not favor one student over the other because of past performance.

5. Use a system so that you do not know what student's paper is being graded. Some sort of simple coding system may be used to ensure anonymity.

6. Score all the answers to one question before going on to the next item. This helps maintain consistency.

7. Establish a method so performance on previous questions is not known. This will help reduce the halo effect.

8. Try to arrange for reevaluation of the papers before returning them. To truly check reliability, each paper should be graded twice by independent graders and the results compared. If this is not feasible, the same teacher may grade the papers with a time interval of sufficient length so that he or she cannot recall prior scores. If there are serious discrepancies in the ratings, the reliability of the scoring is in question.

With these suggestions for increasing the objectivity and reliability of grading essay items, the following recommendations are made for the construction of essay questions:

1. Use appropriate verbs in the phrasing of the question to specify how the question should be answered.

2. Allow sufficient time to plan and construct the essay item. Keep the objectives and instructional content in mind when writing the essay question.

3. Avoid giving the students a choice of questions to answer. All students should respond to the same questions.

4. Use several short essay questions rather than one question that requires a longer response.

5. Consider the time that students will need to plan and write essay answers. If too many questions are given, students will not have time to adequately formulate answers. Fatigue may become a factor.

6. Set limits on the length of responses. Suggested time allotments for individual questions and time limits for the entire exam are often helpful.

7. Make use of essay questions only when instructional content and objectives make them the best choice. If learning objectives can be effectively tested with objective items, then essay questions should not be used.

Administering the Written Test

When done correctly, planning and constructing a written test is a time-consuming process. It takes a substantial amount of effort to write objectives, put together a table of specifications, select a format for test items, and write the test questions. Nevertheless, it is a necessary process to accurately assess student progress toward cognitive objectives in a valid manner. All of this work may be wasted if the test is not assembled and administered properly.

Assembling the Test

When the test is assembled, the questions should be grouped by format. For instance, all the multiple choice items should be put together and all the true/false items should be put together. This will make grading easier and will enable students to work in one format at a time rather than switching frequently. By following this rule, directions for a given format will only have to be stated once.

All instructions should be printed on the examination, making the directions as clear and concise as possible. Directions should be checked to make certain that they include information about how and where to record answers, the basis for selecting answers, and how many points each item is worth. It is also important to provide a space for the name of the student and to remind students to put their names on the exam. They are more likely to remember to put their name on the exam if there is a space provided.

The teacher should attempt to arrange the test items within each section in ascending order of difficulty. Putting the easier items first allows the student to gain confidence and alleviate tension associated with taking a test. If a test has never been given before, it may be difficult to know which items will prove to be more difficult. In these cases, the items should be randomly arranged within each item format. The test should be assembled so that there is adequate space between items and subsections, and each item is distinct from another. When options for multiple choice or matching questions are listed, all options should be on the same page. Similarly, students should not have to go from one page to another to finish reading a true/false or completion item. If court diagrams or other illustrations are used, they should be placed directly above the questions to which they refer and, if possible, the illustration and questions kept on the same page.

After the test is assembled, the teacher should prepare the answer key and make sure there is no pattern of answers and that answers are distributed appropriately in multiple choice and true/false questions. It is important to proofread the test for typographical errors or grammatical mistakes. The exam should be checked for grammatical clues in which elements of one question might answer another. It is a good idea to have another teacher proofread the test to check the clarity of directions and test items as well as to spot any other errors.

Giving the Test

It is the teacher's responsibility to provide an environment that maximizes the probability that the test results are valid indicators of students' knowledge. With this in mind, an atmosphere should be provided that is quiet, well lit, and comfortable. Students should have adequate space to work and should be arranged so that the possibility of cheating is minimized. Control of cheating is crucial to the validity of test scores and to student attitudes about written tests.

The teacher should plan an efficient way of distributing and collecting the examinations. Any ground rules about time limits, restroom policies, sharpening pencils, and so forth, should be discussed before the test is distributed. Suggestions to students about test-taking strategies, such as "Check your answers before you turn in your test" or "Don't spend too much time on one question," should be made before handing out the examinations. Once the students have the test, they are less likely to listen to what the teacher is saying. Immediately after the exams are distributed, the students should be told to check their copies to make certain that all pages are included and to put their names on the exams.

It is important that the teacher actively monitor the exam. Moving throughout the testing area and carefully watching students discourages copying. The teacher can also help the students pace themselves by periodically advising them about how much time is left in the exam period. Any individual questions should be answered at the student's desk in a quiet manner. The teacher must be careful, however, not to give any advantage to the questioning student over others by the answer that is given.

Grading the Test

Many teachers make use of a separate answer sheet when using objective or semiobjective tests, enabling them to grade questions very quickly and efficiently. Suggestions for grading essay tests were discussed at length in a previous section of this chapter. Whatever types of items are included on the test, the answer key should be prepared in advance and checked for mistakes. The tests should be graded and returned to students as quickly as possible; however, test scores of individual students should be kept confidential. Students can decide whether to divulge their own test scores.

Testing Students with Disabilities

It has been mentioned earlier that a teacher must consider the characteristics and needs of students in assessment situations. An excellent example of this is when a written test is administered to a student with a disability. It may be appropriate to design the test and plan the administration of the test with the help of a special education teacher or teacher's aide. It is important to make appropriate accommodations for the student to be able to take the test. Certain types of written tests may not be appropriate. In those cases, alternative tests may need to be developed or other methods of assessing the cognitive domain can be considered.

Analyzing the Test

Regardless of how much time and effort is spent constructing a written test, there will be items on the test that are ambiguous, inappropriate, or invalid in some way. Some problems will not surface until after the test has been administered. For these reasons, it is important that a test be analyzed to check the effectiveness of the examination. In most cases, certain items on the test will need to be modified or deleted. The end result of this process will be a more valid test. **Item analysis** may be done qualitatively or quantitatively. Both methods are valuable in assessing test quality.

Quantitative Item Analysis

Quantitative item analysis is used very effectively with objective test items. It is a numerical procedure for analyzing test items and is particularly appropriate for multiple choice formats, since it will give information about the usefulness of both the distractors and the correct answer. Quantitative analysis is also the most appropriate for a norm-referenced test in which the teacher is interested in determining who learned the material and who did not. A valid test will "discriminate" between those students who know the material and those who do not. The results on such a test will be a spread of grades so that the teacher can determine the true knowledge of various students.

A quantitative item analysis provides information about the difficulty index, the discrimination index, and the item function of all possible responses on a test question. With this information, a test can be edited to improve the quality of test questions before it is administered again.

Difficulty Index

The **difficulty index** refers to the proportion of students who answered the question correctly. This index is calculated by dividing the number of correct responses to a question by the total number of students taking the test. The formula for the difficulty index (p) is:

$$p = \frac{\text{number of correct responses}}{\text{total number of students taking test}}$$

Assume that the test included multiple choice questions with five alternatives. On a given item, 2 students chose alternative A, 3 chose B, no one chose C, 20 chose the correct answer D, and 10 chose E.

A	B	C	D*	E
2	3	0	20	10

Since 20 out of 35 students who took the exam answered the question correctly, the difficulty index would be .57. This is calculated as follows:

$$p = \frac{20}{35} = .57$$

From this information, it immediately becomes apparent that alternative C was not a very good distractor since no one chose it. The item is moderately difficult since 57 percent of the class answered it correctly.

When the difficulty index is above .75, a question is considered relatively easy, while below .25 is considered relatively difficult. Experts in test construction attempt to have most items fall between .20 and .80, with the average being about .50. The ability of a test to discriminate is the greatest when the overall difficulty index is approximately .50 (Kubiszyn and Borich, 1984).

Discrimination Index

The **discrimination index** measures the extent to which a test question discriminates between the students who scored well and those who scored poorly on the overall test. A question can discriminate in one of three ways: (1) If it has a positive discrimination index, then the students who did well on the exam answered the question correctly more than students who did not do well; (2) if it has a negative discrimination index, then the students who did poorly on the exam answered the question correctly more than the students who did well on the overall exam; (3) if both the students who did well and those who did poorly on the exam responded correctly with equal frequency on a particular item, then that item has a zero discrimination index. If an item has a negative or zero discrimination index, then it should be modified or discarded.

Though several methods may be used to calculate the discrimination index of an item, the following procedure is recommended. First, if there is a large number of test papers, such as N = 100, the papers are separated into three groups: the upper 27 percent of the scores, the lower 27 percent of the scores, and the middle 46 percent. According to Ebel (1972), the figure "27 percent" is often recommended, though the percentage used can be anywhere between 25 and 33 percent. If a smaller set of test papers is used, such as N = 35, the papers can be split into the upper 50 percent and lower 50 percent. For each question, the number in the upper group and the number in the lower group that chose the correct answer is tallied. The discrimination index (D) is computed with the following formula (Hopkins and Stanley, 1981):

$$D = \frac{\begin{array}{c}\text{Number who correctly} \\ \text{answered the question} \\ \text{in upper group}\end{array} - \begin{array}{c}\text{Number who correctly} \\ \text{answered the question} \\ \text{in lower group}\end{array}}{\text{Number of students in either group}}$$

In the example used to illustrate the difficulty index, 20 out of 35 students correctly answered the question. Using the same example to illustrate the discrimination index, the scores are separated into an upper 50 percent and a lower 50 percent. Since 35 students took the test, 18 scores are assigned to the upper group and 17 to the lower group. The following information was tallied for the upper and lower groups:

	A	B	C	D*	E
Upper	1	0	0	13	4
Lower	1	3	0	7	6

By inserting the numbers into the formula above, the discrimination index can be calculated. Notice that if the numbers in the upper and lower group are not equal, the larger of the two groups is used in the denominator.

$$D = \frac{13 - 7}{18} = \frac{6}{18} = .33$$

The discrimination index (D) is .33, which is positive. Students who did well on the exam answered this item correctly more often than students who did poorly. Like a correlation coefficient, the value for D can range from –1.00 to +1.00. If D ≥ .40, the item discriminates well. Between .30 and .39, the item is considered acceptable but subject to possible improvement. If D falls between .20 and .29, it is marginal and definitely needs improvement. Below .19 is a poor discriminator and the item in question should be rejected or undergo major revision for improvement (Ebel, 1972).

Safrit (1990) suggests a simple discrimination method that may be used with a single class. First, the teacher identifies the test score that represents the cutoff between the scores in the high group and the scores in the low group. The teacher then leads the class through each question by asking those in the high group to raise their hands if they answered it correctly. This procedure is repeated with the low group. To avoid possible embarrassment, the teacher may want to refer to the groups as A and B. To keep the entire class involved, the teacher may wish to ask for a show of hands from the middle group even though this information is not used in the calculation. If it is a small class, it may be appropriate to identify the middle score and split the class in half in order to complete this procedure. The number of students from each group (high and low) who answered the question correctly is recorded and used in the formula shown previously to calculate the discrimination index.

Several computer programs have been written for quantitative item analysis. If the proper type of optical scan answer sheet is used, the computer can score the exam as well as provide information about the difficulty index, the discrimination index, and total test reliability. Teachers should take advantage of this type of service not only to improve their examinations but also to save the time it takes to grade exams and do a quantitative item analysis by hand.

Item Function

It has been established that the example test question previously discussed has a difficulty index of .57 and a discrimination index of .33. **Item function** refers to the suitability or effectiveness of a test question. What are other things that should be determined about the item function of this test question? It is known that distractor C should be replaced. Are the other distractors acceptable? If more students in the upper group are choosing a distractor than the lower group, the option should be changed. However, in the example, this is not a problem. The alternatives are probably all right, but as the item is used on future exams, the item can be analyzed more accurately with a larger group of students taking the test.

What other information can a quantitative item analysis provide about the effectiveness of a multiple choice item? With a little interpretation and a healthy dose of common sense, checks can be made for mistakes in the answer key, guessing, and ambiguity in the alternatives.

In doing an item analysis, suppose that most students in the upper group were missing a certain question. The first possibility is a mistake in the answer key. Every teacher occasionally miskeys the answer sheet. A sample distribution of this situation might appear as follows:

	A	B	C*	D	E
Upper group	1	13	2	1	1

The answer key shows C to be the correct option when B is actually the correct choice. A distribution from the upper group such as this is a signal to check the answer key.

Some guessing in a multiple choice item is inevitable. However, in the group of students who score well on the exam, guessing should be minimized. When excessive guessing occurs in the upper group, the students respond in an approximate random pattern. That is, the answers are somewhat evenly balanced among the options. The following distribution illustrates this situation:

	A	B	C*	D	E
Upper group	3	4	4	4	3

A response pattern from the upper group such as this signifies a problem with the test question. It usually means that the information was not covered in class or in assigned readings or that the question was so difficult that even the upper group of students had no idea what the answer was.

Ambiguity between options on a multiple choice item should be suspected when the upper group chooses one of the distractors about as frequently as the correct answer. Ambiguity between the correct answer C and alternative A would be suspected in the following example:

	A	B	C*	D	E
Upper group	7	1	7	1	2

In this example, a high percentage of students in the upper group who missed this item are attracted to alternative A. With this sort of distribution, the teacher should investigate the possibility of ambiguity between A and C.

Though quantitative item analysis is a valuable way to analyze questions on a test, it does not point out every type of problem. The only way to determine if a test question is poorly written or reflects lack of mastery on the part of the students is through qualitative item analysis.

Qualitative Item Analysis

Qualitative item analysis should be performed on all test items regardless of format. It is the proper technique for assessing usefulness of semiobjective and essay tests and should be used in conjunction with quantitative item analysis on objective questions. The validity and reliability of a test is greatly improved if a combination of these procedures is used. Whereas quantitative item analysis is based on computations and yields numerical indexes, qualitative item analysis evaluates test items on the basis of matching questions to objectives and editing items that are poorly written. If a question seems ambiguous, promotes excessive guessing, is too difficult or easy, or fails to discriminate in a positive manner, the qualitative item analysis helps to point out these problems so the question can be either discarded or changed.

Qualitative item analysis includes a careful appraisal of test questions based on quantitative results. It requires a healthy dose of common sense as test items are being evaluated. While many of these procedures should be carried out prior to administering the exam, they are also performed after the test is given. The results of the test can provide guidance in improving the validity of the exam. Quantitative item analysis can point out problem areas, but some qualitative item analysis must be made in order to modify the test item.

Another method of qualitative analysis is to elicit feedback from students. Although some student reactions are based on emotion of the moment, there may be some justifiable criticisms that students can offer. By asking students to identify problems, the teacher may be able to pinpoint troublesome test questions in a time-efficient way. Students should write down comments about test questions that they found confusing or unfair, and explain why the question is unclear. Having the students put their comments in writing prevents the teacher from having to make on-the-spot decisions. If a decision to delete a question or accept an alternate response is retroactive to the exam already taken, students should be informed if their score is affected. The important thing is that one other resource has been utilized to help analyze and improve the overall quality of the examination.

Sources for Test Questions

Because most tests given in physical education are teacher-made tests (it would be difficult to find a battery of test questions that matched every teacher's specific objectives), using other sources to provide ideas for test questions may be helpful in constructing an examination. The list below suggests possible sources of test questions for use in physical education. Caution and good judgment must be used in selecting previously constructed test questions to ensure that they are appropriate for a particular situation.

Brown Sports and Fitness Series. Dubuque, IA: Wm. C. Brown Publishers. This series includes titles of paperback textbooks dealing with 44 separate activities. Each booklet contains various types of test questions at the end. For example, Chet Murphy's third edition of *Advanced Tennis* contains 60 true/false, 30 completion, and 10 matching items, while Virginia L. Nance and Elwood Craig Davis include 125 true/false and 50 completion items in their fifth edition of Golf.

Corbin, C., Lindsey, R., and Welk, G. *Concepts of Physical Fitness*. 10th ed. McGraw-Hill (2000). This textbook is designed for college-level classes and has an accompanying teacher's manual that includes multiple choice items for each chapter.

Corbin, C., and Lindsey, R. *Fitness for Life*. 4th ed. Globe Fearon Co. (1997). This textbook is designed for use in the secondary school and has an accompanying teacher's edition that includes suggested multiple choice examination questions covering the material in the textbook.

McGee, R., and Farrow, A. *Test Questions for Physical Education Activities*. Champaign, IL: Human Kinetics Press, 1987. This book provides 250–400 multiple choice questions for each of 15 different physical education activities. Questions cover beginning through advanced levels and are appropriate for junior high through college physical education classes.

Mood, D., Musker, F., and Rink, J. *Sports and Recreational Activities*. 12th ed. McGraw-Hill (1999). Forty-two activities are included in the textbook. A teacher's manual accompanying this book is available and includes written tests on each unit made up of true/false, multiple choice, short-answer, and essay test items.

SUMMARY

The cognitive area of physical education and nonschool programs is often overlooked. Even when cognitive objectives are listed in programmatic goals, there is little articulation between the actual goal and measurement and evaluation strategies. In many cases, no measurements are done to see if goals in this domain are being met. Whereas people outside the discipline might not recognize the cognitive domain as being critical, professionals in school and nonschool settings should not only incorporate cognitive components into their programs, but also become advocates for the expanding body of knowledge that complements activities associated with physical education and exercise science. Though it is important not to stray from the inherent activity-based nature of the discipline, it is equally important to systematically plan, deliver, and evaluate activities designed to meet cognitive goals.

Among the reasons for measuring the cognitive domain in physical education and exercise science programs are evaluating programmatic objectives, monitoring individual progress, accountability, evaluation of components (or units) of a program, and motivation. Additionally, in many school settings, the physical educator is responsible for grading. When a physical educator or exercise specialist administers an instrument (e.g., test, survey, questionnaire) for measuring knowledge, it is important that the instrument used provides a valid indicator of the individual's comprehension of the subject matter. In both school and nonschool settings, much care should be taken in constructing and modifying, as necessary, these instruments. After using the instrument, quantitative and qualitative item analysis should be used to modify and improve the instrument.

In constructing written exams, educators should consider the taxonomy of educational objectives, match test items to objectives, and employ a table of specifications. An understanding and consideration of the relative advantages and disadvantages of various formats is prerequisite to constructing a valid exam. Following proper administrative and grading procedures is also crucial to ensuring valid results. To give written tests that do not possess content validity or to allow improper administrative procedures to bias test results is a waste of valuable class time.

DISCUSSION QUESTIONS

1. What is included in the cognitive domain of physical education and exercise science? Why is proper emphasis on the cognitive domain critical to a quality program?

2. How should assessing the cognitive domain differ between nonschool settings and the school setting? Give reasons for your answer.

3. Discuss reasons that it is important to incorporate sound measurement of the cognitive domain into school and nonschool programs.

4. Why is it important to match test questions to written objectives? How are the

taxonomy of educational objectives and a table of specifications used to construct a written test?

5. List advantages and disadvantages of the following types of test questions: true/false, matching, multiple choice, completion, short answer, essay.

6. What is the difference between the difficulty index and the discrimination index? Why are both important to consider in analyzing a written test?

7. What role does qualitative item analysis play in test analysis? What facets of test construction does qualitative item analysis consider?

REFERENCES

Ayers, S. (2001). Developing quality multiple choice tests for physical education. *Journal of Health, Physical Education, Recreation, and Dance.* 72(6), 23–28, 60.

Bloom, B., Englehart, M., Hill, W., Furst, E., and Krathwohl, D. (1956). *Taxonomy of educational objectives: The classification of educational goals, handbook I: Cognitive domain.* New York: Longmans, Green.

Ebel, R. L. (1972). *Essentials of educational measurement.* Englewood Cliffs, NJ: Prentice-Hall.

Hopkins, K. D., and Stanley, J. C. (1981). *Educational and psychological measurement and evaluation.* 6th ed. Englewood Cliffs, NJ: Prentice-Hall.

Johnson, B. L., and Nelson, J. K. (1986). *Practical measurements for evaluation in physical education.* 4th ed. New York: Macmillan.

Kubiszyn, T., and Borich, G. (1984). *Educational testing and measurement: Class-room application and practice.* Glenview, IL: Scott, Foresman.

Mitchell, M., Barton, G., and Stanne, K. (2000). The role of homework in helping students meet physical education goals. *Journal of Health, Physical Education, Recreation, and Dance.* 71(5), 30–34.

Mood, D. P. (1980). *Numbers in motion: A balanced approach to measurement and evaluation.* Palo Alto, CA: Mayfield Publishing.

Safrit, M. J. (1990). *Introduction to measurement in physical education and exercise science.* 2nd ed. St. Louis, MO: Times Mirror/Mosby.

REPRESENTATIVE READINGS

Gronlund, N. (1998). *Assessment of student achievement* 6th ed. Boston: Allyn and Bacon.

Miller, D. (2001). *Measurement by the physical educator: Why and how.* New York: McGraw-Hill.

Morrow, J., Jackson, A., Disch, J., and Mood, D. (2000). *Measurement and evaluation in human performance.* 2nd ed. Champaign, IL: Human Kinetics Press.

CHAPTER 8

Measuring Affective Behaviors

Key Terms

affective domain

attitude

Likert scale

self-concept

semantic differential

sociogram

sociometry

two-point scale

Objectives

1. Identify areas of individual growth in the affective domain in which quality physical education and exercise programs should make positive contributions.

2. Explain the importance of including assessment of the affective domain in the measurement and evaluation scheme in physical education and the exercise science environment.

3. Compare and contrast similarities and differences of a Likert scale, a two-point scale, and a semantic differential scale.

4. Discuss methods of measuring attitudes toward physical activity interests, motivation, self-concept, and social competence.

5. Understand measurement problems associated with the various methods of evaluating the affective domain.

A mong professionals, there is little disagreement that quality exercise and physical education programs should provide learning opportunities to stimulate growth and development of participants in the physical fitness, psychomotor, cognitive, and affective domains. In movement-based programs, it is apparent that most of the outcomes and program objectives will be directed at the physical fitness and psychomotor domains. Accompanying knowledge and strategies to better understand the how and why of individual activity are associated with the cognitive domain and readily accepted as integral requirements for developing more purposeful movement. Experiencing and understanding movement, developing and maintaining physical fitness, and striving for movement excellence and useful physical skills are practical goals for any physical education and exercise program. Most professionals also contend that their programs contribute to individual growth in the affective domain.

The **affective domain** includes those characteristics associated with an individual's attitudes, interests, values, appreciations, emotions social behaviors, and related personality traits. Textbooks dedicated to curriculum development usually list several program objectives related to changes in affective behavior. Commonly cited affective objectives for physical education and exercise programs are as follows:

1. Through physical education and exercise programs, the individual should develop a positive attitude toward physical activity.

The assumption is often made that physical education is a viable means to promote the growth and development of positive attitudes toward movement and fitness-related activities. Positive feelings about a physical activity should, of course, promote continuance of regular voluntary participation in physical activity. When youth are asked about their attitude toward physical activity, most will state a positive view. Unfortunately, many of these individuals actually subscribe to a sedentary lifestyle. In school and private settings, physical educators must provide instruction and learning experiences that promote good feelings about fundamental movement, fitness-related activities, and sport. Nonschool programs, too, give attention to shaping the attitude participants have toward activity.

2. Through physical education and exercise programs, the individual should develop a desirable self-concept from relevant learning experiences.

Self-concept can be defined as how individuals feel about themselves and their ability to cope with life. Sometimes referred to as self-image or self-esteem, self-concept is developed through the responses of people toward the individual. How teachers, exercise specialists, parents, and friends communicate with an individual suggest feelings of being loved or neglected, capable or incapable, intelligent or ignorant, and so on. Teachers and exercise specialists need to understand students and/or clients and assist them in better understanding themselves.

Through physical activity programs, participants have the opportunity to learn more about themselves. Youngsters can experience success and failure, and adults can face challenging physical tasks. Leading experts in pedagogy and curriculum development recommend that physical educators focus on a student's strong points rather than on weaknesses; that children learn how to accept positive feedback from adults and peers; and that students be encouraged to participate in a variety of activities that provide opportunities for successful experiences (Pangrazi, 2001). Achieving self-satisfying levels of skill competency and physical fitness may help make youngsters feel positive and self-assured. Similarly, programs for adults can offer the satisfaction experienced from fulfillment of personal fitness activity goals.

3. Through physical education and exercise programs, individuals should adopt desirable social standards and ethical concepts.

Social development is often considered one of the foremost of all objectives of physical education. By internalizing and understanding the merits of participation, cooperation, and tolerance, youth hopefully will display qualities of good sportsmanship, leadership, followership, social acceptance, and fair play. The teacher can foster these qualities and assist the students in differentiating between acceptable and unacceptable ways of expressing feelings.

Becoming socially competent is an important objective for all phases of a youngster's formal education. Children need to be aware of how they interact with others and how their behavior influences others' responses to them. If students do not receive feedback about negative behavior from teachers and peers, they may never become aware that some behaviors are strongly resented by others (Pangrazi, 2001).

It is important for children to become socially competent and learn to cooperate. The nature of many competitive games requires cooperation, fair play, and good sportsmanship. Teachers must emphasize these things during learning experiences to promote socially acceptable behavior. Likewise, adults enrolled in exercise programs have numerous opportunities to strengthen social skills.

Thus, it is clear that the development of a positive attitude toward physical activity, positive self-concept, and social competence are worthwhile goals for physical education and exercise programs. All aspects of these programs have a strong impact on promoting behaviors and characteristics associated with affective behavior. How the session is organized, the types of activities presented, how the instructor interacts with the client, or how the children are instructed to interact with one another have a great deal to do with attaining program objectives associated with the affective domain.

Whereas most programs include goals associated with the affective domain and activity instructors in the school and nonschool settings are concerned with the feelings and attitudes of their participants, not all of these practitioners agree on how to assess this area. Because of the challenge of measuring attributes that are often not easily observable, many professionals do not attempt to assess if these objectives are being met. Some argue that if participants are accomplishing cognitive, psychomotor, and health-related fitness goals, the related affective objectives will also be attained. Others point out that it is difficult to measure interests, attitudes, and values. The behaviors and feelings of participants may change very slowly and are formed by inherited personality traits and environmental influences. Further, the accuracy of self-reporting inventories and questionnaires is dependent on honest responses from the participants. Students and adults alike may alter their responses to please their instructor.

Despite these points, it is our feeling that if your program objectives include affective goals, you are obligated to assess your success in meeting these goals. While measurement in the affective area is not as precise as the other domains, it still can be evaluated with reasonable accuracy. To do so, it is important that the practitioner chooses and uses appropriate methods to assess these goals and understand the limitations of each method. In school situations, the teacher should carefully consider how the affective domain will be used in grading and if it should be used at all. Certainly not all student objectives must be used in grading and, if they are used, do not have to be weighted equally.

Thus, we believe that it is important to measure and evaluate progress toward attainment of goals in the affective domain. In the physical fitness, psychomotor, and cognitive domains, this task is relatively straightforward and objective. Assessing progress in the affective domain is more problematic because of the subjective nature of the qualities being measured. For example, what is a "good" attitude toward physical activity and how can it be accurately measured? Or, how close is a youngster to displaying a positive self-concept? Or, where is the line between social competence and social incompetence?

To answer such questions, the following sections provide methods and proce-dures for gathering and analyzing data, followed by selected tests to measure qualities and behaviors associated with the affective domain. Because of the potentially sensi-tive nature of measuring these dimensions, we urge you to proceed cautiously. You should obtain permission from your immediate supervisor and administer these types of tests and interpret the results only after you feel confident that you have the nec-essary skills.

Data Gathering and Analysis

Affective areas are usually measured on scales that require an individual to indicate feelings toward a particular object, person, or policy by providing a response to a writ-ten statement. This is most frequently done by using paper-and-pencil instruments. These instruments may be organized into three categories: (1) the Likert scale, (2) the two-point scale, and (3) the semantic differential.

Likert Scale

Consisting of a series of attitude statements about some person, object, policy, or thing, the **Likert scale** has become one of the most widely used methods of attitude assessment. Respondents indicate the extent to which they agree or disagree with a number of affective statements. Each step of agreement or disagreement is assigned a predetermined numeric value. Totaling the numeric values then suggests whether the individual's attitude is favorable or unfavorable.

The most common Likert scale offers five to seven places along a continuum of descriptors at which the respondent can mark a feeling about a particular statement or object (i.e., agree/disagree). Although it is not particularly important, there is a slight advantage in having an even (4, 6, 8, and so on) rather than an odd number of steps (Nunnally, 1978). Using a scale that has an even number of response locations eliminates the neutral choice necessary with an odd-step scale and forces the respon-dent to favor one descriptor more than the other.

Scoring Procedure: To complete a Likert scale, respondents simply mark the place on the response sheet that most accurately expresses their feelings toward each affec-tive statement. Figure 8.1 provides a sample Likert scale with choices ranging from Strongly Agree to Strongly Disagree and a numeric value assigned to each option. To score the scale, a numeric value is assigned to each space along the continuum, depending on whether the item is worded positively or negatively. For example, the numeric value assigned to the options for item 1 in Figure 8.1, which is worded neg-atively, are SA = 1, A = 2, U = 3, D = 4, and SD = 5. The numeric values for the optional responses associated with item 2, which is positively worded, are: SA = 5, A = 4, U = 3, D = 2, and SD = 1. Summing the numeric values provides the total score for the instrument. Dividing the sum of the scores by the total number of affective statements provides a mean value.

Advantages and Disadvantages: Some advantages and disadvantages of using a Likert scale are listed below.

	Strongly Agree	Agree	Uncertain	Disagree	Strongly Disagree
1. I have a hard time paying attention in class. (negative)	SA (1	A 2	U 3	D 4	SD 5)
2. All students should have to take a course like this one. (positive)	SA (5	A 4	U 3	D 2	SD 1)
3. I like learning new sport skills. (positive)	SA (5	A 4	U 3	D 2	SD 1)
4. I do not enjoy activities in class. (negative)	SA (1	A 2	U 3	D 4	SD 5)
5. I often feel like coming to this class. (positive)	SA (5	A 4	U 3	D 2	SD 1)

Figure 8.1 Sample Likert scale.

Advantages

1. Furnishes a means for primary and consistent assessment of attitudes with well-devised scales.

2. Adaptable to most attitude measurement situations.

3. Easy to administer, score, and transcribe into quantitative data that can be readily entered and analyzed in a computer.

4. Compatible with most optical scan sheet formats. This enables the response sheets to be scored by machine.

Disadvantages

1. As with most self-report surveys, the respondent is able to convey a false impression of his or her attitude.

2. The distance between points on a scale does not represent equal changes in attitude toward a particular affective statement.

3. Multidimensional concepts may be dealt with in a unidimensional manner.

4. Constructing valid and reliable attitudinal instruments requires time and effort.

The Two-Point Scale

The **two-point scale** is a variation of the Likert scale. The primary difference between the scales is the number of response options available to the respondent. The two-point scale features yes/no or agree/disagree options, whereas the Likert scale features five or more options. Because it has only two options, the two-point scale is often referred to as the forced-choice scale.

Scoring Procedure: Deriving a score from the two-point scale is similar to the process used in scoring the Likert scale. Numeric values are assigned to each of the response options. Usually, a positive response is assigned a +1 and the negative response is assigned either a –1 or 0. While using a +1 and –1 is convenient for defining positive and negative attitude (i.e., any summed score above zero reflects a positive attitude and any summed score below zero reflects a negative attitude), using the 0 enables easier interpretation if the data are subjected to statistical analyses (i.e., correlational procedures).

Advantages and Disadvantages: Some advantages and disadvantages of the two-point scale are listed below.

Advantages

1. It is easier to understand than the Likert scale.
2. Theoretically, the forced-choice format causes the respondents to provide a more accurate indication of their attitudinal preferences.
3. The likelihood of respondents accidentally marking the wrong step or misunderstanding the choices is small.

Disadvantages

1. Having only two diametrically opposed options may be irritating to the respondents. Repeated requests to make a definite response about an affective behavior may create sufficient antagonism toward the instrument to reduce the validity of the results.

Semantic Differential Scale

The **semantic differential** is a scale that offers two diametrically opposed alternatives at respective ends of a continuum with various steps in between. Sometimes referred to as a bipolar adjective scale, the semantic differential differs from the previous two scales mainly in that it does not use affective statements. Instead, a word or phrase referring to the person, object, policy, or thing in question is presented, along with a list of adjectives that have opposite meanings. Examples of bipolar adjectives would be good/bad, happy/sad, high/low, and so on. Osgood, Suci, and Tannenbaum (1957) provide an extensive list of bipolar adjectives that can be incorporated into a questionnaire. The adjectives are placed at opposite ends of a continuum with steps between offering the respondent various alternatives at which to indicate feelings toward the item in question. An example of the semantic differential scale used to assess a person's attitude toward physical activity can be found in Figure 8.2.

Scoring Procedure: Scoring the semantic differential may be completed in a variety of ways. Two of the more frequently used methods are explained here. The first way is very similar to the procedures described for the Likert and two-point scales. In Figure 8.2, a numeric weight of 1 is assigned to the most negative response and a numeric weight of 7 assigned to the most positive response. Steps between have been assigned appropriate values. The values are summed and a mean score derived. A score of 3.5 or higher reflects a positive attitude; scores less than 3.5 reflect negative attitudes.

The second approach is one endorsed by Kubiszyn and Borich (1984). Numeric values of 7, 6, 5, 4, 3, 2, and 1 are assigned to each step along the continuum regardless of the type of adjective (positive or negative). All the scores for the pairs with the positive adjectives on the left are added together, and all the scores for the pairs with the negative adjectives on the left are added. Subtract the score for the left negative adjective pairs from the score for the left positive adjective pairs and divide by the

What does the idea in the box mean to you?

> **Physical Activity**

Always think about the idea in the box.

1. high ____ : ____ : ____ : ____ : ____ : ____ : ____ low
2. awkward ____ : ____ : ____ : ____ : ____ : ____ : ____ graceful
3. meaningless ____ : ____ : ____ : ____ : ____ : ____ : ____ meaningful
4. good ____ : ____ : ____ : ____ : ____ : ____ : ____ bad
5. strong ____ : ____ : ____ : ____ : ____ : ____ : ____ weak
6. beautiful ____ : ____ : ____ : ____ : ____ : ____ : ____ ugly
7. painful ____ : ____ : ____ : ____ : ____ : ____ : ____ pleasurable
8. healthy ____ : ____ : ____ : ____ : ____ : ____ : ____ sick
9. small ____ : ____ : ____ : ____ : ____ : ____ : ____ large
10. slow ____ : ____ : ____ : ____ : ____ : ____ : ____ fast

Figure 8.2 Example of semantic differential scale.

number of adjective pairs. If the calculated mean is greater than zero, a positive attitude is reflected. Similarly, if the average is equal to or less than zero, a negative attitude is reflected.

Advantages and Disadvantages: Some advantages and disadvantages of using the semantic differential are listed below.

Advantages

1. The semantic differential can readily be adapted for use in a variety of settings.
2. Its structure allows the evaluation of several different concepts utilizing the same form.
3. The form can be adapted for scoring with an optical scanner.

Disadvantages

1. Selecting appropriate bipolar adjectives can be tedious.
2. Without the assistance of an optical scanner, scoring the semantic differential can be both time consuming and prone to error.

Uses of Attitudinal Scales

Scales to measure attitude can be utilized in activity settings in several ways: (1) to assist the instructor in determining progress toward program or participant's goals, (2) to provide a quantitative database to compare the attitudinal scores of individuals or groups, (3) to compile information that can be used in planning a physical education or exercise program, and (4) to help evaluate the effectiveness of teaching methods and instructional strategies designed to promote the enjoyment of physical activity (Johnson and Nelson, 1986).

Problems Associated with Attitudinal Testing

Several problems are associated with attitudinal testing. The validity of attitudinal scales is sometimes questionable, particularly if individuals have limited experience with certain parts of the program and, thus, cannot make intelligent responses concerning those areas. Many young people, especially below the high school level, lack stability in their attitudes. Young people often will change their attitudes based on recent or new experiences (Johnson and Nelson, 1986). It is important that an instrument measuring attitudes be validated with the population for which it is being used. For example, an attitude survey for preschool children should be validated by (1) experts in the area, (2) test-retest procedures, and (3) concurrent validity tests with an existing instrument. Finally, each statement must be carefully worded to avoid giving any hints of the desired response and to decrease the chance of response distortion by those being measured.

Using Alternative Assessment Strategies

The evaluation of attributes associated with the affective domain can also be accomplished by the use of alternative assessment strategies. The next chapter, Chapter 9, provides a thorough discussion of a variety of alternative assessment techniques and the appropriate ways to implement them. Though paper and pencil inventories can be valuable for assessing the affective domain, alternative assessment can also be effectively used.

Student Logs

The use of student logs or journals is an excellent way to have students reflect on their feelings, attitudes, and perceptions about activities. They can provide insights particular to each participant to the teacher or exercise leader. These logs are sometimes used to monitor activity levels away from physical education class or the nonschool exercise setting. If the participants are pursuing activities away from the formal setting, it is a good indicator that the participant is feeling successful and positive about the activity experience.

Direct Observation

Direct observation by the instructor can also be used as a data source for measuring affective behaviors. Care must be taken to develop appropriate rubrics to ensure the objectivity of observational data (see Chapter 9). Observation of such things as sportsmanship, cooperation, and fair play are possible with well-constructed rubrics. Students can use these same rubrics to observe competitive athletic contests as homework assignments. Anecdotal records can be also be used with direct observation.

Anecdotal Records

Anecdotal records are sequential, brief reports that record a teacher's observation of a student's behavior. The information contained in these records may contribute much toward gaining insight about the conduct exhibited by students. These records usually contain the student's name and space for comments about observed behavior. Because physical education programs provide a variety of social situations, the anecdotal record can be a useful tool in charting progress toward attainment of goals. Recording events as they occur, or shortly thereafter, avoids the pitfall of forgetting. Mood (1980) and Mathews (1978) offer the following suggestions for anecdotal recording:

1. Record the anecdote as soon as possible after the occurrence of the incident. Be sure that the student is unsuspecting of the recording.
2. Describe the incident accurately. Add a note of interpretation of the observation.
3. Include enough background information to give the incident meaning.
4. Be sure the evaluative statement is clearly identified and based on observed behavior.
5. Indicate whether the incident is important because it is representative of the individual or very much different from usual behavior.
6. Record anecdotes frequently in order to establish accurate trends. More frequent recordings result in a better understanding of the student.
7. Establish a system of recording anecdotes so that filing and sorting is easily accomplished. Using a computer may assist in this function.
8. Summarize findings from time to time to determine trends in behavior.
9. The anecdotal record sheet should accompany the student's personnel file throughout the school years.

Checklists
Checklists have long been used as a system of reporting observed behaviors. A regular class list with predetermined behaviors listed across the top of the sheet is a means of monitoring the occurrence of selected behaviors. Frequent tabulation of the tallies can alert the teacher to students who are displaying too much or too little of a selected behavior. Checklists are usually most effective when social behaviors are listed sequentially. In this way, the teacher can direct the teaching process toward diagnosed needs. More information on designing valid checklists is found in Chapter 9.

Rating Scales
Rating scales used in the evaluation of affective behaviors contain certain descriptive criteria of selected traits. In measuring remembered or perceived behavior, the teacher uses an observation system in the form of a rating scale and assesses an individual on one or more characteristics. Assessments are made on the basis of past observations or on the basis of perceptions of what the student is like and how the student will behave. Several traits, such as "ability to get along with others," "listens to instructions," "is viewed favorably by peers," and so on, are common to most rating scales. Usually, the rater scores the student by assigning a numeric ranking (e.g., 0 to 5), which describes the frequency of the social behavior criterion being displayed by the student. For example, in rating a child on good sportsmanship, a score of 5 might be recorded if the youngster is consistent in displaying proper conduct during game-type activities; a score of 2 indicates that the student occasionally displays unsportsmanlike actions.

Rating scales are easy to devise and, more importantly, quick and easy to use. Unfortunately, the apparent ease of construction is deceptive and carries a heavy price: lack of validity due to a number of sources of bias that enter into rating measures (Kerlinger, 1973). Still, with knowledge, skill, and care, rating scales can be a valuable evaluative tool. Steps in developing a valid rating scale are detailed in Chapter 9.

Measuring Attitude Toward Physical Activity

Physical educators and exercise specialists alike recognize the influence attitude has on the performance and exercise behavior of students and clients. Most of the time, the teacher is interested in the student's behavior during active participation in some form of movement experience. For instance, the teacher looks for qualities associated with fair play and genuine interest in physical education class. A coach is interested in the practice and game attitude displayed by athletes. The coach is on the alert to learn about the athlete's sportsmanship and commitment to the strenuous practice regime required for success. An exercise specialist is interested in the attitude of the clients toward physical activity and exercise. They look for attitudinal characteristics that demonstrate a participant's pledge to a planned program of physical activity. Regardless of the exercise or activity environment, the practitioner realizes the influence of attitude on performance and recognizes the value of being able to effectively assess and evaluate attitude toward physical activity. The sections below describe methods and techniques to systematically assess and evaluate individuals' attitudes toward physical activity.

Student attitudes toward physical education have been the focus of attention for a considerable period of time. Attitude studies have been reported in the literature as far back as 1933 with the writings of Lapp. Generally, **attitude** refers to feelings about particular social or physical objects such as types of individuals, significant persons, social institutions, and government policy (Nunnally, 1978). Over the past several decades, a number of studies have been published that address the subject of attitudes toward physical activity. Kenyon (1968a) suggests that, although attitude dynamics are not completely understood, and definition and measurement are problematic, progress has been made to warrant their serious investigation in the realm of physical activity. Mostly, these investigations have focused on examination of attitudes toward physical education (Adams, 1963; Richardson, 1960; and Wear, 1950), intensive competition and sportsmanship (McAfee, 1955), and conditioning (Anderson, 1966). Review of these initial studies reveals several shortcomings. First, the studies were limited to a restricted domain and did not examine the much larger domain of physical activity. Second, proper test construction techniques were not always employed. Third, most of the assessment instruments dealt with multidimensional concepts in a unidimensional manner (Simon and Smoll, 1974). However, as a result of these pioneer efforts, researchers have formulated assessment instruments that are appropriately constructed, view attitude from a multidimensional perspective, and are age specific. Specific tests are described next in this chapter.

The following are examples of testing instruments that can be used to measure attitude toward physical education or physical activity.

Attitude Toward Physical Activity
(Kenyon, 1968a, 1968b)
Purpose: The purpose of the Attitude Toward Physical Activity (ATPA) is to measure various dimensions of an individual's attitude toward physical activity.

HEALTH AND FITNESS SCALE ITEMS

VSA	SA	A	U	D	SD	VSD	Of all physical activities, those whose purpose is primarily to develop physical fitness would *not* be my first choice.
VSA	SA	A	U	D	SD	VSD	I would usually choose strenuous physical activity over light physical activity, if given the choice.
VSA	SA	A	U	D	SD	VSD	A large part of our daily lives must be committed to vigorous exercise.
VSA	SA	A	U	D	SD	VSD	Being strong and highly fit is *not* the most important thing in my life.
VSA	SA	A	U	D	SD	VSD	The time spent doing daily calisthenics could probably be used more profitably in other ways.
VSA	SA	A	U	D	SD	VSD	Strength and physical stamina are the most important prerequisites to a full life.
VSA	SA	A	U	D	SD	VSD	I believe calisthenics are among the less desirable forms of physical activity.
VSA	SA	A	U	D	SD	VSD	People should spend 20 to 30 minutes a day doing vigorous calisthenics.
VSA	SA	A	U	D	SD	VSD	Of all physical activities, my first choice would be those whose purpose is primarily to develop and maintain physical fitness.
VSA	SA	A	U	D	SD	VSD	Vigorous daily exercises are absolutely necessary to maintain one's general health.

MAXIMUM SCORES FOR ATPA DIMENSIONS

	Men	Women
Social	70 (10 Items)	56 (8 Items)
Health and fitness	70 (10 Items)	77 (11 Items)
Vertigo	70 (10 Items)	63 (9 Items)
Aesthetic	70 (10 Items)	63 (9 Items)
Catharsis	63 (9 Items)	63 (9 Items)
Ascetic	70 (10 Items)	56 (8 Items)

Figure 8.3 Attitudes toward physical activity scale.

Reprinted by permission of G. S. Kenyon, University of Lethbridge, Lethbridge, Alberta, Canada.

Description: The ATPA inventory consists of six separate scales designed to measure attitudes toward physical activity as a social experience, aesthetic experience, catharsis, health and fitness experience, ascetic experience, and pursuit of vertigo. Seven-point, Likert-type options ranging from "very strongly agree" to "very strongly disagree" are provided for responses to each of the six subscales. See Figure 8.3 for an example of one subscale.

Instructions: The inventory should be administered in a quiet room free of distractions.

Validity: Face validity for each dimension was established by a panel of experts. Factor analysis procedures were used to verify the six dimensions of attitude toward physical activity. Except for catharsis, scale scores discriminated between those with strong and those with weak preferences.

Reliability: Hoyt reliabilities were calculated for college men and women. Reliabilities ranged from .72 for social experience to .89 for the pursuit of vertigo scale.

Age Level: Males and females high school age and older.

Equipment Needed: Pencils and ample supply of ATPA inventories.

Scoring Procedure: Each scale is scored separately. Therefore, each respondent receives a maximum of six separate scores. Tabulating a quantitative score for each scale is done in the same manner as with any Likert-type scale. The ATPA uses a seven-point scale ranging from "very strongly disagree" to "very strongly agree." It is recommended that the six scores not be summed in an attempt to obtain a composite score. The maximum number of points per scale varies according to the information reported in Figure 8.3. As with other Likert scales, the scoring must be reversed on several items before summing the total score for a particular dimension.

Norms: None available.

Children's Attitude Toward Physical Activity

(Simon and Smoll, 1974)

Purpose: To measure children's attitudes toward physical activity.

Description: The Children's Attitude Toward Physical Activity (CATPA) inventory is based on Kenyon's (1968a, 1968b) conceptual model, which characterizes physical activity as a multidimensional sociopsychological phenomenon, and is modeled after the ATPA. The CATPA, however, employs a semantic differential scale and evaluates each dimension on the basis of eight pairs of bipolar adjectives. This semantic differential is less complex than the Likert-type scale and is more appropriate for elemen-

Figure 8.4 Scale format for CATPA instrument.

Reprinted by permission of the American Alliance for Health, Physical Education, Recreation, and Dance, Reston, Virginia.

tary and middle school children. The CATPA scale format for health and fitness is shown in Figure 8.4.

Instructions: The inventory should be administered in a quiet room free of distractions.

Validity: It was assumed that the original dimensions of the ATPA were equally representative for children. Language modifications of dimension descriptions were made so that each would be more easily understood by children. The resultant subdomains for the CATPA are described as follows:

1. Physical activity as a social experience. Physical activities that give you a chance to meet new people and be with your friends.
2. Physical activity for health and fitness. Taking part in physical activities to make your health better and to get your body in better condition.
3. Physical activity as a thrill but involving some risk. Physical activities that are dangerous. They also can be exciting because you move very fast and must change directions quickly.
4. Physical activity as the beauty in human movement. Physical activities that have beautiful movements. Examples are ballet dancing, gymnastics tumbling, and figure skating on ice.
5. Physical activity for the release of tension. Taking part in physical activities to get away from problems you might have. You can also get away from problems by watching other people in physical activities.
6. Physical activity as long and hard training. Physical activities that have long and hard practices. To spend time in practice you need to give up other things you like to do.

Reliability: Reliability coefficients for the six subdomains ranged from .80 to .89. Higher reliabilities were obtained with this semantic differential instrument than with a Likert-type instrument.

Age Level: Children in grades 4 through 9.

Scoring Procedure: This scaling technique places attitudes on a bipolar continuum. The respondent places a checkmark along the seven-point continuum, which ranges from "extremely favorable" to "extremely unfavorable." The location of the checkmark determines the intensity of the attitude held by the youngster. The scoring procedure assigns the neutral point a score of 0. The extreme ends of the continuum are scored as +3 for "extremely favorable" to –3 for "extremely unfavorable." A +2 score is assigned to checkmarks located in the boxes closest to the "extremely favorable" end of the continuum, while +1 scores were given to checkmarks placed in the boxes closest to the neutral position on the "favorable" side of the continuum. The "unfavorable" side of the continuum follows a similar style of scoring except that minus ranks are assigned to the respective numerals along the scale. The total score for each of the six subdomains is determined by summing all of the scores.

Norms: None available.

CSAPPA: Children's Self-Perceptions of Adequacy in and Predilection for Physical Activity (Hay, 1992)

Purpose: To identify children at risk for hypoactivity and youngsters at risk of becoming obese.

Description: The CSAPPA Inventory is designed to measure an individual's adequacy and predisposition toward physical activity. The choices are structured such that activities for which children may be predisposed are described as enjoyable or preferred. Youngsters who view themselves as inadequate in a particular activity will avoid circumstances requiring that behavior and choose not to make efforts to improve. Perceived adequacy, on the other hand, is viewed as the perception of a person's ability to achieve some acceptable standard of success. Ten items begin with active statements, and 10 begin with inactive statements. Eight items address adequacy, the remainder, predisposition toward physical activity (Figure 8.5).

Instructions: The inventory should be administered in a quiet room free of distractions. Children are instructed to read a pair of sentences and then circle the sentence that is most like them. Once finished, they are asked to decide if the statement circled is "sort of true" for them or "really true" for them, and place a checkmark in the proper location. There are no right or wrong answers. Be sure to complete all questions.

Validity: The inventory was examined using participation questionnaires, teacher evaluations, and motor proficiency.

Reliability: Test-retest reliabilities ranged from .84 (grades 4, 5, 6) to .90 (grades 7, 8, 9).

Age Level: Elementary-age children.

Scoring Procedure: Items are scored 1–4; 1 is low and 4 is high. Students scoring above 60 are considered to have positive self-perception relating to physical activity.

INSTRUCTIONS: In this survey you have to read a pair of sentences and then circle the sentence that you think is <u>more like you</u>. For example:

| | Some kids have one nose on their faces | BUT | Other kids have three noses on their faces! | |

That shouldn't be too hard for you to decide! Once you have circled the sentence that is more like you, then you have to decide if it is <u>SORT OF TRUE</u> for you or <u>REALLY TRUE</u> for you, and put a check mark in the right box. Here is another example for you to try. Remember: <u>First</u> circle the sentence that is more like you and then check off if it is REALLY TRUE <u>or</u> only SORT OF TRUE for you.

REALLY TRUE for me	SORT OF TRUE for me				SORT OF TRUE for me	REALLY TRUE for me
[ ]	[ ]	Some kids like to play with computers.	BUT	Other kids don't like playing with computers.	[ ]	[ ]

Now you are ready to start filling in this form. THERE ARE NO RIGHT OR WRONG ANSWERS, JUST WHAT IS <u>MOST LIKE YOU</u>. Take your time and do the whole form carefully. If you have any questions just ask! If you think you are ready you can start now. BE SURE TO FILL IN BOTH SIDES OF EACH PAGE!

REALLY TRUE for me	SORT OF TRUE for me				SORT OF TRUE for me	REALLY TRUE for me
[ ]	[ ]	Some kids can't wait to play active games after school.	BUT	Other kids would rather do something else.	[ ]	[ ]

Figure 8.5 CSAPPA inventory.   *(continues)*

REALLY TRUE for me	SORT OF TRUE for me				SORT OF TRUE for me	REALLY TRUE for me
[ ]	[ ]	Some kids really enjoy physical education class.	BUT	Other kids don't like physical education class.	[ ]	[ ]
[ ]	[ ]	Some kids don't like playing active games.	BUT	Other kids really like playing active games.	[ ]	[ ]
[ ]	[ ]	Some kids don't have much fun playing sports.	BUT	Other kids have a good time playing sports.	[ ]	[ ]
[ ]	[ ]	Some kids think phys. ed. is the best class.	BUT	Other kids think phys. ed. isn't much fun.	[ ]	[ ]
[ ]	[ ]	Some kids are good at active games.	BUT	Other kids find active games hard to play.	[ ]	[ ]
[ ]	[ ]	Some kids don't like playing sports.	BUT	Other kids really enjoy playing sports.	[ ]	[ ]
[ ]	[ ]	Some kids always hurt themselves when they play sports.	BUT	Other kids never hurt themselves playing sports.	[ ]	[ ]
[ ]	[ ]	Some kids like to play active games outside.	BUT	Other kids would rather read or play video games.	[ ]	[ ]
[ ]	[ ]	Some kids do well in most sports.	BUT	Other kids feel they aren't very good at sports.	[ ]	[ ]
[ ]	[ ]	Some kids learn to play active games easily.	BUT	Other kids find it hard learning to play active games.	[ ]	[ ]
[ ]	[ ]	Some kids think they are the best at sports.	BUT	Other kids think they aren't very good at sports.	[ ]	[ ]
[ ]	[ ]	Some kids find games in phys. ed. hard to play.	BUT	Other kids are good at games in phys. ed.	[ ]	[ ]
[ ]	[ ]	Some kids like to watch games being played outside.	BUT	Other kids would rather play active games outside.	[ ]	[ ]
[ ]	[ ]	Some kids are among the last to be chosen for active games.	BUT	Other kids are usually picked to play first.	[ ]	[ ]
[ ]	[ ]	Some kids like to take it easy during recess.	BUT	Other kids would rather play active games.	[ ]	[ ]
[ ]	[ ]	Some kids have fun in phys. ed. class.	BUT	Other kids would rather miss phys. ed. class.	[ ]	[ ]
[ ]	[ ]	Some kids aren't good enough for sports teams.	BUT	Other kids do well on sports teams.	[ ]	[ ]
[ ]	[ ]	Some kids like to read or play quiet games.	BUT	Other kids like to play active games.	[ ]	[ ]
[ ]	[ ]	Some kids like to play active games outside on weekends.	BUT	Other kids like to relax and watch TV on weekends.	[ ]	[ ]

PLEASE CHECK TO MAKE SURE THAT YOU HAVE ANSWERED ALL THE QUESTIONS!
THANK YOU!

Figure 8.5 CSAPPA inventory *(continued)*.
Reprinted by permission of Dr. John A. Hay.

Feelings About Physical Activity Inventory

(Neilson and Corbin, 1986)

Purpose: To provide information about commitment to physical activity.

Instructions: The statements may or may not describe an individual's feelings most of the time. Physical activity is defined to include all individual, dual, and team sports and all forms of individual exercise. Persons are asked to circle the appropriate letter(s) to indicate how they generally feel about physical activity (Figure 8.6).

Directions: The following statements may or may not describe your feelings about physical activity. Physical activity is interpreted to include all individual, dual, and team sports, and all individual exercises. Please circle the appropriate letter or letters to indicate how well the statement describes your feelings most of the time. There are no right or wrong answers. Do not spend too much time on any one item, but give the answer that seems to describe how you generally feel about physical activity.

SD = STRONGLY DISAGREE   A = AGREE
D = DISAGREE   SA = STRONGLY AGREE
U = UNCERTAIN

THE SCALE

Feelings About Physical Activity					
1. I look forward to physical activity.	SD	D	U	A	SA
2. I wish there were a more enjoyable way to stay fit than vigorous physical activity.	SD	D	U	A	SA
3. Physical activity is drudgery.	SD	D	U	A	SA
4. I do not enjoy physical activity.	SD	D	U	A	SA
5. Physical activity is vitally important to me.	SD	D	U	A	SA
6. Life is so much richer as a result of physical activity.	SD	D	U	A	SA
7. Physical activity is pleasant.	SD	D	U	A	SA
8. I dislike the thought of doing regular physical activity.	SD	D	U	A	SA
9. I would arrange or change my schedule to participate in physical activity.	SD	D	U	A	SA
10. I have to force myself to participate in physical activity.	SD	D	U	A	SA
11. To miss a day of physical activity is sheer relief.	SD	D	U	A	SA
12. Physical activity is the high point of my day.	SD	D	U	A	SA

Scoring: Items 1, 5, 6, 7, 9, and 12 are scored 1 to 5; items 2, 3, 4, 8, 10, and 11 are scored 5 to 1. Thirty-six is the middle score. The following scale gives some interpretative information:

54–60 Very favorable feelings about physical activity

42–53 Favorable feelings

30–41 Neutral feelings

18–29 Unfavorable feelings

12–17 Very unfavorable feelings about physical activity

Figure 8.6 Feelings about activity inventory.

Reprinted by permission of Dr. Charles Corbin, Arizona State University.

Validity: Validity was examined using discrimination indices of item analysis averaged .45.

Reliability: Estimates ranged from 0.88 to 0.91.

Age Level: This inventory is suitable for a broad age range of individuals.

Scoring Procedure: Items 1, 5, 6, 7, 9, and 12 are scored 1 to 5. Items 2, 3, 4, 8, 10, and 11 are scored 5 to 1. Thirty-six is the middle score. The following scale is intended to provide some interpretative information.

54–60	Very favorable feelings about physical activity
42–53	Favorable
30–41	Neutral
18–29	Unfavorable
12–17	Very unfavorable feelings about physical activity

There are other tests that can also be used to measure attitude toward physical activity. However, it is beyond the scope of this chapter to provide detailed information about each test. Short descriptions and reference citations for selected tests are as follows:

- Richardson Scale for Measuring Attitudes Toward Physical Fitness and Exercise (Richardson, 1960)—This instrument is designed for high school and college students and includes two equivalent forms for measuring attitudes toward physical fitness and exercise.

- Wear Attitude Scale (Wear, 1955)—This scale was one of the first developed to assess attitude toward physical education. The instrument was originally designed for college students but can be used with high school students if desired.

- Cheffers and Mancini Human Movement Attitude Scale (Cheffers, Mancini, and Zaichkowsky, 1976)—This pictorial scale is designed for elementary children in grades 1–6. The scale consists of pictures that contain situations or occurrences typical in a physical education class. Children respond by making check marks next to a happy, sad, or neutral facial expression.

Complete reference citations are provided for each instrument at the end of the chapter. You are encouraged to investigate these inventories further if they are of interest to you.

Measuring Activity Interests of Participants

It is logical that program planners in school and nonschool activity environments would want to offer activities in which their participants had interest. Both students and adults will be more motivated to participate in activity if they are offered options that they enjoy. In school settings, surveys done in the spring allow teachers to gather data to help determine curricular offerings for the following fall and spring semesters. We recommend that this type of survey be administered at least every other year. As many students as possible that are representative of all demographic groups in the school should be surveyed to ensure validity. It may be possible to set up a program with the help of computer specialists in your school district to facilitate analysis of the data. Student interest surveys should be analyzed by grade, sex, and racial groups.

The survey instrument should be designed to include all possible physical activities that contribute to the objectives of the program. An example of an activity interest survey is shown in Figure 8.7. This type of survey should be revised regularly to include new activities. This type of activity interest survey can be easily adapted to nonschool activity settings. A primary goal of physical activity programs is to foster a positive attitude toward physical activity. If participants feel that they have input to activities offered and are able to participate in activities they enjoy, then the attainment of this important programmatic goal becomes much easier. Activity interests surveys are simple to construct, administer, and analyze; and they can provide important insights for making programmatic decisions on activities to be offered.

Measuring Motivation

Ostrow (1996) reported that 37 instruments have been developed to measure motivation as related to various types of activity. Some of the areas studied include adherence to exercise programs, adherence to rehabilitation programs, and motives that subjects express for participating in different forms of exercise. As discussed in Chapter 1, large percentages of American youth and adults are inactive. Obesity and adult-onset diabetes have been identified as health problems of epidemic proportions in our country. The reasons that individuals pursue and adhere to activity programs are complicated and not fully understood even by experts who study the phenomenon. Personal attributes, environmental factors, and activity characteristics have been identified as determinants of exercise. Dishman (1990) identified the following determinants of exercise behavior: smoking, occupational level, body composition, exercise history, self-motivation, level of knowledge, positive affect, and perceived exercise capacity. In this section, several psychological instruments used to assess motives of exercise are highlighted.

Self-Motivation Inventory

(Dishman and Ickes, 1981)

Purpose: The purpose of the Self-Motivation Inventory (SMI) is to measure an individual's self-motivation to adhere to exercise programs. It is estimated that approximately 50 percent of all people who start exercise programs drop out in the first 6 months. It would certainly be helpful if the exercise specialists knew what types of persons were more likely to persist or drop out of planned exercise programs.

Description: The SMI has 40 items in a Likert format that asks the subject to rate on a 1–5 scale how characteristic the statement is to the respondent. The scale ranges from "1. Extremely uncharacteristic of me" to "5. Extremely characteristic of me." Figure 8.8 shows the items on the instrument.

Instructions: The instrument should be administered in a quiet room free from distractions.

Validity: The construct validity coefficient was reported as .63.

Reliability: Coefficients for test-retest reliability were .92 and internal reliability was .91 based on a sample of 400 undergraduate men and women.

Age Level: College-aged students and adults.

Physical Activity Interest Survey

Name _____

Grade _____ Age _____ Sex _____

Athletic team _____

Instructions: Which of the following physical activities or sports would you be most interested in taking as a course in the physical education program? Please list your top 5 choices on the line provided. Place a number 1 in front of your highest choice, a number 2 in front of your next choice, and so on, until you reach choice number 5. Remember to make only 5 choices.

Aquatic Activities
_____ Lifesaving, water safety
_____ Skin and scuba diving
_____ Surfing
_____ Swimming, diving
_____ Water sports (polo, volleyball, basketball)

Individual Activities
_____ Archery
_____ Badminton
_____ Fencing
_____ Frisbee
_____ Golf
_____ Gymnastics
_____ Handball
_____ Racquetball
_____ Recreational games (bowling, horseshoes, shuffleboard, etc.)
_____ Roller-skating
_____ Skateboarding
_____ Squash
_____ Tennis
_____ Track and field

Physical Conditioning Activities
_____ Aerobic dance
_____ Body conditioning, weight control
_____ Martial arts (judo, karate, kendo, etc.)
_____ Weight training
_____ Yoga

Outdoor Adventure Activities
_____ Backpacking
_____ Canoeing, kayaking
_____ Cycling (bicycling)

_____ Fishing
_____ Horseback riding
_____ Hunting
_____ Ice skating
_____ Outdoor survival
_____ Orienteering
_____ Rock climbing
_____ Sailing
_____ Skiing (cross country)
_____ Skiing (downhill)
_____ Snow shoeing

Rhythmic Activities
_____ Ballet
_____ Country swing dance
_____ Disco
_____ Folk and square dance
_____ Jazz dance
_____ Modern dance
_____ Social dance

Team Activities
_____ Baseball
_____ Basketball
_____ Field hockey
_____ Flag football
_____ Ice hockey
_____ Lacrosse
_____ Soccer
_____ Softball
_____ Speedball-speed-a-way
_____ Team handball
_____ Volleyball
_____ Wrestling

Directions for the teacher: Remind students to select only 5 choices, using the numbers 1—5 on the lines beside the activities. When analyzing the data, it is helpful to transpose numbers 1 and 5 and numbers 2 and 4. In other words, a 1 becomes a 5 and a 5 becomes a 1. A 2 is worth 4 and a 4 worth 2. The numbers are added for each activity. The activities with the most points are the most popular and those with the least points are popular.

Figure 8.7 Physical activity interest survey.
From Darst and Pangrazi (2002). *Dynamic physical education for secondary school students.* 3rd ed. San Francisco: Benjamin Cummings.

DIRECTIONS; Read each of the following statements and then blacken the appropriate number to the right of the statement to indicate how it best describes you. Please be sure to answer every item and try to be as honest and accurate as possible in your responses. There are no right or wrong answers. Your answers will be kept in the strictest confidence.

CODE: **1** = Very unlike me. **2** = Somewhat unlike me. **3** = Neither like me nor unlike me. **4** = Somewhat like me. **5** = Very much like me.

1. I'm not very good at committing myself to do things. 1 2 3 4 5
2. Whenever I get bored with projects I start. I drop them to do something else. 1 2 3 4 5
3. I can persevere at stressful tasks, even when they are physically tiring or painful. 1 2 3 4 5
4. If something gets to be too much of an effort to do, I'm likely to just forget it. 1 2 3 4 5
5. I'm really concerned about developing and maintaining self-discipline. 1 2 3 4 5
6. I'm good at keeping promises, especially the ones I make to myself. 1 2 3 4 5
7. I don't work any harder than I have to. 1 2 3 4 5
8. I seldom work to my full capacity. 1 2 3 4 5
9. I'm just not the goal-setting type. 1 2 3 4 5
10. When I take on a difficult job, I make a point of sticking with it until it's completed. 1 2 3 4 5
11. I'm willing to work for things I want as long as it's not a big hassle for me. 1 2 3 4 5
12. I have a lot of self-motivation. 1 2 3 4 5
13. I'm good at making decisions and standing by them. 1 2 3 4 5
14. I generally take the path of least resistance. 1 2 3 4 5
15. 1 get discouraged easily. 1 2 3 4 5
16. If I tell somebody I'll do something, you can depend on it being done. 1 2 3 4 5
17. I don't like to overextend myself. 1 2 3 4 5
18. I'm basically lazy. 1 2 3 4 5
19. I have a very hard-driving, aggressive personality. 1 2 3 4 5
20. I work harder than most of my friends. 1 2 3 4 5
21. I can persist in spite of pain or discomfort. 1 2 3 4 5
22. I like to set goals and work toward them. 1 2 3 4 5
23. Sometimes I push myself harder than I should. 1 2 3 4 5
24. I tend to be overly apathetic. 1 2 3 4 5
25. I seldom if ever let myself down. 1 2 3 4 5
26. I'm not very reliable. 1 2 3 4 5
27. I like to take on jobs that challenge me. 1 2 3 4 5
28. I change my mind about things quite easily. 1 2 3 4 5
29. I have a lot of will power. 1 2 3 4 5

Figure 8.8 Self motivation inventory. *(continues)*
Source: R. K. Dishman and W. Ickes. Self-motivation and adherence to therapeutic exercise.
Journal of Behavioral Medicine 4:421—438. 1981. Copyright © Rod K. Dishman, 1978.

CODE: **1** = Very unlike me. **2** = Somewhat unlike me. **3** = Neither like me nor unlike me. **4** = Somewhat like me. **5** = Very much like me.

30.	I'm not likely to put myself out if I don't have to.	1	2	3	4	5
31.	Things just don't matter much to me.	1	2	3	4	5
32.	I avoid stressful situations.	1	2	3	4	5
33.	I often work to the point of exhaustion.	1	2	3	4	5
34.	I don't impose much structure on my activities.	1	2	3	4	5
35.	I never force myself to do things I don't feel like doing.	1	2	3	4	5
36.	It takes alot to get me going.	1	2	3	4	5
37.	Whenever I reach a goal I set a higher one.	1	2	3	4	5
38.	I can persist in spite of failure.	1	2	3	4	5
39.	I have a strong desire to achieve.	1	2	3	4	5
40.	I dont have much self-discipline.	1	2	3	4	5

Figure 8.8 Self motivation inventory *(continued)*.

Equipment Needed: SMI test forms, pencils or pens, and scoring key.

Scoring Procedure: To reduce response bias, there are 19 negatively stated items and 21 positively stated items. Scoring should take into account if the statement is positively or negatively stated and reverse point values for negatively stated items. There is a response scoring range from 40 to 200, with higher scores indicating higher self-motivation.

Norms: None reported.

Physical Estimation and Attraction Scale

(Sonstroem, 1974)

Purpose: The purpose of the Physical Estimation and Attraction Scale (PEAS) is to measure expressed interest in physical activity (attraction) and physical self-esteem relative to physical appearance and performance (estimation). The PEAS is the first social psychological scale designed to measure components of physical self as a motivator of physical activity.

Description: The PEAS consists of 100 randomly ordered statements. Fifty-four of the statements are associated with attraction, 33 with estimation, 2 with socialization, and 11 are neutral. The estimation items require respondents to affirm or deny their physical characteristics, physical fitness, or motor ability. The attraction statements require respondents to affirm or deny their interests in various physical activities. The questionnaire is found in Figure 8.9. The responses to the statements are limited to true (the student agrees with the statement), false (the student disagrees with the statement), or neutral.

Instructions: The inventory should be administered in a quiet room free of distractions.

Keyed response*	Scale†	Attitude statement
X	N	1. I would rather see a play than a movie.
T	A	2. I prefer exercising to reading.
X	N	3. I generally prefer talking with friends to playing a family table game such as Monopoly.
T	A	4. I would much rather play softball than go for a ride in a car.
F	E	5. Most of my friends work harder than I do.
T	E	6. My body is strong and muscular compared to other boys my age.
X	N	7. I would be interested in learning to play a musical instrument.
F	A	8. Most sports require too much time and energy to be worthwhile.
X	N	9. I would have made a good accountant.
T	E	10. I am in better physical condition than most boys my age.
X	N	11. The mechanical properties of motors interest me a great deal.
X	N	12. On a Sunday afternoon, I would prefer to go to a movie rather than to go on a picnic.
T	E	13. I am quite limber and agile compared to others my age.
X	N	14. I often stick up for my own point of view even when no one agrees with me.
X	N	15. I enjoy people who talk a great deal.
T	A	16. I prefer team sports to individual sports because of the experience of playing with different people.
F	A	17. I like to be in sports that don't require a great amount of running.
T	A	18. I know that my health improves when I exercise.
F	E	19. I just don't have the coordination necessary to look like a graceful skier.
X	N	20. I prefer woodworking to tinkering with a motor.
X	N	21. One of my favorite interests is listening to music.
T	A	22. I would enjoy participating in activities such as cross-country skiing and channel swimming.
F	A	23. Music, art, or intellectual pursuits are more refreshing to me than physical activity.
F	A	24. I would rather visit an amusement park than watch a tennis match.
T	A	25. I like the social opportunities afforded by physical activity programs.
T	E	26. I am better coordinated than most people I know.
T	A	27. I would enjoy difficult mountain climbing.
X	N	28. I love to go to jazz or rock concerts.
F	A	29. I don't think that I'd enjoy participating in a judo program.
T	A	30. I enjoy the feeling of physical well-being one gets after a day's tramp in the woods.
F	A	31. I would rather watch a good movie than a hockey match.
T	A	32. I would like to belong to some type of exercise group.
T	E	33. I am a good deal stronger than most of my friends.
F	A	34. I would rather play poker than softball.
F	E	35. Compared to other people I am somewhat clumsy.

Figure 8.6 Physical estimation and attraction scale.   *(continues)*

Keyed response*	Scale†		Attitude statement
T	A	36.	I enjoy hard physical work.
F	A	37.	I like to engage in recreational exercise rather than in organized competitive athletics.
T	E	38.	I am stronger than a good many of my friends.
T	E	39.	Most people I know think I have very good physical skills.
F	E	40.	My friends seem to be more physically active than I am.
F	A	41.	I would rather walk than run through an open meadow or field.
T	A	42.	Sports provide me with a welcome escape from the pressures of present-day life.
T	A	43.	I like the rough and tumble of athletic competition.
F	A	44.	I prefer watching an exciting basketball game to playing it myself.
T	A	45.	I rather enjoy the physical risk involved when I play football.
T	A	46.	I would enjoy participating in a vigorous weight-lifting program.
T	A	47.	Long-distance running would seem to be an enjoyable activity.
F	E	48.	I doubt that I could ever get into good physical condition.
T	E	49.	My legs have as much spring as those of champion high jumpers.
F	A	50.	I don't enjoy doing things that get me sweaty and dirty.
F	A	51.	I prefer not to participate in physical activities that involve risk of injury.
T	A	52.	I would enjoy belonging to a whitewater canoe club.
F	A	53.	When tensions are high, I prefer to lie down and rest rather than to absorb myself in physical activity.
T	E	54.	If I wanted to, I could become an excellent tennis player.
T	A	55.	I enjoy performing gymnastic stunts because of the coordinated movements involved.
F	A	56.	It makes no difference to me how strong or fit I am.
T	A	57.	I would like to meet more people by engaging in various types of physical activities.
F	A	58.	After a day at school, I prefer to take it easy instead of participating in vigorous sport activities.
F	E	59.	It is difficult for me to catch a thrown ball.
T	E	60.	With a fair amount of practice I could maintain a high bowling average.
T	A	61.	I enjoy the discipline of long and strenuous physical training.
T	E	62.	I can run faster than most of my friends.
T	A	63.	Watching an athletic contest provides a welcome relief from the cares of life.
T	E	64.	With practice I could become a very good golfer.
F	A	65.	I have more important things to do than to spend time on developing and maintaining physical fitness.
T	A	66.	I would rather run in a track meet than play badminton.
T	E	67.	I could do better at long-distance hiking than the average boy of my age.
T	E	68.	I exhibit a fair amount of leadership in a sports situation.
F	E	69.	I lack confidence in performing physical activities.

Figure 8.6 Physical estimation and attraction scale *(continued)*.

Keyed response*	Scale†		Attitude statement
F	E	70.	Even with practice I doubt that I could learn to do a handstand well.
T	A	71.	Playing tennis appeals to me more than does golfing.
T	E	72.	I can run for longer distances than most boys of my age.
T	E	73.	I am a natural athlete.
F	A	74.	The thought of getting sweaty and dirty often keeps me from exercising.
T	A	75.	I love to run.
F	A	76.	Getting into good physical shape takes too much effort to be really worth it.
T	E	77.	I have a strong throwing arm for baseball or softball.
T	A	78.	Karate competition must be fun.
F	E	79.	It would be very difficult for me to learn to do a back dive.
F	A	80.	I would prefer to listen to a concert than to watch a gymnastics match.
T	E	81.	I am well-equipped to excel at physical activities.
F	A	82.	Being strong and highly fit is not really that important to me.
T	A	83.	Absorbing myself in a good sport activity provides an escape from the routine of a school day.
F	E	84.	Even with practice I doubt that I could ever learn to do a cartwheel well.
T	A	85.	Exercise relieves me of emotional strain.
F	A	86.	I would play sports more often if I didn't get so tired.
T	E	87.	Probably I could get into good physical condition faster than most fellows my age.
F	E	88.	I often doubt my physical abilities.
T	A	89.	I would rather play touch football than go to an amusement park.
X	S	90.	Participation in physical activity improves me as a social person.
F	E	91.	I'm not very good at most physical skills.
T	A	92.	I enjoy the exhilarated feeling one gets after doing calisthenics.
X	S	93.	I'm not able to meet many worthwhile people through participation in sports.
F	E	94.	Poor timing handicaps me in certain physical activities.
T	E	95.	I am a natural leader in sport activities.
T	A	96.	I would rather play active sports like soccer and basketball than participate in activities like badminton and softball.
T	A	97.	I believe it is important that a person belongs to a group that participates in sport activities together.
T	A	98.	I would rather watch either a baseball or basketball game than visit a museum or art gallery.
F	A	99.	Target archery appeals to me more as an activity than does tennis.
T	A	100.	I believe one of the greatest values of physical activity is the thrill of competition.

Figure 8.6 Physical estimation and attraction scale *(continued)*.

*T when True is the positive response; F when False is the positive response; X when the statement is unscored (neutral).

†E is the physical estimation scale; A is the physical attraction scale; S is social; N is neutral. Reprinted by permission of R. J. Sonstroem, University of Rhode Island, Kingston, Rhode Island.

Validity: The relationships between the estimation scale to actual fitness and self-esteem as measured by the Tennessee Self-Concept Scale are moderate (Sonstroem, 1978). The attraction scale has been reported to correlate with self-reported participation in physical activity (Neale, Sonstroem, and Metz, 1969; Sonstroem, 1976).

Reliability: Coefficients of reliability for internal consistency and stability ranged from .87 to .94 (Sonstroem, 1974; 1976).

Age Level: The validity studies have been conducted primarily with adolescent boys. However, the scale has been used with male and female adults.

Equipment Needed: PEAS forms, pencils or pens, and scoring key.

Scoring Procedure: The answer key, provided with the scale, indicates the response to each statement that demonstrates a positive attitude. Each response consistent with the scoring key receives one point. The total score is the sum of all the individual scores. The higher the score, the more positive the attitude toward physical activity. The estimation and attraction scales can be scored separately.

Norms: None available. Mean scores for the scales as derived from Sonstroem's research are available.

Measuring Self-Concept

One of the primary purposes for all domains of physical education is to enhance the self-concept of students (Pangrazi, 2001; Dauer, and Pangrazi, 2002). Similarly, in the exercise setting it is important for the specialist to strengthen participants' self-concepts through exercise and activity. Developing the self-concept is a slow process that requires participants to observe, differentiate, and select until they can understand and accept the image of who they are.

Physical education, exercise programs, and planned physical activity provide environments that can facilitate the development of self. The ability to establish settings that stimulate achievement, enhance health and physical well-being, allow for risks to be taken, and teach responsibility makes physical activity environments effective in promoting active lifestyles and positive self-images. Orchestrating learning experiences that foster a person's self-image and utilizing teaching techniques that promote a feeling of self-worth require a great deal of preparation and skill. Like any other objective, the development of self should be monitored through assessment and evaluation techniques.

In recent years, interest and concern about the affective behavior of individuals has increased. This increased concern is merited because an individual's affective behavior influences that person's learning and development. The multidimensional characteristics of the self-concept are often cited in the professional literature. Throughout the literature, the self-concept is viewed as a link between observable behavior and the underlying processes of the individual. Some authors contend that self-concept is a directing force for all behavior (Snodgrass, 1977). Others even suggest that it is education's obligation to help youngsters develop better self-concepts (Pangrazi, 1969).

Self-concept is a composite view of how one sees oneself, comprising ideas, attitudes, values, and commitments. Rather than originating from within the individual, self-concept is learned. Its development begins soon after birth and continues throughout life, although it is thought to be relatively stable by the age of 11 or 12 (Fitts, 1971). Children and youth develop a view of themselves from the ways in which they are treated by others. Individuals form their self-concept from the types of experiences they have had in life. Youth develop feelings that they are liked, wanted, accepted, and able from the actual experiences of being wanted, accepted, and successful (Combs, 1965). Many experts believe that a sense of belonging, personal competence, and a sense of worth are important parts of total growth and development (Felker, 1974).

Through physical activity, youth are provided with opportunities to participate in learning experiences designed to develop self-concept. Through exploration, experimentation, and structured learning experiences, youth begin to differentiate their capacities and potentials. Establishing a warm, positive learning environment is crucial, and physical educators and exercise scientists must be prepared to measure and evaluate the changes that occur in self-concept as a result of participation in physical activity.

The following section describes tests suitable for assessing and evaluating the progress of self-concept development.

Cratty Adaptation of Piers-Harris Self-Concept Scale

(Cratty, 1970)

Purpose: To measure how children feel about their physical appearance and motor ability.

Description: The Piers-Harris (1964) scale consists of statements made by children regarding their likes and dislikes about themselves. Using the Piers-Harris scale as a model, Cratty (1970) developed a scale that focuses on children's view of their physical ability and appearance. The resultant self-report inventory classified statements into five categories: feelings about general well-being, social competence, physical appearance, physical ability, and social achievement. Children are asked to respond to the statements by answering yes or no. The statements can be read to children who are unable to read. An example of this instrument is found in Figure 8.10.

Validity: Internal validity was established using item analysis.

Reliability: Test-retest procedures resulted in a reliability coefficient of .82.

Age Level: Kindergarten through grade 6.

Test Area: Any quiet area free of distractions.

Equipment Needed: Self-concept scale and pencils.

Scoring Procedure: One point is awarded for each positive response. The total score is the sum of expected responses for the statements.

Norms: None available.

For Additional Information: To obtain information about the Piers-Harris Self-Concept Scale write to: Piers-Harris Children's Self-Concept Scale, The Way I Feel About Myself, Counselor Recordings and Tests, Box 6186 Acklan Station, Nashville, TN, 37212.

Name _____ Date _____ Grade _____ M _____ F _____			
Scoring Key†			
+	1. Are you good at making things with your hands?	Yes	No
+	2. Can you draw well?	Yes	No
+	3. Are you strong?	Yes	No
+	4. Do you like the way you look?	Yes	No
	5. Do your friends make fun of you?	Yes	No
+	6. Are you handsome/pretty?	Yes	No
	7. Do you have trouble making friends?	Yes	No
+	8. Do you like school?	Yes	No
	9. Do you wish you were different?	Yes	No
	10. Are you sad most of the time?	Yes	No
	11. Are you the last to be chosen in games?	Yes	No
+	12. Do girls like you?	Yes	No
+	13. Are you a good leader in games and sports?	Yes	No

Figure 8.10 Cratty adaptation of Piers-Harris self-concept scale.

†Plus sign (+) indicates questions stated in a positive way. A "yes" response indicates good self-concept. A "no" response on unmarked questions indicates good self-concept.

From B. Cratty, *Movement Activities, Motor Ability, and the Education of Children*, 1970. Courtesy of Charles C. Thomas, Publisher, Springfield, Illinois.

Coopersmith Self-Esteem Inventory

(Coopersmith, 1967)

Purpose: To measure the self-esteem of children.

Description: This inventory is published in either a short or long form. The short form, shown in Figure 8.11, comprises 25 statements about how an individual feels about a particular situation. Students are asked to read each statement and indicate whether the statement describes how they usually feel ("like me") or does not describe how they usually feel ("unlike me"). There are no correct or incorrect answers.

Validity: Face validity is assumed.

Reliability: Test-retest reliability obtained for the Coopersmith Self-Esteem Inventory over a five-week interval with a sample of 30 fifth-grade children was .88, and the reliability after a three-year interval with a different sample of 55 children was .70. The total scores on the long and short forms correlate .86.

Age Level: Ages 8–10.

Test Area: Any quiet area free of distractions.

Equipment Needed: Self-concept scale and pencils.

Scoring Procedure: The score is the total number of responses marked in the direction that indicated high self-esteem. One point is awarded for each positive response.

Norms: None available.

University of California, Davis

Name _____ School _____

Class _____ Date _____

Please mark each statement in the following way:

    If the statement describes how you usually feel, put a check (✔) in the column, "LIKE ME."

    If the statement does not describe how you usually feel, put a check (✔) in the column, "UNLIKE ME."

There are no right or wrong answers.

	LIKE ME	UNLIKE ME
Example: I'm a hard worker.		
1. I often wish I were someone else.		
2. I find it very hard to talk in front of the class.		
3. There are lots of things about myself I'd change if I could.		
4. I can make up my mind without too much trouble.		
5. I'm a lot of fun to be with.		
6. I get upset easily at home.		
7. It takes me a long time to get used to anything new.		
8. I'm popular with kids my own age.		
9. My parents usually consider my feelings.		
10. I give in very easily.		
11. My parents expect too much of me.		
12. It's pretty tough to be me.		
13. Things are all mixed up in my life.		
14. Kids usually follow my ideas.		
15. I have a low opinion of myself.		
16. There are many times when I'd like to leave home.		
17. I often feel upset in school.		
18. I'm not as nice looking as most people.		
19. If I have something to say, I usually say it.		
20. My parents understand me.		
21. Most people are better liked than I am.		
22. I usually feel as if my parents are pushing me.		
23. I often get discouraged in school.		
24. Things usually don't bother me.		
25. I can't be depended on.		

Figure 8.11 Coopersmith self-esteem inventory (SEI).

From *The Antecedents of Self-Esteem* by Stanley Coopersmith. Copyright © 1967 by W. H. Freeman and Company. Reprinted with permission.

Measuring Social Competence

The physical education environment should offer an instructional setting that fosters positive social behaviors and should teach children desirable social standards and ethical concepts (Pangrazi, 2001). Youth must experience and understand the value of cooperation, participation, and patience through guided physical activities. By utilizing proper teaching methodologies, the instructor can help students differentiate between acceptable and unacceptable social behavior.

Physical education is one way that youth become aware of how they interact with others and how others view them. In this environment, students need to receive feedback from significant others about their behavior; otherwise, they may never realize what actions are considered socially inappropriate. A teacher must continually be alert to reinforce youngsters' proper social behaviors and discourage improper actions.

Many factors influence a student's behavior: peer pressure, stages of emotional development, and type of home life are just a few examples. Though teachers cannot control outside factors, they can strive to establish a positive, healthy environment in physical education. By establishing appropriate behaviors for students in activity settings, the teacher can contribute to their development of social competence. Teaching social competence may be difficult, but it is a worthwhile goal. Whatever the outside circumstances, teachers should insist on proper student behavior in class. Progress toward the attainment of this goal should be monitored.

This chapter has discussed the use of paper-and-pencil inventories to assess and evaluate students' attitudes toward physical activity and self-concept. In the case of social competence, however, overt social behaviors are of greater interest than the manner in which experiences have been internalized. Social factors certainly influence learning outcomes of physical education and can be identified. As a consequence, many instruments to measure the social behavior of youth have been developed.

Sociometry

The technique of sociometry was pioneered by Moreno (1934) and Jennings (1948) and has become a popular method of evaluating and understanding social outcomes. **Sociometry** is a scientific method of studying groups and examining the interrelationships among the individuals making up these groups (Kozman, 1951). Data obtained through sociometric technique can be easily quantified and graphically depicted to show the relationships existing at a given time among members of a particular class. Use of a test-retest format allows teachers to note changes in individual and group status. The ability to objectively assess and evaluate social behavior can assist teachers in structuring lessons, managing classes, and evaluating progress toward development of acceptable social behavior.

Basically, sociometric technique asks respondents to choose, based on predetermined criteria, with whom they would like to live, study, work, play, and so on. Questions are written so that each relates to an activity or lesson that the students have experienced. For example, a teacher might ask children to list three classmates they would like to include on their softball team.

Sociometric choices should be organized in an understandable manner if they are to be properly used and interpreted. The matrix chart, or tabulation sheet, shown in

Table 8.1 Sociometric tabulation form.

Chosen → Chooser ↓	Student Number	Thomas 1	Thuy 2	Darius 3	Sarah 4	Manuel 5	Patti 6	Shantrell 7	Ryan 8	Jacob 9	Rolando 10	Choices Used
Thomas	1				(1)*		(2)	(3)				3
Thuy	2						1					1
Darius	3	3				2					(1)	3
Sarah	4	(3)					1			(2)		3
Manuel	5						2		1			2
Patti	6	(1)						(1)		(2)		3
Shantrell	7	(2)			1		(3)					3
Ryan	8						2					2
Jacob	9				(1)		(3)	2				3
Rolando	10			(1)						2		2
Total 1st choices		1	0	1	3	0	2	1	1	0	1	
Total 2nd choices		1	0	0	0	1	3	1	0	3	0	
Total 3rd choices		2	0	0	0	0	2	1	0	0	0	
TOTAL choices		4	0	1	3	1	7	3	1	3	1	

*Circled number indicates mutual choices.

Table 8.1 represents one method to tabulate sociometric results. To design a simple matrix chart, students' names are listed down the left side of the chart and across the top. Each student's level of choice is listed in the appropriate box. From Table 8.1 the following are Sarah's choices:

1. Patti
2. Jacob (mutual choice)
3. Thomas (mutual choice)

Sarah's choices are recorded on the matrix chart next to her name in her horizontal row. The number one is placed in the column under Patti's name; number two is placed in the column under Jacob's name; and so on. When two students select each other in a mutual choice, the numbers are circled. After the tabulating is completed, each choice (regardless of number) is given a point value of one. The total number of choices a student receives on a sociometric question indicates the degree to which the student is accepted by classmates.

Sociogram

Although the matrix chart is useful to organize raw data and determine the level of social acceptance of group participants, it does not provide a total picture of the group's social fabric. The **sociogram** graphically depicts the raw data in a form that is easily understood and interpreted. The sociogram is devised from information contained on the matrix chart. For example, look at the data recorded on the matrix chart in Table 8.1. The sociogram developed from this data is depicted in Figure 8.12. Developing a sociogram from this information requires the following steps:

1. Determine those group members chosen most often and place them near the center of the sociogram. Those chosen least often should be located near the perimeter.

2. Plot the placement of individual cells in pencil and expect to rearrange the location of individuals on the chart.

3. The number assigned to the student on the matrix chart is the identification number for the sociogram.

4. Choices indicated on the matrix chart are represented by lines connecting cells on the sociogram. Arrows (→) from one cell to another indicate choices that are in one direction only. Parallel lines (══) indicate mutual choices.

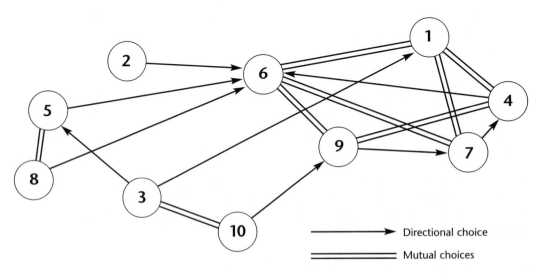

Figure 8.12 Sociogram based on data in Table 8.1.

5. To keep the chart from getting unnecessarily cluttered, plot only mutual and unreciprocated choices.

Sociometric testing can be a valuable tool for the physical education teacher. Using sociometric techniques will assist in better understanding group structure and the behavior of group members.

Problems Associated with Measuring Social Variables

The assessment of social variables can be a difficult and, at times, a time-consuming task. Recognizing the problems associated with collecting information on the social competencies of students will assist teachers in planning and implementing measurement of social factors.

1. The reliability and validity of behavior rating scales is continually questioned. Correlational coefficients indicating the degree of consistency among questions on a scale may be within acceptable limits, yet may prove unreliable over time, especially when the rating involves several different raters.

2. The teacher's assessment of students' behavior probably changes over time. Throughout the school year, it is expected that the teacher's view of students' behavior is, at least, moderately altered. There is no research to suggest that reliable measures of student behavior can be obtained with a few ratings over an extended period of time. Woody (1969) has reported that a student's score is as dependent on the rater's feeling about the student as it is on student's actual behavior. The influence of the "halo effect" on interpreting behavior can be reduced by utilizing trained raters. The availability of video recording equipment also has created an opportunity for teachers to monitor the behavior of students on a regular basis and should provide the means to conduct validation and reliability studies on social behavior scales.

3. Physical educators often are viewed as unskilled in observational techniques, thereby rendering results invalid. Increasingly, studies are being completed by physical educators that utilize well-designed rabrics or systematic observation. Systemic observation is a way of collecting quantifiable data by observing student and/or teacher behaviors. Advances in research methodologies and technology now afford physical educators the means to systematically analyze students' behavior in their classes. More information about these techniques is in Chapter 11.

4. The appearance of some behaviors during formal observation may be fleeting or nonexistent. Students need time to exhibit certain social characteristics. Their ability to get along with classmates may not have a chance to avail itself during self-testing units. Similarly, on-task persistence may not be evident during a large group activity. Regardless, observations of student behavior should be scheduled to allow the student every chance to display the behaviors sought.

5. Social behavior scales are limiting. It is impossible to categorize the many different types of social behaviors that can be displayed in a physical activity setting. Selecting an instrument that includes the behaviors of interest in the assessment is the key to the successful evaluation.

6. The social behaviors being measured may not be related to physical education. The learning experiences in physical education may not provide instruction or activities that foster specific behaviors. If the physical education curriculum is not structured to promote certain behaviors, attempts should not be made to measure those traits.

Selected Social-Psychological Instruments

While it is beyond the scope of this chapter to review instruments used in social-psychological research, it is important that you recognize the breadth of measurement inventories, questionnaires, and scales that are available. Most of these instruments have been developed for research purposes. You should closely analyze how the instrument was validated. Also, recognize that if the instrument was validated on a certain population, it does not automatically mean that it is valid for other populations. For instance, if the instrument is validated with college students 18–22 years of age, then you cannot generalize this validity to adults. The instrument may or may not be valid with adults. Similarly, instruments validated for women may not be valid for men and vice versa. Most of these survey-type instruments used in exercise and sport psychology are relatively easy to administer, but care must be taken in the selection of the instrument and in the analysis of the results.

Ostrow (1996) completed a thorough summary of instruments used in social-psychology of sport, psychology of sport, and psychology of exercise. In this published review, there are 314 instruments placed in 20 different categories. This publication will be a valuable resource if you ever need to locate an instrument to gather social or psychological data in activity settings. The following is a listing of some of the more widely used instruments and is representative of what is available:

Group Environment Questionnaire—measures group cohesion using a multidimensional model that takes into account both task and social cohesion factors.

Carron, A., Widmeyer, W., and Brawley, L. (1985). Assessing the cohesion of teams: Validity of the Group Environment Questionnaire. *Journal of Sport Psychology*. 9:275–294.

Johnson Sportsmanship Attitude Scales—measures the student's attitude toward competition.

Johnson, M. (1969). Construction of sportsmanship attitude scales. *Research Quarterly*. 40:312–316.

Stages of Change Scale for Exercise and Physical Activity—measures and identifies the specific stage of exercise—precontemplation, contemplation, preparation, action, maintenance—at which the subject may be at a particular point in time.

Marcus, B., Selby, V., Niaura, R., and Rossi, J. (1992). Self-efficacy and the stages of exercise behavior change. *Research Quarterly for Exercise and Sport*. 63:60–66.

Sport Competition Anxiety Test—designed to measure competitive trait anxiety, it describes individual differences in how competitive situations are perceived.

Martens, R. (1977). *Sport competition anxiety test*. Champaign, IL: Human Kinetics Press.

Competitive State Anxiety Inventory 2—measures precompetitive state anxiety of the athlete right before competition.

Martens, R., Vealey, R., and Burton, A. (1990). *Competitive anxiety in sport*. Champaign, IL: Human Kinetics Press.

Profile of Mood States—uses six different subscales—vigor, confusion, anxiety, tension, anger, and fatigue—to measure one's emotional state of mind, feeling, inclination, or disposition.

McNair,D., Lorr, M., and Droppleman, L. (1971). *EDITS manual for POMS*. San Diego: Educational and Industrial Testing Service.

Nelson Sports Leadership Questionnaire—measures athletic leadership.

Nelson, D. (1966). Leadership in sports. *Research Quarterly*. 37:268–275.

Test of Attentional and Interpersonal Style—measures the attentional focus and the ability to shift from one attentional focus (broad to narrow and internal to external) to another.

Nideffer, R. (1976). Test of attentional and interpersonal style. *Journal of Personality and Social Psychology*. 34:394–404.

SUMMARY

The affective domain is often overlooked in the measurement and evaluation schemes of physical education and exercise programs. Though program objectives usually include affective goals, the achievement of these goals is rarely assessed. If affective objectives are included, they should be evaluated.

A quality physical education or nonschool activity program can positively influence many areas of the affective domain. This chapter includes selected instruments to measure an individual's attitudes toward physical activity, activity interests, motivation to exercise, self-concept, and social competence. A brief review of the literature, description of instruments, and information concerning advantages and disadvantages of the various methods are included. Alternative assessment strategies are also suggested.

Though measurement and evaluation in the affective domain may not be as precise as in other domains of physical education and exercise science, it is still an important area to assess. By selecting proper instruments, using appropriate alternative assessment techniques, following proper protocols of administration, and carefully interpreting results, practitioners can more thoroughly substantiate their claims of contributing to the affective development of their participants.

DISCUSSION QUESTIONS

1. In what facets of an individual's growth should physical education and exercise science make contributions? Which of these facets can be classified as belonging to the affective domain? What are the problems associated with measurement and evaluation of these affective areas?

2. In your opinion, what area of the affective domain is most important in terms of the contributions that physical education and/or exercise science should make? Give reasons for your answer.

3. Why are measurement and evaluation of affective goals often overlooked in physical education and exercise science? Is it important that this situation change? Why or why not?

4. What are the similarities and differences between the Likert scale, the two-point scale, and the semantic differential scale? What are advantages and disadvantages of each scale?

5. Suppose you are a junior high physical education teacher with coeducational classes. What two instruments would you select to assess attitudes toward physical activity and what instrument would be used to measure the self-concept of students? Briefly describe each instrument and explain why you chose the particular instrument.

6. What is meant by the term "sociometry"? How can sociometric techniques be used to help a teacher understand group dynamics of a class and, in turn, aid in the development of social competence of students?

7. Suppose you are a fitness instructor at a health club. You teach several classes of strength training to adults. What two instruments would you select to assess attitudes toward physical activity, and what instrument would you use to measure the self-motivation of the participants? Briefly describe each instrument and explain why you chose the particular instrument.

8. Explain how alternative assessment strategies can be used to assess the affective domain.

REFERENCES

Anderson, M. L. (1966). *Measurement of changes in attitudes of high school girls toward physical conditioning following an intensified physical fitness program.* Unpublished master's thesis, State University of Iowa.

Cheffers, J. T., Mancini, V. H., and Zaichkowsky, L. D. (1976). The development of an elementary physical education attitude scale. *The Physical Educator* 3:30–33.

Combs, A. W. (1965). *The professional education of teachers.* Boston: Allyn and Bacon.

Coopersmith, S. (1967). *The antecedents of self-esteem.* San Francisco, CA: W. H. Freeman.

Cratty, B. (1970). *Movement activities, motor ability, and the education of children.* Springfield, IL: Charles C. Thomas.

Darst, P., and Pangrazi, R. (2002). *Dynamic physical education for secondary school students.* 3rd ed. San Francisco: Benjamin Cummings.

Dishman, R., and Ickes, W. (1981). Self-motivation and adherence in therapuetic exercise. *Journal of Behavioral Medicine.* 4:421–438.

Dishman, R. (1990). Determinants of participation in physical activity. In Bouchard, C. et al. (Eds.) *Exercise, fitness and knowledge: A consensus of current knowledge.* Champaign, IL: Human Kinetics Press 75–102.

Felker, D. W. (1974). *Helping children to like themselves.* Minneapolis, MN: Burgess.

Fitts, W. H. (1971). The self-concept and self-actualization. *Monograph #3.* Nashville, TN: The Dade Wallace Center.

Hay, J. A. (1992). Adequacy in and predilection for physical activity in children. Clinical *Journal of Sport Medicine,* 2, 192–201.

Jennings, H. (1948). *Sociometry in group relations*. Washington, DC: American Council on Education.

Johnson, B. L., and Nelson, J. K. (1986). *Practical measurements for evaluation in physical education*. 4th ed. New York: Macmillan.

Kenyon, G. S. (1968a). A conceptual model for characterizing physical activity. *Research Quarterly* 39:560–565.

———. (1968b). Six scales for assessing attitudes toward physical activity. *Research Quarterly* 39:566–73.

Kerlinger, F. N. (1973). *Foundations of behavioral research*. New York: Holt, Rinehart and Winston.

Kozman, H. C., ed. (1951). *Group processes in physical education*. New York: Harper & Brothers.

Kubiszyn, T., and Borich, G. (1984). *Educational testing and measurement*. Glenview, IL: Scott, Foresman and Co.

Lapp, V. W. (1933). Pupil objectives in high school physical education. *Research Quarterly* 4:157–67.

Mathews, D. K. (1978). *Measurement in physical education*. 5th ed. Philadelphia, PA: W. B. Saunders.

McAfee, R. (1955). Sportsmanship attitudes of sixth, seventh, and eighth grade boys. *Research Quarterly* 26:120.

Mood D. P. (1980). *Numbers in motion: A balanced approach to measurement and evaluation in physical education*. Palo Alto, CA: Mayfield Publishing Company.

Moreno, J. L. (1934). *Who shall survive? A new approach to the problem of human relationships*. Washington, DC: Nervous and Mental Disease Publishing Co.

Neale, D. C., Sonstroem, R. J., and Metz, K. F. (1969). Physical fitness, self-esteem, and attitudes toward physical activity. *Research Quarterly* 40:743–49.

Neilsen, A. B., and Corbin, C. B. (1986, June). Physical activity commitment. Conference Abstracts, North American Society for the Psychology of Sport and Physical Activity Conference. Scottsdale, AZ, p. 93.

Nunnally, J. C. (1978). *Introduction to psychological measurement*. New York: McGraw-Hill.

Osgood, C., Suci, G., and Tannenbaum, P. (1957). *The measurement of meaning*. Urbana, IL: University of Illinois Press.

Ostrow, A. (1996). *Directory of psychological tests in the sport and exercise sciences*. 2nd ed. Morgantown, WV: Fitness Information Technology.

Pangrazi, R. P. (1969). Developing a climate for success. In *Promising practices in elementary school physical education*. Washington, DC: American Association of Health, Physical Education, and Recreation, pp. 24–28.

Pangrazi, R. P. (2001). *Dynamic physical education for elementary school children*. 13th ed. San Francisco: Benjamin Cummings.

Piers, E. V., and Harris, D. B. (1964). Age and other correlates of self-concept in children. *Journal of Educational Psychology* 55:91–95.

Richardson, C. E. (1960). Thurstone scale for measuring attitudes of college students toward physical fitness and exercise. *Research Quarterly* 31:638–43.

Simon, J. A., and Smoll, F. L. (1974). An instrument for assessing children's attitudes toward physical activity. *Research Quarterly* 45:407–15.

Snodgrass, J. (1977). Self-concept: A look at its development and some implications for physical education teaching. *Journal of Physical Education and Recreation* 48:22–23.

Sonstroem, R. J. (1974). Attitude testing: Examining certain psychological correlates of physical activity. *Research Quarterly* 45:93–103.

_____. (1976). The validity of self-perceptions regarding physical and athletic ability. *Medicine and Science in Sports* 8:126–32.

_____. (1978). Physical estimation and attraction scales: Rationale and research. *Medicine and Science in Sports* 10:97–102.

Wear, C. L. (1955). Construction of equivalent forms of an attitude scale. *Research Quarterly* 26:113–19.

Woody, R. H. (1969). *Behavioral problem children in the schools*. New York: Appleton-Century-Crofts.

REPRESENTATIVE READINGS

Adams, R. S. (1963). Two scales for measuring attitude toward physical education. *Research Quarterly* 34:91–94.

Baumgartner, T., and Jackson, A. (1999). *Measurment for evaluation in physical education and exercise science*. 6th ed. Boston: WCB McGraw-Hill.

Blanchard, B. E. (1936). A behavior frequency rating scale for the measurement of character and personality in physical education classroom situations. *Research Quarterly* 7:56–66.

Edgington, C. W. (1968). Development of an attitude scale to measure attitudes of high school freshman boys toward physical education. *Research Quarterly* 39:505–12.

Miller, David K. (2002). *Measurement by the physical educator: Why and how.* 4th ed. New York: McGraw-Hill.

Morrow, J., Jackson, A., Disch, J., and Mood, D. (2000). *Measurement and evaluation in human performance.* 2nd ed. Champaign, IL: Human Kinetics Press.

CHAPTER 9

Alternative Assessment

Key Terms

alternative assessment

authentic assessment

checklist

event task

instructional alignment

portfolio

rating scale

reliability

rubric

observation

student journal

student log

student project

validity

Objectives

1. Justify the use of alternative assessments in physical education.

2. Identify uses for authentic assessment in evaluating student performance.

3. Analyze and discuss the issues of validity and reliability with respect to alternative assessments.

4. Create a variety of alternative assessments appropriate to a physical education setting.

5. Design rating scales and checklists to be used as rubrics for assessing student performance.

Alternative Assessment

"Not everything that counts can be counted and not everything that can be counted counts." This quote by Albert Einstein is indicative of the dilemma faced by physical educators as they attempt to assess their students.

One of the biggest challenges confronting today's physical educator is that of developing meaningful assessment tools to use not only in evaluating students but also in assigning grades to them. Many standard methods of assessment are available such as skill tests and written tests. However, many physical educators find these traditional methods of assessment to be lacking. Often these traditional forms of assessment are not well matched to the material that has been taught or they do not seem to measure what the teacher is trying to assess. For example, a teacher may have taught a tennis forehand and backhand, serve, volley, doubles positioning and strategy, and scoring to a class. To assess the students, a skill test is given where one student stands at the net and tosses balls for the others to hit. The student being tested hits forehands and back-hands to marked targets on the court. While the skill test may be valid in terms of measuring ability to hit forehand and backhand ground strokes to a target on the court, it may not be a true indicator of the student's ability to play a game of tennis. Also, remember the teacher taught other game skills as well as strategy, positioning, and scoring. Increasingly, physical educators are looking for ways to assess students that take into account the students' ability to play the game, use their knowledge of strategy and positioning, and demonstrate their ability to play within the rules. In response to the needs of teachers to develop assessment procedures that are more meaningful, different forms of assessment have been developed. Several terms have become popular in recent years to refer to these newer forms of assessment. Two of the more common terms are **alternative assessment** and **authentic assessment**. Alternative assessment refers to any type of assessment that differs from a traditional test. Some examples of alternative assessment include projects, portfolios, event tasks, student logs or journals, observations, checklists, and rating scales. Each of these will be described more fully later in the chapter. Authentic assessment emphasizes a test taking place in a "real world setting" (Linn and Gronlund, 1995).

In determining whether or not an assessment is authentic, the following standards have been adapted from Wiggins (1998) and related to a physical education scenario.

An assessment is authentic if it:

1. Is as gamelike as possible. The task enables students to perform as they would in a game.

2. Requires cognitive engagement. Students actively apply cognitive tasks such as rules, strategy, and positioning that have been taught to their game play.

3. Asks students to apply skills. Rather than perform skills in a relatively closed or static environment, students apply skills and knowledge in a dynamic or game-like setting.

Some resources use the terms "alternative" and "authentic" interchangeably. However, in physical education, alternative assessment refers to assessment tools such as portfolios and student logs rather than traditional skills testing and multiple choice tests. Authentic assessment is used to describe assessment that takes into account the context of the game or sport and is more likely to measure students' ability to actually play a game rather than their ability to perform isolated game skills. Thus, authentic assessment is a form of alternative assessment.

The focus of this chapter is to familiarize prospective teachers with new and innovative assessment tools and the issues associated with such tools. Additionally, prospective teachers are provided with guidance in the development of a variety of alternative assessments suitable for grades K–12.

Rationale for Alternative Assessments

Teachers deal with assessment in each lesson they teach. Although they may not always be formally assessing, teachers are constantly making judgments about a student's abilities. At times, this judgment is used for formative assessment. Other times, the judgment is used to determine a student's grade. Teachers may, on occasion, be asked to provide justification for their grading practices. In this section, several reasons for supporting alternative assessments are provided.

Accountability

Today's schools are under increasing pressure to show that students are making progress and learning. Teachers are also under pressure to show that their students are meeting state and national standards. Thus, a physical educator's effectiveness is inextricably linked to demonstrating that learning is occurring in his or her classes. As the field of physical education finds itself in a position of having to be defended from budget and curricular cutbacks, it is vital that physical educators find ways to demonstrate the effectiveness of their programs. One way to do this is by developing meaningful assessment tools that are perceived to be fair, objective, and accurate in their measurement of student learning. Alternative assessment provides the teacher with the tools to make accurate and defensible assessments.

Weaknesses of Standard Testing Practices

There are several reasons why standardized skill tests may not be the best choice to use in assessing student learning. First, standardized tests with validated norms are generally designed for rather specific populations. For example, the AAHPER Football Skills Test, developed in 1966, is designed for boys ages 10–18. Thus, the available norms may not match the age or gender of the students the teacher wishes to assess.

Second, the standardized test may not test the specific content taught by the teacher. As noted in the example above, the test may measure only one skill or aspect of a game when the teacher wants to assess overall play.

Third, standardized tests are typically time consuming to set up and operate. Often, measurements are needed and lines or markers need to be drawn or taped down on the floor. A teacher with multiple classes or little time between classes may be hard pressed to accurately set up and run such a test.

Finally, standardized tests often depend on a contrived environment. A ball will often be tossed or rolled to a stationary student, rather than actually hit from a bat or racket. Whereas an actual game is played in an open environment, a skills test is typically conducted in a closed environment, limiting the authenticity of the test.

That said, standardized tests can be useful as a means of providing formative feedback to students regarding their skills in a particular situation. Skill tests can also be used in station work as a form of self-testing. However, as a means of assessing attainment of all course objectives, their use is somewhat limited.

Authenticity

Most physical educators would agree that an ultimate goal of instruction in team and individual sport activities is to provide students with the skills to allow them to enjoy participation in the actual game. Alternative assessments are the best way for physical educators to evaluate proficiency in game play. It stands to reason that if an educator wants to know how well students can play a game, the teacher should have a systematic way of watching a game and evaluating play. Teachers may be interested in student attainment of various affective instructional goals such as sportsmanship and cooperation. Teachers may also be interested in seeing if students demonstrate knowledge of rules and strategy. Alternative assessments can be developed to make a reasonable assessment of game play, various affective behaviors, and cognitive understanding.

Objectivity

Physical educators who want to assess student proficiency in actual game play may limit themselves to simple observation of play and making a subjective judgment. This is not the fairest way to determine a grade. Simply watching game play, also called "eyeballing," lacks objectivity, is unreliable, and does not guarantee all students an equal opportunity to demonstrate their skills. For example, suppose a teacher is evaluating soccer game play in her high school class. One team has several highly experienced players and, as a result, is on offense for most of the game. Students on that team, whether they are actually skilled or not, will benefit from the perception that their team is performing well and would likely receive a good grade in game play. Likewise, students on the weaker team may not be able to demonstrate their skills if they are not systematically observed. In a similar vein, a weak student is often able to move with the flow of the game and never actually contribute to team play. These students are not evaluated in any kind of objective way when eyeballing is used and thus the accuracy of the grade suffers.

Accuracy

If a teacher wants to assess individual skills rather than overall game play, alternative assessments are also effective. As mentioned above, a standardized skills test is often conducted in a closed environment. Alternative assessments allow the teacher to modify the evaluation and make the environment as dynamic or open as necessary to ensure the accuracy of the test. A variety of instruments such as rating scales or checklists provide the teacher with a systematic method to assess skills, whether in a game or drill setting. Additionally, alternative assessments such as logs or portfolios allow students to demonstrate deeper understanding of course objectives or a level of commitment to activity.

Validity and Reliability

Although alternative assessment offers exciting opportunities in the evaluation of students, two important concepts must be reviewed. **Validity** and **reliability** must be maintained as assessments move toward becoming more authentic. As you will recall from Chapter 4, a test is said to be valid if it accurately measures the attribute that it is designed to measure. A test is said to possess reliability if it gives consistent results. These two concepts must also be kept in mind when developing alternative assessments. According to Wiggins (1998), a simple two-question technique may be used to check the potential validity and reliability of an alternative assessment:

1. Could the student do well at the task for reasons that have little to do with desired understanding or the skill being assessed?

2. Could the student do poorly at the task for reasons that have little to do with the desired understanding or skill?

The goal of asking these questions is to remove the elements of randomness and luck from the testing situation. The teacher's goal is to have an assessment that will only allow someone to score well if they possess the attributes being tested.

Validity Issues

As mentioned previously, standardized skill tests may not always measure the actual content taught by the teacher, leading to validity concerns. The simplest way to check the validity of the assessment is to compare the assessment to the instructional objectives. For example, suppose a physical educator has the following instructional objective:

"The student will be able to perform a tennis forehand groundstroke into the opposing court using good form."

To measure whether or not a student can actually execute a forehand, a checklist or rating scale could be used. The criteria on the assessment tool would correspond to the elements of a forehand groundstroke emphasized in class. This would then be a valid assessment because it measures the instructional objective.

Or:

"The student will be able to perform a tennis forehand groundstroke into the opposing court using good form and appropriate strategy during a doubles game."

In this case, an assessment tool would need to be developed that incorporated the elements listed in the instructional objective—performance of a tennis forehand groundstroke, use of good form, and use of appropriate strategy—that could be used during actual doubles game play.

In each of these instances, the instructional objectives are used as a guide in determining validity of the assessment.

Reliability Issues

Reliability can be a cause for concern in developing alternative assessments. An old maxim of testing states that "To be valid, a test must be reliable." This is also the case with alternative assessment, in that a test may be repeatable, yielding consistent scores over time, yet not be a valid test in relation to the instructional objective. For example, suppose a physical educator is able to devise a basketball checklist for shooting a jump shot. The checklist may be reliable in that over repeated testing, scores remain relatively constant. That alone does not ensure that the assessment is relevant or valid with regard to the instructional objectives of the teacher.

Closely related to the issues of validity and reliability is that of objectivity. Objectivity refers to developing an assessment tool that is as free of bias as possible. Because many assessments of psychomotor skills depend on observation, it is incumbent on the teacher to develop an alternative assessment that is as objective as possible. By clearly describing the desired performance, there is less chance that subjectivity will enter the picture. Limiting subjectivity is the greatest challenge to constructing fair and accurate assessment instruments. Tips for maintaining validity, reliability, and objectivity will be provided as guidelines for developing rubrics are discussed.

Types of Alternative Assessments

This text has mentioned different types of alternative assessments. In this section, each type will be briefly defined. In the next section, guidelines to develop and assess alternative assessments will be examined. Many examples of alternative assessment have been developed to help teachers assess students' learning. An excellent resource for these assessments is *Moving Into the Future: National Standards for Physical Education* (1995), developed by the National Association for Sport and Physical Education (NASPE).

Student Projects

A **student project** refers to a range of activities in which class concepts are incorporated into a finished product following guidelines that have been established by the instructor. A project could include any type of assignment in which students apply what they have learned to produce a solution to a problem, synthesize class material, solve a problem, or apply class concepts to a real-life situation. A project could also require students to integrate material from other disciplines.

Portfolios

Portfolios have been used by artists, photographers, and models for years as a way to portray a body of work. In recent years, portfolios have also become increasingly popular as a form of alternative assessment. A portfolio is defined as a collection of student work compiled over time and reviewed against criteria. Note that the definition uses the term "collection." Some educators have the perception that a portfolio includes *all* work done by a student and for this reason resist any involvement with them. A portfolio should include an adequate representation of student work rather than being simply a collection of all work.

Event Tasks

An **event task** is a performance task that students can complete during a class period. An event task generally asks students to apply what they have learned to a real-world situation. For example, a scenario may be created that asks students to demonstrate their skills in a sport or activity, show an ability to work within a group, plan and rehearse outside of class, or create a routine that incorporates a variety of movements.

Student Logs and Journals

Student logs and **student journals** are somewhat similar and have been grouped together here. A log is simply a record of student work in which progress is noted and measured over time. A journal may include the same information as a log but generally also asks students to share information regarding feelings or attitudes, perceptions, or reflections (NASPE, 1995) with regard to the activity.

Observations

An **observation** of student performance can be done by peers, the student, or the teacher. Observations can be used to measure performance, demonstration of desired affective behaviors, ability to demonstrate strategy in a game setting, or any other observable behavior.

Developing Rubrics

When designing alternative assessments, a physical educator should be concerned with three factors: validity, reliability, and objectivity. Validity and reliability have already been examined. With regard to objectivity, it is imperative that students feel they have been assessed in a reasonable manner and that the test was a fair measure of what they have learned. To help achieve validity, reliability, and objectivity, a physical educator must develop grading guides so that scores are determined equally for all. The guide used to determine a student's score or grade is called a **rubric**. Rubrics are helpful to the students in that they help to specify the work to be done and let students know what the teacher's expectations are for the assessment. Rubrics are helpful to the teacher in that they help the teacher grade fairly and consistently.

Purpose of Rubrics

Herman, Aschbacher, and Winters (1996) list the purpose of rubrics as follows:

1. *Rubrics help teachers define excellence and plan how to help students achieve it.* Picture yourself grading a written assignment that your class of 30 sophomores has turned in. As you begin reading, you notice that some of the assignments are very well written, and free of spelling and grammatical errors, but the information provided is only average. Others have interesting ideas but the ideas are not fully explained or developed. Others are incomplete in that some of the elements in the assignment have not been addressed. How do you differentiate between these assignments? How much weight do you assign to things like spelling and grammar? A rubric provides answers to these questions and helps you to discriminate between grades so that the "A" papers are similar to each other, as are the "B" and "C" papers. Or, picture yourself observing your class play in a soccer tournament at the end of the unit. As you watch, you see differing skill levels. Some students demonstrate complete understanding of the rules, while others don't seem to know basic rules. How do you decide which skills should be assessed? How much should student attitudes like enthusiasm and cooperation count for? A rubric helps assess this range of abilities fairly. Your rubric also helps students understand what your expectations are. Ideally, the rubric would have been shown or given to the students beforehand so that there are no misunderstandings regarding the assessment of their play.

2. *Rubrics communicate to students what constitutes excellence and how to evaluate their own work.* Suppose you ask students to design a floor exercise routine as a culminating event in your gymnastics unit. You'll want to define top levels of performance and let students know where they stand in comparison to others in the class with regard to their grade. Often the teacher has a fairly clear idea of what a top performance is, but details and how to differentiate between levels of performance are not as clear. Your rubric will help you make these decisions in a fair and equitable manner.

3. *Rubrics communicate goals and results to parents and others.* As mentioned earlier in this chapter, teachers must make their grades defensible. While it would seem obvious that students deserve to know how their grade was determined, parents and school administrators are also well served by understanding how a student's grade was decided. A rubric sends a clear message that the teacher has thought through the assignment and how it would be graded.

4. *Rubrics help teachers or other raters be accurate, unbiased, and consistent in scoring.* Using a rubric helps teachers to be accurate, in that the teacher will be looking at the same performance characteristics for each student. Having a standard list to observe keeps the teacher focused and consistent. A teacher may be reluctant to incorporate alternative assessments due to the volume of grading that is anticipated. Many times, this worry can be alleviated by having students learn to assess each other. Students can often learn from each other when they are placed in a position of observing closely enough to assess performance. Students can, and should, be trained to help in assessing student performance. However, this can lead to a second concern. What if the students are inconsistent with their scoring? Will the reliability of the assessment be compromised by having students assess each other? This concern can be eased by developing rubrics with clear standards and easily observable behaviors. Clear standards help all evaluators make important distinctions between levels of performance.

5. *Rubrics document the procedures used in making important judgments about students.* Issuing a grade to a student should never be done arbitrarily or with little thought. For physical education to be taken seriously in schools, the grades issued to students must be based on sound reasoning and should always be well documented. With any type of assessment, it is important for teachers to maintain **instructional alignment**. Instructional alignment refers to the idea of matching each instructional objective to some form of assessment. Writing instructional objectives that a teacher has no way of measuring is poor teaching practice and a disservice to students. In the same vein, assessing students for a behavior that is not articulated in the instructional objectives is blatantly unfair to the students.

The rubric for an alternative assessment must be developed with care. When writing a rubric, teachers should try to develop unique descriptors that will fully differentiate between various levels of performance. Wiggins (1998) cautions against simply using comparative language such as: "very clear, somewhat clear, occasionally clear, not clear" because that type of language is often anything but clear in discriminating between different levels of performance. Wiggins notes that "reliance on comparative language stems from a failure to seek the unique features of performance in different levels of students' work" (p. 172). Comparatives, then, are more likely to describe what a student cannot do rather than providing an accurate assessment of what the student actually *can* do.

Guidelines for Rubrics

The following general guidelines for rubrics have been adapted from Wiggins (1998) to be more relevant to a physical educator.

The best rubrics are those that:

1. *Discriminate among performances in a valid way.* This is done by assessing core elements of the task rather than those that are simply the easiest to count and score. For example, if a teacher is interested in assessing technique in spiking a volleyball, but then simply counts how many balls are hit over the net or how many strike a target on the court, the assessment is not valid. Though it is certainly easier to simply count successful spikes or those that clear the net, the technique is not being evaluated.

2. *Rely on descriptive language rather than comparative language.* For example, different levels of performance are described rather than noted as being "somewhat better" than another. This guideline requires the teacher to fully examine the skill itself and what performers at different skill levels actually look like.

3. *Provide useful discrimination.* Generally teachers find rubrics more useful when the number of levels of their rubric corresponds to the letter grades that they use. For example, if an elementary teacher grades on a scale of "exceeds expectations, meets expectations, or needs improvement," a rubric with three levels may be most appropriate. If a secondary teacher grades on a traditional five-point letter scale of A, B, C, D, or F, then a rubric with five levels may be most helpful. Generally rubrics with more than seven levels tend to be cumbersome to use.

4. *Emphasize the finished product.* Teachers should be wary of over-rewarding the process or effort that a student uses to meet an assessment. If all students are heavily rewarded for effort, the teacher will have no tangible way to separate those who have truly learned or mastered material from those who, though they have tried hard, have simply not reached the desired performance level.

The type of rubrics used most often in alternative assessment in physical education are checklists and rating scales. These can be used to assess all of the types of alternative assessment listed earlier: student projects, portfolios, event tasks, student logs/journals, and observations.

Checklists and Rating Scales

A **checklist** is used to detect the presence or absence of the desired behavior. Checklists generally require a yes/no response and are useful for measuring narrow and concrete dimensions or for measuring attainment of basic skills.

Rating scales are used to determine the degree to which a desired behavior has been observed. Rating scales can be numerical, qualitative, or both (Herman, Aschbacher, and Winters, 1992), depending on whether a number or descriptor is used to assess performance levels. Rating scales can also be analytic or holistic (Lund, 2000).

Checklists

Checklists are generally very straightforward in that the assessor needs only to make a yes or no decision. For that reason, checklists are popular to use when students are assisting with assessment or when the checklist is to be used as a formative assessment. Checklists are also popular to use when the instructional objective states that mastery of a task is needed. Teachers will want to be sure that the checklist is assessing skills in which students have had adequate practice. Box 9.1 shows an example of a checklist for a golf swing.

Box 9.2 shows an example of a checklist for affective behavior. In this case, the behavior of sportsmanship is expected of all students; thus a checklist is very appropriate to use.

Box 9.1 Golf Checklist

Directions: Indicate whether or not the player you are rating consistently does or does not perform the skills listed by circling either Yes or No. The player should take at least three swings for you to evaluate each of the four major headings. Feel free to view the player from different positions to better see the performance.

Setup

Yes No 1. Holds club with a neutral grip (Vs point to chin).

Yes No 2. Feet are shoulder width apart.

Yes No 3. Ball is positioned in the center of the stance.

Yes No 4. A square foot, hip, and shoulder alignment is used.

Yes No 5. The blade of the club is square and perpendicular to target line.

Back Swing

Yes No 1. Arms, hands, and club start back as a unit.

Yes No 2. Weight shifts to rear foot.

Yes No 3. Back faces the target.

Yes No 4. Club shaft is parallel to the ground.

Yes No 5. Target arm is straight.

Forward Swing

Yes No 1. Arms, hands, and club start down as a unit.

Yes No 2. Weight swings to target side.

Yes No 3. Target heel is down.

Yes No 4. Arms and club are extended at contact.

Follow-Through

Yes No 1. Hips turn to face target.

Yes No 2. Weight is on target side.

Yes No 3. Rear shoulder is closer to target (club wraps around body).

Yes No 4. Balanced ending of swing.

Steps in Developing a Checklist

1. *Decide on the behavior or skill to be assessed.* Generally, with a checklist, the behavior or skill to be assessed is something that is concrete or observable. Each element included must be one that is visible to the naked eye. For example, an element commonly seen on a golf swing checklist is "Keeps eye on the ball." However, it's unlikely that an observer can truly note where the student's eyes are actually looking and focusing. Even using a videotape would make an assessment of eye movement close to impossible. To be more accurate, examine what the result of keeping the eye on the ball is. If the student actually does "keep an eye on the ball," the ball will likely not be topped or the student will not miss it

---

Box 9.2 Affective Behavior Checklist

Sportsmanship Checklist

Circle Yes or No based on your observation of the student. The student should consistently display the following behaviors to receive a Yes score.

Yes   No   Makes encouraging comments to classmates.

Yes   No   Recognizes good plays by an opponent.

Yes   No   Shows respect for official's decisions.

Yes   No   Shakes hands with opponent(s) at the game's conclusion.

Yes   No   Through his/her actions, sets a positive example to classmates.

---

entirely. So in preparing the checklist, elements like "ball is struck squarely" or "ball is not topped" would be better representations than "Keeps eyes on the ball." The teacher should focus on one behavior or skill, as trying to combine them would make the checklist ambiguous.

2. *Determine how many elements to include.* The elements of a checklist are the specific indicators to which assessors respond yes or no. Several factors will influence how many elements to include. First, if there are too many elements, the checklist will be difficult to use. A closed skill could potentially have more elements than an open skill. Since closed skills are generally discrete rather than continuous, there will be a definite beginning and end to the movement, making it easier to observe. An open skill is a bit more difficult to assess and the teacher may want to use fewer elements. However, if there are too few elements, the validity and reliability of the checklist could be compromised.

3. *Use vivid language to list each element.* Generally, elements are no longer than one sentence in length. Thus, the description of the element must be clearly stated so the observer can easily determine a yes or no response.

4. *Determine the order of listed elements.* The checklist will be much easier to use if elements are ordered to correspond with how they are typically performed. The assessment is facilitated for the observer since he or she can go through the checklist in a logical sequence. In our golf example in Box 9.1, note how elements related to addressing the ball precede elements for the backswing and forward swing, and conclude with the follow-through.

5. *Use parallel language to describe the elements.* On a checklist, a "yes" signifies correct performance or desired behavior for all elements. A "no" signifies incorrect performance or undesired behavior for all elements. For example, consider these two elements from a golf checklist:
   Keeps arms straight in addressing the ball.
   Lifts head during the swing.
In evaluating the golf swing, keeping the arms straight while addressing the ball

is desired performance and students should be working toward a "yes" score. On the other hand, lifting the head is an undesirable performance and students are working to attain a "no" score.

6. *Pilot the checklist.* Trying out the checklist is a good idea for a number of reasons. First, a trial run with a pilot ensures that directions are clear to the assessors. Second, a pilot test will also help the teacher determine if the elements are representative of the desired performance or behavior. Finally, the pilot test will reveal any logistical concerns that may affect the test situation.

7. *Revise as necessary.* Clearly, if the pilot test reveals ambiguity or difficulty in using the checklist, revise the checklist prior to using it for grading purposes.

Rating Scales

As mentioned previously, rating scales are typically numerical, qualitative, or a combination of the two.

Numerical: A numerical rating scale uses numbers to designate different levels of performance (i.e., 1, 2, 3, 4, 5, etc.). These levels of performance can be thought of as points on a continuum. The number of points on the continuum depends on the needs of the teacher and the type of performance being assessed. There is no ideal number of levels to have on the scale. Regardless of the number used, each number on the scale corresponds to a description of that level of performance.

Qualitative: A qualitative rating scale uses descriptive language to differentiate between levels of performance. These descriptors are also called indicators since they indicate what a performer looks like when performing at a certain level.

Holistic vs. Analytic: Teachers using an analytic trait rubric would evaluate each skill within the overall game. Teachers can use a holistic scale when assessing overall game performance or an overall measurement of affective behaviors. See Boxes 9.3 and 9.4 for examples of analytic and holistic rubrics.

Note that both examples are a combination of numerical and qualitative rating scales. The number identifies the level of performance attained and qualitative descriptors are used to help the assessor visualize desired performance.

Steps in Developing Rating Scales

There are many possible approaches for a teacher who wishes to develop a rating scale. That is, there are no hard and fast rules regarding rating scale construction. The steps listed here are rather straightforward and are listed in an order that should be helpful for beginning teachers or teachers for whom developing rating scales is new.

1. *Decide on the skill or behavior(s) to be assessed.* If evaluating a student's game play ability, the teacher must decide which components of the game should be evaluated. For example, in a badminton unit, the teacher may have taught overhead and underhand clears, overhead and underhand drops, the smash, singles serve, doubles serve, and drive shots. Clearly, trying to evaluate each of these shots would be time consuming. The teacher should reflect on the instructional objectives of the unit and the instructional emphasis placed on the different skills to determine which skills are most crucial to include in the rating scale. Thus, the teacher may decide to include the overhead clear and the doubles short serve in

Box 9.3 Volleyball Analytic Rating Scale

Game Skills: **Passing, serving, setting**

4 = Student executes all skills with good form and accuracy. Balls are passed from the forearms and go to the intended target. Serves are made with an overhead motion, clear the net and land in open spots on the court. Balls are set using the finger-pads of the fingers, from a balanced position, and go to the intended target.

3 = Student executes skills with good form. Passing is sometimes off target due to the ball not contacting the forearms. Setting is sometimes inaccurate or the ball rests illegally in the hands. Serves are made with an overhead motion but are not placed with any accuracy and occasionally do not clear the net.

2 = Student executes few skills with good form. Major skill breakdowns occur in two of the three skills.

1 = Student rarely uses good form. Passes regularly ricochet out of play, serves are underhand and easy to return, sets are slapped or lifted.

Court Movement Skills: **Receive serve, offensive cover, defensive cover**

4 = Student is always in correct formation to receive serve, moves to cover and play behind the offensive spiker, moves to correct defensive position whether blocking or digging.

3 = Student is usually in correct serve receive position, but stays in a stationary position and does not always cover behind the offensive spiker, and is usually in correct defensive position to either block or dig, but not both.

2 = Student is in correct serve receive position for less than half of the six rotations around the court, does not cover the offensive spiker, and occasionally blocks but is out of position for digging.

1 = Student seems unaware of the serve receive positioning, does not cover the offensive spiker, and does not attempt to block or dig balls hit to his/her area.

Cognitive Skills: **Rotation, position responsibilities as hitter or setter**

4 = Student always rotates in a clockwise manner, encourages teammates to do the same, and always assumes hitter and setter responsibilities (as a hitter, does not interfere with the setter; as a setter, gets all second balls and attempts to direct them to a hitter).

3 = Student usually rotates in a clockwise manner, occasionally interferes with the setter taking the second hit, but does usually attempt to hit balls set to him/her; as a setter, does not consistently take charge of the second ball and the sets to hitters are low.

2 = Student rotates in a clockwise manner when reminded, seldom spikes the ball but instead forearm passes it over the net; as a setter, only occasionally takes the second ball and does not direct it to a hitter.

1 = Student must be told which way to rotate, does not attempt to make an offensive play, and is ineffective as a setter.

(Box 9.3 *continues*)

(Box 9.3 *continued*)

***Affective Skills:* Self officiates ball and net contacts honestly, sportsmanship**

4 = Student always calls illegal ball (lifts, double hits) and net contacts on him/herself and consistently encourages teammates.

3 = Student calls illegal net contacts but does not consistently note illegal ball contacts and usually encourages teammates but is often quiet on the court.

2 = Student calls illegal contacts on opponents but not on him/herself, and seldom encourages teammates but occasionally makes unsporting remarks.

1 = Student does not seem to be aware of rules regarding illegal ball or net contact and frequently makes discouraging remarks.

---

the rating scale. The overhead clear may be selected as a good predictor and evaluator of a student's overall power game and the doubles serve as a predictor and evaluator of the student's overall finesse game.

The rating scale may also include cognitive or affective traits, as these have likely also been stressed in the instruction. Cognitive behaviors such as ability to keep score, knowing position responsibilities, and an understanding of rules and strategy could all be considered. Affective behaviors such as working with others, sportsmanship, recognizing good play, and respecting officials could also be considered. Note in Box 9.3 and Box 9.4 that psychomotor, cognitive, and affective skills are all included and addressed.

2. *Determine how many levels of performance to include in the rating scale.* Most resources on alternative assessment give a lot of latitude to the teacher in determining how many levels to include. Herman, Aschbacher, and Winters (1992) recommend considering the following when deciding on the number of levels to include:

   • It's possible to have too many levels. Consider what the rating scale will be used for. Is it being used as formative assessment or to determine a semester grade? Will there be multiple raters? How will this affect the reliability of the scale? There is no need to have 10 levels of performance when the goal of the assessment might be to simply group students into three levels of skill or performance.

   • It's possible to have too few levels. If the scale has only a few levels, it will be hard to distinguish between performance levels. In other words, if you are using only a three-point scale, students who are close to a level above or below may not be properly identified. It becomes much more difficult to discriminate among performance levels when there are too few.

   • Be consistent when multiple behaviors or performances are being assessed. If a teacher is assessing several performances, the same number of scale points should be used for each. This allows for an easier comparison between the scales. For example, a teacher assessing badminton skills would not want to have a four-point scale for the overhead clear, a five-point scale for the serve, and a three-point scale for the smash.

Box 9.4 Volleyball Holistic Rating Scale

Skills: **Passing, serving, setting**

Court Movement Skills: **Receive serve, offensive cover, defensive cover**

Cognitive Skills: **Rotation, position responsibilities as hitter or setter**

Affective Skills: **Self-officiates ball and net contacts honestly, sportsmanship**

4 = Student executes all skills with good form and accuracy. Balls are passed from the forearms and go to the intended target. Serves are made with an overhead motion, clear the net, and land in open spots on the court. Balls are set using the fingerpads of the fingers, from a balanced position, and go to the intended target. Student is always in correct formation to receive serve, moves to cover and play behind the offensive spiker, and moves to correct defensive position whether blocking or digging. Student always rotates in a clockwise manner, encourages teammates to do the same, and always assumes hitter and setter responsibilities (as a hitter, does not interfere with the setter; as a setter, gets all second balls and attempts to direct them to a hitter). Student always calls illegal ball (lifts, double hits) and net contacts on him/herself and consistently encourages teammates.

3 = Student executes skills with good form. Passing is sometimes off target due to the ball not contacting the forearms. Setting is sometimes inaccurate or the ball rests illegally in the hands. Serves are made with an overhead motion but are not placed with any accuracy and occasionally do not clear the net. Student is usually in correct serve receive position, but stays in a stationary position and does not always cover behind the offensive spiker, and is usually in correct defensive position to either block or dig, but not both. Student usually rotates in a clockwise manner; occasionally interferes with the setter taking the second hit, but does usually attempt to hit balls set to him/her; as a setter, does not consistently take charge of the second ball and the sets to hitters are low. Student calls illegal net contacts but does not consistently note illegal ball contacts, and usually encourages teammates but is often quiet on the court.

2 = Student executes few skills with good form. Major skill breakdowns occur in two of the three skills. Student is in correct serve receive position for less than half of the six rotations around the court, does not cover the offensive spiker, and occasionally blocks but is out of position for digging. Student rotates in a clockwise manner when reminded, and seldom spikes the ball but instead forearm passes it over the net; as a setter, only occasionally takes the second ball and does not direct it to a hitter. Student calls illegal contacts on opponents but not on him/herself, and seldom encourages teammates but occasionally makes unsporting remarks.

1 = Student rarely uses good form. Passes regularly ricochet out of play, serves are underhand and easy to return, and sets are slapped or lifted. Student seems unaware of the serve receive positioning, does not cover the offensive spiker, and does not attempt to block or dig balls hit to his/her area. Student must be told which way to rotate, does not attempt to make an offensive play, and is ineffective as a setter. Student does not seem to be aware of rules regarding illegal ball or net contact and frequently makes discouraging remarks.

Linn and Gronlund (1995) recommend using three to seven levels of performance. Lund (2000) suggests using an even number of levels to help ensure a good distribution of scores. She notes that when an odd number of levels is used, the scores tend to regress or cluster to the middle. For a beginning teacher just learning to develop rubrics and rating scales, four levels is probably the ideal number of levels to use. If using four levels, the top level, or Level 4, should describe a top performer, a very skilled student, or the elite athlete. The top level would also represent the ideal performance in terms of cognitive or affective performance, too. Level 3 would represent a level that most students should strive for. It would describe those performers who are above average in their skill level. Level 2 would describe the majority of students in a physical education class. Given some of the common constraints in a typical physical education program (class size, facility limits, amount of equipment, amount of class meeting time), a Level 2 performance is a realistic level to expect of students. Level 1, the lowest level, would represent an unacceptable performance.

3. *Determine the top level of performance.* It is important to identify the top level of performance with clear, descriptive language. To help clarify this level, refer to the instructional objectives for the unit and the types of skills that students should be learning. Here, too, the teacher must consider some of the possible constraints listed above that may exist in the physical education program because these all could have an impact on the top level of performance that can be expected from a student. These factors should be considered in developing the top level.

4. *Create additional levels of performance using parallel language.* Wiggins (1998) suggests that beginning teachers should be as clear as possible regarding the top level and then use comparative language to describe progressively weaker levels of performance. When creating these additional levels, it is helpful to use parallel language in describing performance. Refer to the volleyball rating scale in Boxes 9.3 and 9.4. Note how the language used to describe performance is similar from one level to the next. Keeping the language parallel will help raters discriminate between the various levels. This, in turn, will help increase the reliability of the rating scale.

5. *Pilot the rating scale.* Once a rating scale has been developed, do not assume that it is a finished product. First, try it out on a class. Why?

- Piloting the scale will let the teacher know if the directions for the instrument are clear and easy to follow.

- Piloting the scale will let the teacher know if the descriptors are vivid and accurate enough to depict the students in class. This is especially crucial if students will be helping out as raters.

- Piloting the scale will help the teacher decide if the correct number of levels has been used. If too many students cluster in one level, this is a good indicator that the descriptions are not descriptive enough in discriminating between skill levels.

- Piloting the scale shows the students that the teacher is committed to making the scale accurate. Students can be receptive to your goal of producing a quality assessment tool that will be used in a fair and objective manner to grade them. If the rating scale will be used to help determine a student's final grade, it will be considered a high-stakes assessment. Thus, to be fair to the student, the teacher should be using an assessment tool that is reliable and has had the bugs worked out prior to administering it to students for grading purposes.

6. *Revise as necessary.* Obviously, if clear problems exist with the rating scale, the teacher must make appropriate adjustments prior to using the instrument for grading purposes. Often it is helpful to have a second teacher help with the piloting of the rating scale and assist in possible revisions.

In the next section, you will learn how to develop other alternative assessments. To assess them, teachers will find it helpful to refer to the guidelines for development of checklists and rating scales previously described.

Developing Alternative Assessments

As teachers begin to incorporate alternative assessments into their instruction, it will be necessary for them to make a number of decisions. The following section will help them decide which alternative assessment best fits their situation. Also, guidelines for assigning and assessing these alternative assessments are given.

Student Projects

Development of student projects is only limited by a teacher's imagination. In designing a course and instructional objectives, teachers may find that one or more of their objectives can best be met by some sort of project. Projects are excellent ways to reach higher cognitive levels of thinking and incorporate critical thinking skills into student coursework. Four examples of student projects are included to give teachers a beginning idea of the possibilities that exist for student projects. It is by no means an exhaustive list and teachers are encouraged to apply their instructional objectives to other possible projects.

- **Fitness Plan Project**   Following a fitness unit, students are asked to design a personal fitness plan. The plan would take into account their fitness test results, goals for future fitness levels, and a plan that outlines the types and frequency of fitness activities in which they plan to participate. Students could also be asked to research various fitness facilities in their community to determine which type of facility would help them realize their goals.

- **Playbook Project**   Following a flag football unit, students are asked to design a playbook with an offensive and defensive system of play. Their offensive playbook would include responsibilities listed for each player's position and set a minimum number of running and passing plays to include in the project. Their defensive playbook would include both zone and player-to-player schemes.

- **Aerobic Project**   Following a unit on aerobics in which students have been exposed to a variety of aerobic styles (high/low impact, step, tai bo, kickboxing), students are asked to generate a workout routine using the aerobic style of their choice. Student routines would be designed under guidelines established by the teacher, such as length of the routine, type of music allowed, variety of movement required, and intensity levels.

- **Integration Project** Many opportunities exist for students to integrate physical education course material with other disciplines such as science, biology, geography, or history. Ideally, this type of project would be coordinated with teachers in the other disciplines. Analyzing the history and cultural significance of various sports, examining the biological implications of aerobic and anaerobic activities, and investigating the laws of physics and motion with respect to various sport implements are some possible examples of integration projects.

Guidelines for Assigning Student Projects

The following guidelines have been adapted from Herman, Aschbacher, and Winters (1992) to be used when assigning projects to students. These guidelines will also help teachers ensure that their projects are valid and reliable.

- Does the project match outcome goals the teacher has set for the students? Are complex thinking skills such as analysis and synthesis necessary for the project? Referring to the teacher's instructional objectives will help to answer this question.

- Does the project reflect the types of problems and situations that the students are likely to encounter in the future? The authenticity of the project will be enhanced if the students can see the potential for encountering the problem or situation in real life.

- Is the project fair and free of bias? Will one gender or cultural group have a built-in advantage? All students should have equal access to materials and information. All students should have received enough information in class to allow them to succeed with the project regardless of their prior experience or lack thereof.

- Is the project meaningful and engaging to the students? Students should not perceive the project as an assignment in "busy work," but rather as a project that will enhance their understanding of the subject matter.

- Is the project feasible, given the constraints of the teacher's school? Many factors may affect a teacher's decision to assign a project: class size, amount of class time spent on a particular unit, ability of the teacher to evaluate a project, and availability of and access to library and Internet resources.

Assessing Student Projects

In assessing student projects, a rubric must be designed that takes into account the specifications of the project, the time frame given to students in which to complete the project, the resources available to students, and the amount of time the teacher wants to devote to assigning grades to the project. See Box 9.5 for an example of a generic student project rubric.

Portfolios

As mentioned earlier in the chapter, portfolios have become increasingly popular as a means of assessing student progress and learning. A portfolio can include any number of noteworthy objects to help demonstrate progress and learning. Some possible examples of items to include are the following: workout logs, journals, videotapes of performance, photos, charts of student performance, quizzes and tests, statistical records, checklists, rating scales, and written reports. Before deciding what to include in the

---

Box 9.5 Example of Generic Student Project Rubric

Score	Descriptor
4	All portions of the assignment are completed in exemplary fashion. All ideas are fully explained. Additional resources have been used to strengthen the material presented.
3	All portions of the assignment are complete, but with less detail and thoroughness. No additional material has been added. Some errors in spelling and grammar occur.
2	One or two significant portions of the assignment have not been completed: other portions are brief. Multiple errors in spelling and grammar occur.
1	Project is not completed as assigned.

---

portfolio, Wiggins (1998) suggests determining the use of the portfolio. For example, should the portfolio include the student's best work or simply a representative collection of the student's overall performance? Should the work be selected by the teacher or the student? Should the portfolio be used as a tool to show student growth or as a final assessor of what the student has mastered? Answering these questions will help the teacher determine what to have included in the portfolio. Rink (2002) suggests that the portfolio be used to help the student assume some ownership of the assessment since the student will be compiling the materials. "Ideally the teacher establishes the learning goal and the student decides what goes into the portfolio that would provide evidence of the student's work toward that goal" (Rink, p. 273, 2002). Additionally, the physical educator has other issues to consider with regard to portfolios: At the elementary level, there is often just one physical education specialist for the entire school. If each student is required to keep an extensive portfolio, the grading will be monumental. At any grade level, the nature of activity classes can make collecting and sorting papers cumbersome during class and detract from valuable activity time. For these reasons, care must be taken in terms of what to include, which classes to assess, and how the material will be assessed. The following guidelines for assigning portfolios are intended as a general guide due to the tremendous variety in school scenarios.

Guidelines for Assigning Portfolios

- Select a reasonable number of classes each year to work on portfolios. If classes can be put on a rotational system, each student will perhaps complete a portfolio every two to three years at the elementary level or every two to four years at the secondary level. This will make the grading more manageable for the teacher yet still provide a valuable overview of student learning over time. Kinchin (2001) suggests keeping a team portfolio in which students who are part of a team keep a portfolio recognizing significant team accomplishments.

- Be specific about portfolio entries. Spell out what types of items are appropriate or inappropriate to include. Portfolios become cumbersome when there is simply too much material to sort through.

Box 9.6 Example of Generic Student Portfolio Rubric

Score	Descriptor
4	All portions of the assignment are completed in exemplary fashion. All information is accurate. All portfolio entries clearly communicate an understanding of portfolio requirements. Additional resources have been used to strengthen the material presented.
3	All portions of the portfolio are complete, but with less detail and thoroughness. Limited additional material has been added. Portfolio entries demonstrate a basic understanding of project requirements.
2	One or two significant portions of the portfolio have not been completed; other portions are brief. No additional materials have been utilized. Multiple errors in spelling and grammar occur, limiting the ability of the portfolio to communicate understanding of project requirements.
1	Project is not completed as assigned.

- Be specific about portfolio format. Class portfolios will be much easier to assess if all students are following a similar format. Teachers may find it helpful to create a table of contents for students to follow as they assemble their materials.

- Develop a routine regarding how and when materials are added to a student's portfolio. If students will be asked to submit materials generated during class, establish a time and a routine for the collecting and sorting during class. For example, a teacher may want to include a series of peer checklists to demonstrate student skill level improvement. An efficient means of distributing and collecting paper and pencils must be established.

- Develop a rubric for the portfolios that is shared with students beforehand. As previously mentioned, rubrics are ideally shared with students prior to the assessment process. This helps the student understand how much importance has been assigned to each portion of the portfolio assignment.

Assessing Student Portfolios

In assessing student portfolios, a rubric must be designed that takes into account the purpose of the portfolio, the specifications given to students, and the type, amount, and quality of material to include. See Box 9.6 for an example of a generic student portfolio rubric.

Event Tasks

An event task asks students to demonstrate what they have learned by applying it to a real-life situation. By assigning an event task, the teacher is asking students to synthesize material from class and create a performance which can then be assessed. The assessment indicates the degree to which students are able to take in and use class material. Student development of a routine is one example of an event task. For example, students who have completed a gymnastics, dance, or aerobics class could be assigned an event task and asked to develop a routine. Students would be given basic criteria in terms of length of performance, types of movements required, whether or not the routine would be performed individually or as part of a group, and any other choreography requirements. Another example of an event task would be to have students develop a warm-up routine following a team or individual sport unit. Event tasks can also be assigned that take place outside of school. For example, preparing material for a local fitness or wellness fair would allow students to create materials demonstrating their understanding of fitness principles. Following a jump rope unit, students could be asked to create a jump rope routine that could be performed during a school open house or parent-teacher conference.

Guidelines for Assigning Event Tasks

- Be sure students have received enough information in class to allow them to create a meaningful event task. A short unit with quick exposure to skills and material would not provide a good basis upon which to assign an event task.

- Attempt to include both cognitive and psychomotor elements within the event task. In this way, students will be demonstrating their knowledge and understanding of the material along with their performance of the skills involved.

- Let students know at the start of the unit that an event task will be required of them. This way, students can be thinking about how they will apply material throughout the unit.

- If possible, provide some class time for students to use in preparing their event task. This provides students with an opportunity to ask questions as they begin their task. Also, if the task will be a group event, class time allows students an opportunity to have at least an initial meeting with their peers.

- Provide specific guidelines regarding expected content, length of the event task, and any other criteria.

- Distribute criteria and the rubric that will be used well in advance.

Assessing Event Tasks

Each of the examples listed above would obviously have more than one possible acceptable response. Thus, the assessment of a student task would likely include the initial requirements set out by the teacher and indicate how well students achieved the criteria. Although the teacher is typically the one to assess an event task, part of the process may also include peer and/or self-evaluation of the task. If peer or self-evaluation is used, the teacher or student would need to make arrangements to videotape the event.

Student Logs and Student Journals

Student logs and journals have both been widely used in physical education settings. A student log is simply a record of student work over time. Logs may be used to track students' weight training progress, distance covered in a fitness or jogging unit, laps or distance completed in a swimming unit, or student activity completed outside of class. A student journal typically includes students' thoughts, reflections, and feelings. A journal can be a helpful tool in assessing attitudes toward activity.

Guidelines for Assigning Student Logs and Student Journals

- Establish an efficient management routine for the distribution and collection of written material. Many teachers find it works well to do journal entries at the beginning or end of class. If done at the beginning, paper, notebooks, and pencils can be collected in a box in a designated spot in the gym each day. If done at the end of class, these materials can be quickly distributed prior to the closure of the class and collected as students are dismissed.

- Provide a format for students to follow that coincides with the purpose of the log or journal. For example, if the purpose is to document activity participation outside of class, log headings would include items like the date of activity, type of activity, and length of participation. If the purpose is to assess students' perceptions or attitudes toward an activity, more space for narrative must be provided.

- Identify selected activities, units, or classes in which journals or logs will be used. It is not necessary to maintain logs or journals for every event in the curriculum. This identification will help keep the teacher's assessment responsibilities reasonable.

- Consider including stimulus questions or phrases to help students get started on the reflection process needed to complete a journal entry. For example:

  "My favorite part of this activity was _____."

  "The part of this activity I would most like to change would be _____."

  "Participating with others in this activity was positive or negative (circle one) because _____."

  "I would or would not (circle one) like to continue participating in this activity because _____."

- Reassure students that assessment of their log or journal will be based on completeness of their responses, thoroughness of descriptions, and ability to express themselves in a meaningful way. Their personal reflections will not be viewed as correct or incorrect.

Assessing Student Logs and Student Journals

In assessing this type of alternative assessment, the teacher should let students know that their records of work are being used to assess their participation and therefore, student logs must be accurately kept. If students are also asked to keep a journal with reflections on their thoughts or attitudes, it should be made clear to them that they are free to express their thoughts. That is, the process of completing the journal is assessed, not the content of the journal. If students suspect that their thoughts and attitudes are being judged, they are much more likely to fabricate entries and write what they suspect the teacher wants to hear. When this occurs, the journal ceases to have any usefulness as an assessment tool.

SUMMARY

The focus of this chapter was to familiarize prospective teachers with new and innovative assessment tools and the issues associated with such tools. Alternative and authentic assessment were defined, with examples of each. Issues associated with these newer forms of assessment were presented along with a rationale for their use. The concepts of validity and reliability were reviewed and discussed from the perspective of alternative assessments.

Many types of alternative assessment were defined, including student projects, portfolios, event tasks, and student logs and journals. The ability to develop meaningful rubrics was stressed, along with guidelines for developing checklists and rating scales for assessment purposes.

Finally, practical teaching considerations in assigning and assessing alternative assessments were provided to help beginning teachers learn to include them in their teaching. Physical education should be an important component of every child's education. It is crucial for physical educators to have the skills to allow them to assess children in a meaningful way. This chapter provides them with the terminology and concepts necessary to conduct meaningful assessments of children in an activity setting.

DISCUSSION QUESTIONS

1. What is the purpose of alternative assessment in schools? How does it differ from standardized forms of testing?

2. What is meant by the term "authentic assessment"? Think of a team sport and an individual sport that you have taught. Develop an authentic assessment for each of these activities.

3. Alternative assessments have some unique concerns related to validity and reliability. Briefly discuss them and indicate steps you could take to ensure that your alternative assessments are both valid and reliable.

4. Suppose you are teaching an archery class and you want to incorporate peer assessments into the unit. Create a checklist that would allow students to evaluate each other's technique.

5. Suppose you are teaching at a school that has traditionally used standardized skill tests to evaluate students. You are teaching several soccer classes and want to evaluate students' skill levels, game play abilities, teamwork, and application of game rules. Create a rating scale, either analytic or holistic, that will assess these elements.

6. The principal at your school has asked you to report on your students' fitness knowledge and participation levels by the end of the school year. You have decided to assign an alternative assessment to your students and use that information in your report. Design either a portfolio, event task, or student project that will allow students to demonstrate their fitness knowledge and participation levels.

REFERENCES

American Association for Health, Physical Education, and Recreation. (1966). *AAHPER skills test manual for football.* Washington, DC.

Herman, J. L., Aschbacher, P. R., and Winters, L. (1996). Setting criteria. In R. E. Blum and J. A. Arter, Eds. *A handbook for student performance assessment*, VI 1–4:1–19. Alexandria, VA: Association for Supervision and Curriculum Development.

Herman, J. L., Aschbacher, P. R., and Winters, L. (1992). *A practical guide to alternative assessment.* Alexandria, VA: Association for Supervision and Curriculum Development.

Kinchin, G. D. (2001). Using team portfolios in a sport education season. *Journal of Physical Education, Recreation, and Dance.* 72(2), 41–44.

Linn, R. L., and Gronlund, N. E. (1995). *Measurement and assessment in teaching.* 7th ed. Englewood Cliffs, NJ: Prentice-Hall, Inc.

Lund, J. L. (2000). *Creating rubrics for physical education.* Reston, VA: National Association for Sport and Physical Education.

NASPE. (1995). *Moving into the future. National physical education standards: A guide to content and assessment.* St. Louis, MO: Mosby Publishing.

Rink, J. E. (2002). *Teaching physical education for learning.* 4th ed. Boston, MA: McGraw-Hill Publishing.

Wiggins, G. P. (1998). *Educative assessment: Designing assessments to inform and improve student performance.* San Francisco, CA: Jossey-Bass, Inc.

REPRESENTATIVE READINGS

Hensley, L. D. (2000). Alternative assessment. In Morrow, J., Jackson, A., Disch, J., and Mood, D. *Measurement and evaluation in human performance.* 2nd ed. (pp. 151–174). Champaign, IL: Human Kinetics.

Mabry, L. (1999). *Portfolios plus: A critical guide to alternative assessment.* Thousand Oaks, CA: Corwin Press, Inc.

Melograno, V. (2000). *Portfolio assessment for K–12 physical education.* Reston, VA: National Association for Sport and Physical Education.

Mitchell, S. A., and Oslin, J. L. (1999). *Assessment in games teaching.* Reston, VA: National Association for Sport and Physical Education.

O'Sullivan, M., and Henninger, M. (2000). *Assessing student responsibility and teamwork.* Reston, VA: National Association for Sport and Physical Education.

CHAPTER 10

Grading

Key Terms

checklist

contract grading

criterion-referenced

goals

grade

group goal setting

Individualized education program (IEP)

norm-referenced

peer evaluation

percentage method

percentile equivalent method

performance standards

personal interview

portfolio

self-evaluation

Objectives

1. Discuss the arguments for and against grading in physical education.
2. Understand the intent and use of predetermined performance-based objectives in the decision-making process.
3. Identify and discuss key issues associated with decision making.
4. Differentiate between norm-referenced and criterion-referenced grading.
5. Use various methods to calculate grades.
6. Cite and discuss assorted ways student performance can be exhibited.

P hysical educators are responsible for assessing performance and assigning grades to students. A **grade** is a symbol to denote progress and serves as a permanent record of a student's achievement. Measurement and evaluation are means by which a grade can be quantitatively and qualitatively derived. On the surface, assigning grades may appear relatively simple and straightforward. However, in physical education the process of grading is a source of confusion and controversy, and with the increased emphasis on student performance and program accountability, the confusion and controversy surrounding grading practices have been compounded. Further, the grading procedures for elementary schools differ from those of the middle school, and each of these should differ from the grading practices in high school. As a practitioner you must be sensitive to the impact that grading has on youngsters. Also, you need to become familiar with your school's procedure. Then you need to identify testing and evaluation procedures to fit the scheme. Although most prospective teachers would welcome some foolproof strategies for grading, none are available. Grading requires careful scrutiny and an understanding of the many aspects that contribute to a fair appraisal.

Although the primary focus of this chapter will be on grading in the schools, many of the processes discussed can be applied to other exercise science settings. Practitioners in health clubs, hospital settings, and various other exercise and physical activity programs can assess and evaluate participants for the purposes of decision making. In the schools, this decision-making process commonly results in a grade. In the nonschool setting, the process may result in the formulation of a written individual profile that details progress toward goals, performance relative to other participants, and a general summary of "how things are going." We will discuss possible applications of the evaluation process in the nonschool setting in the section "Other Methods of Determining Grades."

Controversies of Grading

The calculations associated with determining a numerical rating for grading purposes are not that complex. In fact, the steps involved seldom require more than a calculator and a basic understanding of fundamental arithmetic. Recent innovations in computer software have made the calculations of grades accurate and virtually instantaneous. Why, then, is grading such a difficult task for the physical educator? The answer, in large measure, lies in (1) the intricacies associated with the decision-making processes related to how a student is to be evaluated and what criteria are to be used in determining a final grade and (2) the fact that physical education has long been considered separate from the academic mainstream when it comes to grading and, therefore, as a discipline, does not have a strong position on assigning grades to students. The following sections discuss the pros and cons of grading in physical education, elaborate more fully on these two multifaceted problems associated with the grading process, and offer suggestions that may alleviate some of the problems associated with grading.

To Grade or Not To Grade

Physical educators have long debated the issue of whether or not to assign grades to students. Though there appears to be no definitive answer to the dilemma, arguments both for and against the practice of grading in physical education can be cited. Although we do not support all of the following reasons, considering these arguments should assist you in developing a clearer understanding of the issues of grading in physical education.

Reasons Not To Grade

1. Physical education is not an academic subject matter discipline. The assignment of grades to a nonacademic area is unnecessary and inappropriate. Grades should be used only to show achievement in subjects such as math, social studies, history, science, and other knowledge-based subjects.

2. Existing standardized tests and testing procedures for physical education are extremely time consuming. This creates a time management problem for teach-

ers who are already saddled with large classes, restricted activity, and space, limited class time, and inadequate assistance.

3. Physical education should assume a leadership role in an attempt to make sweeping changes regarding the manner in which youth in school systems are evaluated. Elimination of traditional grading practices would be a step in the right direction for educational reform. By leading the way, physical education would improve its image and gain stature within the total educational experience.

4. Due to the conflicting ways physical education teachers view certain tasks, grades become meaningless and in no way reflect a consistent appraisal of performance. Physical educators are unreliable in their assessment of students. Consequently, in response to inconsistencies among teachers in the assessment and evaluation phases of physical education, grades should not be given.

5. Professional preservice and inservice preparation in the area of measurement and evaluation is lacking. This makes it difficult, if not impossible, for practitioners to do an accurate job of assigning grades.

6. Assigning a grade as a result of performance measurement can cause children to become discouraged from active participation in physical activity. If promotion of lifetime activity is the most important outcome of physical education, then grading would be counterproductive for those less skilled and less naturally fit.

7. Grades mean different things to different teachers. The simple fact that individuals view the world differently is evidence enough to support the case that grades are only as good as the teacher who assigns them.

Reasons To Grade

1. Grading is a means to communicate information about student achievement to parents, teachers, administrators, and students. It is an evaluation process that is readily understood by all.

2. Grades have long been, and will continue to be, the common means to signify a student's performance. Grading is an accepted and expected part of school that cannot be altered.

3. By assigning grades, physical education has been able to maintain the status quo within the school environment. The practice of grading is the common denominator for all classes.

4. The current prevalence of criterion-referenced tests makes it easier to assign a grade to a specific performance. Students demonstrate skills and competencies rather than selecting one of several answers on a written exam. This type of assessment allows discrimination among students and opportunities to assign letter grades accordingly.

5. Historically, physical education has been criticized for the indifferent manner in which tests are utilized. Tests selected are oftentimes not specific and lack the objectivity and standardization necessary for accurate measurement. Grading affects this perception and supports the desired image of conscientious instruction.

6. Alternative assessment techniques (see Chapter 9) have been developed and provide more viable options for teachers to consider in grading practices.

7. By not grading, physical education would separate itself even further from the traditional evaluation protocol. Physical education has strived to become an equal partner in the educational mainstream and must continue to follow standards practiced in other subject matter disciplines.

The issues concerning the advantages and disadvantages of grading in physical education are numerous and complex. However, physical educators often become such strong advocates of one point of view about grading that they become overly simplistic and fail to recognize the "bigger picture." As a result, some fundamental realities about the practice of grading in physical education are often ignored. Ironically, it is precisely these realities that must be dealt with in deciding whether or not to grade.

The question of whether or not to grade is usually rendered moot by school policy. Like it or not, physical educators are generally expected to comply with some type of grading practice. After considering the pros and cons, it becomes apparent that currently there are no other viable alternatives to grading. For example, grades serve as a predictor of performance and interest. This information assists teachers and guidance personnel in providing sound advice to students. Parents rely on grades to describe their child's level of achievement. Students have come to view grading as a common practice. As such, it can be of considerable use in formally describing the abilities of a student. State educational agencies and local administrators are imposing mandates on education programs to increase accountability. Grades can serve as a benchmark to verify the strengths and weaknesses of programs.

The practice of grading is not going to disappear. With this in mind, it is inappropriate to ask whether or not we should grade. Rather, it is now time to seek the best ways to evaluate our students' performance in a manner that accurately reflects their performance. Because of the importance placed on grades, using a precise system for grading and reporting marks is imperative.

Issues in Grade Determination

Physical educators are more aware than ever before of the importance of using assessment and evaluation to measure progress toward predetermined program objectives. It is important for practitioners to effectively link grading practices with program goals, unit outcomes, and performance-based objectives (these were generally described in Chapter 2). Doing so not only informs students about what is expected of them, but also demonstrates a logical connection between what is expected and the fundamental goals, unit outcomes, and performance-based objectives. In this day of concern about quality of student performance, it is essential that grading practices reflect an identifiable relationship with expectations and learning experiences. We believe it is a questionable practice to determine a grade based on anything other than measurable performance or observable behavior directly related to predetermined objectives. Clearly defined outcomes, valid and reliable assessment techniques, and sound professional judgment form the basis for acceptable grading procedures.

Educational reform, with its renewed emphasis on accountability, has cemented the link between objectives and evaluation. Debate continues, however, on a variety of issues pertaining to grading. The following sections identify these key issues, offer differing viewpoints associated with the issues, and propose recommendations about grading for consideration.

Educational Objectives versus Student Responsibilities

Goals for physical education are predetermined targets that are distributed among the four learning domains (see Chapter 2): health-related physical fitness domain, psychomotor domain, cognitive domain, and affective domain. It is assumed that grading in physical education should be based on a student's accomplishments relative to stated goals. This, however, appears to be the exception rather than the rule.

Many physical educators ignore objectives and tend to award grades based on student responsibility details such as showering after class, dressing in the appropriate uniform, being in class on time, and various other tasks. The use of affective factors such as attitude and effort seem to form the foundation of the typical practitioner's assessment and evaluation model (Hensley, 1990). In fact, many physical educators opt to base a student's grade solely on participation, meeting the required dress code, and behavior in class (Imwold et al., 1982). These student responsibilities are by no means trivial but are unrelated to progress toward educational objectives. Using the approach that rewards students for complying with school policy (e.g., arriving at class on time) does not promote learning associated with program goals and becomes simply another way of isolating physical education from other curriculum areas within the school. Grading on effort, participation, and improvement is frequently much too subjective and often becomes a self-fulfilling prophecy. Moreover, a norm established in one year would be of questionable validity (Laughlin and Laughlin, 1992).

A problem arises when students receive a grade in physical education that is earned in a manner significantly different from the rest of the school's subject matter disciplines. For instance, performance in a science class is based on academic achievement, not the student's punctuality, attire, or physical appearance. A teacher who has a problem with a student's behavior may seek to improve the situation by visiting with the student's parents or utilizing school policy to reprimand the student. The teacher will not fail the student because of noncompliance with the school's student behavior code if the student has received passing grades on all the course projects, examinations, papers, and so on. Similarly, a student who fails all the requirements for a course but was always in class, tries hard, and displays a positive attitude should not earn a passing grade.

No longer can physical educators base a grade on student responsibilities such as number of absences, the number of times a student was improperly attired, the number of times a student was tardy, or whether a student took a shower after an activity. In this day and age of accountability, even physical education must rely on objective evidence that reflects progress toward goals in determining a grade.

Recommendation: Grades should be awarded on the basis of performance and progress toward stated educational objectives and should not be influenced by behaviors or actions that are enforced through school regulations.

Process versus Product

Another issue to contend with in determining grades is whether the process or the product of education is a more important criterion. This is a difficult issue to resolve and a point of regular debate among professionals. The process involves activity and participation rather than scores and awards. Often, students who focus on the product (i.e., how fast, how far, how long) rather than the process run the risk of early burnout. Those who support the notion of grading on process assert that it is important for students to leave school with a warm and positive feeling toward physical education. The assumption is that students who enjoy the class will take that feeling with them and continue to participate in physical activity on a voluntary basis throughout their lifetimes. Emphasizing product outcomes for children can cause them to become discouraged during their adult years, when they witness slower improvement or a decline in scores (Pangrazi and Corbin, 1993). Most of the time, teachers who subscribe to the process approach to evaluation give more weight to factors such as effort, participation, and attitude in determining a final grade. Process-oriented teachers are more likely to award a higher grade to a poor performer who tries hard than to a skilled performer who puts forth a minimal effort.

On the other hand, there are those educators who endorse the importance of performance and claim that product is the best determinant of a grade. They are quick to point out that students who score highest on history tests receive the highest grade. People on this side of the issue view attainment of performance based on outcome statements as the primary criterion for grading. They further attest that process is important but view it as an expected part of the educational experience. In other words, a teacher is responsible for providing a positive learning environment in which the student can grow through encouragement and a multiplicity of activities. Process is not viewed as something that is deserving of a grade.

The arguments for grading on product and on process are both somewhat defensible. This makes it difficult to resolve the issue to everyone's satisfaction. As Darst and Pangrazi (2002) suggest, perhaps the best solution is to develop a grading system that rewards achievement and to deliver the program in a positive manner. It then would be the instructor's responsibility to explain to students that the performance levels within the class are diverse. Just as in a math, reading, or social studies class, better grades in physical education will be awarded to those students who more closely reach the performance-based objectives. Giving all As cheats the outstanding student. Grades should discriminate among good, fair, and poor students. In this setting, instructors indicate that each student will receive quality instruction within a positive learning environment in order to move them toward stated goals.

Recommendation: Grades should be awarded based on performance, while instruction should be given in an arena filled with encouragement and effective teaching.

Psychomotor Domain versus Health-Related Fitness Domain

Clearly, physical education should provide educational experiences to meet the unique goals of achieving movement excellence and developing health-related physical fitness. Due to such factors as limited space, large class size, and insufficient time allocation for class, physical education programs are forced to establish priorities. Practitioners must make decisions about the relative emphasis to be placed on certain learning experiences. Will more time be directed to health-related fitness activities? Or should more time be spent learning the skills associated with tennis? These are not easy decisions to make. The issue becomes even more problematic when it comes time to determine a grade. Which domain, if either, should receive the greatest weighting?

Practitioners who choose to place more emphasis on skill-related activities in the grading process run the risk of being accused of slighting the fitness dimension. Further, the usually short length of time set aside for each unit is seldom sufficient to significantly improve skill. On the other hand, ignoring skill development and placing a premium on developing fitness is not without problems. Many physical educators believe the heart of any physical education program is skill development. To focus on anything else would be inconsistent with the primary purpose of the profession. In this era of concern about the deteriorating fitness of Americans, however, it seems a major oversight not to focus on fitness development.

Justifying a grade for an individual's performance on fitness tests is also a source of controversy. After all, most health-related fitness qualities are the result of genetic predisposition. To award a grade on someone's "ability to select parents," rather than a legitimate alternative of health-related fitness, is inconsistent with most accepted grading practices.

Recommendation: Any viable physical education program must be able to demonstrate attainment of goals in the psychomotor domain and the health-related physical fitness domain. Somehow practitioners must strike a balance of learning experiences and assessment procedures that relate to each of the domains. It is important, therefore, to consider each factor in the determination of the grade. It is not necessary for all domains or performance objectives to be weighted equally.

Improvement versus Achievement

Many physical educators believe that grades should be based on relative improvement. Relative improvement is the difference between a student's entry- and exit-level performances on a standardized measure of performance. Grading on improvement stems from the teacher's desire to reward those students who put forth the greatest effort in class. However, following this approach to grading can create a situation in which the most highly skilled students do not have an opportunity to receive the best grade. This relative improvement approach to grading contrasts sharply with grading on absolute performance.

For those who choose to grade solely on improvement, it is recommended that they use a method that recognizes that students scoring poorly on the initial test of performance have a much greater potential for improvement than those who display a high level of performance. The following formula takes into account the potential for improvement relative to the highest score in class.

$$\frac{\text{Student's Posttest Score} - \text{Student's Pretest Score}}{\text{Highest Score for All Students} - \text{Student's Pretest Score}} = \text{Improvement Score}$$

For example, a student's pre- and posttest scores on the sit-and-reach test for flexibility are 20 and 40 centimeters, respectively. If the highest attained score in class is 70 centimeters, the equation would look like this:

$$\frac{40 - 20}{70 - 20} = .40$$

This student's 100 percent improvement on raw score would be converted to a more equitable improvement score of .40. By using this approach, the teacher has some flexibility in determining improvement and creates a situation that is more equitable to those students who score high on the pretest (Illinois State Board of Education, 1982).

Grading only on improvement has some serious drawbacks that should be considered before a decision is made about its role in the evaluation process. Grading on improvement is time consuming and requires that the same test be given at the beginning and end of the semester, block, or unit. Devoting this much time to testing detracts from valuable instructional time, creates additional clerical duties for the teacher, and becomes a logistical nightmare if pre- and posttest scheduling is dependent on weather or availability of facilities.

A second problem associated with grading on improvement is that students could be placed in a dangerous situation if asked to perform a pretest before any proper conditioning or skill acquisition has occurred. For example, asking children to complete the 12-minute run on the second day of class in order to obtain a pretest score is ill advised. Similarly, expecting a youngster to perform a test of balance on a beam before gaining some fundamental experience with the apparatus is not prudent teaching and places the child in a potentially hazardous situation.

Third, taking a pretest without the advantage of some knowledge or skill will, in all likelihood, result in inconsistent and inaccurate data. For instance, administering a test of distance and accuracy using a 5-iron to students who have never held a golf club before would not yield the type of results necessary to determine real improvement.

Fourth, once students realize that improvement is the primary criterion for grading, they may be inclined to purposefully decrease their performance on the initial test, thus creating more room for improvement. As we all know, it does not take students long to figure out ways to challenge the system.

Fifth, grading solely on improvement is simply unfair to those individuals who are highly skilled or conditioned performers. Performance is easier to improve at lower levels. Consequently, basing a grade on improvement favors those who have the "longest way to go." A skilled performer may be at a level where improvement is difficult to discern (e.g., how do you measure improvement in a student who made 15 out of 15 on a basketball free-throw pretest?).

Sixth, a youngster's performance on a test of physical fitness skill may improve simply due to physical growth or maturity that occurred between the pretest and posttest. For instance, a child who grows taller and gains weight can certainly be expected to increase performance of measures of strength and endurance. In this case, it becomes difficult to attribute improvement of performance to learning.

Finally, grading on improvement is not in compliance with societal practices or procedures used in other subject matter areas. Society does not reward people for improvement, but rather for achievement. Teachers of English, math, social studies, and the academic disciplines do not base a grade relative to the abilities of the student when they entered the class. The standard in other classes is achievement.

There is an increasing need for schools to demonstrate student achievement. The report card for schools nationwide in most subjects is less than adequate. The achievement of students is being measured against predetermined standards of performance. If we are to have responsible citizens, education must provide learning experiences in all subject disciplines that encourage students to reach higher levels of achievement. In most cases, deriving grades based on established criteria promotes achievement.

Recommendation: Since grading solely on improvement is compromised by inequities and inconsistencies, it should not be given serious consideration in the evaluation process.

Potential versus Observed Performance

Interestingly, some teachers choose to base a grade on potential rather than observed abilities. This type of evaluation is highly subjective and is unfair to those students who are able to perform. The sophisticated testing equipment necessary to even begin to assess potential performance is not available to the practitioner and remains accessible only to a few elite performers. Furthermore, by using potential as a factor in grade determination, teachers place themselves in an indefensible position if challenged on the manner in which the grade was derived.

Recommendation: It is difficult to grade on unobservable characteristics; therefore, observable behavior and performance should be relied on in determining a grade.

Negative versus Positive Point Systems

Employing a point system to determine grades is a common practice. Many educators believe that the practice of assigning a numeric value to a particular activity facilitates the grading process. Determining grades based on a point system is easily adaptable to the physical education environment. Utilizing a point system is an attempt to make a grading system justifiable. In most point systems, both performance-based objectives and administrative details are considered in determining the student's total points. However, as Pangrazi and Darst (1991) suggest, a point system can have a negative effect on students when handled inappropriately. If, for instance, a teacher starts each student with a total number of points and subtracts points each time a student does not meet a standard, students will begin to avoid behavior that can result in the loss of points. This may mean that a youngster loses the initiative to perform tasks that are not point oriented, thereby making the entire learning system dependent on the teacher's grading criteria. This may also lead to the teacher becoming a monitor of behavior and paying more attention to negative behavior, which results in the loss of points, than to positive behavior.

In positive grading systems, students know there will be rewards for performance of tasks and they display behaviors that are in compliance with predetermined objectives or standards. The emphasis is still on performance and behavior but instead of students losing points, a system is established whereby they can earn points. Students are placed in a situation that allows them the opportunity to control their own destiny. They know what behaviors and standards must be met in order to accomplish the goal and understand that the attainment of such is dependent more on them than on the teacher.

Recommendation: Grading systems that utilize points should be structured to reward positive behavior, not to punish undesirable or negative behavior.

Failing Grades versus Social Promotion

One of the more emotional issues associated with the practice of grading is acknowledging a failing student. No teacher finds satisfaction in assigning a grade of F. Many teachers feel a sense of personal failure for each student who fails to meet expected standards. In many cases, this has led to an unwillingness on the part of teachers to give failing grades, and many adopt an attitude that social promotion or advancement is in the best interest of the students.

A failing grade reflects totally unsatisfactory progress toward objectives. A student who receives a failing grade can be affected in one or more of the following ways: (1) the student may be forced to repeat the course and earn a passing grade; (2) the grade may prevent a student from earning the appropriate number of credits necessary to be promoted; and (3) the grade is absorbed within the cumulative grading system and thus reflects overall performance in a particular grade level.

Regardless of the effect, a failing grade represents failure. During the past several decades, many teachers have argued that failing a youngster can cause undue emotional trauma and does not ensure that the child will learn more during a repeat of the failed course. Many educators have subscribed to this notion and have forsaken the failure system in favor of social promotion. Social promotion has shifted the focus from subject matter learning to the conditions and processes associated with education.

Social promotion is rooted in noble intentions. Who can question the uniqueness and importance of each child? Who could enjoy informing a youngster of failure? Who does not want every child to be a success? More fundamental questions, however, are now being raised by state governments, educational agencies, school boards, colleges of education, and school administrations. Is it fair to expect students who are unable to read, write, or perform simple arithmetic to function effectively in our society? Should students learn that achievement is synonymous with performance? Or should teachers simply reinforce the concept of "hang in there, and you will be rewarded"? Throughout the country, these fundamental questions are being answered in the form of educational mandates and legislation directed at applying quality control measures to the students who attend our schools. The public no longer accepts the tenet that there is no failure.

Recommendation: If physical education is to maintain its affiliation with the mainstream of other subject matter areas, it is important to initiate a grading system that attends to the realities of failure and does not acquiesce to the notion of social promotion.

Teaching for Testing versus Teaching for Learning

The increased emphasis on testing programs designed to demonstrate accountability has caused many educators to plan their lessons according to information covered in competency tests. Teaching only material that is included as part of a state or nationally standardized test for the sake of having students rank high on normative comparisons is a practice based on a false assumption. Certainly, teachers are responsible for directing learning toward attainment of mandated outcomes. However, legislated student performance objectives are usually no more than statements linked to broad program goals. It is important for teachers to realize that learning experiences should be developed according to the needs and interests of students and further refined according to the procedures outlined in Chapter 2. Quality learning experiences and effective instruction directed at predetermined goals will result in successful performance on standardized tests.

Recommendation: Physical education programs should use standardized testing programs and legislated performance goals as guidelines for program development and should not "teach for the test."

Single Observation versus Multiple Observation for Grading

A physical educator should not rely on one method of evaluation or a single assessment tool to derive grades. Given the diversity of program and student objectives (see Chapter 2), it would be unfair to grade a student based on performance in only one learning domain. For example, using the results of a written test as the sole evaluative tool in determining a grade for a unit on soccer could be viewed as unfair. Since most of the class time would have been devoted to the practice of soccer skills, it only seems reasonable to include some form of skills assessment in the grading process. It would be a difficult and indefensible task to explain to a highly skilled soccer player who received a lower grade than a lesser skilled soccer player that the grade was based on performance on the sole evaluative criterion, a written test. Teachers place themselves in a more defensible position when grades are based on a variety of evaluative criteria.

Recommendation: Grade determination should be based on proper evaluation technique, which includes assessment in the areas of all four learning domains. Alternative assessment procedures (see Chapter 9) should be considered in developing your grading scheme.

Methods of Grading

Grades should be based on measurable factors that reflect a student's achievement or performance in one or more of the four learning domains. It is the teacher's responsibility to utilize appropriate assessment techniques in determining the student's progress toward goals in the health-related physical fitness, psychomotor, cognitive, and affective domains. In selecting assessment instruments, the teacher should be mindful that it is helpful to the grading process if techniques used to assess level of performance or behavior provide the teacher with information that can be easily quantified. The use of scoring rubrics allows qualitative assessment to be quantified for evaluation purposes. Information that cannot be quantified is often difficult to objectively interpret and usually becomes problematic in the grading process. Determining grades is most commonly accomplished in one of two ways: the norm-referenced approach or the criterion-referenced approach. The following sections explain features of these two methods.

Norm-Referenced Approach

The **norm-referenced** test is sometimes referred to as a test of *relative achievement*. Its purpose is to place students as accurately as possible along a continuum ranging from the lowest to the highest possible scores. This system is based on the normal probability curve that represents a theoretical distribution of data based on a mathematical formula.

As explained in Chapter 3, a normal distribution of interval/ratio data is graphically depicted by the "bell-shaped" curve, in which there is a clustering of scores around the mean and a gradual tapering of scores in the tails of the curve. The entire area under the curve is 100 percent. If you were to divide the area under the curve into sections representing a percentage of the curve, the sum of all sections would still equal 100 percent. The most important consideration in evaluating students based on the norm-referenced approach is careful identification of the areas under the curve that will represent each grade and their corresponding percentages. For the purposes of grading, norm-referenced standards can be used in several ways.

Standard Deviation Method

As discussed in Chapter 3, the standard deviation is a measure of the relative variability of test scores around their mean and is graphically represented as a linear distance along the X-axis of a distribution measured above and below the mean. Mathematically, the standard deviation is defined as the square root of the mean of the squared deviation scores of a distribution. Using this derived measure for purposes of grading requires following several steps. The first step, of course, is to calculate the mean and standard deviation for the group of scores. Secondly, it is necessary to divide the distribution into six sections using the standard deviation values. For example, in Figure 10.1 notice the area under the curve that is 1.5 standard deviations above the mean or higher. Scores falling in this area would receive a grade of A. Assume that the teacher administered a test of softball throw for distance and the mean performance score for the class (N = 30) was 125 feet with a standard deviation of 10. Using Figure 10.1, a score of 132 feet would fall between +0.5 and +1.5 standard deviations above the mean and would fall into the B letter grade range.

It should be clear that grading "on the curve" is often viewed as an unfair practice. The calculated curve may be based on only a small number of students (e.g., a class of 30–40 students). In this case, the distribution of scores might be badly distorted. It is best to pool raw scores and develop standard deviation grading scales from the test results of several classes. Even if this process takes several semesters, the resulting curve will more accurately reflect a normal distribution and will become a more fair way to determine letter grades.

An advantage of using the standard deviation method to determine letter grades is that scores for different types of tests can be converted to a common scale. Since standard deviation units only reflect relationships to the mean scores and not the

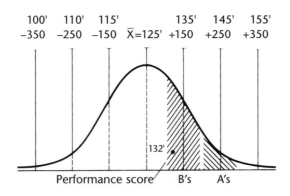

Figure 10.1 Example of grading on a curve for a test of softball throw.

units of measure (e.g., distance in feet and inches, centimeters, number of made free throws), teachers can compare, and even average, letter grades derived via this method on different tests (e.g., motor ability and health-related physical fitness).

A drawback to using the standard deviation method to determine grades is that individual student grades become dependent on the performance of classmates rather than on their own achievement or progress toward performance-based objectives. Remember, this type of grading system implies a normal distribution, and grading is determined by the performance of students, not by criteria the teacher establishes. It may be that the particular group of scores that comprise the total distribution has been obtained from students who are not representative of the normal population. For instance, assume that most students in a given class are members of the cross-country team, and the test is a distance run to measure aerobic ability. Conceivably, students who are not members of the team could perform well when compared to predetermined goals, yet, due to the influence of the team members' scores, they would receive unusually low letter grades.

When using the standard deviation method, many other factors must be considered. Certainly the general level of proficiency of the group itself needs to be taken into account. A low score in a superior group is not the same as a low score in a less able group. The teacher should be prepared to use good judgment in making grading decisions about students who perform well, yet rank at the low end of a highly skilled class.

Percentage Method

Another method of norm-referenced grading is called the **percentage method**. Somewhat similar to the standard deviation method, the percentage method requires the teacher to rank the performance or collective performances on various assignments and/or requirements of all students. The teacher then determines what percentage of the students are to receive As, Bs, and so forth. Usually, this procedure is dependent on the teacher's previous experiences with other classes. For example, if the teacher feels that the overall performance of the present class in various tests of general motor ability exceeds that of the previous class, the teacher may choose to award a higher percentage of high letter grades. On the other hand, if the overall performance is poorer, the percentage of low grades may be increased. The decision about what percent of students in class earn As, Bs, and so on is in this case arbitrary, usually subjective, and depends on the teacher's professional judgment. In any case, this method of norm-referenced grading places more responsibility in the hands of the teacher than the standard deviation method does.

Percentile Equivalent Method

The **percentile equivalent method** is rapidly becoming a popular mechanism to determine letter grades. One reason is that most people have some understanding of percentiles. Simply stated, the percentile rank of a score is defined as the percentage of scores lying below the given score. Further, percentiles provide a quick and convenient means to determine individual achievement compared to others of similar background. For example, we can differentiate performance levels of two 10-year-old male students who ranked in the 75th and 30th percentiles on a test of running speed. The student who performed at the 75th percentile scored better than 75 percent of all other 10-year-old boys who composed the normative database, whereas the youngster ranked at the 30th percentile performed more poorly than 70 percent of all other boys of the same age.

Using percentile equivalents as standard scores (see Chapter 3) also provides a means to compare raw scores from different sets of data. If the mile is run in 12 minutes and 34 seconds, putting the runner in the 15th percentile, and the softball is thrown 175 feet, which places the thrower in the 89th percentile, it is easy to determine the better performance.

Percentile equivalents based on large populations (i.e., national or state norms) are considered valid and provide students with the information necessary to determine their relative performance. Table 10.1 is an example of a percentile table for 10-year-old girls. Test items are from the AAHPERD *Health-Related Physical Fitness Test*. This table is representative of an entire set of norms for youth ages 6–18 years developed as part of a special project funded in part by the Illinois Association of Health, Physical Education, and Recreation. In the example, it is easy for students to locate their scores and relative percentile performance.

For a teacher responsible for grading large numbers of students, conversion from raw scores to standard percentiles can be time consuming and can turn into a logistical nightmare. It used to be that the only way to complete this process was to have a booklet or chart with raw scores and norms available for teachers. It then became their task to make the conversions by hand. From a teacher's perspective, this method of assigning grades is not appealing. Today, however, there are many different types of grading software available that instantaneously convert raw scores to percentile equivalents. There is software that creates normative tables from raw scores. The use of spreadsheet software enables you to use relatively sophisticated grading techniques quite easily. This advance in technology has made the use of percentiles as a method of grading much more realistic.

Advantages of Norm-Referenced Grading

1. This method provides the criteria by which a teacher can group the class for instruction according to ability.

2. It is most appropriate for the first-year or novice teacher who is not yet familiar with appropriate criterion standards for a particular skill, health fitness level, behavior, or cognitive expectation.

3. If the norms are derived from a class (or classes) where poor performance is the result of inferior instruction, then using norm-referenced grading would not penalize students.

4. Norm-referenced grading yields maximum variability among students and the largest possible range of scores.

5. Raw scores can be transformed into standard scores that reflect performance rankings between and among various types of tests.

Disadvantages of Norm-Referenced Grading

1. Since students ultimately set the standard, a letter grade of A may be awarded to students who are not remotely close to a performance level deemed worthy of an A grade by the teacher.

Table 10.1   Percentile table from Illinois health fitness database.

GIRLS: AGE = 10

% Tile	Triceps Skinfold N = (0882)	Sum of Skinfolds (0534)	Sit & Reach (0882)	Sit-Ups (0848)	Mile Run (0828)	% Tile	Triceps Skinfold N = (0882)	Sum of Skinfolds (0534)	Sit & Reach (0882)	Sit-Ups (0848)	Mile Run (0828)
99	5.0	10.0	41	58	6:38	73	9.0	16.0	32	40	9:15
98	6.0	11.0	40	54	7:06	72	9.0	16.0	32	39	9:19
97	6.0	11.0	39	52	7:21	71	9.0	16.0	32	39	9:21
96	6.0	11.0	38	50	7:39	70	9.0	16.5	32	39	9:23
95	7.0	11.5	38	49	7:48	69	9.5	16.5	32	38	9:28
94	7.0	12.0	37	47	7:57	68	9.5	16.5	31	38	9:30
93	7.0	12.5	37	47	8:02	67	10.0	17.0	31	38	9:34
92	7.0	12.5	36	46	8:06	66	10.0	17.0	31	38	9:38
91	7.0	13.0	36	46	8:15	65	10.0	17.0	31	37	9:39
90	7.0	13.0	35	45	8:22	64	10.0	17.0	31	37	9:42
89	7.5	13.0	35	45	8:24	63	10.0	17.0	31	37	9:45
88	8.0	13.5	35	45	8:30	62	10.0	17.0	30	37	9:50
87	8.0	14.0	35	44	8:32	61	10.0	17.0	30	36	9:52
86	8.0	14.0	34	43	8:34	60	10.0	17.5	30	36	9:55
85	8.0	14.0	34	43	8:39	59	10.0	18.0	30	36	9:59
84	8.0	14.0	34	42	8:41	58	10.0	18.0	30	36	10:02
83	8.0	14.0	34	42	8:43	57	10.5	18.0	30	36	10:06
82	8.0	14.0	34	42	8:48	56	10.5	18.0	29	35	10:09
81	8.0	14.5	33	42	8:50	55	11.0	18.5	29	35	10:10
80	8.5	15.0	33	41	8:53	54	11.0	19.0	29	35	10:14
79	8.5	15.0	33	41	8:58	53	11.0	19.0	29	35	10:17
78	9.0	15.0	33	41	9:02	52	11.0	19.0	29	34	10:18
77	9.0	15.0	33	40	9:05	51	11.0	19.0	29	34	10:20
76	9.0	15.0	33	40	9:08	50	11.0	19.5	29	34	10:24
75	9.0	15.5	32	40	9:11	49	11.0	20.0	28	34	10:26
74	9.0	15.5	32	40	9:13	48	11.5	20.0	28	34	10:27

continued

Table 10.1   Percentile table from Illinois health fitness database.

GIRLS: AGE = 10

% Tile	Triceps Skinfold N = (0882)	Sum of Skinfolds (0534)	Sit & Reach (0882)	Sit-Ups (0848)	Mile Run (0828)
47	11.5	20.0	28	33	10:30
46	12.0	20.5	28	33	10:33
45	12.0	21.0	28	33	10:35
44	12.0	21.0	28	33	10:41
43	12.0	21.0	28	32	10:45
42	12.0	21.5	27	32	10:47
40	12.0	22.0	27	32	10:56
39	12.5	22.0	27	31	11:00
38	13.0	22.0	27	31	11:03
37	13.0	22.5	26	31	11:08
36	13.0	23.0	26	31	11:13
35	13.0	23.0	26	30	11:16
34	13.0	23.0	26	30	11:19
33	13.5	23.5	26	30	11:22
32	14.0	24.0	26	30	11:28
31	14.0	24.0	26	30	11:31
30	14.0	24.0	25	29	11:33
29	14.0	24.5	25	29	11:36
28	14.0	25.0	25	29	11:40
27	14.5	25.0	25	28	11:43
26	15.0	26.0	25	28	11:47
25	15.0	26.0	25	28	11:51
24	15.0	26.5	24	28	11:55
23	15.0	27.0	24	27	12:00
22	16.0	27.0	24	27	12:06
21	16.0	28.0	24	27	12:11
20	16.0	28.0	23	26	12:14
19	16.0	28.5	23	25	12:19
18	16.5	29.0	23	25	12:25
17	17.0	30.0	23	25	12:29
16	17.0	30.5	23	24	12:32
15	17.0	31.0	23	24	12:38
14	18.0	32.0	22	24	12:45
13	18.0	32.0	22	23	12:56
12	18.5	34.0	22	23	13:00
11	19.0	35.0	21	22	13:09
10	19.0	36.0	21	22	13:22
9	20.0	37.5	20	21	13:34
8	21.0	38.0	20	20	13:48
7	21.0	39.0	19	20	13:59
6	22.0	40.0	19	19	14:08
5	23.0	42.0	18	18	14:20
4	24.0	45.0	18	17	14:42
3	24.0	46.0	17	14	15:09
2	25.0	52.0	16	12	15:27
1	29.0	56.0	14	6	16:32

From D. N. Hastad, J. R. Marett, and S. A. Plowman, *Evaluation of the Health-Related Physical Fitness Status of Youth in the State of Illinois*, Northern Illinois University, DeKalb, IL. 1983.

2. This type of grading focuses on the rate of learning rather than students' ability to learn, so the quickest learners receive the highest grades.

3. Whereas students vary from semester to semester and year to year, grading on the curve forces teachers to award a certain percentage of each letter grade to a certain number of students. This does not apply to percentile equivalents based on a large sample of students.

4. Grading on the curve is not consistent with evaluation based on performance-based objectives and does not indicate a student's progress toward mastering skills or behaviors.

Criterion-Referenced Approach

The **criterion-referenced** approach to evaluation utilizes measurement of students' performances as they compare with a predetermined standard, such as a score, number of tasks completed, number of successful attempts versus unsuccessful attempts, or difficulty of tasks completed. The criterion, or standard, is established in advance by the teacher and, in most cases, reflects experiences with previous learners in a similar situation. Generally this criterion is set at something less than perfect performance to allow for a certain measure of unreliability in student performance, and stated as a certain proportion or percentage of the items successfully completed on the test, such as 75 percent. Once the performance criterion is established, students scoring above the standard are given a specific grade (such as Pass); those scoring below the standard are given another grade (such as Fail). Since most school districts use the five-point letter grade system, the teacher will be required to identify four cut-off points to determine five grade categories.

Criterion-referenced grading is sometimes referred to as mastery grading and can be used for evaluating student performance or behavior in any of the four learning domains. The success or failure of this method of grading depends on the teacher's ability to set appropriate standards. Standards must be challenging, yet attainable.

The criterion-referenced system is most frequently used as a means of formative evaluation, measurement that occurs during a unit or a course of instruction rather than at the end. Once a letter grade has been determined for a particular unit, it is recorded in the grade book. At the end of the grading period the teacher can weight all the letter grades, convert them to a numerical scale, and arrive at a final letter grade. Suppose a teacher created a grading procedure that weighted skill development (psychomotor domain) and fitness development (health-related fitness) at 35% each and knowledge (cognitive) and social skills and attitude (affective) at 15% each. It would be appropriate to use this sort of weighting if it accurately represented the relative emphasis and time committed in class to the various domains. If a student received a C+ for skill performance, an A for health fitness, a B– for attitude, and a C on the knowledge component, the grade may be determined according to the example shown in Figure 10.2. Following are two methods using the criterion-referenced system for the purpose of determining grades.

Trials Successfully Completed

A common standard in criterion-referenced grading is percentage of items correct or trials successfully completed. Using this method, the teacher establishes the criterion

If a student achieved a C+ on skill, A on fitness, B– on social skills and attitude, C on knowledge, the grade would be averaged as follows:

If A + = 12			35% C+ = .35 x 6 =	2.10
A = 11			35% A = .35 x 11 =	3.85
A – = 10			15% B– = .15 x 7 =	1.05
B + = 9			15% C = .15 x 5 =	.75
B = 8				7.75 = B
B – = 7				
C + = 6				
C = 5				
C – = 4				
D + = 3				
D = 2				
D – = 1				

Figure 10.2 Calculating final grade from multiple criterion-referenced letter grades.

required to earn a particular grade. For example, to receive an A on a written test, a student would have to answer correctly 90 percent, or 90 out of 100, of the questions. Or, to receive an A on a test of free-throw shooting accuracy, a student would have to make 80 percent, or 12 of 15, attempts. Many school districts, particularly at the senior high school level, are using the percentage correct method as a means of evaluating progress toward performance-based objectives.

Performance Standards

Another way to use the criterion-referenced method for grading is by setting **performance standards**. Performance standards are preestablished criteria that must be met to receive a particular grade. Since performance-based objectives are an important part of the curriculum-building process, it is only fitting that we use some form of assessment to evaluate progress toward the successful attainment of these goals. To effectively use performance standards as a means to assign grades, the teacher must first be able to establish realistic, yet challenging, standards. To do so requires a knowledge about the capabilities of the students. For example, requiring 12-year-old girls to run a mile in 8 minutes and 36 seconds to receive an A may be an unrealistic standard. Although this performance would rank at the 75th percentile (meaning that this performance is better than 75 percent of all girls age 12), it may be that these students have not had sufficient opportunity to develop the cardiovascular fitness and running skill necessary to achieve this goal. Likewise, if the teacher is fortunate enough to be teaching a class of students who meet the standard with relative ease, then perhaps the goal is not stringent enough. In this instance, proper standard setting is a more difficult task than the accompanying assessment and evaluation techniques.

The prevailing notion underlying mastery learning is that if the objectives are clearly stated and made known to the students prior to the beginning of instruction, all students will eventually meet the criteria. Instruction will be designed so that *all* students attain *all* stated criteria. The differences among students will be reflected in the time it takes to attain objectives, not the performance differences that exist over a set period of time.

Advantages of Criterion-Referenced Grading

1. This method can be used to evaluate performance or behavior in the health-related physical fitness domain, psychomotor domain, affective domain, and cognitive domain.

2. Once the standards have been determined, the grading system is easily implemented.

3. Grades are not influenced by high or low skill levels of other students in class.

4. This type of grading system is consistent with measuring progress toward performance-based objectives and is a reasonable approach for teachers faced with meeting local or state performance-based outcome statements.

5. Criterion-referenced grading supports the use of programs that are paced to meet the needs of students and is predicated on the positive assumption that all students can master the material.

6. The self-paced format of this approach helps to reduce student anxiety and eliminate subjectivity in grading. In fact, repeated testing is possible and encouraged.

7. Since there are no restrictions on the number of students who can receive high grades (As and Bs), it becomes possible for most students to enjoy a certain amount of success.

Disadvantages of Criterion-Referenced Grading

1. Establishing standards can be problematic in that performance-based goals cannot always be accurately specified before the unit is taught.

2. It is difficult to differentiate clearly between what is passing and what is failing, or to establish cut-off points between letter grades on the five-point grading system.

3. Standards within a school or district may vary among teachers, creating a situation in which erroneous interpretation of scores may be detrimental to students.

4. Motivation to surpass previous performance may be decreased. Students may lower their level of achievement to the minimum standard for passing.

Other Methods of Determining Grades

The norm- and criterion-referenced approaches to evaluation are the two most common methods used to determine a letter grade. But many other means exist to assist the practitioner in assigning grades. While some are merely derivatives of either the norm- or the criterion-referenced approaches, several are unique and merit special attention. The following sections describe five such approaches to grading. The use of any of these approaches is situation-specific and depends on the experience and skill of the teacher. In addition, reference is made to how some of these techniques might be employed in the exercise science setting.

Student Self-Evaluation

It is important for physical educators to provide youth with the requisite levels of fitness, skill, and knowledge to voluntarily participate in physical activity and assume an active lifestyle. An important ingredient in the successful attainment of this goal is the evaluative process. Youth should be given the opportunity to conduct **self-evaluation**. Students who are able to assess and evaluate their personal level of performance are more likely to be active participants in physical activity than those who cannot. With this in mind, it becomes increasingly important to teach students how to assess their abilities in relationship to performance-based objectives. Students should be able to administer self-tests on a variety of fitness- and skill-based goals. Once this procedure is established, it becomes possible to integrate a self-evaluation scheme into the grading system.

When student self-evaluation is used, the instructional approach is closely related to the evaluation technique. Educators need to develop lessons that teach students the proper way to conduct self-assessment techniques. While it can be somewhat time consuming, teaching students how to conduct self-evaluation has long-term benefits for students as well as the program. If done correctly and accurately, self-testing results can be used as a component in determining the overall letter grade. However, it is recommended that self-evaluation be a relatively small percentage of the final grade.

Group Goal Setting

A variation of the self-evaluation approach to grading is allowing the class to develop performance- or behavior-based goals. **Group goal setting** allows the class to decide what is to be accomplished and the manner in which the progress toward goals will be evaluated. This can even include the identification of cut-off points for letter grades. The teacher is responsible for delivering instruction to attain goals. All the students and the teacher are active participants in the evaluation process and determination of the final grade.

Group goal setting can be used in a variety of exercise science settings. For example, an adult swim conditioning class can agree to swim a certain combined distance over a certain period of time. Another illustration might be in a nutrition/weight loss program. The participants could establish a goal to lose a total of 150 pounds during a six-week period. In each of these cases, participants actively determine a group goal. This not only promotes positive interaction among participants and the exercise specialist, but it also establishes a benchmark by which progress can be accurately measured.

Peer Evaluation

Another way to get students actively involved in the grading process is through the use of peer evaluation. **Peer evaluation** gives students an opportunity to evaluate their classmates. Like self-evaluation, peer evaluation makes the students feel more involved in the educational process. Students are more likely to believe that the grading system is fair when it manifests itself through teacher, peer, and self-evaluation (Darst and Pangrazi, 2002). Peer evaluation is useful for the exercise science setting. For example, in a strength training session, participants can be paired and conduct an evaluation of lifting technique. Each would demonstrate selected lifts, while the other observed and provided written and oral commentary about the performance. This type of evaluation can provide yet another bit of evidence to assist the performer in better understanding his/her progress toward predetermined goals.

To be effective, this approach must be well conceived and properly planned. The teacher or exercise specialist must have the goals and process documented and agreed upon prior to beginning the instructional unit. Personality conflicts cannot enter into the evaluation process. This requires that the teacher or exercise specialist be constantly aware of individuals' interactions and able to contend with any biased evaluation that may result from friendship or ego. Depending on the skill of the practitioner and participants, this approach to grading and decision making can be successful even in the upper grades of elementary school. Like self-evaluation, peer evaluation should not be weighted heavily in determining the final grade.

Alternative Assessment

The educational community is constantly seeking methods to assign grades that accurately portray learning and achievement. Alternative assessment is integrated with the teaching effort and provides meaningful information about student learning and achievement (see Chapter 9). This style of assessment is accomplished by focusing on student outcomes and refers to assessment tasks in which students demonstrate skills and competencies rather than selecting one of several predetermined answers. In addition, alternative assessments take place in a real setting, rather than a contrived situation like most psychomotor or health-related fitness test batteries. An example of an alternative assessment would be asking high school students to practically apply their understanding of the physiological principle of overload. Students could choose several ways to respond. They could write about overload, orally describe the principle to the teacher, or actually demonstrate the principle in an exercise setting. Having students maintain a journal describing their exercise habits is another example of alternative assessment. Individuals could record their participation in and feelings about the activity. Journal entries would serve as summaries of performance and behavior. Alternative assessment may also be used in the nonschool setting. A participant in an exercise program could be asked to conduct a self-assessment. This would require that she analyze her personal progress toward goals by rating her performance and participation in a particular sport or exercise regime. This is quite effective with adults.

Alternative assessment supports actual instruction and the goals of a nonschool exercise program. If used properly, it is an effective observational and, at times, subjective technique used to determine students' understanding and performance in a real situation. As such, it becomes another method of assessment to consider when grading or decision making is necessary.

Contract Grading

Contract grading allows students to progress at different rates toward predetermined goals. As with other types of criterion-referenced grading practices, working with contracts creates opportunities for all students to achieve. Though the highly skilled are likely to fulfill the contractual obligations faster than less-skilled students, the less-skilled student is given extra time to practice, receives extra assistance, and ultimately achieves the same level of skill attainment.

As implied, the contract for grading specifies student-based performance or behavior goals that must be accomplished in order to receive a particular letter grade. To avoid potential confusion, performance objectives should be written in behavioral

LACROSSE

Core Objectives (1 point each)

1. With a crosse, throw an overhand shot 4 of 8 times through a target from a distance of 10 yd.
2. Throw an underhand shot 4 of 8 times through a target from a distance of 10 yd.
3. Throw a sidearm shot 4 of 8 times through a target from a distance of 10 yd.
4. Using any throw technique mentioned above, throw the ball through a target 3 of 5 times from a distance of 10 yd.
5. With a partner, catch the ball with an overhand catch 3 of 5 times from a distance of 10–15 yd.
6. Catch the ball with an underhand catch 3 of 5 times from a distance of 10–15 yd.
7. Catch the ball with the backhand catch and reverse pivot 3 of 5 times from a distance of 10 yd.
8. With a partner rolling the ball from a distance of 10 yd, use the side retrieve technique 5 of 10 times.
9. Using the cover retrieve technique, scoop a "dead" ball up 5 of 10 times.
10. Defend 4 of 8 shots taken by a partner from a distance of 10 yd.

Optional Objectives (2 points each)

1. With a partner passing the ball from a distance of 20 yd, use a running side retrieve technique 5 of 10 times.
2. Using the cover retrieve technique, scoop up a "dead" ball 5 of 10 times.
3. With a crosse, throw an overhand shot 4 of 5 times through a target from a distance of 15 yd.
4. Throw an underhand shot 4 of 5 times through a target from a distance of 15 yd.
5. Score 1 of 3 shots past a goalie from a distance of 10–15 yd.

From *Dynamic Physical Education for Secondary School Students*, 2nd ed., by Pangrazi and Darst. Copyright © 1991 by Allyn and Bacon. Reprinted with permission.

Figure 10.3 Grade contract for lacrosse.

terms. Objectives should also be written in order of difficulty, with both the quantity and quality of performance or behavior clearly understood by students. If students are familiar with the goals and understand what is necessary to fulfill each, then it becomes possible for students to monitor their progress toward the objectives and pass quantitative judgment about what grade they have earned. Figure 10.3 shows an example of a contract for students in physical education.

The contract approach to grading has several advantages. First of all, because the measurement techniques are spelled out in quantifiable terms, subjectivity has been eliminated. Grading can be a much more positive and meaningful experience if students are able to establish the pace at which they want to move toward a goal. This not only reduces stress, it also creates the opportunity for students to select different means of learning the necessary skills or behaviors stated in the contract.

The disadvantages of contract grading focus on writing the objectives and the student's ability to accurately assess performance. Because a performance-based objective should be challenging, yet attainable, the teacher must be able to write a contract that is neither too easy nor too difficult. If students realize that the goals are well beyond their level of capability, they will become discouraged. If, on the other hand, the goals are too simple, the students will become bored and the teacher will have been unsuccessful in providing learning experiences that enrich the students' abilities.

PERFORMANCE OBJECTIVE MONITORING FORM															
Name	**Core Objectives**										**Optional Objectives**				
	1	2	3	4	5	6	7	8	9	10	1	2	3	4	5

From *Dynamic Physical Education for Secondary School Students*, 2nd ed., by Pangrazi and Darst. Copyright © 1991 by Allyn and Bacon. Reprinted with permission.

Figure 10.4 Performance checklist monitoring form.

As with any form of criterion-referenced grading, the success or failure of the process depends on the ability to accurately equate a grade with performance. For this reason, contract grading is only recommended for use by experienced teachers who are familiar with the personalities and capabilities of their students.

Using a Checklist for Grading

The **checklist** is a subjective way to assess the performance of students and is viewed by many as suspect. This is particularly true when evaluating elements of the affective learning domain, which include sportsmanship, attitude, and self-concept. Much of the evaluation takes place by observing students and making qualitative judgments about their performance or behavior. The reliability of this form of evaluation is often questioned but can be improved by training observers. By using a checklist or scorecard a teacher can quantify the observed performance and behaviors into usable numerical data, which can be ranked, averaged, and so on. Even though using the checklist will increase the reliability of the data, the overall approach is still viewed as subjective. Figure 10.4 is an example of a checklist used to record the attainment of predetermined core and optional objectives.

Personal Interview

A system closely related to the subjective observation system of grading is the **personal interview**, which occurs when the teacher formally visits with students and asks questions that are related to performance and behavior. From the student's responses, the teacher is able to obtain information that can be used in determining a grade for a particular unit, lesson, or semester. In this setting, students have time to share with the instructor what they have, or have not, learned in class. An obvious advantage of this approach is that it creates an opportunity for the teacher to spend some quality time with each student. A disadvantage is that it is extremely time consuming.

Another potential pitfall of the personal interview is that the final grade may be the result of the quality of the interview rather than the student's knowledge, performance, or behavior. As with the checklist method, the personal interview is more objective if a checklist of questions and performance evaluations is developed prior to each meeting.

From an instructional and counseling standpoint, the personal interview can be a valuable tool. From an evaluation perspective, it should be used judiciously and only in special cases. A teacher has only so much time available for testing and evaluating. A schedule should, therefore, be established and adhered to. Chapter 2 provides examples of implementation strategies for realistic evaluation schemes.

Reporting Student Performance Data

Reporting grades is closely linked to evaluation and can be defined as the process of describing the progress toward goals. Meaningful grade reports to students, parents, and others are extremely important if the program is to maintain credibility. The worth of the program is often judged by the performance of the product. Complete student progress reports may include the following information:

1. The performance-based objective or program goal.
2. The content that was taught to meet the objective or goal.
3. The degree of change exhibited by the student relative to skill performance, behavior, fitness, or knowledge.
4. The student's status relative to continuous progress toward performance-based objectives.
5. The student's status relative to peers.

Though many formats for reporting progress in these areas are available, the four most popular methods seem to be the report card, personal letter, conferences, and student profile.

Report Card

Considerable variation exists in the type and amount of information contained on a traditional school report card. Usually, the report card consists of a listing of the subjects, the letter grades received in those subjects, and relevant personal characteristics of the student. Sometimes, especially with physical education, space will be left to make comments regarding the student's behavior (e.g., sportsmanship, fair play) and general attitude toward the class. The following pieces of information should be included in the report card:

1. The name of the child with all other essential personal information.
2. Absence report.

3. Letter grades, checks, or numerical ratings for selected categories.

4. Space for comments by the teacher(s).

5. A place for the parents to sign, if the card is to be returned.

Most school districts have a standard report card format that is computer generated. This process is certainly advantageous in terms of accuracy, expediency, cost effectiveness, and record-keeping capacity. It does, however, depersonalize the grading process. If we are sensitive to the students' needs and wish to use the evaluative process to enhance learning, then a more personal approach to grading should be considered.

Student Portfolios

Portfolios are becoming a popular alternative assessment method to exhibit student work and performance data. In addition to serving as a means to portray student achievement, the portfolio facilitates teacher and student involvement and still maintains academic integrity by satisfying the need to be accountable. Although relatively new to the education arena, portfolios have been standard fare for displaying the works and achievements of artists, photographers, models, journalists, and other professionals. In recent years portfolios have become a popular means to present students' accomplishments in the areas of reading, writing, art, and other creative and performing subjects. According to Melograno (1994), portfolio implementation in physical education is beginning to emerge in the school setting. Several high schools are employing videotapes of student performance, computer simulations, and fitness progress as artifacts of the student profile.

A portfolio includes many elements and should be designed to meet a variety of important student needs. For example, the portfolio should (1) provide qualitative and quantitative information about student performance that allows students to assess their accomplishments; (2) assist the teacher and student in determining the degree to which learning objectives have been met; and, (3) contain information useful in the placement of students and evaluation of the total program.

Student portfolios can also be characterized as "student-centered" and contain work completed, work in progress, goals, teacher feedback, self-evaluation commentary, reflection on activity and performance goals, and other achievements of students in each of the four learning domains. It is important to keep in mind that these portfolios are to be kept over time and should follow students through their school years. Physical educators should spend time planning and organizing the physical appearance of portfolios and consider potential contents prior to implementing the system in their evaluation scheme.

Personal Letter

One method to personalize the evaluation process is to write a letter to each student. In this letter the teacher can speak directly and uniquely to the individual student and his or her parents. In this type of report, parents and students can get a more accurate and personal appraisal regarding the student's actual performance.

At first, the thought of drafting a personal report to all students may appear to be a clerical nightmare. In most cases, the physical educator teaches more students than does any other subject matter teacher in the schools. This is especially true in the elementary school, in which some specialists are responsible for the evaluation of hundreds of students. The rapid advancement of computer software and hardware capabilities, however, has done a great deal to make the personal report a feasible approach to reporting grades. A standard-form report can be drafted and key sentences that provide the evaluation of the student can be stored and appropriately inserted in each letter so personalized reports can be generated with little time and effort. Most of the instructor's time can be devoted to developing the document and the evaluation statements.

The personal report has some disadvantages. For example, while the report serves the reporting function very well, it is less useful and much more cumbersome as a permanent record. Information cannot be easily quantified and the amount of paper required to print reports for all students can be enormous. Therefore, it is recommended that the report be used to complement the standard school form and be directed at students who require special attention.

Conference

The face-to-face conference is an effective way to report grades to students or parents. It is the most personal way to convey the results of assessment and evaluation. In addition, the conference leaves no room for misinterpretation about the grade and offers the opportunity for students and parents to receive immediate responses to questions they may have about the actual earning of the grade. The teacher has time to clarify any misconceptions that a parent or student may have developed. Also, the conference is likely to lead to better rapport between the teacher and parent. Many schools, especially elementary schools, make parent-teacher conferences a regular part of the school calendar and evaluation process.

One drawback of the personal conference is that, as with the letter, the content is neither easily quantifiable nor readily stored on the student's permanent record. Further, teachers may view the conference more as a public relations effort than an evaluation session. If the interview is the practiced mode of evaluation, the teacher should approach it as such by preparing information relative to the student's progress and relation to peers so that it can be shared with those in attendance at the interview.

Graphic Profile

The graphic profile is a recommended method of illustrating student progress and reporting performance. As shown in Figure 10.5 the graphic profile satisfies many requirements characteristic of meaningful report formats. The old adage "One picture is worth a thousand words" is proven true when using this method. A person can readily observe standards of a student's performance compared to that of other students, percentile equivalents, or the individual's progress over time. Students, parents, and administrators can readily assess the change in performance without having to interpret numerical charts or conversion tables.

Graphic profiles can be generated on a personal computer and printed on most printers. This is advantageous for several reasons. First, the physical task of plotting information is reduced to making a few keystroke entries on the computer and having the software do the work. Software packages that graphically profile data have a storage capacity. As a result, a student's raw scores may be entered and saved for use

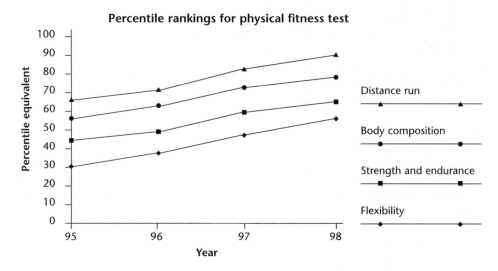

Figure 10.5 Computer-generated graphic profile of performance over time.

at a later date. By using such software, a teacher may follow the progress of a student over time.

Another advantage of the graphic profile is that the burden of obtaining the printout can be placed on the student. In the elementary and secondary schools, the computer is a tool used by all students. It may be that, once they know their scores from a particular test or battery of tests, students can find some computer time during the school day and generate their own profiles. Because the teacher has records of the raw scores, the student can simply show the printed profile to the teacher to check for accuracy. It can then be sent home for the parents to view. Having the students generate their own profiles adds a personal touch to the evaluation process. Students no longer need to rely solely on the teacher; rather, they can assume an active role in determining their progress toward goals. Also, features of graphic profile software now include prescriptive activities and explanations about the current levels of performance. The FITNESSGRAM and ACTIVITYGRAM presented in Chapter 5 are excellent examples of this type of profile.

Grading Students with Disabilities

The Individuals with Disabilities Education Act amendments of 1997 (IDEA) include standards in inclusionary settings for students with disabilities. In physical education classes across the United States, students with disabilities are currently being included. Physical educators must make appropriate modifications in class activities to accommodate these students and also face the challenge of assigning grades in an equitable manner (Churton, Cranston-Gingras, and Blair, 1997). Jansma and French (1994) report that most physical educators feel that their training is inadequate to report grades for students with disabilities. Students with disabilities must receive grades and reports on progress at least as often as do students without disabilities (IDEA, 1997).

Physical education teachers are important members of school personnel teams responsible for educating all students in several curriculum areas. This responsibility, properly performed, is cooperatively implemented with special education and related service staff members (e.g., physical and occupational therapists). Team members' responsibilities include attending staff meetings, planning interdisciplinary and cooperative educational experiences, providing up-to-date and accurate written reports to document attainment of educational goals and objectives, and working together to assist with, and advocate for, the education of students with disabilities.

A major legal requirement for students aged 3–21 who are eligible for special education is the development, implementation, and ongoing evaluation of a written **individualized education program (IEP)**. The term individualized means that each eligible student must have a program specifically written to meet his or her educational needs. Physical education teachers should be active and contributing members of IEP teams. The IEP is prepared by numerous persons, and the content written by physical education teachers is only part of the total information. An IEP can be as short as 3 pages or as long as 15 or more pages, depending on the student's needs. Not all students with disabilities will have a written IEP; some students with disabilities can perform all educational activities without special education assistance or services.

Physical education teachers should communicate with special education staff at the start of and periodically throughout each school year to determine which students have IEPs, and whether physical education requires written documentation (i.e., present levels of performance, long-term or annual goals, and short-term instructional objectives, etc.). Physical education teachers should acquaint themselves with classroom teachers (regular and special education) to determine who is primarily responsible for each student's IEP. This IEP "team leader" should receive written reports on the physical education program for specific students.

The physical educator should also communicate with the principal and/or the appropriate special education supervisor concerning her or his roles with special education pupils and procedures for written IEP reports. A schedule is usually distributed to teachers at the start of the school year regarding deadlines for IEP progress reports. Physical education teachers should be on the distribution list for these schedules. They should determine at the start of the year whether they are expected to attend IEP team meetings, or whether written reports will suffice. The best practice is for physical education teachers to attend and participate in IEP team meetings.

A school or school district may have an adapted or special physical education teacher on staff. In this situation, the regular physical education teacher may assist this specialist with measurement, program planning, and design of goals and objectives for individual special education students. The availability of a specialist will vary from school to school and district to district. Regardless of whether an adapted specialist is on staff, all physical education teachers must understand IEP procedures and be able to perform the roles of measurement, planning, implementing, and evaluating instruction for students with disabilities.

The Written IEP Document

By law, a written IEP must include the following:

1. A statement of the student's present level of educational performance.

2. A statement of annual goals, including short-term instructional objectives.

3. A statement of special education and related services to be provided to the child and the extent to which the child will be able to participate in the regular education program.

4. The projected dates for initiation of services and anticipated duration of the services.

5. Appropriate objective criteria and evaluation procedures and schedules for determining, on at least an annual basis, whether short-term instructional objectives are being achieved.

6. Transition services (beginning no later than age 16, or at a younger age if determined appropriate), to include a statement of the needed transition services and, if appropriate, a statement of each public agency's and each participating agency's responsibilities or linkages, or both, before the student leaves the school setting (Individuals with Disabilities Education Act, Public Law 101-476).

An examination of each of these IEP components will reveal much similarity to measurement and evaluation concepts already presented in this chapter and in Chapter 2.

Grading Alternative

Henderson, French, and Kinnison (2001) suggest an alternative form of grading for students with disabilities. It is directly linked to the learning objectives in the IEP and provides a sound evaluation procedure. It also conforms to standards in IDEA (1997). They suggest contract grading with simple-to-read reports that provide timely feedback on progress the student is making toward IEP goals. Figure 10.6 provides a sample IEP contract.

This type of report can be sent to parents, and student progress can be translated into grades consistent with school policies on grading in the general curriculum. There are advantages and disadvantages to this contract grading approach. Advantages (Sabornie and deBettencourt, 1997) include:

1. Expectations are clearly identified.

2. Teacher objectivity is increased since requirements are stated in advance.

3. Diversity of assignments is encouraged.

4. Because grades are based on individualized criteria, competitiveness is minimized.

5. The student can be involved in goal setting.

6. A more effective learning environment is promoted.

Disadvantages of this type of contract grading (Henderson, French, and Kinnison, 2001) can include:

1. The teacher and student may not agree on goals.

2. Students without disabilities may perceive contract grading as unfair, which, in turn, can cause resentment toward students with disabilities.

3. Contract grading requires more record keeping.

In most cases, the teacher should be able to negotiate successfully with the stu-

Annual Goals	Specific Educational Services Needed	Present Level of Performance	Person Delivering Service
Goal 1. Trevor will improve abdominal strength.	Special physical education consultant services	Performs eight bent-leg sit-ups with assistance	Morgan Stewart, special physical educator
Goal 2. Trevor will improve throwing skills.	Special physical education consultant services	With a tennis ball, Trevor hits a 2' x 2' target five feet away on 2 of 10 trials	Morgan Stewart, special physical educator

Short-Term Objectives	Date Completed	Special Instructional Methods and/or Materials	Grade
Goal 1. Objectives			
1. In the gym, with assistance, Trevor will perform 10 bent-leg sit-ups.	10-12-01	mat; social praise; a performance graph	C
2. In the gym, without assistance, Trevor will perform eight bent-leg sit-ups.	11-7-01	same	B
3. In the gym, without assistance, Trevor will perform 25 bent-leg sit-ups.	Progressing: can do 21	same	A
Goal 2. Objectives			
1. With a tennis ball, Trevor will hit a 2' x 2' target five feet away on 6 of 10 trials.	11-14-01	tennis ball and target	C
2. With a tennis ball, Trevor will hit a 2' x 2' target 10 feet away on 6 of 10 trials.	11-21-01	same	B
3. With a tennis ball, Trevor will hit a 2' x 2' target 20 feet away on 8 of 10 trials.	12-10-01	same	A

SIGNATURES AND TITLES OF APPROPRIATE TEAM MEMBERS: (Signatures indicate approval of this IEP)

_____   _____   _____
(Parent)   (Teacher)   (Administrator/Supervisor)

Source: *Journal of Physical Education, Recreation, and Dance.* August 2001. 72(6), 53. Reprinted by permission of the American Alliance for Health, Physical Education, Recreation, and Dance, Reston, VA.

Figure 10.6 Sample IEP grading contract.

dent on the goals of the contract. With the proper approach with students without disabilities, a positive climate can be developed in class that will minimize resentment. The greatest disadvantage is the additional record keeping. With advances in technology, however, this task has been reduced to some extent.

This contract grading approach for students with disabilities provides a sound approach to grading when these students are mainstreamed into the general physical education setting. Any valid grading procedure links assessment with student learning objectives. This alternative grading system is based on the objectives listed in the student's IEP. Thus, with appropriate modifications on physical activity built into the IEP, the grading procedure has been appropriately adapted as well. For more information on this form of contract grading, please refer to the publication by Henderson, French, and Kinnison (2001).

Summary

Although grading is an integral procedure of teaching, there are differing opinions regarding the relative appropriateness of assigning grades in physical education. Further, a variety of grading practices exist and there is little general agreement among practitioners as to the most appropriate way to grade. The increased attention given to accountability creates a special demand for measurement and evaluation in the physical education curriculum. There needs to be limited, systematic, and objective measurement in the school setting that links goals, outcomes, and objectives with grade determination. This chapter suggests that grading should occur in physical education and cites two basic approaches to determining grades: norm-referenced and criterion-referenced. Norm-referenced tests include the types of assessment that measure relative achievement. Criterion-referenced tests use a single performance and compare it to a predetermined standard. Both types of testing procedures can be used successfully in physical education and the selection of which method to administer is dependent on various factors. In addition to norm- and criterion-referenced tests, other methods may be used to assess and evaluate student performance. The manner of reporting grades is changing with the technological advances in recording, storing, and reporting information, and the computer can now be used to print the traditional report card as well as graphic profiles and personal letters. Alternative procedures for grading students with disabilities were also discussed.

Discussion Questions

1. Explain the basic philosophy underlying your approach to grading in physical education. What constituencies should be permitted to influence the determination of grades?

2. Cite reasons to link grades with program goals, unit outcomes, and performance-based objectives. From a student's perspective, why would this practice be considered useful?

3. Cite the advantages and disadvantages of grading. Based on the information presented, do you think grading should be used in physical education?

4. Which are the most important issues associated with determining grades? The least important? What factors affect the status of these issues?

5. Cite examples of occasions when the norm-referenced approach to grading would be appropriate to use in physical education. When would the criterion-referenced approach be better? Which approach do you think is more compatible with your philosophy of grading?

6. How important is subjective assessment and evaluation in the grading process? Is it a valid means to determine performance? Cite some examples of subjective procedures that you would use in assigning grades.

7. What are the different ways to report grades? In your opinion, which is the best way to communicate performance to the student? Parents? Other teachers?

8. Discuss challenges associated with assigning grades to students with disabilities. Explain how contract grading can be used in this situation.

REFERENCES

Churton, M., Cranston-Gingras, A., and Blair, T. (1997). *Teaching children with diverse abilities*. Boston: Allyn and Bacon.

Darst, P. W., and Pangrazi, R. P. (2002). *Dynamic physical education for secondary school students*. 4th ed. San Francisco: Benjamin Cummings.

Hastad, D. N., Marett, J. R., and Plowman,S. A. (1983). *Evaluation of the health-related physical fitness status of youth in the state of Illinois*. DeKalb, IL: Northern Illinois University.

Henderson, H., French, R., and Kinnison, L.(2001). Reporting grades for students with disabilities in general physical education. *Journal of Physical Education, Recreation, and Dance*, 72 (6), 51–55.

Hensley, L. D. (1990). Current measurement and evaluation practices in professional physical education. *JOPERD*, 61(2): 32–33.

Illinois State Board of Education. (1982). *Tips and techniques: Ability grouping and performance evaluation in physical education*. Springfield, IL: State Board.

Imwold, C. H., Rider, R. A., and Johnson, D. J. (1982). The use of evaluation in public-school physical education programs. *Journal of Teaching Physical Education*, 2(1), 13–18.

Individuals with Disabilities Education Act (IDEA) Public Law 101-476. (1990). 20 U.S.C. Chapter 3 (Available from the Superintendent of Documents, U.S. Government Printing Office, Washington, D.C. 20402).

Individuals with Disabilities Education Act Amendments of 1997, Public Law 105-17. (1997). U.S.C. Title 20, 1400 et seq.

Jansma, P., and French, R. (1994). *Special physical education: Physical activity, sports, and recreation*. 2nd ed. Englewood Cliffs, NJ: Prentice-Hall.

Laughlin, N., and Laughlin, S. (1992). The myth of measurement in physical education. *Journal of Physical Education, Recreation, and Dance*, 63: 83–85.

Melograno, V. J. (1994). Portfolio assessment: Documenting authentic student learning. *Journal of Physical Education, Recreation, and Dance*, 65: 50–61.

Pangrazi, R. P., and Corbin, C. B. (1993). Physical fitness: Questions teachers ask. *Journal of Physical Education, Recreation, and Dance*, 64: 14–18.

Sabornie, E., and deBettencourt, L. (1997). *Teaching students with mild disabilities at the secondary school level*. Columbus, OH: Merrill.

REPRESENTATIVE READINGS

Bosco, J. S., and Gustafson, W. F. (1983). *Measurement and evaluation in physical education, fitness, and sports*. Englewood Cliffs, NJ: Prentice-Hall.

Illinois State Board of Education. (1982). *Tips and techniques: Ability grouping and performance evaluation in physical education*. Springfield, IL: State Board.

Johnson, B. L., and Nelson, J. K. (1986). *Practical measurements for evaluation in physical education*. 4th ed. Minneapolis, MN: Burgess.

Miller, D. (2002). *Measurement by the physical educator*. 4th ed. Boston: McGraw-Hill.

Pangrazi, R. P. (2001). *Dynamic physical education for elementary school children*. 13th ed. San Francisco: Benjamin Cummings.

Wessel, J. A., and Kelly, L. (1986). *Achievement-based curriculum development in physical education*. Philadelphia, PA: Lea and Febiger.

CHAPTER *11*

Using Self-Evaluation to Improve Instruction

Key Terms

Academic Learning Time—Physical Education (ALT-PE)

Arizona State University Observation Instrument (ASUOI)

Behavioral Evaluation Strategy and Taxonomy (BEST)

checklist

duration recording

event recording

eyeballing

group time sampling

instructional time

instructor movement

interobserver agreement (IOA)

interval recording

management

negative modeling

note taking

placheck recording

positive modeling

practice time

rating scale

response latency

System for Observing Fitness Instruction Time (SOFIT)

Objectives

1. Understand problems associated with the measurement and evaluation of teacher effectiveness in physical education.

2. Describe traditional methods of evaluating teachers and explain why these methods lack objectivity and reliability.

3. Identify systematic observation methods used for teacher evaluation and explain the advantages these methods have over the traditional methods.

4. Demonstrate a basic knowledge of the data collection procedures associated with event recording, interval recording, duration recording, and group time sampling.

5. Define interobserver agreement (IOA) and explain why it is critical to establish IOA when using any type of systematic observation.

6. List and describe teacher and student behaviors that can be observed using systematic observation.

Instruction is usually considered in relation to school physical education programs, but instruction takes place in virtually all activity settings. For example, exercise clinicians teach cardiac rehabilitation patients new health and exercise habits and monitor their workouts; athletic trainers provide feedback to athletes during treatment sessions; personal trainers instruct their clients as they oversee their exercise regimens; and coaches at all levels instruct their athletes in the skills and strategies of their sports. Professionals in all activity settings—both school and nonschool—should strive to provide the best instruction possible. Thus, the emphasis on improving instruction in this chapter is targeted at both physical education and exercise science settings. Further, measurement strategies to gather information on behaviors in this wide variety of activity settings stress the use of self-evaluation methods of evaluating instructional effectiveness. A variety of questions arise when considering appropriate self-evaluation strategies.

1. *Why should efforts at improving instruction focus on self-evaluation strategies?* It is recommended that all physical education and exercise science professionals use some form of self-evaluation to monitor and help improve their effectiveness. Whereas a supervisor or administrator may do an evaluation once or twice a year, this is not adequate to provide substantive information about instruction. These evaluations normally use some type of traditional method to gather data. The problems with these traditional methods are detailed in the following section of this chapter. Multiple observations using more objective techniques are needed for meaningful data to be gathered, but time constraints on outside evaluators usually make repeated observations logistically impossible.

Thus, self-evaluation strategies are much more desirable. Self-evaluation alleviates the time constraints of outside evaluators. The use of a portable cassette recorder or VCR camera to record instructional episodes allows for repeated observations and thorough self-evaluation. In many cases, enlisting the cooperation of a colleague in collecting data for self-evaluation is an excellent strategy. A live observer can sometimes gather information difficult or impossible to get from recorded tapes. By working collaboratively with coworkers, you can observe their instruction in exchange for their observation of yours. Insights into particular situations often surface as instructional episodes are discussed with your peers. What better person to involve with your self-evaluation efforts than a peer who understands the special situations and challenges that you face on a daily basis? While periodic observation made by supervisors and administrators certainly should be considered and may provide valuable information, systematic improvement should be based on self-evaluation.

2. *What type of evaluation instrument should be used in analyzing instruction in activity settings?* It is recommended that a systematic observation methodology be used to gather data on instructional episodes. Later in this chapter, specific information on systematic observation techniques is presented in detail. There are many different ways to design observation instruments for different activity settings. While one instrument may be appropriate for an elementary school physical education class, a different or modified instrument likely would be more effective in analyzing instruction in an aerobic dance class at a health club. Whatever instrument is used, information on both instructional behaviors of the practitioner and the nature of activities of the students/clients should be gathered. For instance, what ratio of positive and negative feedback statements does a coach make to his/her athletes? During a workout, what percentage of time is the cardiac rehabilitation patient actually engaged in the prescribed exercise regimen? How many attempts at shooting the basketball does the ninth grade student get during a lesson on shooting? What percentage of instruc-

tions or directions from an aerobic dance instructor are targeted at individuals rather than the entire class? Instruments should be designed to answer questions specific to a given setting. Much care must be taken to ensure that the chosen instrument and data collection procedures provide valid and reliable information concerning the instructional episode.

3. *When should the observations be made?* In general, observations should be made at a variety of times with as many observations as possible. Keep in mind that the data collected should be representative of what goes on in the setting. If self-evaluation is based on only one or two observations, it is possible that what occurs is not representative of normal activities. For example, if a teacher wants to evaluate instruction in a six-week weight training unit, she should videotape one class a week during the unit rather than do six observations in the first two weeks. Coaches should do self-evaluation activities during different times of the season. Exercise clinicians should observe their clients' workout behaviors at different stages of their programs. Observations should be planned and conducted to address the issues of interest in the instructional process.

Whenever observations are made, it is crucial that they be carried out in an unobtrusive, objective, and nonthreatening manner. Multiple observations also serve to ensure that behaviors are not altered on the day of evaluation. While each self-evaluation episode provides information about that particular day, a thorough self-evaluation should look at the accumulation of data over multiple observations to observe trends and make possible a summative self-evaluation. Once a baseline is established from initial observations, then specific behaviors can be targeted for improvement, with subsequent observations made to monitor the improvement. This self-evaluation process should be beneficial to all and improve overall program effectiveness.

In a climate of increased demand for accountability, evaluation in activity settings is sometimes linked to student achievement. Although achievement should not be discounted, this is not the sole criterion by which to evaluate an instructor. Many variables other than instructor performance may affect achievement, including administrative support, class size or number of clients, availability of facilities and equipment, and socioeconomic background of the participants. An instructor has little or no control over these variables; consequently, self-evaluation should emphasize variables the instructor can control.

Professionals have direct control over the behaviors they exhibit while instructing. This chapter will provide a description of traditional methods of evaluation and an in-depth examination of self-evaluation strategies by focusing on the observable and measurable behaviors exhibited in activity settings. The behaviors exhibited during instructional episodes are critical elements that, in great part, determine instructor effectiveness. Because behavior is an instructional variable that can be analyzed and changed, it makes sense that this should be the focus of self-evaluation.

Traditional Methods of Observation

Instruction typically is evaluated by observing the specific setting and using one of several traditional methods of collecting information. The methods detailed below have been used for many years and continue to be employed in many educational and business settings. However, all suffer a major drawback: They are based on the perspective of a single observer making a subjective evaluation.

Eyeballing

A common method of observation is for the evaluator to merely watch what is being taught and then offer comments and suggestions for improvement. Siedentop (1991) used the term **eyeballing** for describing this method. Feedback to the practitioner is usually in the form of a discussion of the performance at the conclusion of the episode. These verbal intuitions passed on by the supervisor normally lack specificity and are based on the subjective opinions of the evaluator. There is no database and no way to determine changes or improvement in subsequent observations. For these reasons, this particular method falls short of meeting criteria for validity, reliability, and objectivity.

Note Taking

An observer using the **note taking** technique writes down comments concerning the instructional effectiveness. These notes may be taken as the class is watched or written from memory at the conclusion of the class. Note taking is an improvement over eyeballing since some visible evidence is provided concerning the formulation of the evaluation. These anecdotal records can vary from a few short phrases to long, detailed notes about the observation. The observer still relies on subjective intuition and opinions, but the perceptions are written down. The value of this method depends on the completeness of the notes used for evaluation.

Though this method is superior to eyeballing, the notes taken may or may not be accurate and usually are written in a less than precise style, which inhibits measuring improvements toward specific objectives. Anecdotal records are valuable as a supplementary evaluation tool, but they do not provide enough objective information on which to base a valid evaluation.

Checklists

A **checklist** is an evaluation tool that offers a series of statements or phrases to which an observer can make yes or no responses. The statements or phrases are characteristics of good instruction, such as "shows enthusiasm" or "good knowledge of subject matter." These characteristics are seldom defined in specific terms, so the observer must interpret each criterion statement. These interpretations inevitably vary from observer to observer, which makes the checklist less than reliable.

The checklist appears to be a more objective evaluation than eyeballing or note taking, but it is still formed by the subjective judgment of a single individual. The evaluation is based on the interpretations and opinions of the observer and offers little in the way of specific information by which to measure future changes (see Figure 11.1). The checklist is valuable for keeping records of steps or jobs completed but should not be used as the major evaluation tool.

Rating Scales

The traditional method that appears to be the most scientific and objective is the **rating scale**. It is similar to the checklist except that it typically allows the observer a

---

EVALUATION FORM

Activity _____ Date _____

Student Teacher_____Elementary _____Secondary_____

College Supervisor _____Cooperating Teacher _____

This evaluation of student teaching serves as a tangible basis for discussion among the cooperating teacher, the college supervisor, and the student. The following symbols will be used: Plus (+) indicates a positive feature of the student teacher's work; minus (–) indicates a need for improvement.

TEACHING COMPETENCIES

☐ Appearance	☐ Planning and organization
☐ Use of language	☐ Execution of lesson-teaching technique
☐ Voice	☐ Knowledge of subject
☐ Enthusiasm	☐ Demonstration of skills
☐ Poise	☐ Appropriate progression
☐ Creativeness	☐ Provisions for individual differences
	☐ Class management/control
	☐ Adaptability, foresight
	☐ Appropriate choice of activity

COMMENTS:

From *Dynamic Physical Education for Secondary School Students*, 2nd ed., by R. Pangrazi and P. Darst. Copyright © 1991 by Allyn and Bacon. Reprinted by permission.

Figure 11.1 Example of a checklist.

greater range than the yes/no decision of the checklist. An evaluator may assign a score from a range of points, typically one to five, for the characteristics included on the rating scale (see Figure 11.2). Thus, for a characteristic such as "shows enthusiasm," the observer has greater flexibility in making the appraisal.

However, the rating scale is plagued by the same problems as the checklist. The observer must still define the characteristic and then make a subjective decision of how to rate the criterion in question. With a five-point scale for each criterion, it becomes even more difficult to demonstrate reliability with this method. If the rating scale has more than five points, such as a 1–10 scale, reliability becomes more of a problem. The fewer points that are involved, the more reliable the ratings become, but by having fewer points, the instrument becomes less precise.

When the rating scale furnishes general information based on only a few rating points for each characteristic, it can be a convenient way to provide supplementary

NAME _____
(Last)   (First)   (Middle)
SUBJECT OR
GRADE LEVEL: _____

Type (X) in the space that indicates your appraisal of the student teacher:	Superior	Above Average	Average	Below Average	Unsatisfactory	Not Known		Superior	Above Average	Average	Below Average	Unsatisfactory	Not Known
Appearance							Innovativeness						
Mental alertness							Communication skills						
Poise and personality							Lesson planning ability						
Enthusiasm							Rapport with students						
Health and energy							Classroom control skills						
Emotional stability							Student motivation skills						
Tact and judgment							Teaching skills						
Desire to improve							Provides for individuals						
Dependability							Understands students						
Professional attitude							Knowledge of subject						
Cooperation							Potential as a teacher						

ADDITIONAL COMMENTS:

(Give this completed and signed form to the student teacher)

Name_____ (Supervising Teacher)_____ Date _____

Name_____ (College Supervisor)_____ Date _____

From *Dynamic Physical Education for Secondary School Students,* 2nd ed., by R. Pangrazi and P. Darst. Copyright © 1991 by Allyn and Bacon. Reprinted with permission.

Figure 11.2 Example of a rating scale.

data on teaching performance. If rating scales are utilized, it is important to understand the weaknesses and limitations of this type of instrumentation.

To summarize, traditional methods of observing and evaluating teacher performance are based on the intuition and opinion of the observer. These methods are of some value if they supplement an evaluatory tool that exhibits validity and reliability. Eyeballing, note taking, checklists, and rating scales are based on the perspective of a single observer and have proven to be ineffective because they lack precision and offer little or no quantifiable data. Because a database is not created, it becomes quite difficult to evaluate improvement from lesson to lesson (Pangrazi and Darst, 1991).

Systematic Observation Methodology

Prior to 1960, most evaluation of instructional effectiveness and research completed on this topic was less than satisfactory because of dependence on inappropriate traditional methodologies. Efforts to observe and evaluate teacher performance were plagued by invalid and unreliable instruments and procedures, some of which were just discussed. As a result, strategies were developed for observing teachers and students in the actual teaching–learning environment in order to obtain more objective and quantifiable information. These tools are called systematic observation instruments.

The advent and growing popularity of systematic observation instrumentation has provided the opportunity to observe, record, measure, and evaluate behaviors in physical education, athletic settings, and clinical exercise environments in a valid and reliable manner. The wide variety of systematic observation instruments allows data to be collected and analyzed on participant and instructor behaviors.

These observational tools range from simple to complex and provide different types of information according to the recording procedures used and the nature of the instrument. The development of these instruments has created new possibilities for improved instructional effectiveness through self-evaluation, improved techniques of supervision, research activities, and innovative models of training and inservice.

Regardless of the complexity or focus of the particular instrument, each observational tool is based on observable behavior categories that are specifically defined to ensure reliability of the observations. Depending on the nature of the instrument, behavioral data can be collected from cassette tapes, from VCR tapes, or by observations made by an on-site data collector. Different recording procedures can be used to collect data—event, interval, duration, and group time sampling. These procedures will be discussed later in this chapter. Such procedures allow a trained observer to observe and record data that produces quantifiable and objective feedback in a variety of activity settings.

Thus, systematic observation allows for the collection of objective data on instructor and participant behaviors. Subsequent analysis of this information can provide critical insights for teachers, coaches, and exercise science professionals to improve their effectiveness. Data collected with systematic observation procedures is collected by live observers or by using audiotapes or videotapes. Information that can be collected on any part of the instructional process includes the following:

- type and quality of instructor feedback
- amount of time devoted to management, instruction, and practice
- number of skill attempts by a student in a given class period

- frequency of instructor using first names of students/clients
- participant off-task and on-task behaviors
- instructor movement patterns during class

To change and improve instructional practices, the practitioner first must be aware of what is taking place in the activity setting. By becoming more cognizant of the relationship of instructor and participant behaviors to an effective teaching–learning activity environment, the instructor can make changes to improve her or his effectiveness. Rink (1993) suggests the following steps in using systematic observation:

1. Decide what to look for.
2. Choose an appropriate observational method.
3. Learn to use the observational method in an accurate manner.
4. Collect data.
5. Analyze and interpret the meaning of the data.
6. Make changes to the instructional process.
7. Monitor changes in instruction over time.

Data Recording Procedures

The use of systematic observation instrumentation provides a way to collect data objectively on instructional effectiveness for purposes of self-evaluation. The methods discussed below have been used not only in studying instructional effectiveness, but also in other areas of research, usually psychological in nature, that examine human behavior. Because of their extensive use, the reliability of these procedures is well documented (Siedentop, 1991).

The following methods are easy to understand and simple to use. The main problem with the use of these methods is deciding which behaviors are to be observed and defining those behaviors in measurable and observable terms. Most problems encountered when using systematic observation systems stem from vague definitions leading to misinterpretations of the behavior categories being observed. The observer must decide on specific definitions of behavior categories, which should be written in a precise manner, preferably with examples, and followed consistently if the data collected are to be accurate and objective. The following represent examples of defined behavior categories that could be used with systematic observation procedures:

Instruction: Verbal statements referring to fundamentals, rules, or strategies of the activity, which can come in the form of questioning, corrective feedback, or direct statements.

> Examples: "In soccer, which player is allowed to use his hands?" or "Next time point your toe when you punt the ball," or "Keep your leg straight on that stretch."

Management: Verbal statements related to organizational details of the activity not referring to strategies, fundamentals, or content of the activity.

> Examples: "Make five lines on the sideline facing me" or "Please complete your weight training circuit in 30 minutes."

Praise: Verbal compliments or statements of acceptance.

> Examples: "Good job moving your feet on defense" or "That is a perfect pace on the Stairmaster."

Scolding: Verbal statements of displeasure.

> Examples: "That was a pitiful effort on defense" or "Stop pushing in the back of that line."

Use of First Name: Using the first name or nickname when speaking directly to a participant.

> Examples: "Nice pass, Bill!" "Smitty, you play on the red team today," or "Betty, you are working hard in aerobics class today."

Learning the different systematic observation methods of data collection usually requires nothing more than one or two practice sessions and a thorough understanding of the behavior categories. The methods can be carried out with simple and inexpensive equipment. Paper, pencil, stopwatch, and sometimes a portable tape recorder are all that is necessary. The use of a videotape recording system can also be quite advantageous in the evaluation process. Portable video cameras are commonplace in contemporary settings and the playback feature creates additional possibilities for self-evaluation. In the following section, several methods for observing and recording instructional behaviors will be discussed.

Event Recording

Event recording is a simple procedure providing precise feedback that can be used in the evaluation process. An observer simply records the number of times predefined behaviors occur during a timed observation period. By gathering information on the frequency of a specific behavior, event recording provides a cumulative record of discrete events occurring during the observation period.

Each discrete event, or behavior, exhibited by the instructor or participant is tallied on a recording sheet (see Figure 11.3). It is typically used to count the frequency of instructor behaviors such as use of first name and feedback statements to skill attempts and student behaviors (Figure 11.13). It is most commonly used to gather and summarize types and frequencies of multiple behaviors. The novice should start by coding a few behaviors at a time because increasing the number of behaviors being recorded makes it more difficult to code the data accurately.

Event recording can also be used to observe participant behaviors. It can be used to count the number of skill attempts (successful and unsuccessful) that students have in a given time period, sometimes called opportunities to respond. Free throws attempted and free throws made is a form of event recording done in basketball statistics. Counting the number of sit-ups a person performed correctly and incorrectly in an aerobics class is a type of event recording. It might be of interest to count how many questions a teacher asked the class or the number of client questions that occurred in a given consultation. Many types of instructor and participant behaviors can be accurately recorded, given a clear definition of the behavior category.

An entire session can be observed using event recording procedures, or it might be decided to collect data in certain timed segments. For example, if an instructional

EVENT RECORDING TALLY SHEET

Date __11/15__   Coach __Davis__   Sport __Basketball__

Categories	Time __10 min.__	Time __10 min.__	Total	RPM	%tage
First Name	ЖЖ ЖЖ IIII	ЖЖ ЖЖ ЖЖ I	30	1.5	15.5
Preinstruction	ЖЖ	II	7	.35	3.6
Concurrent with Instruction	III	I	4	.2	2.1
Postinstruction	ЖЖ ЖЖ ЖЖ ЖЖ ЖЖ ЖЖ ЖЖ II	ЖЖ ЖЖ ЖЖ ЖЖ ЖЖ ЖЖ ЖЖ ЖЖ IIII	81	4.05	41.2
Questioning	IIII	II	6	.3	3.1
Physical Assistance	II		2	.1	1.0
Positive Modeling	III	IIII	7	.35	3.6
Negative Modeling	II	I	3	.15	1.5
Hustle	ЖЖ ЖЖ	ЖЖ III	18	.9	9.3
Praise	ЖЖ	ЖЖ I	10	.5	5.2
Scold	III	III	7	.35	3.6
Management	ЖЖ ЖЖ ЖЖ ЖЖ ЖЖ II	ЖЖ ЖЖ ЖЖ IIII	46	2.3	23.7
Uncodable	II	IIII	3	.15	1.5

TOTAL   __102__   __92__   __194__ __9.7__

Comments   __Preseason practice — 20 minutes total observation__

Figure 11.3 Example of event recording.

session is 40 minutes in length, five segments of three minutes each evenly distributed throughout the session would yield representative behavioral data about the lesson without having to record the entire time period. It is often advantageous to combine event recording procedures with other methods during an observation session.

If segments of a lesson are recorded, the segments should be distributed across the entire session so the data will be representative of the whole class. For example, data collection during the first 15 minutes only of a session typically includes management-type behaviors, such as checking roll, warm-up, and organizing for the day's activity, which would not be indicative of the teaching behaviors exhibited throughout the session. By spreading the observational segments across the session, data more accurately reflect instructional performance.

Calculating Rate per Minute for Behaviors

Whether data are collected for the entire session or for distributed timed segments, it is important to note the total time that observations are made and recorded. When using event recording, a stopwatch should be used to time the length of the observation session to the nearest one-half minute. The results of the event recording data collection can be divided by the number of minutes of observation to calculate the rate per minute (RPM) for each behavior category and a total RPM for all behaviors observed and coded. For instance, if an instructor praises 20 times in 40 minutes of observation, the RPM for the praise category would be calculated as follows:

20 praises divided by 40 minutes = .50 RPM for praise.

This means that the instructor averaged .50 praise per minute during the lesson.

Hopefully, when given this objective information based on systematic observation data, the instructor will realize that future sessions could be made more positive by praising the students more. The instructor could record a future session and count the number of praises used. If 60 praises were recorded in 40 minutes, the RPM (60 praises divided by 40 minutes) for the praise category would be 1.50. Based on this objective method, it is easy to see that the instructor increased the use of praise in the second observation. Subsequent observations should be made to ensure that the RPM for the target behavior is maintained in the future.

Calculating Percentages of Behaviors

When an event recording instrument is designed to record all behaviors of an instructor, the percentage of each independent behavior category should also be calculated. By taking the total number of independent categories and dividing that number into the number of times a specific category was recorded, the percentage for that particular category is ascertained. For instance, if a total of 200 behaviors were recorded, of which 40 were tallied as praise, the percentage of praise behaviors would be figured as follows:

40 praises divided by 200 total behaviors = 20%.

This means that 20 percent of all behaviors were praises.

It should be emphasized that this does not mean that 20 percent of the time was spent praising students. Remember that event recording is based on the number of discrete events, not a unit of time. A teacher might praise a student for 10 seconds and later exhibit a praise behavior for one second. Both are recorded as separate praises. No distinction is made concerning the length of the discrete events. However, a session characterized by discrete behaviors that are lengthy will cause fewer behaviors to be coded, which causes the RPM to be lower.

Consider the practitioner who exhibits only 40 total behaviors in a 40-minute observation. If 20 of these behaviors are in the praise category, then 50 percent of all behaviors (20 praises divided by 40 total behaviors) are praises. Though the figure 50 percent seems high, the RPM for praise is only .50 (20 praises divided by 40 minutes) and the RPM for all observed behaviors is only 1.0 (40 total behaviors divided by 40 minutes). This example illustrates the importance of considering both the RPM and the percentage of a given behavior category when analyzing the data for evaluation purposes.

The use of first name category is often included on event recording instruments. The frequent use of first names reflects more individualized attention and specific feedback for the participants. This category is not an independent behavior since it does not occur by itself; rather, it always accompanies another behavior. Because it is used in combination with an independent behavior, the method for calculating percentage of the use of first name category is handled in a slightly different manner.

By dividing the number of times first names are used by the total number of independent behaviors, the percentage for a first name accompanying an independent behavior is calculated. If 40 first names were coded with 200 total independent behaviors, then 20 percent of all independent behaviors were accompanied by a first name. The use of first name category is a dependent behavior and is handled separately from the independent behavior categories. If the number of first names is included in the calculation of percentages of independent behaviors, the resulting percentage of each other behavior category is decreased, and its true value is distorted. Thus, in calculating percentages, the total of each independent behavior category should be divided by the total number of independent behaviors with the dependent first name category excluded in the total. This treatment of the data yields information that reflects more accurately the behaviors exhibited during the observed teaching performance.

Interval Recording

Another method for collecting meaningful performance data is **interval recording**. Each behavior category is assigned a number for coding purposes. When the behavior is observed, the corresponding number is written on the coding sheet. Each number recorded is considered a data point. In using this technique, behaviors are observed for short intervals of time and then a short period of time is used to code what behavior best categorizes the observed interval. For example, an observer could observe for five seconds and record for five seconds. Each observe-record is considered a data point. According to Siedentop (1991), it is important to have at least 90 data points for validity to be ensured.

For best results, the length of the interval should be 5–12 seconds. If the interval is too short, it cannot be coded accurately. The interval should be as short as possible and still have reliable data. For beginning data collectors, a longer interval allows the observer to become familiar with the technique. As an observer becomes comfortable with the method, the interval can be shortened if desired. When using longer intervals, problems are sometimes encountered when several behaviors occur, and the observer has to decide which behavior to record. The observe-record intervals do not have to be of the same length. For instance, the observation can be five seconds, and the record time can be two seconds. The length of the respective intervals depends on the expertise of the observer and the number and complexity of behavior categories utilized. Usually the observe-record intervals should be the same to avoid confusion.

During field-based interval recording, the observer should use an earphone and portable cassette recorder. A tape with cues to observe and record at the selected time intervals helps the observer with data collection. If a teacher can be taped, coding from a videotape can be advantageous. The videotape can be stopped and reversed if any problems in coding arise. Using a videotape also allows teachers to code themselves. Some VCR cameras have a stopwatch function that can be superimposed on the tape, which is convenient to use with interval recording.

An interval coding sheet (see Figure 11.4) is used to collect the behavioral data. Typically, each behavior category is assigned a number, and each cell on the coding sheet represents a data point. To code behavior, the observer starts at the top, left-hand corner and codes in a vertical direction down the column to the bottom before starting on the second column. If five-second intervals are used, then each cell represents the behavior that characterized that five-second observation interval. If a certain behavior is a lengthy one, it may span several data points. Indications of both frequency and duration of behaviors can be derived with interval recording. The number of intervals coded for each independent behavior indicates frequency, while the number of intervals recorded consecutively indicates the duration of a particular behavior.

Because interval recording is based on time, it is recommended that a silence category be added to the behavior categories. An observation interval can pass without the instructor exhibiting any observable behavior other than monitoring the activity. This interval should be coded as silence, which is not used in event recording.

As discussed previously, the use of first name will always accompany an independent behavior. When the first name category is included, it should be coded in the same cell as the independent behavior it accompanies. If the first name is coded with a 1 and a praise with a 10, then 1/10 would be recorded in the appropriate cell.

Major patterns of behaviors can be derived from interval recording. The behaviors are entered into a matrix system, and a series of steps is followed to determine dominant patterns of behavior. It is beyond the scope of this textbook to detail this procedure, but the reader is referred to the guidelines of the Flanders Interaction Analysis System (Flanders, 1970) for specific information about this process.

Like event recording, a sampling technique can be used in interval recording. For example, interval recording techniques can be used four different times throughout the session, each five minutes in length. Using a six-second interval, this would yield 100 data points from various parts of the session. The selection of the five-minute segments should be carefully made so as not to create bias in the collected data and should be dispersed throughout the time period. Using segments only at certain parts of the session, e. g., at the start of class, could create bias in the collected data. The collected data should be representative of the instructor's behaviors throughout the entire class episode.

INTERVAL RECORDING CODING SHEET

12	14	14	7	4	13	4	14	10	$\frac{1}{12}$	4	3	14	5	14	5	14	14		
12	14	14	12	4	13	10	14	$\frac{1}{10}$	11	4	14	14	14	14	14	14	14		
12	14	14	12	6	12	14	14	14	9	6	14	14	14	14	4	11	14		
13	14	14	11	4	12	14	14	14	2	4	$\frac{1}{3}$	14	4	13	4	4			
12	14	$\frac{1}{3}$	$\frac{1}{3}$	7	12	$\frac{1}{10}$	14	14	2	5	4	14	4	14	10	4			
12	3	5	4	14	12	9	14	14	14	14	4	12	14	14	4	4			
$\frac{1}{5}$	4	14	6	14	2	9	14	14	14	14	5	12	14	14	14	14			
2	4	14	4	14	2	6	14	Rest	14	5	14	12	$\frac{1}{9}$	14	14	14			
2	14	4	4	14	2	7	14	$\frac{1}{10}$	14	14	14	12	14	$\frac{1}{2}$	14	10			
2	14	4	14	14	14	7	14	14	14	10	9	14	14	2	14	4			
7	14	4	14	14	14	3	$\frac{1}{3}$	14	14	14	4	$\frac{1}{4}$	14	14	14	4			
2	$\frac{1}{10}$	9	14	14	14	4	14	12	14	14	7	4	$\frac{1}{10}$	3	14	14			
7	9	7	14	14	$\frac{1}{11}$	4	14	12	$\frac{1}{4}$	14	14	8	4	14	$\frac{1}{10}$	14			
$\frac{1}{5}$	10	8	14	14	4	14	14	12	$\frac{1}{4}$	14	14	7	4	4	14	14			

Coach __Clay__   Date __4-15__

School __Illinois State__   Sport __Tennis (varsity boys)__

Comments __10 min. — Rest — 10 min.; mid-season — day after match__

Behavior Codes

1. Use of First Name	6. Physical Assistance	11. Scold
2. Preinstruction	7. Positive Modeling	12. Management
3. Concurrent Instruction	8. Negative Modeling	13. Uncodable
4. Postinstruction	9. Hustle	14. Silence
5. Questioning	10. Praise	

Figure 11.4 Example of interval recording.

Calculating the Percentage of Intervals

After data are collected on the interval coding sheet, the number of intervals each behavior has been coded is counted and this information is transferred to the interval worksheet (see Figure 11.5). The percentage of intervals should be calculated for each independent behavior category. The number of intervals coded for each individual behavior is divided by the total number of intervals. This number represents the percentage of intervals that each behavior was observed. Though it is not an exact measure, it gives a general idea of the time spent in each behavior category. Percentage of intervals accompanied by a first name can also be calculated.

Duration Recording

Whereas interval recording reveals a general idea of time spent in certain behaviors and event recording yields data about the frequency of behaviors, **duration recording** gives exact information about the amount of time that a behavior takes. Time is the measure of the behavior of interest, and the raw data are expressed in terms of minutes and seconds. Exact time spent in activity, in management, or in instruction can be ascertained with duration recording. In certain instances, this type of systematic observation methodology is more appropriate than event or interval recording.

Suppose that a practitioner wants to know how much time is spent in management activities during a class session. The first step is to clearly define what constitutes management. Checking roll, organizing drills, and transition time between activities are common examples of management time. The observer uses a stopwatch to time each managerial episode throughout the class session. At the end of a 40-minute class, duration recording might indicate that the teacher spent 12 minutes and 30 seconds of time in management behaviors. When first using duration recording, it may be easier to focus on only one behavior. The form shown in Figure 11.6 can be used to identify and time a single behavior such as management. The same type of form could also focus on practice time or instructional time. This is valuable information with which to evaluate and make decisions about improving teacher performance.

Duration recording is also advantageous in measuring such things as instructional time and practice time. Whereas event recording is better for behaviors of short duration, duration recording is best for behaviors that typically occur for longer periods of time. With event and interval recording, an observer can collect data on 12–15 behaviors at once. With duration recording, fewer behaviors are observed, but the data are more exact. After practicing duration recording with one behavior, an observer can use a time line (Figure 11.7) to record multiple behaviors. It is recommended that no more than three behaviors be targeted when using a time line. Typically, the behaviors would be management, instruction, and practice. This allows the teacher to examine the percentages of class time devoted to these activities and make changes as needed.

Calculating Percentage of Total Time

The raw data collected in duration recording is the actual time spent in performing a certain behavior. To say that a teacher spent 12 minutes and 30 seconds in management time means little without knowing the length of observation time. The raw data can be converted into a percentage of time by dividing the time derived from the

CATEGORIES	# OF INTERVALS	% OF INTERVALS
1. Use of First Name	18	7.5
2. Preinstruction	11	4.6
3. Con. Instruction	8	3.3
4. Postinstruction	34	14.2
5. Questioning	8	3.3
6. Physical Assistance	4	1.7
7. Positive Modeling	8	3.3
8. Negative Modeling	2	0.8
9. Hustle	8	3.3
10. Praise	12	5.0
11. Scold	8	3.3
12. Management	19	7.9
13. Uncodable	4	1.7
14. Silence	114	47.5

TOTAL 240

Figure 11.5 Interval recording worksheet.

duration recording by the total observation time. Before this calculation is made, all times are changed into seconds. For example,

$$12 \text{ minutes and } 30 \text{ seconds } = 750 \text{ seconds}$$
$$40 \text{ minutes } = 2400 \text{ seconds}$$

$$750 \text{ seconds of management divided by } 2400 \text{ seconds of total time}$$
$$= 31.25\% \text{ of time spent in management}$$

This conversion to percentage of time permits comparisons between other observations in different settings. Comparisons between classes of different lengths and different instructors can be made. Duration recording offers an excellent way to collect very specific data on behaviors that are essential to effective teaching.

MANAGEMENT TIME

Instructor _____   Observer _____

Class _____   Grade _____   Date and time _____

Lesson focus _____   Comments _____

Starting time _____   End time _____   Length of lesson _____

Total management time _____

Percent of class time devoted to management _____

Number of episodes _____   Average length of episodes _____

Figure 11.6 Duration recording sheet for management time.

Class _____ Grade _____ Date _____

Lesson Focus _____

Comments _____

Length of Lesson _____

Key word or action used to start class and stopwatch _____

Record the word or action used to signal the beginning of the lesson and start the stopwatch. Keep the watch running continuously. Each time you direct the students in one of the following categories, draw a vertical line through the timeline and place the appropriate letter (I, P, M) above the marked section.

I   **Instruction Time:** The initial demonstrations, cues, and explanations that are necessary to get students started on an activity.

P   **Practice Time:** When students are working on specific skills during class time (i.e., warm-up, fitness, rhythms, games).

M   **Management Time:** No instruction or practice takes place during management time. This time includes: giving information, disciplining the class, getting or returning equipment, and the time it takes students to follow those directions.

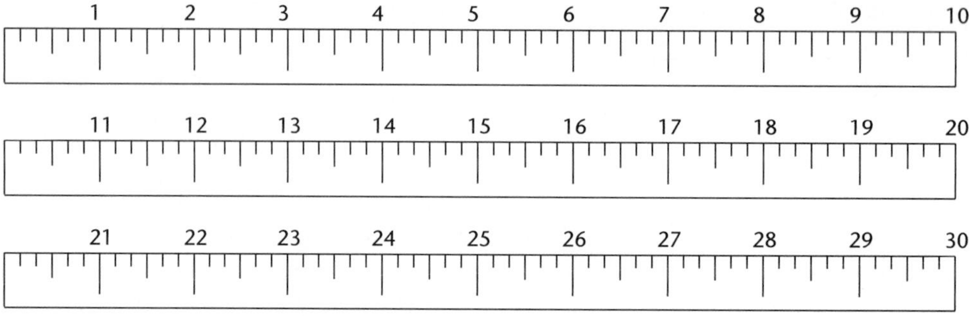

Totals and Percentages: Divide the number of seconds you spent in a category by the number of seconds in class. Multiply by 100 to find the percentage of time spent in each category.

1 = ____ / ____ %   P = ____ / ____ = ____ %   M = ____ / ____ = ____ %

Figure 11.7 Duration recording timeline.

Group Time Sampling

Group time sampling is a method of systematic observation used to collect data on behaviors of all participants over a given time frame. It is similar to interval recording in that observations are made over a given time interval, but is different in that it focuses on the entire group rather than on an individual student. This procedure is sometimes referred to as a **placheck recording** (planned activity check).

At given intervals interspersed throughout the observation session, the coder scans the participants to check how many students are exhibiting a particular behavior of interest. The scan should be done from left to right around the activity setting and can usually be done in about 10 seconds, even with large groups. Once the scan observes a particular person, the observer should not go back if the behavior in question changes. Group time sampling focuses on behaviors that are characterized by such terms as "on task/off task," "appropriate/inappropriate," or "active/inactive" (see Figure 11.8). The objective of this technique is to quickly observe each individual at a certain time and record the number of people engaged in the defined behavior. The behavior should be predefined in specific and observable terms to ensure accuracy of the recorded data.

The observer should know the total number of participants and should count either the number who are engaged in the productive behavior or the number who are not. It is easier to count the alternative to the defined behavior that the least number are exhibiting. To illustrate, assume that the number of participants who are inactive during an aerobics class is smaller than the number who are active. The number of inactive people can easily be subtracted from the total number in class to derive the number of students who are active.

It should take a maximum of 30 seconds to observe and record the data, and it often takes only 10 seconds. The samples should be spaced throughout the lesson at given times. Normally, group time samples are done every three to five minutes. In a 40-minute class, a sample done every four minutes would yield 10 group time observations. If each sample is allotted 30 seconds, only five minutes of observation time would be used with this procedure. If each sample were done in 10 seconds, then only 1 minute and 40 seconds would be used. Even with the five-minute allotment, the time taken for observation is time used wisely to gain valuable information on the behaviors of a group.

Group time samples are normally used in conjunction with another systematic observation procedure. In the time between the samples, for instance, event or interval recording could be used to collect data on teacher behaviors. In this way, an observer would be collecting data on both teacher behavior and the behavior of the class.

Calculating Percentages with Group Time Sampling

As with other techniques, it is advantageous to convert the raw data into a percentage. A percentage figure can be calculated for each group time sample. The number of persons engaged in the productive behavior is divided by the total number to derive this percentage. If 24 participants out of 30 are observed to be active during an observation, then

24 divided by 30 = 80%

PARTICIPANT PERFORMANCE

Instructor_____   Observer _____

Class_____ Grade _____ Date and time_____

Lesson focus _____   Comments _____

Starting time _____ End time _____ Length of lesson _____

_____

Active/inactive

On task/off task

Effort/no effort

_____

Number of plachecks _____

Total number of participants in class_____

Average number of participants not on desired behavior _____

Percentage of participants not on desired behavior _____

From *Instructional Manual for Dynamic Physical Education for Secondary School Students,* 2nd ed., by R. Pangrazi and P. Darst. Copyright © 1991 by Allyn and Bacon. Reprinted with permission.

Figure 11.8 Group time sampling recording sheet.

This calculation shows that 80 percent of all participants were active. By converting data to percentages, classes of different sizes can be compared. By adding the percentages for all samples and dividing by the number of samples taken in a given observation, the mean percentage can be figured for all group time samples observed in that particular class. Group time sampling provides valuable input concerning behaviors of the entire class, which can contribute to a more complete evaluation of instructor performance.

Validity and Reliability of Systematic Observation

As with any data collection procedure, ensuring validity and reliability of the data is critical. Systematic observation instrumentation and data collection procedures must meet the recognized criteria for validity and reliability if the information derived from these processes is to be of any value in self-evaluation.

Validity

As discussed in Chapter 4, validity is the ability to measure the attribute that an instrument is designed to measure. In the case of systematic observation instruments, a valid instrument would measure the instructor and/or participant behaviors that the instrument claims to measure. Validity of systematic observation instruments is established by meeting the criteria of content validity.

The behavior categories included in a chosen systematic observation technique should be representative of behaviors exhibited in the teaching–learning environment. Each category is specifically defined in measurable and observable terms. Whether a systematic observation system is simple or complex, it should satisfy the criteria for content validity.

Reliability

Synonyms for reliability include consistency, repeatability, and precision. A systematic observation system should possess reliability so that confidence can be placed in the collected data. Following established guidelines helps to ensure reliability of data collection procedures. Clear and precise definitions of chosen behavior categories are also crucial. Usually, problems in establishing reliability in systematic observation can be traced to vague or unclear definitions of the behaviors being observed.

When systematic observation procedures are used to determine changes in behaviors, the data must be reliable to ensure that changes are not merely the result of inconsistent data collection by the observer. Confidence in the observations and the resultant evaluation is directly linked to the accuracy and objectivity of the observer.

Interobserver agreement (IOA) checks should be done periodically to ensure the reliability and objectivity of the instrument and coding procedures, as well as the accuracy of the trained observers. To complete an IOA check, two independent observers trained in the chosen observation method and thoroughly familiar with the definitions of the included categories observe the same lesson. Typically, a coworker working on self-evaluation with the practitioner can be used to complete IOA procedures. They should be situated far enough apart so that they cannot see how the other observer is coding, thus making them independent of each other. An IOA can be done in a field-based situation, from an audiotape if nonverbal behaviors are not being recorded, or from a VCR tape if both nonverbal and verbal behaviors are being coded.

According to Siedentop (1991), an IOA of 80 percent is necessary to establish reliability for research purposes. With a low number of observations (12 or fewer), 75 percent is sufficient. A slightly lower rate may be acceptable if the data collected are for feedback on which teachers can base improvement.

In general, the percentage of IOA is calculated using the following formula:

$$\frac{Agreements}{Agreements\ +\ Disagreements} \times 100 = \%\ of\ IOA$$

This formula can be applied to calculate the percentage of IOA for event, interval, duration, and group time sampling recording procedures.

For event recording procedures, IOA should be calculated for each behavior category as well as for the total number of events tallied. For instance, suppose the number of praises occurring in a class period are recorded. One observer tallied 30 praises during the class, while the second observer recorded 34 praises. Thus, the two independent observers agreed on 30 praise behaviors and disagreed on 4. By using the formula above, the IOA is calculated as follows:

$$\frac{30}{30\ +\ 4} \times 100 = \frac{30}{34} \times 100 = 88\%\ of\ IOA$$

If one observer tallied a total of 200 behaviors and the other observed and coded 185, the IOA for all independent behaviors would be as follows:

$$\frac{185}{185\ +\ 15} \times 100 = \frac{185}{200} \times 100 = 93\%\ of\ IOA$$

If interval recording is the selected systematic observation method, the IOA is calculated in a similar way as in event recording, except that rather than looking at agreements and disagreements on separate events, the calculations are based on agreements and disagreements of how many intervals are coded for the defined behavior categories by the independent observers.

If a tape player is used to give auditory cues during the observation, an extra earphone may be spliced into the line with sufficient cord to allow the observers to be situated at least 10 feet apart. A second alternative is to copy the cassette tape being used and equip each observer with a cassette player and earphone.

If duration recording is used to time a behavior of interest, then the time each observer records for the chosen behavior becomes the variable on which to calculate IOA. Assume that two independent observers were timing managerial episodes for a particular class. One observer timed 7:20 while the other observer recorded 9:55 of management time. First, both times should be converted into seconds.

$$7:20 = 440\ seconds$$
$$9:55 = 595\ seconds$$

$$\frac{440}{595} \times 100 = 74\%\ of\ IOA$$

The IOA of 74 percent is too low for any confidence to be put into the accuracy of recording. In a case like this, there is normally some misunderstanding of what constitutes management. A review of the definition and of coding procedures should improve the IOA on the next check. Because of the straightforward nature of duration recording, a high IOA (>90 percent) should be expected (minimum of 80 percent for other methods).

The accuracy of group time sampling should also be checked for IOA. A group time sample done every 4 minutes in a 40-minute class would yield 10 samples for the observation. Assume that there are 30 students in the class being checked for on-task/off-task behaviors. Table 11.1 shows the raw data recorded by the two independent observers for this class.

The number of students that each observer recorded as being on task for the 10 samples is summed. Observer A counted a total of 197 students being on task while Observer B recorded 203 students as on task. IOA is then calculated as follows:

$$\frac{197}{197 + 6} \times 100 = \frac{197}{203} \times 100 = 97\% \text{ of IOA}$$

Whatever observation method is used, it is crucial that the IOA be calculated to ensure the accuracy of the recorded data. It is a waste of time and effort to collect data without being able to place confidence in the information gathered and the resultant self-evaluation. An advantage of these data collection methods is that they reduce the subjectivity of the observer. Reliability of a systematic observation system is established if the IOA is 80 percent or greater. If this is the case, then both the practitioner and the colleague have evidence of the objectivity and accuracy of the data.

Table 11.1 Group time sample data for IOA.

Sample	Observer A	Observer B
1	17/30	19/30
2	21/30	19/30
3	24/30	24/30
4	15/30	14/30
5	19/30	21/30
6	21/30	21/30
7	16/30	18/30
8	23/30	24/30
9	23/30	24/30
10	18/30	19/30

Using Systematic Observation for Self-Evaluation

The process of systematic observation is not complex. Determining and properly defining the behavior categories is the most difficult task. A data collection procedure or combination of procedures must be chosen, and observers need to be trained to collect the data using the established definitions and procedures. Validity and reliability must be established for credibility of the evaluation plan. Once these things are done, the observers can concentrate on collecting data and adhering strictly to the behavior definitions. The raw data are then analyzed and appropriate calculations can be made for input into the final evaluation. The following discussion provides examples of behaviors that can be observed and the data collection procedures that can best be used. Keep in mind that the following represent some possibilities for the use of the previously discussed data collection procedures. It is not an exhaustive discussion. A systematic observation system should be designed specifically to meet the needs of a particular situation.

As discussed earlier in the chapter, the most useful type of evaluation for a practitioner is self-evaluation. By becoming directly involved with collecting your own personal behaviors, you become much more aware of the instruction process in their activity settings. Becoming more aware opens multiple possibilities for studying and modifying personal instructional behaviors in an attempt to increase the participants' enjoyment and achievement.

Effective instructors give participants time to learn by devoting a high percentage of time to the active practice of the skill being taught. Established routines and organizational structures lead to smooth transitions between activities and low rates of management. Effective practitioners actively teach and communicate clear expectations of performance. High rates of specific skill feedback are present, with student progress being monitored closely so that the task can be modified to fit individual needs. The effective teaching–learning environment will communicate warmth through clear, enthusiastic presentations.

Many behaviors occurring in physical education and exercise science settings are linked to these characteristics of effective teaching–learning environments. The following sections will present a variety of possibilities for practitioners to use for self-evaluation purposes. All of them present possibilities of collecting data on the current status of the behavior of interest, analyzing the data to determine how improvements can be made, and implementing new instructional strategies to change the behavior.

Practice Time

For students to achieve in physical education, they must be on task a high percentage of the time. For adults or children to improve their fitness, they must be actively engaged in fitness activities for an appropriate amount of time. **Practice time** refers to the time that participants are practicing skills in an environment that allows them to experience a reasonable amount of success. Generally, the higher the amount of practice time, the better chance participants have to achieve to their potential. Because a participant is in the activity setting for a limited amount of time, it is important that time be used efficiently. Efficient use of time leads to more meaningful periods of physical activity.

To evaluate practice time, an effective method is duration recording. An observer (student, another teacher, administrator) watches the lesson and times the intervals when students practice skills. At the end of the lesson, a certain amount of time will have been spent in practice time. Frequency and length of time of practice episodes, total time of practice, and percentage of practice time can be calculated from duration recording (see Figure 11.7).

Group time sampling can also yield information about practice time. An advantage of group time sampling is that it takes up very little of the total observation period. Event recording can also be utilized to count the number of skill attempts a selected student makes during the observation period. The disadvantage of these two methods is that the data collected are as specific as the information gathered from duration recording.

It should be the instructor's goal to increase the amount of time allowed to practice skills and participate in activity. Decreasing managerial episodes, limiting verbal instructions prior to activity, and creating lessons that encourage maximum participation are ways to increase practice time.

Instructional Time

It is certainly appropriate that instructors spend some time instructing, whether by lectures, demonstrations, or corrective feedback. In this discussion, **instructional time** refers to explanations, demonstrations, and other information that refers to the content of the particular session. Generally, this type of instruction occurs prior to practice time and helps participants get started on the activity.

Though this type of behavior is necessary and desirable, many lessons are plagued by too much instructor talk, which limits the amount of time for active student participation. Instructors must strive to give meaningful instructions succinctly. The right blend of instructional time and practice time differs depending on the type of activity, the maturity and experience of the participants, and whether it is at the start, middle, or end of the unit. These variables must be considered when observing instructional time.

Duration recording can be used to record data on the amount of time spent on instruction. By using a stopwatch and recording the length of instructional episodes, an instructor can receive meaningful feedback about the number of instructional episodes, the average length, and the percent of class time devoted to instruction (Figure 11.7). A general guideline to follow is to employ short instructional episodes frequently rather than to give lengthy instructions. Also, instructors should try not to exceed 45 seconds when giving instructions in physical education settings (Pangrazi and Darst, 1991).

Management Time

The **management** behavior category was defined earlier in the chapter. It includes such things as transition time between drills as participants move into various formations, checking roll, any type of record keeping, distributing or taking up equipment, choosing teams, or suiting up for activity. Good instructors are highly organized and display efficient management behaviors. A well-planned schedule can help decrease the amount of time spent on management activities, thereby allowing more time for instruction and practice.

Some time must be spent on management, and it can be time well invested when it contributes to the organization of the class. Obviously, a large amount of management time would not contribute to effective teaching and would indicate that class procedures need to be streamlined and/or that participants are not responding quickly enough to managerial directions. By using duration recording procedures (Figure 11.7), important information about the length of managerial episodes can be determined. A good goal for management time is that it should not exceed 15 percent of a particular class or exercise session.

If event or interval recording procedures are utilized to collect data on other behaviors, a management category may be included to code the observed management behaviors. Though the data will not be as specific as with duration recording, comparisons to other behavior categories are possible with either event or interval recording. Whatever observation method is used, management behaviors are a crucial aspect of effective instruction and should be carefully monitored and evaluated.

Response Latency

Response latency is the time it takes participants to respond to a signal or direction to start or stop an activity (Pangrazi and Darst, 1991). By using duration recording techniques, the amount of time spent to start or stop an activity after a verbal command or signal can be documented. A decision must also be made as to what percentage of students must respond appropriately before stopping the time. Even a small percentage being off task can lead to a loss of control, so it is recommended that if the criterion is not 100 percent, it should be very near this figure.

As shown in Figure 11.9, the average amount of response latency can be calculated so that the teacher can strive to improve student behavior in future observations. Response latency is wasted time, and class management techniques should be employed to minimize it.

Instructor Movement

Another facet of teaching that can be examined with systematic observation is **instructor movement**—that is, how the instructor moves around the teaching area when giving individualized feedback to participants. Instructors often fall into the unfortunate habit of teaching from one area of the activity area. Students quickly notice where the instructor is located and position themselves according to their particular attitudes toward the instructor and the activity. If the teacher is relatively immobile, then contact with a great number of students is lost. Usually the students who need the most help and attention move away from the instructor. An excellent example of this phenomenon is typical in aerobic dance classes where the instructor teaches only from the front of the room.

This situation can be avoided if the instructor moves throughout the teaching area in an unpredictable manner. The movement by the teacher can be evaluated by dividing the activity area into quadrants and event recording the number of moves from area to area. A move should only be tallied if the instructor interacts with a student or students in some way. Merely jogging through a quadrant should not be recorded as a move. Although active supervision is important, it is also crucial to consider position. The effective practitioner should teach from the perimeter of the activity area as much

RESPONSE LATENCY

Instructor _____   Observer _____

Class _____ Grade _____   Date and time_____

Lesson focus _____   Comments _____

Starting time _____ End time _____   Length of lesson _____

Starting Response Latency

Stopping Response Latency

Total amount of starting response latency _____

Percent of class time devoted to starting response latency _____

Number of episodes _____ Average length of episode _____

Total amount of stopping response latency _____

Percent of class time devoted to starting response latency _____

Number of episodes_____ Average length of episode _____

From *Instructional Manual for Dynamic Physical Education for Secondary School Students,* 2nd ed., by R. Pangrazi and P. Darst. Copyright © 1991 by Allyn and Bacon. Reprinted with permission.

Figure 11.9 Duration recording sheet for response latency.

as possible. This means that the instructor has his or her "back against the wall" most of the time. Therefore, participants are not behind the instructor very often and, thus, can be monitored more effectively. Figure 11.10 offers an example of a simple positioning evaluation tool that can be easily used in all types of settings.

Another possibility for analyzing movement is to use duration recording to time the amount of time spent in each quadrant. The amount of time should ideally be relatively equal for each of the four areas. The type of activity occurring when the teacher moves to a different quadrant can also be recorded. Figure 11.10 illustrates a recording instrument that could be used for this technique. When participants are unable to predict where the instructor will be located, they are more likely to be active in appropriate activities. Thus, analyzing instructor movement and location can provide valuable data.

Specific Instructional Behaviors

Specific instructional behaviors, such as praise, scold, use of first name, and various types of instruction, can be observed and coded by utilizing systematic observation procedures. Typically, event and interval recording procedures are implemented to collect this type of information. Data collection instruments can be designed to record behaviors of interest. With a little practice and precise definitions of behavior categories, an observer can easily record data on a dozen or more behaviors.

Instructional Feedback

A large percentage of behaviors should be instructional in nature. Instructional feedback can take many forms, including nonverbal behaviors such as **positive** and **negative modeling**. Figure 11.11 shows an event recording form designed to code instructional feedback observed in a lesson. Note that ratios for certain types of feedback can be calculated. Totals for all behavior categories are divided by the total minutes of observations to figure the rate per minute (RPM).

Examples of general feedback are comments like "Nice shot" or "Good block," whereas specific feedback provides more information about the behavior, such as "Great job of extending your arm on that shot" or "Billy, you really kept your feet moving on that block." By using first names, the instructor ensures more individualized attention and focuses the comments on the correct students. First name usage can easily be included in the observation data. Since both general and specific feedback can be either positive or negative, positive/negative feedback can also be recorded if desired.

Corrective instructional feedback is also specific by nature. The difference between specific and corrective feedback for the form in Figure 11.11 is that corrective feedback identifies what is incorrect about the skill attempt and also furnishes information about how the skill should be executed. An example would be, "John, you had your head down while you were dribbling. Try to dribble without looking at the ball so you can spot your open teammates." This is a very effective teaching behavior when done in a constructive way. Care should be taken not to comment on every mistake, especially when the teacher feels that the student understands the source of the poor skill attempt. Specific feedback merely furnishes information about the skill attempt but includes no correction.

POSITION AND SUPERVISION EVALUATION FORM

When evaluating yourself from tape, keep track of your position when giving instructions (I), management directions (M), and feedback (FB). Each time you are in a quadrant mark:

I—instructions   Ⓘ—instructions, with students behind you

M—management directions   Ⓜ—management directions, with students behind you

FB—feedback   FB̲ —feedback to students in another quadrant

Instructor _____ Observer (if any) _____

Class _____ Grade _____ Date and time _____

Lesson _____

Starting time _____ End time _____ Length of lesson _____

I	III
II	IV

Perimeter Instructions_____ Perimeter Directions_____

Circled I or M _____ Scans with Feedback (FB)_____

Quadrant Feedback (FB): I _____ II_____ III _____ IV_____ Total _____

Comments_____
_____

Reprinted with permission from *Strategies, A Journal for Physical and Sports Educators*, January 1994. Copyright 1994 by the American Alliance for Health, Physical Education, Recreation, and Dance, 1900 Association Drive, Reston, VA 20191.

Figure 11.10 Recording sheet for teacher movement.

Nonverbal feedback on performance can also be coded. It is sometimes difficult for one person to code both verbal and nonverbal behavior categories. While momentarily recording a verbal behavior, the observer may miss a pat on the back, a frown, or some other nonverbal behavior. The use of videotape can remedy this situation since the tape can be stopped or replayed, or two observers can alleviate the problem in a live situation.

INSTRUCTOR BEHAVIOR EVENT RECORDING

Instructor _____ Observer _____

Class _____ Grade _____ Date and time _____

Lesson focus _____ Comments _____

Starting time _____ End time _____ Length of lesson _____

		3	6	9	12	15	18	21	24	27	30	Event Total
General instructional feedback	+											
	−											
Specific instructional feedback	+											
	−											
Corrective instructional feedback												
First names												
Nonverbal feedback	+											
	−											

Ratio + to −: general instructional feedback _____

Ratio + to −: specific instructional feedback _____

Ratio + to −: nonverbal feedback _____

Ratio + to −: all instructional feedback (verbal and nonverbal) _____

From *Instructional Manual for Dynamic Physical Education for Secondary School Students,* 2nd ed., by R. Pangrazi and P. Darst. Copyright © 1991 by Allyn and Bacon. Reprinted with permission.

Figure 11.11 Event recording sheet for instructor behavior.

The importance of nonverbal behavior in activity settings should not be underestimated. People learn by mirroring the actions of the instructor much faster than by verbal explanation. Try teaching an aerobic dance routine without using nonverbal behaviors. Negative modeling is an excellent way to show mistakes made by participants when executing a skill. Good instructors depend on positive and negative modeling behaviors to communicate effectively with their students. Systematically observing and recording nonverbal behaviors provide added insight to the teaching–learning process.

Praise and Scold

Another way to generate systematic information on positive and negative instructional behaviors is to tally the occurrences of praise and scold behaviors. It should be a goal of every professional to establish a positive climate. Every positive statement is coded as a praise, and every negative statement is coded as a scold. Using this information, self-evaluation of current behaviors can be made and goals for maintaining or increasing positive behaviors can be set.

Of course, instructors can go overboard with positive behavior. More is not always better. If a praise is used too much, positive comments will be taken for granted; consequently, the praise statements will lose their value. The same thing happens to the instructor who constantly corrects and nags students about their actions. The students soon tune out and ignore the comments. A general guideline in activity settings is to have a 4:1 ratio of praises to scolds.

Behavior Feedback

The previous discussion focused on behaviors that are categorized as feedback to skill attempts. Not all feedback is in reaction to skill attempts. A great deal of feedback is in response to student behavior. Examples of this are such statements as "Super job getting into formation today" or "Nancy, stop hitting Doug." Behavior feedback can be classified in the same ways as skill feedback. Some coding forms allow both feedback to skill attempts and to student behavior to be recorded on the same form. Figure 11.12 is an example of this type of form. Self-evaluation of behavior feedback is most appropriate in coaching and physical education settings.

Feedback Statements	Skill Feedback		Behavior Feedback	
	Positive	**Corrective**	**Positive**	**Negative**
Specific				
General				
Total				
Rate per Minute				

From *Developing Teaching Skills in Physical Education*, 3rd ed., by D. Siedentop. Copyright © 1991 by Mayfield Publishing Company. Reprinted by permission of Mayfield Publishing Company.

Figure 11.12 Event recording sheet for skill and behavior feedback.

Selected Instruments for Systematic Observation

Many different systematic observation instruments have been designed and utilized in physical education and athletics. Most of these instruments can be modified to be used with other activity settings as well. An observation instrument should be designed to meet the needs of specific situations. There is no perfect systematic observation instrument. Any instrument will have positive and negative aspects. In considering self-evaluation, decisions about what should be included in the instrument being used must be made. Thought must be given to the behavior categories to be included, how the categories are to be defined, and what recording procedures are to be employed. Using self-evaluation allows the instructor to understand the evaluation procedures more clearly and be less threatened by the process.

Systematic observation instruments vary widely in their complexity. Generally, the more complex the instrument is, the more training is required to use it properly. However, if the instrument is complex, it should yield more sensitive information. An evaluation instrument must be chosen or designed to balance the need for detailed information about instruction with the need for an instrument that can be used in an accurate and reliable manner. Several different systematic observation instruments will be introduced in the following section. Each of the instruments can provide valuable data for evaluating teaching effectiveness, yet they vary in complexity. It is not within the scope of this chapter to give detailed descriptions of the instruments, but references given provide sources for further information. *Analyzing Physical Education and Sport Instruction* (Darst, Zakrajsek, and Mancini, 1989) catalogs over 30 different observational systems, and *Developing Teaching Skills in Physical Education* (Siedentop, 1991, Chapter 16) offers a thorough discussion of instruments for measuring instruction. The highlighting of several instruments in the next section should give the reader a clearer understanding of systematic observation and its many options for self-evaluation.

All-Purpose Event Recording Form (Instructor Behaviors)

Figure 11.13 provides a sample of a completed all-purpose event recording form focusing on instructor reactions to student skill attempts and student behaviors. In nonschool settings, this type of instrument could be used with behavior definitions appropriate for the setting. Note that the observer can change the behavior categories by listing different definitions on the coding sheet. This form limits the observer to four behaviors of interest. Care must be taken to complete demographic data at the top of the sheet, particularly the length of observation. After the frequency of each behavior is totaled, the rate per minute can be calculated by dividing each total frequency by the total length of observation.

All-Purpose Duration Recording Form (Student Time Analysis)

When behaviors of interest can last for extended periods of time, the all-purpose duration recording form may be appropriate. Figure 11.14 shows a sample of a completed all-purpose duration recording form. The focus of this observation is analysis of how students are spending their time. Definitions of behaviors of interest are listed on the coding form. A time line is used for the duration recording of the specified

Instructor: __Longlin__   Date: __3/9__   School: __Desert H.S.__

Activity: __Track__   Time started: __9:05__   Time ended: __9:40__

Length of observation: __35__   Observer: __Cusimano__

Definitions:

1. __Providing exact commendatory information on performance (motor).__

2. __Words supporting students' motor response.__

3. __Providing commendatory statements on behavior, other than motor.__

4. __Teacher comment to terminate behavior.__

1 Pos. Skill Fb. (Specific)	2 Pos. Skill Fb. (General)	3 Behavior Praise	4 Desists
ⅢⅡ ⅢⅡ ⅢⅡ Ⅰ	ⅢⅡ ⅢⅡ ⅢⅡ ⅢⅡ ⅢⅡ ⅢⅡ ⅢⅡ ⅢⅡ ⅢⅡ ⅢⅡ ⅢⅡ Ⅲ	ⅢⅡ Ⅱ	ⅢⅡ ⅢⅡ ⅢⅡ ⅢⅡ Ⅲ

Totals: __16__   __58__   __7__   __23__

Data Summary:

Behaviors	Total frequency	Rate per minute
1 Pos. skill Fb. (S)	16	.45
2 Pos. skill Fb. (G)	58	1.65
3 Praise	7	.20
4 Desists	23	.65

Comments:

* You seem more specific toward male students.

* Let's work on behavior praise! (crucial this time of year)

* Be firm when you desist!!

Figure 11.13 All-purpose event recording form (instructor behaviors).

behaviors. The time line is divided into 30 minutes, with each minute broken down into 10-second segments. When the behavior changes, the observer checks a stopwatch and makes a vertical slash through the time line followed by the appropriate abbreviation. The decision of when the behavior changes is often based on what the

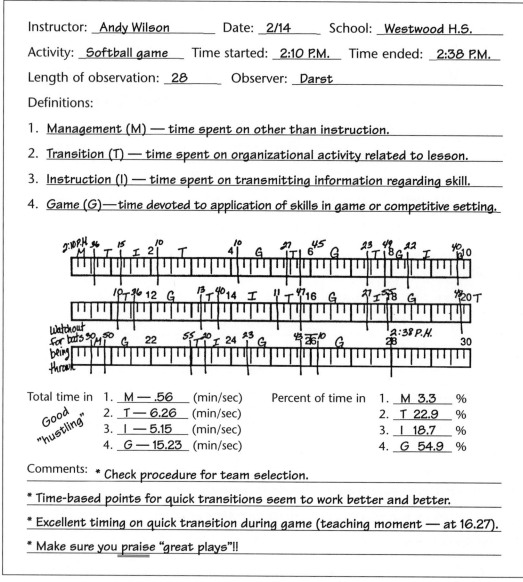

Figure 11.14 All-purpose duration recording form.

majority of the class, or 51 percent, is doing. For instance, in the example depicted in Figure 11.14, students were engaged in management at the start of the class period for 36 seconds, were in transition until 1:15, received instruction until the 2:10 mark, and so on. The same procedure can be used with a targeted student rather than the whole class. Note that the observer can record the exact time of behavior change by writing the exact time directly above the slash mark. The total time for each behavior can be calculated from the time line and the percentage of time in each behavior can then be figured as well.

The all-purpose duration recording form can be adapted easily to nonschool activity settings and can be used for fewer than four behaviors. If an exercise clinician were monitoring the workout of a cardiac rehabilitation patient performing aerobic activities on a variety of exercise machines, duration recording could be used to measure the amount of time spent engaged in exercise, in moving from one exercise machine to another (i.e., treadmill to rowing machine), and in adjusting each exercise machine (i.e., adjusting the seat on a cycle ergometer, setting speed on a treadmill). This information would provide objective feedback to the patient about the effectiveness of the workout. If too much time was spent in moving from station to station or adjusting machines, further observations would tell the clinician and the patient whether exercise times increased appropriately. It would be possible to videotape the patient, and let her do her own duration recording. This likely would raise the awareness of the patient and be an excellent educational experience.

Group Time Sampling Form (Class Analysis)

In some situations, it is desirable to gather information about the activities of the entire class. As described earlier, an observer does group time sampling by making a quick scan of the activity area and counting the number of students who are displaying the defined behavior of interest. In the completed group time sampling form shown in Figure 11.15, several types of student behaviors are observed simultaneously. Appropriate behavior refers to students being on task regardless of the context; the class could be involved in management, instruction, or activity. Engaged behavior denotes that the student is motor-engaged with the subject matter activity. **Academic Learning Time—Physical Education (ALT-PE)** refers to students being motor-engaged with the subject matter activity at a high success rate.

These categories are interconnected in that any given student would have to display "appropriate" behavior to be "engaged." Similarly, "engaged" behavior is a prerequisite of ALT-PE. The observations recorded in Figure 11.15 were made in a class of 30 students. Data were collected every 4 minutes during a 40-minute class, yielding 10 group samples. Across these 10 observations, 78 percent of the class was well behaved (appropriate) and 69 percent was motor-engaged in subject matter activity (engaged), but only 38 percent was motor-engaged at high success rates (ALT-PE). This type of form would also be appropriate to use in adult fitness settings (i.e., aerobic dance class) to ascertain general activity trends of the group.

General Supervision Instrument

Some systematic observation instruments combine several types of coding to produce a more complete view of the behaviors in a physical education class or nonschool

---

PARTICIPANT BEHAVIOR ANALYSIS

Class: **5th Period Volleyball**   Instructor: **Brown**   No. in Class: **30**

Start Time: **1:30**   End Time: **2:10**   Length of Observation: **40 minutes**

Participant Behavior	Appropriate	20	30	28	26	20	30	30	30	30	20
	Engaged	4	26	16	18	20	30	28	26	24	16
	ALT-PE	0	0	14	18	0	24	26	22	0	10

Appropriate = **78%**   Engaged = **69%**   ALT-PE = **38%**

From *Developing Teaching Skills in Physical Education*, 3rd ed., by D. Siedentop. Copyright © 1991 by Mayfield Publishing Company. Reprinted with permission of Mayfield Publishing Company.

Figure 11.15 Group time sampling form.

activity setting. Figure 11.16 shows an instrument that has been used to evaluate student teachers. This system uses event recording to code skill feedback statements and reactions to student behaviors. A group time sample is taken every three minutes to measure the number of students behaving appropriately and the number of students engaged in ALT-PE. A time line is included for duration recording of how much class time is spent in management, instruction, and activity. With practice, a single observer can collect data using all three types of observation techniques. Thus, data are collected on both teacher and student behaviors with the same instrument. The data can be quickly quantified and analyzed using the summary statistics on the form, and the information then immediately shared with the teacher to help evaluate the effectiveness of the lesson and to set behavioral goals for future teaching episodes.

System for Observing Fitness Instruction Time (SOFIT)

The **System for Observing Fitness Instruction Time (SOFIT)** is designed to assess variables associated with students' activity levels and opportunities to become physically fit (McKenzie, Sallis, and Nader, 1991). Though designed for school settings, the instrument could be easily modified to observe activity levels in virtually any setting (i.e., aerobic dance at a health club, a cardiac rehabilitation exercise session, weight training in an off-season athletic workout). SOFIT allows an observer to simultaneously record student activity levels, curriculum context variables, and teacher behaviors. With development and maintenance of physical fitness being a major objective in most physical education programs and many clinical exercise programs, this instrument can be particularly useful for instructors to use to check the activity levels of their students/clients. Many practitioners will be surprised at the low levels of activity that participants exhibit. It is also an interesting instrument to use to code activity levels of students during recess to illustrate the need for structured physical education classes.

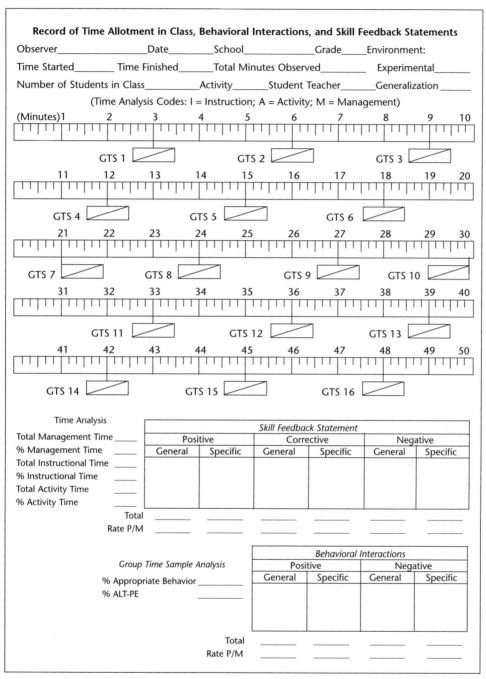

From *Developing Teaching Skills in Physical Education*, 3rd ed., by D. Siedentop. Copyright © 1991 by Mayfield Publishing Company. Reprinted with permission of Mayfield Publishing Company.

Figure 11.16 A general supervision instrument.

This system uses interval recording. A targeted student is observed for 10 seconds and then 10 seconds is allowed for coding. While the observer is learning to use the instrument, it is recommended that initially a longer time period be allowed for coding (perhaps 20 seconds), and the time gradually shortened to 10 seconds.

SOFIT is a three-phase decision system, as shown in Figure 11.17. Phase 1 is coding the activity level of the preselected student to provide an estimate of the intensity of the child's physical activity. Codes 1–4 (lying down, sitting, standing, walking) describe the body position of the child and code 5 (very active) is used when the child is expending more energy than he or she would during ordinary walking. When the student exhibits two or more of these categories during the 10-second observation, code the higher category. The coder must make one of five choices regarding the activity level of the student and move to Phase 2. If desired, only Phase 1 can be used for coding, with Phases 2 and 3 being eliminated. However, if the instrument is so modified, the time allocated for coding decisions should be reduced. It should also be noted that much valuable information is being lost if only Phase 1 coding is completed.

Phase 2 concerns the context of the lesson. For each 10-second observation, a decision is made whether class time is being used for general content (M) such as managerial activities (checking roll, choosing teams, organizing the class, etc.) or for actual subject matter content. If class time is being used for physical education knowledge content, then it can be coded as general knowledge (K) or physical fitness knowledge (P). If the subject being observed is motor active in physical education content, then it should be coded as fitness (F), skill practice (S), game play (G), or other (O). After making a coding decision in Phase 2, the coder moves to Phase 3.

Phase 3 codes teacher behaviors. The first behavior category, promotes fitness (P), is directly related to student involvement in fitness activities and is coded when the teacher prompts or encourages learners for physical fitness engagement. The second category, demonstrates fitness (D), identifies when the teacher models fitness engagement. The four remaining categories—instructs generally (I), manages (M), observes (O), and off task (T)—are only indirectly related to student fitness opportunities, but provide important information on how a teacher spends his or her time.

A sample coding sheet is shown at the bottom of Figure 11.17. This sample shows only two intervals, while a sheet used for actual data collection would include as many intervals as would conveniently fit on the page. When using this instrument, it is recommended that three students be targeted for observation: simply watch student A in the first interval, student B during the second interval, and student C in the third interval, then continue the rotation throughout the observation. The appropriate coding decisions can be circled on the coding sheet. More information on this instrument, which can be used with live observation or videotapes, is available from Dr. Thom McKenzie, Department of Physical Education, San Diego State University.

Arizona State University Observation Instrument (ASUOI)

The **ASUOI** (Lacy and Darst, 1989) is a systematic observation instrument that can be used to collect behavioral data on coaches, physical educators, or exercise science practitioners. It employs 13 behavior categories that can be used with event recording procedures. When interval recording is used, the silence category is added. The behavioral categories are shown in Figure 11.18.

Based on the premise that behaviors of an instructional nature are critical to effective teaching, categories 2–8 are different types of behaviors involved with instruction. This allows an observer to evaluate instructional behaviors in a more sensitive manner. Certainly, the categories could be modified to meet the needs of a particular situation.

Phase 1. **Student activity** decision.
What is the physical nature of an individual learner's engagement? What is his/her activity level?

> Choices:
> 1. lying down   3. standing   5. very active
> 2. sitting   4. walking

Phase 2. **Lesson context level** decision.
What is the general context of the lesson? How is time allocated for the class as a whole (at least 51% of the students)?

> Choices:

General content (M)	Knowlege content	Motor content
transition	physical fitness (P)	fitness (F)
management	general knowledge (K)	skill practice (S)
break	rules, strategy	game play (G)
	social behavior	other (O)
	technique	

Phase 3. **Teacher involvement** decision.
What is the teacher doing?

> Choices:
> (P).   promotes fitness (prompts, encourages, praises, etc.)
> (D).   demonstrates fitness (models)
> (I).   instructs generally
> (M).   manages
> (O).   observes
> (T).   off task

SAMPLE CODING SHEET

Interval	Student Activity	Lesson Context	Teacher Behavior
1	1 2 3 4 5	M K P F S G O	P D I M O T
2	1 2 3 4 5	M K P F S G O	P D I M O T

From F. L. McKenzie, J. F. Sallis, and P. R. Nader, "SOFIT: System for Obsessing Fitness Instruction Time," *Journal of Teaching in Physical Education, vol. 11*, no. 2 (January 1992): 204.

Figure 11.17 Coding phases of the SOFIT instrument.

1. **Use of First Name:** Using the first name or nickname when speaking directly to a student.
2. **Preinstruction:** Initial information given to the student/s preceding the desired action to be executed that explains how to execute a skill, strategy, etc., associated with the activity.
3. **Concurrent Instruction:** Cues or reminders given during the actual execution of the skill, strategy, etc., associated with the activity.
4. **Postinstruction:** Correction, reexplanation, or instructional feedback given after the execution of the skill, strategy, etc., associated with the activity.
5. **Questioning:** Any question to the student/s concerning strategies, techniques, etc., associated with the activity.
6. **Physical Assistance:** Physically moving the student to proper position or through the correct range of motion of a skill.
7. **Positive Modeling:** A demonstration of correct performance of a skill or playing technique.
8. **Negative Modeling:** A demonstration of incorrect performance of a skill or playing technique.
9. **Hustle:** Verbal statements intended to intensify the efforts of the student/s.
10. **Praise:** Verbal or nonverbal compliments, statements, or signs of acceptance.
11. **Scold:** Verbal or nonverbal behaviors of displeasure.
12. **Management:** Verbal statements related to organizational details of practice sessions not referring to strategies or fundamentals of the activity.
13. **Uncodable:** Any behavior that cannot be seen or heard, or does not fit into the above categories.
14. **Silence:** (Used only with interval recording.) Periods of time when the teacher/coach is not talking or modeling, often while monitoring the activity.

Figure 11.18 ASUOI behavior categories.

Though interval recording may be used with the ASUOI, event recording requires less practice to become a reliable coder. The observer tallies the behaviors on a coding sheet as the lesson is being watched. Figure 11.3 shows an example of an event recording tally sheet. Although the ASUOI is designed to concentrate on the behaviors of the teacher, it may be advantageous to combine it with a placheck recording or some other systematic way of gathering information about student behavior to accompany the information collected on the teacher.

It should be noted that the use of first name category is treated as a dependent category because it never occurs by itself, but always accompanies another behavior. All other behaviors are independent categories. For this reason, the totals in Figure 11.3 reflect the total of independent categories. The resulting percentages are calculated by dividing the total of the behavior category by the total of independent behaviors coded. The total number of first names coded are also divided by the total of independent behaviors to calculate the number of independent behaviors that were accompanied by a first name.

The ASUOI is a relatively easy instrument to use. Observers can be easily trained to record teacher behaviors accurately. The instrument can be used in conjunction with videotapes or can be used for field-based coding. More information on the ASUOI is provided in the book *Analyzing Physical Education and Sport Instruction* (Darst, Zakrajsek, and Mancini, 1989).

Behavioral Evaluation Strategy and Taxonomy (Sharpe and Koperwas, 1999)

The observation instruments described previously can be done with stopwatches, paper, and pencil. There are more sophisticated behavior analysis systems that utilize specific software packages. The use of a personal computer or laptop computer in the field enables the practitioner to collect, analyze, and graphically depict the data instantaneously. One such software package is the **Behavioral Evaluation Strategy and Taxonomy (BEST)**.

The BEST software enables the user to record the start and stop times of multiple mutually exclusive and overlapping events. It offers the flexibility to be able to create your own category system to meet your specific observational needs. It also has the capacity to develop multiple different observation systems to be saved for various observational situations. For instance, you can create one system to evaluate teaching in an elementary school physical education setting and design a different system for analyzing coaching and player behaviors in high school basketball practices.

In your activity setting being observed, the BEST software can record and categorize an infinite number of events into as many as 36 categories. It can also record multiple keyed events simultaneously and easily collect data with the observation system represented on screen. In a physical education or coaching situation, some typical behaviors to be analyzed might include events that could be counted, such as use of names, questions, or feedback. These are referred to as discrete trial counts and should be event recorded. Other behaviors might be those that can be timed and these are referred to as duration measures. For example, time spent in activity, management, and instruction is frequently monitored in teaching situations. Other options for recording behaviors include recording response frequency, duration, intervals, time samples, response latency, percentages of time, and count of discrete trials.

The BEST software offers teachers and coaches many options for arranging the computer keyboard in the best configuration for monitoring their particular situation. The practitioner can determine what behaviors to observe and which key is being utilized to code the behaviors. It is recommended that the user become familiar with the options by using a basic setup and then creating a more complex observation plan after becoming comfortable with the features that the BEST program offers.

Figure 11.19 shows a representative keyboard appropriate for learning how to initially use the software that is set up in a rather simple and straightforward way to record a physical education lesson for analysis. Various keys have been configured to monitor discrete trial counts of a teacher's use of names, positive behavior feedback, negative behavior feedback, positive skill feedback, corrective feedback, and questions. For each of these keys, a teacher's use of that behavior can be counted. Thus, each time a teacher uses a name, the "1" key is pressed and that use of a name is recorded and counted. Each time a teacher uses feedback, the type of feedback is noted by pressing keys 3, 5, 7, or 9.

Other keys in Figure 11.19 are set to monitor duration measures. In this configuration, time spent in instruction (teacher talk), activity, and management is recorded. Each of these keys is set to work as a toggle switch. By pressing the "A" key when students begin activity, the observer activates a stopwatch in the program. The program will continue to measure activity time until the "A" key is pressed again

1 Names	2	3 Pos. Beh.	4	5 Neg. Beh.	6	7 Pos. Skl	8	9 Corr. Fb	0
Q Quest.	W	E	R	T Instr. (Tchr Talk)	Y	U	I	O	P
A Activ.	S	D	F	G	H	J	K	L	;
Z	X	C	V	B	N	M Mgmt.	,	.	/

Event Recording	Duration Recording
1 – use of student name	T – instruction (teacher talk)
3 – positive behavior feedback	A – activity
5 – negative behavior feedback	M – management
7 – positive skill feedback	
9 – corrective feedback	
Q – questions by teacher	

Figure 11.19 Representative keyboard for simple setup.

to turn off the stopwatch. Again, other behaviors can also be timed depending on what is warranted by the situation. Please understand that Figure 11.20 is only a sample representative keyboard configuration that can be set up by the user. One of the advantages of the BEST software is that it can be tailored to meet the specific needs of the setting being observed.

Figure 11.20 shows a slightly more advanced keyboard configuration with more keys set so that more behaviors can be monitored. This type of configuration is recommended for use by individuals who have experience with the BEST software. By tracking more behaviors, a finer distinction regarding strengths of the lesson can be observed. In this configuration, cues and demonstrations are also counted. Duration of the class's set and closure is also monitored.

Both the event recording and the duration recording suggested above can be done without the use of a computerized program. However, this software offers the clear advantage of being able to record event and duration data simultaneously with simple keystrokes. A further advantage is that collected data can be analyzed instantaneously and graphically displayed in a variety of ways. For instance, bar graphs and pie graphs can be generated to illustrate event and duration recorded data. Another option for providing a display of multiple measures is the scalable time plot. This graph provides a display of total elapsed time on the X-axis and all of the events mea-

1 Names	2 Cues	3 Pos. Beh.	4 Neg. Beh.	5 Pos. Skl	6 Corr. Fb	7 Demos	8 Quest.	9	0
Q	W	E	R	T	Y	U	I Instr.	O	P
A Activ.	S Set	D	F	G	H	J	K	L	;
Z	X	C Close	V	B	N	M Mgmt.	,	.	/

Event Recording	Duration Recording
1 – use of student name	T – instruction (teacher talk)
2 – instructional cues	A – activity
3 – positive behavior feedback	S – anticipatory set
4 – negative behavior feedback	C – closure
5 – positive skill feedback	M – management
6 – corrective feedback	
7 – demonstrations	
8 – questions by teacher	

Figure 11.20 Representative keyboard for advanced setup.

sured on the Y-axis. Rectangular boxes within the graph indicate the frequency and length of duration measures. Vertical lines indicate the frequency of events measured and place them in the context of the lesson. This provides a visual picture of the sequential nature of events occurring within a lesson. In this view, a teacher could see how feedback was distributed throughout an activity time block or how names and questions were used during an instructional time block. Additionally, a teacher can see if the activity blocks of time were adequate for the lesson. Often upon completing a lesson, teachers have some idea of the amount of time they spent in various areas and their interaction with students. However, their perception of these events and the actual record of these events may be quite different! Seeing their lesson represented graphically can provide teachers with a clear analysis of events and a means by which they can set observable and measurable goals for future lessons.

The BEST software is a powerful software package that offers a variety of options for collecting, analyzing, and displaying behavioral data. The preceding section is a brief description of the program. If desired, more information about the BEST software is available at http://www.scolari.co.uk.

SUMMARY

In the wide range of activity settings in school and nonschool settings, instruction about exercise and activity is a crucial component of any type of program. There are many different methods and systems to provide evaluation of instruction. While evaluation by a school administrator or work supervisor is a necessary and sometimes valuable form of evaluation of instructional effectiveness, this chapter advocates self-evaluation as the best way to improve instruction in all types of activity settings. The best way to conduct this self-evaluation is dependent on the particular setting and on what aspect of instruction is being examined.

The development of systematic observation instrumentation over the past 30 years provides solutions to many methodological problems associated with evaluation of instruction. These observation tools range from simple to complex and can accurately measure many facets of behaviors in activity environments. The use of event, interval, duration, and group time sampling recording offers many options for instructor evaluation. Regardless of the procedure or combination of procedures used, it is essential that the accuracy and objectivity of the data be established by calculating the percentage of interobserver agreement (IOA).

Properly used, systematic observation methods provide feedback that can be used to improve instructional effectiveness. As with any measurement and evaluation procedure, the data collection must be done properly to ensure valid data. It is hoped that more practitioners in all activity settings will realize the weaknesses of traditional methods and the advantages of systematic observation in the measurement and self-evaluation of instructional effectiveness.

DISCUSSION QUESTIONS

1. List four traditional evaluation methods of instructional effectiveness. In terms of measurement and evaluation theory, what weaknesses do these methods have in common?

2. Describe four systematic observation methods that can be used for self-evaluation of instructional effectiveness. Compare and contrast the advantages and disadvantages of these methods.

3. What is interobserver agreement (IOA)? Explain the importance of establishing an IOA when using systematic observation procedures.

4. What type of instructor behaviors can be measured and evaluated with systematic observation methods? Which are most important? Why?

5. What type of participant behaviors can be measured and evaluated with systematic observation methods? Which are most important? Why?

6. What issues must be resolved when a self-evaluation plan is being formulated in regard to instructional effectiveness? If you were designing a self-evaluation, what procedures would you consider the best?

REFERENCES

Darst, P., Zakrajsek, D., and Mancini, V., eds. (1989). *Analyzing physical education and sport instruction.* 2nd ed. Champaign, IL: Human Kinetics.

Flanders, N. A. (1970). *Analyzing teacher behavior*. Reading, MA: Addison-Wesley.

Lacy, A., and Darst, P. (1989). The Arizona State University observation instrument. In P. Darst, D. Zakrajsek, and V. Mancini, eds. *Analyzing physical education and sport instruction*. 2nd ed. Champaign, IL: Human Kinetics.

McKenzie, T. L., Sallis, J. F., and Nader, P. R. (1991). SOFIT: System for Observing Fitness Instruction Time. *Journal of Teaching in Physical Education*. 11, 195–205.

Pangrazi, R., and Darst, P. (1991). *Dynamic physical education for secondary school students: Curriculum and instruction*. 2nd ed. New York: Macmillan Publishing Company.

Rink, J. E. (1993). *Teaching Physical Education for Learning*. 2nd ed. St. Louis: Mosby Publishers.

Sharpe, T., and Koperwas, J. (1999). Behavioral Evaluation Strategies and Taxonomy (Version 3.0) (computer software). London: Scolari Sage Publications.

Siedentop, D. (1991). *Developing teaching skills in physical education*. 3rd ed. Palo Alto, CA: Mayfield Publishing Company.

van der Mars, H. (1989). Basic recording tactics. In P. Darst, D. Zakrajsek, and V. Mancini, eds. *Analyzing physical education and sport instruction*. 2nd ed. Champaign, IL: Human Kinetics.

CHAPTER 12

Measurement and Evaluation in Activity-Based Settings

Key Terms

commercial settings

community settings

clinical settings

corporate settings

exercise adherence

informed consent

Objectives

1. Identify and discuss factors that affect the design of measurement and evaluation models for implementation in school and nonschool settings.

2. Recognize differences in school and nonschool settings that influence assessment strategies.

3. Critique measurement and evaluation models presented in the chapter and recommend any needed modifications.

4. Design measurement and evaluation models for school and nonschool settings not covered in the examples included in this chapter.

The purpose of this chapter is to provide practical examples of measurement and evaluation models in common activity-based settings. The pervading theme of this book is that appropriate measurement and evaluation strategies are absolutely essential to program development and subsequent program revisions. It is hoped that this chapter will vividly illustrate this theme. Section 1 of this chapter will focus on school physical education settings, while Section 2 will highlight assessment models used in nonschool settings with primarily adult populations. The previous chapters have provided information about many aspects of measurement and evaluation. Embedded in this chapter are common scenarios that ask you to consider how you would design an effective measurement and evaluation plan for that particular situation. It is hoped that you will be able to take the information provided throughout this textbook and apply it to the activity-based program that is described to synthesize an appropriate measurement and evaluation plan. The examples provided in Section 1 and Section 2 should provide insights about how to create these assessment plans.

It is hoped that this chapter will help you see how measurement and evaluation theory can be put into practice. With state mandates for program accountability, it is critical that teachers entering the physical education profession be prepared to make knowledgeable decisions about incorporating measurement and evaluation strategies into their teaching. It is equally important that professionals in nonschool settings incorporate sound assessment practices in designing, delivering, and modifying their programs.

A quality physical education school program at any level usually encompasses objectives in each of the learning domains of physical education. Each of these domains has previously been described and various measurement and evaluation techniques detailed with respect to each area: health-related physical fitness (Chapter 5), psychomotor (Chapter 6), cognitive (Chapter 7), and affective (Chapter 8). Similarly, these areas should be considered in activity-based programs outside the school.

Chapter 2 stressed the importance of measurement and evaluation in the program development and assessment process. That chapter introduced the four learning domains and discussed the need to view this process as ongoing and dynamic in order to prevent the program from becoming stagnant and outdated. Step 5 of program development is *evaluating and improving the program*. Turning back to Figure 2.1, the reader will recall that the completion of Step 5 can influence any of the first four steps.

Without a sound measurement and evaluation model in place, the practitioner has no objective data on which to base decisions concerning the program. If there is no way to know how well participants are meeting stated program goals, modifying and improving the program becomes intuitive guesswork at best. By incorporating measurement strategies from each of the four learning domains, you can develop a sound model on which to base evaluation of the program and justification of subsequent programmatic modifications. Therefore, the purpose of this chapter is to present various models of measurement and evaluation as they apply to various activity-based school and nonschool settings.

Section 1—Measurement and Evaluation in School Settings

Guidelines for Effective Measurement and Evaluation

Greater demands are being put on assessment in education at local, state, and national levels. At the same time, traditional forms of measurement and evaluation have been used sporadically or not at all. The reform movement in education includes changing measurement and evaluation activities to fully integrate them with the teaching process and objectives for student achievement. The transformation of these assessment programs is toward performance-based outcomes for students. The use of alternative assessment techniques (Chapter 9) has expanded significantly in the past decade. The measurement and evaluation process should be an ongoing process that assesses student progress toward achieving meaningful learning outcomes.

The following guidelines should be considered in deciding what constitutes effective measurement and evaluation.

- Teacher decisions and grades should be based on a continuous, formative (process) evaluation instead of on a single score on a fitness, written, or skills test.

Evaluation should be integrated into the instructional process, with students being involved with assessment procedures.

- Assessment should be based on clearly defined educational objectives with distinct criteria for measuring student progress. Students should not be evaluated on subjective measures not central to instructional objectives.

- Fitness test scores should be used to help students set personal goals and determine individual progress, not for assigning grades. Self-testing can help students learn to assess their own fitness levels and provide more frequent evaluation than time-consuming formal testing procedures. Students can work with partners and work together to develop fitness profiles. The emphasis on self-testing is on the process rather than the product. Though self-testing will be less accurate than formal testing, the value as an educational endeavor outweighs this disadvantage. Self-testing is not meant to replace the formal testing program required at many schools.

- Use alternative assessments for evaluating skill proficiencies. Formal skills testing can take up too much time, especially with large classes and limited class meetings. A certified physical educator should have the training to apply professional standards to holistically assess student skills. Predetermined performance standards can be used by the teacher, by peers, and by the student for self-evaluation.

- Use a wide variety of measurement and evaluation strategies that include all learning domains of physical education. Skills tests, videotape analyses, qualitative teacher or peer appraisals, formal and self-testing of health fitness, group projects, interviews, student journals, student demonstrations, student interest surveys, and written tests are some of the options.

- Use the results of measurement and evaluation activities for curriculum planning in daily, weekly, and unit objectives. Instruction should be modified as a result of these activities. In too many cases, assessment activities are used for grading but are not considered in curricular decisions.

- Use systematic observation to measure how students spend time in class. If students are to achieve fitness and skill development goals, it is important that they be successfully motor engaged for a high percentage of class time. Using a videotape and stopwatch, teachers should periodically check how much time is spent in activities such as management, transition, listening to the teacher, and appropriate activity. This simple technique can be used to alter teaching strategies in an attempt to increase student engagement. Chapter 11 provided detailed information about how to use systematic observation.

Variables Affecting Measurement and Evaluation Models

Every measurement and evaluation model should be specific to the program with which it is linked. Many of the same variables that are considered in designing a curriculum for a given educational setting will affect the amount and types of measurement and evaluation activities that are included. In fact, these measurement and evaluation strategies should be considered part of the curriculum because they take up class time and provide learning experiences for the students. Just as the curriculum will be different at different schools because so many variables affect curricular decision making, the measurement and evaluation scheme should be specifically tailored for that particular setting. Thus, before presenting the measurement and evaluation models, it is important to consider the many variables that can influence these models.

Characteristics and Interests of Students

The physical, cognitive, and emotional development of students influences the choice of measurement tools. For example, the complexity of measurement instruments changes as students mature physically, cognitively, and emotionally. Thus, the characteristics and interests of students must be considered in designing measurement and evaluation models. While reading the following descriptions of students of different ages, think about the type of instrument that should be used to measure and evaluate the affective, psychomotor, cognitive, and health-related physical fitness domains. Keep in mind that these are general descriptions—there is great variability at every age level in physical and psychological maturity. Pangrazi (2001) and Darst and Pangrazi (2002) provide excellent discussions of characteristics and interests of students. The following discussion concerning the development of students at various grade levels summarizes their thoughts.

Primary Grades (K–2)

Children in grades K–2 have a relatively short attention span. They are naturally curious about what the body can do, enjoy a challenge, and are highly creative. They are beginning to understand and enjoy the concept of teamwork and are becoming curious about how to move effectively. Still, they usually do better in individual and small-group activities.

Children in this age group enjoy physical contact and rough-and-tumble activities. There are few sex differences in terms of their interests or physical capabilities. They like to perform well, work to please the teacher, are basically truthful and straightforward, and freely express individual views and opinions. They also seek personal attention.

Generally enthusiastic about physical activity, students of this age may tire quickly but recover just as quickly. Basic locomotor skills are being developed while sport-related skill patterns are usually immature. Eye-hand coordination and perceptual abilities are developing, but reaction time is still usually slow. They become increasingly interested in fitness and are naturally rhythmic.

Intermediate Grades (3–5)

Students in intermediate grades exhibit a number of unique characteristics and interests. At this age, students begin to question the importance of various activities. They want to know the rules and become interested in strategies of games and sports. They also enjoy learning about the importance of both health-related and sport-related physical fitness.

An intense desire to excel in sport skills and physical capacities normally surfaces. Students in this age group accept more responsibility, are more independent, and become more concerned with being a member of a group. These youngsters enjoy group activities and become increasingly competitive. They have more interest in sports and sports-related activities; consequently, maintaining good sportsmanship needs to be stressed.

Steady growth characterizes this age group, with girls often growing more rapidly than boys and boys becoming rougher and stronger than girls. As their coordination and skills improve, the children become interested in learning more detailed techniques. There are often wide differences in physical capacities and skill development.

Middle School (6–8)

In this age group, students experience a rapid growth spurt that does not follow an even pattern. Usually girls will go through this growth before boys do. Tremendous muscular development occurs along with this erratic growth pattern. These physical developments cause periods of poor coordination because motor abilities increase at a slower rate. Posture is often poor. Boys are stronger than girls, run faster, and have slightly more endurance.

Students become very self-conscious and are strongly influenced by their peer group. They become more socially oriented and are increasingly interested in the opposite sex, which results in concern about physical appearance. Emotions can change rapidly at this age, intellectual capacities increase, and adolescents begin to narrow their interests and focus their attention on particular activities.

High School (9–12)

Students in their high school years continue to mature and develop physically, socially, emotionally, and mentally. Ossification processes are complete and height and weight gains level off. Boys continue to gain musculature and exceed girls in height and weight. Both genders improve their ability to gain motor ability skills.

Students at this age are more secure than their junior high (middle school) counterparts and have more sense of direction. Specialization and narrowing of interests continue. Their moods are more stable, and a great deal of intellectual development occurs with improved capacity for concentration and reasoning. They are still very concerned with social activities and the opposite sex, and the peer group remains a strong influence. Students are able to handle decision-making responsibilities and become more concerned with achievement and possible pay-offs. There is more interest in high risk/adventure activities, certain fitness activities (i.e., aerobic dance, weightlifting), and lifetime sports.

Class Size

Class size is an important consideration in measurement and evaluation models. Many physical education teachers are plagued with the problem of oversized classes. Whereas this should not be an excuse for not testing in physical education, it should be considered when selecting and administering measurement strategies. Measurement and evaluation should be a part of any physical education program, but extremely large classes impose limitations.

Class Time

In planning tests for the various domains of physical education, the amount of time the students spend in class should be considered. Time actually spent in physical education depends on how long the class periods are and how many times per week the class meets. Daily physical education is certainly desirable, but some school districts schedule physical education on an every-other-day basis. Class periods are typically 30 minutes in elementary schools, but may be shorter or longer. Period length at the secondary level is usually 50–55 minutes, but this is not normally all activity time, since students must change clothes at the beginning and end of each class. The result is somewhere around 30 minutes of activity time at junior high and senior high levels. A certain percentage of that time should be spent in testing activities. Some high schools that have adopted block scheduling will have longer class periods. If more time is available in class, then more time can be devoted to measurement and evaluation activities.

Personnel Support

Having people other than the teacher to administer and monitor tests is advantageous to the measurement and evaluation program because more children can be tested in a more efficient manner. Some teachers have teacher aides assigned to physical education. In other instances, more than one physical education teacher may be on staff. Also, it may be possible in some schools to enlist additional personnel support during the administration of measurements. The school nurse can be a valuable resource. Student aides can also be used effectively, as can other teachers. Some teachers have enlisted the help of interested parents. The additional personnel can be used to grade tests, input test scores on optical scan sheets or computers, generate reports to send home with students, or helps administer tests. The use of additional personnel not only help the physical education teacher but also can be an excellent source of good public relations.

Technological Support

Many teachers dislike testing because of the amount of paperwork generated by grading, recording, and reporting the scores. Technological advances can relieve the teacher of much of this tedious work. Word processing makes it possible to create test banks of questions that can be printed quickly for examination. Software is available to average grades, input scores, compute norms, and create individual reports of fitness testing. The personal computer can save many hours of work for the teacher. Optical scan sheets on which students mark their answers allow tests to be machine graded. Some programs also will run an item analysis and provide descriptive statistics concerning test results. The time invested by a physical educator in learning to use these resources will pay dividends of countless hours of work saved in the future. If this type of technological support is available to the teacher, it allows a more thorough measurement and evaluation scheme to be implemented.

State and Local Mandates

Many schools have testing requirements mandated by state agencies or local district policies. Obviously, these mandates affect the planning of a measurement and evaluation model, and a physical education teacher may find that certain evaluation decisions already have been made. For example, it may be the policy of a district to do physical fitness testing in September and May of each year, or the district may have a policy dictating the grading method to be used. Some states or districts may decide to use a certain battery of tests for measuring and evaluating health-related physical fitness. In any case, a teacher must be aware of any legal mandates or local policies when planning a measurement and evaluation model.

Curricular Content

The curricular content of physical education will vary from grade level to grade level. There will be certain similarities between adjoining grade levels, but there should be significant differences when the curricula of diverse grade levels are compared. This is due, in great part, to the differences in student characteristics, needs, and interests. Care should be taken to provide a horizontal progression of learning activities at any given grade level. The proper sequencing of learning activities and units from K–12 grades will provide for vertical progression. A quality curriculum has both horizontal and vertical progression.

Regardless of grade level, a final result of curriculum planning should be implementation of a program of learning experiences selected based on the needs, characteristics, and interests of children. These experiences must be compatible with program objectives. As discussed earlier, the developmental age of the child dictates, in large part, the type of activities to be presented in the program. Although the process of measuring and evaluating progress toward objectives may vary, the program objectives remain virtually the same.

Suggestions for Primary Grades (K–2)

The learning characteristics of children in grades K–2 make it necessary to create an enjoyable as well as an instructional learning environment. Children should find happiness and reward through properly sequenced movement experiences that nurture a positive approach to physical activity that will last a lifetime.

Learning activities for younger children are individualized and focus on divergent movement. Children begin to learn body management, fundamental skills, and other essential movements that provide a foundation for the transition to more specialized skills. Developmental fitness activities must be designed to accommodate the abilities of the child and should be included as part of each lesson.

During grades K–2, children should have ample opportunities to explore and experiment within their environment and create movement activities without fear. Group activities become more prevalent within the programmatic scheme in grade 2. In addition to divergent and educational movement, simple rhythmics, appropriate stunts and tumbling activities, and low-organized games are included in the curriculum throughout the early elementary years.

The selection of activities should be directly linked to program objectives. This approach contrasts with selecting an activity because it is fun or because the teacher is good at it or enjoys it. The program should include varied creative movement experiences that can be performed safely by students and contribute to the physical education of the child (Pangrazi, 2001).

The process we recommend using to make decisions about what specific learning experiences to include in a program is delineated in Pangrazi (2001) and consists of selecting appropriate activities, organizing selected activities into units, allocating units of activity to developmental level, developing a year-long curriculum plan, and delivering a planned daily lesson.

Suggestions for Intermediate Grades (3–5)

The third grade is a transitional period for children, and physical education activities should provide them the fundamental skills and fitness levels necessary to begin to develop specialized movements. Sports skills are introduced in third grade and are intended to establish a foundation that can be built upon during the coming years. Throughout the fourth and fifth grades, the program shifts to an increased emphasis on sports skills and the refinement of previously learned movement competencies. Basketball, football, soccer, softball, track and field, and volleyball become an integral part of the program. This increased emphasis on sports skills prompts a renewed focus on quality of movement and correctness of patterns. Physical fitness development remains a priority, with increasing emphasis on vigorous aerobic activity. During the intermediate grades, the categories of activities remain the same (rhythmics, stunts and tumbling, games, and so on), but the time allocated to each changes.

Suggestions for Middle School (6–8)

The middle school curriculum often gets overlooked in curriculum planning. Many curricula are designed specifically for elementary and high schools, but in most cases, the middle school curriculum is an adaptation of one or the other. Because of the unique characteristics of the middle school student, the curriculum should be specifically designed for these students.

Most middle school students have a wide variety of interests, so the curriculum should offer the opportunity to participate in many different activities. The curriculum should be balanced with a diversity of team sports, fitness activities, lifetime sports, dance, outdoor adventure activities, and aquatics. The units should be short and may be repeated at different times of the year if student interests so dictate. It is recommended that no unit be longer than three weeks, with many activities being only one or two weeks in duration. This allows students to explore many activities, allows greater chance of success, and alleviates boredom.

Suggestions for High School (9–12)

Senior high school programs may vary a great deal from state to state and from large schools to small schools, with differences in facilities and in size of staff. As students mature and narrow their focus in physical activity, they desire more in-depth, specialized instruction. Whereas the middle school curriculum should provide exposure to a variety of activities, the senior high school curriculum should give students as many choices as there are teachers in a given class period.

With increased specialization and student interest, the units should be at least six weeks long. Some schools have nine-week units, while others offer single activities for entire 18-week semesters. More emphasis should be on activities that can be included in an active lifestyle throughout a lifetime.

Examples of School Measurement and Evaluation Models

As previously discussed, there are underlying guidelines that provide the foundation for effective measurement and evaluation strategies. It would be a good idea to review these guidelines before proceeding in this chapter. Many of the variables that affect measurement and evaluation decisions have been delineated as well. When determining what percentage of class time will be devoted to assessment activities, keep in mind that many of these activities should be infused as learning experiences in the curriculum. For instance, peer assessment of the tennis serve can provide feedback as to student progress in serving, but also can be a learning experience in analyzing the important components of this skill. Asking students to keep a daily log of activities outside of physical education class provides an opportunity to assess exercise patterns away from class and makes students more aware of their regular activity patterns. This type of activity could be a starting point for making positive interventions in exercise away from class. Also, keep in mind that there are many different measurement and evaluation activities that can be utilized that are not included in these case studies. Assessment should be continuous. The suggestions in the case studies only highlight the type of activities that can be used; they are not meant to be inclusive.

The case studies that follow are representative of common physical education environments. Careful examination of these case studies will provide insights into the degree and type of testing that are feasible in certain teaching situations. Each case study is illustrated as a yearly plan with suggested measurement and evaluation activities included in each of the four learning domains: health-related physical fitness (HRPF), psychomotor (PM), affective (AFF), and cognitive (COG).

Although there are physical education classes (usually elementary) in which the student-to-teacher ratio may be 60:1 or higher, these are abhorrent situations that are unfair to both the teacher and the students. Measurement and evaluation procedures are severely limited, as is the entire program, by this type of scheduling. Physical educators should have the same number of students as the classroom teacher. The gym is not an oversized classroom, and the scheduling of excessively large classes should not be tolerated.

With excessively large classes, it is tempting to abandon measurement and evaluation. Admittedly, they can be laborious and time consuming in these settings. However, measurement and evaluation activities are critical to any program, and should not be omitted from the curriculum. Rather, the teacher must choose carefully the types of measurement and evaluation tools and thoroughly organize the administration of the selected tests. Alternative assessments, self-testing, and peer assessment are a few strategies that can be employed in these situations.

The resourceful physical educator should enlist the administrator who schedules the large classes to help with the testing. Other volunteers may come from older children at the school, other teachers, and parents. By giving these volunteers first-hand experience with oversized classes, the physical educator can turn a negative situation into a positive opportunity to inform them of the multitude of problems associated with overcrowded classes. Oftentimes, results of various tests will show that students are scoring below acceptable standards. The oversized classes and resultant shortage of active learning time and individual attention can be pinpointed as major factors in the lack of student achievement. The results of the measurement and evaluation activity can provide important information by which to justify hiring additional physical educators and/or changing the schedule to permit more manageable class sizes.

Case Study #1—Elementary School Model

The setting is an elementary school (grades K–5) with a physical education instructor assigned to the school. The coed classes meet daily for 30 minutes with 30+ children per class. Ample indoor facilities are available, as well as outdoor space. Figure 12.1 illustrates a measurement and evaluation model for this situation.

In this model, health-related physical fitness testing is completed twice a year for all grades. The testing done in September serves as a needs assessment and the results, in the form of a graphic profile, are sent home to parents at the end of the first grading period. Sending a graphic profile depicting the student's performance is an excellent way to communicate with the parents. These baseline data provide the information needed to set goals and establish activity schedules for the upcoming year. Students in grades 4–5 should be taught how to self-test themselves on all health-related physical fitness items and encouraged to periodically check their own progress.

During the fall, skill-related physical fitness tests are administered to children in grades K–2. These tests serve as screening devices to identify youngsters who need special assistance. Time in the spring term is devoted to administering skill-related test batteries to the entire school population. The progress of younger students (K–2) is

	HRPF	PM	AFF	COG
Aug.– Sept.	Health-related fitness testing (K–5)		Survey—attitude toward activity (3–5) Sociometric test (3–5)	Written quizzes, activity logs, group projects, etc. (3–5) as needed for certain units
Oct.		Skill-related fitness testing (K–2)		
Nov.				
Dec.	Self-testing (3–5)		Student interest survey (3–5)	
Jan.				
Feb.	Self-testing (3–5)			
Mar.		Skill-related fitness testing (K–5) or teacher observation	Student journal (3–5)	
Apr.	Health-related fitness testing (K–5)			
May– June			Survey—attitude toward activity (3–5)	

Figure 12.1 Suggested measurement and evaluation model for case study #1.

determined, and the older children (grades 3–5) are evaluated against nationally recognized standards. Formative assessment may be appropriate for this assessment. Rubrics can be developed to assess motor skills of students using teacher observation checklists or rating scales.

A pre- and posttest approach to monitoring the attitudes of older children toward physical activity is suggested. The surveys give the instructor insight into children's feelings about what they do in physical education. The mid-year interest survey gives the instructor time to make alterations in the yearly program base. The sociometric test early in the year gives the physical education instructor and classroom teachers opportunities to identify youngsters who do not seem to fit in with the class.

Daily physical education classes offer ample time for learning experiences associated with concepts of physical fitness. Time is devoted to written examinations or quizzes that give the instructor an opportunity to assess learning. Periodic quizzes during the fall and spring periods are recommended.

CHECKING YOUR UNDERSTANDING

The setting is an elementary school (K–5) with a physical education instructor assigned to the school. The coed classes meet twice a week for 30 minutes with 30+ children per class. There are ample indoor facilities and outdoor space available.

In this scenario, physical education teaching has been reduced 60 percent compared to the first case study. However, measurement and evaluation continue to be an important part of the yearly program. Using Figure 12.1 as your format, how would you alter the yearly measurement and evaluation model to match the situation described in this elementary school physical education setting?

Case Study #2—Middle School Model

The setting is a middle school with grades 6–8. There are four instructors in physical education. Classes meet daily for 55 minutes, with about 40 coed students per instructor. Students dress out each day. Units are no longer than three weeks. There is a small weight room, a gymnasium, and ample field space. Figure 12.2 illustrates a measurement and evaluation model for this situation.

Health-related physical fitness testing is done twice yearly. Testing in September serves as a needs assessment, and results are sent home with students at the end of the first grading period. The second test administration is done in late April or early May and shows final fitness levels and improvement for the year. This report also is sent to parents and forms the basis for evaluating program objectives in this domain. Students may self-test themselves during the year to check their status in the various components of health-related fitness.

With units no longer than three weeks, time for formal sports-skills testing is minimal. Alternative assessments are used, and students evaluate their own proficiency during certain drills (e.g., "Shoot 10 free throws and see how many you can make."). Some units, such as weight training or jogging, lend themselves to testing more easily than others. Peer testing and teacher observation using checklists or rating scales can be used.

	HRPF	PM	AFF	COG
Aug.–Sept.	Health-related fitness testing	↑	Survey—attitude toward activity	↑
Oct.		Alternative assessments as needed (self-testing, peer testing, teacher observation, etc.)	Sociometric test	
Nov.	Self-testing			Written tests every 3 weeks, group projects, daily logs, demos, etc.
Dec.			Student interest survey	
Jan.			Sociometric test	
Feb.	Self-testing			
Mar.			Student journal	
Apr.	Health-related fitness testing		Survey—attitude toward activity	
May–June		↓	Student interest survey	↓

Figure 12.2 Suggested measurement and evaluation model for case study #2.

Sociometric tests are done early in each semester so that instructors are aware of the social dynamics of the class. Some sort of survey concerning attitudes toward activity is administered at the beginning and at the end of the year. Finally, a student interest survey is given at the end of each semester to help instructors evaluate their curricular offerings and plan for future units. Each of the tests in the affective domain can be administered in one class period.

Written tests are administered about every three weeks. Normally, tests are given at the end of a unit. If several short units (one or two weeks in length) are taught, those two units are combined into one test. Multiple choice questions are usually appropriate for these tests. Other alternative assessment options for evaluating the cognitive domain are used as well.

CHECKING YOUR UNDERSTANDING
The setting is a middle school for grades 6–8. There are two physical education instructors. The classes alternate with the health class, so they occur every other day. There is a 55-minute class period with 35 minutes of actual

activity, since the students change clothes at the beginning and end of each period. The coed classes have 30–35 students. There is a small weight room, a gymnasium, an activity room, and ample field space. The activity units are a maximum of three weeks long. This model differs from the previous middle school model because there are fewer class periods as a result of meeting on alternate days. Using Figure 12.2 as your format, how would you alter the yearly measurement and evaluation model to match the situation described in this middle school physical education setting?

Case Study #3—High School Model

The setting is a high school with grades 9–12. There are six instructors per class period, which meets daily for 55 minutes. Students dress out each day. The coed classes have 30–35 students, who are given a choice of activity. Each activity lasts six weeks, and students are not allowed to enroll for any single activity more than twice during the school year. There is a weight room, swimming pool, activity room, two gymnasiums, and ample field space. Figure 12.3 illustrates a measurement and evaluation model for this situation.

Formal testing in the health-related physical fitness domain is done at the start of the school year and again at the end of the year. Students are given the opportunity to assess their status with self-testing procedures in the middle of the school year.

Sports-skills testing is performed after each six-week unit. With units of this length, adequate time is available to test the proficiency of each student. In some units, such as gymnastics or dance, alternative assessment stategies are more appropriate. Alternative assessment is ongoing in other units as well. Peer and self-assessments are used effectively. When alternative assessment is used, students are told the criteria on which the evaluation is based. Sound rubrics are necessary.

Because students are given a choice of unit each six weeks, the composition of each instructor's class changes. Thus, sociometric testing is done at the start of each six-week unit. Attitude surveys are taken at the beginning and end of the school year. A student interest survey is administered at the end of the year to help instructors evaluate their curriculum and plan modifications for the upcoming year.

A major written test is given during each six-week unit. Quizzes are administered on a weekly basis. Outside projects, homework assignments,and other alternative assessments can be used effectively in units of this length.

CHECKING YOUR UNDERSTANDING

The setting is a high school for grades 9–12. There are 4 instructors per class period, which meets daily for 55 minutes. Students dress out each day. The coed classes have about 30–35 students, who are given a choice of activity. Each activity chosen lasts for 1 semester, or 18 weeks. Students must sign up for 4 semesters of physical education credit during high school and cannot take any activity more than twice. There is a weight room, activity room, one gymnasium, and ample field space. Using Figure 12.3 as your format, how would you alter the yearly measurement and evaluation model to match the situation described in this high school physical education setting?

	HRPF	PM	AFF	COG
Aug.–Sept.	Health-related fitness testing	↑	Survey—attitude toward activity	↑
Oct.		Multiple alternative assessments		Quizzes weekly, written tests, projects, daily logs, demos, etc.
Nov.	Self-testing	Sports-skills test at end of 6-week unit		
Dec.			Sociometric test at the start of each 6-week unit	
Jan.				
Feb.	Self-testing			
Mar.			Student journal	
Apr.	Health-related fitness testing		Survey—attitude toward activity	
May–June		↓	Student interest survey	↓

Figure 12.3 Suggested measurement and evaluation model for case study #3.

Measurement and Evaluation for Students with Disabilities

The models previously presented in this chapter did not include information on assessing students with disabilities. Whenever necessary, teachers should make appropriate accommodations for the particular student involved. Modifications of the test are made depending on the nature of the disability. Some tests offer suggestions for appropriate modifications. For instance, the FITNESSGRAM offers a modified test battery for special populations to assess health-related physical fitness (see Chapter 5). Other tests specific to testing the psychomotor domain are available (see Chapter 6).

Chapter 10 provides in-depth discussion about grading issues. Material pertaining to designing an individualized education program (IEP) for students with disabilities was included in that chapter. An IEP provides an integrated model for measurement and evaluation of the student. IEPs are developed in conjunction with special education teachers and adapted physical education specialists. The IEP includes evaluation criteria, procedures, and timelines. A sample IEP is illustrated in Figure 12.4.

Physical education, specially designed or adapted if necessary, is required by federal law, with which all states and public school districts must comply, for all eligible

SCHOOL DISTRICT OF LA CROSSE
OFFICE OF STUDENT SERVICES
807 East Avenue South
La Crosse, WI 54601
(608) 789-7688
(608) 789-7603 FAX
(608) 789-7694 TDD

INDIVIDUALIZED
EDUCATION
PROGRAM

Page 1 of ___15_____

Current IEP Dates
From _____ to _____
           M/D/Yr   M/D/Yr

Name of Student		D.O.B.	Age	Sex	Race/Ethnic	Grade	Building
Marissa Jones		3/23/87	9	F	Caucasian	4	State Ridge

Parent or Legal Guardian		Address	Telephone
Martha Jones		1111 Willow Way South	608-000-0000

District of Residence	For Transfers: District of Original Placement	IEP Beginning Date	IEP Ending Date
Lamont	Ona Sparta	(M/D/YR) 10-15-96	(M/D/YR) 10/1/98

Area of EEN (Handicapping Condition)	X For School Calendar Term	___ For Summer Term
Cognitive Delay		From:

Document efforts to involve parents in IEP (Dates/Methods/By Whom)   Parents attended 11-14-97
1. 11-3-97 B. Smith, Call | 2. 11-7-97 B. Smith, Letter| 3. meeting

For students transferring between school districts within the state, IEP Adopted: _____
                                                                      (Date)   (Name & Title of District Representative)

A.   Extent to which student will participate in regular education programs, and nonacademic and extracurricular services and activities;
     (Describe any modifications the child requires to participate in the regular education programs). (List schedule: Amount of time and
     Frequency of each class.)

          Attend regular art class (2 days per week – 45 minutes each)
          Attend regular music class (2 days per week – 40 minutes each)
          Attend regular computer lab (2 days per week – 40 minutes each)
          Attend regular physical education class (3 days per week – 45 minutes each)
          Attend regular language arts classes (5 days per week – 45 minutes each)

B.   Please state the specific special education services and the amount of time for each service. (List schedule; Amount of time and
     Frequency of each class.)

          Marissa will participate in the EEN (cognitive delay) elementary class
          for ½ of each school day. This will include instruction in math, reading,
          science, and social studies.

C.   Justification for removal from regular education or regular education environment (include nature and severity of handicap and any
     potential harmful effects on the child or on the quality of services. (Add additional page(s) as necessary.)

          Testing and observational data reveal that Marissa has a cognitive delay.
          Her present needs will be best met in the EEN elementary class at State
          Ridge school. Much of each day will be spent in regular education
          settings. Marissa has very good social and language skills, and has no
          behavior problems.

     Are any related services **required** to assist the child to benefit from special education?   ☒ Yes   ☐ No

                    FREQUENCY/DURATION   FREQUENCY/DURATION

☐ Occupational Therapy   _____   ☐ Psychological Services   _____
☐ Physical Therapy   _____   ☐ Recreation   _____
☒ Transportation   everyday/45 minutes   ☐ School Health Services   _____
☐ Counseling   _____   ☐ Social Work Services   _____
☐ Audiology   _____   ☐ Parent Counseling/Training   _____
☐ Assistive technology   _____   ☐ Rehabilitation Counseling Services _____
                                                   ☐ Other (specify):   _____

Rev. 8/95   WHITE: EEN Teacher   YELLOW: EEN file   PINK: Parent

Figure 12.4 Sample school district IEP.   *(continues)*
Courtesy of the School District of La Crosse.

If visually handicapped, does the student need braille instruction?   ☐ Yes ☐ No   (Justify):

Physical Education   ☒ Regular   ☐ Specially designed

Vocational Education   ☒ Regular   ☐ Specially designed

Are transition services required?   ☐ Yes ☒ No (If Yes, include transition activities within the goals and objectives, and complete the Summary of Transition Services.)

Will the student participate in standardized testing?

Fourth, Eighth or Tenth grade testing under s.118.30, Wis. Stats.,	☒ Yes ☐ No	☒ With Modifications _____
Competency based testing	☐ Yes ☐ No	☐ With Modifications _____
Achievement testing (i.e., CTBS)	☐ Yes ☐ No	☐ With Modifications _____
Third grade Reading Test	☒ Yes ☐ No	☒ With Modifications _____

Date of IEP meeting __9–14–97__	Date of IEP Review __10–1–98__
IEP meeting participants	IEP meeting participants
LEA Representative/Title	LEA Representative/Title
Teacher/Title	Teacher/Title
Teacher/Title	Teacher/Title
Parent/Guardian	Parent/Guardian
Private School Representative (when required)	Private School Representative (when required)
WSD or WSVH* Representative (when required)	WSD or WSVH* Representative (when required)
Community Agency Representative/Title (when required)	Community Agency Representative/Title (when required)
Student (if appropriate)	Student (if appropriate)
Other/Title	Other/Title
Interpreter (when required)	Interpreter (when required)

This form interpreted by _____ on _____

*Wisconsin School for the Deaf (WSD), Wisconsin School for the Visually Handicapped (WSVH)

Rev. 8/95

Figure 12.4 *(continued)*

INDIVIDUALIZED EDUCATION PROGRAM   Page __6_ of _15_

Name of Student

Marissa Jones   (Physical Education objectives)

Present levels of educational performance

Marissa can run 1 mile in 13 minutes and 36 seconds (1-9-97)

Annual goal

Marissa will increase her cardiovascular endurance

Short-term Objectives	Evaluation Criteria (Expected level of performance)	Evaluation Procedures (Data collection)	Evaluation Schedule When will this objective be reviewed?
Following the teacher's directions, Marissa will run 400 meters in less than 2 minutes and 45 seconds.	Run 400 meters in less than 2:45.	Physical Education teacher will observe and time Marissa during physical education class.	3-10-97
Marissa will ride a stationary bicycle on 3 consecutive days for 15 minutes without stopping.	3 consecutive days of nonstop stationary cycling for 15 minutes per session.	Physical education teacher will observe and time cycling sessions in gymnasium.	2-28-97
Marissa will run 1 mile in less than 12 minutes on the outdoor 400 meter track.	Run 1 mile in less than 12 minutes.	Physical education teacher will observe and time Marissa as she runs.	4-20-97

Titles of specific educational staff and related services personnel who will contribute to meeting this goal:

Ryan Cole, regular physical education teacher
Barb Smith, adapted physical education consultant

Parents agreed on importance of this goal - approved   9-14-97

Action taken on this goal at IEP review: Date:

Figure 12.4 *(continued)*

SUMMARY OF TRANSITION SERVICES

Date Student Invited and Method of Invitation _____

Transition Services Included in the IEP: (indicate the page and objective number on IEP)

Yes	No	
☐	☐	* Instruction
☐	☐	* Community Experiences
☐	☐	* Employment Objectives
☐	☐	* Post School Adult Living Objectives
☐	☐	** Acquisition of Daily Living Skills
☐	☐	** Functional Vocational Evaluation

* If not included as annual goals and short term objectives in the IEP, write an annual statement of needed services <u>or if not needed, write a statement regarding the basis upon which the service(s) were excluded.</u>

** If not included as goals and objectives in the IEP, these require an annual statement of needed services, if appropriate.

If the child did not attend the IEP meeting, what steps were taken to ensure that the child's interests and preferences were considered in the planning?

Is a statement of each public agency's and each participating agency's responsibilities or linkages, or both, needed?   ☐ Yes ☐ No

Participating Transition Service Agencies	Date Agency Representative Invited and Method of Invitation	Statement of Responsibilities/Linkages Related to Each of the Needed Transition Skill Areas

If an invited agency representative did not attend the IEP meeting, what steps were taken to obtain the participation of the agency in the planning of transition services?

Figure 12.4 *(continued)*

students with disabilities. Furthermore, proper assessment or testing procedures are required under this mandated physical education (Dunn and Fait, 1989; Wisconsin Department of Public Instruction, 1988). Providing quality physical education services for students with disabilities should not be justified solely on the basis of fulfilling a legal mandate, however. Students with disabilities have physical education needs no different from those of their nondisabled peers, and these needs must be met through the same provision of appropriately planned, implemented, and evaluated programs (National Association for Sport and Physical Education, 1995). Obviously, there will be times when the equipment, activities, or methods used to achieve program goals, or the goals themselves, should be modified for specific students. Knowledge of proper techniques and strategies for measurement and evaluation is an important basis for achieving appropriate programming (Fisher, 1988).

Many terms are used by educators, parents, and the general public to describe students with disabilities. Included are words such as *impaired, disabled, handicapped, exceptional, special,* and *unique.* Each of these terms has a meaning that is determined by the knowledge and experiences of the user. However, whatever term is used, the identity of the person should not be hidden in the descriptor. The person should always be described first (i.e., a person with a disability, a student with a unique educational need, or a child with a hearing impairment). This shifts the focus from the disability to the person as an individual with unique physical education interests and needs.

Regular physical education teachers are responsible for K–12 students with disabilities who are appropriately mainstreamed for inclusion into their classes (persons interested in physical activity programming for adults with disabilities should consult Lasko-McCarthey and Knopf, 1992; Rimmer, 1994; and Shepard, 1990. The material in this textbook is introductory in nature, and it is recognized that regular physical education teachers may at times need the assistance of an adapted or special physical education teacher. Consulting with an adapted physical education specialist is helpful when the severity and nature of a student's disabilities prevent safe and successful participation in all regular physical education instruction. Most undergraduate programs feature specific courses in adapted physical education.

Recognition of when and where to seek assessment and programming assistance regarding students with disabilities is important. Regular physical education teachers should remember that persons with expertise in adapted physical education are often available from local special education service centers or programs. Many school districts and/or regional special education programs have adapted specialists on staff for the purposes of providing consultation and/or direct teaching services. Physical educators should never isolate themselves in the gymnasium. Contact and communication with professionals in other disciplines should be a routine activity for all regular teachers, including those in physical education (Lavay, 1988).

The use of testing or assessment for placement decisions is common when working with students who have special or adapted physical education needs. Persons interested in more detailed information about adapted physical education assessment and programming should refer to comprehensive and specialized resources such as texts by Auxter, Pyfer, and Heuttig (1993), Jansma and French (1994), Kelly (1995), Eichstaedt and Kalakian (1993), Sherrill (1993), Seaman and DePauw (1989), Werder and Kalakian (1985), Wessel and Kelly (1986), and Winnick (1995). It is also recommended that persons responsible for testing many students with disabilities enroll in courses that will provide the skills and knowledge necessary to appropriately work in this specialized area.

Measurement and Evaluation Models for Teaching Effectiveness

Although the models included earlier in this chapter do not address planned self-evaluation of teaching effectiveness, Chapter 11 went into great detail on a variety of options that can be used to assess teaching. The effectiveness of your teaching should be grounded in how your students are spending their time. Your goal is to have students optimally engaged with learning activities directly linked to student learning objectives. Thus, systematically assessing what percentage of time your students are engaged in appropriate motor activity, what percentage they are listening to you talk, and what percentage they are involved with managerial activities (including waiting in line) is critical. Figures 11.13 and 11.15 provide simple but effective models for assessing critical time variables. Even more simply, pick a student at random and videotape that student for an entire class period. Go back and review that tape and collect data on how that student spent her or his time. Group time sampling (Figure 11.14) is also a good way to get insights to how your students are spending their time.

Specific teacher behaviors directly impact how students spend their time. Teachers who are positive, enthusiastic, and actively monitor their students will logically cause students to be more actively engaged in appropriate tasks. Thus, checking your movement patterns while instructing (Figure 11.9) and your verbal feedback (Figures 11.10, 11.11, 11.12) are important self-evaluation procedures as well.

Other possibilities for simple models for evaluating teaching effectiveness would be the System for Observing Fitness Observation Time (SOFIT) and the Arizona State University Observation Instrument (ASUOI) described in Chapter 11. Finally, a more sophisticated computer-based program is the Behavior Evaluation Strategy and Taxonomy (BEST) that is also illustrated in Chapter 11. The BEST system would provide ultimate flexibility and options for self-evaluation if you have access to this software program.

It is suggested that teachers should plan to measure and evaluate their teaching effectiveness on several occasions throughout the academic year. At a minimum, teachers should plan a self-evaluation of some aspect of their teaching once a semester. Teachers should target different aspects of their teaching in these self-evaluations. Perhaps one self-evaluation would focus on positive versus negative verbal behaviors, while the next one would target increasing the amount of time students are in activity during a particular unit. This self-evaluation should be done early enough in the semester that the teacher has the opportunity to modify behaviors as necessary. October and February would be good months to plan a self-evaluation. To check for successful changes in student or teacher behaviors, there will need to be more than one data collection. Some teachers may choose to evaluate more than twice a year, particularly if they want to check how effectively different units are being taught.

SECTION 2—MEASUREMENT AND EVALUATION IN NONSCHOOL SETTINGS

Since the early 1980s, physical activity programs have flourished in a variety of non-school settings. The nonschool settings that commonly sponsor physical activity and fitness programs designed to enhance health-related physical fitness can be grouped into four broad categories: **corporate, community, commercial,** and **clinical**. Corporate, or worksite, fitness programs are offered by an employer, and membership is usually limited to the employees of the organization. University- and college-sponsored programs also fall into the corporate setting category. Community programs cater to the local population and are commonly sponsored by not-for-profit agencies such as YMCAs, YWCAs, Boys' and Girls' Clubs, and churches. Commercial settings are those in which fitness programs are the primary component and are run for a profit, such as in private health clubs. Commercial settings also cater to the local population but tend to be more costly than community programs. The clinical settings that sponsor fitness programs are primarily hospitals, but may also include physical therapy, chiropractic, athletic training or other sports rehabilitation organizations. Clinically sponsored fitness programs are usually open to patients or previous patients and may or may not be open to the public.

The role of measurement and evaluation is as important in each of the nonschool settings as it is in school settings. The development and success of an exercise prescription and fitness program is dependent upon measurement and evaluation techniques. As an example, consider the function of pre- and posttraining fitness testing. Fitness testing is usually performed early in an exercise program in order to establish baseline fitness levels, and is repeated at various time points throughout the program to monitor progress. Without the initial measurement, development of an individualized exercise prescription/program would be impossible. As you know, multiple measurements are needed to provide the information necessary to render an evaluation. Therefore, without follow-up measurements, evaluation and modification of the exercise program would also be impossible.

In comparing the function of measurement and evaluation between school and nonschool settings, it seems clear that the fundamental purposes of measuring and evaluating are the same in both settings. There are, however, some key differences between the two settings that may influence measurement and evaluation procedures. Some of these differences are listed below for your consideration.

1. Nonschool settings focus mostly on exercise programs for adult populations. However, programming for children and older adults in these settings is growing, as is the need for exercise professionals who have experience working with those populations.

2. Because of the focus on adult populations, prescreening and risk stratification (see Chapter 5) are a must.

3. The focus of exercise programs in nonschool settings is on enhancement of health-related physical fitness. Although usually not labeled as such, the cognitive domain is gaining more attention in nonschool settings as exercise specialists have realized the importance of ensuring that clients are knowledgeable in equip-

ment use and exercise technique. Similarly, affective domain measurements such as exercise belief and perception have also become more common in nonschool settings. However, very little, if any, attention is paid to enhancing physical skills.

4. Development and modification of individualized exercise programs is more practical in nonschool settings than in school settings. Most clients who participate in nonschool sponsored exercise programs expect personalized testing and an individualized exercise prescription.

5. Participation in exercise testing and exercise programs in nonschool settings is voluntary, as is nonparticipation. Conversely, students are required to participate and attend physical education classes.

6. Overcrowding, time limits, and space constraints are less of a problem in nonschool settings than in school settings. Unlike school settings, where students may have infrequent and short sessions, participants in nonschool settings can select the times for their exercise sessions, as well as the type and duration of activity.

7. Many nonschool settings have greater resources than school settings, which results in better access to equipment and technology.

8. Fitness programs in nonschool settings continue year round, and clients may begin at any time throughout the year.

Considerations for Measurement and Evaluation In Nonschool Settings

Though the guidelines for applying measurement and evaluation techniques are similar in school and nonschool settings, there are some special considerations that relate specifically to nonschool settings. Measurement and evaluation techniques will differ among corporate, community, commercial, and clinical settings and can differ widely within any of these four categories. The procedures chosen for each facility depend on a number of variables, some of which are listed below. As you read through the following considerations, think about how each one could affect the number and types of measurement and evaluation procedures performed in each of the nonschool settings.

Program Goals

When comparing different nonschool settings, the program goals will vary immensely. The goal of many clinical programs is to improve functional capacity and quality of life and to reduce impairment and the risk of future illness. The goal of most community and commercial fitness programs is to promote physical activity and to assist individuals in achieving their personal fitness goals. The goal of most corporate fitness centers is similar to the previous goal, except that these facilities may also have additional, worksite-specific goals, such as reducing sick days or improving productivity. Each goal necessitates different measurement and evaluation techniques. For instance, assessing the 1 RM for a client who has recently undergone bypass surgery is not only dangerous but also irrelevant to the improvement in functional capacity early on in a cardiac rehabilitation program. In a corporate setting, an office ergonomic assessment may be included as part of the measurement and evaluation procedures to help eliminate potential causes of neck and back pain, which could result in lower productivity and time off from work.

Client Goals and Preferences

If you have several testing options, the client's goals may have some impact on the tests you choose. For instance, if the client is particularly interested in gaining upper-body muscular strength, then it might be wise to perform a bench press 1 RM test, which provides a better assessment of upper-body strength than the handgrip test. If a client does not like to run and does not plan to run as part of his fitness program, then the 1.5-mile run test may not be a good choice. The Rockport Fitness Walking test would be an easy option in this case.

Target Populations

As mentioned above, nonschool programs focus mostly on adults. However, within the adult population are subpopulations that may require special measurement and evaluation techniques. The most obvious subpopulation is found in clinical settings, where the fitness program may stem from a hospital cardiopulmonary rehabilitation center. The clients in these programs are often current or previous hospital patients who have or are at high risk for cardiovascular or pulmonary disease, and who may be limited in the types of activities they can perform. Many of the fitness tests described in Chapter 5 will not be appropriate for this population. While it is beyond the scope of this text to discuss clinical exercise testing, you should be aware that measurement and evaluation techniques in clinical settings may differ substantially from those in other nonschool settings. Other examples of subpopulations that may become involved in exercise programs in nonschool settings and that would require special measurement and evaluation procedures include individuals with visual impairment, obesity, hypertension, arthritis, osteoporosis, or diabetes, to name a few. Exercise specialists in nonschool settings should be prepared to modify testing procedures and be familiar with the guidelines for testing adults who may present with special conditions. For more information on specialized exercise testing, please refer to ACSM (1997).

Risk Stratification

In Chapter 5, you learned that it was imperative to evaluate the risk of an untoward event occurring during exercise for each client. Clients are classified as low, moderate, or high risk based on age, previous medical history, and risk factors for disease. The resulting risk stratification will determine if exercise testing is appropriate for your client. If so, the risk stratification will also determine the type of testing that is appropriate and whether or not a physician should be present during the testing. It is recommended that exercise specialists in nonschool settings refer to the *ACSM Guidelines for Exercise Testing and Prescription* (ACSM, 2000) to learn more about how risk stratification affects exercise testing and evaluation procedures.

Client Age

As discussed in Chapter 5, the assessments for older adults may differ from those of younger adults, particularly for older adults whose goal is to improve functional fitness. However, there are many adults over the age of 65 years who already have high levels of fitness and whose goal is to improve or maintain their fitness levels. For these individuals, the ACSM or YMCA test batteries may be more appropriate. Being familiar with the physiological changes that are associated with aging will help you to make sensible choices regarding measurement and evaluation for older adults.

Revenue Generation

Unlike the school setting, most nonschool settings are not funded by tax dollars. Often, the measurement procedures are performed at a cost to the client, either through membership dues or through an additional fee. For this reason, the testing and evaluation procedures need to appeal to the clients and provide them with valuable information. Additionally, for continued cash flow, members should be consulted about the type of information that would be useful to them. One way to do this is through a written or oral interest survey. Clients can be asked if they would prefer to know more about their body composition, dietary intake, cholesterol levels, etc. This information could be used as a guide for adding or developing new measurement and evaluation procedures that would benefit the clientele and generate revenue for the facility.

Equipment

The available equipment at your facility clearly influences your choice of measurement procedures. This is, of course, influenced by the facility's budget. Because of the importance of measurement and evaluation to program design, nonschool settings should at least have a stopwatch, calculator, scale, mat, yardstick, and masking tape. With this equipment, you can assess the five health-related fitness components using the ACSM Fitness Battery or separate tests, including the Rockport Fitness Walking test or the 1.5-mile run test, body mass index, timed sit-up test, push-up test, and the sit-and-reach test. Many nonschool settings will have more testing equipment than this, however. If given the opportunity to purchase equipment, you should evaluate what pieces of equipment are most valuable for your facility based on available funds, client interests, and functionality. For instance, obtaining a weight bench or cycle ergometer would not only allow you to perform additional types of testing, but would also provide an additional piece of equipment for your clients.

Support Personnel

When choosing exercise tests, you should consider the availability and expertise of support personnel. The 1 RM test and the Astrand-Rhyming and YMCA cycle ergometer tests are difficult to perform with only one tester, and each of these tests requires at least 10–15 minutes to complete. Not all facilities will be able to assign two employees every time a client is tested. Additionally, the expertise of the employees affects the tests that can be performed. Certain assessments (e.g., blood pressure, skinfold measurements, hydrostatic weighing) require knowledge, practice, and expertise to perform. All personnel should be certified in CPR and be familiar with the facility's emergency procedures.

Time

Time may be a testing consideration, both for you and the client. Total test time in nonschool settings should be limited to 60 minutes or less. The cycle ergometer, Rockport

Walk, and 1.5-mile run tests listed in Chapter 5 will take at least 10–15 minutes to complete. Strength assessment using 1 RM testing can be very time consuming, particularly if maximum lifting abilities are substantially underestimated. In the interest of time, it may be wise to include only one "long" test ($\geq$15 minutes) in your testing battery.

Monitoring Progress

The exercise specialist's job is not over once the exercise prescription is developed. In order for your clients to keep improving health-related physical fitness, programs need to be monitored and updated periodically. The best way to monitor progress is by keeping accurate and up-to-date records on all participants. This could be as simple as having clients keep exercise journals or logs that can be reviewed periodically by an exercise specialist. Ideally, the tools for recording exercise sessions should be provided by the facility.

Measuring the Cognitive and Affective Domains

Throughout this textbook, it has been suggested that cognitive and affective measurement and evaluation should be a consideration for activity programs in nonschool settings. As such, a discussion of assessment in these domains is relevant here.

The format for measuring and evaluating the cognitive domain will differ between school and nonschool settings. Written exams and homework will probably not be used in a nonschool setting. Nonetheless, it is important to ensure that clients understand the key elements of an exercise program. Clients should have knowledge regarding the differing benefits of aerobic, resistance, and flexibility exercises, the safe use of all exercise equipment, and proper exercise technique. In addition, clients should know the procedures for monitoring exercise intensity, using both heart rate and ratings of perceived exertion (RPE). The client's understanding of the use of the perceived exertion scale is a component of the cognitive domain, even though the scale itself assesses how the participant feels during exercise. A carefully constructed checklist would be an appropriate instrument for assessing and monitoring the knowledge acquired by the client throughout the exercise program. The checklist should be specific to the nonschool setting in which it is used and include all of the important cognitive elements of the specific exercise program.

Most exercise specialists would agree that part of their job is to ensure that clients stay interested and continue to participate in the program. To be successful at this, exercise specialists must measure the affective domain. The design of an exercise program should take into consideration the client's interests and attitudes toward exercise, as well as the factors that act as motivators or barriers to exercise. Of course, these factors must be measured and evaluated in order to take them into account when designing an individualized exercise program.

Assessing client interest can be as simple as asking a client to choose favorite activities from a checklist of activities that the facility provides. A sample physical fitness interest survey is shown in Chapter 8, Figure 8.6. Although this survey is specific to a physical education program, it could easily be modified to be relevant to any nonschool setting.

Chapter 8 also includes several tools for measuring attitudes toward physical activity (Attitudes Toward Physical Activity inventory, Feelings About Activity inventory, and exercise logs) and motivation for exercise (Self-Motivation inventory) that would be appropriate for adult populations. The written questionnaire shown in Figure 12-5 is used to assess current physical activity status, motivation and potential barriers to physical activity. This questionnaire also provides you and the client with strategies for dealing with the common barriers to exercise associated with each physical activity status. Addressing low self-motivation, negative attitudes toward exercise, and other potential barriers early in an exercise program can increase **exercise adherence.** Exercise adherence, the participant's compliance with the exercise program, is a major challenge for exercise clinicians. Many clients will start an activity program but fail to maintain a regular exercise regime. Thus, not only must you motivate people to start an exercise program, but you must also motivate your clients to make activity a lifestyle habit so that they will stick to their exercise regimen. This should be of the utmost importance to you as an exercise specialist, not only because it is important for your client's health and well-being, but also because you do not want to see your well-designed, individualized exercise program go to waste!

Example of a Nonschool Measurement and Evaluation Model

Each nonschool setting has unique characteristics, target populations, and program goals that may affect measurement and evaluation techniques. Most nonschool settings do not formally assess the psychomotor domain. Nonschool programs are year-round, with no clear starting or ending point. For these reasons, it is more difficult to establish models exactly like those provided earlier in this chapter for school settings. However, we have devised a recommended model that provides a guide for measurement and evaluation procedures in nonschool activity programs. Figure 12.5 illustrates the general plan for this model. This model assumes that there will be two assessment sessions during Week One, one session during Week Two, and at least one follow-up session. The timeline begins the day a client becomes a member of a nonschool activity program and continues for the duration of that client's membership.

As you look at the model, you may realize that it is most appropriate for commercial, community, and corporate settings. As mentioned previously, measurement and evaluation procedures in clinical settings can vary substantially from those in the other three categories of nonschool settings. We believe that the general model we present below is usable in clinical settings, but that some modification of the time line and assessment type may be required.

Week One (Sessions One and Two)

Session One should be scheduled early in the first week of membership, if not on the first day. This session should consist of a tour of the facility and completion of initial paperwork, including prescreening tools (i.e., PAR-Q, medical history form) and an interest survey. At this time, testing procedures should be explained and a testing session scheduled, also preferably within the first week of membership. A risk stratification and evaluation of the client's predicted fitness level should be developed immediately so that future testing decisions can be made.

Week One			
	HRPF	**AFF**	**COG**
Session One	Prescreening	Activity interest survey	
Session Two	Health related fitness testing	Attitude toward physical activity	Informed consent
		Assess barriers to physical activity	Rating of perceived exertion scale
		Self-motivation assessment	

Week Two			
	HRPF	**AFF**	**COG**
Session Three		Exercise log continued for every workout	Checklist
			Heart rate assessment

Week Six to Week Ten			
	HRPF	**AFF**	**COG**
Follow-Up Session	Health related fitness retesting	Attitude toward physical activity reassessment	Checklist
		Self-motivation reassessment	
		Exercise log continues	

Ongoing Measurements			
	HRPF	**AFF**	**COG**
	Individual or group health related fitness testing as needed	Reassess attitudes, barriers, interests as needed	Checklist as needed
		Exercise log continues	

Figure 12.5 General model for measurement and evaluation in nonschool settings.

When the client arrives for Session Two, re-explain all of the testing procedures, including an explanation of the use of the RPE scale. Ask if the client has any questions, and answer these completely. Have the client complete an **informed consent** document that explains the risks and benefits of the exercise testing. Most facilities that perform exercise testing will have a prepared informed consent document. This is also a good time to have the client complete surveys related to physical activity attitudes, motivations, and barriers. Once the paperwork is complete, and provided that exercise has been determined to be safe for this individual, fitness testing can begin. The client should sit quietly for five minutes prior to resting heart rate and blood pressure assessment. Perform testing for the five health-related fitness components in the order described in Chapter 5. If testing for functional fitness in an older adult, perform the test battery for older adults as described in Chapter 5. Once the testing procedures are complete, you may decide to evaluate and discuss the results at that time or to wait until the next meeting. You should schedule Session Three at this time, ideally within a few days.

Week Two (Session Three)

During Session Three, you should discuss the results of the fitness testing if you did not do it during Session Two. You should provide the client with a beginning exercise prescription, and suggest possible program options based on the client's interests. You should also discuss the barriers indicated by the client and some possible strategies to overcome them. Your explanation of the exercise prescription/program should include an explanation of how to assess exercise intensity, operate the exercise equipment, perform exercises correctly, and track progress and attitudes toward exercise using exercise logs. These are the types of skills that should be included on a checklist as part of the cognitive assessment. Finally, your client should be encouraged to use an exercise log to briefly describe the nature of each workout, to note the intensity and duration of workout, and to record feelings about the workout. Your client should also log activity sessions that may take place away from your facility. Dietary logs can also be incorporated if desired. Using the exercise log should continue every week throughout the program.

Weeks Six through Ten (Follow-Up Session)

Follow-up testing should be performed soon enough in an exercise program to be motivating to the client, but not before improvements would be expected. A good time to reassess health-related physical fitness is six to ten weeks after initiation of the exercise program, assuming regular participation in the program. The best time to reassess will vary depending upon the client's initial fitness level and frequency and intensity of activity. A client who is new to exercise will probably make noticeable gains in fitness relatively soon in the program (i.e., between six and seven weeks). Conversely, a veteran exerciser may take longer to adapt to the program. Generally, both the new and veteran exerciser will experience relatively greater gains as the intensity and frequency of the activity increases.

The assessments performed during the follow-up session should be the same assessments performed during the initial testing session in order to make valid comparisons. A reassessment of attitudes toward physical activity may be prudent at this time because it can provide insight into the client's feelings about the exercise program. A review of the exercise log can also provide information on exercise attitudes as well as participation in the exercise program, which may explain the magnitude of the changes in health-related physical fitness. For instance, if the client has not been performing resistance exercise, you would not expect to see much change in muscular strength. The exercise log may also provide information as to why the client has not been performing resistance exercise. The results from all of the follow-up measurements should be used to evaluate the success of the fitness program and to make modifications accordingly.

Ongoing Measurements

Additional individual follow-up sessions can be included as desired by the client, within reason. You should explain to clients that improvement in health-related physical fitness could plateau after the client becomes more fit, and there is no need to have formal re-assessments at one- to two-week intervals. As your client becomes a more educated consumer, he or she should be able to perform some informal self-assessments to monitor progress. A formal reassessment planned every three to six months will be appropriate for most clients. As a convenience to both clients and the exercise specialist who performs the testing, many facilities offer special fitness testing sessions for all members periodically throughout the year. Examples include blood pressure assessments the first Monday of every month or body composition assessments the third Wednesday of each month.

Sample Case Study

No two nonschool settings are exactly alike in the types of clients or equipment available. It is important that you understand that there are many factors that determine the measurement and evaluation procedures in a given nonschool setting. Knowing that measurement and evaluation are critical to effective program design, you must assimilate all the factors and make a professional decision as to the best procedures for a particular setting. We have provided a sample case study below that includes the type of client and equipment common to many nonschool settings. Figure 12.6 illustrates the measurement and evaluation plan for this client.

Client:	35-year-old female
Risk Stratification:	Low risk
Equipment:	Sphygmomanometer, stethoscope, cycle ergometer, perceived exertion scale, indoor running track, bench step, weight bench, mats, sit-and-reach box, skinfold calipers, tape measure, stopwatch, calculator

In this model, the prescreening tools were administered and the client was determined to be in the low risk category. The results of her interest survey indicate that she is primarily interested in aerobic dance classes and weight training. Because of her interest in weight training, we chose to perform a 1-RM test. Since the 1-RM can be lengthy, we chose shorter tests to assess the remaining health-related fitness components. During Session One, this client indicated that she currently performs aerobic exercise, is highly motivated to exercise, and enjoys exercise. Thus, we chose to forgo the ATPA and Self-Motivation Surveys, but included the Current Physical Activity Questionnaire to help her review her current aerobic exercise program and anticipate and deal with future barriers. The exercise log is included in primarily to monitor her weight training activities. The cognitive assessments we chose are the informed consent, checklist, and procedures for assessing exercise intensity using heart rate and RPE. RPE was introduced in Session Two because the subject will need to understand how to use the scale during health-related physical fitness testing. Being a veteran exerciser, the client may not need the checklist or the explanation of heart rate and RPE, but we included these assessments to be certain. Follow-up testing was scheduled for week eight. At minimum, we would expect to see muscular strength and endurance adaptations and may want to modify her weight training program based on her increased muscular fitness. We also reviewed her exercise log

Week One			
	HRPF	**AFF**	**COG**
Session One	Prescreening	Activity interest survey	
Session Two	Heart rate Blood pressure Skinfold test 3-min. step test 1-RM Timed sit-up Sit-and-reach	Assess barriers to exercise	Informed consent Rating of perceived exertion scale

Week Two			
	HRPF	**AFF**	**COG**
Session Three		Exercise log—continues every workout	Checklist Heart rate assessment

Week Eight			
	HRPF	**AFF**	**COG**
Follow-Up Session	Repeat as listed in Session Two Evaluate progress and modify	Review exercise log Review interests Review barriers	Checklist

Ongoing Measurements			
	HRPF	**AFF**	**COG**
	Individual or group health-related fitness testing as needed	Reassess barriers and interests as needed Exercise log continues	Checklist as needed

Figure 12.5 General model for measurement and evaluation in nonschool settings.

to assess resistance exercise adherence and interests and barriers to ensure that neither had changed.

CHECKING YOUR UNDERSTANDING

Client:	50-year-old male
Risk Stratification:	Moderate risk
Equipment:	Mats, stopwatch, tape measure, calculator, bench step, sit-and-reach box, and running track

Using the assessment model presented in the previous case study, what measurement and evaluation plan should be designed for this client?

Measurement and Evaluation in Athletic Training

Athletic training is rapidly becoming a popular choice for students interested in pursuing a health-related profession. This is due in large measure to its affiliation with competitive sports. Potential athletic trainers undergo intensive education designed to provide the requisite knowledge and skills to gain employment in public schools, colleges, or professional sports. Some states require licensure for athletes trainers. Further, it is highly recommended that trainers become board-certified by the National Athletes Trainers Association. To do so requires successful completion of a standard examination. An athletic trainer's primary responsibilities are to prevent, recognize, and treat sports injuries. In addition, trainers must provide assessment, rehabilitation, program organization, and education of the athlete. As might be expected, familiarity with and understanding of measurement and evaluation techniques is essential if trainers are to perform their responsibilities effectively. The assessment of sports injuries is a competency that all athletic trainers must possess. Both on and off the field, the athletic trainer is required to render accurate and detailed assessment and evaluation of a variety of circumstances.

Central to the responsibilities of athletic trainers is the ability to prescribe and oversee an appropriate rehabilitation program for an injured athlete (see Figure 12.7). Several criteria must be measured at the beginning, during, and at the end of this process. The following criteria should be considered when determining the status of an injury:

1. strength of each muscle group
2. power of each muscle group
3. endurance of each muscle group
4. balance between antagonistic muscle groups
5. flexibility of the muscles around the rehabilitated joint (Roy and Irvin, 1983).

The assessment and evaluation of sports injuries is the primary function of athletic trainers. Each trainer must develop a systematic approach to measuring and evaluating the extent of an injury. According to the American Academy of Orthopaedic

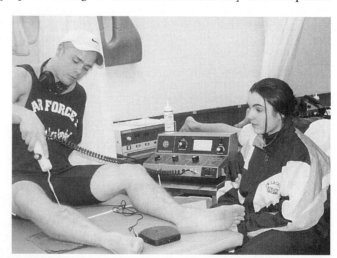

Figure 12.7 Treatment of injury.

Surgeons (1984), there are three distinct evaluations associated with a sports injury. First is the primary, or on-site, inspection and evaluation. This phase consists of providing necessary first aid, the determination of serious injuries, and the proper disposition of the athlete. Second is the off-site evaluation, during which the trainer sequences the procedures that determine the nature, location, and seriousness of the injury. The last phase consists of a treatment regimen, including therapy and, of course, a follow-up exercise program. Once treatment of the injury has been completed, it is the responsibility of the athletic trainer to design a program of exercise to rehabilitate the injured area. An instrument used to aid in the development of an exercise program to rehabilitate an injury is the Cybex (see Figure 12.8). This instrument calculates the strength of a muscle or muscle group and can be used to compare the injured area with its uninjured counterparts.

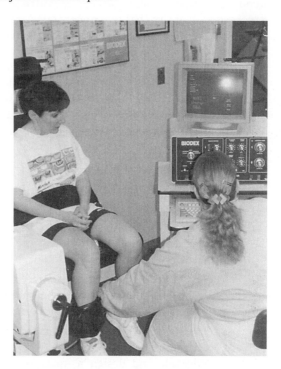

Figure 12.8 The Cybex.

In addition to aiding in the exercise plan, measurement and evaluation techniques are used to assist the athletic trainer in a number of other tasks. Valid, reliable sports injury data can materially help decrease sports-related injuries. Properly interpreted, this type of data can be useful in modifying rules and in assisting coaches and teachers to better understand risks associated with participation in certain sports. Quantitative record keeping can also aid in evaluating products designed to protect athletes. In this era of accountability, the public needs to understand the risks inherent in sports.

In sum, the profession of athletic training depends heavily on measurement and evaluation techniques. To be effective in their multiple duties, trainers must continually assess and evaluate situations ranging from on-the-scene analysis of an injury to analysis of data accrued over time.

SUMMARY

This chapter has provided suggestions for developing measurement and evaluation models for application in typical school physical education programs and in nonschool activity programs found in corporate, community, commercial, and clinical activity settings. Case studies and checks for student understanding were included in both major sections of the chapter.

Section 1 of the chapter focused on school settings. Variables that impact the design of appropriate measurement and evaluation models were presented. Examples of measurement and evaluation models at the elementary, middle, and high school levels were provided. Issues pertaining to measurement and evaluation strategies used with students with disabilities were addressed. Suggestions were also made about appropriate techniques for measuring and evaluating teaching effectiveness.

Section 2 of the chapter concentrated on practical measurement and evaluation issues in nonschool activity settings. Because there are many differences in the nature of school and nonschool settings, the nature of measurement and evaluation changes substantially. Considerations for assessing clients participating in different types of nonschool adult fitness programs were detailed. A general model for measurement and evaluation in nonschool settings was presented, followed by a more specific case study using this model. This section summarized the importance of measurement and evaluation in the athletic training setting as well.

DISCUSSION QUESTIONS

1. Which of the four learning domains merits the most and the least measurement and evaluation time in the school physical education setting? Defend your opinion.

2. In considering the health-related physical fitness, cognitive, and affective domains, which merits the most and the least measurement and evaluation time in adult fitness settings? Defend your opinion.

3. Select one of the case studies presented in this chapter. What concerns would you have about implementing this measurement and evaluation model? Suggest changes that would eliminate your concerns.

4. The setting is a high school that offers units lasting a full 18-week semester. Classes are coed and average 30 students. Choose a lifetime sport about which you are knowledgeable and design a measurement and evaluation model that would complement the curricular activities of that sport.

5. The setting is a community fitness program for senior citizens. Your client is a 65-year-old male with moderate risk stratification. Your client's goal is functional fitness. Assuming the normal range of equipment found in this sort of setting, design a specific measurement and evaluation plan for this client that includes assessment in the health-related physical fitness, cognitive, and affective domains.

6. Compare and contrast the characteristics of school and nonschool settings that impact measurement and evaluation models.

REFERENCES

American Academy of Orthopaedic Surgeons. (1984). *Athletic training for sports medicine.* Chicago: American Academy of Orthopaedic Surgeons.

American College of Sports Medicine (2000). *ACSM's guidelines for exercise testing and prescription.* 6th ed. Baltimore, MD: Lippincott Williams & Wilkins.

American College of Sports Medicine (1997). *ACSM's exercise management for persons with chronic diseases and disabilities.* Champaign, IL: Human Kinetics.

Auxter, D., Pyfer, J., and Heuttig, C. (1993). *Principles and methods of adapted physical education and recreation.* 7th ed. St. Louis, MO: Mosby.

Bartz, D., Anderson-Robinson, S., and Hillman, L. (1994). Performance assessment: Make them show what they can know. *Principal,* 73 (3): 11–14.

Darst, P., and Pangrazi, R. (2002). *Dynamic physical education for secondary school students.* 3rd ed. San Francisco: Benjamin Cummings.

Dunn, J., and Fait, H. (1989). *Special physical education: Adapted, individualized, developmental.* 6th ed. Dubuque, IA: Brown.

Eichstaedt, C., and Kalakian, L. (1993). *Developmental/adapted physical education: Making ability count.* 3rd ed. New York: Macmillan.

Fisher, J. (1988). Measurement in adapted physical education. In P. Bishop, ed. *Adapted physical education: A comprehensive resource manual of definition, assessment, programming, and future directions.* Kearney, NE: Educational Systems Associates.

Jansma, P., and French, R. (1994). *Special physical education: Physical activity, sports, and recreation.* 2nd ed. Englewood Cliffs, NJ: Prentice-Hall.

Kelly, L. (Project Director, NCPERID). (1995). *Adapted physical education national standards.* Champaign, IL: Human Kinetics.

Lasko-McCarthey, P., and Knopf, K. (1992). *Adapted physical education for adults with disabilities.* 3rd ed. Dubuque, IA: Bowers.

Lavay, B. (1988). The special physical educator: Communicating effectively in a team approach. In P. Bishop, ed. *Adapted physical education: A comprehensive resource manual of definition, assessment, programming, and future predictions.* Kearney, NE: Educational Systems Associates.

National Association for Sport and Physical Education (AAHPERD). (1995). *Moving into the future—National physical education standards: A guide to content and assessment.* St. Louis: Mosby.

Pangrazi, R. (2001). *Dynamic physical education for elementary school students.* 13th ed. San Francisco: Benjamin Cummings.

Rimmer, J. (1994). *Fitness and rehabilitation programs for special populations.* Dubuque, IA: Brown.

Roy, S., and Irwin, R. (1983). *Sports medicine: Prevention, evaluation, management, and rehabilitation.* Englewood Cliffs, NJ: Prentice-Hall.

Seaman, J., and DePauw, K. (1989). *The new adapted physical education: A developmental approach.* 2nd ed. Palo Alto, CA: Mayfield Publishing Company.

Shepard, R. (1990). *Fitness in special populations.* Champaign, IL: Human Kinetics.

Sherrill, C. (1993). *Adapted physical activity, recreation, and sport: Cross-disciplinary and lifespan.* 4th ed. Dubuque, IA: Brown.

Werder, J., and Kalakian, L. (1985). *Assessment in adapted physical education*. Minneapolis, MN: Burgess.

Wessel, J., and Kelly, L. (1986). *Achievement-based curriculum development in physical education*. Philadelphia, PA: Lea and Febiger.

Winnick, J. (1995). *Adapted physical education and sport*. 2nd ed. Champaign, IL: Human Kinetics.

——. (1988). *Physical education for exceptional educational needs students*. Information Update Bulletin No. 88.2, December 1988. (Available from Wisconsin DPI, 125 S. Webster St., PO Box 7841, Madison, WI 53707-7841.)